# A History of
# English Literature

# Macmillan Foundations

*A series of introductory texts across a wide range of subject areas to meet the needs of today's lecturers and students*

*Foundations* texts provide complete yet concise coverage of core topics and skills based on detailed research of course requirements suitable for both independent study and class use – *the firm foundations for future study.*

## Published

*Biology*
*Chemistry*
*Contemporary Europe*
*Economics*
*A History of English Literature*
*Physics*
*Modern British History*
*Politics*

## Forthcoming

*British Politics*
*Economics for Business*
*Mathematics for Science and Engineering*
*Modern European History*
*Nineteenth Century Britain*
*Sociology*

# A History of English Literature

**MICHAEL ALEXANDER**

First published 2000 by
MACMILLAN PRESS LTD
Houndmills, Basingstoke, Hampshire RG21 6XS
and London
Companies and representatives
throughout the world

ISBN 0–333–91397–3 hardcover
ISBN 0–333–67226–7 paperback

A catalogue record for this book is available
from the British Library.

This book is printed on paper suitable for recycling and
made from fully managed and sustained forest sources.

10   9   8   7   6   5   4   3   2   1
09   08   07   06   05   04   03   02   01   00

Typeset by Footnote Graphics, Warminster, Wilts
Printed in Great Britain by
Antony Rowe Ltd, Chippenham, Wilts

# Contents

## PART 3

# Augustan and Romantic

## PART 4

# Victorian Literature to 1880

# *Acknowledgements*

Having decided the scope of this history, and that it would be narrative but also critical, the task of selection imposed itself. In order to sharpen my focus, I then invited, at a preliminary stage, twenty university teachers of English literature each to send me a list of the twenty works which they believed would have to receive critical discussion in such a history. Some of those who replied evaded my rigour by including Collected Works in their list. But I thank them all. I have a much longer list of colleagues to thank for answering more scholarly queries. I name only Michael Herbert, George Jack, Christopher MacLachlan, Rhiannon Purdie and Michael Wheeler, who each read a chapter for me, as did Neil Rhodes, to whom I turned for advice more than once.

Thanks also to Frances Arnold and Margaret Bartley at Macmillan, who invited me to write this book; I enjoyed the reading, and the rereading. Thanks to Houri Alavi, who has patiently shepherded the monster forward into the arena. Thanks most of all to my family, especially to Mary and Lucy for reading many pages, and for listening.

The book itself is also a kind of thank you – to those who wrote what is now called English literature; to scholars, editors, critics; to the English teachers I had at school; to fellow-students of literature, especially at Stirling and St Andrews; to all from whom I have learned. I still have much to learn, and thank in advance any reader who draws to my attention any errors of fact.

## Illustrations

AKG Photo, London, pp. 94, 110, 133, 150, 241; E.T.Archive, pp. 21, 28, 45, 207, 202; The British Library, p. 190; The British Museum, pp. 23, 27; J. Burrow and T. Turville-Petre, *A Book of Middle English*, Blackwell Publishers, p. 37; Camera Press, London, p. 349; Corbis Collection, p. 340; Corpus Christi College, Oxford, UK/The Bridgeman Art Library, p. 50; Courtauld Institute of Art, London, p. 138; Judy Daish Associates, p. 364; Norman Davies, *The Isles*, Macmillan, p. 12; The Dickens House Museum, London, p. 277; The Dorset Country Museum, p. 301; Edifice, pp. 170, 248; Mark Gerson, p. 367; The Hulton Getty Picture Collection Ltd, pp. 270, 317, 321, 347, 372; Image Select International, pp. 96, 139, 185, 335, 338; The National Portrait Gallery, pp. 98, 212, 223, 273, 374, 379; Nottingham County Library, The D. H. Lawrence Collection, p. 326; RIBA Library Photographs Collection, p. 255; Ann Ronan at I.S.I., pp. 54, 62, 79, 106, 232, 242, 251, 263, 268, 278, 282, 287, 291, 298, 300; John Timbers, Arena Images, p. 363; Utrecht University Library, p. 108; The Victoria and Albert Museum, pp. 64, 168, 213.

Every effort has been made to trace all copyright holders, but if any have been inadvertently overlooked the publishers will be pleased to make the necessary arrangement at the first opportunity.

# *Preface*

This *History* is written for two audiences: those who know a few landmark texts of English literature but little of the surrounding country; and those who simply want to read its long story from its origins to the present day.

The history of English writing begins very early in the Middle Ages and continues through the Renaissance, the Augustan and Romantic periods to the Victorian age, the twentieth century, and down to the present. This account of it is written so as to be read as a coherent whole. It can also be read in parts, and consulted for information. Its narrative plan and layout are clear, and it aims to be both readable and concise. Attention is paid to the greater poets, dramatists, prose writers and novelists, and to more general literary developments. Each part of the story gains from being set in literary and social contexts. Space is given to illustrative quotation and to critical discussions of selected major authors and works.

Minor writers and movements are described rather than discussed, but a great deal of information about them is to be found in the full apparatus which surrounds the narrative. This apparatus allows the *History* also to be used as a work of reference. A look at the following pages will show the text supplemented by a set of historical tables of events and of publications; by boxed biographies of authors and their works; and by marginal definitions of critical and historical terms. There are some sixty illustrations, including maps. There are also suggestions for further reading, and a full index of names of the authors and works discussed.

# *Abbreviations*

| | |
|---|---|
| ? | uncertain |
| Anon. | anonymous |
| b. | born |
| *c.* | *circa*, about |
| d. | died |
| ed. | edited by |
| edn. | edition |
| et al. | and others |
| etc. | and other things |
| fl. | flourished |
| Fr. | French |
| Gk. | Greek |
| Lat. | Latin |
| ME | Middle English |
| med. Lat. | medieval Latin |
| MS., MSS. | manuscript, manuscripts |
| OE | Old English |

# Introduction

England has a rich literature with a long history. This is an attempt to tell the story of English literature from its beginnings to the present day. The story is written to be read as a whole, though it can be read in parts, and its apparatus and index allow it to be consulted for reference. To be read as a whole with pleasure, a story has to have a companionable aspect, and the number of things discussed cannot be too large. There are said to be 'nine and twenty ways of reciting tribal lays', and there is certainly more than one way of writing a history of English literature. This Introduction says what kind of a history this is, and what it is not, and defines its scope: where it begins and ends, and what 'English' and 'literature' are taken to mean.

'Literature' is a word with a qualitative implication, not just a neutral term for writing in general. Without this implication, and without a belief on the part of the author that some qualities of literature are best appreciated when it is presented in the order in which it appeared, there would be little point in a literary history. This effort to put the most memorable English writing in an intelligible historical perspective is offered as an aid to public understanding. The reader, it is assumed, will like literature and be curious about it. It is also assumed also that he or she will want chiefly to know about works such as Shakespeare's *King Lear* and Swift's *Gulliver's Travels*, the poems of Chaucer, Milton and T. S. Eliot, and the novels of Austen and Dickens. So the major earns more space than the minor in these pages; and minor literature earns more attention than writing stronger in social, cultural or historical importance than in literary interest.

## Literary history

Literary history can be useful, and is increasingly necessary. Scholars specialize in single fields, English teachers teach single works. Larger narratives are becoming lost; the perspective afforded by a general view is not widely available. Students of English leave school knowing a few landmark works but little of the country surrounding them. They would not like to be asked to assign an unread writer to a context, nor, perhaps, to one of the centuries between Chaucer and the present. 'How many thousands never heard the name/Of Sidney or of Spenser, or their books!', wrote the Elizabethan poet Samuel Daniel. This history offers a map to the thousands of people who study English today. University students of English who write in a final exam 'Charles Dickens was an eighteenth-century novelist' could be better informed. A reader of this book will gain a sense of what English literature consists of, of its contents; then of how this author or text relates to that, chronologically and in other ways. The map is also a journey, affording changing perspectives on the relations of writing to its times, of one literary work to another, and of the present to the past. Apart from the pleasures of discovery and comparison, literary history fosters a sense of proportion which puts the present in perspective.

## What's included?

The historian of a literature tries to do justice to the great things in its tradition, while knowing better than most that classical status is acquired and can fade. As for literary status itself, it is clear from *Beowulf* that poetry had a high place in the earliest English world that we can know about. The first formal assertion of the classical potential of writing in a modern European vernacular was made about 1307 by the Italian poet Dante. Such a claim was made for English by Philip Sidney in his *Defence of Poetry* (1579), answering an attack on the theatre. Puritans closed the public theatres in 1642. After they were reopened in 1660, literature came to take a central role in English civilization. From 1800, Romantic poets made very great claims for the value of poetry. Eventually the Victorians came to study English literature alongside that of Greece or Rome.

Literature has also had its enemies. The early Greek writer-philosopher Plato (*c*.429–347 BC), in banning poets from his imaginary ideal Republic, acknowledged their power. The English Puritans of the 17th century, when they closed the theatres, made a similar acknowledgement. After 1968, some French theorists claimed that critics were more important than writers. Some Californian students protested, at about the same time, that dead white European males were over-represented in the canon.

## Tradition or canon?

A canon is a selection from the larger literary tradition. The modern English literary tradition goes back to the 15th century, when Scottish poets invoked a poetic tradition with Chaucer at its head. As the Renaissance went on, this tradition was celebrated by Sidney, Spenser, Shakespeare, Jonson, Milton and their successors. Tradition implies participation and communication: it grows and fades, changing its aspect every few generations. When scholars first looked into English literary history in the 18th century, they found that the medieval phase was stronger and longer than had been realized. In the 19th century, the novel became stronger than drama.

Writing and literature continue, as does the study of English. Since about 1968, university English departments have diversified: literary tradition has to contend with ideology and with research interests. Other writing in English had already come in: American, followed at a distance by the writing of other former colonies. Neglected work by women writers was uncovered. Disavowing literature, 'cultural studies' addressed writing of sociological or psychological interest, including magazine stories, advertising and the unwritten 'texts' of film and television. Special courses were offered for sectional interests – social, sexual or racial. The hierarchy of literary *kinds* was also challenged: poetry and drama had long ago been joined by fiction, then came travel writing, then children's books, and so on. Yet the literary category cannot be infinitely extended – if new books are promoted, others must be relegated – and questions of worth cannot be ignored indefinitely. Despite challenge, diversification and accommodation, familiar names are still found at the core of what is studied at school, college and university. Students need to be able to put those names into an intelligible order, related to literary and non-literary history. This book, being a history of the thirteen centuries of English literature, concerns itself with what has living literary merit, whether contemporary or medieval.

## Priorities

Although this history takes things, so far as it can, in chronological order, its priority is literary rather than historical. Shakespeare wrote that 'So long as men can read and eyes can see,/So long lives this, and this gives life to thee'. The belief that literature outlives the circumstances of its origin, illuminating as these can be, guides the selection. Ben Jonson claimed of Shakespeare that he was 'not of an age, but for all time'. This distinguishing characteristic is at odds with historicizing approaches which have sought to return literature to social or political contexts, sometimes with interesting results. Beliefs and priorities apart, not many of these 190,000 words can be devoted to the contexts of those thirteen centuries. The necessary contexts of literary texts are indicated briefly, and placed in an intelligible sequence. Critical debates receive some mention, but a foundation history may also have to summarize the story of a novel. Another priority is that literary texts should be quoted. But the prime consideration has been that the works chiefly discussed and illustrated will be the greater works which have delighted or challenged generations of readers and have made a difference to their thinking, their imaginations or their lives.

But who are the major writers? The history of taste shows that few names are oblivion-proof. In Western literature only those of Homer, Dante and Shakespeare are undisputed, and for ages the first two were lost to view. Voltaire, King George III, Leo Tolstoy, G. B. Shaw and Ludwig Wittgenstein thought Shakespeare overrated. Yet ever since the theatres reopened in 1660 he has had audiences, readers and defenders. So continuous a welcome has not been given to other English writers, even Milton. This is not because it is more fun to go to the theatre than to read a book, but because human tastes are inconstant. William Blake and G. M. Hopkins went unrecognized during their lives. Nor is recognition permanent: who now reads Abraham Cowley, the most esteemed poet of the 17th century, or *Sir Charles Grandison*, the most admired novel of the 18th? The mountain range of poetry from Chaucer to Milton to Wordsworth has not been eroded by time or distance, though a forest of fiction has grown up in the intervening ground. Prose reputations seem less durable: the history of fictional and non-fictional prose shows whole kinds rising and falling. The sermon was a powerful and popular form from the Middle Ages until the 19th century. In the 18th century the essay became popular, but has faded. In the 18th century also, the romance lost ground to the novel, and the novel became worthy of critical attention. Only after 1660 did drama become respectable as literature. In the 1980s, while theorists proved that authors were irrelevant, literary biography flourished. As for non-fiction, the Nobel Prize for Literature was awarded in 1950 to the philosopher Bertrand Russell and in 1953 to Winston Churchill as historian. Thereafter, non-fictional writing drifted out of the focus of literature, or at least of its professional students in English departments in Britain. There are now some attempts to reverse this, not always on literary grounds.

## What is literature?

What is it that qualifies a piece of writing as literature? There is no agreed answer to this question; a working definition is proposed in the next paragraph. Dr Johnson thought that if a work was read a hundred years after it had appeared, it had stood the test of time. This has the merit of simplicity. Although favourable social, cultural and academic factors play their parts in the fact that Homer has lasted twenty-seven centuries, a work must have unusual merits to outlive the context in which it appeared, however vital its relations to that context once were. The contexts supplied by scholars – literary, biographical and historical (not to mention theoretical) – change and vary. A literary text, then, is always more than its context.

This is a history of a literature, not an introduction to literary studies, nor a history of literary thought. It tries to stick to using this kitchen definition as a simple rule: that the merit of a piece of writing lies in its combination of literary art and human interest. A work of high art which lacks human interest dies. For its human interest to last – and human interests change – the language of a work has to have life, and its form has to please. Admittedly, such qualities of language and form are easier to recognize than to define. Recognition develops with reading and with the strengthening of the historical imagination and of aesthetic and critical judgement. No further definition of literature is attempted, though what has been said above about 'cultural studies', academic pluralism and partisanship shows that the question is still agitated. In practice, though the core has been attacked, loosened and added to, it has not been abandoned.

In literary and cultural investigations, the question of literary merit can be almost indefinitely postponed. But in this book it is assumed that there are orders of merit and of magnitude, hard though it may be to agree on cases. It would be unfair, for example, to the quality of a writer such as Fanny Burney or Mrs Gaskell to pretend that the work of a contemporary novelist such as Pat Barker is of equal merit. It would be hard to maintain that the Romantic Mrs Felicia Hemans was as good a poet as Emily Brontë. And such special pleading would be even more unjust to Jane Austen or to Julian of Norwich, practitioners supreme in their art, regardless of sex or period. It is necessary to discriminate.

The timescale of this history extends from the time when English writing begins, before the year 680, to the present day, though the literary history of the last thirty years can only be provisional. The first known poet in English was not Geoffrey Chaucer, who died in 1400, but Cædmon, who died before 700. A one-volume history of so large a territory is not a survey but a series of maps and projections. These projections, however clear, do not tell the whole story. Authors have to be selected, and their chief works chosen. If the discussion is to get beyond critical preliminaries, authors as great as Jonathan Swift may be represented by a single book. Half of Shakespeare's plays go undiscussed here, though comedy, history and tragedy are sampled. Readers who use this history as a textbook should remember that it is selective.

## Language change

As literature is written language, the state of the language always matters. There were four centuries of English literature before the Anglo-Saxon kingdom fell to the Normans. Dethroned, English was still written. It emerged again in the 12th and

13th centuries, gaining parity with French and Latin in Geoffrey Chaucer's day. With the 16th-century Reformation, and a Church of England for the new Tudor nation-state, English drew ahead of Latin for most purposes. English Renaissance literature became consciously patriotic. John Milton, who wrote verse in Latin, Greek and Italian as well as English, held that God spoke first to his Englishmen.

English literature is the literature of the English as well as literature in English. Yet Milton wrote the official justification of the execution of King Charles I in the language of serious European communication, Latin. Dr Johnson wrote verse in Latin as well as English. But by Johnson's death in 1784, British expansion had taken English round the world. Educated subjects of Queen Victoria could read classical and other modern languages. Yet by the year 2000, as English became the world's business language, most educated English and Americans read English only.

## Other literatures in English

Since – at latest – the death of Henry James in 1916, Americans have not wished their literature to be treated as part of the history of English literature. Walt Whitman and Emily Dickinson are not English poets. For reasons of national identity, other ex-colonies feel the same. There are gains and losses here. The English have contributed rather a lot to literature in English, yet a national history of English writing, as this now has to be, is only part of the story. Other literatures in English, though they have more than language in common with English writing, have their own histories. So it is that naturalized British subjects such as the Pole Joseph Conrad are in histories of English literature, but non-Brits are not. Now that English is a world language, this history needs to be supplemented by accounts of other literatures in English, and by comparative accounts of the kind magnificently if airily attempted by Ford Madox Ford, who called himself 'an old man mad about writing', in his *The March of Literature: From Confucius to Modern Times* (1938).

The exclusion of non-Brits, though unavoidable, is a pity – or so it seems to one who studied English at a time when the nationality of Henry James or James Joyce was a minor consideration. In Britain today, multi-cultural considerations influence any first-year syllabus angled towards the contemporary. This volume, however, is not a survey of present-day writing in English, but a history of English literature. The author, an Englishman resident in Scotland for over thirty years, is aware that a well-meant English embrace can seem imperial even within a devolving Britain.

The adoption of a national criterion, however unavoidable, presents difficulties. Since the coming of an Irish Free State in 1922, Irish writers have not been British, unless born in Northern Ireland. But Irish writing in English before 1922 is eligible: Swift, Berkeley, Sterne, Goldsmith, Burke, Edgeworth, Yeats and Joyce; not to mention drama. There are hard cases: the Anglo-Irish Samuel Beckett, asked by a French journalist if he was English, replied '*Au contraire*'. Born near Dublin in 1906, when Ireland was ruled from Westminster, Beckett is eligible, and as his influence changed English drama, he is in. So is another winner of the Nobel Prize for Literature, Seamus Heaney, though he has long been a citizen of the Republic of Ireland, and, when included in an anthology with 'British' in its title, protested: 'be advised/My passport's green./No glass of ours was ever raised/To toast *The Queen*'. Born in 1939 in Northern Ireland, he was educated at a Catholic school in that part of the United Kingdom and at Queen's University, Belfast.

Writing *read* in Britain today becomes ever more international, but it would have been wholly inconsistent to abandon a national criterion after an arbitrary date such as 1970. So the Bombay-born British citizen Salman Rushdie is eligible; the Indian Vikram Seth is not. Writing in English from the United States and other former colonies is excluded. A very few non-English writers who played a part in English literature – such as Sir Walter Scott, a Scot who was British but not English – are included; some marginal cases are acknowledged. Few authors can be given any fullness of attention, and fewer books, although the major works of major authors should find mention here. Literary merit has been followed, at the risk of upsetting partisans.

## Is drama literature?

Drama is awkward: part theatre, part literature. Part belongs to theatre history, part to literary history. I have rendered unto Cæsar those things which are Cæsar's. Plays live in performance, a point often lost on those whose reading of plays is confined to those of Shakespeare, which read unusually well. In most drama words are a crucial element, but so too are plot, actors, movement, gesture, stage, staging and so on. In some plays, words play only a small part. Likewise, in poetic drama not every line has evident literary quality. King Lear says in his last scene: 'Pray you undo that button.' The request prompts an action; the button undone, Lear says 'Thank you, sir.' Eight words create three gestures of dramatic moment. The words are right, but their power comes from the actions they are part of, and from the play as a whole.

Only the literary part of drama, then, appears here. It is a part which diminishes, for the literary component in English drama declines after Shakespeare. The only 18th-century plays read today are in prose; they have plot and wit. In the 19th century, theatre was entertainment, and poetic drama was altogether too poetic. The English take pride in Shakespeare and pleasure in the stage, yet after 1660 the best drama in the English tongue is by Irishmen: Congreve, Goldsmith, Sheridan, Shaw, Wilde and Beckett.

## Qualities and quantities

'The best is the enemy of the good,' said Voltaire. As the quantity of literature increases with the centuries, the criterion of quality becomes more pressing. Scholarly literary history, however exact its method, deals largely in accepted valuations. Voltaire also said that ancient history is no more than an accepted fiction. Literary histories of the earliest English writing agree that the poetry is better than the prose, and discuss much the same poems. Later it is more complicated, but not essentially different. Such agreements should be challenged, corrected and supplemented, but not silently disregarded. In this sense, literary history is critical-consensual, deriving from what Johnson called 'the common pursuit of true judgement'. A literary historian who thought that Spenser, Dryden, Scott or Eliot (George or T. S.) were overrated could not omit them: the scope for personal opinion is limited.

The priorities of a history can sometimes be deduced from its allocation of space. Yet space has also to be given to the historically symptomatic. Thus, Thomas Gray's *Elegy written in a Country Churchyard* (1750) is treated at length because it shows a century turning from the general to the personal. This does not mean that the *Elegy* is worth more than the whole of Old English prose or of Jacobean drama, which are summarily treated, or than travel writing, which is not treated at all. Space is given to Chaucer and Milton, poets whose greatness is historical as well as personal. Where there is no agreement (as about Blake's later poetry), or where a personal view is offered, this is made clear.

## Texts

The best available texts are followed. These may not be the last text approved by the author. Line references are not given, for editions change. Some titles, such as *Shake-speares Sonnets*, and Dryden's *Mac Flecknoe*, keep their original forms; and some texts are unmodernized. But most are modernized in spelling and repunctuated by their editors. Variety in edited texts is unavoidable, for well-edited texts can be edited on principles which differ widely. This inconsistency is a good thing, and should be embraced as positively instructive.

# Further reading

### Primary texts

Blackwell's Anthologies of Verse.

Longman's Annotated Anthologies of Verse.

Penguin English Poets, and Penguin Classics as a whole.

Oxford Books of Verse.

Oxford and Cambridge editions of Shakespeare.

Oxford University Press's World's Classics.

### Secondary texts

Drabble, M. (ed.). *The Oxford Companion to English Literature*, revd edn (Oxford: Oxford University Press, 1998). The standard work of reference.

Rogers, P. (ed.). *The Oxford Illustrated History of English Literature* (Oxford: Oxford University Press, 1987; paperback, 1990). Well designed; each chapter is by an expert scholar.

Jeffares, A. N. (general ed.). *The Macmillan History of English Literature* (1982–5) covers English literature in 8 volumes. Other volumes cover Scottish, Anglo-Irish, American and other literatures.

*The Cambridge Companions to Literature* (1986–). Well edited. Each *Companion* has specially-written essays by leading scholars on several later periods and authors from Old English literature onwards.

PART
I

# Medieval

• • • • • • • •

# Old English Literature: to 1100

# CHAPTER 1

## Overview

The Angles and Saxons conquered what is now called England in the 5th and 6th centuries. In the 7th century, Christian missionaries taught the English to write. The English wrote down law-codes, and later their poems. Northumbria soon produced Cædmon and Bede. Heroic poetry, of a Christian kind, is the chief legacy of Old English literature, notably *Beowulf* and the Elegies. A considerable prose literature grew up after Alfred (d.899). There were four centuries of writing in English before the Norman Conquest.

## Contents

## Orientations

### Britain, England, English

> the cliffs of England stand
> Glimmering and vast, out in the tranquil bay.
>
> Matthew Arnold, 'Dover Beach' (*c*.1851)

The cliffs at Dover were often the first of Britain seen by early incomers, and have become a familiar symbol of England, and of the fact that England is on an island. These cliffs are part of what the Romans, from as early as the 2nd century, had called the Saxon Shore: the south-eastern shores of Britain, often raided by Saxons. The Romans left Britain, after four centuries of occupation, early in the 5th century. Later in that century the Angles and Saxons took over the lion's share of the island of Britain. By 700, they had occupied the parts of Great Britain which the Romans had made part of their empire. This part later became known as *Engla-land*, the land of the Angles, and its language was to become English.

It is not always recognized, especially outside Britain, that Britain and England are not the same thing. Thus, Shakespeare's *King Lear* ends by the cliff and beach at Dover. But Lear was king not of England but of Britain, in that legendary period of its history when it was pre-Christian and pre-English. The English Romantic poet William Blake was thinking of the legendary origins of his country when he asked in his 'Jerusalem'

**St Bede** (676–735) Monk of Wearmouth and Jarrow, scholar, biblical commentator, historian.

> And did those feet in ancient time
>     Walk upon England's mountains green?
> And was the holy Lamb of God
>     On England's pleasant pastures seen?

Blake here recalls the ancient legend that Jesus came with Joseph of Arimathea to Glastonbury, in Somerset. One answer to his wondering question would be: 'No, on Britain's.'

Literature is written language. Human settlement, in Britain as elsewhere, preceded recorded history by some millennia, and English poetry preceded writing by some generations. The first poems that could conceivably be called 'English' were the songs that might have been heard from the boats crossing the narrow seas to the 'Saxon Shore' to conquer Britannia. 'Thus sung they in the English boat', Andrew Marvell was to write.

The people eventually called the English were once separate peoples: Angles, Saxons and Jutes. **St Bede** recounts in his Latin *Historia Ecclesiastica Gentis Anglorum* (*Ecclesiastical History of the English People*, 731) that the Jutes were invited into Kent in 449 to save the British kingdom from the Saxons and Picts. The Jutes liked what they saw, and by about 600 the lion's share of Britannia had fallen to them, and to Saxons and Angles. The Celtic Britons who did not accept this went west, to Cornwall and Wales. The new masters of Britain spoke a Germanic language, in which 'Wales' is a word for 'foreigners'. Other Britons, says Bede, lived beyond the northern moors, in what is now Strathclyde, and beyond them lived the Picts, in northern and eastern Scotland. English was first written about the year 600 when King Æthelred of Kent was persuaded by St Augustine of Canterbury that he needed a written law-code; it was written with the Roman alphabet.

The coming of the Angles, Saxons and Jutes in the 5th, 6th and 7th centuries

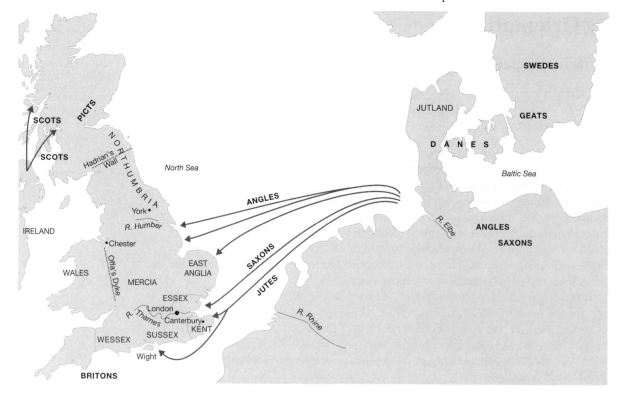

The peoples to be called the English lived in a mosaic of small tribal kingdoms, which gradually amalgamated. The threat of Danish conquest began to unify a nation under King Alfred of Wessex (d.899). Under his successors, *Angel-cynn* (the English people and their territory) became *Engla-lond*, the land of the English, and finally England. English literature, which had flourished for four centuries, was dethroned at the Norman Conquest in 1066, and for some generations it was not well recorded.

After 1066 the English wrote in Latin, as they had done before the Conquest, but now also in French. English continued to be written in places like Medehamstead Abbey (modern Peterborough), where the monks kept up *The Anglo-Saxon Chronicle* until 1152. Not very much English writing survives from the hundred years following the Conquest, but changes in the language of the Peterborough *Chronicle* indicate a new phase. 'Anglo-Saxon' (AS) is a Renaissance Latin term, used to designate both the people and the language of pre-Conquest England. The modern academic convention of calling the people Anglo-Saxons and their language **Old English** should not detract from the point that the people were English, and that their literature is English literature.

Linguistically and historically, the English poems composed by Cædmon after 670 and Bede (673–735) are the earliest we know of. Manuscripts (MSS) of their works became hard to read, and were little read between the Middle Ages and the reign of Queen Victoria, when they were properly published. Only then could they take their place in English literary history. Old English is now well understood, but looks so different from the English of today that it cannot be read or made out by a well-educated reader in the way that the writings of Shakespeare and Chaucer can: it has to be learned. Linguistically, the relationship between the English of AD 1000 and that of AD 2000 might be compared to that between Latin and modern French. Culturally, the English of 1000 had none of the authority of Latin.

In terms of literary quality – which is the admission ticket for discussion in this history – the best early English poems can compare with anything from later periods. Literature changes and develops, it does not improve. The supreme achievement of Greek literature comes at the beginning, with the *Iliad* of **Homer** (8th century BC); and that of Italian literature, the *Commedia* of Dante (d.1321), comes very early. Any idea that Old English poetry will be of historical interest only does not survive the experience of reading Old English poetry in the original – though this takes study – or even in some translations.

Old English literature is part of English literature, and some of it deserves discussion here on literary merit. Besides merit, it needed luck, the luck to be committed to writing, and to survive. The Angles, the Saxons and the Jutes were illiterate: their orally-composed verses were not written unless they formed part of **runic** inscriptions. The Britons passed on neither literacy nor faith to their conquerors. The English learned to write only after they had been converted to Christ by missionaries sent from Rome in 597. Strictly, there is no Old English writing that is not Christian, since the only literates were clerics.

## Oral origins and conversion

It would be a mistake to think that oral poetry would be inartistic. The Germanic oral poetry which survives from the end of the Roman Empire, found in writings from Austria to Iceland, has a common form, technique and formulaic repertoire.

**Old English** Historical linguists speak of *Old English* (OE), 450–1100; *Middle English* (ME), 1100–1500; and *Modern English,* after 1500.

**Homer** (8th century BC) The author of two magnificent verse epics: *The Iliad,* about the siege of Troy and the anger of Achilles; and *The Odyssey,* about the adventures of Odysseus as he makes his way home from Troy to Ithaca.

**runes** A Germanic alphabetic secret writing. Runic letters have straight lines, which are easier to cut. See Franks Casket.

Places of interest in Old and Middle English Literature

Oral poetry was an art which had evolved over generations: an art of memorable speech. It dealt with a set of heroic and narrative themes in a common metrical form, and had evolved to a point where its audience appreciated a richly varied style and storytelling technique. In these technical respects, as well as in its heroic preoccupations, the first English poetry resembles Homeric poetry. As written versions of compositions that were originally oral, these poems are of the same kind as the poems of Homer, albeit less monumental and less central to later literature.

Just as the orally-composed poetry of the Anglo-Saxons was an established art, so the Roman missionaries were highly literate. Bede's *Ecclesiastical History of the English People* makes it clear that the evangelists sent by Pope Gregory (in 597) to bring the gospel (*godspel*, 'good news') to the Angles were an élite group. Augustine was sent from Gregory's own monastery in Rome. His most influential successor, Theodore

(Archbishop from 664), was a Syrian Greek from Tarsus, who in twenty-six years at Canterbury organized the Church in England, and made it a learned Church. His chief helper Hadrian came from Roman Africa. Theodore sent Benedict Biscop to Northumbria to found the monastic communities of Wearmouth (674) and Jarrow (681). Benedict built these monasteries and visited Rome six times, furnishing them with the magnificent library which made Bede's learning possible. Throughout the Anglo-Saxon period, clerics from Ireland and England travelled through western Europe, protected by the tonsure which marked them as consecrated members of a supranational church with little regard to national jurisdictions.

English literature, as already noted, is both literature in English and the literature of England. In the 16th century, England became a state with its own national church. Before this, English was not always the most important of the languages spoken by the educated, and loyalty went to the local lord and church rather than to the state. Art historians use the term 'Insular' to characterize British art of this period. Insular art, the art of the islands, is distinctive, but of mixed origins: Celtic, Mediterranean and Germanic. The blended quality of early English art holds true for the culture as a whole: it is an Anglo-Celtic-Roman culture.

This hybrid culture found literary expression in an unmixed language. Although Britannia was now their home, the English took few words from the languages of Roman Britain; among the exceptions are the Celtic names for rivers, such as Avon, Dee and Severn, and the Roman words 'wall' (*vallum*) and 'street' (*strata*). Arriving as the Roman Empire faded, the Saxons did not have to exchange their Germanic tongue for Latin, unlike their cousins the Franks, but Latin was the language of those who taught them to read and write. As they completed their conquest of Britain, the Saxons were transformed by their conversion to Catholicism. Gregory's mission rejoined Britain to the Judaeo-Christian world of the Latin West.

## Aldhelm, Bede, Cædmon

Although Cædmon is the first English poet whose words survive at all, the first known English poet is **Aldhelm** (*c*.640–709). King Alfred thought Aldhelm unequalled in any age in his ability to compose poetry in his native tongue. There is a tradition that Aldhelm stood on a bridge leading to Malmesbury, improvising English verses to the harp in order to attract his straying flock. Aldhelm's English verse is lost; his surviving Latin writings are exceedingly sophisticated.

Aldhelm (*c*.640–709), the monastic founder of Malmesbury, Frome and Bradford-on-Avon, was the star pupil of Hadrian's school at Canterbury, and became Bishop of Sherborne. His younger contemporary Bede wrote that Aldhelm was 'most learned in all respects, for he had a brilliant style, and was remarkable for both sacred and liberal erudition'. Aldhelm's brilliance is painfully clear, even through the dark glass of translation, as he reproaches an Englishman who has gone to Ireland:

The fields of Ireland are rich and green with learners, and with numerous readers, grazing there like flocks, even as the pivots of the poles are brilliant with the starry quivering of the shining constellations. Yet Britain, placed, if you like, almost at the extreme edge of the Western clime, has also its flaming sun and its lucid moon …

Britain has, he explains, Theodore and Hadrian. Aldhelm wrote sermons in verse, and a treatise in verse for a convent of nuns, on Virginity. He also wrote an epistle to his godson, King Aldfrith of Northumbria, on metrics, which is full of riddles and

## Dates of early writings and chief events

| Date | Author and title | Event |
| --- | --- | --- |
| AD 43 | | Conquest of Britain by Emperor Claudius |
| 98 | Tacitus: *Germania* | |
| 313 | | Toleration of Christians |
| 314 | | Council of Arles |
| 330 | | Constantinople founded |
| | | St Helena finds True Cross |
| 384 | St Jerome: Vulgate edition of the Bible | |
| 410 | | Legions recalled from Britain |
| 413 | St Augustine of Hippo: *The City of God* | |
| 417 | Orosius: *History of the World* | |
| 430 | | St Patrick in Ireland |
| | | St Ninian in N. Britain |
| **449** | | **Hengest** and Horsa: Conquest by Angles, Saxons and Jutes begins |
| *c.*500 | | British resistance: Battle of Mons Badonicus; St David in Wales |
| *c.*521 | | Hygelac the Geat (d.) |
| 524 | Boethius: *Consolation of Philosophy* | |
| 529 | | St Benedict founds Monte Cassino |
| | | Legendary reign of Beowulf |
| *c.*547 | Gildas: *Conquest of Britain* | |
| 563 | Venantius Fortunatus: Hymns of the Cross | St Columba on Iona |
| 577 | | Battle of Dyrham: British confined to Wales and Dumnonia |
| 591 | Gregory of Tours: *History of the Franks* | |
| **597** | Aneirin: *Y Gododdin* | **Gregory sends Augustine to Canterbury** |
| | | St Columba (d.) |
| *c.*615 | | Aethelfrith King of Bernicia defeats Britons at Chester |
| 616–32 | | Edwin King of Northumbria |
| 627 | | Edwin converted by Paulinus |
| 632 | | (?) Sutton Hoo ship burial |
| 635 | | Oswald King of Northumbria defeats Cadwallon at Heavenfield |
| 643 | From this date: early heroic poems: *Widsith, Deor, Finnsburh, Waldere* | Mercia converted |
| 664 | | Synod of Whitby accepts authority of Rome |
| 657–80 | Cædmon's *Hymn* | Hilda Abbess of Whitby |
| | Cædmonian poems: *Genesis A, Daniel, Christ and Satan* | |
| **669–90** | | **Theodore of Tarsus** Archbishop of Canterbury; Wearmouth and Jarrow founded |
| 678 | Earliest date for composition of *Beowulf* | |
| 688 | (?) *Exodus* | |

## Dates of early writings and chief events *Continued*

| Date | Author and title | Event |
|---|---|---|
| 698 | Eadfrith: *Lindisfarne Gospels* | |
| | First linguistic records | |
| | Ruthwell Cross | |
| **731** | **Bede**: *Historia Ecclesiastica Gentis Anglorum* | |
| 756–96 | | Offa King of Mercia |
| 782 | (?) The Poetic Elegies | Alcuin at Charlemagne's court |
| 793 | | Vikings sack Lindisfarne |
| 800 | After this date: Cynewulf: *Christ II*, *Elene*, *Juliana*, *Fates of the Apostles* | Charlemagne crowned Emperor |
| 802 | | Egbert King of Wessex |
| 851 | (?) *Genesis B* | Danes spend winter in England |
| 865 | | Danish army in East Anglia |
| **871–99** | (?) *Andreas* | **Alfred** King of Wessex, the only kingdom unconquered by Danes |
| 878 | Alfredian translations: *Pastoral Care*, *Ecclesiastical History*, Orosius, Boethius, *Soliloquies*; *Anglo-Saxon Chronicle* begun | Alfred at Athelney<br>Defeat of the Danes: Treaty of Wedmore |
| 909 | (?) *Beowulf* composed by this date | |
| 910 | | Abbey of Cluny founded (Burgundy) |
| 911–18 | (?) *Judith* | |
| 919 | (?) *The Phoenix* | Mercia subject to Wessex |
| 924–39 | | Athelstan King of Wessex |
| 937 | *Brunanburh* in *Anglo-Saxon Chronicle* | Battle of Brunanburh: Athelstan defeats Scots and Vikings |
| 954 | | End of Scandinavian kingdom of York: England united under Wessex |
| 959–75 | | Reign of Edgar |
| **960–88** | Monastic revival | **Dunstan** Archbishop of Canterbury |
| 973 | | Coronation of Edgar |
| 978–1016 | The major poetry manuscripts: Junius Book, Vercelli Book, Exeter Book, *Beowulf* MS | Reign of Ethelred II |
| 991 | After this date *The Battle of Maldon* | Battle of Maldon |
| **990–2** | **Aelfric**: *Catholic Homilies* | |
| 993–8 | Aelfric: *Lives of the Saints* | |
| 1003–23 | | Wulfstan Archbishop of York |
| 1014 | Wulfstan: *Sermo Lupi Ad Anglos* | Swein of Denmark king of England |
| 1017–35 | | Reign of Cnut |
| 1043–66 | | Reign of Edward the Confessor |
| **1066** | | Harold king |
| | | Battle of Stamford Bridge |
| | | **Battle of Hastings** |
| | | William I king |
| 1154 | End of Peterborough *Chronicle* | |

word games. Even if Aldfrith and the nuns may not have appreciated Aldhelm's style, it is clear that 7th-century England was not unlettered.

More care was taken to preserve writings in Latin than in English. Bede's Latin works survive in many copies: thirty-six complete manuscripts of his prose *Life of St Cuthbert*, over one hundred of his *De Natura Rerum*. At the end of his *Historia Ecclesiastica Gentis Anglorum* Bede lists his ninety Latin works. Of his English writings in prose and in verse, only five lines remain. As Ascension Day approached in 735, Bede was dictating a translation of the Gospel of St John into English, and he finished it on the day he died. Even this precious text is lost. On his deathbed, Bede sang the verse of St Paul (Hebrews 10:31) that tells of the fearfulness of falling into the hands of the living God. He then composed and sang his 'Death Song'. This is a Northumbrian version:

> Fore thaem neidfaerae    naenig uuirthit
> thoncsnotturra,    than him tharf sie
> to ymbhycggannae    aer his hiniongae
> hwaet his gastae    godaes aeththae yflaes
> aefter deothdaege    doemid uueorthae.

Literally: Before that inevitable journey no one becomes wiser in thought than he needs to be, in considering, before his departure, what will be adjudged to his soul, of good or evil, after his death-day.

The 'Death Song' is one of the rare vernacular poems extant in several copies. Its laconic formulation is characteristic of Anglo-Saxon.

Bede is one of the five early English poets whose names are known: Aldhelm, Bede, Cædmon, Alfred – two saints, a cowman and a king – and Cynewulf, who signed his poems but is otherwise unknown. Oral composition was not meant to be written. A poem was a social act, like telling a story today, not a thing which belonged to its performer. For a Saxon to write down his vernacular poems would be like having personal anecdotes privately printed, whereas to write Latin was to participate in the lasting conversation of learned Europe. Bede's works survive in manuscripts across Europe and in Russia. The modern way of dating years AD – Anno Domini, 'the Year of Our Lord' – was established, if not devised, by Bede. Bede employed this system in his *History*, instead of dating by the regnal years peculiar to each English kingdom as was the custom at the time. His example led to its general adoption. Bede is the only English writer mentioned by Dante, and the first whose works have been read in every generation since they were written. The first writer of whom this is true is Chaucer.

English literature is literature in English; all that is discussed here of Bede's Latin *History* is its account of Cædmon. But we can learn something about literature from the account of the final acts of Bede, a professional writer. This shows that composing came before writing: Bede composed and sang his 'Death Song' *after* singing the verse of St Paul upon which it was based. Composition was not origination but re-creation: handing-on, performance. These features of composition lasted through the Middle Ages, and beyond.

**Cædmon** was the first to use English oral composition to turn sacred story into verse; the English liked verse. Bede presents the calling of this unlearned man to compose biblical poetry as a miraculous means for bringing the good news to the English. He tells us that Cædmon was a farmhand at the abbey at Whitby, which was presided over by St Hilda (d.680), an old man ignorant of poetry. At feasts when all in turn were invited to compose verses to the harp and entertain the company, Cædmon,

when he saw the harp coming his way, would get up from table and go home. On one such occasion he left the house where the feast was being held, and went out to the stable where it was his duty that night to look after the beasts. There when the time came he settled down to sleep. Suddenly in a dream he saw a certain man standing beside him who called him by name. 'Cædmon', he said, 'sing me a song.' 'I don't know how to sing,' he replied. 'It was because I cannot sing that I left the feast and came here.' The man who addressed him then said: 'But you shall sing to me.' 'What should I sing about?' he replied. 'Sing about the Creation of all things,' the other answered. And Cædmon immediately began to sing verses in praise of God the Creator that he had never heard before, and their theme ran thus.

Bede gives Cædmon's song in Latin, adding 'This the general sense, but not the actual words that Cædmon sang in his dream; for verses, however masterly, cannot be translated word for word from one language into another without losing much of their beauty and dignity.' The old man remembered what he had sung and added more in the same style. Next day the monks told him about a passage of scriptural history or doctrine, and he turned this overnight into excellent verses. He sang of the Creation, *Genesis*, and of Exodus and other stories of biblical history, including the Incarnation, the Passion, the Resurrection, the Ascension, Pentecost and the teaching of the apostles, and many other religious songs. The monks surely wrote all this down, though Bede says only that 'his delightful renderings turned his instructors into auditors'.

In 1655 the Dutch scholar Junius published in Amsterdam 'The monk Cædmon's paraphrase of Genesis etc.', based on a handsome Old English manuscript containing *Genesis*, *Exodus*, *Daniel* and *Christ and Satan*. The poems are probably not by Cædmon, but follow his example. John Milton knew Junius and read Old English, so the author of *Paradise Lost* could have read *Genesis*. He calls Bede's account of the calling of the first English poet *perplacida historiola*, 'a most pleasing little story'.

In the margins of several of the 160 complete Latin manuscripts of Bede's *Ecclesiastical History* are Old English versions of 'Cædmon's Hymn', differing in dialect and in detail, as usual in medieval manuscripts. Their relation to what Cædmon sang is unknown. Here is my own translation.

> Praise now to the keeper of the kingdom of heaven,
> The power of the Creator, the profound mind
> Of the glorious Father, who fashioned the beginning
> Of every wonder, the eternal Lord.
> For the children of men he made first
> Heaven as a roof, the holy Creator.
> Then the Lord of mankind, the everlasting Shepherd,
> Ordained in the midst as a dwelling place
> – The almighty Lord – the earth for men.

English is a stressed language, and the Old English verse line is a balance of two-stress phrases linked by **alliteration**: the first or second stress, or both, must alliterate with the third; the fourth must not. Old English verse is printed with a mid-line space to point the metre. Free oral improvisation in a set form requires a repertory of formulaic units. The style is rich in formulas, often noun-phrases. Thus in the nine lines of his 'Hymn' Cædmon has six different formulas for God, a feature known as variation. The image of heaven as a roof and of the Lord as protector is characteristically Anglo-Saxon.

**alliteration** The linking of words by use of the same initial letter. In Old English verse, all vowels alliterate.

## Northumbria and *The Dream of the Rood*

Many of the manuscripts which perished in the 1530s in Henry VIII's destruction of the monasteries (see Chapter 3) may have been in Old English. About 30,000 lines of Old English verse survive, in four main poetry manuscripts. These were written about the year 1000, but contain earlier material. Much is lost, but three identifiable phases of Old English literature are the Northumbria of the age of Bede (d.735), the programme of Alfred (d.899), and the Benedictine Revival of the late 10th century.

The artistic wealth of Northumbria is known to us through Bede, but also through surviving illuminated books such as the Lindisfarne Gospels and the Codex Amiatinus, and some fine churches, crosses and religious art. The Ruthwell Cross is from this period: in 1642 this high stone cross near Dumfries, in Scotland, was smashed as idolatrous by order of the General Assembly of the Kirk of Scotland. In 1823, however, the minister reassembled and re-erected it, and it now stands 5.7 metres tall. It was an open-air cross or rood, covered with panels in deep relief showing scenes from the life of Christ, each with an inscription in Latin. On it is also carved in runic characters a poem which in a longer MS. version is known as *The Dream of the Rood*. This longer text in the Vercelli Book (*c*.1000) has 156 lines. The Ruthwell text, which once ran to about 50 lines, is itself a great poem. If carved *c*.700, it may be the first substantial English verse to survive.

The Dreamer in the poem sees at midnight a glorious cross rise to fill the sky, worshipped by all of creation. It is covered with gold and jewels, but at other times covered with blood. The Dreamer continues:

> Yet lying there a long while
> I beheld, sorrowing, the Healer's Tree
> Till it seemed that I heard how it broke silence,
> Best of wood, and began to speak:
> 'Over that long remove my mind ranges
> Back to the holt where I was hewn down;
> From my own stem I was struck away,
>     dragged off by strong enemies,
>
> Wrought into a roadside scaffold.
>     They made me a hoist for wrongdoers.
> The soldiers on their shoulders bore me
>     until on a hill-top they set me up;
> Many enemies made me fast there.
>     Then I saw, marching toward me,
> Mankind's brave King;
>     He came to climb upon me.
> I dared not break or bend aside
> Against God's will, though the ground itself
> Shook at my feet. Fast I stood,
> Who falling could have felled them all.
>
> Almighty God ungirded Him,
>     eager to mount the gallows,
> Unafraid in the sight of many:
>     He would set free mankind.
> I shook when His arms embraced me
>     but I durst not bow to ground,
> Stoop to Earth's surface.
>     Stand fast I must.

I was reared up, a rood.
>I raised the great King,
Liege lord of the heavens,
>dared not lean from the true.
They drove me through with dark nails:
>on me are the deep wounds manifest,
Wide-mouthed hate-dents.
>I durst not harm any of them.
How they mocked at us both!
>I was all moist with blood
Sprung from the Man's side
>after He sent forth His soul …

These last lines appear on the Rood at Ruthwell. The Ruthwell Cross is an expression of the veneration of the Cross which spread through Christendom from the 4th century. Constantine had been granted a vision of the cross, which told him that in that sign he would conquer. Victorious, the new emperor declared toleration for Christianity, and built a basilica of the Holy Sepulchre on Mt Calvary. In excavating for the foundations, fragments of what was believed to be the Cross of the crucifixion were discovered, and miraculous cures were attributed to it. The emperor's mother Helena was later associated with this finding of the Cross. Encased in reliquaries of gold and silver, fragments of the Cross were venerated all over Europe. One fragment was presented by the Pope to King Alfred, and is now in the 10th-century Brussels Reliquary, which is inscribed with a verse from *The Dream of the Rood*.

In warrior culture, it was the duty of a man to stand by his lord and die in his defence. But the lord in *The Dream* is an Anglo-Saxon hero, keen to join battle with death. The cross is the uncomprehending but obedient participant in its lord's

'Carpet' page from the Lindisfarne Gospels, a Latin Gospel Book (see page 20), written and painted on vellum by Eadfrith in 698, who became Bishop at Lindisfarne, founded indirectly from the Irish monastery on Iona. The 'carpet' design of the Cross may have come to Ireland from Egypt. The close detail is in the Insular style of inlaid metalwork, a Celtic/Mediterranean/Anglo-Saxon blend.

death: 'Stand fast I must.' The cross yields his lord's body to his human followers, who bury him. The three crosses are also buried. But 'the Lord's friends learnt of it: it was they who girt me with gold and silver.' In a devotional conclusion, the cross explains that it is now honoured as a sign of salvation, and commands the dreamer to tell men the Christian news of the Second Coming, when those who live under the sign of the cross will be saved.

The poem exemplifies both the tradition of the vision, in which a bewildered dreamer is led from confusion to understanding, and the medieval 'work of affective devotion', affecting the emotions and moving the audience from confusion to faith. It boldly adapts the Gospel accounts to the culture of the audience, employing the Old English riddle tradition, in which an object is made to speak, and telling the Crucifixion story from the viewpoint of the humble creature. The poem fills living cultural forms with a robust theology, redirecting the heroic code of loyalty and sacrifice from an earthly to a heavenly lord.

## Heroic poetry

Early literatures commonly look back to a 'heroic age': a period in the past when warriors were more heroic and kings were kings. The Christian heroism of *The Dream of the Rood* redirected the old pagan heroism which can be seen in fragments of Germanic heroic poetry. *Waldere*, an early poem, features the heroics of Walter's defence of a narrow place against his enemies. *Finnsburh*, another early poem set on the continent, is a vividly dramatic fragment of a fight in *Beowulf*. Such poems recall times before the Angles came to Britain in the 5th century, as do the minstrel poems *Widsith* and *Deor*. Widsith (meaning 'far-traveller') is the name of a *scop* (poet), who lists the names of continental tribes and their rulers, praising generous patrons. Deor is a *scop* who has lost his position; to console himself, he recalls famous instances of evil bringing forth good, and after each stanza sings the refrain *Þæs ofereode, thisses swa mæg*: 'That went by; this may too.' *Deor* is one of only three stanzaic poems. The first stanza goes:

> Wayland knew the wanderer's fate:
> That single-willed earl suffered agonies,
> Sorrow and longing the sole companions
> Of his ice-cold exile. Anxieties bit
> When Nithhad put a knife to his hamstrings,
> Laid clever bonds on the better man.
>
> That went by; this may too.

This story of the imprisonment of Wayland, the smith of the gods, has the (heathen) happy ending of successful multiple vengeance. The hamstrung Wayland later escaped, having killed his captor Nithhad's two sons and raped his daughter Beadohild; Beadohild bore the hero Widia, and was later reconciled with Wayland. A scene from this fierce legend is carved on an 8th-century Northumbrian whalebone box known as the Franks Casket: it shows Wayland offering Nithhad a drink from a bowl he had skilfully fashioned from the skull of one of Nithhad's sons; in the background is a pregnant Beadohild. Little of the unbaptized matter of Germania survives in English. The Franks Casket juxtaposes pagan and Christian pregnancies: the next panel to Wayland, Nithhad and Beadohild shows the Magi visiting Mary and her child.

Although English writing came with Christianity, not everything that was written was wholly Christian. Pope Gregory, according to the story in Bede, saw some fair-

The front of the Franks Casket, a small carved whalebone box given by Sir A. Franks to the British Museum. Runic inscription: 'This is whale bone. The sea cast up the fish on the rocky shore. The ocean was troubled where he swam aground onto the shingle.' For a key to the lower panels, see page 22. Left, adoration of the Magi; right, Wayland.

haired boys for sale in the Roman slave market: on hearing that they were Angles and heathen, he sent Augustine to convert the Angles, to change them so that, in a famous papal wordplay, the Angles would become worthy to share the joys of the angels. Cædmon converted the traditional praise of heroism performed by poets such as Widsith and Deor to spreading the Gospel. But so strongly heroic was the poetic repertoire that the Angles at times seem to translate the Gospel back into heroic terms, as *The Dream of the Rood* had, but without reconceiving heroism. Here is the opening of *Andreas* in the translation of C. W. Kennedy:

> Lo! We have heard of twelve mighty heroes
> Honoured under heaven in days of old,
> Thanes of God. Their glory failed not
> In the clash of banners, the brunt of war,
> After they were scattered and spread abroad
> As their lots were cast by the Lord of heaven.

Eleven of the twelve heroic apostles were martyred – St Andrew by Mermedonian cannibals, according to *Andreas*, the Acts of the apostle Andrew. Much Old English prose and verse is given to the Saint's Life, a genre popular with Anglo-Saxons of AD 1000. Miraculous, sensational and moralistic stories still abound today in daily newspapers, although they rarely feature heroic Christians. Sophisticated pagans of Constantine's day expected miracles as much as simple Christians did.

Most of the official and popular writing of the medieval period is of interest to later generations for historical and cultural rather than literary reasons – as is true of most of the writing of any period.

## Christian literature

The dedicated Christian literature of Anglo-Saxon England is of various kinds. There are verse paraphrases of Old Testament stories, such as Cædmon's: *Genesis* and *Exodus*, *Daniel* and *Judith*. They emphasize faith rewarded. There are lives of saints such as Andrew or Helena; or the more historical lives of contemporaries such

**liturgy** (Gk) A religious service; the words for the prayers at a service.

as St Guthlac (an Anglian warrior who became a hermit), of Cuthbert of Lindisfarne, or of King Edmund (martyred by Danes). And there are sermons, wisdom literature, and doctrinal, penitential and devotional materials – such as *The Dream of the Rood*.

The New Testament is principally represented in translation and liturgical adaptation. Translation of the Bible into English did not begin in the 14th or the 16th centuries: the Gospels, Psalms and other books were translated into English throughout the Old English period; parts of several versions remain. The Bible was made known to the laity through the liturgical programme of prayers and readings at Mass through the cycle of the Christian year. The **liturgy** is the source of poems like *Christ*, and contributes to *The Dream of the Rood*. Modern drama was eventually to grow out of the worship of the Church, especially from re-enactments such as those of Passion Week. *Christ* is a poem in three parts also known as the *Advent Lyrics*, *Ascension* and *Doomsday*. The seventh of the lyrics based on the liturgy of Advent is *Eala ioseph min* ('O my Joseph'), in which Mary asks Joseph why he rejects her. He replies with delicacy and pathos:

> 'I suddenly am
> Deeply disturbed, despoiled of honour,
> For I have for you heard many words,
> Many great sorrows and hurtful speeches,
> Much harm, and to me they speak insult,
> Many hostile words. Tears I must
> Shed, sad in mind. God easily may
> Relieve the inner pain of my heart,
> Comfort the wretched one. O young girl,
> Mary the virgin!'

It is from liturgical adaptations like this that the drama developed.

Parts 2 and 3 of *Christ* are signed 'Cynewulf' in a runic acrostic. The approach is gentler than that in *Andreas*. *Ascension*, for example, is addressed to an unknown patron. Cynewulf begins:

> By the spirit of wisdom,    Illustrious One,
> With meditation    and discerning mind,
> Strive now earnestly    to understand,
> To comprehend,    how it came to pass
> When the Saviour was born    in purest birth
> (Who had sought a shelter    in Mary's womb,
> The Flower of virgins,    the Fairest of maids)
> That angels came not    clothed in white
> When the Lord was born,    a Babe in Bethlehem.
> Angels were seen there    who sang to the shepherds
> Songs of great gladness:    that the Son of God
> Was born upon earth    in Bethlehem.
> But the Scriptures tell not    in that glorious time
> That they came arrayed    in robes of white,
> As they later did    when the Mighty Lord,
> The Prince of Splendour,    summoned his thanes,
> The well-loved band,    to Bethany.

**Cynewulf**, an unknown cleric of the 9th century, is the only Old English poet to sign his poems.

Names and dates are almost wholly lacking for Old English verse. The four chief verse manuscripts are known as the Junius Book, the Exeter Book, the Vercelli Book and the *Beowulf* manuscript. Each is a compilation of copied and recopied works by different authors, and each is of unknown provenance. Though composed earlier, these manuscripts were written about the year 1000 during the Benedictine Revival, the period of the prose writers Ælfric and Wulfstan, and of a few late poems such as *Judith* and *The Battle of Maldon*. We turn now from the golden age of Northumbria, the lifetime of Bede (d.735), to the age of Alfred (d.899).

**Alfred** (d.899) King of Wessex from 871, who defended his kingdom against the Danes and translated wisdom books into English.

## Alfred

Bede and Ælfric were monks from boyhood, Cædmon was a farmhand. The life of **Alfred** casts an interesting light on literacy as well as on literature. The fourth son of the king of Wessex, he came to the West-Saxon throne in 871 when the Danes had overrun all the English kingdoms except his own. Though Danes had settled in east and north England, an area known as the Danelaw, the Danes whom Alfred defeated turned east and eventually settled in Normandy ('the land of the northmen'). Alfred wrote that when he came to the throne he could not think of a single priest south of the Thames who could understand a letter in Latin or translate one into English. Looking at the great learning that had been in the England of Bede, and at the Latin books which were now unread, the king used the image of a man who could see a trail but did not know how to follow it. Alfred was a great hunter, and the trail here is that left by a pen.

Riddle 26 in the Exeter Book elaborates what a book is made of:

> I am the scalp of myself, skinned by my foeman,
> Robbed of my strength, he steeped and soaked me,
> Dipped me in water, whipped me out again,
> Set me in the sun. I soon lost there
> The hairs I had had. The hard edge
> Of a keen-ground knife cuts me now,
> Fingers fold me, and a fowl's pride
> Drives its treasure trail across me,
> Bounds again over the brown rim,
> Sucks the wood-dye, steps again on me,
> Makes his black marks.

At the end the speaker asks the reader to guess his identity; the answer is a Gospel Book, made of calf-skin, prepared, cut and folded. The pen is a quill (a 'fowl's pride'); the ink, wood-dye. Writing is later described as driving a trail of 'successful drops'. And to read is to follow this trail to the quarry, wisdom. Reading is an art which Alfred mastered at the age of twelve; he began to learn Latin at thirty-five. Having saved his kingdom physically, Alfred set to saving its mind and soul. He decided to translate *sumæ bec, tha the niedbethearfosta sien eallum monnum to wiotonne* ('those books which be most needful for all men to know') into English; and to teach the freeborn sons of the laity to read them so that the quarry, wisdom, should again be pursued in Angelcynn, the kindred and country of the English.

Old English verse was an art older than its written form. Old English prose had been used to record laws, but in *The Anglo-Saxon Chronicle* for 757 we find evidence of narrative tradition in the story of Cynewulf and Cyneheard. In authorising versions of essential books from Latin into English prose, however, Alfred established English as a literary language. The books he had translated were Bede's *Ecclesiastical*

**Alfred's needful authors**
Alfred's wise authors were
Augustine (354–430), Orosius
(early 5th century), Boethius
(c.480–524), and Gregory
(c.540–604).

*History*, Orosius' *Histories*, Gregory's *Pastoral Care* and *Dialogues*, Augustine's *Soliloquies* and Boethius' *Consolation of Philosophy*, later to be translated by both Chaucer and Elizabeth I. Alfred also translated the Psalms. It was in his reign that *The Anglo-Saxon Chronicle (ASC)* began: the only vernacular history, apart from Irish annals, from so early a period in Europe. The early part draws on Bede; the West-Saxon *Chronicle* then records Alfred's resistance to the Danes. The *ASC* was kept up in several monastic centres until the Conquest, and at Peterborough until 1154. It used to be regarded as the most important work written in English before the Norman Conquest, a palm now given to *Beowulf*.

Here is the entry for the climactic year of the Danish campaign, written by a West-Saxon.

878  In this year in midwinter after twelfth night the enemy came stealthily to Chippenham, and occupied the land of the West Saxons and settled there, and drove a great part of the people across the sea, and conquered most of the others; and the people submitted to them, except the king, Alfred. He journeyed in difficulties through the woods and fen-fastnesses with a small force …

And afterwards at Easter, King Alfred with a small force made a stronghold at Athelney, and he and the section of the people of Somerset which was nearest to it proceeded to fight from that stronghold against the enemy. Then in the seventh week after Easter, he rode to 'Egbert's stone' east of Selwood, and there came to meet him all the people of Somerset and of Wiltshire and of that part of Hampshire which was on this side of the sea. And they rejoiced to see him. And then after one night he went from that encampment to Iley, and after another night to Edington, and there fought against the whole army and put it to flight …

Alfred stood sponsor at the baptism of the defeated King Guthrum at the treaty of Wedmore (878).

The Somerset marshes are also the scene of the story of Alfred hiding at the hut of an old woman, and allowing the cakes to burn while he was thinking about something else – how to save his country. Alfred's thoughtfulness is evident in his two famous Prefaces, to the *Pastoral Care* and the *Soliloquies*. His resolute and practical character was combined with a respect for wisdom and its rewards. Alfred added to his Boethius the following sentence: 'Without wisdom no faculty can be fully brought out: for whatever is done unwisely can never be accounted as skill.'

In his Preface to his later translation of the *Soliloquies* he seems to be looking back on his career as a translator when he writes:

Then I gathered for myself staves and posts and tie-beams, and handles for each of the tools I knew how to use, and building-timbers and beams and as much as I could carry of the most beautiful woods for each of the structures I knew how to build. I did not come home with a single load without wishing to bring home the whole forest with me, if I could have carried it all away; in every tree I saw something that I needed at home. Wherefore I advise each of those who is able, and has many waggons, to direct himself to the same forest where I cut these posts; let him fetch more there for himself, and load his waggons with fair branches so that he can weave many a neat wall and construct many an excellent building, and build a fair town, and dwell therein in joy and ease both winter and summer, as I have not done so far. But he who taught me, to whom the forest was pleasing, may bring it about that I dwell in greater ease both in this transitory wayside habitation while I am in this world, and also in that eternal home which he has promised us through St Augustine and St Gregory and St Jerome, and through many other holy fathers …

Alfred builds a habitation for his soul with wood taken from the forest of wisdom. In the next paragraph he asks the king of eternity, whose forest this is, to grant the soul a charter so that he may have it as a perpetual inheritance. The simple metaphysical confidence with which this metaphor is handled shows that Alfred's later reputation for wisdom was not unmerited. Later writers also call him *Englene hyrde, Englene deorlynge* ('shepherd of the English, darling of the English').

Alfred's educational programme for the laity did not succeed at first but bore fruit later in the Wessex of his grandson Edgar, who ruled 959–76. After the Ages of Bede and Alfred, this is the third clearly-defined Age of Anglo-Saxon literature, the Benedictine Revival, under Dunstan, Archbishop of Canterbury 960–88, himself a skilled artist. Bishop Æthelwold made Winchester a centre of manuscript illumination. In its profusion of manuscripts the Wessex of Dunstan, Æthelwold and Ælfric is better represented today than the more remarkable early Northumbria of Bede. In this period English prose became the instrument for a flourishing civilisation, with scientific, political and historical as well as religious interests. It was in this second Benedictine age, towards AD 1000, that the four poetry manuscripts were made: the Vercelli Book, the Junius Book, the Exeter Book and the *Beowulf* mansucript.

## Beowulf

Like Greek literature, English literature begins with an epic, a poem of historic scope telling of heroes and of the world, human and non-human. Compared with the epics of Homer, *Beowulf* is short, with 3182 verses, yet it is the longest as well as the richest of Old English poems. Like other epics, it has a style made for oral composition, rich in formulas. The poem is found in a manuscript of the late 10th century, but was composed perhaps two centuries earlier, and it is set in a world more than two centuries earlier still, on the coasts of the Baltic. This was the north-west Germanic world from which the English had come to Britain. The coming of the Saxons is recalled in a poem in the *ASC* for 937.

> ... from the east came
> Angles and Saxons up to these shores,
> Seeking Britain across the broad seas,
> Smart for glory, those smiths of war
> That overcame the Welsh, and won a homeland.

The first great work of English literature is not set in Britain. *Beowulf* opens with the mysterious figure of Scyld, founder of the Scylding dynasty of Denmark, who would have lived *c*.400, before England existed. A Hengest mentioned in a sub-story of the poem may be the Hengest invited into Kent in 449 (see page 13). The Offa who is mentioned may be an ancestor of Offa, king of Mercia in the 8th century.

*Beowulf* showed the English the world of their ancestors, the heroic world of the north, a world both glorious and heathen. Dynasties take their identity from their ancestors, and the rulers of the English kingdoms ruled by right of ancestral conquest. The date and provenance of *Beowulf* are uncertain, and its authorship unknown, but the poem would have had ancestral interest to such a ruler. West-Saxon genealogies go back to Noah via Woden; they include three names mentioned in *Beowulf* – Scyld, Scef and Beow. When in the 7th century the English became Christian they sent missionaries to their Germanic cousins. The audience for poetry was the lord of the hall and the men of his retinue. Such an audience was proud of its ancestors – even if, as the poem says of the Danes, 'they did not know God'.

The text of *Beowulf* is found in a manuscript in the West-Saxon dialect of Wessex

The sceptre from the ship burial at Sutton Hoo, Suffolk. A bar of fine-grained stone two feet long, tapered to a terminal knob with a human face on each side; on a bronze stand, and surmounted by a bronze ring bearing a stag. The ship may have been the grave of Rædwald, King of East Anglia (d. *c*.625).

The opening of *Beowulf* in the manuscript of *c*.1000 in the British Library:

HWÆT WEGARDE
na in gear dagum theod cyninga
thrym ge frunon hu tha æthelingas ellen fremedon …

Word-for-word:

Listen! We of the Spear-Danes
in days of yore, of the kings of the people
the glory have heard, how those princes did
deeds of valour.

The irregular outline of the leaf is due to fire-damage in 1731.

which had become the literary standard. All the texts in the manuscript are about monsters, but the prime concern of *Beowulf* is not with monsters or even heroes but with human wisdom and destiny. It recounts the doings over two or three generations about the year 500 of the rulers of the Danes and the Swedes, and of a people who lived between them in southern Sweden, the Geats. The name Beowulf is not recorded in history, but the political and dynastic events of the poem are consistent with history. Beowulf is the nephew of Hygelac, King of the Geats, who died in a raid on the northern fringe of the Frankish empire. This key event of the poem is recorded in two Latin histories as having happened in about 521.

Hygelac fell in a raid in search of booty. In attacking the Frisians on the Frankish border, Beowulf's uncle was asking for trouble, says the poem. The Franks took from Hygelac's body a necklace of precious stones, a treasure previously bestowed on Beowulf by the Queen of the Danes as a reward for having killed the monster, Grendel (see below). On his return from Denmark, Beowulf had presented this prize to his lord, Hygelac, but the necklace was lost in this needless attack. Beowulf stopped the enemy champion, Dayraven, from taking Hygelac's armour by crushing him to death with his bare hands. Beowulf returned with the armour of thirty soldiers, and declined the throne, preferring to serve Hygelac's young son. But when this son is killed for harbouring an exiled Swedish prince, Beowulf became king and ruled the Geats for 'fifty years'.

The poem has a mysterious overture in the arrival of Scyld as a foundling child, sent by God to protect the lordless Danes, his victorious life and his burial in a ship. His great-grandson Hrothgar inherits the Danish empire and builds the great hall of

Heorot, where he rewards his followers with gifts. At a banquet, Hrothgar's poet sings the story of the creation of the world. The sound of music, laughter and feasting is resented by the monster Grendel, who comes from the fens to attack Heorot when the men are asleep. He devours thirty of Hrothgar's thanes. Beowulf hears of the persecution of the Danes and comes to kill Grendel, in a tremendous fight at night in the hall. The next night, Grendel's mother comes to the hall and takes her revenge. Beowulf follows her to her lair in an underwater cave, where with God's help he kills her. Finally, in old age, he has to fight a dragon, who has attacked the Geats in revenge for the taking of a cup from his treasure-hoard. Beowulf faces the dragon alone, but can kill it only with the help of a young supporter; he dies of his wounds. The poem ends with a prophecy of the subjection of the Geats by the Franks or the Swedes. The Geats build a funeral pyre for their leader.

> Then the warriors rode around the barrow
> Twelve of them in all, athelings' sons.
> They recited a dirge to declare their grief,
> Spoke of the man, mourned their King.
> They praised his manhood, and the prowess of his hands,
> They raised his name; it is right a man
> Should be lavish in honouring his lord and friend,
> Should love him in his heart when the leading-forth
> From the house of flesh befalls him at last.
>
> This was the manner of the mourning of the men of the Geats,
> Sharers in the feast, at the fall of their lord:
> They said that he was of all the world's kings
> The gentlest of men, and the most gracious,
> The kindest to his people, the keenest for fame.

The foundation of Germanic heroic society is the bond between a lord and his people, especially his retinue of warriors. Each will die for the other. Beowulf's epitaph suggests an ethical recipe for heroism: three parts responsibility to one part honour. The origin of Beowulf's life-story, in the folk-tale of the Bear's Son and his marvellous feats, is transmuted by the poem into a distinctly social ideal of the good young hero and the wise old king.

The heroic world is violent, but neither *Beowulf* nor Beowulf is bloodthirsty. The poem shows not just the glory but also the human cost of a code built upon family honour and the duty of vengeance. This cost is borne by men and, differently, by women. In this aristocratic world, women have honoured roles: peacemaker in marriage-alliances between dynasties, bride, consort, hostess, counsellor, mother, and widow. In *Beowulf* the cost of martial honour is signified in the figure of the mourning woman. Here is the Danish princess Hildeburh at the funeral pyre of her brother Hnæf, treacherously killed by her husband Finn, and her son, also killed in the attack on Hnæf. Shortly after this, Finn is killed by Hengest.

> Hildeburgh then ordered her own son
> To be given to the funeral fire of Hnæf
> For the burning of his bones; bade him be laid
> At his uncle's side. She sang the dirges,
> Bewailed her grief. The warrior went up;
> The greatest of corpse-fires coiled to the sky,
> Roared before the mounds. There were melting heads

> And bursting wounds, as the blood sprang out
> From weapon-bitten bodies. Blazing fire,
> Most insatiable of spirits, swallowed the remains
> Of the victims of both nations. Their valour was no more.

The heroic way of life – magnificent, hospitable and courageous – depends upon military success. It can descend into the world of the feud, violent and merciless. The heroic code involves obligations to lord, to family and to guest, and heroic literature brings these obligations into tension, with tragic potential.

A comparison can be made between Beowulf and the Achilles of the *Iliad*. When Achilles' pride is piqued, he will not fight, rejoining the Greeks only after his friend and substitute is killed. Achilles takes out his anger on the Trojan Hector, killing him, dishonouring his corpse and refusing to yield it for burial, until at last Hector's father humiliates himself before Achilles to beg his son's body. Achilles is reminded that even he must die. Homer's characterisation is more dramatic, brilliant and detailed; the characters of *Beowulf* are types rather than individuals. Yet the ethos is different. Beowulf devotedly serves his lord Hygelac, and his people the Geats. His youthful exploits in Denmark repay a debt of honour he owes to Hrothgar, who had saved Beowulf's father Edgetheow, paying compensation for the life of a man Edgetheow had killed. Like Achilles, Beowulf is eloquent, courageous, quick to act, unusually strong. But Beowulf is considerate, magnanimous and responsible. As Hrothgar points out, he has an old head on young shoulders; he makes a good king. Yet as the poem makes clear in a series of stories marginal to Beowulf's own life, most warriors from ruling families fall far short of Beowulf's responsibility and judgement. *Beowulf* is both a celebration of and an elegy for heroism. The ideal example set by Beowulf himself implies a Christian critique of an ethic in which honour can be satisfied by 'the world's remedy', vengeance.

Grendel envies the harmony of the feast in Heorot and destroys it. He is a fiend: *feond* means both enemy and malign spirit. He is also in man's shape, though of monstrous size. He is identified as a descendant of Cain, the first murderer, who in Genesis is marked and driven out by God from human society. Fratricide was an occupational hazard in ruling Germanic families, since succession was not by primogeniture but by choice of the fittest. In the heroic age of the north, sons were often fostered out, partly to reduce conflict and risk, but fraternal rivalry remained endemic. In *Beowulf* the greatest crimes are treachery to a lord and murder of kindred. The folklore figure of Grendel embodies the savage spirit of fratricidal envy. The dragon is a brute without Grendel's human and demonic aspects. He destroys *Beowulf*'s hall by fire in revenge for the theft of a golden cup from his treasure. The dragon jealously guards his hoard underground, whereas the king shares out rings in the hall.

*Beowulf* commands respect by the depth and maturity of its understanding. Although its archaic world of warriors and rulers is simple, the poem is often moving in its sober concern with wisdom and right action, the destiny of dynasties, the limits of human understanding and power, and with the creative and the destructive in human life. Its style has reserve and authority.

## Elegies

The most striking early English poems are the Elegies of the Exeter Book: 'The Wanderer' and 'The Seafarer' are heroic elegies, as is 'The Ruin'. A second group of love-elegies is 'The Husband's Message', 'The Wife's Complaint' and 'Wulf and Eadwacer'. The Elegies are dramatic monologues whose speaker is unnamed and whose situation is implied rather than specified. In the first two poems the speaker is an exile who lacks a lord; his soliloquy moves from his own sufferings to a general lament for the transitoriness of life's glory, expressed in 'The Wanderer' and 'The Ruin' in the image of a ruined hall. All three poems are informed by a Christian view of earthly glory; 'The Ruin' is set in the ruins of a Roman city with hot baths, usually identified as Bath. The Wanderer's painful lack of a lord and companions can be remedied, as the poem indicates quietly at its ending, by turning to a heavenly lord. 'The Seafarer' fiercely rejects a comfortable life on land in favour of the ardours of exile on the sea, and then turns explicitly towards the soul's true home in heaven. Ezra Pound's spirited version of 'The Seafarer' (1912) expresses the isolation and the ardour. It should be read for the feel of the verse rather than for the poem's Christian sense, which Pound thought a later addition and cut out.

'The Wanderer' and 'The Seafarer' are passionate and eloquent. They are conveniently self-explanatory, have been well edited, and fit into the social and intellectual background suggested by other poems. They also appeal because they read like dramatic soliloquies of a kind familiar from Romantic literature, in which the reader can identify with the self-expression of the speaker. The situations of the speakers are, however, imaginary, and all three poems appropriate heroic motifs for the purpose of a Christian wisdom. If 'The Seafarer', like *The Dream of the Rood*, is affective devotion, 'The Wanderer' might be called affective philosophy.

The second trio of elegies is less self-explanatory. Not evidently Christian or stoic, they express secular love, not devotion between men. The enigmatic 'Wulf and Eadwacer' is spoken by a woman married to Eadwacer but bearing the child of her lover Wulf. The speaker of 'The Wife's Complaint' (or 'Lament') is banished to a cave.

> 'Some lovers in this world
> Live dear to each other, lie warm together
> At day's beginning; I go by myself
> About these earth caves under the oak tree.
> Here I must sit the summer day through,
> Here weep out the woes of exile …'

Passionate feelings voiced in a desolate landscape are typical of the elegies. 'The Husband's Message' departs from type: in it a man expresses a tender love for his wife and calls her to a happy reunion.

## Battle poetry

In *Germania* (AD *c*.100), the Roman historian Tacitus says that German warriors recited poetry before battle; and Beowulf recalls his victories before going into fight. *Waldere* and *Finnsburh* are early battle poems; but even when England had been long settled, invasion renewed the occasion for battle poems.

Two survive from the 10th century, *Brunanburh* and *Maldon*. *Brunanburh* is the entry for 937 in the *ASC*, a record of the crushing victory of the West-Saxons over an invading force of Scots, Picts, Britons and Dublin Vikings. It is a panegyric in praise of the victorious king Athelstan, and was translated by Tennyson in 1880. Although it deploys time-honoured motifs such as the birds of prey, it has a historical purpose, and ends with a reference to written histories (quoted above on page 27), claiming Brunanburh as the greatest victory won by the English since their original conquest of Britain five hundred years earlier. *Maldon* is also traditional, with clashing swords, brave words and birds of prey, but with more historical details of battlefield topography, tactics and the names of local men who took part, names recorded in Essex charters. We hear of words spoken at 'the meeting-place' rather than in the mead-hall of poetic tradition. Maldon was a defeat of the East-Saxon militia by Vikings in 991, and after it the *ASC* says that the English paid the Danes to go away. The purpose of *Maldon* is not so much documentary, to record things said and done and give reasons for defeat, as exemplary, to show right and wrong conduct on the field, and how to die gloriously in defence of your lord and of Christian England. Much of the detail is symbolic: for example, before the battle Byrhtnoth sent the horses away, and one young man 'Loosed from his wrist his loved hawk;/Over the wood it stooped: he stepped to battle'. There was to be no retreat; the time for sport was over.

The text of *Maldon* breaks off as defeat is imminent. An old retainer speaks:

> 'Courage shall grow keener, clearer the will,
> The heart fiercer, as our force grows less.
> Here our lord lies levelled in the dust,
> The man all marred: he shall mourn to the end
> Who thinks to wend off from this war-play now.
> Though I am white with winters I will not away,
> For I think to lodge me alongside my dear one,
> Lay me down at my lord's right hand.'

This clear and attractive poem shows that the old ways of conceiving and describing the ethos and praxis of battle still worked.

## The harvest of literacy

Alfred's translation programme had created a body of discursive native prose. This was extended in the 10th century, after the renewal of Benedictine monastic culture under Archbishop Dunstan, by new writing, clerical and civil. The extant prose of Ælfric (*c*.955–*c*.1020) and **Wulfstan** (d.1023) is substantial. Over one hundred of Ælfric's *Catholic Homilies* and scores of his Saints' Lives survive, primarily for use in the pulpit through the church's year. He is a graceful writer, intelligent, clear and unpedantic, a winning expositor of the culture of the Church, the mother of arts and letters throughout this period. His homilies are called 'catholic' not for their orthodoxy but because they were designed to be read by all, lay as well as cleric.

We have impressive political and legal writings by Wulfstan, a *Manual* on computation by Byrhtferth of Ramsey, and some lives of clerics and kings. Ælfric translated Genesis at the command of a lay patron. This prose provided the laity with the religious and civil materials long available to the clergy in Latin. By 1000 the humane Latin culture which developed between the renaissance of learning at the court of Charlemagne, crowned Holy Roman Emperor in 800, and the 12th-century renaissance (see Chapter 2) had found substantial expression in English.

Among the many manuscripts from this time are the four main poetry manuscripts. There was, however, little new poetry after *Maldon*. Changes in the nature of the language – notably the use of articles, pronouns and prepositions instead of final inflections – made verse composition more difficult. There were too many small words to fit the old metre, and the historical verse in the *ASC* shows faltering technique.

The millennium was a period of cultural growth but of political decline. The reign of Ethelred II (978–1016) saw an artistic revival, especially at Winchester, a bishopric and the capital of Wessex and of England: work in metal and gems, book production, manuscript illumination, embroidery, architecture and music. But there were disunity and Danish invasions. Alphege, Archbishop of Canterbury, martyred by Vikings in 1012, and Wulfstan, Archbishop of York in the early 11th century, were better leaders of the English than their king. In *Sermo Lupi ad Anglos* ('The Word of Wulf to the English'), Wulfstan raised his voice against the evils flourishing in the social breakdown caused by the Danish invasions. His denunciations ring with the conviction that he spoke for the whole community.

The conquest of England by Danish and then by Norman kings disrupted cultural activity, and changed the language of the rulers. Latin remained the language of the church, but the hierarchy was largely replaced by Normans, and English uses were done away with. William the Conqueror made his nephew Osmund the first bishop in the new see of Salisbury. Osmund seems, however, to have been persuaded to keep one English usage, which has survived. The words in the wedding service in the *Book of Common Prayer* – 'I take thee for my wedded wife, to have and to hold from this day forward, for better for worse' and so forth – employ Old English doublets. Like the names of the parts of the body and the days of the week, they are an instance of the survival of Old English at a level so basic that it is taken for granted.

# Further reading

Alexander, M. *Old English Literature* (Basingstoke: Macmillan, 1983; Peterborough, Ontario: Broadview, revd edn 2000). A simple introduction with translations.

Bede. *Ecclesiastical History of the English People*, trans. L. Shirley-Price, revd R. E. Latham, ed. D. H. Farmer (Harmondsworth: Penguin, 1990). The primary source for early Anglo-Saxon history.

Campbell, J. (ed.). *The Anglo-Saxons* (Oxford: Oxford University Press, 1982; Harmondsworth: Penguin, 1991). An outstanding historical conspectus, very well illustrated.

Mitchell, B. and F. C. Robinson. *A Guide to Old English*, 5th edn (Oxford: Blackwell, 1995). A grammar, reader and study-guide for students.

# Middle English Literature: 1066–1500

## Overview

Literature in England in this period was not just in English and Latin but in French as well, and developed in directions set largely in France. Epic and elegy gave way to Romance and lyric. English writing revived fully in English after 1360, and flowered in the reign of Richard II (1372–99). It gained a literary standard in London English after 1425, and developed modern forms of verse, of prose and of drama.

## ■ The new writing

### Handwriting and printing

Medieval writing was done by hand. For the scribes, the period began and ended with the unwelcome arrivals of two conquerors: Normans in 1066, and the printing press in 1476. English literature survived the first conquest with difficulty. The record is patchy, but the few surviving manuscripts show that it was some generations before native literature recovered. Three centuries after 1066 it recovered completely, flowering in different dialects under Richard II. One generation later, London English offered a more stable literary medium.

Historians of English and of England agree that a period ends with the 15th century. When the first printed English book appeared in 1476, the phase of Middle English (ME) was virtually over: the language had assumed its modern form, except in spelling. Soon afterwards, the Wars of the Roses, a long dynastic struggle between supporters of Lancastrian and Yorkist claimants to the throne, ended in the victory of the Lancastrian Henry Tudor in 1485. Henry made a politic marriage with Elizabeth of York; they called their first son by the British name of Arthur. In 1492 Ferdinand and Isabella drove Muslims out of Spain and backed the voyage of Columbus to the Indies. In 1503 their daughter Katherine was married to Arthur, who died; then to his brother Henry, who became Henry VIII. Henry divorced her in 1533, leading to the break with Rome and a separate English nation-state with strong central rule and a state Church following the Protestant doctrines of the Reformation (see page 78).

As printing and Protestantism established themselves, the manuscripts in which **vernacular** writing survived, outdated and possibly suspect, were neglected. By 1700 some manuscripts were being used as firelighters or worse; Alexander Pope refers to 'the martyrdom of jakes and fire' ('jakes': lavatory). Survival was chancy: some of Chaucer's works have been lost, and *Sir Gawain and the Green Knight* was not printed until 1839.

Even if much more had survived, the story would be neither simple nor clear. Literature survived in three languages: Latin lived alongside Norman French and an 'English' which was a welter of dialects, spoken rather than written. English writing was local, with too few authors and dates for positive literary history. Only after 1360 did English win parity with French as a literary medium; the English which 'triumphed' was Frenchified in language and culture. Avoiding these complexities, short histories of English literature focus on the modern, leap over its first millennium, land at the Renaissance with relief, and do not look back. This simplification ignores a vast amount of good writing, and allows the Renaissance to take credit for earlier developments. In the **Middle Ages**, the English language evolved its modern nature and structure. Literature too found modern forms in the medieval period: prose in Julian of Norwich and Malory in the 15th century, verse in Chaucer and his many peers in the 14th century, and drama as early as the 12th century. Drama had been popular for ten generations before Shakespeare.

**vernacular** (Lat. *verna*, slave) The native language; West-European languages other than Latin.

**Middle Ages** Historically, the English *Middle Ages* is the period *c.*500–*c.*1500. The period after 1100 is often called the *later Middle Ages*; in English political history, this runs from 1066 to 1485. In European cultural history the 13th century is often regarded as the *High Middle Ages*. It is not entirely fanciful to see the 12th century as the spring of the later Middle Ages, the 13th century as summer, the 14th century as autumn, and the 15th century as winter.

## The impact of French

The Conquest of England in 1066 by William of Normandy displaced English as the medium of literature, for the language of the new rulers was French. William the Conqueror tried to learn English, but gave up; Saxons dealing with him had to learn French, and French was the language of the court and the law for three centuries. The Normans spoke Norman French; the Norman French of England is called Anglo-Norman. By 1076 all bishops were Normans, except Wulfstan of Worcester. Clerics, writing in Latin as before, recorded some 'English' stories: Alfred burning the cakes, or the Saxon resistance of Hereward the Wake. Educated men for the next three centuries were trilingual, and many homes bilingual.

Literature in English suffered a severe disruption in 1066. Classical Old English verse died out, reviving later in a very different form, but prose continued: sermons were still written in English and *The Anglo-Saxon Chronicle* was kept up in monasteries. When the new writing appeared, it was in an English which had become very different from that of the 11th century. The reasons for this include the lack of any written standard to discourage dialectal variety; scribal practice; linguistic change; and a new literary consciousness.

## Scribal practice

With the disestablishment of the English of Winchester and Wessex as the literary standard, a uniform West-Saxon was not available to scribes, who now used forms nearer to their own dialects. With the Winchester standard gone, dialectal divergence became apparent, with a bewildering variety of spellings, word-forms and grammatical forms. This variety was dialectal and geographical, but also structural and progressive; fundamental changes in grammar and stress kept the language in a ferment for four centuries after the Conquest.

**Reigns and major events 1066–1399**

| | |
|---|---|
| 1066 | William I (the Conqueror) |
| 1087 | William II (Rufus) |
| 1100 | Henry I |
| 1135 | Stephen |
| 1154 | Henry II (Plantagenet) |
| 1170 | murder of Thomas Becket, Archbishop of Canterbury, by agents of the King |
| 1189 | Richard I on Third Crusade (see page 40) |
| 1199 | John |
| c.1216 | Henry III |
| 1272 | Edward I |
| 1307 | Edward II |
| 1314 | The Battle of Bannockburn (Scots defeat invading English army) |
| 1327 | Edward III |
| 1346 | The Battle of Crécy (English victory in France) |
| 1348–9 | Black Death |
| 1377 | Richard II |
| 1381 | Peasants' Revolt |
| 1399 | Henry IV |

## Dialect and language change

Even when English had attained full literary parity with French in the reign of Richard II (1372–98), there was no standard literary English: the great writers of that reign – Geoffrey Chaucer, William Langland and the author of *Sir Gawain and the Green Knight* – wrote three different forms of English. Chaucer wrote in a London English, Langland in a Worcestershire English, and the *Gawain*-poet in an English of the Stafford–Cheshire border. There are Middle English works in Yorkshire English, Kentish English, Norfolk English and other varieties of English; and much writing in Scots, known as *Inglis*.

William the Conqueror had made London the capital of England, and it was not until 1362 that Parliament was opened in English instead of French. But London English was itself a mixture of dialects, changing during this period from Southern to East Midland. The Midland dialect area, as can be seen from the map on page 37, had borders with the other four chief dialect areas and was understood in each. In the 15th century, London's changing English became the national standard. Printing, introduced in 1476, helped to spread this literary standard under the Tudors (1485–1603). The King's English was eventually disseminated by such centrally-issued works as the Prayer-Book (1549, 1552, 1559) and the Authorized Version of the Bible (1611). Spelling was fully standardized only after Dr Johnson's *Dictionary* of 1755.

In contemporary British English, regional variation is more a matter of accent than of word and idiom, but the passages quoted in this chapter show Middle English dialects differing in vocabulary and grammar. The absence of standard spelling makes Middle English dialectal divergence seem even greater. Danish settlement in the north and east of England in the 10th century had brought Scandinavian speech-forms to English, similar in stem but different in **inflection**. The resulting confusion

**inflection** A word's ending, as distinct from its (usually invariable) stem; a grammatical variation in the final syllables, indicating a word's case and number.

1  *The Peterborough Chronicle*
2  *The Owl and the Nightingale*
3  Layamon's *Brut*
4  *Ancrene Wisse*
5  *Sir Orfeo*
6  *The Cloud of Unknowing*
7  Langland: *Piers Plowman*
8  *Sir Gawain and the Green Knight*
9  Gower: *Confessio Amantis*
10  The York Play of the Crucifixion
11  Chaucer: *The Parliament of Fowls*

The dialects of Middle English (drawn after J. Burrow and T. Turville-Petre (eds), *A Book of Middle English*. Oxford: Blackwell, 1996), with probable places of composition of some works.

encouraged a loss of inflection. Element-order became the indicator of syntax and of sense: subject–verb–object now became more common than subject–object–verb. All forms of early Middle English show the reduction of most final inflections towards -*e*, leading to the survival of only two standard inflections in nouns, -*s* plural and -*s* possessive.

The Conquest eventually added thousands of French words to English, sometimes taking the place of Old English words (for example, OE *theod* gave way to ME *people* and *nation*), but often preserving both Germanic and Latin-derived alternatives (*shire* and *county*). The cross with French almost doubled the resources of English in some areas of vocabulary. The Saxon base was enriched with French, especially in such areas as law and manners; Latin kept its clerical–intellectual prestige. English, the language of the majority, was in ferment.

## Literary consciousness

Middle English writing blossomed in the late 14th century, and developed a literary self-consciousness. A clear example of this comes at the end of Chaucer's *Troilus and Criseyde*: he speaks to his poem in the intimate second person, *thee*:

> And for ther is so gret diversite
> In Englissh and in writyng of oure tonge,
> So prey I God that non myswrite the,            thee
> Ne the mysmetre for defaute of tonge.           lack of language

He prays that no scribe will miscopy his words, nor substitute a variant form and spoil the metre. *Diversite in Englissh* refers to dialect difference, but Chaucer had earlier warned his audience about change over time: 'Ye know eke [also] that in fourme of speche is chaunge.' Diversity and change were enemies to this new hope that English verse might attain the beauty and permanence of the classics.

Just before these lines Chaucer had taken leave of his poem in an *envoi*: 'Go, litel bok, go, litel myn tragedie …/And kis the steppes where as thow seëst pace/Virgile, Ovide, Omer, Lucan, and Stace.' These lines draw on a scene in Dante's *Inferno*. In

### Writers in Romance languages

**Provençal** Bernart de Ventadorn (flourished *c*.1150–80); Arnaut Daniel (flourished *c*.1170–1210)

**French** Benoît de Ste-Maure, *Roman de Troie* (*c*.1160); Marie de France, *Lais* (?*c*.1165–80; Chrètien de Troyes (*c*.1170-91), *Erec, Yvain, Lancelot, Perceval*; Guillaume de Lorris, *Roman de la Rose* (completed *c*.1277 by Jeun de Meun).

**Italian** The Italian Trecento (the 14th century): Dante (1265–1326), *Commedia* (*c*.1304–21); Petrarch made poet laureate (1341); Boccaccio, *Decameron* (*c*.1351).

Limbo, at the threshold of the underworld, Dante and his guide Virgil meet the spirits of Omer (Homer), Horace, Ovid and Lucan (Chaucer substitutes Stace, the epic poet Statius, for Horace). The poets welcome Virgil, and beckon Dante to join them. In instructing his poem to 'kiss the steps' of Homer and the poets of the Western classical tradition, Chaucer joins the queue of Italian aspirants to poetic fame: Dante, Petrarch and Boccaccio, from all of whom he had translated.

Chaucer's ambitions for vernacular poetry had been raised by reading the Italian poets of the 14th century, the Trecento. He identifies himself as a European poet, the first to write in English. Furthermore, Chaucer wrote in English only; his senior contemporary John Gower (?1330–1408), to whom he dedicates *Troilus*, wrote in English, French and Latin. After Chaucer, poetry in English is part of the modern European tradition – though Chaucer's ease and wit are not found again until the Latin prose of Thomas More's *Utopia* in 1517.

## New fashions: French and Latin

Chaucer had begun to write in the French fashions native in England since the 12th century. We must now turn back to the French conquest of English. Within two generations of the arrival of this romance language came new literary forms and the humanism of the 12th-century Renaissance, when first Norman and then Gothic churches arose in England. Poems were about knights, and then about knights and ladies. For the 12th and 13th centuries a history of English writing has to discard its English monocle, for writing in the Anglo-Norman kingdom of England was largely in Latin and French.

Writers had to be maintained, either by the Church or by secular patrons, who spoke French. Eleanor of Aquitaine, granddaughter of the first troubadour, William IX of Aquitaine, was the dedicatee of some of the songs of the troubadour **Bernart de Ventadorn** (flourished *c.*1150–80). Eleanor married first Louis VII of France, then Henry Plantagenet of Anjou, Henry II of England. Kings of England spoke French rather than English. The first English king to insist that the business of the court be done in English was Henry V (1413–22), who claimed to be king of France as well as of England, Ireland and Wales. Much Middle English writing derives from French writing, which in turn derives largely from Latin.

### Anglo-Latin and Anglo-Norman authors

**Latin**
The Italian-born monk of Bec, St Anselm, Archbishop of Canterbury (1093–1109) and theologian: *Cur Deus Homo?* ('Why did God become Man?').

**12th-century Benedictine chroniclers** Orderic Vitalis, an English monk in Normandy, *Historia Ecclesiastica*; William of Malmesbury (d.1143); Jocelin de Brakelonde; Henry of Huntingdon; Geoffrey of Monmouth, *Historia Regum Britanniae* (1135).

**Humanists** John of Salisbury, *Policraticus* (1159); Walter Map, *De Nugis Curialium* ('Courtiers' Trifles', 1181–92); Matthew Paris (13th century).

**Anglo-Norman**
(Anglo-Norman is the French spoken by Normans in England.)

Marie de France and Chrètien de Troyes may have written some of their Arthurian romances in England; Wace, *Roman de Rou* (1172).

As literacy spread in western Europe, the international Latin clerical culture was rivalled, from Iceland to Sicily, by vernacular writing, often on secular themes and sometimes by laymen. Writers and readers were mostly men, but some of the new vernacular literature, religious and non-religious, was written for women who had the time to read but knew no Latin. Some of these vernacular books were about, as well as for, women; a few were *by* women, for example Marie de France (late 12th century) and Julian of Norwich (*c.*1343–1413/29).

## Epic and romance

The change in literary sensibility after 1100 is often characterized as a change from epic to **romance**. William I's minstrel Taillefer is said to have led the Normans ashore at Hastings declaiming the *Chanson de Roland*. This *chanson de geste* ('song of deeds') relates the deeds of Roland and Oliver, two of the twelve peers of the emperor Charlemagne, who die resisting a Saracen ambush in the Pyrenees. Roland scorns to summon the aid of Charlemagne until all his foes are dead. Only then does he sound a blast on his ivory horn, the *olifans*. Primitive romance enters with some emotion-heightening detail: three archangels come to conduct Roland's soul to heaven; later his intended bride, *la bele Aude*, appears for a few lines to hear of his death and die of shock. In treating death, Northern epic is reticent where romance is flamboyant: compared with Roland's death, the death and funeral of Beowulf are sombre, his soul's destination not clear.

The first extant Middle English writing to be noted here is **Layamon**'s *Brut* (*c.*1200), a work in the Old English heroic style: this is based on the French *Roman de Brut* by Wace, a Norman from Jersey who in 1155 dedicated the work to Eleanor of Aquitaine. Wace, a canon of Bayeux, had in turn based his work on the Latin *Historia Regum Britanniae* (*c.*1130–6) by **Geoffrey of Monmouth** (d.1155). In Geoffrey's wonderful *History*, the kings of Britain descend from Brutus, the original conqueror of the island of Albion, then infested by giants. This Brutus is the grandson of Aeneas the Trojan, from whom Virgil traced the kings of Rome. Brutus calls Albion 'Britain', after his own name; the capital is New Troy, later called London. The Romans conquer Britain, but the Britons, under Lucius, reconquer Rome. They fight bravely under King **Arthur** against the Saxon invader, but Arthur, poised to conquer Europe, has to turn back at the Alps to put down the revolt of his nephew Mordred. Fatally wounded at the battle of Camlann, Arthur is taken to the island of Avalon, whence, according to the wizard Merlin's prophecies, he shall one day return. Geoffrey stops in the 6th century at King Cadwallader, after whom the degenerate Britons succumbed to the Saxons.

Geoffrey of Monmouth started something. 'Everything this man wrote about Arthur', wrote William of Newburgh in *c.*1190, 'was made up, partly by himself and partly by others, either from an inordinate love of lying, or for the sake of pleasing the Britons.' The Britons *were* pleased, as were the Bretons and their neighbours the Normans. It was in northern France that the legends of Arthur and his Round Table were further improved before they re-crossed the Channel to the northern half of the Norman kingdom. The Normans had conquered southern Scotland, Wales and Ireland, which were now included in the Arthurian story. Geoffrey's confection was popular history until the Renaissance, and popular legend thereafter. It is in Geoffrey that we first read of Gog-Magog, of Gwendolen, of King Lear and his daughters, of King Cole and of Cymbeline, not to mention Arthur, the Round Table

**romance** A kind of medieval story, originally from stories written in *romauns*, or vernacular French; 'romance' is the adjective for languages deriving from Latin. As a genre term, it means 'marvellous story'; its adjective is also 'romance', to avoid confusion with 'Romantic', a late-18th-century term for writing which imitates medieval romance. (The use of 'romance' for 'love-story' is modern.)

**Arthur** If he was historical, Arthur defeated the pagan Saxons in battle at Mons Badonicus (*c.*510). The Arthur of literature belongs to the age of chivalry and the Crusades after 1100.

**feudalism** The codification of the roles, land-rights, privileges and duties of the Germanic warrior-class, the French-speaking Normans who ruled Britain and, with the Franks, much of Europe during the period of the Crusades.

**Crusades** The series of expeditions from western Europe to the eastern Mediterranean to recapture Jerusalem, taken by the Turks from the Byzantines in 1071. First Crusade, 1095–1104 (Jerusalem taken in 1099); Second Crusade, 1147–9; Third Crusade, 1189–92 (Jerusalem lost in 1187, recovered in 1229, lost in 1291). The Crusades ended in defeat by the Turks at Nicopolis (1396).

**knight** The Old English *cniht* was simply a boy or youthful warrior, as in *Maldon*, line 9. 'Knight' began to acquire its modern sense only after the success of the mounted warrior.

**chivalry** (from Fr. *chevalerie*, from med. Lat. *caballus*, 'horse') A system of honourable conduct expected of a knight or 'gentle' (that is, noble) man, involving military service to Christ and king, protection of the weak, and avoidance of villainy (from Fr. *vilain*, base; ME *villein*, a churl).

and Merlin, and the moving of Stonehenge from Ireland to Salisbury Plain. Geoffrey's legendary history of the Island of Britain was put into English by Layamon. His 14,000-line *Brut* makes no distinction between the British and the English, thus allowing the English to regard Arthur, their British enemy, as English.

Layamon was a priest from Worcestershire, an area where old verse traditions lasted. His talent was for narrative, and his battles have a physicality found later in Barbour's *Bruce* (1375) and in the alliterative *Morte* (c.1400). These qualities came from Old English verse, but Layamon's metre is rough, employing the old formulas with less economy, mixing an irregular alliteration with internal rhyme. Arthur's last words are:

> 'And Ich wulle varen to Avalun,    to vairest alre maidene,
> to Argante there quene,    alven swithe sceone,
> and heo scal mine wunden    makien alle isunde,
> al hal me makien    mid haleweiye drenchen.
> And seothe Ich cumen wulle    to mine kineriche
> and wunien mid Brutten    mid muchelere wunne.'

And I shall fare to Avalon, to the fairest of all maidens, to their queen Argante, the very beautiful elf-lady; and she shall heal all my wounds, make me whole with holy infusions. And afterwards I shall come to my kingdom and dwell with the Britons with much rejoicing.

Whereas Beowulf's body is burnt, and Roland's soul is escorted to heaven by angels, Arthur's body is wafted by elf-ladies to Avalon to be healed – and to return. This promise is repeated in Malory's *Morte Darthur* (c.1470).

The change during the 11th–13th centuries from *Gestes* (songs of *res gestae*, Lat. 'things done', 'doings') to romances of chivalry is part of the rise of **feudalism**. A **knight**'s duty to serve God and the King had a religious orientation and a legal force; it was not just an honour-code in literature. **Chivalry** was historical as well as literary; its cultural prestige was spread through Romance.

Romances were tales of adventurous and honourable deeds – deeds of war, at first; but knights also fought to defend ladies, or fought for ladies, introducing a new ethos. Although romance took popular forms, it began as a courtly genre, a leisure pursuit – like feasting, hunting, reading, playing chess, or love itself. The warrior gave way to the knight, and when the knight got off his horse he wooed the lady. In literature the pursuit of love grew ever more refined.

## Courtly literature

The distance between *chevalier* and *vilain*, or *knight* and *churl*, widened and became hereditary; a literature for the court developed. The French rulers, ruling by conquest, enjoyed romances of antiquity, about Thebes, Aeneas, Troy and Alexander. In 1165 Benoît de Sainte-Maure produced a 30,000-line *Roman de Troie* at the court of Eleanor of Aquitaine. Such popular stories of antiquity were 'the matter of Rome' – that is, of classical antiquity. The romances of Alexander were full of marvels, and the *romans* of Aeneas took the part of Queen Dido, whom Aeneas abandoned in order to go and found Rome. But Arthurian romance, 'the matter of Britain', was more popular with ladies. Chaucer's Nun's Priest swears, of his 'Tale of the Cock and Hen': 'This storie is also trewe, I undertake,/As is the book of Launcelot de Lake,/ That wommen holde in ful greet reverence.'

The first developments of Geoffrey's Arthurian material were in French. After Wace came Marie de France, the first known French woman poet, who lived in England in the late 12th century and wrote a number of *lais* – a *lai* is a Breton minstrel's tale. Marie turns these songs into verse stories, brief and mysterious Celtic fairytales. An English example of this genre is *Sir Orfeo*, a romance of Orpheus. Marie de France should be distinguished from Marie de Champagne, daughter of Eleanor of Aquitaine. It was for Marie de Champagne that Chrètien de Troyes wrote the French Arthurian romances, *Erec et Enide*, *Cligès*, *Yvain*, *Lancelot*, and *Perceval*, the first vernacular story of the quest for the Grail (the legendary vessel used by Christ at the Last Supper). Chrétien was the first to turn the *matière de Bretagne*, the matter of Britain, from legend into literature; his couplets have a French economy and a light touch. Some of Chrétien and Marie was translated into English.

To go from Chrétien to English romance is to enter a simpler world. Famous examples of this large category are *King Horn* (*c.*1225), *Floris and Blancheflour* (early 13th century), *Havelok the Dane* (*c.*1300), *Bevis of Hampton* and *Guy of Warwick*. In octosyllabic rhyming couplets, Christian knights prove themselves against the Saracen. The most skilful and magical early romance is *Sir Orfeo*, found in the Auchinleck manuscript of *c.*1330, which Chaucer may have known. The Greek Orpheus and Eurydice become English. Sir Orfeo is lord in Winchester; he loses Dame Heurodis to a Fairy King who abducts her from her orchard to a Celtic underworld. After ten years grieving in the wilderness, Orfeo follows a fairy hunt through a hillside into the underworld, where he wins back Heurodis with his harping. He returns to Winchester disguised as a beggar, and plays so well that the Steward asks about the harp. When told that the harper had found it by the corpse of a man eaten by wolves, the Steward swoons.

| King Orfeo knew wele bi than | that |
| His steward was a trewe man | |
| And loved him as he aught to do, | |
| And stont up, and seyt thus: 'Lo! | |
| Yif ich were Orfeo the king, | If I |
| And hadde y-suffred ful yore | long ago |
| In wildernisse miche sore, | |
| And hadde y-won mi quen o-wy | away |
| Out of the lond of fairy, | |
| And hadde y-brought the levedi hende | gracious lady |
| Right here to the tounes ende …' | |

These *ifs* end in recognition and reunion, and Orfeo and his queen are joyfully restored to the throne.

| Harpours in Bretaine after than | Brittany   that |
| Herd hou this mervaile bigan, | |
| And made her-of a lay of gode likeing, | popular |
| And nempned it after the king. | named |
| That lay 'Orfeo' is y-hote: | called |
| Gode is the lay, swete is the note. | sweet |

The romance is a lasting legacy of the Middle Ages, not only to works of fantasy such as Edmund Spenser's *Faerie Queene* or the Gothic novel, but also to such marvellous but pseudo-realist works as Daniel Defoe's *Robinson Crusoe* and Samuel Richardson's *Pamela* in the early 18th century, and to the happy endings of the novels of Jane Austen in the 19th century. Fantasy flourished again in the novel of the late 20th century.

## Medieval institutions

Having seen some of the effects of the submersion of English by French, and before approaching the flowering of English poetry in the reign of Richard II (1372–98), we should look at institutions and mental habits which shaped this new English literature.

Foremost of these is the Church. Modern literature is largely concerned with secular life and written by lay people. But for a thousand years, the thought, culture and art of Europe were promoted by the Church. The clergy were the source of education, arts and literature – including anti-clerical satire. Bishops and priests living in the world – 'seculars' – brought the Word and the sacraments to the people. Higher education and culture were provided largely by 'religious': monks, nuns and, later, friars. Monastic cathedrals in cities, as at Winchester, Canterbury or Westminster, not far from London, had schools.

From the 12th century, intellectual initiative began to pass from these schools to universities. At universities in Paris or Oxford (founded *c.*1167), the teachings of the Fathers and Doctors of the Church were modified by new learning. There was in the 12th century a revival of classical learning and a new systematic thinking about God, man, civil society and the universe: a Renaissance. At the 12th century School of Chartres, France, this learning and philosophy were humanist (see page 75), valuing human life in itself as well as as a preparation for heavenly life.

Intellectual activity in the new universities was led less by secular clergy than by **friars**, members of the new orders founded by St Dominic and St Francis to evangelize the growing cities. Dominic's Order of Preachers, distinguished in logic and intellectual enquiry, revived professional academic philosophy and theology. 'Scholasticism', the philosophy of the university Schools such as that of Thomas Aquinas (*c.*1225–74), was later regarded as too theoretical by students of natural philosophy and northern European humanists. But it had reintroduced the systematic thinking

### Latin Fathers of the Church

**Jerome** (*c.*342–420), whose Latin translation of the Bible from Greek and Hebrew into the vulgar tongue of the Roman Empire, known as the Vulgate, became the Bible of the West.

**Augustine of Hippo** (354–430) was the chief influence on western theology until the 13th century.

**Ambrose of Milan** (*c.*340–97).

**Pope Gregory the Great** (*c.*540–604).

### The chief orders of monks

**Benedictines** follow the Rule of St Benedict of Nursia (480–*c.*550), the foundation of Western monasticism

**Carthusians** were founded by St Bruno at La Grande Chartreuse (1084).

**Cistercians** (from Cîteaux, where the order was founded in 1098) were popularized by St Bernard, Abbot of Clairvaux in 1153.

**The four Orders of Friars** (Lat. *frater*, Fr. *frère*, brother):

**Franciscans**, **Friars Minor** or **Grey Friars**, founded by St Francis of Assisi in 1210.

**Dominicans**, **Order of Preachers** or **Black Friars**, founded by St Dominic in 1216.

**Carmelites** or **White Friars**, founded in 1154.

**Austin Friars** were founded in 1256: they follow a rule based on the precepts of St Augustine.

of Aristotle, whose works came into Europe via Spain, retranslated from Arabic translations. The Scholastics dealt with the problems of theology and philosophy, of ontology and epistemology, of mind and language. They enquired into and debated truths by methods of proposition and logical testing still used in philosophy today.

The more humane Christianity of the 12th century, in which the incarnation of Christ made the physical universe speak of its divine origin, encouraged a further development of all the arts beyond what had been seen in 10th-century Winchester. What the Church did is largely still visible in the 10,000 medieval churches which survive in England. She was the patroness of architecture, sculpture, wood-carving, wall-painting, stained glass and enamel, fabrics, book-production, writing, illumination and music. These arts enhanced the services which enacted and proclaimed the life of Christ and his teachings through the feasts of the Christian year. The fabric of a church was a physical icon for all, *laered* or *lewed*, literate or illiterate. The 15th-century French poet François Villon wrote for his mother a *Ballade* as a prayer to Our Lady. What she says of herself was true of most medieval people: *onques lettre ne lus* ('not one letter have I read').

> Femme je suis povrette et ancienne,
> Qui riens ne scay; onques lettre ne lus.
> Au moustier voy dont suis paroissienne
> Paradis peint, ou sont harpes et lus,
> Et ung enfer ou dampnez sont boullus.

A poor old woman am I, who knows nothing; I've never read a letter. At the church of which I am a parishioner, I see paradise painted, where there are harps and lutes, and a hell, where the damned are boiled.

Literacy came through the Church, since the man who held the pen was a clerk (Fr. *clerc*, Lat. *clericus*). For three hundred years after 1066, monks copied Latin works; English texts were less worth preserving. The clerical monopoly weakened, but when Middle English is found in manuscripts before 1350, it is usually devotional. Yet in a Christian world, all writing had, or could gain, a Christian function. The Latin chroniclers, for example, wrote a providential and moral history, modelled on biblical history. Much of the best English writing was wholly religious, such as that of the mystic Julian of Norwich, or William Langland's *Piers Plowman*. Medieval drama and much medieval lyric was created to spread the gospel to the laity. Clerical thinkers, usually academics, gave philosophy priority over poetry – a priority challenged later at the Renaissance.

## Authority

Academic intellectual authority was vested in certain authors (Lat. *auctores*), as Augustine in theology or Boethius in philosophy. Writers, whether religious or secular, Latin or vernacular, invoked earlier authors: authority came from *auctores*. Authors' names are still powerful and can still mean more than their books. Chaucer names *Franceys Petrak, the lauriat poete* and *Daunte, the wyse poete of Ytaille* as sources, but claims that his *Troilus* is based not on his true source, the *Filostrato* of Boccaccio, a lesser name than Petrarch or Dante, but on *myn auctor, Lollius*. The name of Lollius is to be found in the first line of an Epistle by the Roman poet Horace: '*troiani belli scriptorem, maxime lolli, … relegi*'. Horace was writing *to* Lollius Maximus that he had been reading *the* writer on Troy, that is, Homer. This was

misunderstood as: 'I have read Lollius again, the greatest writer on the Trojan War
…'. Lollius is named as the authority on Troy by the 12th-century philosopher John
of Salisbury, a pupil of Abelard and a witness of Becket's murder.

Another aspect of medieval literary thought is allegory, the making out of deeper
meanings below the surface of literature or of life, meanings of a moral or spiritual
sort. Allegory developed from the Hebrew and Christian use of biblical prophecy as
the key to events. Allegory is a function of the principle of analogy, the correspondence of physical and spiritual in a universe which was a set of concentric spheres with
the earth at the centre. Hell was inside the earth, heaven above it. In the hierarchy of
creation, man was at a midpoint between angels and animals. Allegory could be
expressed in composition or in interpretation. Dante set out a scheme of the four
kinds of meaning to be found in a text. Allegorists quoted Augustine's saying that all
that is written is written for our doctrine. This agreed with the often-cited classical
maxim that literature should teach and delight. Classical ideas persisted strongly in
the Middle Ages, often in unclassical forms: one significant survival was the classifying of literature as composition, a branch of Rhetoric, originally the art of public
speaking.

Such academic attitudes inspired clerical literature, as in *The Owl and the
Nightingale* (early 13th-century), a debate between two birds, a wise Owl and a
pleasure-loving Nightingale, dusty Wisdom and appealing Song. That youth and
age are often *at debaat* was proverbial, but *debaat* was sharpened by the rise of
universities with few masters and many students. In *The Owl*, Latin academic debate
is refreshed by the beast-fable form and English idiom. The birds' spirited quarrel
becomes philosophical; all that they can agree on is an arbitrator of their dispute,
one Nicholas of Guildford. They fly to Portisham, Dorset, to see this clerk; but here
the author breaks off, saying that he cannot tell how their case went. He leaves us to
decide between owl and nightingale.

## Lyrics

The nightingale had become the bird of love in Provençal lyrics of the early 12th
century. In these first lyrics of courtly love, the service due to a feudal lord was transferred to a lady. Whatever the relation of this literary cult to real-life wooing, it is
not found in classical literature. The refinement and abundance of Provençal song-
literature is unmatched in North French and English lyric. Yet the love-song of birds
echoes clearly in the lyrics of the early-14th-century Harley manuscript. 'Alysoun'
opens:

| | |
|---|---|
| Bitwene March and Averil, | |
| When spray beginneth to springe, | |
| The litel foul hath hire wil, | bird |
| On hyre lede to synge. | her language |
| I live in love-longinge, | |
| For semeliest of alle thynge, | |
| She may me blisse bringe, | |
| Ich am in hire baundoun. | control |
| An hendy hap ich have y-hent, | lucky chance   received |
| Ichot from hevene it is me sent, | I know |
| From alle wommen my love is lent | has gone |
| And light on Alysoun. | alighted |

From a French late 15th-century manuscript showing the Labours of the Month. '*Aprilis habet dies xxx*': '(The month of) April hath thirty days'. April's activity is courting in a garden.

The little bird has *hire wil* to sing in *hyre lede*. To love Alysoun, a local beauty, is *a hendy hap*, a lucky chance; the singer's love has gone *From alle wommen* to her. In contrast, the *domna* (lady) of a Provençal lyric is unique and superior; her troubadour has not previously loved *alle wommen*. The English poet claims later that he will die unless Alysoun takes pity on him – but his refrain dances. French ways are cheerfully domesticated.

Secular lyrics survive not in fine manuscripts but incidentally, as in preachers' examples of frivolities to avoid – fugitive scraps, without music. Although the cultivation of stanzaic song implies art, the English lyric is lively rather than refined. Another Harley lyric ends:

> Ich wolde Ich were a thrustelcok,
> A bountyng other a laverokke;
> Swete bryd,
> Bitwen hire kirtel and hire smok
> Ich wolde ben hid.

I would I were a thrush, a bunting or a lark – lucky bird! I would I were hidden between her skirt and her shift.

The poet's desire to be a pet bird, close to the beloved, is playful: *bryd* is 'bird' or 'girl'.

The Harley manuscript, like the 13th-century Digby manuscript, is a miscellany of French, Latin and English. Some secular lyrics survive in margins. A late scrap reads:

> Western wind, when will thou blow,
> The small rain down can rain?
> Christ, if my love were in my arms
> And I in my bed again.

Lyrics such as this or 'Maiden in the mor lay' are anonymous and, compared with those of a Bernart de Ventadorn, simple. The natural world is glimpsed in 'Sumer is icumen in/Lhude [loud] sing, cuccu!' and 'Mirie it is while sumer ilast/With fugheles [birds'] song/Oc [but] nu neghest [comes near] wintres blast/With weder strong.' These two survive with complex music – they are not folk songs. Shepherds, housewives and labourers sang; but the lyrics were written by clerks. More than one is entitled *De clerico et puella* ('The Clerk and the Girl'); in others, a knight dismounts to talk to a girl:

| | |
|---|---|
| As I me rode this endre day | was riding   other |
| On mi playinge | |
| Seigh I where a litel may | saw   maid |
| Bigan to singe: | |
| 'The clot him clinge!' | may the earth cover him |

The singer does not get far with this sharp-tongued shepherdess.

Hundreds of medieval lyrics remain in manuscripts which can be roughly dated, but composition and authors are usually unknown. There are popular songs like 'The Nut-Brown Maid', drinking songs, Robin Hood ballads, and mnemonics like 'Thirty days hath September,/April, June and November'. There are a few political poems, like those written at the time of the Peasants' Revolt (1381): 'When Adam delved and Eve span/Who was then the gentleman?' and 'The ax was sharp, the stock was hard/In the fourteenth year of King Richard'. But most lyrics are religious, including the two earliest lyrics: from the 12th century we have 'Merie sungen the muneches binnen Ely …' ('Merrily sang the monks within Ely when King Canute rowed thereby. The men rowed near the land, and we heard the monks sing'); and the other is the hymn of St Godric (d.1170):

> Sainte Marie virgine
> Moder Jesu Cristes Nazarene,
> Onfo, schild, help thin Godrich,
> Onfang, bring heghilich with the in Godes riche.

Holy virgin Mary, Mother of Jesus Christ of Nazareth, receive, protect, help thy servant Godric; take, bring [him] highly with thee into God's kingdom.

Rhyme is first found in Church hymns; this song is translated from Latin, and ends in a pun on the author's name. We know from a full Latin Life that Godric, after many adventures and pilgrimages, became a hermit at Finchale near Durham, dying at the age of 105. Late religious lyrics are discussed below, with 15th-century literature.

## English prose

Another saint's life of the early 13th century is that of St Katherine, which gives its name to the Katherine Group of texts, written for nuns in Herefordshire. It includes lives of St Margaret and St Juliana, and the *Ancrene Riwle*, a Rule for Anchoresses, later rewritten for general use as the *Ancrene Wisse*, or Anchoresses' Guide. These are the first substantial works in early Middle English prose.

The *Riwle* is addressed to three well-born sisters 'of one father and one mother in the blossom of your youth', choosing to withdraw from the world to a life of prayer and contemplation. It prescribes regular reading and meditation, directed to the inner life and the love of Christ. The sisters should keep two maids, so as not to have to shop or cook. Ladies with letters but no Latin were often the patrons and the readers of devotional writing in English. The life they chose was the kind of life which gave rise to 14th-century mystical writing.

The impulse to spiritual perfection was not confined to the religious: much devotional writing is for the laity. The Fourth Lateran Council of the Church (1215) decreed personal confession at least once a year. Confession and conscience abound in Ricardian poetry (the poetry of the reign of Richard II). The Council also required the preaching of a homily at Mass after the gospel. It was chiefly in church that unlettered people heard speech composed with art.

# ▌ The fourteenth century

## Spiritual writing

Spiritual writing, seeking a discipline of the spirit to become closer to God, begins in Middle English with **Richard Rolle** (*c*.1300–49). Such writing had revived with Bernard of Clairvaux, although there had been mystical writing in English since *The Dream of the Rood* in the 8th century. Rolle had studied at Oxford and Paris, and his Latin works were much read in Europe. His English writings include the *Ego Dormio* ('I sleep') a meditation on the Old Testament *Song of Songs* as an allegory of Christ's love for the Church and the soul, and a Psalter with an allegorical commentary. Poems and prose marked by a musical rhetoric poured out from his Yorkshire hermitage. His *Form of Living* celebrates the solitary's direct experience of the divine, especially through devotion to the holy name of Jesus: 'It shall be in thine ear joy, in thy mouth honey, and in thy heart melody.'

Very different is the anonymous 'book of Contemplacyon the which is clepyd *the Clowede of Unknowyng* in the which a soule is onyd [united] with God'. This union comes by self-surrender: 'God wil thou do but loke on hym, and late [let] Him al one.' Looking on Him and leaving Him alone to work leads to darkness, 'and as it were a cloude of unknowyng, thou wost never what, savyng that thou felist in thi wille a naked entent unto God'. God is felt in and through this necessary cloud, not behind it. The novice asks 'How schal I think on himself, and what is hee?' The master replies, 'I wote never' ('I know not'). In this kind of negative theology, God is loved but cannot be imagined. *The Book of Privy Counselling* and *Dionise Hid Divinitie* may be by the author of *The Cloud*.

*The Scale* (or *Ladder*) *of Perfection* of **Walter Hilton** (d.1379) is addressed to a contemplative, and to all who wish to live the spiritual life. The self's imperfection must be known before the gift of God's love can be perceived.

A soule that hath yyft of love thorw [through] gracious byholdynge of Jesu ... he is naght besye [busy] forto streyne hymself over his myght ... Therfore preyeth he, and that desyreth he, that the love of God wolde touchen hym with hys blesside lyght, that he myghtte seen [see] a litel of hym by his gracious presence, thenne ssolde [should] he love hym; and so by thys way cometh the yyft of love, that is God, into a soule.

## Julian of Norwich

**Julian of Norwich** (*c*.1343–*c*.1413/27) is the finest English spiritual writer before George Herbert, and the first great writer of English prose. She says that she had her *Revelations* during a near-fatal illness in 1373, when she was thirty; Margery Kempe visited her in Norwich in 1413. Dame Julian set down her 'showings', meditated on them, and later expanded them.

She had prayed God for three things: remembrance of his Passion; a sickness to hasten her union with him; contrition, compassion and longing for him. In May

1373 she had a 'showing' of the Passion. Her next 'showing' was of Our Lady, 'a simple mayden and a meeke, yong of age, a little waxen above a chylde, in the stature as she was when she conceivede.' The new-born Christ child 'shewed a littel thing, the quantitie of an haselnott, lying in the palme of my hand … and it was as rounde as a balle. I looked theran with the eye of my understanding, and thought, What may this be? And it was answered generaelly thus: It is all that is made.' The littleness of created things must be reduced to nought if we are to come to the creator. 'It liketh God that we rest in him … he hath made us only to himself.'

Again she has a 'bodily sight' of the Passion: the blood falling as fast as raindrops fall from eaves and as round as herring scales. 'I saw him, and sought him, and I had him, and I wantyd [lacked] him … .' 'And after this I saw God in a poynte; that is to say in my understandyng, by which syght I saw he is in al thyng.' 'He was hangyng uppe in the eyer as men hang a cloth for to drye'. The flesh under the thorns was 'rympylde [rumpled] with a tawny coloure, lyke a drye bord'. Christ tells her that the wound in his right side is 'large inow for alle mankynde that shalle be savyd to rest in pees and love'. He also tells her 'that alle shalle be wele, and alle shalle be wele, and alle maner of thynge shalle be wele'. Of Christ's compassion she writes: 'Ech kynde compassion that man hath on hys evyn-Cristen [fellow-Christian] with charyte, it is Crist in hym. Hys love excusyth us; and of hys gret curtesy he doth away alle our blame and beholdeth us with ruth and pytte as children innocens and unlothfulle.' Christ explains: 'I it am, I it am. I it am that is hyghest. I it am that thou lovyst. I it am that thou lykyst, I it am that thou servyst. I it am that thou longest. I it am that thou desyryst. I it am that thou menyste. I it am that is alle.' And 'Oure lyfe is alle grounded and rotyd [rooted] in love, and without love we may nott lyve.'

These brief extracts indicate Julian's focus on central Christian teachings and the purity of her style; but not the richness of the Showings, nor of her meditations in the mystical tradition of the Bible from Augustine to Bernard. Among other women mystics of the 14th century was St Bridget of Sweden (1303–73).

The Bohemian reformer John Hus said that **John Wyclif** (*c*.1330–84) translated all the Bible into English, but no extant English text is now ascribed to this Oxford theologian. (His followers produced an English Vulgate so literal as to be almost unreadable.) It was not the first Bible in English – there are Old English versions. But before lay literacy, the Word could not be spread except by mouth, which was the role of the Church.

Wyclif's attacks on Church abuses won support, but his denial of the Real Presence of Christ in the Eucharist was heresy; his followers, known as Lollards, were repressed, and his own polemics suppressed. Wyclif was a reformer, not a writer of English. The Bible his followers produced lacks the qualities which made Luther's version the exemplar of modern German.

## Secular prose

Since the end of the Peterborough Chronicle in 1154, English secular prose – non-religious prose – had been used for practical matters, but in Richard II's reign English came into general use. **John Trevisa** translated a French encyclopedia and a Latin world history; adding that, as grammar-school teaching was now (1385) in English rather than in French, children know no more French than does their left heel.

The **Sir John Mandeville** who wrote his *Travels* at this time may have been as fictional as most of his stories. Although he claims as his own experiences the travellers' tales he translated from French, he advances his more exotic claims with a disarming hesitancy. The chief 'travels' are to the Holy Land, thrice visited by Chaucer's Wife of Bath, twice by St Godric, and once by **Margery Kempe**. Margery (*c.*1373–*c.*1440), a Kings Lynn housewife, dictated *The Book of Margery Kempe*, revising it in 1436. In a mental crisis after the birth of the first of her fourteen children, she had a religious conversion; her confessional testament is fascinating and artless. The Paston Letters, the correspondence of a 15th-century Norfolk family, have a similar human interest.

### Ricardian poetry 1377–99

| Events | | Literature | |
| --- | --- | --- | --- |
| 1337–1453 | Hundred Years War, between England and France | | |
| 1346 | Edward III's victory at Crécy | | |
| 1348–9 | Black Death | | |
| 1356 | Victory at Poitiers | | |
| | | *c.*1370 | Geoffrey Chaucer, *The Book of the Duchess* |
| 1377 | Richard II's accession | *c.*1377 | William Langland, *Piers Plowman* (B Text) |
| 1381 | Peasants' Revolt | *c.*1382–5 | Chaucer, *Troilus and Criseyde* |
| | | *c.*1387 | Chaucer begins *Canterbury Tales*; John Gower begins *Confessio Amantis* |
| | | | Popularity of Mystery plays evident from Chaucer's 'Miller's Tale' |
| | | *c.*1390 | *Gawain* manuscript; Anon., Stanzaic *Morte* |
| 1399 | Richard II deposed by Henry IV | *c.*1400 | Anon., Alliterative *Morte* |

## Ricardian poetry

The reign of Richard II saw the arrival of a mature poetic literature in Middle English. Besides lyric and religious prose of the highest quality, we have spirited Arthurian verse romances in the Stanzaic *Morte* and the Alliterative *Morte*. The revival of English alliterative verse produced at least two great poems, *Piers Plowman* and *Sir Gawain and the Green Knight*, with three other fine poems in the *Gawain* manuscript. Verse drama was also popular, although surviving texts are 15th-century.

The historic development, however, is the appearance of an assured syllabic verse in the long poems of **John Gower** (?1330–1408), and Geoffrey Chaucer's establishment in English of the decasyllabic verse of France and Italy: in the *Troilus* stanza and the couplets of the *Canterbury Tales*. Chaucer's importance is not merely historical. He is as humane as any English non-dramatic poet, with a versatility and narrative skill never exceeded. Gower wrote in three languages, Chaucer in English only, an instrument with a richer tone and a deeper social reach than French or Latin. Chaucer (*c.*1342–1400) was a bright star in a sky with many bright stars; his importance was recognized at his death.

### Piers Plowman

*Piers Plowman* is a dream poem in the alliterative style. It opens on the Malvern Hills in Worcestershire:

| | |
|---|---|
| In a somer seson,   whan soft was the sonne, | |
| I shope me in shroudes | I put on outer clothes |
| as I a shepe were, | as if I were a shepherd |
| In habite as an heremite | in the garb of a hermit |
| unholy of workes | not holy in conduct |
| Went wyde in this world   wondres to here. | marvels   hear |
| Ac on a May mornynge   on Malverne hulles | but   hills |
| Me byfel a ferly, | A wonder befell me, |
| of fairy me thoughte; | from fairyland it seemed to me |
| I was wery forwandred | tired out with wandering |
| and went me to reste | |
| Under a brode banke   bi a bornes side, | broad   stream's |
| And as I lay and lened   and loked in the waters, | leaned |
| I slombred in a slepyng, | |
| it sweyved so merye. | flowed along so sweetly |

The author is said in a manuscript of *c.*1400 to be **William Langland** (*c.*1330–*c.*1386), probably from near Malvern. A married cleric in minor orders, he writes more about London and Westminster than Malvern. He revised his great work several times; it survives in fifty-two manuscripts and three or four versions, known as the A, B, C and Z texts; the above quotation is from the B text.

The Dreamer falls asleep:
'And as I lay and lened
and loked in the wateres,
I slombred in a slepyng,
it sweyved so merye'.

From MS CCC 201 f.1 Historical initial depicting the dreamer (parchment) Piers Plowman (15th century)

The sleeper dreams that the world is a fair field full of folk, between the tower of Truth and the dungeon of Hell:

| | |
|---|---|
| Than gan I to meten   a merveilouse swevene, | dream vision |
| That I was in a wildernesse,   wist I never where. | knew |
| As I bihelde into the Est,   and heigh to the sonne, | up |
| I seigh a toure on a toft   trielich ymaked; | a tower on a hill, truly built |
| A depe dale binethe,   a dongeon thereinne | |
| With depe dyches and derke   and dredful of sight. | to see |
| A faire felde ful of folke   fonde I there bytwene, | I could see |
| Of alle maner of men,   the mene and the riche, | humble |
| Worchyng and wandryng   as the world asketh. | requires |
| Some putten hem to the plow, | themselves |
|               pleyed ful selde … | very seldom |

One such worker is Piers (Peter) the Plowman, after whom the poem is called. Langland follows this Prologue with a series of Passus (Lat. 'steps') in a pilgrimage. The dreamer is a learner: we share his experiences, learning from his visions and encounters with Reason, Anima, Holy Church and Lady Meed. The didactic allegory is complex, and its progress is less predictable than in its continental predecessors. Each dream is a fresh start on old problems: collective neglect of God and neighbour; how to live well and find personal pardon and salvation in Christ's redemption of mankind.

The poem is colloquial, its verse rough and its architecture Gothic, abruptly changing from direct social satire to symbolic allegories of salvation. Langland does not want to reform the structures or ideals of Church and society, but our hearts and behaviour. This was the hope of those who shouted lines from *Piers Plowman* in the Peasants' Revolt. What is new in his work is its Gothic existentialism, its dizzying structure, and its deep engagement. In atmosphere, though not setting and convention, it parallels Dostoevsky's *Brothers Karamazov* (1880). Its scheme is like that of Bunyan's *Pilgrim's Progress* (1684), but less straightforward; its sweep like that of Ezra Pound's *Cantos* (1917–59), but theological. This very English poem, more of its time than Chaucer's, is often hard work, but it seizes its audience. Evangelical and prophetic, it breathes in theology and breathes out the Latin of the Vulgate and the liturgy.

The climax is the account of the Redemption, in Passus 18. On Palm Sunday Christ entered Jerusalem as a knight clad in 'our' arms (*humana natura*), 'somdel [somewhat] like to Piers Plowman'. But one of the soldiers at the Crucifixion called out 'Hail, master' and struck him with reeds:

| | |
|---|---|
| '*Ave, rabby*,' quod that ribaude,   and threw redes at hym, | scoffer   reeds |
| Nailled hym witth thre nailles   naked on the rode, | cross |
| And poysoun on a pole   thei put up to his lippes, | |
| And bede hym drynke his deth-yvel; | death-drink |
|             his dayes were ydone. | |
| 'And yif that thow sotil be,   help now thi-selven. | if   clever |
| If thow be Cryst and kynges sone,   come downe of the rode; | off |
| Thanne shul we leve that Lyf the loveth | believe   Life loves thee |
|             and wil nought lete the dye.' | |
| '*Consummatum est*,' quod Cryst | It is finished |
|             and comsed for to swowe; | began to swoon |
| Pitousliche and pale,   as a prisoun that deyeth; | prisoner |

> The lord of lyf and of light
> tho leyed his eyen togideres.          closed his eyes
> The daye for drede withdrowe    and derke bicam the sonne.
> The wal wagged and clef                shook   split
> and al the worlde quaved.              trembled

The dreamer sees Christ harrowing hell to free mankind. The four Daughters of God (Mercy, Truth, Righteousness and Peace) dispute the justice of the Redemption, but at last are reconciled: 'Tyl the daye dawed this demaiseles daunced/That men rongen to the resurexion …' ('These maidens danced until day dawned and men rang out Easter'). The bells awake the dreamer. Piers, his wife Kit and his daughter Kalote kiss the cross and put the fiend to flight.

## Sir Gawain and the Green Knight

Clerical and romance traditions meet in *Sir Gawain and the Green Knight*, the finest English verse romance. *Sir Gawain* is found in a manuscript with three other poems, *Patience*, *Cleanness* and *Pearl*, all in alliterative measure and a late 14th-century Cheshire dialect, presumably by the one author. Each poem is strikingly original and intelligent, but *Gawain* must stand here for all.

It has a typical romance opening, an outrageous challenge to the knights at King Arthur's court at Christmas; the challenge is accepted, and a knight of the Round Table rides forth on his quest, surviving adventures and a fearful final encounter, to return to Camelot a year later. The themes of prowess and gallant conduct are combined with that of the Grail-quest, chastity. *Gawain* is a romance of rare economy and zest. It displays chivalry – brave knights and fair ladies, magnificent hospitality in the castle, courage in the field and fine language – in a plot combining adventure, excitement and surprise. It is full of festive fun and games, a masque-like entertainment, yet it raises questions about chivalry, that bonding of a military code onto the Gospel, which maintained Christendom. The preaching of the Crusades in the 12th and 13th centuries refined the ethic of chivalry and consecrated it as a religious rule of life. The knightly code, devoted to Christ, protecting the rights of the weak (especially ladies) and treating antagonists with honour, was a calling. Invoked in ceremony and literature, it often fell short in practice.

The Green Knight, a green giant with a huge axe, offers to take a blow from the axe – in exchange for a return blow in a year's time. Gawain volunteers, to save the honour of his uncle Arthur and of the Round Table. Beheaded by Gawain, the Green Knight picks up his severed head from among the feet of the diners, and remounts his green horse, causing consternation:

> For the hede in his honde he haldes up even,
> Toward the derrest on the dece he dresses the face;
> And hit lyfte up the yye-lyddes, and loked ful brode,
> And meled thus much with his muthe …

For he holds up the head upright, he turns the face to the highest on the dais; and it lifted up the eye-lids and looked broadly, and spoke as follows with its mouth …

The mouth now tells Gawain to keep his bargain at the Green Chapel on New Year's Day, or be a coward. By the following Christmas, Gawain has made his way through the wilderness. He fights bulls, bears, boars and giants (all in one line), but finds the cold worse: 'Near slain with the sleet, he slept in his irons'. The running water 'hanged high over his head in hard *iisse-ikkles*'. He prays to Mary, and a wonderful castle appears, so battlemented and pinnacled 'That pared out of paper purely [exactly] it semed'. Gawain, who has a reputation as a gentleman, especially with the ladies, is welcomed to the castle by its hearty lord. The host proposes that while he hunts in the mornings, Gawain should sleep in to recover his strength; in the evenings they shall exchange their winnings. Early each morning the radiant lady of the castle comes to Gawain's chamber and locks the door after her. She flirts with him, pressing him to take a kiss and other tokens of love. Gawain plays well, declining without refusing; but is obliged to take a kiss, and the next day two kisses. These he gives to the lord in exchange for the deer and a boar the lord wins in his hunting. On the third day Gawain is persuaded to take three kisses – and also a sash from the lady which makes the wearer invulnerable. He gives the lord the kisses but conceals the sash, receiving in exchange the skin of an old fox.

On New Year's morning at the Green Chapel the Green Knight appears; he threatens huge blows but gives Gawain a slight cut on the neck. Gawain exults. Then the Green Knight reveals that he is the lord of the castle, and that he and his wife have been testing Gawain. The cut on his neck is a token punishment for concealing the sash: 'for ye loved your life; the less I yow blame.' Furious and ashamed, Gawain loses his famous courtesy for a moment. He rides home to Camelot, wearing the sash; he confesses his fault, blushing with shame. The court laugh with relief, declaring that they will all wear the sash for Gawain's sake: 'For that was acorded the renoun of the Rounde Table/And he honoured that hit had evermore after.'

Life and death thus depend upon integrity in private sexual and social conduct. Gawain the impeccable breaks his word; it is a venial sin. Yet the Round Table wear the mark of their fellow's fault as a mark of honour. At the end of the poem, another hand has written HONY SOYT QUI MAL PENCE, a motto which suits the open-endedness of the poem and resembles the motto of **the Order of the Garter**. *Gawain* has gusto and wit: a poem which is itself a Christmas game, it celebrates chivalry while asking how Christian it is.

## John Gower

**John Gower** (?1330–1408) wrote his *Mirour de l'Omme* ('Mirror of Mankind'), a long didactic poem in French, in the 1370s. His Latin poem *Vox Clamantis* cries out against the social evils of the day. His English *Confessio Amantis* ('A Lover's Confession') survives in fifty manuscripts and three versions, the last completed in 1393. A gentleman landowner in Suffolk and Kent, Gower was on terms of trust with Chaucer, who submitted *Troilus* to him for correction. At the end of Gower's *Confessio Amantis*, Venus in turn says, 'And gret wel Chaucer when ye mete/As mi disciple and mi poete …'. Caxton printed both poets, and the critic George Puttenham in 1589 called them the first masters of the 'art of English poesy'.

The *Confessio* is a narrative in dialogue form: Genius, a priest in the religion of courtly love, hears the confession of Amans, 'the Lover'. To examine the conscience of the Lover, Genius takes him through the Seven Deadly Sins, giving examples of each in its five aspects by telling cautionary tales from antiquity, often from Ovid. Although a priest of Venus and of the benign goddess Nature (found also in Chaucer's *Parlement of Fowls*), Genius is also a true priest and eventually persuades the aging Amans to give up courtly love, however refined and refining, for a higher love and wisdom. The *Confessio*, like all Ricardian poetry, addresses the role of Christianity in a Christian world which remains *the* world.

Some of Gower's tales are told again by Chaucer: his Wife of Bath tells Gower's

**The Order of the Garter**
Edward III in 1348 founded the Order of the Garter, the first European order of chivalry, modelled on the fellowship of knights of Arthur's Round Table. Its members vow loyalty to their lord and to defend the right. Its motto is *Honi soit qui mal y pense*: at a ball at Calais, the King danced with the young Countess of Salisbury; when she dropped her garter Edward bound it on his own knee with the words: 'Shame on him who thinks evil of it.' The words are on the Garter worn as a device by the twenty-four members of the Order at St George's Chapel, Windsor. The Knights of the Garter feasted at a Round Table made in the 13th century, still to be seen in Winchester Castle.

tale of the Loathly Bride, and Chaucer's Man of Law tells that of Gower's Constance. Another tale told by both is Ovid's Ceyx and Alcyone. This is how Gower describes the embraces of Alcyone (who has turned into the Halcyon bird):

> Hire wynges bothe abrod sche spradde,
> And him, so as sche may suffise,     *as well as she could*
> Beclipte and keste in such a wise,     *embraced*
> As sche was whilom want to do:     *formerly*
> Hire wynges for hire armes tuo     *two*
> Sche tok, and for hire lippes softe
> Hire harde bile, and so ful ofte     *bill*
> Scho fondeth in hire briddes forme,     *tries*
> If that sche mihte hirself conforme,
> To do the plesance of a wif,
> As sche dede in that other lif.

If Chaucer has more variety and power, both have graceful verse, an engaging narrative voice and a light touch.

Chaucer riding on his pilgrimage; the figure is adapted from a standing portrait. The pen-case shows he is a writer. He points to the beginning of the tale he tells about Melibee. From the Ellesmere Manuscript of the *Canterbury Tales* of c.1410.

# Geoffrey Chaucer

Geoffrey Chaucer was born about 1342 in the Vintry, the vintners' street, in London's walled City; with nearby Westminster, this then had *c.*30,000 inhabitants. His father and grandfather were wine merchants, but Geoffrey became a king's man, a professional royal servant, holding a series of posts, including Collector of Customs and Clerk of the King's Works. He was also a diplomat, who travelled on the king's business, often to France, once to Spain, twice to Italy. His name occurs four hundred times in the records, not as a poet. He lived in London and in Kent, surviving the Black Death, the French wars, the Peasants' Revolt, the Lords Appellants' challenge to Richard II, and Richard's deposition by Henry IV. Chaucer's writing reveals nothing of these, nor of his personal life. His mother married three times. He himself married Philippa, daughter of a Flemish knight; her sister later became John of Gaunt's third wife. Geoffrey's sister was a nun. Long after he died in 1400, his son Thomas became the most important royal servant in England.

Geoffrey's career as a king's man was not unusual, but he was unusually good at his other calling, writing English verse. His first lines show his command: 'It is the Romance of the Rose/In which the art of love I close.' He enjoys his chosen task, the translation of *Le Roman de la Rose*, the famous 13th-century love-encyclopedia. Its dreamer dreams that he wakes early and goes out into a May landscape, with a garden whose outer wall is painted with figures: Avarice, Envy, Age, and Poverty. The gate is kept by the porter, Idleness. Within is the exclusive Garden of Love, with Gladness, Mirth, Beauty, Riches and other courtiers, the God of Love, and the Rose. Chaucer stopped at line 1704, others continued the work.

The early poems are based on French dream visions: *The Book of the Duchess* is based on Guillaume de Machaut. Eustache Deschamps called Chaucer *le grand translateur*. Chaucer cannot sleep; he reads to

> drive the night away;
> For me thoughte it beter play
> Than play either at ches or tables.      draughts
> And in this bok were written fables
> That clerkes had in olde tyme,
> And other poets, put in rime …

He falls asleep reading Ovid's story of Queen Alcyone, who dreamed that she sought her dead husband King Seys. He dreams that he awakes in a May dawn, in a chamber whose stained glass tells of Troy and of *The Romance of the Rose*. Going out, he sees a

## Chronology of Chaucer's works

| | |
|---|---|
| before 1372 | The first part of *The Romaunt of the Rose* |
| 1368–72 | *The Book of the Duchess* |
| 1378–83 | *The House of Fame* |
| 1380–2 | *The Parlement of Fowls* |
| 1382–6 | *Boece* and *Troilus and Criseyde* |
| 1380–7 | *Palamon and Arcite* |
| *c.*1387 | *The Legend of Good Women* |
| 1388–1400 | *The Canterbury Tales* |

hunt, and is led by a hound into a wood where he meets a man in black, a king who complains eloquently about his beloved, one 'goode faire White'. Chaucer asks sympathetic questions, which lead to the revelation that White is dead. The hunting horn blows, the black king rides back to 'A lang castel with walles white/By seynt Johan'. This identifies him as John of Lancaster, whose wife Blanche had died. Chaucer wakes with a book in his hand, Ovid's *Metamorphoses*.

*The House of Fame* is a three-part vision in which the dreaming poet finds himself in a Temple of Venus, its glass walls engraved with the story of Dido and Aeneas. In Book II, Chaucer is carried up in the air by an Eagle who discourses on the theory of sound, to the House of Fame (Rumour, but also Poetry), a bewildering place described in Book III. The poem breaks off as Chaucer meets a man whose name he cannot give: 'But he semed for to be/A man of gret auctorite …'.

## The Parlement of Fowls

Chaucer's first completed work is a dream, his second a broken dream; his next, *The Parlement of Fowls*, is a dream ending in a puzzle. The poet seeks to understand Love, which, so books say, has bewildering effects. He has been reading Cicero's *Scipio's Dream*, in which Africanus explains how the immortal soul can attain the heavens only by working for the common good. Chaucer sleeps, and dreams of Africanus, who takes him to a paradisal Garden of Love, containing a dark Temple of Venus. Out in the Garden, the goddess Nature presides over the Parliament of Birds: it is St Valentine's Day, when fowls, birds, chose their mates. Three noble eagles seek the hand of a beautiful female, the *formel*, each protesting that he will die if she will not have him. The common birds lose patience, the goose saying: 'But [unless] she wol love hym, lat hym love another.' When the sparrowhawk says that this is the remark of a goose, 'the laughter aros of gentil fowles alle'. '"Nay, God forbede, a lovere shulde chaunge!"/The turtle [dove] seyde, and wex for shame al red.' The duck and cuckoo mock this gentil sentiment, the noble birds of prey defend it. Nature calls a halt and asks the *formel* to decide. 'If I were Resoun', she says, I'd counsel you to take the royal eagle. But the *formel*, granted a free choice, speaks as follows: 'Almyghty queen! unto this yer be gon,/I axe respit for to avise me,/And after that to have my choys al fre …'.

The *formel* uses here the words with which the king declined a Bill presented by Parliament: *le roi s'avisera*, 'the king will think it over'. She 'wol nat serve Venus ne Cupide,/Forsothe as yit …'. Nature dismisses the Parliament. The birds, except for the royal eagles, embrace their mates.

> But fyrst were chosen foules for to synge,
> As yer by yer was alwey hir usaunce        their
> To synge a roundel at here departynge,        their
> To don to Nature honour and plesaunce.
> The note, I trowe, imaked was in Fraunce,        tune    believe
> The wordes were swiche as ye may heer fynde,
> The nexte vers, as I now have in mynde.
>
> 'Now welcome, somer, with thy sonne softe,
> That hast this wintres wedres overshake        storms shaken off
> And driven away the longe nyghtes blake.'

The roundel interlaces its verses, ending with the lines with which it began.

| | |
|---|---|
| And with the shouting, whan the song was do | done |
| That foules maden at here flyght awey, | their |
| I wok, and othere bokes tok me to, | |
| To reed upon, and yit I rede alwey. | |
| I hope, ywis, to rede so som day | |
| That I shale mete som thyng for to fare | dream   so as to get on |
| The bet, and thus to rede I nyl nat spare. | better |

The poet, awakened by the dawn chorus, returns to his books. *The Parlement* has philosophy, a love-vision, a beast-fable, a debate, and a light and intriguing manner. Chaucer mixes genres and attitudes: he is a bookworm seeking enlightenment about love, an owl who will never be a nightingale. Boethius, Dante, Langland and the poet of *Pearl* dream to seek enlightenment, but Chaucer's comical self-presentation is disarmingly different.

A learner in love requires not a book but a beloved. If we re-run the dream backwards, the *formel* calls the bluff of her noble suitors the eagles, who will not die. She keeps them waiting until *she* chooses. The farmyard birds know that love is physical; but humans should do better than birds. The Temple of Venus is hot with idolized sexual pleasure. *Scipio's Dream* says that love of the common good leads to immortality, unlike the love of *likerous folk*. Extremes of lust and of idealization are, then, to be avoided. Yet human nature is not very reasonable: love remains a puzzle, insoluble to those who take themselves too seriously. Such a fresh, elegant presentation of complex issues is dazzlingly new in English. The *Parlement* is not equalled in French until Pierre de Ronsard in the early 16th century or in English until the late 16th century.

Chaucer's work drew on Latin, and, in modern languages, on models in French (*The Book of the Duchess*) and Italian (*Troilus*). He brought modern European modes into English. He seems to have read Langland, but not *Gawain*.

The *Prologue* to the *Legend of Good Women* is Chaucer's last love-vision, written in the first decasyllabic couplets in English. It opens in a May landscape, full of flowers; the courtly May Day love-cult involved flowers, especially the daisy. Chaucer is found kneeling by a daisy by the God of Love, attended by his Queen and her train, who sing a ballade in her praise: 'Hyd, Absalon, thy gilte tresses clere'. Love asks why his flower is venerated by Chaucer, an enemy to love:

| | |
|---|---|
| 'Thou maist yt nat denye, | |
| For in pleyn text, withouten nede of glose, | gloss |
| Thou hast translaat the Romaunce of the Rose, | |
| That is an heresye ayains my lawe, | |
| And makest wise folk from me withdrawe …; | |
| Hast thou nat mad in Englysh ek the bok | also |
| How that Crisseyde Troylus forsok, | |
| In shewynge how that wemen han don mis?' | amiss |

The Queen of Love defends Chaucer:

| | |
|---|---|
| 'This man to yow may wrongly ben acused, | be |
| Ther as by ryght hym oughte ben excused. | |
| Or elles, sire, for that this man is nyce, | foolish |
| He may translate a thyng in no malyce, | |
| But for he useth bokes for to make, | is accustomed |
| And taken non hed of what matere he take, | to take no heed |
| Therefor he wrot the Rose and ek Crisseyde | |
| Of innocence, and nyste what he seyde…. | innocently   knew not |

The Queen is Alceste, who offered to die in the place of her husband, and has been turned into a daisy: a new metamorphosis. She bids Chaucer make a Legendary of the lives of the saints of love. He tells nine legends of love's 'martyrs' – Cleopatra, Dido, Lucrece, Ariadne *et al.* – in penance for his 'heresies'. The *Prologue* is the most 'autobiographical' of Chaucer's visions, and his last charade in the worship of Love. The Victorians loved it. Today it seems a try-out for the *Canterbury Tales*.

### Troilus and Criseyde

'How that Crisseyde Troylus forsok' is told in *Troilus and Criseyde*, a work of marked symmetry. It opens:

> The double sorwe of Troilus to tellen
> That was the king Priamus sone of Troye,
> In lovynge, how his aventures fellen
> From wo to wele, and after out of joie,
> My purpos is, ere that I parte fro ye.

The poem, set in Troy in the tenth year of the siege, is in 8239 lines and five books. In Book I, Prince Troilus falls in love with Criseyde, the widowed daughter of the seer Calcas who has defected to the Greeks. In II Pandarus brings together his neice Criseyde and the prostrate Troilus. In III their love is consummated with *joie* at Pandarus' house. In IV the Trojans agree to swap Criseyde for the captured Antenor. In V Criseyde 'allone, among the Grekis stronge' accepts the protection of Diomede. Troilus trusts her to return, and when her infidelity is proved, is killed. The sorrow is *double*: the *tragedye* has four books of sorrow, one of joy. In its 'rhyme royal' (a stanza rhyming *ababbcc*), *Troie* often rhymes with *joie*, and *Criseyde* with *deyde*. The end is foreknown: interest lies in its detailed unfolding.

This story had been developed in Boccaccio's *Filostrato* from the 'Troy books' elaborated in the Middle Ages out of Homer, Virgil and Statius. Chaucer's version is the supreme English example of a doomed story of courtly love. The literary dignity of its opening, quoted above, relaxes with *ere that I parte fro ye*, an 'oral' gesture to the audience. Chaucer seems innocent and slightly foolish, and the teller's quick sympathy towards the lovers complicates interpretation. When their love is consummated, he exclaims:

> O blisful nyght, of hem so longe isought,     them
> How blithe unto hem bothe two thow weere!
> Why nad I swich oon with my soule ybought,     had I not such a one
> Ye, or the leeste joie that was theere?     Yes

His willingness to sell his soul for a kiss comes back into the mind when at the end we read this appeal:

> O yonge, fresshe folkes, he or she,
> In which that love up groweth with youre age,
> Repeyreth hom fro worldly vanite,     home
> And of youre herte up casteth the visage
> To thilke God that after his ymage     that same
> Yow made, and thynketh al nys but a faire     consider   fair
> This world, that passeth soone as floures faire.     flowers

The young are next told to trust Jesus, who *nyl falsen no wight* ('will not betray anyone') – unlike human lovers. After the teller's sympathy, it is a surprise to be told that the lovers' joys were unreal.

The surprise has been prepared. Each book opens with a lofty invocation in the manner of Dante, and the action is punctuated by comments from a work which Chaucer had translated, Boethius' *Consolation of Philosophy*, a medieval handbook to classical philosophy. Boethius speaks for a puzzled, suffering humanity, but eventually accepts Lady Philosophy's austere arguments. The five books of *Troilus* follow the revolution of Fortune's wheel: sexual bliss is fleeting and temporary, less real than eternal truths, and hence *fals*.

On the human level, the lovers' predicament is real enough. The smitten Troilus complains upon his bed. The lovers come together only through the scheming of Pandarus, who has to push the swooning Troilus into Criseyde's bed. When Troilus tells her she must yield, she replies: 'Ne hadde I er [Had I not before] now, my swete herte deere,/Ben yelde, ywis [indeed], I were now nought [not] here.' She has 'been yielded': she does not yield herself. Pandarus, her supposed protector, has indeed worked tirelessly to get her to yield, and in his house. But uncle and neice have a knowing relationship; next morning, she calls him a fox. Troilus too colludes in Pandarus' lie that he, Troilus, is about to die of jealousy – a ruse to get him into Criseyde's room. Deceit and fidelity are part of the secrecy of courtly love. But Troilus' pretended jealousy turns into real jealousy, and her sincere promises are broken by events. Once they are parted, *sorwe* begins to bite.

Criseyde's characterization is ambiguous and opaque, a matter of suggestion and interpretation, closer to Samuel Richardson and Henry James than to *Le Chanson de Roland*. Readers differ over the culpability of Criseyde; the narrator excuses her as 'tendre-herted, slydyng of corage', terms which also fit him. But when Criseyde gives Diomede Troilus's love-token, the narrator says 'Men seyn – I not – that she yaf hym her herte' ('They say – I don't know – that she gave him her heart'). The narrator does not know, but the author invites a guess. The blind pagan lovers are at the mercy of events: the God of Love makes Troilus fall for Criseyde as a punishment for laughing at love. Criseyde is exchanged willy-nilly for Antenor, who is to betray Troy to the Greeks. Readers are free to choose sides, since each personage is presented from its own perspective. Romantics can identify with Troilus, or with Criseyde, or pity the pair of them, broken by circumstance. 'Pite renneth sone in gentil herte' is a line that comes five times in Chaucer. If we do not pity, the ending has no sting, and the poem fails. But the reader can see the folly of love, and the lovers punished by their passions. After the slow revolution of Fortune's wheel, Troilus is killed in one line – 'Despitously him slew the fierse Achille.' His spirit looks down from the heavens at those weeping at his funeral, and 'in himself he lough'. Sudden death and laughter: a Gothic change of perspective.

## The Canterbury Tales

Chaucer's last work, *The Canterbury Tales*, is today his most popular. Its opening 'When that April with his shoures soote' is the first line of English verse that is widely known. The sweet showers of April that pierce to the root the dryness of March are a *reverdie*, a celebration of Spring renewal. This opening, a welcome to April showers and to the classical god of the West Wind, is often taken as a starting point for 'Eng. Lit.' (In 1922 T. S. Eliot began his lament for civilization, *The Waste Land*, with 'April is the cruellest month', reversing Chaucer's *reverdie*.) It would be better to take Chaucer's opening line as confirming that English poetry, already seven centuries old, had successfuly domesticated new European literary traditions.

Chaucer tells how he was joined in the Tabard Inn, Southwark, by a company of 'sondry folk,/And pilgrims were they alle'. Spring is the pilgrimage season in Christendom:

> And specially from every shires ende
> Of Engelond to Caunterbury they wende
> The hooly blisful martir for to seeke              *blessed   seek*
> That hem hath holpen when that they were seeke.   *helped   sick*

The innkeeper proposes a tale-telling game to pass the time on the two-day ride to the shrine of St Thomas Becket of Canterbury, killed by agents of Henry II in 1170 at the altar of his Cathedral. The thirty pilgrims are each to tell two tales on the way and two on the way back; the teller of the tale *of best sentence* [moral import] *and most solaas* [comfort, pleasure] wins a supper at the Tabard paid for by the others.

The game creates the *Tales*; pilgrim tales were proverbially known as 'Canterbury tales'. The pilgrims tell twenty-four tales of popular kinds: saints' lives, moral fables, rude jokes, beast fables, sermons, penitential treatises. Most often read today are the General Prologue and the tales of the Knight, the Miller, the Wife of Bath, the Merchant, the Franklin, the Pardoner and the Nun's Priest; less often, those of the Cook, the Reeve, the Man of Law, the Friar, the Summoner, the Clerk, the Shipman, the Prioress and 'Sir Thopas'. The moral tales are neglected; we prefer the clowns. The pilgrims do not behave well: they banter and tease, interrupt and quarrel; the Knight stops the Host attacking the Pardoner. Some do not tell tales; Chaucer tells two, since the Host halts his first. The Knight prevents the Monk from finishing the thirteenth of his tragedies.

The *Tales* are found in around eighty manuscripts, in separate sections or Fragments. The best manuscripts have ten Fragments, each with one or more tales. If some Fragments are incomplete, the *Tales* have a conclusion. As the shadows lengthen, with Canterbury in sight, the Host jocularly asks the Parson to speak last and 'knytte up wel a greet mateere'. He responds with 'a myrie tale in prose … To shewe yow the wey, in this viage,/Of thilke parfit glorious pilgrymage/That highte Jerusalem celestial'. His Tale is a confessor's manual based on the Seven Deadly Sins: a fitting end to a pilgrimage, and a comprehensive answer to its parliament of fools.

The First Fragment has the General Prologue, and the *Tales* of the the Knight, the Miller, the Reeve and the Cook. It is a polished introduction to and sample of the narrative of the *Tales* as a whole. Between the Spring opening and the Host's takeover of the pilgrimage, the roll of pilgrims in its colour, chat and variety is a miniature of English society. Chaucer joins his 'sondry folk': 'And shortly, whan the sonne was to reste,/So hadde I spoken with hem everichon/That I was of hir felaweshipe anon'. The diplomat wins the confidence of his puppets.

The pilgrims are types familiar from medieval social satire, but Chaucer makes them speak to him and through him to us: their voices animate their sparkling two-dimensional portraits. Medieval satirists reproved obstinate vice, but the pilgrim Chaucer praises his creatures, letting us see the imperfections to which they are blind. He loves the Prioress's ladylike table-manners and admires the fat Monk's beautiful boots. When the Monk disputes a text which says that a monk out of his cloister isn't worth an oyster, Chaucer agrees: 'And I seyde his opinion was good'. The bookish author enjoys the Monk's scorn at the absurd idea that he should do the work prescribed to monks:

> What sholde he studie and make hymselven wood,    *Why  mad*
> Upon a book in cloystre alwey to poure,            *pore*

| Or swynken with his handes, and laboure, | toil |
| As Austyn bit? How shal the world be served? | Augustine bade |
| Lat Austyn have his swynk to him reserved! | toil reserved to himself |

Chaucer's disciple Lydgate testified that Chaucer *seide alwey the beste*. This courtesy sharpens his irony, often directed at professional avarice. He says of the Lawyer, 'Nowher so bisy a man as he ther nas,/And yet he semed bisier than he was.' The Doctor is 'esy of dispense' [slow to spend money] – for 'He kepte that [what] he wan in pestilence' [Plague]. Chaucer's casual comments, usually innocent, are sometimes deadly. He wrote of 'the smylere with the knyf under the cloke'. He is an **ironist**, not a **satirist**; his comedy flickers between human sympathy and an absolute morality. His Knight, Parson and Plowman are ideal: defender of the faith, pastor, worker. His Clerk of Oxford, too, is an ideal:

| Noght o word spak he more than was neede. | one |
| And that was seyd in forme and reverence, | |
| And short and quyk and ful of hy sentence; | ethical truth |
| Sownynge in moral vertu was his speche, | Tending to |
| And gladly wolde he lerne and gladly teche. | |

The first tale, the Knight's, is a chivalric romance in which the princes Palamon and Arcite fall for the fair Emelye, whom they espy from their prison as she roams and sings in a garden below. They escape and fight over her, a fight stopped by Theseus, who ordains a tournament in which Emelye's hand is the prize. Before it, Arcite prays to Mars for Victory, Palamon to Venus for Emelye, Emelye to Diana not to marry; or, if she must, to wed 'hym that moost desireth me'. When Arcite has won, Emelye gives him a friendly look. His prayer has been answered. But Saturn sends an infernal fury, which makes Arcite's horse throw him in the moment of triumph; he dies in Emelye's arms. After years of mourning, Palamon and Emelye marry, on Theseus' advice. Chivalry tries to mend the injustice of the world.

After this attempt to settle a love-contest without bloodshed, the Host asks the Monk to speak, but has to give way to the drunken Miller. In the first funny story in English, the attractions of Alysoun drive three men mad, two young Oxford clerks and John, her old husband. The Miller makes fun of the Knight's tale, also provoking the Reeve (a carpenter) by making John (also a carpenter) incredibly stupid. The Reeve tells how a Miller is doubly cuckolded by two Cambridge students. The Cook then tells of a London apprentice dismissed for riotous living. He moves in with a friend whose wife kept a cookshop for the sake of appearances but *swyved for her sustenance*, the last line of the Fragment: 'for her living, she fucked'. The pilgrimage, with its April aspiration, communal devotion to the *blisful* saint, dawn start and chivalric romance, falls to sexual comedy in Oxford and farce in Cambridge. Instead of Canterbury or *Jerusalem celestial*, it has returned to the City, and to a knocking-shop. Love-contest gives way to love-making, then to sexual congress, then to sexual commerce. The Prodigal Son has rolled to the bottom of the stairs, and Chaucer stops.

The tone goes up in the Man of Law's Fragment II, down with the Wife of Bath in Fragment III, up with the Clerk in IV and down with the Merchant, then up in V with the Squire and the Franklin. In the second half of the *Tales*, moral *sentence* predominates over the mirthful *solaas* of the Shipman, 'Sir Thopas' and the Nun's Priest. In VIII, a Canon's Yeoman rides up to tell the pilgrims about his master's fraudulent alchemy. In IX, near 'a litel toun/Which that ycleped is Bobbe-up-and-doun', the

'A good Wif was ther of beside Bathe': Chaucer's Wife of Bath, an illustration from the *de luxe* Ellesmere manuscript of the *Canterbury Tales* (*c.*1410). She rides astride, carries a whip, and is looking for a sixth husband.

drunken Cook falls from his horse, and in X the Parson knits up the unravelling pilgrimage, telling how human faults can be forgiven and mankind saved.

For all its brilliant particulars, *The Canterbury Tales* makes us aware of general issues and typical destinies. Exceptionally a tale reveals the character of its teller, as with the Wife of Bath and the Pardoner, who have self-explaining Prologues and self-illustrating tales. Yet even they are not individuals but animated caricatures. Some tales reveal their tellers; others do not. The Nun's Priest's Tale, of a cock and his seven hens, is told by the one man in a house of women. Each tale can stand alone; relation to teller signifies less than relation to other tales. The *Tales* exemplify human conduct, self-deceiving or saintly, and its animal, rational and spiritual bases. The whole is a debate and drama of ideas and humours.

Chaucer is an author who makes fun of authority. The tales he himself tells, Sir Thopas and Melibee, would not have won the supper. 'Sir Thopas' is a parody of popular tail-rhyme romance, full of silly conventions, empty phrases and bad rhymes. The Host, missing the point, cuts him off with the comment that his rhyming 'is not worth a turd'. Chaucer then tells 'a litel thyng in prose', the lengthy moral fable of Melibeus and Prudence. The author, dismissed by his puppet, the Host, shows him the way to wisdom with many a sentence. Chaucer repositions himself with the speed of a hummingbird. The detail of the General Prologue does not lead to social realism; there is no steady moral viewpoint. Chaucer's Gothic switches of genre and tone are allowed by his comprehensive conception of life, physical, social, moral and metaphysical, shown from a variety of viewpoints. As his final Retractions show, Chaucer's humanity has a theological dimension.

## The fifteenth century

Chaucer and Gower were buried outside the City of London, in the churches in Westminster and Southwark next to which each had lived. The grave of the

### Fifteenth-century events and literature

| Events | | Literature | |
|---|---|---|---|
| 1399–1413 | Henry IV | ?1369–1426 | Thomas Hoccleve |
| | | ?1370–1449 | John Lydgate |
| 1413–22 | Henry V | *c.*1405 | *The Castle of Perseveraunce* |
| 1415 | Victory at Agincourt | | |
| 1422 | Henry VI succeeds as a minor. | | |
| | Deposed 1461 | *c.*1430 | Wakefield Play Cycle |
| 1453 | Defeat at Castillon ends Hundred | | |
| | Years War; Turks take Constantinople | | |
| 1455–85 | Wars of the Roses | | |
| 1461–83 | Edward IV | *c.*1465 | *Mankind* (play) |
| 1483 | Edward V | 1478 | William Caxton prints *The Canterbury Tales* |
| 1483–5 | Richard III | 1485 | Thomas Malory's *Le Morte Darthur* printed |
| 1485–1509 | Henry VII (Tudor) | 1513 | Thomas More's *History of Richard III* |

author of *Piers Plowman* is unknown. The name of the author of *Gawain* is unknown. It was not until 1599, when poetry had claimed a public role, that **Edmund Spenser** was buried near Chaucer in Westminster Abbey in what became Poets' Corner. Of Chaucer's avowed followers, only the Scots and Spenser approach his quality.

There was good English writing in the 15th century, in lyric and drama and prose, but no major poet. **Thomas Hoccleve** (?1369–1426) called Chaucer his 'father'. He scratched his living as as a copyist at Westminster, lacking his master's skill and his diplomacy. Academics have recently found a vividness in Hoccleve's complaints about his boring job, exigent employers, deteriorating eyesight, depression and poor pay.

Unlike poor Hoccleve, **John Lydgate** (?1370–1449), a monk of Bury St Edmunds, did well out of English verse. He had grand commissions: his *Troy Book* was written for Henry V; his version of *The Pilgrimage of the Life of Man* for the Earl of Salisbury; his *Fall of Princes* for Humphrey, Duke of Gloucester. Here is a stanza from 'As A Midsummer Rose':

| | |
|---|---|
| Floures open upon every grene, | |
| Whan the larke, messager of day, | |
| Salueth th'uprist of the sonne shene | greets   rising   bright |
| Most amerously in Apryl and in May; | amorously |
| And Aurora ageyn the morwe gray | Dawn at the approach of morn |
| Causith the daysye hir crown to uncloose: | open |
| Worldly gladnes is medlyd with affray, | mingled   fear |
| Al stant on chaung like a mydsomer roose. | is at the point of change |

Stanza-form, image and phrase are from Chaucer; the sonorous moral refrain is Lydgate's. Most of Lydgate's 145,000 lines say the expected thing in a decorated style without Chaucer's rhythm, verve and intelligence.

The decasyllable lost its music in the 15th century, as words altered in accent and inflection. English topped up with prestige words from Latin and French. Doubling its resources, its eloquence took the form of reduplication, pairing English and Romance synonyms, as later in *Othello*'s 'exsufflicate and blown surmises'.

# Drama

## Mystery plays

English drama is Catholic in origin. After the 10th century, liturgical drama spread over Europe, representing Biblical history in Latin and in local tongues. These plays are known as Miracle or Mystery plays. An early one is the Anglo-Norman *Mystère d'Adam*, probably written in England *c.*1140. Suppressed at the Reformation, these plays continued in Catholic Europe, as in the Passion Play at Oberammergau, Bavaria. They were revived in 20th-century England in Nativity plays, in Benjamin Britten's *Noyes Fludde* and in Tony Harrison's *Mysteries*.

The Mystery plays were cycles of religious dramas performed by town guilds, craft associations of a religious kind. The term 'Mystery' may derive from two words: *mètier* (Fr.) or *ministerium* (Lat.), meaning 'craft'; and *mysterium* (Lat.), 'what was performed'. As Greek tragedy began in religious rite, so medieval European drama began with the representation of the central Christian story in the Mass, and in the annual cycle of services developed by the early Church. There were Christmas plays, beginning with the angel's declaration to Mary, her reply, and dialogues with Joseph (see page 24), and with shepherds and kings. The Easter plays began with the entry of Christ into Jerusalem, with procession and palm branches. In Holy Week, the Gospel accounts of the Passion of Christ were recited, with clerics and congregation taking parts, as in Catholic churches today. The resurrection was acted by the women coming to the empty tomb, where they were met by the angel with the question, 'Whom do you seek?', also put to the shepherds at the manger in Nativity plays. From this seminal question grew a forest of representations, liturgical, musical and artistic – church windows, carvings, paintings and manuscript illustrations – as well as dramatic.

Drama began in church, with clerics as authors and chief players. The congregation got into the act with performances on the *parvis* outside the west door. These dramatizations of the Bible, from Creation to Doomsday, were popular. Records survive from France, Italy, Spain, Germany, Ireland and Scotland. A Cornish cycle survives, and plays from several English towns, with complete 15th-century cycles from Chester, Wakefield and an unknown town ('the N. Town cycle'). The York cycle has 48 plays. After 1311 the feast of Corpus Christi, celebrating the Real Presence of Christ in the Eucharist, was held on 29 June; this was a long day, upon which a cycle, *The Play Called Corpus Christi*, was performed. Each guild staged its play on a pageant-wagon through the streets. They were amateurs, but payments are recorded. In a Cain and Abel play, God (who earned one penny) is greeted by Cain's question to Abel: 'Who is that hob [clown] o'er the wall?'

The rich quality of these short plays resists quotation. Much admired are the York Butchers' Play of the Crucifixion and the Wakefield Second Shepherds' Play, in which the sheep-rustler Mak (a Scot?) tries to hide a sheep he has stolen in the manger of the Christ-child. The Wakefield Master writes complex stanzas in broad Yorkshire for his shepherds; the raciness of his sacred drama recalls Langland. Chaucer's Miller's Tale often refers to the plays: Absolon, the parish clerk, a girlish treble, likes to play Herod, a raging tyrant; John the Carpenter has forgotten Noah's Flood, a Carpenters' play with a comic Mrs Noah. More subtly, Absolon travesties

The pageant-wagon of the Annunciation. From illustrations of a Brussels pageant of 1615.

the angel of the Annunciation, his wooing of Alysoun echoes *The Song of Songs*, and the gullible wife-worshipping carpenter recalls the foolish Joseph of the Nativity plays. The familiarity of religion encouraged comedy, even what now seems blasphemy. Every summer the citizens acted out the drama of human history; the Mystery plays were communal (see the illustration on page 64).

## Morality plays

The Morality plays of the 15th and 16th centuries, which showed the fate of the single human person, were played by travelling companies. *The Castle of Perseveraunce* (*c*.1405) is a spectacle with a cast of thirty-six, to be played in a large open-air arena, dramatizing the life of Human Kind from birth to death, with a tournament of virtue and vice, as at the end of *King Lear*. *Mankind* (1465) and *Everyman* (1495) show the lives of representative humans in dialogue with persons such as Fellowship and Good Deeds. Knowledge says, 'Everyman, I will go with thee and be thy guide,/In thy most need to go by thy side.' (This was adopted as the motto of Everyman's Library; alas, Knowledge deserts Everyman before death.)

The Moralities survive in Marlowe's *Dr Faustus*, with its soliloquizing protagonist, its Good and Bad Angels, and its final moral. But it is to the Mysteries that Elizabethan drama owes a long-established communal participation in religious drama, civic comedy and secular drama, recorded but not extant. The Mysteries did not 'wane' at the Reformation; along with other popular forms of piety, they were suppressed. The Coventry plays were last performed in 1580. Scriptural drama was banned from the stage, returning in Milton's *Paradise Lost* and in Handel's *Messiah*.

## Religious lyric

Religious lyric derived from Latin songs and hymns. Hymns came into the Latin church in the 4th century, bringing in accentual rhythm and rhyme from popular song. These hymns swing, unlike quantitative classical verse. There is a large literature of Latin song, sacred and profane, from every century.

Vernacular songs often adapt secular themes. For example:

| | |
|---|---|
| Where beth they beforen us weren, | are they who were before us |
| Houndes ladden and havekes beren | (who) led   hawks bore |
| And hadden feld and wode? | owned field and wood |

'Where are they now' is an old question, asked sadly in the Old English *Wanderer* (see page 31). Now a sharp answer is provided:

| | |
|---|---|
| Men kneleden hem biforen | knelt before them |
| They beren hem wel swithe heye | bore themselves very proudly indeed |
| And in a twincling of an eye, | |
| Hoere soules weren forloren. | their   lost |

Pride comes before a fall. Equally 'medieval' is the doctrine of Adam's 'happy fault' leading to the Redemption.

| | |
|---|---|
| Adam lay y-bownden, | bound |
| bownden in a bond, | |
| Fower thousand wynter | years |
| thought he not to long. | too |

Sweetly clear exemplification of doctrine is the aim of some lyrics, as it was of the paintings of Fra Angelico. A perfect one is:

> I syng of a mayden
>> that is makeles,         *without peer*
> Kyng of alle kynges
>> to here sone she ches.         *chose*
>
> He cam also stille         *as silently*
>> there his moder was         *where*
> As dew in Aprille
>> that falleth on the gras.
>
> He cam also stille
>> to his moderes bowr         *bower*
> As dew in Aprille
>> that falleth on the flour …

The coming of the dew is likened to the Holy Ghost, who comes to the Virgin Mary with the delicacy and reverence of a courtly wooer.

English religious painting was whitewashed at the Reformation, but Italian painting offers a parallel to the wealth of the English lyric. Lyrics on Christmas and on the Crucifixion combine the theological poise of 'I syng of a mayden' with the human dignity of the panels of Duccio's *Maestà* in Siena. Others have the emotional realism of Giotto. Friars used lyrics to induce pity and repentance; the preaching book of the Franciscan **John of Grimestone**, made in 1372, contains almost 250 such lyrics, chiefly penitential, as notes or illustrations for sermons. But most lyrics are Anon.

Some have refrains, as in the Corpus Christi Carol: 'Lully lullay, lully, lullay,/The faucon hath borne me make [love] away.' Another is the complaint of Christ the lover of mankind:

> In the vaile of restles mynd         *vale*
>> I sought in mounteyn and in mede,         *meadow*
> Trustyng a trewe love for to fynd.
>> Upon an hyll than toke I hede,         *took I heed*
>> A voice I herd (and nere I yede)         *nearer I went*
> In gret dolour complaynyng tho,         *grief   then*
>> 'See, dere soule, my sides blede,         *bleed*
> Quia amore langueo.'         *Because I am sick for love*

This stanza shows how well a rhyming stanza can use alliteration to link and shape syllabic phrases. The refrain, from *The Song of Songs*, is found in other lyrics. In the religious lyric, as in the 'Showings' of Julian of Norwich, the keynote is the personal love of of the Saviour for each member of humankind.

## Deaths of Arthur

The oldest prose narrative still familiar in English, apart from those in scripture, is *Le Morte Darthur* (1470) of Sir Thomas Malory. Geoffrey of Monmouth's history branched into many romances of chivalry: of these, the most remarkable in English between *Gawain* and Malory are the Stanzaic *Le Morte Arthur* (contemporary with *Gawain*, and from the same area) and the *Morte Arthure* of *c*.1400, known as the Alliterative *Morte*, from Lincolnshire. These derive from the French prose *La Mort*

*Artu* and were among Malory's sources. The Stanzaic *Morte* skilfully develops the division in Lancelot's allegiance which leads to Arthur's death. Wounded, Lancelot sends a message to Arthur: 'Grete welle [greet well] my lorde I yow pray,/And tell my lady how I fare,/And say I wille come whan I may.'

Simple messages of double meaning haunt the pages of Malory. But implication, and love, play small parts in the Alliterative *Morte*, devoted to Arthur's campaigns. This fierce 4350-line epic has a physical force. The glamour given to chivalric combat in the *Chronicle* of **Jean Froissart** (d.1410), best known in the translation of Lord Berners (1523–5), is corrected by the fighting in the Alliterative *Morte*. Here is the end of the fight between Gawain and Mordred:

> Than Gawayne gyrde to the gome    and one the groffe fallis –
> Alls his grefe was graythede,    his grace was no bettyre.
> He shokkes owtte a schorte knyfe    schethede witth silvere
> And sholde have slottede hym in,    but no slytte happenede:
> His hand slepped and slode    o slante one the mayles,
> And the tother sleyly    slynges hym undire.
> With a trenchande knyfe    the trayttoure hym hyttes
> Thorowe the helme and hede,    one heyghe one the brayne.
> And thus Sir Gawayne es gon,    the gude man of armes.

Then Gawain sprang at the man and fell face downward; so his misfortune was arranged, he had no better luck. He pulls out a short knife sheathed with silver, and should have cut his throat, but no cut happened: his hand slipped and slid slantwise on the rings of mail, and the other man cunningly throws himself under. With a sharp knife the traitor hits him through the helmet and the head upward into the brain. And thus went that good warrior Sir Gawain.

The author of *Le Morte Darthur* tells us that he is **Sir Thomas Malory**, and is writing in prison. He is probably the Sir Thomas Malory from Warwickshire who in the 1440s was charged with crimes of violence, and spent most of the 1450s in jail, escaping twice. This was in the Wars of the Roses between Lancastrian and Yorkist claimants to the throne. In 1468 he was jailed again, on charges of plotting against Edward IV. He tells us he finished his book in 1469; he died in 1471. In 1485 William Caxton printed *Le Morte Darthur*, editing it into twenty-one books. A manuscript with a better text was found in 1934 in the Fellows' Library of Winchester College (founded 1378; motto 'Manners makyth man'). In this manuscript of the 1470s Malory tells the story of Arthur's life in eight self-contained but linked books.

Malory acknowledges the French (prose) books on which he draws, but not his English verse sources. His is the first prose close enough to modern English to be read with ease, and the *Morte* is the first great work of English prose fiction. He writes with the directness and confidence of a practised storyteller. His straightforward narration creates the chivalric world and its conflicting loyalties.

As Book Seven opens, Arthur proclaims a tournament at Camelot, 'otherwyse callyd Wynchester'. Lancelot comes disguised, borrowing the shield of the son of his host, Sir Barnard of Ascolot.

So thys olde barown had a doughtir that was called that tyme the Fayre Maydyn of Ascolot, and ever she behylde Sir Lancelot wondirfully. And, as the booke sayth, she keste such a love unto Sir Launcelot that she cowde never withdraw hir loove, wherefore she dyed; and her name was Elayne le Blanke. So that as she cam to and fro, she was so hote in love that she besought Sir Launcelot to were uppon hym at the justis [jousts] a tokyn of hers.

Lancelot demurs, then decides to bear her token, 'that none of hys bloode thereby myght know hym'. Wearing Elayne's sleeve of scarlet silk, Lancelot receives a near-fatal wound; she nurses him back to health. When he is ready to leave, she says

'have mercy uppon me, and suffir me nat to dye for youre love.' 'Why, what wolde you that I dud?' seyde Sir Launcelot. 'Sir, I wolde have you to my husbande,' seyde Elayne. 'Fayre demesell, I thanke you hartely,' seyde Sir Launcelot, 'but truly,' seyde he, 'I caste me [am resolved] never to be wedded man.' 'Than, fayre knyght,' seyde she, 'woll ye be my paramour [lover]?' 'Jesu defende me!' seyde Sir Launcelot. 'For than I rewarded youre fadir and youre brothir full evyll for their grete goodnesse.' 'Alas, than,' seyde she, 'I must dye for youre love.'

Sir Lancelot offers to settle upon her and a future husband a thousand pound yearly. She declines; he departs. After ten days she dies, and her body is placed in a black barge which comes down the Thames to Westminster, 'and there hitt rubbed and rolled too and fro a grete whyle or [before] ony man aspyed hit'. This is the basis of Tennyson's *The Lady of Shallott*.

Malory's prose is rhythmical, and there is a larger narrative rhythm to his scenes. His well-paced narrative, with its dramatic exchanges, tells of conflict and loss in a world both marvellous and everyday. Malory begins his book with Arthur's begetting, his miraculous youth, and his foreign conquests. The Hundred Years War fought by the English against the French had been lost when Malory was in his prime, and he knew well that the chivalry he portrays in his central books of Sir Gareth, Sir Tristram and the Grail was not to be found. Nor were loyalty to the king and courtesy between knights found in the Wars of the Roses, in which Malory had fought.

The imprisoned author ends the *Morte* with the break-up of the Round Table and the death of Arthur. In the feud that follows the discovery of his adulterous love for Guenevere, Lancelot kills Gareth, Gawain's brother, and leaves the Round Table for his native France. Gawain, with Arthur his uncle, seeks vengeance on Lancelot, and in their absence the traitor Mordred claims the throne. Many side with him against Arthur, and Malory, a Lancastrian, exclaims: 'Alas! thys ys a greate defaughte of us Englysshemen, for there may no thynge us please no terme [for any length of time].' Without Lancelot, Arthur loses. The close, with the deaths of Arthur, Lancelot and Guenevere, is full of mistrust and regret. Arthur's last knight Sir Bedwere falsely tells him that all he had seen at the lake was water lapping and dark waves: 'watirs wap and wawys wanne'. Arthur replies 'A, traytour unto me and untrew … now hast thou betrayed me twyse!' Bedwere puts Arthur into the barge in which the ladies are to take him away to the vale of Avylyon to heal him of his grievous wound. Then Bedwere cries: 'A, my lorde Arthur, what shall become of me, now ye go frome me and leve me here alone amonge myne enemyes?' Malory gave the ramifying Arthurian story its classic form. 'Many men say' that there is written upon Arthur's tomb: HIC IACET ARTHURUS, REX QUONDAM REXQUE FUTURUS ('Here lies Arthur, the once and future king').

## The arrival of printing

The status of *Le Morte Darthur* owes much to its printing by **William Caxton** (?1422-91), an entrepreneur who had learned printing in Cologne and Bruges and set up a press near Westminster Abbey in 1476. Most of the eighty books he printed were religious, but the first was his translation of a history of Troy; he also printed a *Canterbury Tales* in 1477. He translated from French works such as *The Book of the Order of Chivalry*, a guide to knightly conduct, addressed 'not to every comyn man … but to noble gentylmen'. Common men could not read, but 'quality' marketing had begun. Chivalry was dying, but manners could be learned.

## Scottish poetry

In the late 15th century the best poetry in English came from Scotland. This kingdom, united under Malcolm Canmore in the late 11th century, had four tongues: Highland Gaelic, lowland English, clerkly Latin, and lordly Anglo-Norman French. Since the 7th century, English had been spoken on the east coast from the River Tweed to Edinburgh. Its speakers called the tongue of the Gaels, who since the 5th century had come into Argyll from Ireland, *Scottis*. A Gael was in Latin *Scotus*, a name then extended to Lowlanders, who called the northern English they spoke *Inglis*. After the 14th century, a century of war with England, the Lowlanders called their speech *Scottis*, and called the Gaelic of the original Scots *Ersche*, later *Erse* (Irish).

The first *Scottis* literature is the *Brus* of **John Barbour** (*c.*1325–95), an archdeacon of Aberdeen who studied in Oxford and Paris. The *Brus* (*c.*1375) is a heroic life of Robert the Bruce, whose defeat of Edward II at Bannockburn in 1314 made him King of Scotland. This lively chronicle has nearly 14,000 octosyllabics, the most quoted of which is 'A! fredome is a noble thing!' This echoes the Scots' Declaration of Arbroath (1320), a Latin appeal to the Pope: 'It is in truth not for glory, nor riches, nor honours that we are fighting, but for freedom – for that alone, which no honest man gives up but with life itself.' Bruce tells his men before Bannockburn that they have three advantages: 'The first is, that we have the richt;/And for the richt ilk man suld ficht [each man ought to fight].' The second is that 'we' will have the great wealth the English have brought with them – 'Gif that we wyn, as weill may fall.'

> The thrid is, that we for our lyvis
> And for our childer and our wifis,
> And for the fredome of our land,
> Ar strenyeit in battale for to stand …     obliged

Right, profit, family feeling and independence – a good Lowland Scots combination.

Universities were founded: St Andrews in 1411, Glasgow in 1451, Aberdeen in 1495. The successors of the *Brus* include the *Kingis Quair* (*c.*1424), Sir Richard Holland's *Boke of the Howlat* [Owlet] (*c.*1460) and Blind Harry's *Wallace* (*c.*1460), inferior to the *Brus* but more popular. Then come Henryson, Dunbar and Douglas, sometimes called 'Scottish Chaucerians'. They call Chaucer their father and their

## Scottish poetry

| Events | | Literature | |
|--------|--|-----------|--|
| 1306 | Bruce crowned | | |
| 1314 | The Battle of Bannockburn | *c.*1325–95 | John Barbour, *Brus* (1375) |
| | | ?1424–?1506 | Robert Henryson |
| | | ?1460–?1513 | William Dunbar |
| 1513 | James IV dies at Flodden | ?1475–1522 | Gavin Douglas |

language *Inglis*, yet their only imitative poem is the fine *Kingis Quair*, a poem in southern English deriving from Chaucer's *Knight's Tale*, supposedly written by King James I of Scotland during his stay as a hostage in England. (Chaucer's Scots admirers wished not to rival him but to master the 'international' style. Another hostage, found alive among the dead on the field of Agincourt, was a greater poet, **Charles d'Orlèans** (1394–1465), who wrote in English as well as French, but is not called a 'French Chaucerian'.)

**Robert Henryson** (?1424–?1506), **William Dunbar** (?1460–?1513) and **Gavin Douglas** (?1475–1522) each has a considerable body of work. These are writers as good as Burns or Scott, but they are little read in Scotland today.

## Robert Henryson

Robert Henryson was a schoolmaster at Dunfermline, Fife. His *Fables* are his great achievement, but *The Testament of Cresseid*, a sequel to Chaucer's *Troilus*, is his most famous work. His decasyllabic and often stanzaic verse is as quiet as Gower's.

His *Testament* has a very medieval divinity and morality. Parted from Troilus, Cresseid took up with Diomede; yet 'Quhen Diomeid had all his appetyte,/And mair, fulfillit of this fair Ladie,/Upon ane uther he set his haill [whole] delyte …'. 'And mair' is deadly. Cresseid became a whore and was afflicted with leprosy. An old leper quotes at her a proverb familiar from Chaucer:

| | |
|---|---|
| I counsail the mak vertew of ane neid. | thee   necessity |
| To leir to clap thy Clapper to and fro, | learn |
| And leve after the law of lipper leid. | live   leper folk |

One day Troilus passes this half-blind beggar:

| | |
|---|---|
| Then upon him scho kest up baith hir ene, | eyes |
| And with ane blenk it came into his thocht | |
| That he sumtime hir face befoir had sene. | |
| But scho was in sic plye he knew hir nocht; | plight |
| Yit than hir luik into his mynd it brocht | then   look |
| The sweit visage and amorous blenking | |
| Of fair Cresseid, sumtyme his awin darling. | |

Neither recognizes the other; he gives alms out of 'knichtlie pietie'. The measured turning of the *Troilus* stanza renders the encounter objectively but with compassion.

The Fable of the Preaching of the Swallow is less pathetic than the *Testament*, but a more universal moral example. In the humorous Fable of the Uponlondis Mous and the Burges Mous (Country Mouse and Town Mouse), Henryson makes Aesop at home in a Fife full of humble natural detail.

## William Dunbar

William Dunbar has a courtier's sense of the world's variability:

| | |
|---|---|
| The stait of man does change and vary; | |
| Now sound, now seik, now blith, now sary, | sick   sorry |
| Now dansand mery, now like to dee: | dancing   die |
| *Timor mortis conturbat me.* | |

'The fear of death distresses me.' As a priest, Dunbar will have pronounced this refrain as a Response in the Office of the Dead.

> That strang unmercifull tyrand
> Takis, on the moderis breist sowkand,　　　　sucking
> The bab, ful of benignite:　　　　　　　　　baby　good will
> *Timor mortis conturbat me.*

The poem begins 'I that in heill [health] was and gladness'; it is known as *Lament for the Makaris* (makers, poets). The recurrence of the Black Death made Death a recurrent topic.

> He has done petuously devour　　　　　　　pitiably
> The noble Chaucer, of makaris flour,　　　flower of poets
> The monk of Bery and Gower, all thre:　　i.e. Lydgate
> *Timor mortis conturbat me.*

Chaucer had died a century earlier. After the English trio, Dunbar names twenty Scots poets: 'In Dunfermlyne he has done roune [whispered]/With Maister Robert Henrisoun.' He concludes: 'Sen [since] for the deid remeid [remedy] is none,/Best is that we for dede dispone [prepare for],/Eftir our dede that lif [live] may we.'

'Remeid' for *timor mortis* is found in Dunbar's poem on the Harrowing of Hell, Christ's descent into hell after the Crucifixion to release the souls of the good:

> Done is a battell on the dragon blak;
> Our campioun Christ confoundit hes his force　　champion
> The yettis of hell ar brokin with a crak;　　　gates
> The signe triumphall rasitt is of the croce.　　raised
> The divillis trymmillis with hiddous voce;　　　devils tremble　voice
> The saulis ar borrowit and to the bliss can go;　saved
> Chryst with his blud our ransonis dois indoce　　endorses our ransoms
> *Surrexit Dominus de sepulchro.*

The refrain comes from the Mass for Easter Day: 'The Lord is risen from the tomb'.

Dunbar's proclamation of victory has a personal sense of drama and a rhythmic drive which anticipate John Donne (1572–1631). His poems are often set in the Renaissance court of James IV, the last of the Stewarts to speak Gaelic. James died in a medieval raid on England at the disastrous defeat of Flodden in 1513. Dunbar shows another side in his vigorous 'flyting' (a duel of insults) with the Gaelic poet Walter Kennedy. His invective is best seen in his burlesque on a friar who attempted to fly from the walls of Stirling Castle, and his conversation piece 'Twa maritt Wemen and the Wedo', members of the Wife of Bath's *secte*. But the poems of Dunbar read by non-Scots are his hymns and lyrics of personal complaint.

## Gavin Douglas

Gavin Douglas, Bishop of Dunkeld, produced the first version of Virgil's *Æneid* in any variety of English, working from the edition of Ascensius (Paris, 1501). The range and raciness of Douglas's style makes him the equal of Dunbar, but his sprightly translation has been neglected in favour of the vivid Prologues to each book of the *Æneid*, especially those referring to the tongue and landscapes of Scotland. Going to bed in December, he wrapped up his head, 'kest on clathis thrynfald [threw on three layers of clothes]/For to expell the peralus persand cald'. In autumn, he sees the cranes, birds which then spent the summer in Scotland, flying in a Y formation. This 'Northern' realist detail is new.

The Prologue to a 13th book, a happy ending to the *Aeneid* written by Mapheus

Vegius, an Italian humanist, in 1428, is brilliantly entertaining. Glad to have finished Virgil, Douglas walks in a garden in June, 'and in a sege down sat,/Now musing apon this and now on that.' An old man comes to him in a dream, 'Lyk to sum poet of the ald fasson [old guise]' and reproaches him for not including his – thirteenth – book. Douglas replies:

| | |
|---|---|
| 'Mastir,' I said, 'I heir weill quhat yhe say | what you |
| And in this cace of perdon I you pray – | pardon |
| Not that I have you onything offendit | in any point |
| But rathir that I have my tyme misspendit | |
| So lang on Virgillis volume …' | |

He tells Vegius that some think his thirteenth book unnecessary:

| | |
|---|---|
| As to the text accordyng never-a-deill | not a bit |
| Mair than langis to the cart the fift quheill. | belongs   wheel |

At this Vegius strikes him twenty times with his club – much as an old-fashioned author excluded from this history might cudgel its author. Douglas resumes his task.

## ■ Further reading

Benson, L. D. (ed.). *The Riverside Chaucer* (Boston: Houghton Mifflin, 1987; Oxford: Oxford University Press, 1988). The standard edition.

Burrow, J. and T. Turville-Petre (eds). *A Book of Middle English*, 2nd edn (Oxford: Blackwell, 1996). A textbook anthology, well designed and annotated.

Cooper, H. *The Canterbury Tales* (Oxford: Oxford University Press, 1989). A well-judged critical introduction.

Pearsall, D. (ed.) *Chaucer to Spenser: An Anthology* (Oxford: Blackwell, 1999). Well-chosen and annotated.

Schmidt, A. V. (ed.). *The Vision of Piers Plowman* (London: Everyman, 1978). A well-annotated text.

# PART
# 2

# Tudor and Stuart

# Tudor Literature: 1500–1603

# CHAPTER 3

## Overview

The hopes of the humanists and the writers of the early Renaissance were cut short by the turmoil of the Reformation and the despotism of Henry VIII. A literary Renaissance was triumphantly relaunched in the late 1570s by Sidney and Spenser, and the 1590s produced – besides the drama – an unprecedented abundance of non-dramatic poets and translators. This Elizabethan golden age also saw a variety of prose, artful, lively and dignified.

## ▉ Renaissance and Reformation

### The Renaissance

In 1550, the painter Georgio Vasari wrote of a *rinascità* in the arts in his native Florence and in Italy in the 15th century, a 'rebirth'. The French 19th-century historian Jules Michelet extended this idea of a 'renaissance' from the Italian 15th century, the Quattrocento, to a general cultural renewal in western Europe beginning earlier. Michelet's idea has proved very popular with historians.

The turn towards classical models of verse began with a man whom Chaucer calls 'Fraunceys Petrak, the lauriat poete'. On Easter Sunday 1341, Petrarch ('Petrak') was crowned with a wreath of laurel in Rome before Robert, King of Naples. The Renaissance revived classical cultural models, such as the laureation of poets. Greek had died out in the West, but returned after 1400 with the arrival of Byzantine scholars in Italy, who in 1440 founded a Platonic Academy in Florence. After the Turks took Constantinople in 1453, Greek scholars brought manuscripts to Italy. Petrarch, a **humanist**, collected classical manuscripts. Aldus Manutius (1449–1515) printed elegant classical texts at his Aldine press in Venice. The Renaissance is sometimes called the 'Revival of Learning', yet the classical texts it 'discovered' had survived because they had been copied into medieval manuscripts. The contrast between Renaissance learning and medieval ignorance is often exaggerated.

The Renaissance spread from 15th-century Italy to France, Spain and beyond. The Northern Renaissance was, except in the Low Countries, more intellectual than artistic; it was set back by the Reformation (see page 78). The art of the Italian

**humanist** A student of *humanitas* (Lat. 'humanity'; also 'literature'); a lover of *litterae humaniores* ('more humane letters'); an admirer of classical models derived from antiquity; a writer following such models. (Later meanings – such as promoter of humane values, believer in 'the religion of humanity', atheist – date from the 19th century.)

## Renaissance artists and authors

**Architects**

Filippo Brunelleschi (1377–1446)

Leon Battista Alberti (1402–72)

**Painters**

Piero della Francesca (1410/20–92)

Sandro Botticelli (1444–1510)

Andrea Mantegna (1431–1506)

**High Renaissance**

Leonardo da Vinci (1452–1519)

Michaelangelo Buonarotti (1475–1564)

Raffaello Sanzio (Raphael) (1483–1520)

Albrecht Dürer (Germany) 1471–1528)

**Humanist authors**

*Netherlands*

Desiderius Erasmus (1466–1536)

*England*

Thomas More (1478–1535)

*Italy*

Francesco Petrarca (1304–74)

Ludovico Ariosto (1474–1533)

Torquato Tasso (1554–95)

*France*

François Rabelais (1494–1553)

Pierre de Ronsard (1524-85)

Michel de Montaigne (1533–92)

*Spain*

Francisco Ximenes (1436–1517)

Jorge de Montemayor (1519–61)

Miguel de Cervantes (1547–1616)

*Portugal*

Luis de Camoens (1524–80)

Renaissance is today better known than its literature. The High Renaissance trio of **Leonardo da Vinci, Michaelangelo Buonarotti** and **Raffaello Sanzio (Raphael)** typify its characteristics: Leonardo was a painter, an anatomist, a scientist and inventor; Michaelangelo a sculptor, an architect, a painter and a poet; and Raphael's paintings in the Vatican gave classic form to the long flowering of Italian art.

The change from medieval to Renaissance was at first more formal than substantial; literature changed less than art and architecture, although the content of all three remained Christian. Celebrated icons of the High Renaissance are Michaelangelo's gigantic David in Florence, his central design for St Peter's Basilica in Rome, and its Sistine Chapel. In Italy the Renaissance had intellectual origins, drawing on the study of Plato (*c.*427-348 BC) and his followers. It also found civic expression in the Florence of the Medici and the Rome of Leo X (Pope 1513–21), as well as many smaller city-states.

## Expectations

The Renaissance held a higher and more heroic idea of human capacity than had been allowed for by the ascetic side of medieval thought. **Pico della Mirandola**'s *Of the Dignity of Man* (1486) emphasizes the human capacity to ascend the Platonic scale of creation, attaining a heavenly state through a progressive self-education and self-fashioning; his idea of the perfectibility of Man was Christian. The sculpture of Michaelangelo is neither nobler nor more beautiful than the French romanesque of Moissac or the French Gothic of Chartres, but its pride in naked physical beauty, though based on classical models, is new. His youthful David is a giant superman in comparison with human figures in medieval art.

Ambition is a theme of the drama of **Christopher Marlowe** (1564–93): his protagonists, Tamburlaine and Dr Faustus, scorn conventional norms, though they overreach and fall. Marlowe was fascinated also by *The Prince* (1513), in which

Machiavelli (1469–1527) had anatomized the cynical means by which Cesare Borgia had kept power. Machiavelli advises the Prince to be feared rather than loved. His failure to condemn shocked and fascinated the English subjects of Henry VIII; his moral irony went unnoticed.

## Investigations

Contemporary with the Renaissance were physical discoveries by Iberians, of the West Indies by **Christopher Columbus** (1492) and of the western sea route to India by **Vasco da Gama** (1498); **Ferdinand Magellan** rounded the world in 1521.

Scientific developments, as in anatomy, were less dramatic, but the changing approach to natural philosophy announced by **Francis Bacon** (1561–1626) called for a more experimental science, and a more secular outlook. In a universe in which man seemed less limited and heaven less near, the bounds to human achievement were not moral but natural: time and mortality. Life was less wretchedly a preparation for the life to come.

Since the Fall of Rome in the 5th century, historians have found renaissances in the 8th century under Charlemagne, and in the 12th century; but the 15th-century revival of classical models made the Gothic seem deficient. The period between the Fall of Rome and the Renaissance was first termed a *medium ævum*, a 'middle age', by a Neo-Latin writer in 1604.

Conceptions of the physical universe changed. Scholastic theory had to give ground to empirical testing: Galileo (1564–1642) verified with his telescope the heliocentric theory of Copernicus (1474–1543); anatomists dissected the human body; and Machiavelli described power-politics at work.

Ideals changed: medieval saint and warrior gave way to Renaissance hero, courtier, gentleman. Christianity may have remained, but Christendom, a western Europe united rather than divided by religion, ended at the Reformation. The humanist ideal is expressed by Hamlet: 'What a piece of work is man! How noble in reason! How infinite in faculty! In form and moving how express and admirable! In action, how like an angel! In apprehension how like a god! The beauty of the world! The paragon of animals …!' And yet,' Hamlet concludes, in words less often quoted, 'And yet, to me, what is this quintessence of dust? Man delights not me.'

Humanist disappointment at human actuality is pungent in the last line of Shakespeare's Sonnet 94: 'Lilies that fester smell far worse than weeds.' The Renaissance began in hope but ended in a disillusion, first expressed in the 1590s in England; scepticism came later. It was not until the 17th century that some thinkers in England came to regard metaphysics with scepticism and Christianity with reserve.

## England's place in the world

The Spanish and Portuguese discovery of the New World meant that England was no longer at the end of Europe but at its leading edge. The centralization of power in the Crown and of finance in London enabled her to take advantage of this. England gained in power in the 16th century; her defeat of the Spanish Armada in 1588 showed that with God's help David could beat Goliath. In 1603, with the accession of King James I, the Scottish crown came to England; Britain was poised for empire. The spring signalled by More's *Utopia* (1517) and the verse of Wyatt had been blighted by the disruption of religion in the 1530s, its fruition put back forty years. In 1564, the year of Michaelangelo's death and Shakespeare's birth, the Italian

Renaissance was over, but the English Renaissance had hardly begun. By 1579 a renewed cultural confidence was clear in Sir Philip Sidney's *Defence of Poesy*; and the achievement of Spenser, Marlowe and Shakespeare followed.

English literary history cherishes the poetry of **Sir Thomas Wyatt** (1503–42) and **Henry Howard, Earl of Surrey** (1517–47), and such humanist writings as *The Governor* (1531) by Thomas Elyot and *The Schoolmaster* (1558) of Roger Ascham, who became tutor to Queen Elizabeth. The achievements of the sixty-two years between *Utopia* and 1579 would include the refoundation of humanist schools, the development of a critical prospectus for English poetry, the establishment of its metre, and the writing of the first blank verse, some fine lyrics and songs, and the first Elizabethan plays. These preparations eventually led up to that Renaissance man, Sir Philip Sidney. Yet Sidney's *Defence of Poesy* (1579) found little to praise in English writing to date. The establishment of the Tudor state under Henry VII and Henry VIII and of a national church under Elizabeth I necessitated a consciously national literature, so that English might compete with Latin, Greek, French, Spanish and Portuguese. It was too late to compete with Italian: as late as 1638, the Puritan John Milton went to Italy to complete his education.

By 1579, when English was about to 'burst out into sudden blaze', French already had the poems of Du Bellay and Ronsard to rival those of Petrarch. English writers had been unlucky under Henry VIII, who beheaded More and Surrey. Wyatt, a lover of Ann Boleyn, escaped the axe, but his son rebelled against Mary Tudor and lost his head. Mary burnt many Protestants as heretics; her father Henry, brother Edward and sister Elizabeth executed fewer Catholics, including in 1587 Mary Queen of Scots, as traitors. After 1581, Catholicism was considered as treason; Elizabeth also executed four Puritans.

> Hops, heresy, bays and beer
> Came into England all in one
> year
> A rhyme of *c.*1525

## The Reformation

The Protestant Reformation had begun in 1517 with Martin Luther's attacks on the Church's penitential system, order and doctrine. The Reformation, like the Renaissance, was an outcome of a gradual transfer of authority away from weaker central and communal structures to stronger local individual ones, and an accompanying transfer from external to internal ways of thinking, feeling and representing.

These changes towards modern nation-states and individualism had begun in the 12th century, but the final stages were not gradual: after decades of turmoil and long wars in the north, Europe divided into states either Catholic or Protestant. In 1519 Henry VIII wrote the first book by an English king since King Alfred, though in Latin not English. His Latin *Defence of the Seven Sacraments*, against Luther, was rewarded by Rome with the title of *Fidei Defensor* ('Defender of the Faith': a title retained on modern coinage as '*F.D.*'). Henry had had some help with the book from Thomas More. Failing to produce a male heir by Catherine of Aragon, Henry asked Rome for a divorce; he wanted to marry Ann Boleyn. Rome hesitated, Ann fell pregnant, Henry went ahead with the marriage, Rome excommunicated him, and Henry made Thomas Cranmer Archbishop of Canterbury. When in 1533 Henry made himself Supreme Head of the Church, now the Church of England, More, who had resigned as Chancellor, declined to take the Oath of Supremacy legitimizing Henry's coup. More was beheaded in 1535. By 1540 the three thousand religious houses of England were suppressed, and their abbeys, plate and lands taken by the Crown and sold off.

Shrines were ransacked for gold and jewels, notably that of the Archbishop who in 1170 had stood up for Church against Crown, Thomas Becket.

Henry held to Catholic doctrines, but in the six years under his young son Edward VI (1547–53), reform was imposed; there were now only two sacraments. For the next six years, under Mary (Henry's legitimate daughter by Catherine of Aragon), Catholicism returned with much support. Mary began gently, recalling the Benedictines to Westminster Abbey, but not touching monastic lands. But her marriage to Philip II of Spain was unpopular, and after a rebellion led by the son of the poet Wyatt, orthodoxy was in peril. Cranmer and others were burnt to death for heresy.

Elizabeth I (1558–1603), Ann Boleyn's daughter, gradually imposed a compromise between Protestant teaching and Catholic practice. The Queen liked Catholic liturgy, and strongly believed in bishops. There was a major Catholic Northern Rising, but Catholics lost ground when in 1570 Rome declared the Queen illegitimate (as her father's Parliament had done in 1536).

The divisions of the Reformation can still be seen in Europe and in the United Kingdom. The effects on popular worship, on social provision, and on general culture, were disastrous. The leading Northern humanist **Desiderius Erasmus** (1466–1536) had advocated reform of Church, education and society, but recoiled from the mayhem Luther unleashed. In Spain, Cardinal Ximenes turned from liberal humanism to the defence of orthodoxy, as did More in England.

## Sir Thomas More

**Thomas More** (1478–1535), a lawyer's son, wrote a new kind of book, the life of a new kind of writer, Pico della Mirandola, a Platonist aristocrat who withdrew from court and cloister to study and write *Of the Dignity of Man* (1486). Humanists shared a new faith in education: a classical education which taught bright lads, and the princes and princesses they would serve, how to write. In theory, a boy familiar with the examples and warnings of classical history should make a good prince, statesman or adviser.

Rhetoric, the art of persuasive public speaking and of literary composition, was the tool of these new ideals. Rhetoric challenged the medieval sciences of logic and theology. Greek was taught in the élite schools and colleges founded by early English humanists, such as the school founded by the Dean of St Paul's Cathedral, John

Sir Thomas More (1478–1535), after Hans Holbein.

Colet (1466–1519) and Bishop Fox's Corpus Christi College, Oxford (1516). The humanists were serious Christians: Colet wanted the boys at St Paul's School to be 'taught always in good literature both Latin and Greek and good authors such as have the very Roman eloquence joined with wisdom, especially Christian authors that wrote their wisdom with clear and chaste Latin either in verse or in prose, for my intent is by the school specially to increase knowledge and worshipping of God and Our Lord Jesus and good Christian life and manners'. Erasmus taught Greek at Cambridge for five years. He dedicated to his friend More his Latin work *Encomium Moriae* (1507). The title means both *Praise of Folly* and *Praise of More*, as the Greek for a fool is *moros*.

More's Latin *Utopia* was brought out by Erasmus in Louvain in 1517. It was not 'Englished' until 1551; in 1557 appeared More's unfinished English *History of King Richard III* (see page 113). *Utopia* describes an ideal country, like Plato's *Republic* but also like the witty *True History* of Lucian (AD *c*.115–*c*.200). Raphael Hythloday is a travelling scholar, who in Book II tells of his visit to a far-off geometrical island run like a commune with an elected, reasonable ruler. There is no private property, gold is used for chamber pots, vice is unknown, and priests are few and virtuous; some are female. Clothes are uniform; marriage is preceded by mutual naked inspection in the presence of a respected elder. *Utopia* (Gk: 'nowhere') is thus most unlike the Christian, feudal, passionate England of Book I, where starving men who have stolen food are unreasonably punished. Hythloday and a character called Thomas More discuss whether a scholar should advise the prince directly, or indirectly by his pen; More says directly, Hythloday indirectly. But to the European élite for whom *Utopia* and *Praise of Folly* were written, the learned traveller's name would suggest an angelic dispenser of nonsense. 'More' means moron; the king is called Ademos (Gk: 'without a people'). More tells Hythloday that while Utopian communism sounds interesting, it would never do in England.

Such jokes, and the ironical mode of *Utopia* as a whole, make it, like *Praise of Folly*, proof against a censor seeking to ascertain the author's teaching on a particular point. This learned joke released into the European think-tank such absurd ideas as basing society on reason alone. But such ideas could be disowned, as *Utopia* is clearly a spoof of travellers' tales, an elaborate joke. Shakespeare used fools to tell truths, and systematic irony was to be powerfully used in Swift's *Gulliver's Travels*. At the heart of this great in-joke was a serious issue for humanists: the choice of life. More chose justice, Erasmus his books; both died Catholics, Erasmus in his bed.

The Reformation made it clear that a humanist education would not restrain the passions of men. Lord Chancellor More defended orthodoxy against freethinking heresy, repressing Protestant versions of the Bible; he died as 'the king's good servant, but God's first.'

### The Courtier

The Tudors gave their subjects openings for the practice of wit on the scaffold. To make light of difficulty was expected of the complete gentleman, a Renaissance ideal well known by 1535. Its classic embodiment, Castiglione's *Il Cortegiano* (1528), was translated into Spanish in 1534 and French by 1538. Although read in England, it reached print only in 1561 in Sir Thomas Hoby's version, *The Boke of the Courtier*.

How does the new courtesy differ from the medieval ideal? Chaucer's 'parfit gentil Knyght' is *curteis* and his Squire has the physical and social skills; the 15th-century princes Charles d'Orléans and James I of Scotland were fine poets; the young King

Henry VIII was a champion athlete who composed songs and motets, and also wrote a treatise in Latin. The Renaissance gentleman was more consciously Christian, more highly educated, more skilled in speech.

Castiglione set his dialogue at the court of Federigo of Urbino, patron of the painters Piero della Francesa, Botticelli and Raphael and the humanist Pietro Bembo. Castiglione's Urbino, in which ladies preside, remains attractive. After a discourse of Cardinal Bembo on the ladder of Platonic Love,

The Lord Gaspar began to prepare himself to speak to the Duchess. 'Of this,' quoth she, 'let M. Peter [Bembo] be judge, and the matter shall stand to his verdict, whether women be not as meet for heavenly love as men. But because the plead between you may happen be too long, it shall not be amiss to defer it until tomorrow.'

'Nay, tonight,' quoth the Lord Cesar Gonzaga.

'And how can it be tonight?' quoth the Duchess.

The Lord Cesar answered: 'Because it is day already,' and showed her the light that began to enter in at the clefts of the windows. Then every man arose upon his feet with much wonder, because they had not thought that the reasonings had lasted longer than the accustomed wont, saving only that they were begun much later, and with their pleasantness had deceived so the lords' minds that they wist not of the going away of the hours. And not one of them felt any heaviness of sleep in his eyes, the which often happeneth when a man is up after his accustomed hour to go to bed. When the windows then were opened on the side of the palace that hath his prospect toward the high top of Mount Catri they saw already risen in the east a fair morning like unto the colour of roses, and all stars voided, saving only the sweet governess of the heaven, Venus, which keepeth the bounds of the night and the day, from which appeared to blow a sweet blast that, filling the air with a biting cold, began to quicken the tunable notes of the pretty birds among the hushing woods of the hills at hand. Whereupon they all, taking their leave with reverence of the Duchess, departed toward their lodgings without torch, the light of the day sufficing.

The courtier is a layman, well grounded in classical literature and history, and in the arts; a skilled fencer and rider; a composer and performer of music and song; he converses well. He is trained to rule, and with magnanimity. Accomplishment must seem natural, worn with *sprezzatura*, an effortless grace. Ophelia says that Hamlet has 'the courtier's, scholar's, soldier's eye, tongue, sword': the ideal of Castiglione in the rhetoric of the humanist. Sir Philip Sidney was the pattern of this ideal. He described his vast *Arcadia* as a trifle. As he lay dying on the battlefield, he is said to have given his water-bottle to a common soldier, saying, 'Take it, for thy necessity is yet greater than mine.' Sidney had been christened Philip after his god-father, the Queen's husband; he died attacking Philip II's troops in the Spanish Netherlands in 1586, aged 32.

## Sir Thomas Wyatt

Two generations before Sidney, the first English literary Renaissance is summed up in Surrey's 'Epitaph on Sir Thomas Wyatt' (1542), praising the parts of the first English gentleman-poet. Among them:

> A tongue that served in foreign realms his king,
> Whose courteous talk to virtue did inflame
> Each noble heart: a worthy guide to bring
> Our English youth by travail unto fame.
> An eye whose judgment no affect could blind,      feeling
> Friends to allure and foes to reconcile,
> Whose piercing look did represent a mind
> With virtue fraught, reposèd, void of guile.

Wyatt is said to have a courtier's eye, a scholar's tongue, and a hand that, according to Surrey, 'taught what may be said in rhyme,/That reft [stole from] Chaucer the glory of his wit'. Poetry is only one of Wyatt's parts; Surrey goes on to praise his patriotism, his virtue, his soul. A belief in moral example is typical of Tudor poetics; so is the boast that Wyatt has stolen Chaucer's glory. Chaucer had more modesty and discernment when he told his 'litel boke' (*Troilus and Criseyde*) to 'kiss the steps' of the classical poets (see page 37). Renaissance poets were publicists for poetry; ambition made them envious of past glory and present competition. Compared with the medieval John Gower, gentle as a man and as a poet, Wyatt is tense and modern.

**Sir Thomas Wyatt** (1503–42) was a courtier, a diplomat in France and Spain. He celebrated his return home to a more honest country in 'Tagus farewell, that westward with thy streams'. He translated sonnets from Petrarch and Alamanni; one example runs:

> Whoso list to hunt, I know where is an hind,          whoever desires
> But as for me, alas, I may no more.
> The vain travail hath wearied me so sore
> I am of them that farthest cometh behind.
> Yet may I, by no means, my wearied mind
> Draw from the deer, but as she fleeth afore
> Fainting I follow. I leave off therefore,
> Since in a net I seek to hold the wind.
> Who list her hunt, I put him out of doubt,
> As well as I, may spend his time in vaine.
> And graven with diamonds in letters plain
> There is written, her fair neck round about,
> '*Noli me tangere*, for Caesar's I am,
> And wild for to hold, though I seem tame.'

This poem (pub. 1815) adapts a **sonnet** of Petrarch: the dear 'deer' is identified as Ann Boleyn, whose pursuit Wyatt had to give up. Hunting was a royal prerogative, and the verse on her collar (itself an adaptation of two of Christ's sayings) casts Henry VIII as Caesar. Wyatt was twice in prison, but his coolness got him out. (Other suspected lovers of Ann Boleyn's were less lucky: 'The axe is home, your heads be in the street', Wyatt wrote to them.)

His own pride can be scented elsewhere in his verse, for example in 'They flee from me that sometime did me seek/With naked foot stalking in my chamber.' Only in his songs is he the conventional Petrarchan lover:

> My lute, awake! Perform the last
> Labour that thou and I shall waste,
> And end that I have now begun;
> For when this song is sung and past,
> My lute, be still, for I have done.

The grave grace of his lines has a conscious art quite unlike the rapid social verse of his predecessor at court, **John Skelton** (1460–1529): Wyatt's metrical control makes the learned Skelton, a gifted satirist, sound a casual entertainer. The Renaissance set high standards of conscious art. Wyatt reft Skelton the glory of his wit, even in satire. When Wyatt was banished from court in 1536, he wrote a verse letter to a friend: 'Mine own John Poins, since ye delight to know/The cause why that homeward I me draw/And flee the press of courts ...'. The letter, adapted from a satire by

**sonnet** (It. *sonnetto*, 'little sound') A verse form of (classically) 14 lines, rhyming 8 and 6. It is found in Italy in the 13th century, and was used by Dante and especially by Petrarch, whose *Canzoniere*, with 317 sonnets in a narrative/dramatic sequence, set a European fashion. The English or Shakespearean sonnet usually rhymes 4,4,4,2.

**Alamanni** (1495–1556), contrasts the flattery and corruption of court with the moral health of country life. The innocence of rural retirement, a theme of the Roman poet **Horace** (65–8 BC), is naturalized.

> This maketh me at home to hunt and hawk,
> And in foul weather at my book to sit,
> In frost and snow then with my bow to stalk.
> No man does mark whereso I ride or go ...

This seems timelessly English. But Wyatt's conclusion has a new kind of Englishness:

> I am not now in France, to judge the wine,
> With sav'ry sauce those delicates to feel;       delicacies
> Nor yet in Spain, where one must him incline,    bow, humble himself
> Rather than to be, outwardly to seem.
> I meddle not with wits that be so fine;
> Nor Flanders' cheer letteth not my sight to deem  drink preventeth
> Of black and white, nor taketh my wit away
> With beastliness, they beasts do so esteem.
> Nor am I not where Christ is given in prey
> For money, poison, and treason – at Rome
> A common practice, usèd night and day.
> But here I am in Kent and Christendom,
> Among the Muses, where I read and rhyme;
> Where, if thou list, my Poins for to come,
> Thou shalt be judge how I do spend my time.

The effects of Reformation and Renaissance on England show here. Christendom is now not Europe but a state of mind. In a newly assured but local poetry, the xenophobic superiority of an Englishman to beastly Flemings and corrupt sophisticated Latins is proclaimed – in a tissue of echoes from Alammani and Horace. Yet Wyatt's voice is independent and personal. He was not the last to resent the ingratitude of princes; one of his poems translates a gloomy chorus from Seneca. A comparison with More's Christianity is instructive.

## The Earl of Surrey

**The Earl of Surrey** (1517–47), eldest son of the Duke of Norfolk, head of the nobility of England, printed his epitaph on Wyatt. Normally, gentlemen did not print verse but circulated it in manuscripts. Wyatt and Surrey were first printed in 1557 in Tottel's *Miscellany* of Songs and Sonnets. Thus it was in Mary's reign that two modern verse-forms reached print: the sonnet, and an unrhymed **iambic pentameter**, first used in Surrey's versions of Virgil's *Aeneid* II and IV, known as 'blank verse'.

Surrey's songs and sonnets were more popular than Wyatt's; poets found their regular movement easier to imitate. Surrey's version of a poem by Petrarch begins, 'Love, that doth reign and live within my thought'. Wyatt's begins, 'The long love that in my thought doth harbour'. Surrey found 'doth' and 'within' metrically convenient. Twentieth-century critics preferred Wyatt, who has a voice, and more to say, although Surrey dared to glance at Henry VIII in 'Th'Assyrian king, in peace with foul desire'. Surrey was beheaded on a false charge, aged 30.

Surrey's major achievement is his Virgil, not just because it pioneered blank verse. In the Renaissance, as in the Middle Ages, translation was not wholly distinct from composition, although Renaissance philology produced better texts

**iambic pentameter**
Classically, a line of ten alternating unstressed and stressed syllables, beginning with an unstress: for example, Wyatt's 'I *am* not *now* in *France* to *judge* the *wine*'. Variations on this regular pattern are permitted.

and stricter notions of fidelity. As Latin, Europe's old vernacular, faded, educated readers were eager for writings in the new national vernaculars. There was a need and a new prestige for translation and for the modernizing kind of adaptation known as imitation.

Surrey had the example of the *Eneados* of Gavin Douglas (*c*.1513; see page 71). The comparison is instructive: Surrey has no prologues, fewer fireworks, more fidelity. Douglas turns each line of Virgil into a lively couplet; Surrey's pentameters have a Latin concision. His version of the Fall of Troy in *Aeneid* II has tragic dignity. Here Hector's ghost tells Aeneas to leave the ruins of Troy and found a new empire:

> from the bottom of his breast
> Sighing he said: 'Flee, flee, O goddess' son,
> And save thee from the fury of this flame.
> Our en'mies now are masters of the walls,
> And Troyë town now falleth from the top.
> Sufficeth that is done for Priam's reign.          that which
> If force might serve to succour Troyë town,
> This right hand well mought have been her defence.   might
> But Troyë now commendeth to thy charge
> Her holy reliques and her privy gods.
> Them join to thee, as fellows of thy fate.
> Large walls rear thou for them: for so thou shalt,
> After time spent in th' o'erwandered flood.'        sea

He left this regular stately verse to Sidney and Marlowe to perfect.

## Religious prose

In the push to develop a native vernacular English, prose was first required. Prose is merely written language; the Bourgeois Gentleman of the French comic playwright Molière (1622–73) was surprised to discover that he had been speaking prose all his life. Whereas verse chooses to dance in metre, and take on rhyme and other patternings, prose walks with no rules other than those of syntax.

Prose has such a variety of tasks that its history is not readily summarized, and its qualities are not well indicated in brief quotation. Chaucer's prose is unformed compared with his verse, but the prose Shakespeare gave Falstaff shows how much ground had been made up. Yet posterity has awarded all the literary prizes to Tudor verse (drama was chiefly in verse), except in one area central to the life of 16th-century England.

### Bible translation

The Reformation created an urgent need for a religious prose. Luther wanted to put the word of God into the ploughboy's hand; his German Bible (finished in 1545) helped to form not only German Protestants but also the German language. The English Bible, in the Authorized Version (AV) of 1611, although less decisive in the evolution of the language, played a similar role in the culture of English-speaking countries; it was adopted in Presbyterian Scotland and later in the Empire. More generally, the Reformation gave the book and the word a privileged place in Protestant lands, and the non-verbal arts a lower place. The spreading of the Word was the task of the apostles, given the gift of tongues. The Bible, put into Greek before the time of Christ, has overwhelmingly been read ever since in translation. The aim of its translators has been fidelity. Fidelity was the rule of Jerome (c.342–420) when he translated the Bible from Greek and Hebrew into Latin, the language of the people of the West. Jerome's Vulgate was in the vulgar tongue, and, like the 16th-century translators, he wrote to be read aloud.

St Augustine (358–430) says in his *Confessions* that he was astonished to see Ambrose of Milan read without moving his lips. Though a practised orator, Augustine had not seen this before. The Protestants who practised the private un-guided reading of which the Church disapproved also moved their lips or heard the words in their heads.

By 1539 **Miles Coverdale** (1488–1568), producer of the the first complete printed English Bible, knew that his words formed part of the services of the Church of England. Translators producing texts for such a use did not neglect rhythm and rhetorical spoken quality: they wrote for the tongue to perform and for the ear to hear. Very different is the situation of modern Bible translators, translating for speedy silent readers in a world where there is too much to read. Their gift of tongues is an expertise in ancient languages.

The psalms, gospel, epistles and Old Testament lessons were part of church services, as before, but were now in English. Under Elizabeth, church attendance on Sundays was required by law. As important to Anglicans as the Bible was the Book of Common Prayer (BCP, 1549) with its still largely Catholic liturgy, translated under Cranmer from the Church's Latin. For centuries the words and cadences of the AV and the BCP conducted English people from the cradle to the altar to the grave, and through the Christian year, as Latin had done for a millennium. In the 1920s, T. S. Eliot's titles 'The Burial of the Dead' and 'Ash-Wednesday' needed no footnotes; they had been in the BCP since the 16th century.

Such words were for many the words of life; for all, an example of public English. There are biblical allusions in the early English poems *The Dream of the Rood* and *Beowulf*, but the Bible-version which has contributed most to the language is the AV.

## English Bible Translations

The first English translation of the Bible we know of is by Bede, who finished his version of the gospels in 735 (see page 18). Aelfric (d.c.1020) translated Genesis and other parts of the Old Testament. Parts of several Old English translations survive; there were also Middle English versions, notably those produced by disciples of Wyclif (d.1384; see page 48).

The first English Bible translated from Greek and Hebrew rather than Latin was by the gifted **William Tyndale**, who in 1523, in exile, began a New Testament. He was martyred in 1536. The first complete printed English Bible was published in 1535 by **Miles Coverdale** in Zurich. In 1540 the Great Bible, adding Coverdale to Tyndale, was placed in churches.

In 1560 came the Geneva Bible, by Protestant refugees with a Calvinist commentary. In 1568 the less Protestant Bishops' Bible was issued in England. Catholic refugees produced a New Testament in Rheims (1582) and an Old Testament at Douai (1610); the Douai-Rheims Bible is translated from the Vulgate.

In 1604, King James authorized 'a more exact Translation into the *English Tongue*', avoiding the errors of Papists and also of 'self-conceited Brethren'. Under the chairmanship of Lancelot Andrewes, teams of scholars produced in 1611 the Authorized Version (AV) or King James Version. It was based on the original tongues and drew on earlier English versions, especially Tyndale's. It was not revised until 1881–5.

Gospels and psalms were best known, but for a sample of the AV's grand simplicity, Ecclesiastes 12:1–7 will serve:

Remember now thy Creator in the days of thy youth, while evil days come not, nor the years draw nigh, when thou shalt say, I have no pleasure in them; while the sun, or the light, or the moon, or the stars, be not darkened, nor the clouds return after the rain: in the day when the keepers of the house shall tremble, and the strong men shall bow themselves, and the grinders cease because they are few, and those that look out of the windows be darkened, and the doors shall be shut in the streets, when the sound of the grinding is low, and he shall rise up at the voice of the bird, and all the daughters of musick shall be brought low; also when they shall be afraid of that which is high, and fears shall be in the way, and the almond tree shall flourish, and the grasshopper shall be a burden, and desire shall fail: because man goeth to his long home, and the mourners go about the streets: or ever the silver cord be loosed, or the golden bowl be broken, or the pitcher be broken at the fountain, or the wheel broken at the cistern. Then shall the dust return to the earth as it was: and the spirit shall return unto God who gave it.

This prose for God was not built in a day, but was the work of generations. The emergence of a weekday prose for man is not so simply traced.

## Instructive prose

*Le Morte Darthur*, that masterpiece of 15th-century prose, perfects a storytelling mode originally oral. Renaissance prose had more abstract and prescriptive tasks: the titles *The Prince*, *The Governor*, *Toxophilus*, *The Courtier* and *The Schoolmaster* propose ideal secular roles. The roots of these words are not Old English: Latin, with its romance derivatives, had honeycombed English, and was again the source of new words. Fifteenth-century scholars had borrowed from Latin to meet a technical need or to add weight; Latin duplicates added choice, sonority or play. Patriotic humanists wanted English to replace Latin as the literary medium, but it was Latin which provided both the new words and the stylistic models. Writers about language, whether grammarians or humanists, took their ideas of style from **Cicero** (106–43 BC) and **Quintilian** (AD *c*.35–*c*.100). Latin-derived words poured into 16th-century English in quantities which worried linguistic patriots. Adventurers in elaborate new styles fought conservatives resisting 'inkhorn' terms too obviously taken from books. An example of plain Tudor prose is Roper's *Life of More*, written in Queen Mary's reign.

The first significant prose writers were tutors to the great. **Sir Thomas Elyot** (*c*.1490–1546) served Cardinal Wolsey; at Wolsey's fall, he wrote his *Governor* (1531), dedicated to Henry VIII. Its theme is the necessity for governors, and for governors to be educated – in classical literature. Elyot says that Henry praised him for not introducing any Latin or French words too hard to understand; he was made an ambassador. The humanist **John Cheke** (1514–57) became tutor to Edward VI.

**Roger Ascham** (1515–68) taught Greek at Cambridge, but it was sport rather than Greek which brought him leisure. He dedicated his *Toxophilus* (1545) to Henry, which earned him a pension. *Toxophilus* (Gk: 'bow-lover') is a treatise on how to use the longbow, the weapon that had won at Agincourt. At home in Kent and Christendom, Wyatt had stalked with his bow in the winter. Ascham has a good page on wind-drag in winter:

That morning the sun shone bright and clear, the wind was whistling aloft and sharp according to the time of the year. The snow in the highway lay loose and trodden with horses' feet: so as the wind blew, it took the loose snow with it, and made it so slide upon the snow in the field which was hard and crusted by reason of the frost overnight, that thereby I might see very well the whole nature of the wind as it blew that day.

Archery made for pure English.

Ascham became tutor in 1548 to Princess Elizabeth, and served Queens Mary and Elizabeth as Latin secretary, a job which Milton performed for the Commonwealth a century later. Ascham says in his *Schoolmaster*, posthumously published in 1570, that he preferred writing Latin or Greek to writing English. On schoolmastering, Ascham is humane and sensible, but otherwise partisan. Thus, he finds good Lady Jane Grey reading Plato at home while her family are hunting in the park. Good Queen Elizabeth (his pupil) is more learned than all but one or two of her subjects. But, rather than the Bible, Ascham says, our forefathers preferred reading Malory, in whom 'those be counted the noblest knights that do kill most men without any quarrel and commit foulest adulteries by subtlest shifts.' Italy is the source not of Platonic learning but Catholic vices.

Lady Jane, a 17-year-old put on the throne for nine days in an attempted coup in 1553, is also a heroine in the vividly partisan *Book of Martyrs* (1563) by John Foxe (1516–87). As an act of state propaganda, a copy of Foxe, illustrated with lurid woodcuts, was placed in English churches on the lectern, next to the Bible. Foxe reports that the last words of Hugh Latimer, burnt at the stake under Mary, were (to a fellow-martyr): 'Be of good comfort, Master Ridley, and play the man: we shall this day light such a candle by God's grace in England as, I trust, shall never be put out.'

## Drama

The spiritual and cultural trauma of the Reformation may account for the fact that the major literature of the period 1540–79 was in the translation of religious texts. The proceeds of the suppression of the monasteries and their schools did not go into education. As England lurched from Luther to Calvin to Rome to her own compromise, the crown was an unsafe patron. But poets needed patrons. Before the Elizabethan theatre opened, there was no paying profession of writing. University men tried vainly to bridge the gap between uncommercial 'gentle' status and scribbling for a tiny market. Yet in this fallow period secular drama began.

The Mystery and Morality plays (see page 64) continued, the Mysteries until Shakespeare's day; his Falstaff and Shylock owe something to the antic Vice in the Mysteries, who entertained the audience before his dismissal. As guilds clubbed together to buy pageant waggons and costumes, Mysteries became dearer. The civic link slackened; companies of players travelled between inns and great houses (as in *Hamlet*). The Mysteries were Corpus Christi plays, summer plays. A new kind of play, the **interlude**, was now played between courses in big houses at Christmas and Easter.

A moral entertainment, the interlude involved debates similar to the one Thomas More reports in *Utopia*, set in the household of Cardinal Morton, where More had been a page. Morton's chaplain Medwall wrote the first interlude we have, *Fulgens and Lucrece*, played at Christmas 1497 before the ambassadors of Flanders and Spain; Lucrece has two suitors, a nobleman and a comic servant. Roper's *Life* tells us that as a page More would 'suddenly sometimes step in among the players, and never studying for the matter, make a part of his own there presently among them'.

Drama became a family habit: More's brother-in-law **John Rastell** (?1470–1536) had a stage in his garden in Finsbury Fields, London. He printed *Fulgens* on his own press; also his own interlude *The Four Elements*, with the first printed music. Rastell's daughter married **John Heywood** (c.1497–1580), author of the farcical interlude, *The Four Ps*. In this, a Palmer, a Pardoner, a 'Pothecary and a Pedlar compete to tell

**interlude** (Lat. 'between'+'game') A moral play offered between courses.

the biggest lie; the Palmer wins by claiming that he had never known a woman lose her temper.

Roman comedies by Plautus and Terence were adapted by humanist school-masters for their pupils: the first English comedy to survive, *Ralph Roister Doister*, was written by **Nicolas Udall** (1504–56), headmaster of Eton in the 1530s; it crosses Plautus with popular tradition. (The Pyramus-and-Thisbe interlude in *A Midsummer Night's Dream* borrows from Udall a joke based on mispunctuation.) At Christmas, university students appointed a Lord of Misrule, and put on plays in King's College Chapel, Cambridge, and the hall of Christ Church, Oxford. *Gammer Gurton's Needle*, performed at Christ's, Cambridge, in the early 1560s, is neater, if lower, than Udall's play. (The grandmother's needle, lost when mending the breeches of Hodge, a rustic in love, is eventually found when Diccon, a rogue, kicks Hodge, driving it into his backside; it is funnier than it sounds.)

John's son **Jasper Heywood** (1535–98), a Jesuit (and uncle to John Donne), pub-lished in 1559 a translation into English of Seneca's *Troas*, and, with others, *Seneca his Ten Tragedies* (1581). ('Seneca his' = 'Seneca's'; the expansion of the possessive ending is mistaken pedantry.) Seneca was tutor, then minister to the emperor Nero, executing his atrocious whims – such as feeding Christians to lions. When Nero turned against him, Seneca gathered his friends and, in AD 69, committed a philo-sopher's suicide. His fall recalls those of Wolsey, More and Cromwell. His 'closet' drama – written for the study or recital, not for the stage – places reason above passion, human dignity above inscrutable fate. What Boethius was to the Middle Ages, Seneca became to the Elizabethans; Greek tragedies were not yet available. Breaking the classical rule that horror must be off-stage, the English enacted what Seneca reported. His characters moralize blackly and at length about unseen atrocities and the vengeance of the gods, but Elizabethans saw what Romans read about. Sidney praised Thomas Sackville and Thomas Norton's blank-verse tragedy *Gorboduc* (1561) as 'full of stately speeches and well sounding Phrases, clyming to the height of *Seneca* his style, and as full of notable moralitie.' Sackville had already

## Tudor translations

William Tyndale: New Testament, 1525

Ralph Robinson: More's *Utopia*, 1551

Sir Thomas Hoby: Castiglione's *Boke of the Courtier*, 1561

Arthur Golding: Ovid's *Metamorphoses*, 1565

William Adlington: Apuleius' *The Golden Ass*, 1566

George Gascoigne: Ariosto's *Supposes*, 1567

Jasper Heywood *et al.*: *Seneca his Ten Tragedies*, 1581

Richard Stanyhurst: *The First Four Books of Virgil his Æneis*, 1582

Sir John Harington: Ariosto's *Orlando Furioso in English Heroical Verse*, 1591

Sir Thomas North: *Plutarch's Lives of the Noble Grecians and Romans*, 1595

John Chapman: Homer's *Iliad*, 1598

Christopher Marlowe: *Hero and Leander*, 1598; *All Ovids Elegies*, 1600

Mary Herbert, Countess of Pembroke: The Psalms (pub. 1863)

Edward Fairfax: Tasso's *Gerusalemme Liberata*, 1600

John Florio: Montaigne's *Essays*, 1603

(Lancelot Andrewes *et al.*: The Authorized Version of the Bible, 1611)

contributed to the 1559 *Mirror for Magistrates*, a best-selling multi-authored continuation of Lydgate's *Fall of Princes*.

A writer in this bad time for writers was George Gascoigne (1539–78), a gentleman-poet who lost his money and tried his pen at most things, including *Supposes*, a play adapted from Ariosto, a source for Shakespeare's *The Taming of the Shrew*. This is the period also of Chronicles by Edward Hall and Raphael Holinshed, which, like North's *Plutarch* of 1579, provided material for tragedies and history plays. Hoby's *Courtier* and Arthur Golding's *Ovid* are enjoyable works of this period. Shakespeare liked Golding's version of Ovid's *Metamorphoses*, which still pleases, despite the seven-foot lines in which it was written and the stiff moral allegory prefixed to each book. Many of the original poems of this century are also translations; the converse is true as well.

# Elizabethan literature

## Verse

After the fallow, the flower: in 1552 were born Edmund Spenser and Walter Ralegh, and in 1554 Philip Sidney, John Lyly and Richard Hooker. This generation began what was completed by Christopher Marlowe and William Shakespeare (b.1564), and John Donne and Ben Jonson (b.1572).

Sidney and Spenser were the pupils of humanist schools, and their writing shows a new conscious art and formal perfection. There are perfect single Middle English lyrics, such as 'I sing of a maiden' (page 66), but literature was not its author's vocation. With the exception of lyrics by Chaucer, such as 'Hyd Absolon thi gilte tresses cleere', metrical perfection was not an aim. The instability of Middle English did not help. English verse had learned French syllabic metres in the 12th century, and had adapted them to its own stress-based rhythms; but Chaucer was right to worry that change in the form of speech would cause scribes to *mismetre* his verses (page 37). Linguistic changes such as the loss of the final -*e* made many 15th-century poets lose their metre. The printer Richard Tottel tried to regularize Wyatt's metre. Chaucer's music was inaudible to Tudor ears (its secret was rediscovered by Thomas Tyrwhitt in 1775). The metrical basis of English verse was re-established by Sidney and his circle.

In the 1580s, the musical regularity of poems such as Marlowe's 'Come with me and be my love' was admired. In the 1590s, with Spenser and Campion, it had become usual. Sidney's verse set a standard to the Elizabethans, as they in turn did to Herbert and Milton and their successors. Late-Elizabethan verse is too exuberant to be classical in the way of Horace or Virgil, but its formal perfection made it classical for future English poets. Despite its pretensions, and one implication of the word Renaissance, Elizabethan verse was not neo-classical. Neo-classical concision in English is first found in Jonson's Jacobean verse.

### Sir Philip Sidney

The fame of Spenser's *Faerie Queene* (Books I–III, 1590; IV–VI, 1596) should not conceal the primacy in non-dramatic poetry of **Sir Philip Sidney**, to whom Spenser dedicated his apprentice work, *The Shepheardes Calender* (1579): 'Goe little booke: thy selfe present,/As child whose parent is unkent:/To him that is the president/Of noblesse and of chevalree'. Sidney's glamour, death and legend have obscured his writing, widely circulated but printed posthumously; his verse was edited properly only in 1962.

Sidney led a group which sought to classicize English metre; called the Aeropagus, it met at Leicester House, Strand, the home of Sidney's uncle Leicester, the Queen's favourite. Its members included the poets Edward Dyer and Fulke Greville. After Shrewsbury School and Oxford, Sidney made a three-year tour, visiting Paris at the time of the St Bartholomew's Day massacre of Protestants (1572), and also Germany, Vienna, Padua, Venice (where his portrait was painted by Veronese), Prague, Poland and Holland. Here William the Silent offered to marry his daughter to Sidney, in a Protestant alliance, but Queen Elizabeth vetoed this. Sidney was out of favour for three years when he opposed the Queen's proposed marriage to a Catholic. (A commoner who published a pamphlet against the marriage had his right hand cut off.)

Sidney, son of the Governor of Ireland, had public ambitions, of which his writing was a part; Greville said that 'his end was not writing, even while he wrote'. In three years, Sidney wrote three books, each of a kind new in English: *Arcadia*, a romance; a formal *Defence of Poesy*; and a sonnet sequence, *Astrophil and Stella*. Sidney's apparently private sonnets had a more literary end. The *Arcadia* is an entertainment for family and friends, offering positive and negative moral and public ideals to the governing class to which they belonged. It is an amusement for serious rulers, as Jane Austen's novels later were for the gentry. It is in prose divided by verse eclogues, singing competitions between shepherds. These trial pieces in classical quantitative metres and modern Italian forms proved that an English poem could be formally perfect.

In a prefatory letter to his sister Mary, Sidney describes the *Arcadia* as 'but a trifle, and that triflingly handled. Your dear self can best witness the manner, being done in loose sheets of paper, most of it in your presence; the rest by sheets sent unto you as fast as they were done.' In 1577, when he began the first version, he was 25 and Mary 16; he finished it in 1580 at Wilton, Wiltshire, the home of the Earl of Pembroke, whom she had married. In 1580 he wrote his *Defence* and in 1582–4 rewrote the first half of *Arcadia*; this was published in 1590, but superseded in 1593 by his sister's composite version, *The Countess of Pembroke's Arcadia*, in which it has since been read. *Arcadia*'s success was in part a tribute to the author; mourned in two hundred elegies, he was buried in St Paul's Cathedral as 'England's Mars and Muse'.

The Countess of Pembroke continued her brother's work, revising *Arcadia* and completing his translation of the *Psalms* with her own excellent versions in free and inventive forms. Here is a stanza from her Psalm 58:

> Lord, crack their teeth; Lord, crush these lions' jaws,
>     So let them sink as water in the sand.
> When deadly bow their aiming fury draws,
>     Shiver the shaft ere past the shooter's hand.
> So make them melt as the dis-housed snail
>     Or as the embryo, whose vital band
> Breaks ere it holds, and formless eyes do fail
>     To see the sun, though brought to lightful land.

The *Arcadia* draws on Greek, Italian, Spanish and French romances; its story is in five prose acts divided by verses. Its splendid scale prefigures *The Fairie Queene*, but *Arcadia* was finished, then half-rewritten, whereas Spenser's poem is far from complete. Sidney's romance tells the story of two princes shipwrecked on the shore of

Arcadia, the home of pastoral poetry. They disguise themselves and fall in love with the daughters of Basileus (Gk: 'king'), who has withdrawn to live with shepherds in order to avoid the oracle's prophecy: that his elder daughter Pamela shall be seduced; his younger succumb to an unnatural love; he commit adultery with his own wife; and his sons-in-law be accused of his murder. After fantastic adventures, some tragic, and denouements like those of Shakespeare's romances, the oracle is technically fulfilled; yet all ends well. *Arcadia* is high-spirited play – its persons are princes, its plot improbable, its prose artificial. Its fortunes fell as the nobility fell, and romance gave way to the novel, the more plausible diversion of plainer folk.

In his *Defence* Sidney says that 'Nature never set forth the earth in as rich tapestry as divers poets have done … . Her world is brazen, the poets only deliver a golden.' Accordingly, in Arcadia:

There were hills which garnished their proud heights with stately trees; humble valleys whose base estate seemed comforted with refreshing of silver rivers; meadows enamelled with all sorts of eye-pleasing flowers; thickets, which, being lined with most pleasant shade, were witnessed so to by the cheerful deposition [testimony] of many well-tuned birds; each pasture stored with sheep feeding with sober security, while the pretty lambs with beating oratory craved the dams' comfort; here a shepherd's boy piping as though he should never be old; there a young shepherdess knitting and withal singing, and it seemed that her voice comforted her hands to work and her hands kept time to her voice's music.

The elaborately patterned rhetoric is alleviated by Sidney's sense of fun: birds testify and sheep are sober. Prince Musidorus is described as having

a mind of most excellent composition, a piercing wit quite void of ostentation, high erected thoughts seated in a heart of courtesy, and eloquence as sweet in the uttering as slow to come to the uttering, a behaviour so noble as gave a majesty to adversity, and all in a man whose age could not be above one and twenty years …

Love's adversity soon dents this majesty; the action is often tragicomic. Among the eclogues are much-imitated poems, such as 'My true love hath my heart and I have his' and 'Ring out your bells'. Sidney's 286 extant poems try out 143 stanza-forms. He was a virtuoso in rhetoric and metre, in symmetrical structure and paradoxical perspectives – qualities we accept more easily in verse than in prose.

*Astrophil and Stella* is a suite of 108 sonnets of various kinds, moments in the love of Starlover (*Astrophil*: Gk., masculine) for Star (*Stella*: Lat., feminine). The set-up is literary, but *Phil* is Sidney's name (a character in *Arcadia* is called Philisides), and Stella is modelled on Penelope Devereux, who married Lord Rich. The first sonnet, 'Loving in truth, and fain in verse my love to show', climbs a long ladder of logic and rhetoric, only to fall off in the last line: ' "Fool," said my muse to me; "look in thy heart and write." ' Sincerity is hard work.

This is the first sonnet sequence in English, a robust variation on Petrarch's *Canzoniere*, interspersed with songs. It has gravely perfect sonnets, such as 'Come sleep, O sleep, the certain knot of peace' and 'With how sad steps, O moon, thou climb'st the skies'. Its lightest virtuosity comes in its Eighth Song, 'In a grove most rich of shade'. Astrophil speaks:

'Stella, in whose body is
Writ each character of bliss;
Whose face all, all beauty passeth,
Save thy mind, which yet surpasseth:

> Grant, O grant – but speech, alas,
> Fails me, fearing on to pass;
> Grant – O me, what am I saying?
> But no fault there is in praying:
>
> Grant, O dear, on knees I pray' –
> (Knees on ground he then did stay)
> 'That not I, but since I love you,
> Time and place for me may move you …'

She, with less self-deception and bathos, declines:

> 'Tyrant honour thus doth use thee,
> Stella's self might not refuse thee.'
>
> Therewithal away she went,
> Leaving him so passion-rent
> With what she had done and spoken
> That therewith my song is broken.

Sidney returns to the first person and his foolish heart.

Artful in strategy and rhetoric, Sidney is simple in diction. In his *Defence* he commended Spenser's *Shepheardes Calender*, but added 'That same framing of his style to an old rustic language I cannot allow.' Elsewhere: 'I have found in divers smally learned courtiers a more sound stile, then in some professors of learning.' The *Defence* is the first classic of English literary criticism, and Sidney the first in a line of poet-critics: Dryden, Johnson, Coleridge, Arnold, Eliot. It defends poetry against Stephen Gosson's *The School of Abuse* (1579), a Puritan attack on the stage, dedicated

---

### The Arcadia

#### Publication

1 *The Old Arcadia*, completed in 1580 (first pub. 1912): five books divided by pastoral eclogues in verse.

2 *The Countesse of Pembrokes Arcadia*, published by Fulke Greville (1590), known as the *New Arcadia*. Although Sidney rewrote less than half of the story, the revision is 50,000 words longer than the 180,000 words of the *Old*.

3 'The Countesse of Pembroke's Arcadia … Now since the first edition augmented and ended … 1593.' This joins the first half of the *New* with Mary's revision of the second half of the *Old*.

4 In a 5th edition (1621), Sir William Alexander wrote thirty pages to join the *New* to the *Old*; this ran to nine editions. In 1725 a 14th edition appeared; and also an edition rewritten in modern English. Selections appeared throughout the 18th century.

#### Reception

1649 At his execution, King Charles I repeated Pamela's prayer in prison.

1740 Richardson called his first novel *Pamela*.

1810 Hazlitt called it 'one of the greatest monuments of the abuse of intellectual power upon record.'

1860 Dickens' *Great Expectations* has as hero Pip, who vainly pursues Estella, borrowing names and features from *Arcadia* and its title from *Astrophil and Stella* 21.

1977 First complete modernized-spelling edition, ed. M. Evans (London: Penguin): 790 pages, *c*.320,000 words.

to a Protestant patron, Sidney himself. The *Defence* is elaborate, patterned on a classical oration and full of humanist learning. Yet it begins with a digression on horsemanship, and, compared to its Italian predecessors, it canters along, humanized by touches of humour and *sprezzatura*. Its argument is that poetry (that is, literature) imitates the golden Idea, what should be, rather than the brazen actuality, what is. It delights and moves us to virtue, unlike tedious philosophy or unedifying history. Plato's charge that poets lie and corrupt applies to bad poets only. Contemporary poetry is full of abuses; ideally it would promote heroic virtue.

The *Defence* is also a prospectus. English literature to date did not satisfy Sidney; had he lived to be sixty, he could have seen all of Shakespeare's plays. His moral idealism is an attractive if simple version of the role-model theory, animated by an enthusiasm for heroic literature. Yet for all the ardour and exuberance of his twenty-five years, Sidney was no utopian: 'our erected wit maketh us know what perfection is, and yet our infected will keepeth us from reaching unto it' (*Defence*). The sobriety of northern Christian humanism informs the rewriting of *Arcadia* undertaken after the *Defence*: showing the follies of love, and the worse follies of honour and pride, to be avoided rather than imitated. Sidney's inventive play has hidden his sanity and seriousness. He was an original writer as well as an origin.

## Edmund Spenser

Henry's closing of religious houses had caused what Ascham called 'the collapse and ruination' of schools; Sir Thomas Pope, founder of Trinity College, Oxford, in Mary's reign, described Greek as 'much decayed'. Only in the 1560s did good schools revive, including Shrewsbury, attended by Sidney, or Merchant Taylors, London, attended by Spenser. **Edmund Spenser** (b.1552) was a scholarship boy at Cambridge, where he translated sonnets by Petrarch and Du Bellay. In 1579 he wrote the *Shepheardes Calender*. From 1580 he was a colonist in Ireland, writing *The Faerie Queene*. At Ralegh's prompting, he published three books in 1590 (and got a pension), adding three more in 1596. Spenser dedicated his heroic romance to the Queen. It is now the chief literary monument of her cult.

After the reigns of her little brother, and a sister married to Philip II, Elizabeth came to the throne – handsome, clever and 25. It was a truth universally acknowledged that such a queen was in want of a husband. Dynastic marriage and the succession had dominated the century since Prince Arthur's death in 1502. Yet Elizabeth turned this truth to her advantage, not only in foreign diplomacy; each year on Accession Day there was a tournament at which she presided, a lady whose bright eyes rained influence. In the tournament in Chaucer's Knight's Tale (reprinted by John Stow in 1561), Emelye was the prize. The prize at Accession Day tournaments was access to Elizabeth. The Philip Sidney who rode in the lists, devised court masques and wrote 'Having this day my horse, my hand, my lance/Guided so well, that I obtained the prize', died of a bullet wound.

As marriage negotiations succeeded each other, the legend of the Virgin Queen grew, unsullied by her real-life rages when her favourites Leicester and Ralegh fell to ladies of the court. Elizabeth's birthday was on the feast of the Nativity of the Virgin Mary, and some of the cult was transferred to her. There was a cult of virgins: Diana, huntress; Cynthia, mistress of the seas; Astræa, goddess of justice. The stories of Sir Walter Ralegh laying his cloak on a puddle in the Queen's path, and of Sir Francis Drake finishing his game of bowls in sight of the Spanish Armada, are true to the theatricality of public life. As the Armada approached, Elizabeth addressed her

Queen Elizabeth I: the 'Ermine' portrait
(1585), attributed to William Segar.
The ermine is an emblem of chastity.

troops at Tilbury, armed as a knight. The Queen, her advisers and her courtier-writers knew about images. The armed lady Britomart in *The Faerie Queene* is a figure of Elizabeth uniting Britain and Mars.

Sir Walter Ralegh (pronounced 'Rauley'), colonist of Ireland and Virginia and – had he found it – El Dorado, wrote Elizabeth a long poem, *The Ocean to Cynthia*, of which only the first book survives. A sample suggests the mythopoeia of Elizabeth's court:

> To seek new worlds, for gold, for praise, for glory,
>   To try desire, to try love severed far,
> When I was gone, she sent her memory,
>   More strong than were ten thousand ships of war,
>
> To call me back, to leave great honour's thought,
>   To leave my friends, my fortune, my attempt,
> To leave the purpose I so long had sought,
>   And hold both cares and comforts in contempt …

The Queen figures as the cruel beloved, the poet-hero as a knight-errant serving his imperial and imperious mistress; this politic recreation of courtly love also informs Spenser's adoption of chivalric romance as the form of his epic. Medieval Arthurianism had enjoyed a new popularity in Italy at the court of Ferrara, in Ariosto's *Orlando Furioso* (1532) and Tasso's *Rinaldo* (1562). The Puritan Spenser wanted to 'overgo' these poems, to build a national myth: the Tudors were descended from British kings, of whom Arthur was the greatest.

Spenser's first three books are prefaced by a letter to Ralegh: 'Sir: knowing how doubtfully all allegories may be construed, and this book of mine (which I have entitled *The Faerie Queene*), being a continued allegory or dark conceit, I have thought good … to discover unto you the general intention … to fashion a gentle-man or noble person …'. This is the aim of Sidney's *Defence*, using the 'historical fiction … of King Arthur', following 'the antique poets historical: first Homer, who in the persons of Agamemnon and Ulysses hath exampled a good governor and a virtuous man …; Virgil … Aeneas; Ariosto … in his Orlando; and lately, Tasso …. By example of which excellent poets, I labour to portrait in Arthur, before he was king, the image of a brave knight, perfected in the twelve private moral virtues, as Aristotle had devised – the which is the purpose of these first twelve books …'. [If accepted, he plans a further twelve on the *pollitique vertues*.] Arthur, he goes on,

'I conceive to have seen in a dream or vision the Faerie Queene, and … went to seek her forth in Fairyland. In that Faerie Queene, I mean 'glory' in my general intention; but in my particular, I conceive the most excellent and glorious person of our sovereign Queen, and her kingdom in Fairyland … She beareth two persons (the one of a most royal Queen or Empress, the other of a most virtuous and beautiful lady), this latter part in some places I do express in Belphoebe: fashioning her name according to your own excellent conceit of Cynthia – Phoebe and Cynthia being both names of Diana … In the person of Prince Arthur, I set forth magnificence.

This last princely virtue contains the twelve moral virtues, of which 'I make twelve other knights the patrons, for the more variety of the history, of which these three books contain three: the first, of the knight of the Red Cross, in whom I express Holiness; the second, of Sir Guyon, in whom I set forth Temperance; the third, of Britomartis, a lady knight, in whom I picture Chastity …'

The complexity of the project is apparent. Elizabeth's other name in the poem, as 'most royal Queen and Empress', is Gloriana; the twelfth book was to have described the twelve days of Gloriana's annual feast. Spenser wrote three further books, of Friendship, Justice and Courtesy. Two Cantos of Mutability from the Seventh Book appeared posthumously. There are six books of twelve cantos, each of about fifty nine-line stanzas; the poem runs to about 33,000 lines: shorter than *Arcadia* or Byron's *Don Juan* or Dickens' *David Copperfield*, but longer than the *Iliad* and three times as long as Milton's *Paradise Lost*. Spenser wrote only half of 'these first twelve books', one quarter of the grand plan, but he died in 1599.

*The Faerie Queene* and the *Arcadia*, both printed in 1590, are the first major works in English literature since *Le Morte Darthur*. Hugely ambitious, their scale and accomplishment give them an importance which posterity has confirmed in different ways. Spenser's complex long poem, imitative of early Chaucer, was drawn on by Milton, Wordsworth and Keats. But the popularity of *Arcadia* ended with the 18th century; its prose was too artful for Hazlitt. In these two works, which have the megalomania of the Elizabethan great house, scholars have recently found rich intellectual schemes.

Spenser's craft is the admiration of poets. Canto I, Book I of *The Faerie Queene* begins:

> A Gentle Knight was pricking on the plaine,          cantering
>     Y cladd in mightie armes and siluer shielde,
>     Wherein old dints of deepe wounds did remaine,
>     The cruell markes of many a bloudy fielde;

The iambic beat is regular, speech accent coinciding with metrical accent; nouns are accompanied by suitable epithets. Smooth verse and decorous diction are conspicuous features of a style remarkable for its ceremony and harmony, creating the poem's unique atmosphere.

Red-Crosse Knight and Dragon: a woodcut from the first edition of the first three books of Spenser's *The Faerie Queene* (1590). The shield bears the cross of St George of England.

'Fairyland' is a word first found in Spenser. Book I begins with 'a faire Ladye in mourning weedes, riding on a white Asse, with a dwarfe behind her leading a warlike steed'. This is the world of Ariosto: knights, enchantresses, hermits, dragons, floating islands, castles of brass. The legacy of Spenser is his style, which enchants us into this world. His aim was not to lull us to sleep but to allow us to dream. Dreams contain surprises: the next line is 'Yet armes till that time did he neuer wield.' The old armour worn by this new knight is (as Spenser told Ralegh) 'the armour of a Christian man specified by Saint Paul *v.* Ephes.' ('Put on the whole armour of God, that ye may be able to stand against the wiles of the devil' – Ephesians 6:11: the shield of faith and the helmet of salvation.) Spenser's dream is the outward sign of inward religious truths. To chivalric romance he adds medieval allegory; the glamour gilds the pill of truth.

The ethical truths beneath Spenser's 'continued allegory or dark conceit' are 'doubtfully construed'. Teachers have used allegory since Plato's dialogues and Jesus's parables. In the Middle Ages, allegory grew elaborate, exposing agreed truths in a universe of analogy. But a mode of exposition which has a surface story and a deeper meaning runs the risk – if the reader lacks the assumed mentality – that the 'true' meaning may be missed or mistaken; Spenser's twelve private moral virtues have not been found in Aristotle. Allegory, like irony, was useful to humanists: a deeper meaning which proved displeasing to authority could be denied. The unified metaphysic of the medieval order was gone, and there were several new ones. The allegorical keys to Spenser are therefore 'doubtful'.

His moral sense, however, is usually clear and often simple. An example is the episode of Guyon and the Bower of Bliss. Guyon, the hero of Book II, represents Temperance. At the end of the Book he reaches the island of Acrasia (Gk: 'unruliness'), an earthly paradise of erotic love. At the gates he is tempted by two wanton girls sporting in a fountain, who 'shewed him many sights, that courage cold could reare.' Inside the Bower, he sees Acrasia leaning over a sexually conquered knight, and hears a voice sing a 'lovely lay' encouraging him to pluck the rose of love. Its second stanza runs :

> So passeth, in the passing of a day,
>    Of mortall life the leafe, the bud, the flowre,
>    Ne more doth flourish after first decay,
>    That earst was sought to decke both bed and bowre,
>    Of many a Ladie, and many a Paramowre:
>    Gather therfore the Rose, whilest yet is prime,
>    For soone comes age, that will her pride deflowre:
>    Gather the Rose of loue, whilest yet is time,

The stanza of eight pentameters rhyming *ababbcbc* turns slowly, pausing as the point of balance is reached in the central couplet rhyming 'bowre/Paramowre'. Against this ground (repeated 3700 times in the poem) the unfolding chain of sense is decorated by various patterns and repetitions. Sound and sense are equal, or, where the theme is familiar as here, sense is the weaker. But to the existing octave Spenser added a ninth line of twelve syllables, an alexandrine: 'Whilest loving thou mayst loved be with equall crime.' The asymmetry of this longer line is marked by rhyme: 'crime/time' makes the closing couplet lopsided and slows the galleon still further. The stanza becomes a lyrical frame to be contemplated in itself, and Time seems to stand still.

'Crime' breaks the sensuous spell. The captive knight's warlike arms, 'the idle instruments/Of sleeping praise', hang on a tree. Guyon and his guide, the Palmer, rescue the knight, and Guyon breaks down the bowers 'with rigour pittilesse'. Acrasia's sleeping beasts are turned back into men (as in the episode of Circe in the *Odyssey*). But one beast, a hog 'hight Grille by name' (Gk: 'pig'), wishes to remain a pig.

> Said *Guyon*, See the mind of beastly man,
>    That hath so soone forgot the excellence
>    Of his creation, when he life began,
>    That now he chooseth, with vile difference,
>    To be a beast, and lacke intelligence.
>    To whom the Palmer thus, The donghill kind
>    Delights in filth and foule incontinence:
>    Let *Grill* be *Grill*, and have his hoggish mind,
> But let vs hence depart, whilest wether serues and wind.

A lucid epitome of the humanist doctrine of self-fashioning – man can choose to perfect himself or to ruin himself: his physical form shows his spiritual nature.

For Spenser, ethics, religion and politics coalesce, since in its ideal 'conceit' England was a united Protestant, virtuous nation. Thus, Red-Crosse is not seduced by duplicitous Duessa (the Catholic Church) but prefers honest Una (the English Church). Unity had been imposed on England, but not on the British Isles: the conquest of Ireland did not go smoothly. Sir Walter Ralegh was involved in some bloody episodes, and Spenser was burnt out of his home. As *The Faerie Queene* went on, the gap between ideal and real was such that the proclaimed perfection of an ideal England can be read ironically. In his remaining years, Spenser wrote a few stanzas on Time and Mutability, the last of which is a prayer to 'rest eternally'.

*The Faerie Queene* is its age's greatest poetic monument, and one can get lost in its musical, pictorial and intellectual delights. Historically, it is Spenser's major work, and takes precedence over lesser but delightful works such as the wedding hymns *Prothalamion* and *Epithalamion*, poems of wonderful musical vigour, and the *Amoretti* (containing perfect sonnets, such as 'One day I wrote her name upon the strand').

Spenser was loved by Milton and the Romantics, but in the 18th century his influence faded. Poets followed the simpler clarity of Ben Jonson, who remarked of Spenser, 'In affecting the ancients, he writ no language.' This echoes Sidney's objection to the 'old rustic' style of *The Shepheardes Calender*, and anticipates Dr Johnson's strictures upon Milton's style. In humanist theory, decorum was 'the grand masterpiece to observe', yet they objected to Spenser's adoption of a style suited to 'medieval' romance, preferring a modern elegance to Gothic extravagance. Gothic poems which used or adapted Spenser's stanza were James Thomson's *Castle of Indolence*, William Wordsworth's *Resolution and Independence*, Lord Byron's *Childe Harold's Pilgrimage*, and John Keats's *Eve of St Agnes*. A recent editor called the poem *The Fairy Queen* and did away with Spenser's old spelling where he could; but antiquity was part of Spenser's aim.

## Sir Walter Ralegh

The inaugurators of the golden age of English verse present a historic contrast. Sidney was a nobleman who did not print, yet his work survives in many manuscripts. None of Spenser's verse survives in manuscript. He was a scholarship boy, who for all his professionalism depended upon the Crown for employment and patronage. The next stage is marked by Marlowe (b.1564), a poor scholar at Kings School, Canterbury, and Cambridge. He too worked for the Crown but achieved precocious theatrical

Sir Walter Ralegh (1552–1618)
with ruff, and lace in his hair.
A miniature by Nicholas Hilliard,
4.8 cm × 4.2 cm.

success with *Tamburlaine* in 1587. The middle-class Shakespeare (also b.1564) did
not attend university, but made a living out of acting and writing for the commercial
theatre, sharing in its profits, publishing verse only when the theatres were closed.
Great gentlemen and ladies wrote, but not for a living: Henry VIII, Elizabeth I and her
Earls of Oxford and of Essex all wrote well, and the Earl of Surrey and the Countess
of Pembroke better than well. But writing was one of their many parts; Henry wrote
good music; Elizabeth translated Boethius and wrote a fine Italian hand.

The conviction that the gentle do not write for a living is exemplified in **Sir Walter
Ralegh** (*c*.1552–1618), the son of a country gentleman, who spoke broad Devonshire
all his life. A national figure, he was a poet of huge talent who hardly printed, an
amateur. His thirty surviving poems are scattered gestures surrounding a large personality. Some cannot be extricated from career and patronage, such as *The Ocean to
Cynthia* (pub. 1870) and 'Methought I saw the grave where Laura lay'. This claims
that, thanks to *The Faerie Queene* (addressed to Ralegh), Elizabeth's fame eclipses
that of Petrarch's Laura.

The poems Ralegh printed advertise ambition foiled. A bold soldier and chief
colonist of Virginia, he became the Queen's favourite and was knighted in 1584. But
in 1592 an affair with a maid of honour lost him favour. Briefly in the Tower, he
wrote 'Like truthless dreams, so are my joys expired', and his finest poem, 'As you
came from the holy land':

> As you came from the holy land
>    Of Walsinghame,
> Met you not with my true love
>    By the way as you came?
>
> How shall I know your true love,
>    That have met many one
> As I went to the holy land,
>    That have come, that have gone?

> She is neither white nor brown,
>   But as the heavens fair,
> There is none hath a form so divine
>   In the earth or the air.

The pilgrim returning from Walsingham (a Norfolk shrine to the Virgin Mary), recognizes this 'she': Elizabeth's hair was red. Ralegh's ballad (in anapaests) manages to be energetic, dignified and plaintive. Decisive movement marks the reproaches of 'The Lie' ('Go, soul, the body's guest,/Upon a thankless errand'), containing the memorable *envoi*:

> Say to the court it glows
>   And shines like rotten wood;
> Say to the church it shows
>   What's good, and doth no good:
>     If church and court reply,
>     Then give them both the lie.

Condemned to death for plotting against James's accession, Ralegh was let out of the Tower in 1616 to lead an expedition to the golden kingdom of El Dorado, which he claimed to exist in Guiana. Not finding it, his men burnt a Spanish settlement; on his return in 1618 he was beheaded. Some poems from the Tower, like 'Even such is Time', go beyond his disappointments to re-express the moral conviction of earlier Tudor verse in the simpler forms in which he excelled. The similar moral verse of 'The Passionate Man's Pilgrimage', formerly Ralegh's, has recently been reattributed to an anonymous Catholic recusant.

> Give me my scallop-shell of quiet,
> My staff of faith to walk upon,
> My scrip of joy, immortal diet,
> My bottle of salvation,
> My gown of glory, hope's true gage,
> And thus I'll take my pilgrimage.

Ralegh's sombre *History of the World* (1614) has a justly famed conclusion:

O eloquent, just, and mighty Death! Whom none could advise, thou hast persuaded; whom none hath dared, thou has done; and whom all the world hath flattered, thou hast cast out of the world and despised; thou hast drawn together all the far-fetched greatness, all the pride, cruelty, and ambition of man, and covered it all over with these two narrow words: *Hic jacet!* [Here lies ...]

The dramatic commonplace is near the heart of Elizabethan literature. Ralegh, who embodied the extremes of his age's ambition, fell, tried to recover, and then wrote and rewrote its epitaph.

## The 'Jacobethans'

After Sidney and Spenser, the harvest. Leaving Shakespeare aside, the 1590s are perhaps the richest decade in English poetic history. Suddenly 'well over thirty poets of at least some talent were known to be writing' (Emrys Jones) – among them John Donne, who wrote satires, elegies and some libertine verse before 1600.

The decade 1600–10 is almost as good, even without drama. The great outbursts of English poetry come in 1375–1400, 1590–1610 and 1798–1824. The Ricardian

| Non-dramatic poets of the 1590s | |
| --- | --- |
| Sir Walter Ralegh (c.1552–1618: executed) | Christopher Marlowe (1564–93: killed) |
| John Lyly (c.1554–1606) | William Shakespeare (1564–1616) |
| Fulke Greville (1554–1628) | Thomas Nashe (1567–1601) |
| George Chapman (?1559–1634) | Thomas Campion (1567–1620) |
| Robert Southwell SJ (1561–95: executed) | Sir John Davies (1569–1626) |
| Samuel Daniel (c.1563–1619) | John Donne (1572–1631) |
| Michael Drayton (1563–1631) | Ben Jonson (1572–1637) |

and Romantic constellations have stars as great (if Shakespeare is left out of account), but there are fewer of them than of the 'Jacobethans'.

In *Hamlet* (1601) the Prince wears an inky cloak; Jacobean tragedy is very black indeed. The 'golden' phase of Elizabethan poetry passed in 1588. After Gloriana's zenith, writers addressed less ideal subjects. Marlowe wrote of naked will and ambition's fall; Donne mocked human folly; Bacon's essays reduced human pretension. A sceptical, analytical mood coincided with a more Calvinist temper in the face of Catholic Europe. The Elizabethan plantation of Munster brought the harshness of empire nearer home.

## Christopher Marlowe

Christopher Marlowe's plays tower over his poems. But his 'Come live with me and be my love' was a favourite, answered in Ralegh's 'The Nymph's Reply to the Shepherd' and much parodied. It gracefully reworks Latin lyric themes, as do Ralegh's own 'Serena' and other lyrics of the time. Of Renaissance kinds, the lyric was closest to its classical exemplars.

Besides his Ovid, Marlowe also translated the first book of Lucan into blank verse. The Elegies from Ovid are polished and witty, but the Ovidian *Hero and Leander* has a brilliance of a new kind. This Epyllion (a short epic) draws on Ovid's *Heroides*, but is based on a later Greek version of the tale of Leander's swimming of the Hellespont to woo Hero. Before the advent of the University wits – Lily, Lodge, Greene and Marlowe – Ovid's tales were moralized, as in Golding's *Metamorphoses*. *Hero and Leander*, however, is erotic rather than epic. Marlowe's Acrasia-like delight in sex becomes high fantasy:

> Even as delicious meat is to the taste,
> So was his neck in touching, and surpassed
> The white of Pelops shoulder. I could tell ye
> How smooth his breast was, and how white his belly,
> And whose immortal fingers did imprint
> That heavenly path with many a curious dint
> That runs along his back, but my rude pen
> Can hardly blazon forth the loves of men,
> Much less of powerful gods …

The archness of this mock-modesty is as new to English verse as are Leander's 'curious dints'. (One couplet runs: 'There might you see the gods in sundry shapes,/Committing heady riots, incest, rapes.' Could Golding have seen that such lasciviousness is also comic?) Marlowe added homoeroticism to the Greek original.

He was to exploit his discovery of 'classical' sexual glamour in his drama. Of more general note, however, is the sheer assurance of the couplets. By line 818, when he stopped, Marlowe had lost control of the tone, though not of the verse; its lines include 'Whoever loved that loved not at first sight.' Chapman finished the story, more weightily. Epyllion was fashionable in the 1590s; Shakespeare's effort, *Venus and Adonis*, is inferior to *Hero and Leander*, which Marlowe may have written as an undergraduate.

# Song

This was a great time for the 'twin-born harmonious Sisters, Voice and Verse', Milton's baroque phrase for the sung poem or art song. English music was famed in the 15th century, but poems-with-music survive in numbers from the 16th century. Singing was heard at work, in home and in tavern, at court and in church.

Sung words must be singable and their sense taken in at one hearing, yet the words of 16th-century and 17th-century songs are not, like those of many later art songs, vacuous, except in refrains such as 'Hey, nonny, nonny', or in this song to Spring:

> Spring, the sweet spring, is the year's pleasant king;
> Then blooms each thing, then maids dance in a ring,
> Cold doth not sting, the pretty birds do sing:
> Cuckoo, jug-jug, pu-we, to-witta-woo!

('jug-jug, pu-we, to-witta-woo!' represents the songs of the nightingale, the peewit and the owl.) This song is from a play by Thomas Nashe, as is 'Litany in Time of Plague', with its line 'Brightness falls from the air'. Shakespeare often uses songs in his plays, as in *Love's Labour's Lost*, *As You Like It*, *Twelfth Night* and *The Tempest*. Most of his songs have an art which conceals art. There is plenty of anonymous song, from the drinking song 'Back and Side Go Bare, Go Bare' to the artful madrigal 'My love in her attire doth show her wit.'

Literary history can say little about the anonymous poems which fill the popular lyric anthologies, from *Tottel's Miscellany* (1557) through *A Paradise of Dainty Devices* and *A Gorgeous Gallery of Gallant Inventions* to *England's Helicon* (1601). These numbers are often unfolksy: 'Thule, the period of cosmography' and 'Constant Penelope sends to thee, careless Ulysses', in catchy metrical hexameters. Ferocious linguistic schooling encouraged delight in language.

## Thomas Campion

Of all song-writers, **Thomas Campion** (1567–1620), inventive composer and masque-maker, wrote the best quantitative verse. His 'Rose-cheeked Laura, come', in praise of an ideal woman dancing, is the classic example. In later versions of this theme, the dancer, an emblem of Platonic harmony, sings. Campion's Laura is accompanied only by her own silent music (and his verbal intelligence):

> Rose-cheeked Laura, come,
> Sing thou smoothly with thy beauty's
> Silent music, either other
>     Sweetly gracing.
>
> 5  Lovely forms do flow
> From concent divinely framèd:       *musical concord*
> Heav'n is music, and thy beauty's
>     Birth is heavenly.

> These dull notes we sing
> 10    Discords need for helps to grace them;
> Only beauty purely loving
>      Knows no discord,
>
> But still moves delight,
> Like clear springs renewed by flowing,
> 15    Ever perfect, ever in them-
>      Selves eternal.

The matching of syllable-length to metrical stress in a trochaic pattern is broken twice: by lines 9–10, which act out the singer's pretended clumsiness; and by the iamb in line 13, where 'still' is both 'unmoving' and 'perpetually'. Another Campion poem imitating musical effect is 'When to her lute Corinna sings'. His 'My sweetest Lesbia, let us live and love' is one of several fine contemporary versions of Catullus' *vivamus, mea Lesbia, atque amemus*.

## Prose

### John Lyly

One outcome of the revived grammar schools was an art prose of a kind used by Sidney. Its acme was *Euphues* (1578) by **John Lyly** (*c*.1554–1606), grandson of the author of the standard Latin grammar. Euphues (Gk: 'well-endowed') 'dwelt in Athens, a young gentleman of great patrimony, and of so comely a personage, that it was doubted whether he were more bound to Nature for the lineaments of his person, or to Fortune for the increase of his possessions.'

The balancing of 'patrimony' and 'personage', 'Nature' and 'Fortune', 'person' and 'possessions', and other elements of composition, suggests the delight taken in pattern and parallelism, alliteration and artifice. The court took up the fashion, and the style is still visible in the prose of John Milton, generations later. The recommended rhetorical model was the style of Cicero, with a use of balanced tropes and rhythms, but Renaissance Ciceronianism is far more artificial than Cicero. It runs to playful excess, as, in the moral sphere, does the exemplary hero, Euphues.

It happened this young imp to arrive at Naples (a place of more pleasure than profit, and yet of more profit than piety) the very walls and windows whereof shewed it rather to be the Tabernacle of Venus, than the Temple of Vesta [goddess of chastity]. There was all things necessary and in readiness that might either allure the mind to lust, or entice the heart to folly, a court more meet for an atheist than for one of Athens, for Ovid than for Aristotle, for a graceless lover than for a godly liver: more fitter for Paris than Hector, and meeter for Flora [a fertility goddess] than Diana.

This antithetical style is parodied when Falstaff catechizes Prince Hal. The part of the schoolmaster in the style-wars of this period is shown by the pedants lovingly caricatured in Udall's Rhombus and in Sir Nathaniel in Shakespeare's *Love's Labour's Lost*: 'Thou hast been at a great feast of languages and stol'n away the scraps.'

### Thomas Nashe

**Thomas Nashe** (1567–1601) carries Marlowe's undergraduate irreverence further. His extravagance is suggested by his titles: *Pierce Penniless his Supplication to the Divell* (the complaint of a poor writer), *Christs Teares over Jerusalem* (an apocalyptic satire), *The Terrors of the Night* (a study of nightmares), *The Unfortunate Traveller. Or The Life of Jacke Wilton* (escapades abroad), *Have with you to Saffron-walden, Or Gabriel Harveys Hunt is up* (a pamphlet controversy), *The Isle of Dogs* (a lost play), *Nashe's Lenten Stuffe* (a mock encomium of the red herring, including a parody of *Hero and Leander*), and *Summers Last Will and Testament* (a comedy).

Pierce Penniless defends drama against Puritans:

> Our players are not as the players beyond sea, a sort of squirting bawdy comedians, that have whores and common courtesans to play women's parts, and forbear no immodest speech or unchaste action that may procure laughter; but ... honourable and full of gallant resolution, not consisting like theirs of pantaloon, a whore, and a zany [stock parts in the Italian *Commedia dell'Arte*]

In *The Unfortunate Traveller* Nashe deplores Italian influence on the English visitor: 'From thence he brings the arts of atheism, the art of epicurising, the art of whoring, the art of poisoning, the art of sodomitry.' Despite his Sunday-newspaper censoriousness, Nashe was at war with puritans, especially Spenser's friend Gabriel Harvey. Such was his invective that the Church authorities ordered that 'all Nashe's books and Doctor Harvey's books be taken wheresoever they may be found and that none of their books be ever printed hereafter.'

### Richard Hooker

Puritans had attacked the Church of England in the anonymous 'Marprelate' tracts (prelate=bishop), taking their tone from prayers such as 'Lord, crack their teeth' (Psalm 58). A better effort at loving his puritan neighbour was made by **Richard Hooker** (1553–1600) in his *Laws of Ecclesiastical Polity*, a defence of the apostolic episcopal order and doctrine of the Church of England, appealing to natural law as well as the Bible. His closely-reasoned moderation is suggested in this passage:

> The best and safest way for you therefore, my dear brethren, is to call your deeds past to a new reckoning, to re-examine the cause ye have taken in hand, and to try it even point by point, argument by argument, with all the diligent exactness ye can; to lay aside the gall of that bitterness wherein your minds have hitherto over-abounded, and with meekness to search the truth ...

Hooker's treatise and Ralegh's *History* are major works of a new English discursive prose.

## Further reading

Braunmuller, A. R. and M. Hattaway (eds). *The Cambridge Companion to English Renaissance Drama* (Cambridge: Cambridge University Press, 1990).

Jones, E. (ed.), *New Oxford Book of Sixteenth-Century Verse* (Oxford: Oxford University Press, 1992). A fresh and generous selection.

Kraye, J. (ed.), *The Cambridge Companion to English Renaissance Humanism* (Cambridge: Cambridge University Press, 1994).

Lewis, C. S., *Poetry and Prose in the Sixteenth Century, Excluding Drama* (Oxford: Oxford University Press, 1954). A clear, bold, provocative introduction.

# Shakespeare and the Drama

## Contents

## Overview

Shakespeare's family, early marriage and obscurity. First mentioned as a London player and playwright at the age of 28, he came in on the crest of a wave of new poetic drama. Kyd and Marlowe died, leaving the stage to him. He averaged two plays a year for twenty years: first comedy and history (a form he perfected), then tragedy, and finally romance. He retired early, half of his plays being preserved only in the First Folio, introduced by his successor, Jonson.

## William Shakespeare

### Shakespeare's life

**William Shakespeare** was born in 1564 at Stratford, a market town on the river Avon in Warwickshire. He was the eldest son and the third of eight children of John Shakespeare, a glover, and Mary Arden, a landowner's daughter. In 1568 John was bailiff (mayor) of Stratford.

Education at Stratford school was based on Latin grammar, rhetoric and composition; to speak English was forbidden in the upper forms. At church, Holy Trinity, which William attended by law with his father, he would also have learned much. At home there were three brothers and a sister (three sisters died as children), and around the home there were river-meadows, orchards and parks. He saw the public life of the town, too, although his father's part in this declined. Strolling players visited Stratford, and at nearby Coventry there was a performance of the cycle of Mystery plays on the feast of Corpus Christi.

He left school, probably at 15, and at 18 married Anne Hathaway, eight years his senior. At the time of the church wedding she was expecting a child, born in 1583 and christened Susanna. In 1585 Anne had twins, Hamnet and Judith. When next we hear of William, in 1592, he is in the London theatre, attacked in print by a university writer who warns other graduates against an 'upstart crow' who 'supposes he is as well able to bombast out a blank verse as the best of you'. This upstart is 'in his own conceit the only Shake-scene in a country.' *Shake-scene* is Shakespeare, whose name is found in various forms, some of them playful.

How had he lived between 1579 and 1592, the 'lost years'? Nothing is known, but in 1681 an actor whose father had known Shakespeare told John Aubrey that Shakespeare 'had been in his younger years a schoolmaster in the country'. Shakespeare may be the William Shakeshaft, apparently a player, who in 1581 was left money in the will of Alexander Houghton, a Catholic landowner in Lancashire. Houghton's neighbour, John Cottom, was master of Stratford school when William was there. There were notable Catholics at Stratford school: after John Cottom left Stratford, his brother was executed as a priest, with Edmund Campion, in 1582. Perhaps John Cottom went back to Catholic Lancashire and found a place as a tutor in Houghton's very Catholic household for 'Shakeshaft'; who could then have joined a company of players which came to London.

Unproven possibilities. But the old faith was strong locally, and the Shakespeares had Catholic loyalties. The poet's mother, Mary Arden, came from a noted Catholic family; a cousin was hanged, drawn and quartered in 1583. Shakespeare's father, John, lost his municipal positions in the 1580s and was reported for recusancy (not going to church) in 1592. In 1757 a bricklayer working on the Shakespeare house found hidden under the tiles a 'soul testament', a lengthy declaration of faith prepared for Catholics likely to die without a priest, signed 'John Shakespeare' at the head of each paragraph. This document, since lost, was published in 1790.

The Catalogue of 'the First Folio' of Shakespeare's plays, published by his fellow actors Heminges and Condell in 1623, in which eighteen of the plays were printed for the first time. *Cymbeline* is listed as a tragedy rather than a comedy.

William Shakespeare may have had Catholic sympathies, but occasionally gone to church, as did many 'church papists'. He was not a recusant, but nothing recorded is inconsistent with crypto-Catholicism. His daughter was reported as being 'popishly affected': she did not take communion at Easter 1606, a few months after the Gunpowder Plot. (On 5 November 1605 a plot by Catholic extremists to blow up Parliament had been unmasked; the plot had Warwickshire links.) Her father was later said to have 'dyed a papist'. The writings show a positive Christian understanding together with a questioning Renaissance humanism. The plays are full of symbolic ways of representation; they show no signs of anti-symbolic Reformation theology.

William kept up his links with Stratford, but his professional life was in London, writing and acting. He was a partner in the leading company of actors, the Lord Chamberlain's Men, founded in 1594. It played at Court and in the theatre, the Curtain, and in its own Globe theatre, built in 1599. Shakespeare shared in the substantial profits of what in 1603 became the King's Men. They played at Court as well as at the Globe and, from 1608, at the indoor Blackfriars theatre, especially in the winter. In 1596 William's son Hamnet died, aged 11. In 1597 William bought the largest house in Stratford, New Place. In 1601 his father died. In 1607 his daughter Susanna married; she bore a daughter in the following year. In 1609 his mother died. From 1610 he spent more time in Stratford. In February 1616 his daughter Judith married, and on 23 April 1616 he died: he was buried in the chancel of Holy Trinity, Stratford. There, before 1623, his monument was erected.

## The plays preserved

At his death in 1616, half of Shakespeare's plays had not been printed, but in 1623 two of his fellow-actors brought out a collected edition: thirty-six plays in a book

The title-page of the First Folio, with a portrait engraved by Martin Droeshout. One of two authoritative representations of Shakespeare; the other is the monument in Holy Trinity Church, Stratford.

of nearly nine hundred double-column pages in a large **Folio**, entitled *Comedies, Histories, and Tragedies.* In the poet's lifetime, nineteen plays had come out in little **Quartos**, pirated versions which provoked the players to bring out better quartos. Later they also brought out quartos of much-performed plays.

There is no sign that the author corrected texts set up from his papers. Without the Folio, English literature would have been very different. Without the Authorized Version of 1611, England would still have had a Bible. But if Shakespeare's friends not printed his plays, half of them (including *Macbeth* and *The Tempest*) would have been lost; the Folio is his true monument. (The suggestion that the plays must have been written by someone else, a man of rank or with a university degree, reveals something about those who entertain it.)

The Folio is prefaced by a poem by Ben Jonson (1572–16), who in 1616 had published his own *Works* as if he were a classical author. In *To the memory of my beloved, the author Mr William Shakespeare: and what he hath left us,* Jonson prefers Shakespeare to earlier English poets, and wishes he could show the tragedies to Aeschylus, Euripides and Sophocles. But in comedy his Shakespeare could stand the comparison:

> Of all, that insolent *Greece*, or haughtie *Rome*
> Sent forth, or since did from their ashes come.
> Triumph, my *Britaine*, thou hast one to showe,
> To whom all Scenes of *Europe* homage owe.
> He was not of an age, but for all time!

The conclusion is an apotheosis: Shakespeare, hailed as 'Sweet Swan of Avon', is raised to the heavens as a 'constellation', the 'Starre of *Poets*'. This is a witty poetic puff. But the claim that Shakespeare is not only the greatest European dramatist but also 'for all time' stands up well. Jonson had a high idea of poetry, and was a critic hard to please. He wrote of Shakespeare that he 'loved the man, and do honour his memory, on this side idolatry, as much as any'. John Milton wrote in the Second Folio (1632) of the 'deep impression' made by Shakespeare's 'delphick lines' and echoes Jonson in calling him '*my* Shakespeare'.

Writers adopted Shakespeare early, critics followed later. The idolatry Jonson eschewed dates from the Stratford Jubilee in April 1769, led by David Garrick and James Boswell, when false relics of 'the Bard', as he was called, were sold by the thousand. Thereafter Jonson's witty promotion of Shakespeare to semi-divine status was taken seriously in Germany and even in France. In 1818 Keats entitled a poem 'On sitting down to read *King Lear* once again'. The Bard was now more read than performed.

## Luck and fame

But Shakespeare lives because he is a playwright: his plays are re-created in daily performance in and beyond the English-speaking world. He joined the theatre as it entered its great period, a time of general intellectual ferment, cultural confidence and linguistic exuberance. Materials were to hand – classical and European literature re-created in translation – and models of English verse in Sidney and Spenser, and of lively drama in Lyly, Kyd and Marlowe.

Shakespeare has been lucky in that his English remains largely intelligible. Chaucer's 'verray parfit gentil knyght' can be misunderstood: *verray* meant true, *parfit* complete, and *gentil* noble. Compared with Chaucer, Shakespeare takes more

**folio** Leaf of paper. A printer's term for a large-format book made of leaves of 14" by 20", folded once to make 2 leaves (4 pages). In a **quarto** book each leaf is folded twice, making 4 leaves (8 pages).

risks with words; yet senses have changed less since his day. He also lived at the beginning of the modern age: his ideas of the world were shaped by the Christian and humanist ideals which have fed most of what has so far followed. Lucky in his school and home, he then had to make his way in the world. At the age of 20 he was himself a father of three. The theatre offered him a living.

## The drama

It was two centuries since drama had moved out of the church and into the street, although the Mystery plays, which dramatized biblical stories in all-day cycles on summer holy days, continued into Shakespeare's time. The Reformation had transferred much pageant and spectacle to the State. The Church was cowed, and the theatre was the chief place where the concerns of the day could, with care, be ventilated. There was public appetite for drama, which explored the interests of a large new audience. Theatres were erected by commercial joint-venture companies outside the City, chiefly on the South Bank of the Thames, the home of diversions not permitted in the City.

### The commercial theatre

Strolling players did not make money: audiences melted away as the hat went round. In London inn-yards of the 1550s, the spectator put his penny in a box at the entrance (hence 'box-office'). Then in 1576 James Burbage, a carpenter-actor-impresario, built The Theatre for the Earl of Leicester's players, who had a Royal Patent. This was the first purpose-built permanent public theatre. Although its title (and perhaps its shape) echoed classical theatre, Burbage would have been surprised to learn that what passed on the stages he built is valued more than the non-dramatic poetry of his day.

Drawing of the Swan Theatre, London: a copy of a drawing of *c.*1596 by Johannes de Witt, a Dutch vistor to London.
*tectum* roof
*porticus* gallery
*sedilia* seats
*ingressus* entry
*mimorum ædes* the house of the actors
*proscænium* fore-stage
*planities sive arena* flat space or arena.

In 1599 the new Globe stood three storeys high, near Southwark Cathedral, surrounded by other theatres, houses, inns, churches, shops, brothels, cockpits and bearpits. Puritans feared the theatre; the Court watched it; plays were licensed. Built by Shakespeare's company out of the old timbers of The Theatre, the Globe could hold 3000 – a huge audience, although the atmosphere of the rebuilt modern Globe (opened in 1996) is surprisingly intimate. There were then five other big theatres in a London of about 200,000 inhabitants. Ten days counted as a long run, and revivals were unusual; new plays were always needed.

The plays were put on in the afternoon in this enclosed yard with its roofed stage and thatched galleries. Shakespeare mentions 'the two hours' traffic of the stage': there was no scenery to change. As one scene ended, another would begin: an actor would enter saying 'This castle has a pleasant seat' or 'Is this a dagger that I see before me?', so that the audience would know what to imagine. The audience did not suspend disbelief within a darkened theatre: it collaborated in daylight make-believe. Plays did not pretend to be real: the sultry, mature Cleopatra was played by a boy, as were all women. Verse is itself a convention, as is the soliloquy and the aside. So is invisibility: in broad daylight an actor would whisper 'I am invisible'. He was not invisible to the 'groundlings', who stood on the ground at his feet visible, audible and inhalable, crowding round the stage. Each of those who paid one penny to stand cannot have heard or grasped every flying word. But high-sounding and patterned language appealed in itself; crowds flocked to hear ornate sermons. Theatre was popular; the Globe could hold a sizeable fraction of Londoners free to attend. They participated, as at a provincial Italian opera, a Spanish bull-fight or a British pantomime. The cultural mix meant that popular vigour and crudity rubbed shoulders with poetry and intelligence.

Shakespeare came in on a rising tide. After 1594 Marlowe and Kyd were dead, and he was the leading playwright, sharing in the profits of his Company. He began with the sexual knockabout of *The Taming of the Shrew*, the classical atrocities of *Titus Andronicus*, and the martial pageantry of *Henry VI*, but in his romance comedies combined action with literary high spirits. Public drama was crude and refined, sensational and complex; private theatres were indoor, smaller, quieter. But the theatres drew high and low, fine and coarse: it was the popular draw which gave the medium its cultural power, without which its enactment of current and recurrent human issues would have lacked the structure of humanist thinking, and drama might have lacked humour.

## Predecessors

Chapters 2 and 3 followed drama from Mystery and Morality through interlude to academic Roman comedy and Senecan tragedy. As for Shakespeare's immediate exemplars, Jonson wrote: 'how far thou didst our Lyly outshine,/Or sporting Kyd, or Marlowe's mighty line'. After *Euphues*, **Thomas Lyly** (1554–1606) wrote for schoolboys and the choristers of the Chapel Royal, who played in a private theatre made in the ruins of Blackfriars. His *Campaspe* (1583) told how Alexander loved a beautiful captive but allowed her to wed the artist Apelles, whom he had commissioned to paint her. A humanist debate, conducted in elegant prose with choral interludes, showed greatness giving way to art. But the great Gloriana proved a mean patroness to Lyly, and the theatre and the press did not support subsequent university wits: **Robert Greene** (1558–92), whose play *Friar Bacon and Friar Bungay* gave hints to Marlowe for *Dr Faustus*; and **Thomas Lodge** (1558–1625), whose prose romance

*Rosalynde* was the source for *As You Like It*. Lyly is polite, but Greene, Lodge and Nashe wrote for new middle-class patrons of mixed tastes.

'Sporting' is not the obvious epithet for **Thomas Kyd** (1558–94), author of *The Spanish Tragedy; or, Hieronymo is Mad Again*; perhaps Jonson thought his art immature. Kyd pioneered the revenge play; the performance of his tragedy at the Rose in 1592 may have been a revival. It has an isolated, agonized avenger, lurid characters and a brilliantly intricate plot. In the prologue a ghost cries out for vengeance, and the mad Hieronymo uses a play-within-a-play to avenge his son Horatio. The stilted end-stopped lines build little momentum, but the bloody ending is successfully horrific; it was hugely popular. Kyd may also have written a lost play about Hamlet.

## Christopher Marlowe

Shakespeare outshone Kyd, but learned from his own contemporary, **Christopher Marlowe** (b.1564), who was killed in a tavern in 1593. Marlowe announced his talent in *Tamburlaine the Great* (1587):

> We'll lead you to the stately tent of war,
> Where you shall hear the Scythian Tamburlaine
> Threatening the world with high astounding terms,
> And scourging kingdoms with his conquering swords.

The 'mighty line' was the blank pentameter, not used since *Gorboduc* (1561). Its might comes from the rhythmic energy which allowed Marlowe to launch each 'astounding term' like a rocket. Each of the lines has a final stress which begs to be shouted.

The shepherd Tamburlaine rose to rule the Mongol empire, humiliating the rulers of Persia, Turkey, Egypt and Babylon with a savagery softened only at the request of his beloved, the 'divine Zenocratë'. His hubris in challenging the gods is not punished; he merely dies. Like the protagonists of Marlowe's *Jew of Malta* and

The title-page of the sixth printing of Marlowe's play, showing Faustus conjuring spirits: a devil rises from the trapdoor.

*Dr Faustus*, Tamburlaine is an arrogant upstart who scorns human limits. A Romantic view of the Renaissance saw Dr Faustus as transcending worn-out teachings like Galileo, or as an emblem of human aspiration like Goethe's Faust. But Faustus doesn't believe in hell, and sells his soul for twenty-four years of fun. The knowledge he seeks is paltry, and he wastes his powers on schoolboy tricks. 'Farce' means stuffing, and although the beginning and end of *Faustus* are golden, its middle is stuffed with the jests of the Vice of the old Moralities; a form which also provides a Good and an Evil Angel, and devils who finally claim the unrepentant sinner.

> Cut is the branch that might have grown full straight,
> And burnèd is Apollo's laurel bough,
> That sometime grew within this learned man.
> Faustus is gone! Regard his hellish fall ...

The orthodox moral of the Epilogue is transformed by a might and music of language quite new to the English stage. Earlier Faustus has summoned up an image of Helen of Troy:

> 'Is this the face that launched a thousand ships
> And burnt the topless towers of Ilium?
> Sweet Helen, make me immortal with a kiss:
> Her lips sucks forth my soul, see where it flies.'

Aspiration turns into delusion: the Doctor's 'immortal' soul falls mortal prey to a demonic succuba he has himself conjured up. Marlowe specializes in the glamour of desire: 'O thou art fairer than the evening air,/Clad in the beauty of a thousand stars.' He gives the same rhetorical projection to Christian lines: 'See, see, where Christ's blood streams in the firmament!' cries the despairing Faustus. Sin leads to hell; which makes sensational theatre. Marlowe's mighty line echoes; but the extinguished aspiration seems sardonic rather than providential.

The protagonist of *The Jew of Malta* is called Barabas, like the thief in the Gospel whom the mob spared in preference to Jesus. A cunning trickster, he blows up a convent of nuns (including his convert daughter) with devilish glee; but finally falls into a cauldron of boiling oil he had prepared for his guests. Marlowe exploits the revulsion of his audience, who see that the Catholic defenders and Turkish attackers of Malta are as amoral as Barabas, and lack his cynical zest. The overreacher drops into hell; yet this play is less tragic than blackly comic, an exposé of hypocrisy. The Prologue, spoken by Machiavel, has the gleefully impious couplet: 'I count religion but a childish toy,/And hold there is no sin but ignorance.' The wicked Machiavel also says: 'Admired I am by those who hate me most'. Although 'admired' means 'wondered at', this suggests Marlowe's fascination. The final screams of Barabas show that the sin of ignorance is universal.

Screams also end *Edward II*, Marlowe's most workmanlike play, a study in the operation of power: the weak king loses his throne to rebel nobles who resent his homosexual infatuation with the low Gaveston and conspire with his wife to depose him. The murder of Edward suggested a pattern of pathos to Shakespeare for *Richard II*. In comparison, Marlowe is disturbing, sensationalistic, lacking in tragic complexity; but his sulphuric brilliance is not outshone.

## The order of the plays

Shakespeare wrote on average two plays a year between *c.*1588–90 and 1611, except in 1592–4 when bubonic plague shut the theatres. His contemporaries saw or read

## Order of composition of the plays

Compiled from the *Oxford Shakespeare*, ed. S. Wells and G. Taylor (1988). The dates of the early plays are conjectural.

| | | | |
|---|---|---|---|
| 1590–1 | *Two Gentlemen of Verona* | 1599 | *Julius Caesar* |
| 1590–1 | *The Taming of the Shrew* | 1599–1600 | *As You Like It* |
| 1591 | *2 Henry VI* | 1600–1 | *Hamlet* |
| 1592 | *3 Henry VI* | 1601 | *Twelfth Night* |
| 1592 | *1 Henry VI* | 1602 | *Troilus and Cressida* |
| 1592 | *Titus Andronicus* | 1593–1603 | *The Sonnets* |
| 1592–3 | *Richard III* | 1603 | *Measure for Measure* |
| 1592–3 | *Venus and Adonis* | 1603–4 | *Othello* |
| 1593–4 | *The Rape of Lucrece* | 1604–5 | *All's Well That Ends Well* |
| 1594 | *The Comedy of Errors* | 1605 | *Timon of Athens* |
| 1594–5 | *Love's Labour's Lost* | 1605–6 | *King Lear* |
| 1595 | *Richard II* | 1606 | *Macbeth* |
| 1595 | *Romeo and Juliet* | 1606 | *Antony and Cleopatra* |
| 1595 | *A Midsummer Night's Dream* | 1607 | *Pericles,* |
| 1596 | *King John* | 1608 | *Coriolanus* |
| 1596–7 | *The Merchant of Venice* | 1609 | *The Winter's Tale* |
| 1596–7 | *1 Henry IV* | 1610 | *Cymbeline* |
| 1597–8 | *The Merry Wives of Windsor* | 1611 | *The Tempest* |
| 1597–8 | *2 Henry IV* | 1613 | *Henry VIII* |
| 1598 | *Much Ado About Nothing* | 1613–14 | *Two Noble Kinsmen* |
| 1598–9 | *Henry V* | | |

Shakespeare play by play, as we do in the theatre or at school. But the Folio gave Shakespeare as a whole to readers, and before approaching representative plays the order of his writing is worth a look, both chronologically and in terms of genre.

He began with comedies of love, and chronicle-plays. The first decade produced nine plays called after kings of England, ten comedies of love and two non-historical tragedies. The second decade shows more critical comedies, with tragedies and Roman plays, followed by four romances, ending with *The Tempest*. Ten years after Elizabeth's death he worked with Fletcher on *Henry VIII* and on *Two Noble Kinsmen*.

## Histories

The Folio classification by kinds is rough (the Greek and Roman histories are classed as tragedies) and has caused trouble, for Shakespeare did not follow the classical division of dramatic experience into comedy and tragedy. He often put comedy into tragedy and vice versa, upsetting the classically-minded. The history, perfected and defined by Shakespeare's example, is not a pure or classical kind of play. He wrote ten English histories in all, listed in the Folio in the order of the reigns of the kings in their titles. But the order of reigns was not the order of composition. The first **tetralogy** – the three parts of *Henry VI* and *Richard III* – was written in 1590–3. We shall look at the second tetralogy – *Richard II*, *Henry IV parts 1 and 2*, and *Henry V* – composed in 1595–9.

The three *Henry VI* plays are loosely-constructed pageant-like epic drama –

**tetralogy** A set of four works.

patriotic, military and spectacular. In contrast to these dramatized chronicles, *Richard III* is a drama. The Quarto title was *The Tragedy of Richard of York*, and it has tragic form. Compared with what followed, it is relatively crude, as are *The Comedy of Errors*, *The Shrew* and *Titus Andronicus*, early plays based on unsentimental classical precedents. *Richard III* is based on More's prose *History of Richard III* (written in 1513 in Latin and English), a study in tyranny. Shakespeare's twisted plotter comes from More (see page 80). Compared with medieval chroniclers who construct their narratives in terms of divine providence and personal character, humanists like More wrote analytic history in the mode of the Roman historian **Tacitus** (AD 55–after 115). Although he is modelled on the Vice figure from the Morality plays, Richard is not merely malignant. A central figure whose soliloquies show internal consciousness is found in the Morality play *Everyman*, but Richard is the first Shakespearean protagonist to soliloquize.

Shakespeare's reigns-on-stage stop with *Richard III* and the advent of the Tudors. Henry VIII's three children had each in turn reversed preceding religious policy. As Shakespeare began writing, Mary Queen of Scots – mother of Elizabeth's heir-apparent, James VI of Scotland – lost her head. Dynastic historiography was dangerous. From 1547 the Tudors made sure that their subjects heard regularly from the pulpit about their duty to obey the Crown. Church attendance was the law, and nine times a year homilies were read on the divine appointment of kings and the duty of subjects to order and obedience. The manuscript of a play of *c*.1594 on *Sir Thomas More* survives, with contributions by six hands, one thought to be Shakespeare's; it was not staged in the Queen's lifetime. It was ten years after Elizabeth's death that Shakespeare collaborated in a *Henry VIII*. The portrayals of More and of Katherine of Aragon are sympathetic.

Shakespeare's histories draw on the *Chronicles* of Holinshed (1587), and on plays such as *Woodstock*, about the murder of Thomas Woodstock, uncle of Richard II. On the afternoon before his attempted coup in 1601, supporters of the Earl of Essex commissioned a special performance of *Richard II*. The players at first demurred, saying that the play was stale. The Queen said on this occasion that it had been played forty times (that is, since 1595). It was not stale, however, for she also said 'I am Richard II, know ye not that?' Richard had been deposed (and murdered) by Lancastrians, from whom the Tudors inherited their right to the throne. Essex was executed.

## *Richard II*

*Richard II* is a historical tragedy, modelled on Marlowe's *Edward II* in its set-up and its manipulation of our sympathies. In each play the king's irresponsibility and unfitness is clear, but once he is deposed we are made to pity him. Edward neglects his country for the favours of Gaveston; Edward's noble opponents are less likeable even than he; his wife and son conspire against him. Marlowe shows the unedifying workings of power, relieved by the flares of homosexual infatuation. After a red-hot poker and screams, the play closes with the 'reassuring' young Edward III. In such history there is no moral significance.

In marked contrast, *Richard II* is rich in poetry and in ideas. Through John of Gaunt, Duke of Lancaster, Shakespeare provides a poetry of England as a Christian kingdom, this 'other Eden', this 'blessed plot', but watered with the blood and tears of civil war. The king is 'the deputy anointed by the Lord', and the play is symbolic, sacramental, symphonic. It opens with mutual chivalric defiance (which Richard calls off, exiling the combatants) and continues with formal, ceremonial verse almost throughout. The keynote is Gaunt's dying vision of England as it ought to be, and then as it currently is, leased out to Richard's tax-farming cronies. Time-honoured Lancaster's feudal music ends with his death; Richard smartly announces that 'we seize into our hands,/His plate, his goods, his money and his lands'. The disinheriting of Lancaster's son, Henry Bolingbroke, strikes down the principle of succession by which the king holds his throne, and gives the returning Bolingbroke the perfect slogan for his march through England: 'I come for Lancaster'.

Action is symbolic and symmetrical. Richard weeps to stand upon his kingdom once again, but sits to hear sad stories of the death of kings; the sun rises, but Richard, whose symbol is the sun, falls: 'down, down I come, like glistering Phaeton,/Wanting the manage of unruly jades'. He has a series of arias lamenting his fall, deploying the sacred language which at Gaunt's bedside had made him yawn. At Flint Castle, the cross-over point, Richard has to 'come down' to the aspiring Bolingbroke. There follow the symbolic garden scene, and the self-deposition arranged in Westminster Hall so that Henry may 'proceed without suspicion' – a scene cut from the Quarto as too dangerous. Henry says that in God's name he ascends the royal throne. The Bishop of Carlisle points out that he lacks God's blessing, which Henry acknowledges. He deals with quarrelling nobles firmly, unlike the petulant Richard of Act I. Henry ends the play with a vow to go as a pilgrim to Jerusalem to purge the guilt of Richard's murder. The Lord's anointed is succeeded by an efficient pragmatist. Richard invoked divine sanctions and did nothing; the usurper uses the language of rights and does not put a foot wrong. The end has justified the means, but the 'silent king' cannot now invoke the old sanctions; and he finds that he cannot sleep.

*Richard II* is a foundation for the three-play sequence topped out by *Henry V*. It is also a tragedy, but Richard is not a noble tragic hero; he likens his passion to Christ's, but we pity him less than he pities himself. Shakespeare, however, did not observe the tragic norms which Renaissance theorists derived from Aristotle. History is raw and untidy, and has to be cooked and shaped to fit the moulds of comedy and tragedy. Also, as Sidney noted, history shows that the wicked prosper, although Shakespeare's chronicle sources had found in it a providential sense of design. The purpose of the tetralogy is revealed by the dying speech of Henry IV, who tells his son that 'the soil of the achievement [the guilt of usurpation]/Goes with me into the earth', and that his son's succession is 'plain and right'. For Henry V was not only the heroic victor of Agincourt: he paved the way for the Tudors. He married Kate of France, brought her to England and died, whereupon Kate married Owen Tudor, who was the grandfather of Henry VII, Elizabeth's grandfather.

### Henry IV

Shakespeare took care with his foundation for the tetralogy. *Richard II* draws on seven different sources, and transcends them; it is modelled on *Edward II*, but it makes Marlowe look flat.

Shakespeare's resourcefulness shows in *1* and *2 Henry IV* and *Henry V*, plays very different from *Richard II*. They mingle verse and prose, high and low, court and tavern, royal camp and rebel camp in a many-sided representation of the life of England. Falstaff's first words, 'Now, Hal, what time of day is it, lad?' create character as decisively as Henry's opening line, 'So shaken as we are, so wan with care'. Falstaff's hangover, his familiarity with his Prince, and his neglect of time are Theme as well as Character. Shakespeare turns to profit the problem of Hal's legendary wild youth by creating a gloriously attractive drinking companion in Falstaff. Prince Hal studies the common people he will have to lead in war; he learns their ways and speech, and the part he will have to play. The rebel Hotspur scorns 'the king of smiles' and his efforts at 'popularity'. But acting has now become part of political life: Henry sends into the battlefield at Shrewsbury men dressed as himself, duplicate kings whom Douglas kills. These multiplied images admit that the monarchy has lost its sacredness, that kingship is a role, with Hal as understudy. Hal transforms into Prince Henry at Shrewsbury, kills the honourable Hotspur and, as in a fairy tale, allows Falstaff to take the credit. Shakespeare has worked a trick whereby Hal has touched pitch and is not defiled.

In *2 Henry IV* we see less of Hal and less of the comic and festive side of unruly popular life, more of its disease and low tricks. We also see trickery and suspicion in high places. Prince John cheats; King Henry wrongly accuses Prince Henry of wanting him dead so that he can have the crown. In their last interview he advises his son to 'busy giddy minds/With foreign quarrels': Agincourt a diversion! The rogues of Eastcheap will serve in *Henry V* as a foil to the noble King. In a rich invention, Mr Justice Shallow reminisces in his Gloucestershire orchard with Falstaff about their naughty youth and how their days of wenching and boozing will return when Falstaff is Lord Chief Justice. When Falstaff accosts the new King as he comes from his crowning, he has to be banished; but this most lovable of Vices was to ride again in *The Merry Wives of Windsor*.

## Henry V

*Henry V* begins by telling us that it is a chronicle turned into a play, set within 'this wooden O' (the Globe), with prologues and chorus and reference to 'the story'. It is a pageant with heroic tableaux. Henry coolly plays his legendary role for all it is worth, but on the night before Agincourt we see him pray and suffer, and, in disguise as a common soldier, take the king's part in an argument with other soldiers. We see him dealing with nobles, traitors, enemies, soldiers, captains, the French court, the princess. But he never meets the denizens of Eastcheap, and Falstaff dies offstage.

Throughout *Henry V* we see the seamy side of the tapestry of history alternate with the public side. Immediately before the wooing of Kate of France we hear that Doll Tearsheet is dead and that Bardolph will run a brothel. The daughters of Harfleur are threatened with rape, so that the town should yield; Kate learns English so that she may yield. Henry's clemency is followed by his angry killing of the prisoners, and a joke about Alexander 'the Pig'. The play is a carefully mounted study of how to be king, and of what it costs; but for all his courage and splendid words Henry is due admiration rather than the unmerited love which animates the Hostess's account of the death of one of the 'gentleman in England now abed' of whom Henry speaks at Agincourt, Sir John Falstaff. Mrs Quickly:

Nay, sure he's not in hell. He's in Arthur's bosom, if ever man went to Arthur's bosom. A made a finer end, and went away an it had been any christom child. A parted ev'n just between twelve and one, ev'n at the turning o' th'tide – for after I saw him fumble with the sheets, and play with flowers, and smile upon his finger's end, I knew there was but one way. For his nose was as sharp as a pen, and a babbled of green fields. 'How now, Sir John?' quoth I. 'What, man! Be o' good cheer.' So a cried out, 'God, God, God', three or four times. Now I, to comfort him, bid him he should not think of God; I hoped there was no need to trouble himself with any such thoughts yet. So a bade me lay more clothes on his feet. I put my hand into the bed and felt them, and they were cold as any stone. Then I felt to his knees, and so up'ard and up'ard, and all was as cold as any stone.

The sacred ideals of England and of kingship, set up at the start of *Richard II* and turned into theatre by Richard at Flint Castle, were betrayed by him in practice. His usurping successor could not claim these ideals, fair and firm though his rule was. England is at last led to foreign victory by a king who succeeds by right, and who is shown to have well studied his people and his role. But the new relationship between England and her king is based on a providential combination of succession and success. As the Epilogue points out, Harry of Agincourt was soon succeeded, as King of France and England, by the infant Henry VI, 'Whose state so many had the managing/That they lost France and made his England bleed.'

In both artistic and human terms, Shakespeare's histories reach their best in *Henry IV*, a play which mixes Henry's brooding distrust of his wild son with the comic irresponsibility of Eastcheap to produce a romance outcome: Hal's apparent wildness is Henry V's apprenticeship. The father–son conflict is rehearsed comically in Part I, with Falstaff as the King, and in near-tragic earnest in Part II. Shakespeare's inclusion of all sorts and ranks in his historical representation of England helped to enrich and universalize his later tragedies, notably *King Lear*.

## Comedy

Shakespeare's early plays are mostly comedy and history, kinds of play more open and inclusive than tragedy. Comedy came easily to Shakespeare. Half of his dramatic output is comic, and his earlier critics, from Jonson to Johnson, preferred his comedy.

The writing in his earliest surviving play, *Two Gentlemen of Verona*, is already accomplished. It is a love-comedy with familiar ingredients: a duke, young rivals, a father called Antonio, a daughter who dresses as a boy to follow her lover, a ring, a glove, a friar's cell, comic servants, a song ('Who is Silvia?'). Plot is stronger in *The Comedy of Errors*, based on a Roman comedy by Plautus (*c*.254–184 BC) which Shakespeare would have studied at school, about identical twins with the same name, Antipholus. Shakespeare is confident enough to give the Antipholus twins identical twin servants called Dromio, and to manage the complications.

Comedy was easier to write than history: there was a repertory to hand in Roman comedy and medieval romance, and the humanist wit and polish of Lyly. To write a history, Shakespeare had to turn chronicle into drama, but in comedy he had a stock of devices already proven on the stage – disguise, mistaken identity, the contrasting perspectives on love of men and women, parents and children, masters and servants. Alternation of perspective, contrast and variety became a structural principle in all his plays.

In comparison with *Two Gentlemen*, the *Henry VI* plays are elementary, though *Richard III*, like *The Shrew*, is a strong stage-play. But nothing in the first histories prepares us for the brilliance of *Love's Labour's Lost* and the maturity of *A Midsummer Night's Dream*, plays without direct sources for the plot. In *Love's Labour's Lost* the King of Navarre and three friends vow to forswear the company of women for three years while they pursue wisdom in a 'little academe'. The Princess of France and three of her ladies arrive; the men fall in love but daren't tell each other; the ladies disguise themselves and make the men look foolish. Their decision to break their vows and woo the ladies is rationalized by the witty Biron:

> From women's eyes this doctrine I derive.
> They sparkle still the right Promethean fire.
> They are the books, the arts, the academes
> That show, contain and nourish all the world.

At an Interlude of the Nine Worthies, put on by characters from a comic subplot, news comes of the death of the Princess's father. The comedy ends not in four weddings but in a funeral and a year's mourning. The men's efforts to continue their wooing are repulsed; Biron is reminded by his lady Rosaline that 'A jest's prosperity lies in the ear/Of him that hears it, never in the tongue/Of him that makes it.' She sends him to do charitable work, and 'jest a twelve-month in a hospital'. The play closes with the cuckoo's song of Spring, answered by the owl's song of Winter.

This 'conceited comedy' is carried off by a play of language and ideas so high-spirited that its sudden stop, the loss of love's labour in death, is a shock. After the gallantry and laughter, the black clothes of the Messenger tell the Princess his news before he speaks. To make action comment upon words thus at the climax shows mastery of theatre. Death interrupts the interlude, and the dismissal of love's labourers is followed by the cuckoo and the owl. Rosaline is the first typically Shakespearean heroine – a woman of sounder understanding than the man who swears love to her. Love is folly, but necessary folly; for foolish mistakes are the only way to learning. Biron: 'Let us once lose our oaths to find ourselves/Or else we lose ourselves to keep our oaths.'

## A Midsummer Night's Dream

Shakespeare's wit and complexity go even further in *A Midsummer Night's Dream*, a play involving four marriages and 'a most rare vision'. Duke Theseus of Athens is to wed the Amazon Queen, Hippolyta; two young Athenian couples (after much confusion in a wood near Athens) also marry. The King and Queen of the Fairies, Oberon and Titania, quarrel passionately over an Indian boy; Oberon makes Titania fall in love with Bottom, a weaver who is rehearsing (in another part of the wood) a play for the Duke's wedding.

The source for the Athenian part of the story is Chaucer's Knight's Tale; Shakespeare adds to the triangle of young lovers a second woman, in love with a man who scorns her. (A foursome permits a happy ending without loss of life.) Puck, servant to the classical Oberon and Titania, is a creature from English folklore. Bottom and his friends, straight from the streets of Stratford, choose to play Pyramus and Thisbe, a love-tragedy from Ovid's *Metamorphoses*. With great assurance, Shakespeare choreographs these disparate elements in an action on four levels: fairy king and queen, legendary hero and heroine, fashionable young lovers, and English tradesmen.

Puck adds supernatural confusion to the effects of love and midsummer moonlight. Directed by Oberon, he puts an ass's head on Bottom, and squeezes the love-inducing juice of a magic herb onto Titania's eyelid. She wakes and loves the first creature she sees – the asinine Bottom, whom she carries off to her bower. The love-juice causes operatic mayhem among the four young lovers in the wood. But Jack shall have Jill: Oberon makes Puck put everything right in time for the wedding. The wedding-eve of the Duke (and the lovers) is taken up with the play of Pyramus and Thisbe, lovers who, each convinced the other is dead, commit suicide. The innocent artisans' efforts at tragedy are met by the laughter of the court, and audiences always laugh at the lovers' suicide; 'very tragical mirth'. It is a brilliantly unsuitable play for a wedding. Shakespeare used a similar tragedy of errors to end his next play, *Romeo and Juliet*.

If comedy is tragedy averted, it is often in Shakespeare averted narrowly. The passions of the lovers in the wood read conventionally, but this predictability and interchangeability is intended by Shakespeare – as is brought out in Benjamin

Britten's 1960 opera of the play, where the four voices sing duets of love and hate, which turn into a final harmonious ensemble. The fierce jealousy of the fairies is expressed in a sumptuously baroque poetry, while the irrationality of sexual possession is suggested only lightly in the love of the goddess Titania for Bottom. The unimaginative Bottom says when he wakes up:

'I have had a most rare vision. I have had a dream past the wit of man to say what dream it was. Man is but an ass if he go about t'expound this dream. Methought I was – there is no man can tell what. Methought I was, and methought I had – but man is but a patched fool if he will offer to say what methought I had. The eye of man hath not heard, the ear of man hath not seen, man's hand is not able to taste, his tongue to conceive, nor his heart to report what my dream was. I will get Peter Quince to write a ballad of this dream. It shall be called "Bottom's Dream", because it hath no bottom …'

The earthy Bottom puts his enjoyment of the fairy queen in terms that parody St Paul's account of Heaven (1 Corinthians 2:9). Bottom's bottomless dream is the subject of the play: love, moonlight and madness. Hippolyta observes: ''Tis strange, my Theseus, that these lovers speak of.' Theseus replies:

> More strange than true. I never may believe
> These antique fables nor these fairy toys.
> Lovers and madmen have such seething brains,
> Such shaping fantasies, that apprehend
> More than cool reason ever comprehends.
> The lunatic, the lover, and the poet
> Are of imagination all compact.
> … And as imagination bodies forth
> The forms of things unknown, the poet's pen
> Turns them to shapes, and gives to airy nothing
> A local habitation and a name …

To the Athenian reason of Theseus, the story of the night is incredible; to Hippolyta it testifies to something real.

> HIPPOLYTA:  But all the story of the night told over,
>     And all their minds transfigured so together,
>     More witnesseth than fancy's images,
>     And grows to something of great constancy.

They exchange roles in their reactions to the Interlude.

> HIPPOLYTA:  This is the silliest stuff that ever I heard.
> THESEUS:  The best in this kind are but shadows, and the          *shadows* actors
>     worst are no worse if imagination amend them.
> HIPPOLYTA:  It must be your imagination, then, and not theirs.
> THESEUS:  If we imagine no worse of them than they of themselves, then
>     they may pass for excellent men.

This pair of exchanges tells us much about Shakespearean drama. The play-within-a-play was a device he favoured: the players become spectators at a play; the playhouse audience are both godlike spectators and foolish shadows. Hippolyta, who found truth in dreams, cannot accept the play; whereas her rational lord lends his imagination to complete the inadequacy of the images. Are dream and play the same? Which can we trust?

That all the world's a stage, and all the men and women merely players, as Jaques says in *As You Like It*, was a common conceit. A poem by Ralegh puts it neatly:

> What is our life? a play of passion,
> Our mirth the musicke of division,
> Our mothers' wombs the tiring-houses be,
> Where we are drest for this short Comedy,
> Heaven the judicious sharp spectator is,
> That sits and marks still who doth act amiss,
> Our graves that hide us from the searching sun,
> Are like drawn curtains when the play is done,
> Thus march we playing to our latest rest,
> Only we die in earnest, that's no jest.

At the last, in *The Tempest* Prospero predicts that the stage, 'the great globe itself', will dissolve.

Shakespeare now produced a series of more mature comedies in which averted tragedy comes much closer, as in *The Merchant of Venice* and *Much Ado About Nothing*. He wrote the love-tragedy *Romeo and Juliet* and the political tragedy *Julius Caesar*. *Hamlet* was written about 1600, as was *As You Like It*.

*Twelfth Night*, written in 1601, is discussed next as the example of a mature love comedy. In order of composition, there follow what late 19th-century critics called the 'problem plays', *Measure for Measure* and *All's Well that Ends Well*, bitter-sweet love-comedies, and *Troilus and Cressida*, a harshly satirical version of Trojan love and Greek heroism. While most plays address a problem, the moral conundrums which these plays address are not resolved by the weddings with which they end; their spirit is satirical, baffling rather than comic.

*Measure for Measure* addresses sexual crime and punishment. Chastity is exemplified by the aspirant nun Isabella and the puritan magistrate Angelo, appointed to clean up the vices of Vienna. She pleads for the life of her brother Claudio, forfeit for having made his fiancée pregnant; the price Angelo asks is Isabella's maidenhead. The Duke of Vienna disguised as a friar works a 'bed-trick', in which Angelo sleeps with his fiancée Mariana, thinking her Isabella; and a 'head-trick', in which a murderer is executed instead of Claudio. In the denouement the Duke unties the knot by tying four other knots, marrying Isabella himself. Marriage is better than convent or brothel: but the theatricality of the Duke's measure points to the intractability of the issues. The tragedies that follow *Hamlet* also address intractable problems: the justifiability of tyrannicide; the corruption of personal honour by ambition and power; and the fate of goodness in the world.

## Twelfth Night

*Twelfth Night*, which marks the mid-point of Shakespeare's career, is a ripe love-comedy with a happy ending. Shipwrecked separately on the coast of Illyria are twins, Viola and Sebastian, each thinking the other drowned; each ends up marrying well.

As in most Shakespeare plays about love, the protagonist is a girl, Viola. She disguises herself as a boy (Cesario), to evade detection rather than to pursue a young man. Cesario (Viola) is employed by the young Duke Orsino to carry his love to the young Olivia. Both Olivia and Viola mourn a brother. Viola falls in love with Orsino, however, and Olivia falls for Cesario. Orsino's opening words had announced the theme of longing:

> If music be the food of love, play on,
> Give me excess of it that, surfeiting
> The appetite may sicken and so die.
> That strain again, it had a dying fall.
> O, it came o'er my ear like the sweet sound
> That breathes upon a bank of violets,
> Stealing and giving odour. Enough, no more,
> 'Tis not so sweet now as it was before.

This play is as much music as action: the players dance to a series of variations upon love. Orsino and Olivia overdo the love-sickness. When Orsino says that women's hearts lack retention, Viola disagrees:

> My father had a daughter loved a man
> As it might be, perhaps, were I a woman
> I should your lordship.
> ORSINO:                    And what's her history?
> VIOLA: A blank, my lord. She never told her love …

Viola's love is discreet, patient, unpossessive, undisclosed. Beneath the plangent strings there is a scherzo of wind instruments led by Sir Toby Belch, who sits up late guzzling the cakes and ale of his niece Olivia, and singing loud catches, to the disgust of Malvolio. Olivia's steward, as his name suggests, is 'sick of self-love'. He is tricked by a forged letter written by another servant, Maria, into thinking that his mistress wants him to woo her. In a very funny scene, Malvolio's declarations convince Olivia he is mad. Olivia is herself tricked into marrying Viola's lost twin Sebastian. Viola reveals herself to her restored Sebastian. Maria marries the undeserving Toby, and Viola her wonderful Orsino. The humiliated Malvolio is unmated; as is the clown Feste, who sings the songs, 'O Mistress mine, where are you roaming?', 'Come away, come away death' and 'When that I was and a little tiny boy'.

Feste is one of Shakespeare's best fools. Henry VIII and James I kept licensed fools; the Popes kept one until the 18th century. Shakespeare developed the jester into a choric figure. His fools joke and sing, and make fun of their betters – as did the Lord Chamberlain's Men. Feste's songs are sad, and there is a balance in the play between those things which make romance and fairy tale – discoveries, recognitions, the promise of love fulfilled, the restoration of a lost twin – and a sense of a time-governed world in which these wished-for things do not happen. Viola and Sebastian are identical brother and sister; Shakespeare was the father of such twins, of whom the boy died, aged 11.

Sexual possessiveness is a theme of *A Midsummer Night's Dream* and *Much Ado*. It becomes more insistent in the 'problem plays' and *Hamlet*, *King Lear* and *Antony and Cleopatra*, and is the subject of *Othello* and half of *The Winter's Tale*. Among the many variations of love explored in *Twelfth Night* there is no jealousy; it is Shakespeare's last innocent play.

## The poems

What Shakespeare wrote before he was 28 does not survive. His best non-dramatic poems are found in the volume entitled *Shake-speares Sonnets*, published in 1609. His sonneteering began in 1593–4, the year in which he also published *Venus and Adonis* and *The Rape of Lucrece*, longish verse-narratives of sexual passion, modelled on Ovid.

In a tale adapted from the *Metamorphoses*, Venus pursues the unwilling youth Adonis, who dies; sexual desire and love are exemplified and discussed. In a tragic episode from early Roman history, Tarquin rapes the noble matron Lucretia, who commits suicide. Shakespeare finds it difficult to take either story quite seriously throughout: playful erotic comedy is more successful in Marlowe's *Hero and Leander* than in *Venus and Adonis*. In the Shakespeare poems, rhetoric calls attention to itself at the expense of narrative. Resistance to sexual passion is comic in Adonis, admirable in Lucrece, but the achievement of the poems lies less in the narrative than in the dramatic depiction of Tarquin's mental state as he approaches his crime. 'Tarquin's ravishing strides' are later applied to Macbeth.

The sonnet (see page 82) carried the medieval doctrines of love into modern European poetry; the first sonnet in English is found in Chaucer's *Troilus and Criseyde*, and sonnets appear in early Shakespeare plays as love-tokens. The dramatist followed the example of other sonneteers in composing his love-sonnets as a sequence. He had allowed some of them to circulate 'among his private friends' before 1598. Their apparently unauthorized publication in 1609 may not have been against his will.

Secrecy was part of the convention of sonneteering, and much in this unconventional sequence is not transparent; yet it projects an intelligible story. There are 126 sonnets to a fine young man, followed by 26 to a dark woman. The love-poems to the young lord at first beg him to have children so that his beauty will not die. The poet then claims that the lovely boy's beauty will not die since these poems will keep him alive until the end of time. The man's physical beauty, it emerges, is not matched by his conduct. The poet's love is ideal and unselfish, but the addressee coolly exploits the devastating effect of his looks and his rank. The poet attempts to believe the best, but his unease grows and breaks out in disgust: 'Lilies that fester smell far worse than weeds'. In the twelve-line sonnet 126, the poet drops his claim that poetry will preserve youthful beauty – and unselfish love – against Time and death.

If it is a surprise to discover that the *Sonnets* express an ideal love for a beautiful man, it would have been more of a surprise for sonnet-readers to find that the poet's mistress is neither fair, young, noble, chaste nor admirable. His love for the 'woman coloured ill' is sexual and obsessive. Her sexual favours make her 'a bay where all men ride', yet the poet's illicit relation with her requires mutual pretences of love. Finally, in sonnet 144, 'Two loves I have, of comfort and despair', the lovely boy and the dark woman come together in a sexual union which doubly betrays the poet. The sequence ends in humiliated revulsion, and is followed by two frigid **epigrams** on the burns inflicted by Cupid, and also a stanzaic narrative of 329 lines, *A Lover's Complaint*, which some now think to be by Shakespeare, and part of the design of the *Sonnets* volume. In it, a shepherdess complains of being seduced and abandoned by a young man of extraordinary beauty and eloquence. This anti-idyll clarifies the design and the theme of the *Sonnets*, for the 'Lover' is the chateau-bottled seducer of 1–126, as experienced by one of his victims.

The volume has, then, four main *personae*: the lovely boy, the dark woman, the poet, and the ruined maid. The volume explores love unsatisfied. Neither of the poet's loves can be satisfied: the worship of the young man, because he is a man; the love of the woman, because it is lust. *A Lover's Complaint* shows the predatory nature of sexual desire, a theme of Shakespeare's non-dramatic poems. The 'Com-

**epigram** Short sharp pointed poem.

plaint' completes the sequence in so schematic a way as to disable simple biographical interpretations. Neither of the poet's loves has the normal end of sexual love, the procreation of children. Yet this unspoken orthodoxy makes sense of the insistent advice to 'breed' with which the sequence opens: 'From fairest creatures we desire increase'. But there is no increase.

*Shake-speares Sonnets* is a puzzling volume, and at first the series seems less than the sum of its parts; but the opposite is the truth. The *Sonnets* imply a story both complex and unhappy. This surprises those who know the anthology pieces – love's sensuous appeal in 'Shall I compare thee to a summer's day' (18); the noble sentiments of 'Let me not to the marriage of true minds' (116); the emotion of 'When to the sessions of sweet silent thought' (30); the grandeur of 'Like as the waves make toward the pebbled shore' (60); the melancholy of 73:

> That time of year thou mayst in me behold
> When yellow leaves or none or few do hang
> Upon those boughs which shake against the cold,
> Bare ruined choirs where late the sweet birds sang.

The appeal of such poems is not to be denied; compared with other sonneteers, Shakespeare writes a mightier line in a simpler rhyme-scheme, giving a more dramatic delivery. But these excessively beautiful poems, taken together, are rich not only in art and expression, but also in dramatic intelligence. Their generous idealism is gradually penetrated by an understanding of love's illusions.

Sonnet 73 ends: 'This thou perceiv'st, which makes thy love more strong/To love that well which thou must leave ere long.' This compliments the young man for continuing to cherish the ageing poet. But this courteous acknowledgement of inequalities in age, rank and love also recognizes that such kind attentions cannot last. The end conceals a reproach: 'well' may be a play on the poet's name, Will. Two later sonnets are entirely devoted to plays on 'Will' as Desire. Such signatures encourage us to take the 'I', the writer-speaker, as Shakespeare himself; yet the detectives identifying the poet's loves and the rival poet are all in the dark. The sonnets move between the poles of autobiography and Sidneian romance. Although Shakespeare sounds as if he is speaking openly, the relationships are always dramatized, and they are menaced by rivalries which remain cryptic. 'Will' names itself and himself, but gives no names to his loves.

There is one area in which the dramatized voice may be personal. 'Shall I compare thee to a summer's day' ends: 'So long as men can breathe and eyes can see/So long lives this and this gives life to thee.' The claim is that *this* poem will live to the end of time, or for as long as men read English verse aloud. The brag is Shakespeare's. Yet the claim has to be surrendered. The poet concedes in 126 that the 'lovely boy' must be rendered by Nature to Time, the enemy of human love. Two Christian sonnets, 55 and 146, look beyond death and Doomsday, but the series is this-worldly. *Shake-speares Sonnets* may contain our finest love-poems, but the note is not often that of 'the lark at break of day arising'. The sequence dramatises the misery of love in this world more than its splendours.

## Tragedy

*Julius Caesar* is based on Thomas North's 1579 version of Plutarch's *Lives of the Noble Grecians and Romans*. It is a play of rhetorical power and unusual lucidity, if with a double focus. The murder of Caesar exemplified the medieval idea of tragedy: the downfall of a great man. Dante had put the assassins Brutus and Cassius alongside Judas in the lowest circle of hell, for treason to one's lord was then the worst sin. But Brutus is the other hero of the play, an honourable man who makes a tragic mistake. Reformers like John Knox (1513–72) justified tyrannicide. But the noble Brutus, for what seems to him a good reason, commits murder, and his murder and treason haunt him. He is, however, accorded the introspective soliloquies characteristic of Shakespeare's tragic heroes. More generally characteristic of Shakespeare's dramaturgy is the double dramatic focus on Caesar *and* Brutus. This doubleness, with implicit comparison and transfer of sympathy, was first seen in *Richard II*, is in many of the plays, and in the title of *Antony and Cleopatra*.

The four great tragedies – *Hamlet*, *Othello*, *King Lear* and *Macbeth* – do not conform strictly to a defined type, except that each ends in the death of the hero, just as the comedies end in marriage. Each finds the noble protagonist in an evil plight. Hamlet exclaims, 'The time is out of joint. O cursed spite!/That ever I was born to set it right.' Such a mismatch is one basis of tragedy: Hamlet is a humanist prince in a Mafia family; Othello is a warrior in a world of love and intrigue; Coriolanus is a Homeric Achilles in modern politics. In the Britain of *Lear*, goodness has to go into exile or disguise if it is to survive. But Lear is partly responsible for his own tragedy, and Macbeth almost entirely so: it is he who disjoints the time.

Shakespeare did not adhere to one model of tragedy, despite the continuing popularity of A. C. Bradley's 'tragic flaw' theory. In his *Shakespearean Tragedy* (1904), Bradley famously proposed that each of the tragic heroes has such a flaw: ambition in Macbeth, jealousy in Othello. This misapplies the *Poetics* of Aristotle, who did not speak of the protagonist's character except to say that he should be noble but not so noble that we cannot identify with him. Aristotle's penetrating analysis was based on action, finding that tragedy proceeds from a tragic error – as when Oedipus marries his mother in ignorance – rather than a character-flaw such as jealousy. The tragedies can be understood without Aristotle, even if Shakespeare knew of Aristotle's notion that a tragedy would inspire feelings of 'pity and fear' – as is suggested by the words 'woe or wonder' in Horatio's lines at the end of *Hamlet*: 'What is it you would see;/If aught of woe, or wonder, cease your search.' Shakespeare does not exemplify Aristotle's admired singleness of focus or unity of action: *Hamlet* is exceedingly complex, and in Gloucester and his sons *King Lear* has a secondary plot.

## Hamlet

Whatever ideas he had of tragedy, Shakespeare learned the genre from the tragedies he saw when he came to London, such as the revenge plays of Thomas Kyd. These were influenced by the example of the 'closet drama' of the Roman Seneca, written to be read, not performed. Thomas Nashe wrote in 1589 that 'English Seneca read by candlelight yields many good sentences as "Blood is a beggar", and so forth: an if you intreat him fair in a frosty morning, he will afford you whole *Hamlets*, I should say handfuls of tragical speeches.' Shakespeare's *Hamlet* is such a handful, and it relies on familiarity with a previous play about Hamlet, probably by Kyd and now lost. Horatio's final summary gives the recipe that made tragedy popular:

> you shall hear
> Of carnal, bloody, and unnatural acts,
> Of accidental judgements, casual slaughters,
> Of deaths put on by cunning and forced cause;
> And, in this upshot, purposes mistook
> Fallen on th'inventors' heads.

The world of Seneca and of Elizabethan and Jacobean tragedy is morally corrupt, their incident and language sensationalistic: malignant plotting, cunning death, madness. *Hamlet* has all this, and its complex plot is conducted with the usual dexterity. Yet it is an entirely new kind of play, for in his long soliloquies we are given unprecedented access to the thoughts and feelings of Hamlet, an admirable hero in a horrible world. The Prince is 'the expectancy and rose of the fair state', the ideal Renaissance prince lamented by Ophelia. The heir-apparent knows of the humanist ideal of human nature: 'What a piece of work is a man!' But in practice, in the prison of Denmark, 'man delights not me'. Hamlet ponders, tests out the king's guilt, outwits those set to watch him, and reproaches his mother, but does not act. His madness is feigned, but he is poisoned by the evil around him, mistreating Ophelia, sparing the life of Claudius when he finds him praying, in case Claudius should be saved from eternal punishment. (A reason for not taking revenge 'too horrible to be read or uttered' – Johnson.) Revenge tragedy is premised upon action, and action so extremely deferred increases suspense. Only when Hamlet is sent to England to be killed can he defend himself. He is relieved when he is challenged to a duel; once put out of his misery, he can act. The audience share his relief. The concatenation of deaths in the last scene of *Hamlet* also produces the strange aesthetic satisfaction peculiar to tragedy: if such dreadful things must be, this is how they should happen.

*Romeo and Juliet* and *Julius Caesar* are based on preceding plays or types of play. Shakespeare's later tragedies are more original. By reason of its domestic focus, *Othello* may be for modern audiences the closest of the tragedies. *Macbeth* is the most intense, sudden, economical; *Antony and Cleopatra* the most expansive in language and sentiment. But there is space to discuss only Shakespeare's starkest tragedy.

### King Lear

*King Lear* is larger than the other tragedies in its moral scope. It is a play of good and evil, a parable with little psychology of character. It begins like a fairy tale: the old king asks his three daughters to say which loves him best. His youngest, Cordelia, loves him but is not prepared to outbid her sisters to gain a richer portion of the kingdom. The subplot also has a fairy-tale ending, in which the good brother Edgar defeats the evil brother Edmund in single combat. Virtue triumphs here, but not in the main plot. This ends with a brief scene introduced by the stage direction: '*Enter Lear, with Cordelia in his arms.*' Lear asks:

> Why should a dog, a horse, a rat, have life,
> And thou no breath at all? Thou'lt come no more,
> Never, never, never, never, never.
> Pray you, undo this button. Thank you, sir.

Samuel Johnson (1709–84) edited Shakespeare in his middle fifties. He relates that he was many years ago so shocked by Cordelia's death that 'I know not whether I ever endured to read again the last scenes of the play' – until he had to edit it. For 'Shakespeare has suffered the virtue of Cordelia to perish in a just cause, contrary to the natural ideas of justice, to the hope of the reader, and what is yet more strange, to the faith of the chronicles.' Johnson's reaction was uncommon only in its strength; Nahum Tate had adapted *Lear* in 1681 to give it a happy ending in which Edgar marries Cordelia, and this version of the play held the stage until the early 19th century. Why does Shakespeare depart from his sources and have Cordelia hanged?

In this play Shakespeare seems to have wished to show the worst pain and the worst evil that could be felt and inflicted by human beings. As usual with him, this is put in terms of the family. What 'the worst' is is asked by Edgar, and when Lear carries the dead Cordelia onstage, Kent asks 'Is this the promised end?' – a reference to Doomsday. Evil persecutes good through most of the play. Lear's sufferings when cast out into the storm by his daughters Goneril and Regan drive him mad. Lear's son-in-law Cornwall puts out the eyes of the loyal Duke of Gloucester, sending him 'to smell his way to Dover'. These elder daughters are monsters of cruelty and lust. Edmund, the bastard son of Gloucester, destroys his brother and his father. The tirades of Lear on the heath, his meeting with Gloucester on the beach, and the play's last scene are terrible to read or to see. There is nothing in English to equal the scenes of Lear, the Fool and Edgar on the heath. Stretches of *Lear* reach a sublimity beyond anything in secular literature.

Virtue does not triumph in *Lear*, yet vice fails miserably. Cordelia, Kent and Edgar are as good as Goneril, Regan, Edmund and Cornwall are evil. After Cordelia is hanged, Lear dies and Kent is about to follow his master. Edgar is left to say the last lines:

> The weight of this sad time we must obey,
> Speak what we feel, not what we ought to say.
> The oldest hath borne most: we that are young
> Shall never see so much, nor live so long.

We feel what Edgar says, having seen the most suffering that man can bear. Yet evil has lost: Edgar defeats Edmund; Goneril kills Regan and herself. Good at last prevails, at the cost of the lives of Gloucester, Lear, Cordelia and Kent. Much earlier the Duke of Cornwall suffered a mortal wound from a servant loyal to the Duke of Gloucester – who saw this with his then-remaining eye. Cruelly-treated children preserve the lives of their parents: Edgar succours his blinded father, Cordelia her mad father.

In his preface to *Tess* (1891), Thomas Hardy supposes that Shakespeare endorses the words of the blinded Gloucester: 'As flies to wanton boys are we to the gods. They kill us for their sport.' But Gloucester speaks these words in the presence of his wronged son Edgar, who, disguised as a beggar, cares for his father, twice saving him from despair and suicide. He at last discloses himself to his father, whereat, on hearing the true story of his son's conduct, Gloucester's heart 'burst smilingly'. This wincing paradox offers the audience a cue: not woe or wonder, but woe *and* wonder.

Earlier the maddened and exhausted Lear has been rescued, tended, allowed to sleep, washed, dressed in new garments, and, to the sound of music, brought back to life by his daughter. He feels unworthy and foolish and twice asks forgiveness. When they are recaptured by their enemies, and sent to prison together, Lear is delighted: 'Come, let's away to prison:/We two alone will sing like birds i' th' cage:/When thou dost ask me blessing, I'll kneel down/And ask of thee forgiveness.' He adds: 'Upon such sacrifices, my Cordelia,/The gods themselves throw incense.' Edgar had said to the defeated Edmund: 'Let's exchange charity.' Johnson notes: 'Our author by negligence gives his heathens the sentiments and practices of Christianity.' Edmund repents – too late to save Cordelia. Lear thanks a man for undoing a button, and calls him Sir.

The play is a struggle between good and evil – a play rather than a tract, but one in which despair is resisted. Christianity does not pretend that goodness is rewarded in this world. Johnson says that the virtue of Cordelia perishes in a just cause: it would be truer to say that Cordelia perishes, but that her virtue does not. That is where Shakespeare leaves the argument, at the point of death, between this world and the next.

It is useful at this point to analyse the penultimate scene of *Lear*, a glimpse of Shakespeare at work. Before the battle between the army of Cordelia and Lear on the one hand and that of Cornwall, Goneril and Regan on the other, Edgar asks his father, Gloucester, to wait for him.

> ACT V, SCENE 2: *Alarum within. Enter with drum & colours Lear, Cordelia,*
> *& soldiers over the stage; Exeunt.*
> *Enter Edgar disguised as a peasant, guiding the blind Duke of Gloucester.*
>
> EDGAR:  Here, father, take the shadow of this tree
>   For your good host; pray that the right may thrive.
>   If ever I return to you again I'll bring you comfort.
> GLOUCESTER: Grace go with you, sir.          *Exit Edgar*
>
> *Alarum and retreat within. Enter Edgar*
> EDGAR:  Away, old man. Give me your hand. Away.
>   King Lear hath lost, he and his daughter ta'en.          5     are taken
> GLOC:  No further, sir. A man may rot even here.
> EDGAR:  What, in ill thoughts again? Men must endure
>   Their going hence even as their coming hither.
>   Ripeness is all. Come on.
> GLOC:                        And that's true too.          10
>                        *Exit Edgar guiding Gloucester*

Edgar's farewell in line 3 means that he will do or die. Yet the blind Gloucester's prayers, if any, are not answered; Edgar brings him no comfort. Gloucester wishes to stay; he cares not if he is captured, like Lear. But Edgar will not let his father despair; he reminds him that men must be ready to die, not choose the moment of their death. The brunt of the scene is given in lines 5 and 10. But the tree adds much: the tree, linked with the words 'rot' and 'ripeness', raises the kindness of lines 1–4 and the wisdom of lines 8–9 to something consciously Christian. The tree helps Edgar remind us that men, like fruit, do not chose to enter the world; and that men must not choose to fall and rot, but be ready for the death God sends. With a tree and some simple words – and with no mention of trees in Eden or on Calvary – much can be done in ten lines.

Shakespeare went no deeper in tragedy than *King Lear. Macbeth, Antony* and *Coriolanus* are later, not darker. Although Macbeth's vivid soliloquies take us so intensely into his mind, his evil is far graver than Lear's arrogance, and the poetic justice refused at the end of *Lear* is inevitable in *Macbeth*.

## Romances

Shakespeare ended his career with romance and tragicomedy. His plays do not state his views, but his choice of subject indicates changing interests. In his last plays, he fixes on the relation of father and daughter. The strong and often subversive role played by sexual attraction in Shakespeare's writing, from *Hamlet* onwards, takes a different turn after *Antony*. In the *Sonnets, Measure for Measure, Troilus, Hamlet, Othello* and *Lear*, the power of sexual passion to destroy other ties is shown. Hamlet's attacks on the honour of women show that his mind has been tainted. In his madness, Lear reasons that since his children have persecuted him there should be no more children, no more procreation. When Macbeth hesitates to kill Duncan, his wife taunts him with lack of manliness. Iago tests Othello's masculine honour with tales of Desdemona's adultery. *Antony* weighs honour and sexual love in a more tragicomic balance. The relation of children to the protagonist is crucial only in *Lear* and *Macbeth*, but is to become central.

In *Lear*, the sexual effect of Edmund upon Goneril and Regan reveals monstrosity, whereas Cordelia's forgiving care for her father is exemplary, pure, sacred. She revives him, brings him, as he says, back out of the grave. The moral resurrection of a father by means of a daughter better than he deserves is a theme in four of the last five plays Shakespeare wrote before he retired to Stratford: *Pericles, Cymbeline, The Winter's Tale* and *The Tempest*. Sexual jealousy is a major theme only in *The Winter's Tale*, where Leontes' jealous suspicion of his wife's fidelity is (unlike the jealousy of earlier plays) without any excuse. Leontes asks Hermione to persuade his old friend to stay, then madly misconstrues one of their exchanges. In a jealous fit he destroys his family. The gods declare him mistaken; he does penance for many years; then is miraculously restored. Women act as angels and ministers of grace. Their names are clearly symbolic: Cordelia, Marina, Innogen, Perdita, Miranda. The generations were changing: in 1607 Shakespeare's first child Susanna married a Stratford physician, and produced the first grandchild, Elizabeth. His mother Mary died in 1609.

If *The Winter's Tale* is the richest of these plays, *The Tempest* is the most perfect. All four are improbable in plot and unrealistic in mode. They are theatrical fairy tales, like the indoor masques at the court of **James I**, full of special effects, songs and dances. In each, tragedy is eventually averted by providential or divine intervention: father and daughter are reunited in a pattern of rescue, healing, restoration and forgiveness. The pattern is that of the medieval romances which contribute to the plots: stories where deep human wishes come true. The lost are found, wrongs can be righted, death is not separation, families are reunited in love. The happy endings are providential in a Christian-humanist sense: they come by means of grace embodied as forgiveness and loving-kindness. The plane of action is natural, human and familial, but with explicitly supernatural interventions, pagan in name but with Christian meaning. Although staunchly virtuous characters such as Kent, Edgar or Paulina are necessary, the transformative effect of the recovered daughters, and of Hermione, comes as a grace rather than from merit on the part of the father. The persistent Christianity of these plays is not allegorical or moral but sacramental and providential.

## The Tempest

The three predecessors of *The Tempest* begin with tragedy and end in comedy: the father is eventually restored to and by the daughter. But in this play the tragic matter is already in the past. Twelve years have passed since Duke Prospero was overthrown, and put into a rotten boat with his three-year-old daughter. Her presence saved him: 'A cherubin/Thou wast, that didst preserve me.' Divine Providence brings them to a desert island, and *The Tempest* addresses the central question of Christian humanism: how far education and upbringing can improve nature.

The play is original in its fable, and observes the unities of time and place. Prospero has educated his daughter, but failed to educate an earthy goblin he found on the island, Caliban, 'a devil … in whose nature nurture will never stick'. Caliban had tried to rape Miranda. Prospero uses his magic to raise the tempest and bring onto the island those who overthrew him: his brother Antonio and Alonso King of

**James I** James Stuart, James VI of Scotland, succeeded Elizabeth I in 1603 as James I of England. In 1625 he was succeeded by his son Charles I. Stuarts ruled England, on and off, until 1714.

Naples; with Alonso's brother Sebastian and son Ferdinand. He uses the spirit Ariel to trick and test these noble castaways: Ferdinand proves worthy of Miranda's hand; Alonso repents his crime; but Antonio and Sebastian do not wish to reform. They are like Spenser's Gryll, who prefers to remain a pig: 'Let Gryll be Gryll, and have his hoggish mind.' They joke about how much money they might make out of exhibiting Caliban as a freak. At the end of the play Caliban (who has also been tested, and has failed) resolves (unlike the hoggish nobles) 'to be wise hereafter,/And seek for grace.' Prospero resigns his magic, and will return to Naples to see the wedding of Ferdinand and Miranda, 'And thence retire me to my Milan, where/Every third thought shall be my grave.'

The Tempest stands first in the Folio, with more stage-directions than any other play; it has been taken as a testament, for its author then retired to Stratford. (The last surviving play in which he had a major hand, *Henry VIII*, was written from retirement.) Prospero is unprecedented. The Duke in *Measure for Measure* plays Providence in disguise, but Prospero is a magician who openly creates and directs the action. It is hard not to liken him to his creator, the actor-impresario-author who had often likened the world to a stage. After the masque of Hymen (with Iris, Ceres and Juno) which Prospero puts on for the benefit of Ferdinand and Miranda, Prospero says:

> Our revels now are ended. These our actors,
> As I foretold you, were all spirits, and
> Are melted into air, into thin air;
> And like the baseless fabric of this vision,
> The cloud-capped towers, the gorgeous palaces,
> The solemn temples, the great globe itself,
> Yea, all which it inherit, shall dissolve;
> And, like this insubstantial pageant faded,
> Leave not a rack behind. We are such stuff
> As dreams are made on, and our little life
> Is rounded with a sleep.

We should see a reference in 'the great globe itself' to the Globe theatre. Prospero later abjures his 'rough magic' and drowns his book. Gonzalo then invokes a blessing on the young couple, using a theatrical metaphor: 'Look down, you gods,/And on this couple drop a blessed crown,/For it is you that have chalked forth the way/Which brought us hither.' Directors still use chalk to 'block' on the boards of the stage the moves the actors are to make. If the world is a stage, the author is a god who makes the Providence of the plot.

The Tempest and A Midsummer Night's Dream are both plays which rely greatly upon the image-making powers of language and use the transforming power of music. The earthy speech in which Caliban describes the island, though it draws on Golding's version of Ovid's *Metamorphoses*, is an original invention. Caliban's airy counterpart Ariel is, like Puck, a spirit who sings and works the transformations commanded by his master. At the end of the play he is released, and Prospero's final words to the audience ask to be set free.

## Conclusion

### Shakespeare's achievement

Shakespeare had extraordinary gifts, and the luck to find in the theatre the perfect opening for them. What he achieved still seems wonderful. Like Mozart, he found composition easy, but did not repeat himself. He preferred to transform existing plays and stories, inventing when he had to. He perfected the new genre of the history play, and developed new forms of romance and sexual comedy.

Each play is different; this is especially true of his tragedies. To read through Shakespeare's plays is to meet an unprecedented range and variety of situations and behaviour, and to improve understanding of human surfaces and depths. Dr Johnson pronounced in his *Preface* that by reading Shakespeare a 'hermit could estimate the transactions of the world'. Since Johnson's day the novel has added detail and breadth to our idea of the world's transactions. But the novel has also added length, and unless Johnson's hermit had the patience of an accountant, he would miss the concentrated force of drama, and the play and metaphor of Shakespeare's language.

## His supposed point of view

Keats was to praise Shakespeare's 'negative capability', his non-partisan and un-ideological capacity. Shakespeare has been claimed as a supporter of the most diverse points of view, political and social, and actors' lines cited in evidence. But a play does not *have* a point of view – it is neither tract nor argument nor debate, but a play: a complication of the initial situation. The dramatist imagines and gives words to the participants; ventriloquism is one of his skills. Shakespeare lived in contentious times, and set only one play, *The Merry Wives of Windsor*, in his own England. Some since Keats have thought that they knew Shakespeare's point of view; earlier he had been suspected of not having had one. 'He is so much more careful to please than to instruct, that he seems to write without any moral purpose' (Johnson: *Preface to Shakespeare*).

At the end of Evelyn Waugh's *A Handful of Dust* (1934), the hero is forced to read aloud to a madman in the jungle the complete works of Dickens; once he has finished he has to start again. To reread Shakespeare would be less of a penance. Thanks to him we can better understand how we live and think. We also share in his linguistic omnipotence; language was to him as Ariel was to Prospero – he could do anything with it.

# Ben Jonson

**Ben Jonson** (1572–1632), eighteen years Shakespeare's junior, knew him well; they acted in each others' plays. As playwright, poet, critic and man of letters, Jonson dominated his generation. He was a great poet and a great dramatist. Jonson and Marlowe belong with Shakespeare; other Jacobeans appear in the next chapter.

Jonson wrote that Shakespeare was the greatest of writers, and that he 'loved the man, this side idolatry'; he also mentioned his 'small Latin and less Greek' and his carelessness. Ben Jonson was at Westminster School under the antiquarian William Camden (1551–1623), author of *Brittania* (1587). He then worked with his step-father, a bricklayer, and served as a soldier in the Low Countries, killing an enemy champion in single combat. In 1598 he killed a fellow-player in self-defence. Converted in prison, he was 'twelve years a Papist'. He played Hieronimo in Kyd's *Spanish Tragedy* in 1601. Questioned about the Gunpowder Plot in 1605, in 1606 he (and his wife) were charged with recusancy. After the publication of his Folio *Works* in 1616, James I gave him a pension. We know Jonson through his moral satire, criticism, social verse and self-portraits. He tells us of 'my mountain belly and my rockie face'; and that he weighed nearly twenty stone (170 kilogrammes). In 1618–19 he walked to Scotland to win a bet; his table-talk there was recorded by his host, Drummond of Hawthornden. He wrote plays, verse and court masques, and died in 1637.

Jonson's education gave him a classical idea of literature, valuing sanity, concision and integrity. He took the old masters as 'guides, not commanders', which, as Oscar Wilde remarked, 'made the poets of Greece and Rome terribly modern'. But those poets are not known now as they were to Wilde; and terrible modernity is not obvious in Jonson's sombre *Sejanus* (1603) and *Catiline* (1611). These Roman tragedies are less alive than Shakespeare's; the toga hides the topicality of their political satire.

Satire is the motive of Jonson's comedy also: *Every Man in His Humour* (1598) is set in Florence (Shakespeare is listed in the cast), and *Volpone* (1605) in Venice; but London is the scene of *Epicœne, or the Silent Woman* (1609), *The Alchemist* (1610), *Bartholomew Fair* (1614) and other plays. Jonson's ridicule of the deformations of contemporary life is ferocious but farcical: although he held that comedy does not derive from laughter, we laugh more, and harder, at his comedies than at Shakespeare's. Jonson has the Renaissance idea that comedy laughs us out of vices and follies. 'Comedy is an imitation of the common errors of our life, which he representeth in the most ridiculous and scornful sort that may be, so as it is impossible that any beholder can be content to be such a one.' – Sidney.

Jonson's comedy-of-humour characters are caricatures ruled by a single idea. In physiology a 'humour' was a bodily fluid, an excess of which unbalanced the temperament, making it phlegmatic, bilious, sanguine, melancholy, choleric, and so on. Jonson extended this purgative approach to ruling passions and monomaniac fixations. (This 'humour' tradition goes from Chaucer to Dickens *via* Henry Fielding and the caricaturist Hogarth in the 18th century. Dickens liked to act the part of Bobadil in *Every Man in his Humour*.) In Jonson's grotesque world, avarice is the chief vice, ahead of pride, lust and gluttony; folly is everywhere. Jonson's London bubbles most anarchically in *Bartholomew Fair*, the action centring on the tent of the pig-woman, Ursula, where pig and human flesh are on sale, and hypocrisy is unmasked. Although he later wrote more for the Court than for the public, Jonson does not mock the citizen more than the courtier. His ideal remained an integrity, artistic, intellectual and moral; he hated fraud, personal, moral or social.

Jonson gave his abundant spirits a classical focus. *Epicœne* has a brilliantly simple plot. *Volpone* and *The Alchemist* share a simple base in the confidence tricks played by two fraudsters on a series of greedy gulls. The deception-machine spins faster and faster until the tricksters overreach themselves and the bubble bursts. Jonson makes Marlowe's theme of aspiration comic rather than tragic.

### The Alchemist

In *The Alchemist* Sir Epicure Mammon plans the sexual conquests he will enjoy after taking the elixir of youth: 'I will have all my beds blown up, not stuffed;/Down is too hard.' As for diet:

> Oiled mushrooms; and the swelling unctuous paps
> Of a fat pregnant sow, newly cut off,
> Dressed with an exquisite and poignant sauce;
> For which, I'll say unto my cook, 'There's gold;
> Go forth, and be a knight.'

The alchemist's stone, supposed to turn base metal into gold, attracts the parasites of London: epicurean merchants, but also such brethren as Tribulation Wholesome. Tribulation's Deacon, Ananias, has a line – 'Thou look'st like Antichrist in that lewd hat!' – which strikes the note of crazed disproportion which delighted Jonson. He is the first critic of puritan capitalism, yet his critique of human nature, though 'terribly modern', is as old as the view of Rome taken by the first-century poet Martial.

### *Volpone*

*Volpone* is darker than *The Alchemist*, but the rich Volpone (Italian for 'old Fox') is a cousin of Sir Epicure. He begins with 'Good morrow to the day; and next, my gold!/Open the shrine, that I may see my saint.'

He and his servant Mosca (Fly) trick a series of fortune-hunters, Voltore, Corbaccio and Corvino: each makes him a gift in the hope of becoming his heir. Corvino (Raven) is persuaded that the bedridden Volpone is so deaf that he must be at death's door: Mosca yells into Volpone's ear that his 'hanging cheeks … look like frozen dish-clouts, set on end.' Corvino tries comically hard, but cannot match Mosca's Cockney insults. Mosca suggests Corvino invite Volpone to enjoy his young wife Celia. Before taking advantage of Corvino's generosity, Volpone sings a sprightly song, adapted from Catullus: 'Come, my Celia, let us prove/While we may, the sports of love./Cannot we delude the eyes/Of a few poor household spies?' His rape is foiled, but his fantastic tricks come to an end only when, in order to enjoy the discomfiture of the birds of carrion, he makes Mosca his heir and pretends to die. Mosca tries to double-cross Volpone, and so, in a court-room climax, Volpone has to prove he is alive. Put in irons until he is as ill as he pretends to be, he exits with: 'This is called mortifying of a Fox.' This savagely moral caricature on avarice is also wonderfully entertaining; Volpone is allowed to speak the witty Epilogue.

## Further reading

Bate, J. *The Genius of Shakespeare* (London: Picador, 1997).

Gurr, A. *The Shakespearean Stage 1574–1642*, 3rd edn (Cambridge: Cambridge University Press, 1992).

Wells, S. (ed.) *The Cambridge Companion to Shakespeare Studies* (Cambridge: Cambridge University Press, 1986).

# Stuart Literature:
# to 1700

## Contents

## Overview

The 17th century is divided into two by the outbreak of the Civil War in 1642 and the temporary overthrow of the monarchy. With the return of Charles II as King in 1660, new models of poetry and drama came in from France, where the court had been in exile. In James I's reign, high ideals had combined with daring wit and language, but the religious and political extremism of the mid-century broke that combination. Restoration prose, verse, and stage comedy were marked by worldly scepticism and, in Rochester, a cynical wit worlds away from the evangelicalism of Bunyan. When Milton's *Paradise Lost* came out in 1667, its grandeur spoke of a vanished heroic world. The representative career of Dryden moves from the 'metaphysical' poetry of Donne to a new 'Augustan' consensus.

## The Stuart century

The Stuart century was concerned with succession. James VI of Scotland ruled England as James I from 1603 until 1625. James's son, Charles I, ruled until civil war broke out in 1642. Monarchy was restored in 1660, and Charles II ruled until 1685, followed by his brother, James II. In 1688 James fled before his invading son-in-law, the Dutchman who became William III. William and Mary were succeeded by Mary's sister, Anne (1702–14). There was thus an eighteen-year interval between reigns, 1642–60, or Interregnum, when first Parliament and then Oliver Cromwell ruled. This was bisected by the execution of Charles I in 1649. Regicide was a new departure in the history of Europe. It 'cast the kingdom old/Into another mould,' as Andrew Marvell put it in his *Horatian Ode*. When England became a kingdom again, her literature too fell into other moulds.

Charles I's execution also bisected the career of the poet John Milton. In 1644 he had written: 'I cannot praise a fugitive and cloistered virtue, unexercised and unbreathed, that slinks out the race where that immortal garland is to be run for, not without dust and heat'. 'That garland' is the heavenly prize of virtue in the race of life. Milton left poetic laurels in Italy for the 'dust and heat' of prose controversy. He

Detail from 'View of London', engraved by Claes Jan Visscher, 1616. The view is from above the South Bank, looking north across the Thames (*Thamesis*) to Old St Paul's. Donne was then Dean of the Cathedral, and Milton a new boy at St Paul's School. Foreground (right) is the Globe theatre.

became Latin Secretary to the Council of State, losing his eyesight in 1652 while writing the Council's defence of its regicide. Milton's secretaries were to include Marvell and John Dryden. In the second edition of *Paradise Lost* (1674), Milton defended its blank verse against the 'bondage of rhyming'. Yet in this same year, the last of his life, he gave Dryden leave to turn it into rhyme – for an opera. Changed times, and for Milton fallen times.

As a boy at St Paul's School, Milton could have heard its Dean, John Donne, preach in the Cathedral. Donne was writing before 1600, the year of *Twelfth Night*. John Dryden died in 1700, the year of William Congreve's *The Way of the World*. Thus Donne, Milton and Dryden together take us from 1600 to 1700. The prose of these poets shows the differences of their eras: Donne's sermons, Milton's polemic, Dryden's literary criticism. Donne's tomb survived the Fire of London in 1666, and stands in the cool spaces of Christopher Wren's new St Paul's Cathedral in London as a reminder of more dramatic days (see page 138). 'The Stuart century' is a convenient historical label, pasting the name of a twice-disrupted dynasty onto a round number. (The first century to call itself a century was the 19th century.) Literary history also needs less tidy period-names: the English Renaissance extends from More's *Utopia* in 1517 to Milton's last works in 1671.

The execution of Charles I changed England. After Charles and Cromwell, any regime, monarchical or republican, which believed itself to be divinely ordained was not trusted. Regicide had made it clear that 'the ancient rights … do hold or break,/ As men are strong or weak' (Marvell: *Horatian Ode*). After 1660, Christianity is less

**Jacobean** Of the reign of
James I (Lat. *Jacobus*),
1603–25.

explicit in polite writing. Charles II concealed his Catholicism. When his brother
James II tried to restore an absolute monarchy, it was his Catholic appointments that
were unacceptable.

## Drama to 1642

Marlowe, Shakespeare and Jonson are the giants of English Renaissance drama. The
chief **Jacobean** plays are listed below. Public theatres also flourished under Charles I,
until Parliament closed them in 1642. Plays were not always printed, and authors are
sometimes unknown. Some were prolific: Thomas Heywood (?1570–1632) claimed to
have written two hundred plays and Philip Massinger (1583–1649) fifty-five. Thomas
Dekker, Sir Francis Beaumont, John Fletcher and John Ford also wrote copiously.

### Comedy

The comedy of this period continued into the comedy of manners of the 18th
century. *The Merry Wives of Windsor* (1597) is Shakespeare's one 'citizen comedy', a
genre whose archetype is Dekker's *The Shoemaker's Holiday* (1599). This celebrates a
jolly shoemaker mayor of London, without satire and with some sentiment. Rude
jokes disarm serious expectations; Dekker's hero tells his wife that one of her maids
'hath a privy fault: she farteth in her sleep'. Such jests are found in Dekker's source,
stories by Thomas Deloney in *The Gentle Craft* (1597). This 'citizen' tradition feeds
not only the popular comedy of the 18th century, but also Dickens and modern
situation comedy; it relies on stock characters and laughable situations. *A Chaste
Maid in Cheapside* (1611, revived in the rebuilt Globe in 1997), by Thomas Middleton
(1580–1627), is more satiric, with Yellowhammer, a goldsmith, and Sir Walter
Whorehound, a gentleman rake. Beaumont's highly theatrical *Knight of the Burning
Pestle* makes fun of the simplicity of well-to-do grocers at the theatre, who send their
apprentice up onto the stage to be as good a knight as any they see there.

Jonson scorned the artless comedy of the town, and grew disenchanted with the
Court masque. High and low had attended the Globe, but the popularity of drama
allowed theatre audiences to separate. Masque had elegant verse, music, gods and
goddesses (played by the royal family, though they did not speak) and an allegory
which upheld hierarchy. These shows paid well; the one performance of Thomas
Carew's *Coelum Britannicum* (1634) cost £12,000. But the money went on design:
sets, costumes, spectacle; Jonson took offence on behalf of Poetry. The designer was
the first British neo-classical architect, Inigo Jones (1573–1652). He built the Ban-
queting Hall in Whitehall, from which Charles stepped to his execution. Jonson's
masques had crystalline lyrics and high doctrine, and were imitated by Milton. But a
masque was the ancestor of modern opera and ballet, a show not always requiring
intelligent attention.

### Tragedy

Jacobean tragedy continued the vein of Kyd's *The Spanish Tragedy* of a generation
earlier. The best of John Marston (?1575–1634), Cyril Tourneur (?1575–1626), John
Webster (*c.*1578–*c.*1632) and Thomas Middleton (*c.*1580–1627) is sometimes read
with Shakespeare's tragedies. Typically, the revenger, a man of unrecognized talent,
is hired to avenge a private wrong involving both murder and sexual honour. Perverse crimes are horribly punished; virtue, its oppressors, and the revenger die. Like
films about the Mafia, the revenge play has a recipe: take one incestuous Cardinal,

## Stuart dramatists to 1642

With best-known plays and approximate date of first performance.

George Chapman (?1559–1634), *Bussy D'Ambois* (1607)

Thomas Dekker (?1570–1632), *The Shoemaker's Holiday* (1599)

Thomas Heywood (?1574–1641), *A Woman Killed with Kindness* (1603)

John Marston (?1575–1634), *The Malcontent* (1604)

Cyril Tourneur (?1575–1626), *The Atheist's Tragedy* (1611)

John Webster (c.1578–c.1632), *The White Devil* (1609), *The Duchess of Malfi* (1612–13)

John Fletcher (1579–1625) with Shakespeare, *Henry VIII* (1613) and *Two Noble Kinsmen* (1613–14); several plays with Beaumont

Thomas Middleton (1580–1627), *(?)The Revenger's Tragedy* (1607), *The Changeling* (1622, with Rowley), *A Chaste Maid in Cheapside* and *A Game at Chess* (1624), *Women beware Women* (1620–7)

Philip Massinger (1583–1649), *The Fatal Dowry* (1618), *A New Way to Pay Old Debts* (1625)

Sir Francis Beaumont (1584–1616), *The Knight of the Burning Pestle* (?1607), *The Maid's Tragedy* (c.1610, with Fletcher)

John Ford (1586–after 1639), *'Tis Pity She's A Whore* (1633)

---

one malcontent avenger, poison the skull of the Duke's murdered mistress/her Bible/his saddle-bow; set to simmer in Mantua for two hours; add a good lady to taste. These intensely dark plays are lit by candle flames of virtue and moments of passion in language that briefly recalls Shakespeare. Vice bubbles on the hob of a Catholic court. In comparison *Hamlet*, which transcends the Revenge formula, is a large and various play.

The best of the revenge tragedies is Webster's *Duchess of Malfi*, with a strong heroine in its widowed Duchess. Her secret marriage to her steward makes her brothers, a Duke and a Cardinal, try to drive her mad. When their ingenious cruelties fail, she faces execution calmly. The Duke, her twin, says after she has been strangled: 'Cover her face; mine eyes dazzle; she died young.'

The revenge plays are successfully frightening, but their forty-year popularity suggests a fascination with human malignity which calls for explanation. Old ideas of human nature had been shaken by the imposition of four religious regimes in four decades. If comedy is social, showing the challenge to old social values from new mercantile values, tragedy is metaphysical. Theology may be relevant here: Thomas Aquinas (1225–74) had thought man good but stupid, whereas Martin Luther (1483–1546) found man bad but clever. The doctrine of John Calvin (1509–64) that most are damned gained ground early in James's reign. Whatever the source of the pessimism of Jacobean tragedy, it is hard to take most of it as seriously as it seems to take itself.

There is intelligence and interest in human motive in *The Changeling*, by Middleton, with a subplot possibly by William Rowley. Beatrice-Joanna, an heiress, hires De Flores to kill her unwanted fiancé. The killer then claims her as his reward. Repulsed, he replies: 'Push! You forget yourself!/A woman dipp'd in blood, and talk of modesty!' She admits the attraction of the repulsive De Flores, and succumbs to him. The 'comic' subplot in Bedlam (the Bethlehem mad-house) reflects these themes. Middleton is a disciplined and versatile dramatist, whose secular realism can sound very modern.

# John Donne

**John Donne** (1572–1631) is the most striking of 17th-century poets. In the 1590s he wrote elegy and satire. The elegies are amorous and urbane, like Ovid's, but have more attack. In Elegy 16, 'On his Mistress', Donne, about to go abroad, warns her not to

> fright thy nurse
> With midnight's startings, crying out, 'Oh, oh
> Nurse, O my love is slain, I saw him go
> O'er the white Alps alone; I saw him, I,
> Assailed, fight, taken, stabbed, bleed, fall and die!'

This nightmare would be frightening if it were not over so quickly.

This tragicomedy in five lines suggests that Donne, 'a great frequenter of plays', had the dramatist's capacity to take us by the throat. His poems open 'What if this present were the world's last night?' or 'I wonder by my troth what thou and I/Did till we loved!' or 'Batter my heart, three-personed God.' Such first-person address invites identification with the speaker, and of the speaker with Donne, lending immediacy. But the speaker contradicts himself in the next poem. Grave, passionate love-poems, such as 'The Anniversary', 'A Nocturnal: for St Lucy's Day' or 'A Valediction: Forbidding Mourning', are followed by libertine flippancy, as in 'I can love both fair and brown,/Her whom abundance melts, and her whom want betrays', or 'Love's Alchemy', which ends: 'Hope not for mind in women; at their best/Sweetness and wit, they are but mummy, possessed' (once sexually enjoyed, no more than preserved dead flesh). Many of his best poems mix amorous protestation with a hyperbole inviting disbelief, as in these lines from 'The Ecstasy': 'All day, the same our postures were,/And we said nothing, all the day'.

Donne's gifts for drama and controversy developed early. Schooled in rhetoric and logic, he came from a family devoted to the memory of Sir Thomas More, his mother's great-uncle. He was brought up by his mother, a Catholic to her death in 1631. Her father and grandfather wrote interludes, and her brother Jasper translated Seneca's plays. Jasper Heywood and his brother were **Jesuits**; Jasper, head of the Jesuit mission in England 1581–3, was exiled under sentence of death. Educated at Oxford and Cambridge, Donne became Master of the Revels at Lincoln's Inn in 1593. His brother, held in Newgate Prison for harbouring a priest, died there. Donne left the Catholic Church. He sailed to Cadiz with Ralegh and to the Azores with Essex, found office and became a Member of Parliament. But in 1602 a rash secret marriage to the young neice of his patron ended his career – 'John Donne, Ann Donne, Undone', he said once. His exclusion worsened when the Jesuits were (incorrectly) blamed for the Gunpowder Plot (1605), a Catholic conspiracy to blow up King and Parliament. Donne attacked Catholic extremism in *Pseudo-Martyr* (1610) and *Ignatius His Conclave* (1611), yet still found no office. He wrote a treatise in defence of suicide. The King urged him to take Holy Orders, and he became a priest in the Church of England in 1615, then a royal chaplain, and in 1621 Dean of St Paul's and a famous preacher.

Donne's first prose was *Paradoxes* – 'That Only Cowards Dare Die' – *and Problems* – 'Why hath the common Opinion afforded Women Soules?' His valedictory poem, telling his wife not to fear for him when he is abroad, begins, unconsolingly, 'As virtuous men pass quietly away/And whisper to their souls to go …'. Paradox was a habit confirmed by exclusion. The difficulties of anyone who is not a convinced

**Jesuits** The Society of Jesus is a religious order founded in Paris in 1534 by the Basque Ignatius Loyola: it aimed to take a reformed Catholicism throughout the world, and to counter Protestantism. Edmund Campion and Robert Southwell were Jesuits.

Protestant are strenuously argued in *Satire III*, a search for the true Church. He strenuously adjures his audience to

> Seek true religion. O where? Mirreus          Scented one
> Thinking her unhoused here, and fled from us,
> Seeks her at Rome, there, because he doth know
> That she was there a thousand years ago.

'He loves her rags so,' he continues, 'as we here obey/The statecloth where the Prince sate yesterday'. (Papists reverence the sacrament, but we English bow to a cushion.) Donne nails reformers, conformists and free-thinkers, then turns on the reader and on himself: 'unmoved thou/Of force must one, and forced but one allow./And the right' ('forced' means 'tortured').

> Be busy to seek her, believe me this,
> He's not of none, nor worst, that seeks the best.
> To adore, or scorn an image, or protest,
> May all be bad; doubt wisely, in strange way          an unknown road
> To stand enquiring right, is not to stray;
> To sleep, or run wrong, is. On a huge hill,
> Cragged and steep, Truth stands, and he that will
> Reach her, about must, and about must go;
> And what the hill's suddenness resists, win so;          steepness
> Yet strive so, that before age, death's twilight,
> Thy soul rest, for none can work in that night.

The need to find the true Church confronts the politic rule, observed throughout Europe, that a country adopt the religion of its ruler. Will it help at 'the last day'

> To say a Philip, or a Gregory,          Philip II of Spain   Pope
> A Harry or a Martin taught thee this?          Henry VIII   Luther
> Is not this excuse for mere contraries,
> Equally strong; cannot both sides say so?
> That thou mayest rightly obey power, her bounds know;
> Those past, her nature, and name is changed; to be
> Then humble to her is idolatry.

Donne was known to the public as a preacher. His verse was privately admired ('the first man in the world, in some things', said Jonson), but published only after his death. Twentieth-century critics were struck especially by such love poems as 'The Sun Rising', 'The Anniversary' and 'The Good Morrow'. Just as fine are his *Holy Sonnets*, *Hymns* and 'Good Friday, 1613: Riding Westward', and his translation 'The Lamentations of Jeremy'.

Donne argues aloud to define, dramatize and project a moment's mood. Theatrical improvisation is the basic impulse, giving his writing compression and bravura. His most sustained paradoxes come in 'Good Friday, 1613: Riding Westward': 'I am carried towards the west/This day, when my soul's form bends towards the east.'

> Yet dare I almost be glad, I do not see
> That spectacle of too much weight for me.
> Who sees God's face, that is self life, must die;
> What a death were it then to see God die? ...
> If on these things I durst not look, durst I
> Upon his miserable mother cast mine eye,
> Who was God's partner here, and furnished thus

Half of that sacrifice, which ransomed us?
Though these things, as I ride, be from mine eye
They are present yet unto my memory,
For that looks towards them; and thou look'st towards me,
O Saviour, as thou hang'st upon the tree;
I turn my back to thee, but to receive
Corrections …

Although religious and metaphysical categories are central to his thinking, Donne's love poems are not truly metaphysical. They use logic to justify claims such as: 'She is all states, and all princes, I,/Nothing else is!' ('The Sun Rising') – not a philosophical proposition but a dramatic gesture. Donne is not a sceptic nor a romantic egotist of the emotions. It is rather that he forced the language of 1590s drama into lyric. His love poems are Jacobean in style: although a master of verse, he avoided Elizabethan melody, natural imagery and classicized beauty. Idea dominates word; and the words have what he called 'masculine persuasive force'.

John Donne's monument, by Nicholas Stone (1631–2). The Dean of St Paul's Cathedral stands in his shroud above his urn. The monument survived the 1666 fire at Old St Paul's (see page 154) and stands in Wren's new Cathedral (see page 170).

Donne had a 'Hydroptique immoderate desire of human learning and languages'. He often took images from the new discoveries in anatomy and geography. He hails a very literary naked mistress with: 'O my America, my new found land!' The physicians who examine him in bed 'are grown/Cosmographers, and I their map'. Despite such contemporary reference, he never escaped from the soul/body problem of medieval scholasticism, nor from the Four Last Things on which Christians were to meditate: Heaven, Hell, Death and Judgement. Even his love-poems are concerned with the resurrection of the body. If his unease was new, its cause was not. In 'A Hymn to God the Father', he wrote: 'I have a sin of fear, that when I have spun/My last thread, I shall perish on the shore;/But swear by thy self, that at my death thy son/Shall shine as he shines now …'. The theologian who knew that the promise of redemption is universal asks the Father to repeat it for him personally.

Eternal destiny, general and personal, is never far from Donne's Sermons and Divine Meditations. 'No man is an *Iland*, intire of itselfe; every man is a peece of the *Continent*, a part of the *maine*; if a *Clod* bee washed away by the *Sea*, *Europe* is the lesse, as well as if a *Promontorie* were, as well as if a *Mannor* of thy *friends*, or of *thine owne* were; Any Mans *death* diminishes *me*, because I am involved in *Mankinde*; And therefore never send to know for whom the *bell* tolls; It tolls for *thee*.' Despite its last gesture, this famous passage is communal. Donne's sermons rehearse his 'sin of fear' in order to make the hearers identify with his guilt, fear, repentance and rapture. The preacher was their representative in the pulpit, as the priest had been at the altar.

If Donne's poems read dramatically, his sermons were drama both audible and visible. Conspicuous in his raised pulpit, his chief stage-prop was the preacher's hourglass: 'we are now in the work of an houre, and no more. If there be a minute of sand left, (There is not) If there be a minute of patience left, heare me say, This minute that is left is that eternitie which we speak of; upon this minute dependeth that eternity.' In days when kings could be rebuked from the pulpit, the public were not spared. At Donne's sermons, women fainted and men wept: 'like guilty creatures sitting at a play', to apply the words of Shakespeare's Hamlet.

Donne often imagined his own death. He did not die in the pulpit, but he managed to preach his last sermon dressed in his shroud, as shown in the frontispiece of the sermon printed as *Death's Duell*, 1632. His biographer **Isaak Walton** (1593–1683) wrote that 'Dr Donne had *preach't his own Funeral Sermon*.' His ashes were buried in an urn, his statue showing him in his shroud, vertical, ready for take-off at the General

Resurrection. This tomb survived the Fire of London and Old St Paul's. Donne's final piece of one-upmanship exhibits a medieval 'good death' in the Renaissance guise of world-as-theatre. This was not a philosophical 'virtuous man' passing 'mildly away', but a sinner dying in exemplary hope. Marvell describes Charles I as 'the royal actor' on the 'tragic scaffold': Charles's end on 'that memorable scene' was the last instance of the Renaissance understanding of life as exemplary display, one which gives this phase of English life and literature a special resonance.

Charles the Martyr. The frontispiece to *Eikon Basilike. The Pourctraicture of his Sacred Majestie in his Solitudes and Sufferings* (1649). The text was put together from the king's notes. Having put off the earthly crown, he takes the crown of thorns, looking up to the heavenly crown which awaits him. Latin labels explain the emblems. The book reads 'My Hope is in Thy Word.'

## Prose to 1642

The cool evenhandedness of Marvell contrasts with Donne's histrionic urgency. During the 17th century prose became plainer, less elaborate. Its stylistic model was not the artful Cicero but the shorter Seneca; and there were English exemplars of this. The first major writers to choose succinctness were Ben Jonson, and **Sir Francis Bacon** (1561–1626) in his *Essays* of 1597.

In his *Advancement of Learning* (1605), Bacon advocated that the truths about natural phenomena should be established by experiment. This empiricism gained ground in philosophy as well as science. The founders of the Royal Society (1662) acknowledged Bacon as their master, and its Secretary wanted to reduce style to 'a mathematical plainness'. Then the cadences of **Lancelot Andrewes** (1555–1628), of the antiquarian **Robert Burton** (1577–1640), and the physician **Thomas Browne** (1605–82) gave way to a style whose business was to state its business: not only in the politics of **Thomas Hobbes** (1588–1679) and the epistemology of **John Locke** (1632–1704), but in fields outside philosophy. The two styles are worlds apart, and the difference is connected with the move from first causes to second causes, from Donne's angels and the metaphysical doctrine of analogy to Newton's apple and the physical law of gravity.

## Sir Francis Bacon

Francis Bacon rose under James I to become Lord Chancellor. Dismissed in 1621 for corruption, he spelled out his plans for systematizing the pursuit of knowledge, dividing the supernatural truths of biblical revelation from the truths of nature. After the *Advancement of Learning* he proposed in his Latin *Novum Organum* (1620) a 'new instrument' for human understanding: 'not of a sect or doctrine, but of human utility and power,' words which strikingly define the priorities of the modern world. But King James did not invest in research, nor found a College of Science, as further proposed in *The New Atlantis* (1627).

For all the repute of his other works, only Bacon's *Essays* have been much read since. The spectator who liked *Hamlet* but had not realized it was so full of quotations stumbled on a clue to much Renaissance writing: its love of nuggets. Its favourite book was Erasmus's *Adagia* (1500), a collection of classical sayings with witty commentary. Adages and proverbs, decorations on the sponge-cakes of the 1580s, stuff the plum-puddings of the 1590s, the decade of gists, piths and aphorisms. Donne practised this contraction – as did Jonson, in saying that Donne 'for not being understood, would perish' and that 'Shakespeare wanted art'.

Bacon's *Essays* are a little like the *Essais* of **Montaigne** (1533–92), translated by John Florio in 1603. Bacon settles a topic in three pages. A professional demolisher, he knew the value of an initial blow: '*Reuenge* is a kinde of Wilde Justice; which the more Mans Nature runs to, the more ought Law to weed it out' or 'He that hath *Wife* and *Children*, hath giuen Hostages to Fortune; For they are Impediments, to great Enterprises, either of Vertue, or Mischiefe'. The essays interweave experience and authorities; their close sententiousness has the scepticism of Montaigne but without his engaging explorativeness. Reading them is like playing chess with a superior opponent.

## Lancelot Andrewes

The central assumption, even of natural philosophers before the Civil War, is religious. Deism, acknowledging the Author of Nature rather than the God of Revelation, is first found by Lord Herbert of Cherbury. On completing his *De Veritate*, Herbert tells that he knelt and asked for a sign from heaven as to whether he should publish it: 'a Loud though yet Gentle noise' from a clear blue sky assured him that he should.

His younger brother, the poet George Herbert (1593–33), was a friend of Donne and of **Lancelot Andrewes** (1555–26). Andrewes, the chief Anglican writer after Donne, followed Richard Hooker (1554–1600) in finding his Church a *via media*, a middle way, between Rome and Geneva, holding both the apostolic succession of the Catholic Church and the doctrines of reform. The doctrine of the Elizabethan Church was Swiss, not Roman, but Hooker steered the national church to the centre of the stream. The acceptance of the *via media* is clear in George Herbert's 1620s poem 'The British Church': his 'dearest mother', neither Geneva nor Rome, whose 'fine aspect in fit array/Neither too mean nor yet too gay/Shows who is best'. Andrewes' learning allowed the English Church to dispute with Rome on better terms. He was linguistically the most learned of the Authorized Version's translators, and his sermons expound the text with surgical skill.

## Robert Burton

Bacon's curt method and Andrewes' incisiveness are not found in Burton's *Anatomy of Melancholy, What it is, With all the kinds, causes, symptomes, prognostickes, & severall cures of it. In three Partitions, with their severall Sections, members & subsections, Philosophically, Medicinally, Historically opened & cut up*. This museum of the milder forms of mania has not since the 18th century been consulted for its science but dropped into, like an old secondhand bookshop, for the atmosphere. **Robert Burton** (1577–1640), an Oxford don in an age of accumulating specialist knowledge, confessed that he had read many books but 'to little purpose, for want of a good method'. Burton was a collector, self-deprecating and sceptical; fond of a Latin authority, opinion or argument; unsure whether it is worth sticking to the point. He was liked by Sterne and Lamb, connoisseurs of anticlimax, and appeals to lovers of the strange and the quaint.

## Sir Thomas Browne

The style of **Sir Thomas Browne** (1605–82) is more metaphysical than Burton's, and his *Religio Medici* ('A Doctor's Faith') has lasting value for its peaceable and humane tone:

For my religion, though there be several circumstances that might persuade the world I have none at all, as the general scandal of my profession, the natural course of my studies, the indifferency of my behaviour … yet in despite hereof I dare, without usurpation, assume the honourable style of a Christian.

Browne was himself 'of that reformed, new-cast Religion, wherein I dislike nothing but the name,' a loyal Anglican. He studied medicine in Europe, where, he tells us, he 'wept abundantly' at Catholic devotions, 'while my consorts, blind with opposition and prejudice, have fallen into an access of scorn and laughter'. He held the neglected Christian idea that 'no man can justly censure or condemn another, because indeed no man truly knows another'. In matters of fact and interpretation, he has a medical practitioner's reliance on evidence, and a Christian belief that nature had a code, which he tried to read, though without much trust in reason. Sense and sympathy coexist with speculation: 'I love to lose myself in a mystery,' he confides, 'to pursue my reason to an *o altitudo* [O the height (of God's ways)!].'

Wonderful depths are found in his late work, *Urn-burial*, a meditation on the vanity of earthly fame, prompted by the discovery of ancient burial-urns near Norwich.

What name the Sirens sang, or what name Achilles assumed when he hid himself among women, though puzzling questions, are not beyond all conjecture. What time the persons of these ossuaries entered the famous nations of the dead, and slept with princes and counsellors, might admit a wide solution. But who were the proprietaries of these bones, or what bodies these ashes made up, were a question above antiquarism; not to be resolved by man, nor easily perhaps by spirits, except we consult the provincial guardians, or tutelary observators. Had they made as good provision for their names as they have done for their relics, they had not so grossly erred in the art of perpetuation. But to subsist in bones, and be but pyramidally extant, is a fallacy in duration.

One fascination of his style, which here approaches self-parody, is its perilous balancing of the metaphysical, the moral and the scientific. By the end of the century, physics and metaphysics were separate pursuits.

## Poetry to Milton

### Ben Jonson

Donne's wit was admired by those who read it; but extravagance was cut short with Charles I, or took a quieter form. Later non-dramatic poets followed neither Donne nor Milton but Jonson (1572–1637), a professional poet as well as playwright. His clarity, edge and economy lie behind the wit of Andrew Marvell, the polish of Alexander Pope, and the weight of Samuel Johnson. Jonson's *Works* (1616) begin with 'To the Reader': 'Pray thee take care, that tak'st my book in hand,/To read it well; that is, to understand.'

Jonson's natural ferocity was balanced and ground to a point by a lifetime's reading, which transmuted classical phrases, lines and whole poems into English literature. He imitated especially the caustic and lyric epigrams of the Roman poets, Catullus, Horace and Martial. Jonson's verse is social, directed at a person, a topic, an occasion. Its function, civil, moral or aesthetic, is as clear as its sense. He wrote short, highly-crafted poems in a variety of styles across a range of subjects. His non-dramatic verse matches his writing for the stage, and he carved out a role for the poet as the arbiter to civilized society, an ideal which lasted for a century and a half.

Jonson's social ideal is exemplified in 'To Penshurst', a thank-you letter to the Sidney family for their hospitality at their estate in Kent: 'Thou art not, Penshurst, built to envious show.' The unpretentious birthplace of Sir Philip Sidney offers country hospitality to all, the commoner and the king. Golden-age fancy mingles with actuality:

> The blushing apricot and wooly peach
> Hang on thy walls, that every child may reach.
> And though thy walls be of the country stone,
> They are reared with no man's ruin, no man's groan;
> There's none that dwell about them wish them down;
> But all come in, the farmer and the clown,              yokel
> And no one empty-handed, to salute
> Thy lord and lady, though they have no suit.            fine dress/favour to beg
> Some bring a capon, some a rural cake,
> Some nuts, some apples; some that think they make
> The better cheeses bring them …

The dry humour of 'think' and 'no suit' gains credit for the ideal implied in Jonson's compliments: reciprocal rights and duties, harmonious hierarchy. Penshurst was the home of a patron; but Jonson was not a reliable flatterer: 'His children thy great lord may call his own,/A fortune in this age but rarely known.' His own idea of hospitality is defined in 'On Inviting a Friend to Dinner', which ends: 'No simple word/That shall be uttered at our mirthful board/Shall make us sad next morning; or affright/The liberty that we'll enjoy tonight.' (Young poets used to sup with Jonson at the Mermaid tavern in London. **Robert Herrick** (1591–1674) is the best-known of the Sons of the Tribe of Ben, as Jonson called them.) The first line of Jonson's masque *Pleasure Reconciled to Virtue* is 'Room, room! make room for the bouncing belly!'

Another side to the bear-like Jonson is seen in 'On My First Son' (who died aged seven): 'Farewell, thou child of my right hand, and joy;/My sin was too much hope of thee, loved boy' (the son's name was also Benjamin: 'child of my right hand' in Hebrew). Deliberate wit, couplet-rhyme and formal compression were to Jonson means of self-control. An impersonal craft is seen in the flawless songs in his masques, such as 'Queen and huntress, chaste and fair' or 'See the chariot at hand here of Love,/Wherein my lady rideth.' A final sample of Jonson's classical balance, on another early death:

> It is not growing like a tree
> In bulk, doth make man better be;
> Or standing long an oak, three hundred year,
> To fall a log at last, dry, bald and sere:
> A lily of a day
> Is fairer far, in May,
> Although it fall and die that night;
> It was the plant and flower of light.
> In small proportions we just beauty see,
> And in small measures life may perfect be.

## Metaphysical poets

Dr Johnson identified a 'race of poets' between Donne and Cowley, since known as the 'metaphysical poets'. The term was not an admiring one. Dryden had said that Donne 'affects the metaphysics' in his love poems, perplexing 'the fair sex' with 'nice speculations of philosophy'. As 'affects' suggests, these metaphysics are not offered seriously. Johnson objected to the relentless ingenuity of Donne's comparisons, citing 'A Valediction: Forbidding Mourning', which compares parted lovers to a pair of compasses. Sincerity, said Johnson, would express itself more simply.

In his 'Elegy' for Donne, Thomas Carew wrote 'Here lies a king, that ruled as he thought fit/The universal monarchy of wit.' Donne had subjects, Jonson disciples. Later poets learned from both, but none had Donne's wit or impropriety. Henry King wrote in his 'Exequy' to his dead wife:

> But hark! My pulse, like a soft drum
> Beats my approach, tells thee I come;
> And, slow howe're my marches be,
> I shall at last sit down by thee.

King, Herbert, Crashaw and Vaughan have the paradoxes of their Christian perspectives; that of Carew and the Cavalier poets (see below) is smarter and blander; they did not have to try as hard as Donne or Jonson. The English poetry of Charles's

**Metaphysical poets**

Henry King (1592–1669)
George Herbert (1593–1633)
Thomas Carew (1594–1640)
Henry Crashaw (1612/13–49)
John Cleveland (1613–58)
Abraham Cowley (1618–67)
Andrew Marvell (1621–78)
Henry Vaughan (1621–95)
Thomas Traherne (1637–74)

reign is mature. With all the skill of the previous generation, it has more warmth, flexibility and joy, without loss of penetration or of the tragic sense. The sureness of Herbert and Marvell is found in minor writers, such as Robert Herrick, Thomas Carew or Edmund Waller, who are not eclipsed by their greater contemporaries. Few poets of any age have as many good lyrics as Herrick in his *Hesperides.*

A history cannot overlook poems such as Carew's 'Ask me no more where Jove bestows/When June is past, the fading rose' or Waller's 'Go Lovely Rose': 'Go, lovely Rose,/Tell her that wastes her time and me,/That now she knows,/When I resemble her to thee,/How sweet and fair she seems to be.' It ends:

> Then die, that she
> The common fate of all things rare
> May read in thee:
> How small a part of time they share
> That are so wondrous sweet and fair.

'The common fate of all things rare' is perfect without effort. In quality and quantity, the minor poetry of the 17th century is unequalled. So general a quality comes from the life of the time.

## Devotional poets

Between the crises which began James's reign and ended his son's, **George Herbert** (1593–1633) wrote devotional verse. The accomplished Herbert, a younger son of a gifted family, not finding a career, became a village parson. The poems of this country priest have made him an unofficial saint of Anglicanism. His *Life* – told with piety and charm by Izaak Walton, author of *The Compleat Angler* – describes an ideal rather more gentlemanly than Chaucer's pilgrim Parson.

Herbert's poems are homely in imagery and simple in language, and often about the church; his volume is called *The Temple*. These prayer-poems differ from similar poems by Donne, Marvell, Crashaw, Vaughan or Traherne, being personally addressed to God in an intimate tone. Christ was for Herbert a human person to whom one speaks, and who may reply. This medieval intimacy became rare after Herbert; for Milton, God 'hath no need/Of man's works or his own gifts' ('On his Blindness'). This remoteness was increased for rational Anglicans by the Puritan enthusiasm of the 1640s. Herbert's simple faith was not simple-minded; Renaissance Christianity did not lack mind or drama. Herbert, formerly Public Orator of Cambridge University, spoke fluent Latin. His is the studied simplicity of the parables. Words danced for him: 'Lovely enchanting language, sugarcane,/Honey of roses, whither wilt thou fly?' (from 'The Forerunners'). He could, when he wished, astonish. 'Prayer' is an arc of metaphors, ending: 'The milky way, the bird of paradise,/Church bells beyond the stars heard, the soul's blood,/The land of spices, something understood.'

Herbert's usual note is given in the openings of 'Virtue' – 'Sweet day, so cool, so calm, so bright' – and of 'The Flower': 'How fresh, oh Lord, how sweet and clean/Are thy returns! even as the flowers in spring.' Later in 'The Flower', after a barren time:

> And now in age I bud again,
> After so many deaths I live and write;
> I once more smell the dew and rain,
> And relish versing.

**Caroline** Of the reign of Charles I (Lat. *Carolus*), 1625–42 (executed 1649).

The verses are often complaints – unresolved in 'Discipline', or distressed, as in 'Deniall': '*Come, come, my God, O come!*/But no hearing.' 'The Collar' ends,

> But as I raved and grew more fierce and wild
> At every word,
> Methought I heard one calling, *Child!*
> And I replied, *My Lord.*

The title is both the clerical collar and *choler*, a fit of temper. *The Temple* leads up to 'Love (III)', a eucharistic prayer. Herbert likens taking Communion to a visit to a tavern. It begins, 'Love bade me welcome; yet my soul drew back' and ends, 'You shall sit down, says Love, and taste my meat:/So I did sit and eat.'

Donne, Herbert and Traherne had Welsh connections. Herbert's disciple **Henry Vaughan** (1621–95) was Welsh. His Christianity was Platonic: 'My soul, there is a country/Far beyond the stars' and 'I saw eternity the other night/Like a great ring of pure and endless night.' 'They are all gone into the world of light!' contains the verse:

> I see them walking in an air of glory,
> Whose light does trample on my days:
> My days, which are at best but dull and hoary,
> Mere glimmering and decays.

Mystical vision is stronger in the work of **Thomas Traherne** (1637–74), whose wonderful poems and *Centuries*, prose meditations, were printed only in 1908. Vaughan and Traherne, like Herbert, were devotional poets who wrote no secular verse. An earlier 'son' of Herbert was **Richard Crashaw** (1613–49). An Anglican priest turned out by Parliamentary Commissioners, Crashaw wrote his baroque *Steps to the Temple* before exile and Catholicism. These Anglican pietists lack Herbert's stamina and syntax; Vaughan's second couplet (quoted above) falters.

From this date the educated wrote less about heaven. **Anne Finch**, Countess of Winchilsea (1661–1720), wrote that the soul 'Joys in the inferior world' of natural scenes. In the light of sense and reason, vision glimmered and decayed.

## Cavalier poets

A quietist reaction to religious and political revolution had begun in the 1640s. With the Civil War, high Anglican devotion became private. The gallant secular verse of 'Cavalier poets' such as **Sir John Suckling** (1609–42) and **Sir Richard Lovelace** (1618–58) came to an end or rusticated itself, as in Lovelace's 'The Grasshopper', a delightful poem of friendship written to Charles Cotton. Abraham Cowley also wrote a 'Grasshopper'; Izaak Walton's Angler is an Anglican version of the retiring Roman poet Horace. Most cavaliers did not join Charles II in France but joined the clergy in the country, sending (like grasshoppers) chirpy signals to their short-lived fellows. The Civil War overwhelmed some good writers. Court and Church had been patrons of fine literature before the War; the alliance survived, but sacred and profane verse diverged.

The most astonishing poems from the country were by **Andrew Marvell** (1621–78), written 1650–1 but published posthumously. Opposing the execution of the king, Sir Thomas Fairfax, Lord General of the Parliamentary forces, had retired to his Yorkshire estate. Marvell tutored his daughter there, then taught at Eton. A moderate parliamentarian, he was later a Member of Parliament and a diplomat.

Marvell's poems have Donne's wit and Jonson's neatness, with a lighter touch and a social, detached tone. 'Society is all but rude/To this delicious solitude,' he wrote in 'The Garden', not claiming a philosopher's dignified calm but a poet's pleasure in 'the garlands of repose': 'Annihilating all that's made/To a green thought in a green shade.' Contemplation, scorned by Milton in 1644 as 'fugitive and cloistered virtue', is defended at length in 'Upon Appleton House'.

> But at my back I always hear
> Time's wingéd chariot hurrying near,
> And yonder all before us lie
> Deserts of vast eternity.

These lines from 'To his Coy Mistress' condense the Renaissance apprehension of time to a metaphysical conception of eternity as infinite empty space. Like Herrick in 'Gather ye rosebuds while ye may', Marvell makes mortality an argument for sexual love: 'The grave's a fine and private place,/But none I think do there embrace.' In this casual epigram, 'fine' and 'private' keep their Latin senses, 'narrow' and 'deprived'. His poems play discreetly on words, a finesse boldly used in his 'Horatian Ode upon Cromwell's Return from Ireland', a remarkable analysis of the contemporary crisis. It praises Cromwell's strength, then his art – suggesting that he let the king escape so that he should be recaptured and tried:

> That thence the royal actor borne,
> The tragic scaffold might adorn;
>         While round the arméd bands
>         Did clap their bloody hands.
>
> *He* nothing common did or mean
> Upon that memorable scene,
>         But with his keener eye
>         The axe's edge did try. …

Praise for Charles – or for a good performance? Ambiguity is systematic: 'clap', applaud *or* drown his words; 'mean', base *or* intend; 'scene', stage *or* platform; 'edge' (Lat. *acies*), eyesight *or* edge; 'try', assess for sharpness *or* for justice.

After Cromwell's Irish victories, 'What may not others fear/If thus he crown each year?/A Caesar, he, ere long to Gaul,/To Italy a Hannibal.' Lofty comparisons! Yet Caesar was assassinated, Hannibal defeated. A final exhortation and warning:

> But thou, the war's and fortune's son,
> March indefatigably on,
>         And for the last effect
>         Still keep thy sword erect:
> Besides the force it has to fright
> The spirits of the shady night,
>         The same arts that did gain
>         A power must it maintain.

Marvell, a satirist on the Parliamentary side, wrote after the Civil War that 'the Cause was too good to have been fought for. Men ought to have trusted God; they ought and might have trusted the King with the whole matter.'

The keenness of Marvell's mind recalls that of the French mathematician and theologian **Blaise Pascal** (1623–62). In 'The Mower to the Glowworms' and other poems, Marvell uses aesthetic appeal to express the unreason of mortal love:

> Ye living lamps, by whose dear light
> The nightingale does sit so late,
> And studying all the summer night
> Her matchless songs does meditate …

Marvell's grave religious poem 'The Coronet' is in the **baroque** style, which always has a kind of displayfulness about it. 'Bermudas', on Puritan migrants to America – 'Thus sung they in the English boat,/An holy and a cheerful note' – has similarly marvellous imagery: 'He hangs in shades the orange bright,/Like golden lamps in a green night'. Marvell's poems are lucid, decorative, exquisite and penetrating, but also enigmatic.

**baroque** A term in art history for the ornate style which succeeded the classicism of the High Renaissance.

## Crisis, Civil War, Commonwealth, Restoration

1629  Parliament, refusing further taxes, is dissolved.

1633  Laud, Archbishop of Canterbury, acts against the Puritans.

1634  Charles I imposes Ship Money to raise revenue.

1635  Attempt to impose the Anglican liturgy in Scotland is resisted.

1638  Scots sign a National Covenant to resist episcopacy.

1639  Charles's army proves unreliable against the Scots Covenanters.

1640  Short Parliament is called; and refuses taxes. The Scots invade. The Long Parliament is called (and sits till 1653).

1641  Charles's minister, Strafford, is tried by Parliament and executed; the Star Chamber court is abolished; Grand Remonstrance at royal excesses; Puritan legislation; a rising in Ireland.

1642  The King leaves London after conflicts with Parliament. Royalist and Parliamentary armies fight at Edgehill. The Puritans close public theatres.

1643  Many battles. Parliament imposes Presbyterianism in England.

1644  Cromwell defeats Prince Rupert at Marston Moor.

1645  Cromwell's New Model Army triumphs at Naseby. Laud executed.

1646  Charles surrenders to the Scots. Levellers proclaim the people sovereign.

1647  Scots hand over Charles to Parliament for £400,000. Parliament's attempt to disband the Army fails. Charles intrigues.

1648  Scots, invading on Charles's behalf, defeated at Preston. Parliament purged of its Presbyterian majority by the Army. Rump Parliament votes for the trial of the King.

1649  Charles I tried and executed. The Rump abolishes the monarchy and the House of Lords, and proclaims England a Commonwealth. The Levellers suppressed. Royalist Protestants join Catholics in Ireland: rising crushed by Cromwell.

1650  Charles II lands in England. Cromwell defeats Scots at Dunbar.

1651  Scots crown Charles II king. Defeated at Worcester, he goes to France.

1652  War with Holland (to 1654). The Army petitions for a new Parliament.

1653  Cromwell replaces remaining elected members with a group of nominees, the Barebones Parliament. Proclaimed Lord Protector.

1655  Major-Generals rule England in eleven military districts.

1657  Parliament offers Cromwell sovereign powers.

1658  Cromwell dies, and is succeeded by his son Richard.

1659  Richard retires. General Monck marches the Army down from Scotland to restore Parliament.

1660  Charles II invited back to restore the old form of government.

## John Milton

Poetry in the 17th century came from the Court, the Church, the gentry or the theatre. The grand exception is the late work of **John Milton** (1608–74), after the great crisis of the Civil War. He wrote for a spiritual élite. *Paradise Lost*, he prayed, would 'Fit audience find, though few', echoing Christ's saying that many are called but few are chosen (Matthew 20:16). He invoked for his epic the Spirit 'that dost prefer/Before all temples the upright heart and pure.' A Puritan, he chose to rewrite the Bible as it might have been written with the benefit of a humanist English education. If this does not conform to our ideas of Puritans, not all Puritans were like Shakespeare's Malvolio or Jonson's Tribulation Wholesome.

Milton was not a conformist. His father's career illustrates the link between Protestantism and capitalism: turned out of the house for reading the Bible in his room, he became a scrivener (legal writer) and moneylender in London. He stuck to his books, gaving his eldest son the education of a scholar and a gentleman: St Paul's School (stiff); Cambridge University (disappointing); five years of private study; a grand tour of Italian literary patrons. Education moulded the life and work of England's most influential poet.

It was an upbringing in the high Protestantism of Spenser. St Paul's gave its pupil a humanist faith in the powers of the mind and in the lofty role of poetry. He read widely in Latin, Greek, Hebrew and modern languages, and was remarkable for learning in an age when a reader could know virtually all that was known. His first poem was a version of Psalm 114, 'When Israel went out of Egypt'. This becomes 'When the blest seed of Terah's faithful son …'. A 'fit' audience would know of God's promises to Abraham and his descendants. The few who knew that Abraham was the son of Terah would see that 'faithful' distinguishes the son's faithfulness from the father's idol-worship, and would be saved from folly. Milton's 'faithful' father had left an idolatrous home. As one of the 'blest seed', Milton would claim that God 'spoke first to his Englishmen', the new chosen people.

Humanist ideals shape the early poems: poetic aspiration in 'At a Vacation Exercise' and 'What needs my Shakespeare for his honoured bones'; impatience in 'How soon hath time, the subtle thief of youth/Stol'n on his wing my three and twentieth year.' Other early works are in pastoral modes or lighter moods: the rejoicing baroque ode *On the Morning of Christ's Nativity*, and the playful debate of *L'Allegro* and *Il Penseroso*. Young Milton is already master of medium and form, and his joy in the exercise of his art is infectious. L'Allegro, the cheerful man, likes comedy: 'Then to the well-trod stage anon/If Jonson's learnéd sock be on,/Or sweetest Shakespeare, fancy's child/Warble his native woodnotes wild.' The thoughtful Penseroso prefers tragedy; he goes to church alone:

> But let my due feet never fail,
> To walk the studious cloister's pale,      enclosure
> And love the high embowéd roof,
> With antic pillars massy proof,
> And storied windows richly dight,      decorated
> Casting a dim religious light.
> There let the pealing organ blow
> To the full-voiced choir below,
> In service high, with anthems clear,
> As may with sweetness, through mine ear,
> Dissolve me into ecstasies,
> And bring all heaven before mine eyes.

A joyous response to nature and to art enlivens the early work. The 'dim religious light' is Anglican, and the 'ecstasies' almost Italian. After Milton left the Church of England in the mid-1630s he would do with words what the Church did with stained glass and music. But for years he was part of the high Caroline culture, an artistic consensus between Church and Court, writing courtly masques. The figuration of the *Nativity Ode* is distinctly baroque. Peace, he writes,

> crowned with olive green, came softly sliding
> Down through the turning sphere
> His ready harbinger,                                    [God's]
>   With turtle wing the amorous clouds dividing,
> And waving wide her myrtle wand,
> She strikes a universal peace through sea and land.

The olive crown of Peace is both classical and biblical, for the turtledove brought an olive branch to the Ark. The appearance of Peace is now likened to the chariot of Venus, drawn by doves; 'amorous' is an epithet transferred from the goddess of love to the clouds clinging to her. The Love she symbolizes is divine, not pagan. Such a use of classical symbolism was common form in Europe.

Milton's early Protestant ideals were at odds with his sophisticated Italianate style. At court, Charles I patronized the baroque sculptor Bernini. This style, far from Puritan plainness, displays its art with the confidence of the Catholic Reformation. Milton wrote six sonnets in Italian, and English verse in an Italian way. The title *Paradise Lost* answers that of Tasso's epic, *Gerusalemme Conquistata* (1592), 'Jerusalem Won'. Milton embraced Renaissance and Reformation, Greek beauty and Hebrew truth. This embrace was strained in the 1630s as England's cultural consensus came apart. In 1639 Milton abandoned a second year in Italy, returning from the palace of Tasso's patron in Naples to write prose in London. Although John Donne called Calvinist religion 'plain, simple, sullen, young', the first Puritan writer who was truly plain and simple was John Bunyan (1628–88).

Strains begin to appear in *Comus* (1634), a masque for a noble family. It owes something to Jonson's *Pleasure Reconciled to Virtue* (1618), but Milton's virtuous Lady rejects the (sexual) Pleasure eloquently urged by Comus, the 'bouncing belly' of Jonson's masque. Virtue is Chastity (that is, obedience to divine Reason). The earnest argument of *Comus* shows its author's ambition.

*Lycidas* (1637) is an ambitious pastoral elegy for a Cambridge contemporary, a priest and poet who drowned in the Irish Sea. *Lycidas* is the longest poem in a collection otherwise in Latin and Greek. Nature mourns the young shepherd-poet, and the parts of the classical **pastoral elegy** are displayed. Renaissance pastoral convention allows Milton to discuss poetic fame, and to criticise the pastoral care of bishops. He shows his poetic skill, and his horror at the early loss of a poetic talent. Apollo tells him that Jove (that is, God) will judge his fame in heaven, a Reformation answer in a Renaissance form. The crisis comes after the list of flowers brought 'to strew the laureate hearse where Lycid lies./For so to interpose a little ease/Let our frail thoughts dally with false surmise.' The 'false surmise' is the poem's pagan pretence. Since the body was not recovered, there was no hearse to strew: 'thee the shores, and sounding seas/Wash far away, where'er thy bones are hurled ...'. Then:

> Weep no more, woeful shepherds weep no more,
> For Lycidas your sorrow is not dead,
> Sunk though he be beneath the watery floor,

**pastoral elegy** An elaborate classical form in which one shepherd-singer laments the death of another.

So sinks the day-star in the ocean bed,
And yet anon repairs his drooping head,
And tricks his beams, and with new spangled ore,
Flames in the forehead of the morning sky:
So Lycidas sunk low but mounted high,
Through the dear might of him that walked the waves.

He is now with heaven's 'sweet societies/That sing, and singing in their glory move,/And wipe the tears forever from his eyes.' Revealed faith consoles, unlike nature's myth. Yet the poetry of nature returns:

Henceforth thou art the genius of the shore,          guardian spirit
In thy large recompense, and shalt be good
To all that wander in that perilous flood.
Thus sang the uncouth swain …

This unknown shepherd (Milton) sings a far from uncouth song.

And now the sun had stretched out all the hills,
And now was dropped into the western bay;
At last he rose, and twitched his mantle blue:
Tomorrow to fresh woods, and pastures new.

The beauty of the close does not end the discord of 'where Lycid lies', a deliberate false note. Such passionate question-and-answer is to mark all of Milton's mature work.

Personal concerns also obtrude in the prose to which, in an abrupt change of plan, Milton now devoted himself. In London in 1641–2 he published five anti-episcopal tracts; and in 1642, shortly after the outbreak of the Civil War, he married Mary Powell, a girl half his age who soon went back to her Royalist family. Milton wrote four tracts in favour of divorce, then attacks on the king, and then the government's *Defences* of its regicide. At Cromwell's death, Milton called again for a republic and liberty of conscience, publishing *The Ready and Easy Way to Establish a Free Commonwealth* as Charles II returned.

### Paradise Lost

Milton's prose might today be little read if he had not written *Paradise Lost*. The first principles of politics and religion were being debated in Parliament, at open-air meetings, and in tracts. None appealed to principles more grandly than Milton, although he abused opponents. He had come to notice when he argued that Scripture allowed the putting away of a wife found to be incompatible. Then, in an attack on episcopacy, *The Reason of Church Government* (1642), he confessed to an 'inward prompting which now grew daily upon me, that by labour and intense study (which I take to be my portion in this life), joined with the strong propensity of nature, I might perhaps leave something so written to aftertimes as they should not willingly let it die.'

He resolved 'to be an interpreter and relater of the best and sagest things among mine own citizens throughout this island in the mother dialect.' He outlined his plans:

Time serves not now, and perhaps I might seem too profuse to give any certain account of what the mind at home, in the spacious circuits of her musing, hath liberty to propose to herself, though of highest hope and hardest attempting; whether that epic form whereof the two poems of Homer and those other two of Virgil and Tasso are a diffuse, and the book of Job a brief model; or whether …

John Milton, aged about 62, when he had been blind for 10 years. Engraved by William Faithorne for *The History of Britain*, 1670.

But poetry was postponed. Satan's address to the Sun, written in 1642, appeared in *Paradise Lost* in 1667. The brief epic *Paradise Regained* and the tragedy *Samson Agonistes* followed in 1671.

The only prose which has escaped from the 'dust and heat' of controversy is *Areopagitica*, called after the Areopagus, the hill of Ares where the Athenian parliament met. This *speech for the liberty of unlicensed printing to the Parliament of England* is couched in the form of a classical oration, beginning with a quotation from Euripides: 'This is true liberty, when free-born men,/Having to advise the public, may speak free …'. *Areopagitica*, however, defends not free speech but a free press. It asks Parliament to stop the pre-publication 'licensing' of books, a practice begun by Henry VIII, abolished in 1641, but reimposed in 1643. A particular kind of liberty was one of Milton's ideals, and his speech has noble sentences:

as good almost kill a man as kill a good book: who kills a man kills a reasonable creature, God's image; but he who destroys a good book kills reason itself, kills the image of God, as it were, in the eye. Many a man lives a burden to the earth; but a good book is the precious life blood of a master-spirit, embalmed and treasured up on purpose to a life beyond life.

He ends with a vision of England as Samson: 'Methinks I see in my mind a noble and puissant nation rousing herself like a strong man after sleep, and shaking her invincible locks.'

*Areopagitica* used to be seen as a classic of liberalism, prophetic of religious and civil toleration. Its advocacy transcends its occasion. But Milton would not have allowed Catholics to publish, and he never argued against censorship after publication: 'if [books] be found mischievous and libellous, the fire and the executioner will be the timeliest and the most effectual remedy.' Mischievous books would be burnt, and their printers and authors would suffer cropped ears or slit noses. Parliament was unmoved; Milton later acted as a censor for Cromwell. Among his other prose, *Of Education* is still read. A Latin *On Christian Doctrine* found in the censor's office in 1823, translated and published in 1825, makes his unorthodoxy, darkly visible in *Paradise Lost*, crystal clear.

The poet's plan of 1642 was fulfilled twenty-five years later. He may have worked on *Adam Unparadis'd*, a drama which became *Paradise Lost*, and on *Samson*, but he returned fully to poetry only after Cromwell's death in 1658. His causes had failed, the millennial Rule of the Saints prophesied in Revelations had not come, the English had returned to their regal and episcopal vomit. He had lost his eyesight in 1652, his wife and only son in 1653, a daughter in 1657, and his beloved second wife in 1658. He was 50. He had advised the public, in vain. There remained his poetic talent.

At the Civil War, Milton turned from poetry to reforming prose, and toughened his argumentative powers. In his late poetry he dallied less with the 'false surmise' of the classical poems which had charmed his youth and formed his style. Instead, he mythologized himself. After the Restoration and amnesty, he presents himself as 'In darkness and in dangers compassed round,/And solitude; yet not alone', for he was visited by the Heavenly Muse. This is from the Invocation to *Paradise Lost*, Book VII. The Invocations to Books I, III and IX put epic to plangent personal use, creating a myth of the afflicted poet as a blind seer, or as a nightingale, who 'in shadiest covert hid,/Tunes her nocturnal note'.

In the sonnet 'When I consider how my light is spent', he fears that 'that one talent which is death to hide' was now 'lodged with him useless'. He asks 'Doth God exact day-labour, light denied'? He hears: 'God doth not need/Either man's work or his own gifts'; he is to 'stand and wait'. His sonnet 'Methought I saw my late espousèd saint' ends:

> Love, sweetness, goodness in her person shined
> So clear, as in no face with more delight.
> But O as to embrace me she inclined
> I waked, she fled, and day brought back my night.

In the Invocation to III he again makes personal protest at his blindness:

> Thus with the year
> Seasons return, but not to me returns
> Day, or the sweet approach of even or morn,
> Or sight of vernal bloom, or summer's rose,
> Or flocks, or herds, or human face divine.

He later identifies with the faithful angel Abdiel: 'Among the faithless, faithful only he;/ Among innumerable false, unmoved,/Unshaken, unseduced, unterrified' (III.897–9).

*Paradise Lost* follows the Renaissance idea that poetry should set an attractive pattern of heroic virtue. Holding a humanist belief in reason and in the didactic role of the word, Milton turned argument back into poetry. In the European conversation of the Renaissance, his was the last word. As well as relating the Fall, he attempted a more difficult task: 'to justify the ways of God to men'. He would retell the story of 'Man's first disobedience' so as to show the justice of Providence. The result is, in its art, power and scope, the greatest of English poems. Dr Johnson, no lover of Milton's religion, politics or personality, concluded his *Life* thus: 'His great works were performed under discountenance, and in blindness, but difficulties vanished at his touch; he was born for whatever is arduous; and his work is not the greatest of heroick poems, only because it is not the first.' *Paradise Lost* is a work of grandeur and energy, and of intricate design. It includes in its sweep most of what was worth knowing of the universe and of history. The blind poet balanced details occurring six books apart.

*Paradise Lost* begins with the fall of the angels, Satan's plan to capture God's newly created species, and a Heavenly foresight of the future. In Book IV we meet Adam and Eve in the Garden. Raphael tells Adam of Satan's rebellion, the war in Heaven, the fall of the angels, the creation of the universe, and of Man and of his requested mate, and warns him of the tempter. In IX Satan deceives Eve, and Adam resolves to die with her; the Son conveys God's doom and promises redemption. In X, Satan boasts of his success, but he and his angels are transformed to serpents. In XI and XII Raphael shows the miseries of mankind until the Redemption, whereafter Adam will have 'a paradise within thee, happier far'.

The 'heroic poem' exemplified right conduct. There are several heroisms: Adam and Eve, like the Son, show 'the better fortitude/Of patience and heroic martyrdom' (IX.31–2), – not the individual heroism of Achilles or the imperial duty of Aeneas, nor yet the chivalry of the Italian romantic epics. The magnificence of Satan's appearance and first speeches turns into envy and revenge. At the centre of the poem is an unglamorous human story, although 'our first parents' are ideal at first, as is their romantic love:

> So hand in hand they passed, the loveliest pair
> That ever since in love's embraces met,
> Adam the goodliest man of men since born
> His sons, the fairest of her daughters Eve.

In IV Eve says that Paradise without Adam would not be sweet. In IX the Fall elaborates the account in Genesis. Eve, choosing to garden alone, is deceived by the serpent's clever arguments. She urges Adam to eat. 'Not deceived', he joins her out of love:

> How can I live without thee, how forgo
> Thy sweet converse and love so dearly joined,
> To live again in these wild woods forlorn?

Eve leads Adam to sin but also to repentance; blaming herself for the Fall, she proposes suicide.

Milton types the sexes traditionally ('He for God only, she for God in him') but also allegorically – Adam is intellect, Eve sense. He likes cosmology, she prefers gardening. Although the sexes are not equal, the presentation of sexual love and of marriage is positive and new. Central to *Paradise Lost* is the first good marriage in English literature. When Adam and Eve are expelled from the Garden:

> Some natural tears they dropped, but wiped them soon.
> The world was all before them, where to choose
> Their place of rest, and Providence their guide:
> Thus hand in hand, with wandering steps and slow,
> Through Eden took their solitary way.

Milton's endings display his mastery of verse, syntax and sense. The sole humans, having lost God and angel guests, are 'solitary' yet hand in hand; wandering yet guided; needing rest yet free to choose. The balance is, as Milton said poetry should be, 'simple, sensuous and passionate'.

Milton's Christian humanism depends on human reason, and for him 'Reason also is choice'. Right reason freely chooses to recognize the truths of God. Eve freely chooses not to accept Adam's reasoned warning; Adam freely chooses to die with her; the Son freely chooses to die for Man. Milton held that 'just are the ways of God,/And justifiable to men', yet made God justify himself and blame mankind. 'Whose fault?' asks the Father, 'Whose but his own? Ingrate, he had of me/All he could have; I made him just and right,/Sufficient to have stood, though free to fall' (III.97–9). The point is clear, but so is the crossness. Here, 'God the Father', as Alexander Pope said, 'turns a school divine' (an academic theologian). To represent God the Father as conducting his own defence was a mistake. Mysteries, as Donne wrote, are like the sun, 'dazzling, but plain to all eyes'. Milton explains the dazzle. The invented scene of the Son's promotion to 'Vice-Gerent', which prompts Satan's revolt, is a blunder. To portray 'what the eye hath not seen and the ear hath not heard' is almost impossible: in Milton the life of Heaven is too like that of Homer's Olympus: 'Tables are set, and on a sudden piled/With angels' food, and rubied nectar flows … They eat, they drink, and in communion sweet/Quaff immortality.' Dante does it better.

The faults are the obverse of Milton's strength of purpose. *Paradise Lost* does in compact form what the Mystery cycles had done. Its Bible story is rational, as the Renaissance wished, and pictorial, in the style of Italian ceiling painters. The energy and grandeur of *Paradise Lost* strike even those readers who do not know the Bible. It is like hearing Handel's *Messiah* in the Sistine Chapel; or, more precisely, how a blind man might hear a *Messiah* by Henry Purcell (1659–95), had he composed one.

*Paradise Regain'd* is not about the Redemption but about the temptation in the desert. The Son's rejection of Satan's offer of the (pagan) learning of Athens stands out in a dry landscape. *Samson Agonistes* is a tragedy to be read, not acted. ('A dialogue without action can never please like a union of the narrative and dramatick powers' – Johnson.) Its form is Greek, with protagonist and chorus; its subject the fate of Israel's champion, 'eyeless in Gaza at the mill with slaves'. Samson speaks: 'Why was my breeding ordered and prescribed/As of a person separate to God/Designed for great exploits; if I must die/Betrayed, captived, and both my eyes put out?'

> O dark, dark, dark, amid the blaze of noon,
> Irrecoverably dark, total eclipse
> Without all hope of day!
> O first-created beam, and thou great word,
> Let there be light, and light was over all;
> Why am I thus bereaved thy prime decree?
> The sun to me is dark
> And silent as the moon,
> When she deserts the night
> Hid in her vacant interlunar cave.

Milton's self-vindication turns scripture and tragedy into autobiography. For example, Dalilah betraying Samson to the Philistines recalls the first Mrs Milton. Finally the persecuted hero pulls down the temple, slaying all his foes at once: 'the world o'erwhelming to revenge his sight' (Marvell). The last chorus, both Greek and Christian, begins: 'All is best, though we oft doubt/What the unsearchable dispose/Of highest wisdom brings about'. It ends:

> His servants he with new acquist
> Of true experience from this great event
> With peace and consolation hath dismissed,
> And calm of mind, all passion spent.

Milton left an example to English poets of dedication to his art, but also of passionate self-assertion.

## ■ The Restoration

The restored monarchy inaugurated a new temper, and a cultural style which lasted. Although things sobered up under King William, Congreve's *The Way of the World* (1700) is still a 'Restoration comedy'. Charles II's return gave literature chances it had not had for eighteen years. The theatres opened, determined to reject Puritan earnestness. The king's friends came back from France with a more secular, sceptical and 'civilized' tone, and neo-classical ideas. The Church of England was re-established. Charles patronized the Royal Society, the Royal Observatory, the theatre and the opera. In 1665–6 the Plague and the Great Fire destroyed much of London. Sir Christopher Wren designed fifty-one new churches; his St Paul's Cathedral was completed in 1710. London 'society' took shape in the new quarter of St James's. Tea, coffee and chocolate were drunk in places of public recreation. Horse-racing became a fixture in a social calendar. It became 'civilized' for men to be agreeable, not to converse on religion and politics, and to speak gallantly of 'the fair sex'.

There were wars with Protestant Holland, then with Catholic France. The expulsion

## Events 1660–1700

| | |
|---|---|
| 1660 | The Monarchy is restored: Charles II passes the Act of Oblivion. |
| 1662 | Charles marries Catherine of Braganza (they have no children). Act of Uniformity excludes Nonconformist ministers. |
| 1665–6 | Great Plague of London. |
| 1666 | Great Fire of London. |
| 1666 | Dutch raid the naval port of Chatham, near London. |
| 1670 | Secret Treaty of Dover: in return for a subsidy, Charles II agrees to help Louis XIV of France against Holland. |
| 1672 | Declaration of Indulgence towards Catholics and Nonconformists. |
| 1673 | Test Act excludes Catholics from public office. |
| 1677 | William of Orange marries Mary, daughter of James, Duke of York. |
| 1678 | Titus Oates invents a 'Popish Plot'; Catholics persecuted. |
| 1680 | Crisis over the Exclusion Bill to exclude James, Duke of York, from the succession on the grounds of his Catholicism. (His second wife was the Catholic Mary of Modena, and they produced a son and heir.) |
| 1683 | Failure of the Rye House Plot to kill Charles and James. |
| 1684 | Monmouth, Charles's bastard son, is implicated in the Rye House Plot. |
| 1685 | Charles I dies; James II accedes. Louis XIV allows persecution of French Protestants. |
| 1687 | James's Declaration of Indulgence for Liberty of Conscience. |
| 1688 | Seven bishops refuse to swear to a Second Declaration. The so-called Glorious Revolution: William of Orange is invited to help depose James, who flees to France; William III and Mary II rule. |
| 1689 | The Bill of Rights; toleration of Nonconformists. James lands in Ireland; William's war with France continues. |
| 1690 | William defeats James at the Battle of the Boyne in Ireland. |
| 1691 | Jacobites are defeated at the Battle of Aughrim (Ireland). |
| 1693 | National Debt is begun. |
| 1694 | Bank of England is established. |

in 1688 of James II, Charles II's Catholic brother, led to the exclusion by Act of Parliament of Catholics from the succession. In Scotland the Presbyterian Church was established by law; should the monarch come north, he was assumed to change religion as he crossed the border (as today). Monarchy was limited by Parliament, and the City's commercial interests; the wounds of the Civil War slowly healed. The governmental balance struck in the Bloodless Revolution of 1688 prevailed in England until the extension of the franchise in the Great Reform Bill of 1832. Writing took its tone not from the Court but from a polite society defined by rank, property and, increasingly, money. New ideas were diffused in journals. By 1700 a book trade had begun to support writers, and to cater for readers of leisure, some of 'the fair sex'. Journalism began, sensational or smart. There was also a literature of religious and social dissent.

In literature the Restoration was a period of novelty, change and refoundation rather than of great writing. Apart from *Paradise Lost* and the 1662 Anglican Prayer Book, the only books from these forty years to have been read in every generation since are Bunyan's *The Pilgrim's Progress* (1678–9), some poems by John Dryden,

**Augustus** (31 BC–AD 14)
Among the poets of Augustus
were Virgil (70–19 BC),
Horace, (65–8 BC), Propertius
(54/48–c.16 BC), and Ovid (43
BC–AD 17/18).

and the better Restoration comedies. The faith of Bunyan, the philosophy of John Locke, and the mathematics and optics of Sir Isaac Newton had more lasting cultural impact than any literary work of the period in verse, prose, or drama. An exception can be made for Dryden's *Absolom and Achitophel* (1681), the model for a century of couplet satire. In a period of recurrent public crisis, writing was topical, allusive and factional, and the theatre was taken up with current affairs, political, ecclesiastical, and sexual. The newspaper and the novel were at hand.

The 'heroic' tragedy of the Restoration has not lasted well, but its comedy is often staged today. It was the source of the comedy-of-manners tradition in English writing: Henry Fielding, Oliver Goldsmith, Richard Sheridan, Jane Austen, W. S. Gilbert, Oscar Wilde and much since. Dryden was the leading poet of the period, excelling in all its forms, especially satire and translation. He also wrote the best critical prose of an age in which prose moved towards conversation.

If the Restoration period produced no writer of the first rank, it gave secular literature new importance. It is notable that Charles II's tolerance extended to the great writer who was the public apologist for his father's execution. Milton's absoluteness was recognized rather than welcome in an age of compromise and crisis management. After a sunset of 'heroic' gestures, poetry subsided into the verse of the smooth sons of the 'Sons' of Ben Jonson: Suckling, Denham and Waller. The civil, secular, social culture of the Restoration period is often called Augustan: its writers saw parallels between the restored monarchy and the peace restored by the Emperor **Augustus** after civil war and the assassination of Caesar had ended the Roman republic. Charles I was no Caesar and Charles II no Augustus, but he was 'civilized': he shared his cousin Louis XIV's esteem for *les beaux arts et les belles lettres.* He patronized the Royal Society, the theatre, and actresses. The English Augustans prized peace and order – and envied the prestige, patronage and polish of the first Augustans.

Augustanism ruled from Dryden's maturity in the 1680s until the death of Alexander Pope in 1744, but its ideals guided Dr Johnson (d.1784), and schooled Jane Austen (1775–1817). Literary history sometimes includes the Restoration in the 18th century, for 'eighteenth-century' qualities can be found in literature from 1660 to 1798, the publication date of Wordsworth and Coleridge's *Lyrical Ballads*.

Augustan verse was typically in the rhymed pentameter couplet, as for example in Pope's epigram:

> Nature and Nature's laws lay hid in night;
> God said, *Let Newton be!* and all was light.

The 'heroic couplet', so called from its use in Restoration heroic tragedy, was less about ancient virtue than about its modern absence. This example typically recalls a higher text, the creation of light in Genesis. The theoretical prestige of 'the heroick poem' was maintained by criticism, as in Joseph Addison's appreciation of *Paradise Lost* in *The Spectator* in 1712. Another homage to the heroic was translation. Dryden's *Aeneid* (1697) and Pope's *Iliad* (1720) echo Milton, but they moderate and modernize their exemplars. These heroic frames put into perspective the tameness of everyday life; which was also explored less critically in prose.

The Restoration consensus was an agreement to disagree. Charles II managed to govern without parliament and rode out his troubles, but James II rekindled old conflicts and in 1688 was forced out. An Act of 1662 had re-established Anglican Uniformity, banishing to the nonconformist wings both Catholics and the dissenting heirs of the Puritans. The new centrists could laugh at Samuel Butler's *Hudibras* (1678), a satire on a Presbyterian knight, one

> of that stubborn crew
> Of errant saints whom all men grant
> To be the true Church Militant:
> Such as do build their faith upon
> The holy text of pike and gun;
> Decide all controversies by
> Infallible artillery,
> And prove their doctrine orthodox
> By apostolic blows and knocks;
> Call fire and sword and desolation
> A godly, thorough reformation,
> Which always must be carried on,
> And still be doing, never done;
> As if religion were intended
> For nothing else but to be mended.

## The Earl of Rochester

A less simple reaction to the reversal in social mores in 1660 is found in the libertine wit of John Wilmot, **Earl of Rochester** (1648–80), son of a Cavalier hero and a Puritan mother. The libertine enjoyment of poetic sex, found in Ovid and classical poets, and in Marlowe and Donne, was a convention of gallant Cavalier verse. Rochester, however, is ferocious. Like other Restoration writers, he disliked righteous sentiment and sexual hypocrisy, but was also a sceptic about human reason.

Renaissance humanists imagined that Reason would choose to go up rather than down the scale of creation, though Erasmus, Montaigne, Jonson and Pascal had doubts. Scepticism had been applied to the theory of the state by Thomas Hobbes. In his *Leviathan* (1651), written in exile in France, the natural brutality of man needs the control of an absolute ruler. This scepticism is the starting point of Rochester's *Satyr against Reason and Mankind*:

> Were I (who to my cost already am
> One of those strange, prodigious creatures, man)
> A spirit free to choose, for my own share,
> What case of flesh and blood I pleased to wear,
> I'd be a dog, a monkey or a bear,
> Or anything but that vain animal
> Who is so proud of being rational.

To envy a dog is to recall the Greek Cynics, and Rochester was a cynic as well as a sceptic. His Interregnum childhood had caused him to doubt the rational perfectibility of man. Rochester 'blazed out his youth and health in lavish voluptuousness' (Johnson). He had a rake's disrespect for love: 'Love a woman! You're an ass!/'Tis a most insipid passion/To choose out for your happiness/The silliest part of God's creation.' The King fared no better:

> His sceptre and his prick are of a length,
> And she may sway the one, who plays with th'other,
> And make him little wiser than his brother.
> Restless he rolls about from whore to whore,
> A merry monarch scandalous and poor.

Charles II had seventeen acknowledged bastards.

Rochester's outrageousness could be light as well as gross, as in 'Song of a Young Lady: To Her Ancient Lover': 'Ancient person, for whom I/All the flattering youth defy,/Long be it ere thou grow old,/Aching, shaking, crazy cold;/But still continue as thou art,/Ancient person of my heart.' The style of his wit, both Metaphysical and Augustan, was admired by Marvell and Dryden. He turned to God on his deathbed.

## John Bunyan

Another kind of conversion was that of **John Bunyan** (1628–88). A tinker's son and a soldier in the Parliamentary Army, his *Grace Abounding to the Chief of Sinners* (1666) recounts the effect of reading Luther, and the stages of Protestant spiritual autobiography: conviction of sin, realization of the redemption, spiritual rebirth, calling. He became an unlicensed Baptist preacher, was imprisoned in 1660, and continued to preach and write in Bedford Jail; in prison again, he wrote *The Pilgrim's Progress* (1678, 1679), *The Life and Death of Mr Badman* and *The Holy War*. *Pilgrim's Progress* has been a most successful religious allegory, for reasons which are easily seen.

As I walked through the wilderness of this world, I lighted on a certain place where was a Den, and I laid me down in that place to sleep; and, as I slept, I dreamed a dream. I dreamed, and behold I saw a man clothed with rags, standing in a certain place, with his face from his own house, a book in his hand, and a great burden upon his back. I looked and saw him open the book and read therein; and as he read, he wept, and trembled; and not being able longer to contain, brake out with a lamentable cry, saying, 'What shall I do?' In this plight, therefore, he went home and refrained himself as long as he could, that his wife and children should not perceive his distress; but he could not be silent long, because that his trouble increased.

[This man is called 'Christian'. Christian tells his wife and children that all in their city will be burned by fire from heaven; they think he is mad.] Now I saw, upon a time, when he was walking in the fields, that he was (as he was wont) reading in this book, and greatly distressed in his mind; and as he read, he burst out, as he had done before, crying, 'What shall I do to be saved?'

[A man named Evangelist gave him a parchment] …and there was written within, 'Fly from the wrath to come.' The man therefore read it, and looking upon Evangelist very carefully [sorrowfully], said, Whither must I fly? Then said Evangelist, pointing with his finger over a very wide field, Do you see yonder wicket-gate? The man said, No. Then said the other, Do you see yonder shining light? He said, I think I do. Then said Evangelist, Keep that light in your eye, and go up directly thereto; so shalt thou see the gate; at which when thou knockest it shall be told thee what thou shalt do.

So I saw in my dream that the man began to run. Now, he had not run far from his own door, but his wife and children perceiving it, began to cry after him to return; but the man put his fingers in his ears, and ran on, crying, Life! life! eternal life! So he looked not behind him, but fled towards the middle of the plain.

On his way from the City of Destruction to the Celestial City, Christian goes through the Slough of Despond and Vanity Fair, and meets Mr Worldly Wiseman; the piercing simplicity of the narrative brought it home to many for as long as England was a strongly Protestant country. When in 1847 the worldly-wise Thackeray chose for his novel the title *Vanity Fair*, he sharpened its moral perspective.

Bunyan challenges the idea that literary judgment is unaffected by belief. He made his English plain and pure so that it might save souls. Readers who do not look to be saved in Christian's way, or who cannot put biblical revelation so far above reason, recognize the power of Bunyan's storytelling, and enjoy his homely shrewd-ness. But compared with the other English allegory of salvation, *Piers Plowman*, Bunyan is terribly simple. A milder Puritanism is found in the works of **Richard Baxter** (1615–91).

The chasm between Bunyan and Rochester was not to be bridged by Church or State. Puritans attacked the new theatres, where marriage, the marriage-market and extra-marital intrigue were played for laughs. Playwrights replied that comedy selects the ridiculous in order to satirize. Actresses became the public mistresses of public men: Nell Gwynn went from the bed of the actor Charles Hart to that of the rakish poet-dramatist Sir Charles Sedley, and then to that of Charles II, whom she called 'Charles the Third'.

## Samuel Pepys

A panorama of London life is found in the diary kept by **Samuel Pepys** from 1660 to 1669. Pepys (1633–1703) was 'clerk of the King's ships' during the Dutch war. At his death, his fellow diarist John Evelyn (1620–1706) wrote of him as 'a very worthy, industrious and curious person, none in England exceeding him in knowledge of the navy ... universally beloved, hospitable, generous, learned in many things, skilled in music, a very great cherisher of learned men.' The diary shows Pepys as a faithful government servant, social, fond of plays and music, conventionally religious, proud of his country, his profession, his family, his wife and his home. He disarmingly records everything, including his own infidelities. The diary was deciphered and part-published in 1825. Its interest lies not just in its accounts of the Plague, the Fire and the Dutch at the doors in 1665–7, but in its detail. It shows that public life was, like social life, marked by public infidelity and venality. In previous reigns, the un-edifying life of the Court led to comment, not to public laughter. No one laughed at Henry VIII.

## The theatres

The London theatres opened to plays by the older dramatist Sir William Davenant (1608–68) and to adaptations of pre-Civil War drama, but there were no pro-fessional actors, and the new plays were different. Two public companies licensed by the King acted in purpose-built theatres rather like modern theatres. Davenant's at Lincoln's Inn Fields and Dorset Garden, and Killigrew's at Drury Lane were covered; they had proscenium arches, curtains, scenery, lighting and music. They offered lightly classicized entertainments of a semi-operatic kind to the Court and its friends. Noble arms and noble love strut and fret their heroic conquests, and debate the problems of honour in symmetrical couplets. These English tragedies lack the focus of French tragedy. It is hard to see them staged, but Dryden's *All for Love* (1678) reads well. It is a tidy version of *Antony and Cleopatra*, in a dignified blank verse which works better than the heroic couplets of Dryden's previous tragedies.

Shakespeare now became the stage's standby: his plots, language and morals were trimmed to suit fashions influenced by the plays of Pierre Corneille (1616–84) and Jean Racine (1639–99), seen at Paris. A neo-classical criticism was imported, with 'rules' requiring the three 'unities' of action, place and time: that the action should happen in one place in no more than three hours. Shakespeare had ignored these rules, but they are worth understanding. The critics turned Aristotle's point that most good tragedies have a single plot into a rule; and added the unities of place and time. These doctrines are economically put by Dryden in his prologue to his play *Secret Love* (1665):

> He who wrote this, not without pains and thought
> From *French* and *English* Theaters has brought
> Th'exactest Rules by which a Play is wrought:
>
> The Unities of Action, Place and Time;
> The Scenes unbroken; and a mingled Chime
> Of *Johnsons* humour, with *Corneilles* rhyme.     i.e. Ben Jonson's

Drama now tried to be purely comic or purely tragic, and critics also embraced Aristotle's commendation of artistic unity, singleness of effect, and philosophic truth. To his doctrine that art should imitate the permanent traits in human nature, they added the principle that it should show virtue rewarded. These aims are irreconcilable in tragedy. In Nahum Tate's 1681 version of *King Lear*, Cordelia survives to marry Edgar. Johnson, writing on *Lear* in 1765, approved:

> A play in which the wicked prosper and the virtuous miscarry may doubtless be good because it is a just representation of the common events of human life: but since all reasonable beings naturally love justice, I cannot easily be persuaded that the observation of justice makes a play worse; or that if other exellencies are equal the audience will not always rise better pleased from the final triumph of persecuted virtue. In the present case the public has decided. Cordelia from the time of Tate has always retired with victory and felicity.

Shakespeare leaves Edgar and Albany to sustain 'the gored state', but in 1681 England was still a gored state; Charles's legitimate heir was his strong-minded brother. The only neo-classical tragedy whose appeal survived the 18th century was Thomas Otway's *Venice Preserv'd* (1682).

## Restoration comedy

Restoration comedy showed the seamy sexual side of the smooth social world. The leading comic writers of Charles's reign were Sir George Etherege (?1634–?91) and

---

### Restoration plays

With dates of first performances.

Sir George Etherege: *Love in a Tub* (1664), *She Would if She Could* (1668), *The Man of Mode; or Sir Fopling Flutter* (1676).

John Dryden: *The Indian Queen* (1664), *Marriage à-la-Mode* (1672), *The Conquest of Granada* (1669), *Aureng-Zebe* (1675), *All for Love* (1678).

William Wycherley: *Love in a Wood, or, St James's Park* (1671), *The Country Wife* (1675), *The Plain Dealer* (1676).

George Villiers, Duke of Buckingham: *The Rehearsal* (1672).

Aphra Behn: *The Rover* (1677).

Thomas Otway: *Venice Preserv'd* (1682).

Sir John Vanburgh: *The Relapse* (1696), *The Provok'd Wife* (1697).

William Congreve: *Love for Love* (1695), *The Way of the World* (1700).

George Farquhar: *The Recruiting Office* (1706), *The Beaux' Stratagem* (1707).

William Wycherley (1641–16); among the second rank is Aphra Behn (1640–89), the first woman to make a living by her pen. The wit and teasing amoralism of these comedies was by 1700 found gross, and it changed: Sir John Vanburgh (1654–1726) is lighter, William Congreve (1670–1729) more polished, George Farquhar (?1677–1707) more genial – trends which continued in the 18th century. Charles Lamb (1775–1834) argued that the artificial comedy of the Restoration, no longer staged in the early 19th century, had nothing to do with real life. The Victorian historian T. B. Macaulay found it immoral; the 20th-century critic L. C. Knights found it dull; today it amuses once more, though the sex-comedy of the 1670s is more bawdy than witty.

Restoration comedy takes a pleasure in the vices it caricatures: it shows 'the way we live now', pushing current trends to logical extremes. The hero of Wycherley's *The Country Wife* is said to be impotent from venereal disease, and no threat to womankind. His name, Horner, was then pronounced the same as 'honour', a word heard often in the play. Horner uses his safe reputation to dis-honour the women of the play and give their husbands cuckolds' 'horns'. We are not to condemn the play's morals but to admire its plot, wit and repartee. Old ideals had been smashed in the Civil War. Before it, faith had been supported by reason; after it, reason was distrusted equally by Rochester and Bunyan.

# John Dryden

The Duke of Buckingham's *The Rehearsal* (1672) was a hugely successful prose burlesque of the theatrical conventions of the 'heroic' tragedies of the 1660s, spiced with partisan and personal attacks known as 'lampoons', in the manner of the modern *Private Eye*. One target of its mockery was **John Dryden** (1631–1700), who put on five plays in 1667. When Davenant died in 1668, Charles II, a keen patron of the theatre, made Dryden Poet Laureate.

It was a time of class, party and faction. Rochester, Buckingham and Sedley scorned Dryden as a social inferior. Others who wrote for a living acknowledged his superiority by attacking him. He was called 'Bayes', after his Laureate crown of bay leaves. When Royalist politics and religion lost favour in the 1680s, Dryden turned to satire, and then to translation. He wrote in every kind, but posterity has liked best the non-dramatic work of his later career: his satire, his prose and his Virgil.

We have very full materials for Dryden's life. His long literary career is a commentary on his times. At Westminster School, near London, where his Puritan family had sent him for a classical education, he was, when the King lost his head, a

## John Dryden's chief writings

| | |
|---|---|
| *Astraea Redux* (1660) | *To the Memory of Mr Oldham* (1684) |
| *Annus Mirabilis* (1667) | *The Hind and the Panther* (1687) |
| *Essay on Dramatic Poesy* (1668) | *A Song for St Cecilia's Day* (1687) |
| *Absolom and Achitophel*, part I (1681) | *Alexander's Feast* (1697) |
| *The Medal, A Satire against Sedition* (1681) | Virgil: *Works* (1697) |
| *Mac Flecknoe* (1682) | *Fables, Ancient and Modern* (1700) |
| *Religio Laici* (1682) | |

**anti-Catholicism** In 1678 the Monument to the Fire of London was erected. Its inscription said that the Fire was started 'by the treachery and malice of the popish faction ...to introduce popery and slavery'. These words, removed under James II, were re-cut under William and stood until 1831. They enshrined the Whig myth of a Popish Plot to kill Charles II in 1678, a 'plot' fabricated by Israel Tonge and Titus Oates, perjurers who sent twenty innocents to their deaths.

King's Scholar. After Cambridge, he returned to London to live by writing for the stage and the Court. Though a gentleman, he was a slave to the pen, writing twenty-five plays, some with collaborators. His politics sharpened into satire, and his religion deepened into the Anglican *Religio Laici* ('A Layman's Faith'), and *The Hind and the Panther*, in which he reasoned his way into Catholicism. He stuck to this faith in William III's reign, a time of **anti-Catholicism**, to the material disadvantage of self and family.

Dryden's faith went from Puritan to Catholic; his style went from Metaphysical to baroque to something clearer. His theatrical flourish settled in the 1670s into a way of discoursing in verse, less heroic and more urbane. Extravagance ripened into complexity. Charles wanted heroic tragedies to be in rhyming couplets, as in France, but the second edition of *Paradise Lost* (1674) carries a defence by Milton of 'English heroic verse without rhyme', and a commendatory poem by Marvell, including the lines:

> Well mightst thou [Milton] scorn thy Readers to allure
> With tinkling Rime, of thy own sense secure;
> While the *Town-Bayes* writes all the while and spells,
> And like a Pack-horse tires without his bells.

Milton had just given Dryden leave to 'tag his verses': to put *Paradise Lost* into rhyme for a semi-opera. The result, *The State of Innocence*, was printed but never staged, though Dryden learned much in reducing Milton's 10,000 lines to 1400. *Bayes* did indeed write 'all the while', but the persuasive verse prologues, and the prose accompanying the printed plays, show that he also thought all the while.

Marvell sneered in rhyme: rhyme lends point in a closed couplet. Dryden found that the English closed couplet was too neat for tragedy, and made it instead the vehicle for satire. He also used open couplets, and triplets, as in the famous opening of *Religio Laici* (1682):

> Dim, as the borrow'd beams of Moon and Stars
> To *lonely, weary, wandring* Travellers,
> Is *Reason* to the *Soul*: And as on high,
> Those rowling Fires *discover* but the Sky
> Not light us *here*; So *Reason's* glimmering Ray
> Was lent, not to *assure* our *doubtfull* way,
> But *guide* us upward to a *better Day*.

This 'layman's religion' relies less on glimmering Reason than on the light of Faith, yet its language is quietly witty. Dryden has a reasoned response to the historical criticism of scripture:

> More Safe, and much more modest 'tis, to say
> *God wou'd not leave Mankind without a way*:
> And that the *Scriptures*, though not *every where*
> Free from Corruption, or intire, or clear,
> Are uncorrupt, sufficient, clear, intire,
> In *all* things which our needfull *Faith* require.

If this is not the faith of George Herbert, it at least makes sense in an area where reason could not help either Bunyan or Rochester.

## Satire

In *Mac Flecknoe* Dryden found his true vocation, verse satire. The aged Richard Flecknoe, a Catholic priest and a tedious writer, has long ruled the empire of Dulness:

> All human things are subject to decay,
> And when fate summons, monarchs must obey.
> This Flecknoe found, who, like Augustus, young
> Was called to empire, and had governed long:
> In prose and verse, was owned, without dispute,
> Through all the realms of Nonsense, absolute.

Seeking a successor, Flecknoe – like Augustus – adopts an heir (*Mac* means 'son'), the playwright Shadwell:

> 'Sh—— alone my perfect image bears,
> Mature in dullness from his tender years:
> Sh—— alone, of all my sons, is he
> Who stands confirmed in full stupidity.
> The rest to some faint meaning make pretence,
> But Sh—— never deviates into sense …'

The poem, composed in 1679, was published in 1682, when Shadwell had become a political opponent.

*Mac Flecknoe* reverses the aims and methods of heroic tragedy, turning heroic into **mock-heroic** and converting the rhyming couplet to new ends: magnifying the littleness of pretension. 'There is a vast difference,' Dryden wrote in a *Discourse concerning the Original and Progress of Satire*, 'between the slovenly Butchering of a Man, and the fineness of a stroak that separates the Head from the Body, and leaves it standing in its place.' Dryden used the sharp edge of praise. Whereas Donne, Jonson, Milton and Butler employ the harsh ridicule of classical satirists, Dryden preferred 'fine raillery', intelligent teasing. Flecknoe's 'deviates' is a 'fine stroak'; we are amused, not outraged. Such writing is easy, yet full of comparison, metaphor, allusion, wordplay. Dryden made the couplet so efficient a instrument of satire that Swift, Pope and Johnson used no other. Pope re-used *Mac Flecknoe*'s Empire of Dulness in his *Dunciad*.

The subject of *Absolom and Achitophel* is the rebellion of Charles's illegitimate son, the Duke of Monmouth, prompted by the Earl of Shaftesbury, leader of the Whigs. Dryden parallels this failed rebellion with that of the biblical Absolom against his father David, the great king of Israel; Israel, as in the sermons Dryden heard as a boy, means England. Nonconformists thought that Charles's infidelities had made God send the Plague, the Fire and the Dutch in 1666–7. Achitophel (Shaftesbury) was supported by City merchants who believed that 'Kings were useless, and a Clog to Trade'. The brave David (Charles II), humane to his enemies, was a King beloved in Israel. He loved God – but also music, song, dance, and beautiful women. Dryden grasps this nettle with glee:

> In pious times, e'er Priest-craft did begin,
> Before *Polygamy* was made a sin;
> When man, on many, multiply'd his kind,
> E'er one to one was, cursedly, confin'd:
> When Nature prompted, and no law deny'd

**mock-heroic** (mock' = 'pretend') A mode which does not ridicule heroism, but uses heroic style to belittle pretension. Less misleading is Pope's term for *The Rape of the Lock* (1713), 'Heroi-Comical'.

Promiscuous use of Concubine and Bride;
Then *Israel*'s Monarch, after Heaven's own heart,
His vigorous warmth did, variously, impart
To Wives and Slaves: And, wide as his Command,
Scatter'd his Maker's Image through the Land.

Dryden launches his complex fable with astonishing ease, confidence and humour. Criticism of Absolom is wrapped in praise: 'What faults he had (for who from faults is free?)/His Father could not, or he would not see.' Achitophel is a Miltonic tempter, offering Monmouth

'Not barren praise alone, that gaudy flower
Fair only to the sight, but solid power;
And nobler is a limited command,
Given by the love of all your native land,
Than a successive title, long and dark,
Drawn from the mouldy rolls of Noah's ark.'

The biblical David grieved bitterly for his son Absolom, killed running away; but Monmouth survived.

This dexterous poem, published during Shaftesbury's trial for treason, ends with David's mercy to the rebels – and to his sons. But it warns the King, the country, and any future rebels against a second civil war. Charles had prevented Parliament's exclusion of James Duke of York from his 'successive title'. Parliament took revenge, however: when James was deposed, Dryden lost the Laureateship to Shadwell. Dulness had succeeded.

Literary succession was on Dryden's mind in his moving poem in memory of the younger poet John Oldham, and again in his late work: his musical Odes, his Preface to the Fables, and his Virgil. It is the theme of his 1693 epistle 'To my dear friend Mr Congreve on his comedy called *The Double Dealer*':

Well then, the promis'd Hour is come at last;
The present Age of Wit obscures the past:
Strong were our Syres, and as they fought they Writ,
Conqu'ring with Force of Arms and Dint of Wit:
Theirs was the Giant Race before the Flood ...

The realism of this retrospect is as remarkable as its tone. Making way for Congreve, Dryden finds his own generation weaker than its predecessor. Charles had brought refinement, but the likes of Shakespeare and Jonson would not come again. There had been giants on earth in those days, before the 'Flood' of the Civil War.

Our age was cultivated thus at length,
But what we gain'd in Skill we lost in Strength.
Our Builders were with Want of Genius curst;
The second Temple was not like the first.

The rebuilt temple was English Augustanism. 'O that your brows my Lawrel had sustain'd,' says Dryden to Congreve: 'Well had I been depos'd if you had reign'd!'

Latin translation would cultivate the English, as Greek translation had cultivated Rome. The success of Dryden's *Sylvae* (1685), a selection from Horace, Theocritus, Lucretius and Virgil, encouraged him to do a complete Virgil for Tonson the bookseller. Couplets could at last be properly heroic:

Arms, and the Man I sing, who, forc'd by Fate,
And haughty *Juno*'s unrelenting Hate;
Expell'd and exil'd, left the *Trojan* Shoar:
Long labours, both by Sea and Land, he bore;
And in the doubtful War, before he won
The *Latian* Realm, and built the destin'd Town;          Latium, in Italy
His banish'd gods restor'd to Rites Divine,
And setl'd sure Succession in his Line;
From whence the Race of *Alban* Fathers come,             rulers descended from Aeneas
And the long Glories of majestick *Rome*

The proclamatory flourish of this opening recalls the fanfares of Henry Purcell (1659–95), Dryden's collaborator in these years, or the ornate woodcarving of Grinling Gibbons (1648–1721). 'I looked on Virgil,' Dryden wrote in the preface to the *Sylvae*, 'as a succinct and grave majestic writer, who weighed not only every thought, but every word and syllable: who was still aiming to crowd his sense into as narrow a compass as possibly he could …'. Yet in his *Aeneid* Dryden chose to 'pursue the excellence and forsake the brevity', for English is less compact than Latin. The preface to the *Sylvae* gives his policy:

a translator is to make his author appear as charming as possibly he can, provided he maintains his character, and makes him not unlike himself. Translation is a kind of drawing after the life; where everyone will acknowledge there is a double sort of likeness, a good one and a bad. 'Tis one thing to draw the outlines true, the features like, the proportions exact, the colouring itself perhaps tolerable; and another thing to make all these graceful, by the posture, the shadowings, and, chiefly, by the spirit which animates the whole.

This animating spirit can be felt in the prophecy in which Aeneas's father exalts the rule of Rome above the arts of Greece:

'Let others better mould the running mass
Of metals, and inform the breathing brass,
And soften into flesh a marble face;
Plead better at the bar; describe the skies,
And when the stars ascend, and when they rise.
But, Rome! 'tis thine alone, with awful sway,
To rule mankind, and make the world obey:
Disposing peace and war thy own majestic way.
To tame the proud, the fettered slave to free,
These are imperial arts, and worthy thee.          (VI.1168–77)

England too is to excel in empire rather than art. Dryden's artful *Dedication* can also be read sideways, as accepting the rule of William III. Ever a political writer, he read his times and his readers well, as in the last jocular Chorus to the *Secular Masque* (1700):

All, all, of a piece throughout:
     Thy Chase had a Beast in View;
Thy wars brought nothing about;
     Thy lovers were all untrue.
'Tis well an Old Age is out,
     And time to begin a New.

At the end of a century where monarchical succession had twice been broken and restored, Dryden was buried in Chaucer's grave. 'What was said of Rome, adorned by Augustus, may be applied by an easy metaphor to English poetry embellished by Dryden,' wrote Dr Johnson: "he found it brick, and he left it marble."' If Dryden made English verse more elegant, he also left it more usable than when he had found it.

## Prose

Dryden was equally a master of what he called 'the other harmony of prose'. Although musical, he contrives to sound as if he is talking to an intelligent friend. This civilized tone became general over a range of English discourse, including humbler genres: diary, familiar letters, the essay, the 'character'; romance and auto-biography; history, criticism, philosophy, political thought, religion and natural science.

The Royal Society of London was the nursery of English science, its members in-

### A chronology of Restoration prose

1662   Revised Version of The Book of Common Prayer; Joseph Glanvill, *The Vanity of Dogmatizing*

1664   John Evelyn, *Sylva*

1665   Izaak Walton, *Life of Richard Hooker* (La Rochefoucauld, *Maximes*)

1667   Thomas Sprat, *History of the Royal Society of London for the Improving of Natural Knowledge*

1668   John Dryden, *Essay of Dramatic Poesie*; John Wilkins, *Towards a Real Character, and a Philosophical Language*

1669   Bp. Gilbert Burnet, *Conference between a Conformist and a Non-conformist*

1670   Walton, *Lives* (Pascal (d.1662), *Pensées*)

1672   Andrew Marvell, *The Rehearsal Transprosed*

1674   Thomas Rymer, *Reflections on Aristotle's Treatise of Poesie*

1675   Thomas Traherne, *Christian Ethics*

1677   (Spinoza (d.1677), *Ethics*)

1678   John Bunyan, *The Pilgrim's Progress*

1679   Burnet, *History of the Reformation of the Church of England*

1680   Sir Roger l'Estrange, *Select Colloquies of Erasmus* (trans.)

1685   Charles Cotton, *Montaigne's Essays* (trans.)

1686   Lord Halifax, *Letter to a Dissenter*

1687   Isaac Newton, *Principia Mathematica* (Latin)

1688   Aphra Behn, *Oronooko, or the Royal Slave*; Halifax, *Character of a Trimmer*

1689   John Locke, *Two Treatises on Government*; *First Letter on Toleration*

1690   Locke, *An Essay Concerning Human Understanding*

1692   Sir Richard Temple, *Miscellenea*

1693   Rymer, *A Short View of Tragedy*

1695   Locke, *The Reasonableness of Christianity*; Archbishop Tillotson (d.1694), *Works*

1696   John Aubrey, *Miscellanies*; Richard Baxter (d.1691) *Reliquiae Baxterianae*; John Toland, *Christianity not Mysterious*

1697   William Dampier, *Voyages*

1698   Jeremy Collier, *A Short View of the Immorality and Profanity of the Stage*

1701   John Dennis, *The Advancement and Reformation of Modern Poetry*

1703   Lord Clarendon (d.1674), *The History of the Rebellion and the Civil Wars*

cluding Wren, Boyle, Hooke, Locke and Newton. Its secretary Thomas Sprat, writing in *History of the Royal Society*, wished to make language fit for science:

Of all the Studies of Men, nothing may be sooner obtain'd than this vicious Abundance of Phrase, this Trick of Metaphor, this Volubility of Tongue, which makes so great a Noise in the World … They [the Royal Society] have therefore been more rigorous in putting in Execution the only Remedy, that can be found for this Extravagance; and that has been a constant Resolution, to reject all the Amplifications, Digressions, and Swellings of Style; to return back to the primitive purity and shortness, when Men deliver'd so many Things, almost in an equal number of Words. They have exacted from all their Members, a close, naked, natural way of Speaking; positive expressions, clear Senses; a native Easiness; bringing all things as near the mathematical Plainness as they can; and preferring the Language of Artizans, Country-Men, and Merchants, before that of Wits, or Scholars.

This is propaganda: the Society's royal patron much preferred the language of Wits. Nor did Sprat cure all the members of metaphor, although such ideals may have helped in the clarification of prose. His puritan suspicion of figurative language was taken to a logical extreme in John Wilkins's *Philosophical Language*, satirized in Jonathan Swift's Academy of Projectors in *Gulliver's Travels* (1726), where the projectors, instead of using words to represent things, carry the things themselves.

As the titles in the chronology indicate, the Restoration ushered in an age of reasonableness. The Society was social as well as scientific, beginning in informal meetings of Oxford savants and writers, not all of whom had the scientific interests of Abraham Cowley. It was an early example of a club, meeting to discuss things of interest. Talk, Sprat's 'natural way of speaking', informs Restoration prose, allowing for difference but inviting agreement. The presumption that language is for civil exchange made for reasonableness. Civilization and urbanity spread from the city and the Court to the professions and the gentry. Women begin to make a substantial contribution to writing. But this civilization excluded middle-class dissenters, and the Society had few 'Artizan' members.

There is much pleasurable minor prose: Izaak Walton's *Lives*; the diaries of Samuel Pepys and John Evelyn; the *Memoirs of Colonel Hutchinson* by his daughter Lucy; the account of the assassination of Buckingham in John Aubrey's *Brief Lives*. Dorothy Osborne began a letter to her future husband William Temple: 'Sir, If to know I wish you with me pleases you, 'tis a satisfaction you may always have, for I do it perpetually.'

Another new form was the 'character', a brief biography. An example is Lord Shaftesbury's Character of Henry Hastings, 'the copy of our nobility in ancient days in hunting and not warlike times':

he was low, very strong and very active, of a reddish flaxen hair, his clothes always green cloth, and never all worth when new five pounds … Not a woman in all his walks of the degree of a yeoman's wife or under, and under the age of forty, but it was extremely her fault if he were not intimately acquainted with her … The upper part of [the parlour] had … a desk, on the one side of which was a church Bible, on the other the Book of Martyrs; on the tables were hawks' hoods, bells, and such like, two or three old green hats with their crowns thrust in so as to hold ten or a dozen eggs, which were of a pheasant kind of poultry he took much care of and fed himself; tables, dice, cards and boxes were not wanting. In the hole of the desk were store of tobacco-pipes that had been used. One side of this end of the room was the door of a closet, wherein stood the strong beer and wine, which never came thence but in single glasses, that being the rule of the house exactly observed, for he never exceeded in drink or permitted it. On the other side was a door into an old chapel not used for devotion; the pulpit, as the safest place, was never wanting of a cold chine of beef, pasty of venison, gammon of bacon, or great apple-pie, with thick crust extremely baked ... He lived to a hundred, never lost his eyesight, but always wrote and read without spectacles, and got to horse without help. Until past fourscore he rode to the death of a stag as well as any.

## John Locke

**John Locke** (1632–1704) was a key figure in British cultural history. An Oxford academic, he became physician to Lord Shaftesbury, moved to Holland in the Monmouth crisis and returned with William of Orange. Publishing after 1689, he formulated an empirical philosophy which derived knowledge from experience and a theory of government as a contract between governor and the governed.

He preferred to derive Christianity from reason rather than from revelation, yet exempted Catholics from his advocacy of religious toleration. His *Essay concerning Human Understanding* held that at birth the human mind was 'a white Paper, void of all Characters, without any Ideas': a blank written upon by experience. Knowledge comes from the reason reflecting upon sense-impressions, and monitoring the association of ideas. This epistemology and psychology, drawing on the mechanics and optics of Sir Isaac Newton, became part of the common sense of the 18th century.

## Women writers

Among women writers of the 17th century not yet acknowledged are the poets Anne Bradstreet (*c.*1612–72) and Katherine Philips, 'the matchless Orinda' (1631–64); Anne Killigrew (1660–85) and Anne, Lady Winchilsea (1661–1720). Mary Astell (1666–1731) and Delarivière Manley (1663–1724) wrote variously and at length, as

Anne Bracegirdle, one of the first actresses on the Restoration stage, playing the Indian Queen in Aphra Behn's *The Widow Ranter* (1689). A mezzotint in the Victoria and Albert Theatre Museum, London.

did Aphra Behn (1640–89), thrown into authorship by the early death of her Dutch husband. The merry banter of Behn's sex comedies gave scandal, though not to other playwrights, with whom she was on good terms, nor to Nell Gwynn, to whom she dedicated *The Feign'd Curtezans*. She shows the other side of libertinism, notably in *The Rover*, where Angellica Bianca, a 'famous courtesan', truly loves but experiences the disappointments of free love. Behn's adventures as a colonist in Surinam, a royal spy in Antwerp, and a woman of the Restoration theatre also got into her fiction. Her 'novel', *Oroonoko, or the History of the Royal Slave*, is an ideological romance: a noble African prince cruelly enslaved by colonists is redeemed by the love of 'the brave, the beautiful and the constant Imoinda'.

# William Congreve

The literary century closed with Congreve's comedy *The Way of the World*, a classic intrigue of manners, love, money and marriage. **William Congreve** (1670–1729) polishes the mirror of society to a new brilliance. Mirabell woos Millamant, neice of the widow Lady Wishfort, while being gallant to the aunt. This the aunt is kindly told by Mrs Marwood, whose advances Mirabell has rejected. Lady Wishfort now hates Mirabell 'worse than a quaker hates a parrot', and will disinherit Millamant if she marries him. A plot by Mrs Marwood and Fainall, Lady Wishfort's son-in-law, to get the inheritance, is foiled by an entertaining counterplot involving servants, a country cousin ('rustick, ruder than Gothick'), and a late legal surprise. Love and virtue outwit villainy, though wit shines more than virtue. In this double-dealing world, integrity (when in love) has to assume the mask of frivolity. The audience need the clues in the characters' names, yet the lovers' names are unclear. How does Millamant treat her 'thousand lovers'? What besides wit is 'admirable' in Mirabell?

In the Proviso scene, the lovers negotiate the rules of their marriage:

MILLAMANT: … I won't be called names after I'm married; positively I won't be called names.
MIRABELL: Names!
MILLAMANT: Ay, as wife, spouse, my dear, joy, jewel, love, sweetheart, and the rest of that nauseous cant, in which men and their wives are so fulsomly familiar – I shall never bear that – Good Mirabell, don't let us be familiar or fond, nor kiss before folks … Let us never visit together, nor go to a play together, but let us be very strange and well bred: let us be as strange as if we had been married a great while; and as well bred as if we were not married at all.
MIRABELL: Have you any more conditions to offer? Hitherto your demands are pretty reasonable.

Yet the sophisticated Millamant soon confesses to Mrs Fainall: 'If Mirabell should not make a good husband, I am a lost thing; for I find I love him violently.' The mask of wit slips to reveal true love.

Ushering Mrs Marwood into her closet to overhear a conversation, Lady Wishfort says: 'There are books over the chimney – Quarles and Pryn, and *Short View of the Stage*, with Bunyan's works to entertain you.' Quarles was a quaint old moralizer; Prynne an enemy of stage plays; Bunyan died in 1688. Congreve tries thus to laugh off the recent attack on himself, among others, by Jeremy Collier in *A Short View of the Immorality and Profaneness of the English Stage* (1698). Collier was not a Puritan but a principled Anglican clergyman who refused to swear the oath to William and Mary.

The new St Paul's, built to replace Old St Paul's (see page 133), the Cathedral of the City of London. Begun in 1675, completed in 1711. The architect, Sir Christopher Wren, had wanted a dome on a central drum, but had to incorporate a traditional long 'Gothic' nave.

*The Way of the World* was not a hit, and Congreve wrote no more plays. George Farquhar stuck to the formula, but Collier's distaste was prophetic. Alexander Pope (1688–1744), whose own wit could be risqué, was soon to disapprove of the kind of Restoration comedy in which 'obscenity was wit'.

# Further reading

Corns, T. N. (ed.) *The Cambridge Companion to English Poetry, Donne to Marvell* (Cambridge: Cambridge University Press, 1993).

Danielson, D. (ed.) *The Cambridge Companion to John Milton* (Cambridge: Cambridge University Press, 1999).

Parry, G. *The Seventeenth Century: The Intellectual and Cultural Context of English Literature, 1603–1700* (Harlow: Longman, 1989).

# Augustan and Romantic

# Augustan Literature: to 1790

# CHAPTER 6

## Overview

After the brilliant achievements of Pope, literary civilization broadened to include more of the middle class and of women. The aristocratic patron gave way to the bookseller. After mid-century, the Augustan 'sense' of Swift, Pope and Johnson was increasingly supplemented by Sensibility, with 'Ossian', Gray and Walpole. The novel flourished in the 1740s, with Richardson, Fielding and Sterne. The latter part of the century saw major achievements in non-fictional prose, with Johnson, Gibbon and Boswell, a brief revival of drama (Goldsmith, Sheridan), and a retreat of poetry into privacy and eccentricity.

## Contents

## The eighteenth century

The course of the 18th century presents a broad contrast to the disruption and change of the 17th. A desire for rational agreement, and an increasing confidence, mark literary culture for a century after 1688. There were cross-currents, exclusions and developments: the novel arrived in the 1740s, and Augustanism was increasingly in dialogue with other modes.

England and her empire within the British Isles prospered by improvements in agriculture and industry, and by trade with her overseas empire, at first commercial, then territorial. In 1740 the Scottish poet James Thomson exhorted Britannia to rule, and especially to 'rule the waves'. Having contained Louis XIV in Europe and eclipsed Holland, Britannia defeated France in India and North America, and dominated the far South Pacific. With more leisure at home, literature gained a reading public, and through the book trade, periodicals, salons and libraries reached beyond the Church, the gentry and the professions, and beyond London, Dublin and Edinburgh. Yet most of the population – nine million, by the end of the century – could not read.

Much of the religion of a rational Church of England settled into duties, social and private, though there was the evangelical revival known as Methodism. Dissenters and Catholics had civil disabilities, but were tolerated: Dissenters with condescension, Catholics with mistrust. Toleration was extended to Jews (expelled from England in 1290) and atheists.

## Hanoverian England

(1714–1830) George I, James I's grandson, was Elector of the German state of Hanover, and he and his successors, George II, III and IV of England, are Hanoverians. So were their successors, William IV and Victoria, but 'Hanoverian England' usually refers to the reigns of the four Georges.

**Enlightenment** (German: *Aufklärung*): a period of intellectual progress in the 18th century, when it was hoped that Reason would clear away the superstition of darker ages.

### Public events of the time of Pope

| | |
|---|---|
| 1702 | William dies. Anne reigns (to 1714). |
| 1704 | Marlborough defeats the French and the Bavarians at Blenheim. |
| 1706 | Marlborough defeats Louis XIV at Ramillies. |
| 1707 | Union of the Scottish Parliament with that of England at Westminster. |
| 1710 | Fall of the Whigs. Christopher Wren's St Paul's Cathedral completed. Act of Copyright. |
| 1713 | Treaty of Utrecht ends the War of Spanish Succession. British gains. |
| 1714 | Anne dies. The **Hanoverian succession**: George I reigns (to 1727). |
| 1715 | Fall of the Tories. Jacobite rising defeated. |
| 1721 | Walpole Chancellor of the Exchequer and First Lord of the Treasury (to 1742). |
| 1727 | George I dies. George II reigns (to 1760). |
| 1730 | Methodist Society is begun in Oxford. |
| 1734 | Lloyd's List (of shipping) begins. |
| 1743 | War of Austrian Succession: George II defeats the French at Dettingen. |
| 1745 | Jacobite army reaches Derby, then withdraws. |

Periodicals carried literary essays on civilized neutral topics, including literature itself. The status of literature is shown also by the sums subscribed for editions of Prior and Pope, and the authority accorded to Addison, Chesterfield, Burke, Gibbon and Johnson. Johnson's *Dictionary* was a monument to English letters, as were his edition of Shakespeare and his *Lives of the English Poets* – in sixty-eight quarto volumes. There were literary crazes, for Sterne's *Tristram Shandy*, Macpherson's 'Ossian', and Gothic fiction. The neo-classicism prevailing until mid-century held that Art should imitate Nature or reality; but the success of literature became such that Nature began to imitate Art. Country estates were designed to look 'natural' or pleasingly wild; owners put up picturesque hermitages and ruins in which to experience literary feelings.

Much 18th-century literature has a polite or aristocratic tone, but its authors were largely middle-class, as were its readers. The art of letters had social prestige, and poets found patrons among the nobility, who also wrote. Congreve, Prior and Addison rose high in society, and so, despite his disadvantages, did Pope: 'Above a patron, though I condescend/Sometimes to call a minister my friend'. The booksellers who commissioned Johnson's *Lives of the Poets* asked him to include several noblemen alongside Milton, Dryden, Swift and Pope. Fiction was less polite and more commercial than poetry. In Johnson's *Dictionary* the prose writer most cited is Samuel Richardson, a joiner's son who became a printer and finally a novelist. Johnson himself was a bookseller's son. The pioneer realist, Daniel Defoe, was a hack journalist who lived by his pen. Defoe and Richardson had a concern with individual consciousness, which evolved out of the Protestant anxiety about personal salvation, found in John Bunyan. Defoe and Richardson were Dissenters. Henry Fielding, an Anglican, scorned Richardson's concern with inwardness and attacked social abuses.

## The Enlightenment

**The Enlightenment** is a name given by historians of ideas to a phase succeeding the Renaissance and followed (though not ended) by Romanticism. The Enlightenment believed in the universal authority of Reason, and in its ability to understand and explain, as in Pope's line: 'God said, *Let Newton be*, and all was light.' It favoured toleration and moderation in religion, and was hopeful about the rational perfectibility of man. Among English writers, scepticism rarely reached to the Deism of anticlericals such as the Frenchman Voltaire and the virtual atheism of the Scot David Hume: 'Enlightenment' is a term which fits France and Scotland better than England. Edward Gibbon (1737–94) is one of the few English writers who are wholly of the Enlightenment, though by the time of the French Revolution (1789) the term fits political thinkers such as William Godwin and Tom Paine, and writers such as Maria Edgeworth. When Horace Walpole, himself indifferent to religion, went to France in 1765, he found its rational godlessness uncomfortable. Early in the century, the third Earl of Shaftesbury advocated enlightened self-interest, holding that multiple self-interest would work together to the good – a benign view scorned by Jonathan Swift (1667–1745), for whom Christianity was a necessary curb to human unreason. The realist Bernard de Mandeville (1670–1733) held that self-interest leads to competition, not co-operation.

## Literature at the time of Pope

1704  Isaac Newton, *Optics.*

1705  (The playwright Sir John Vanburgh designs Blenheim Palace for the Duke of Marlborough.)

1706  George Farquhar, *The Recruiting Officer.*

1707  Farquhar, *The Beaux' Stratagem*; Isaac Watts, *Hymns.*

1708  3rd Earl of Shaftesbury, *Letter concerning Enthusiasm.*

1709  Sir Richard Steele, *The Tatler*; Berkeley, *A New Theory of Vision*; Prior *Poems*; Nicholas Rowe (ed.), *The Works of Mr William Shakespeare* (6 volumes to 1710).

1710  Bishop Berkeley, *Treatise on the Principles of Human Knowledge*; Shaftesbury, *Advice to an Author.*

1711  Joseph Addison, *The Spectator*; Shaftesbury, *Characteristics.*

1713  Addison, *Cato.*

1714  John Gay, *The Shepherd's Week*; Bernard de Mandeville, *Fable of the Bees.*

1715  (Handel, *Water Music*.)

1716  Gay, *Trivia* and *Three Hours after Marriage* (Hawksmoor designs St Mary Woolnoth, London).

1719  Daniel Defoe, *Robinson Crusoe.*

1722  Thomas Parnell (d.1718), *Poems*; Daniel Defoe, *Moll Flanders.*

1726  James Thomson, *Winter*; Gay, *Fables.*

1728  John Law, *A Serious Call to a Devout and Holy Life*; Gay, *The Beggar's Opera*; Ephraim Chambers, *Cyclopaedia.*

1729  Thomson, *Britannia.*

1730  Thomson, *The Seasons*; Henry Fielding, *Tom Thumb.*

1731  *The Gentleman's Magazine.*

1732  *The London Magazine.*

1735  Samuel Johnson, *A Voyage to Abyssinia* (Hogarth, *A Rake's Progress*).

1736  Bishop Butler, *The Analogy of Religion.*

1737  William Shenstone, *Poems*; John Wesley, *Poems and Hymns*; Lady Mary Wortley Montagu, *The Nonsense of Common-Sense.*

1738  Johnson, *London.*

1739  John and Charles Wesley, *Hymns and Sacred Poems*; David Hume, *A Treatise of Human Nature*

1740  Samuel Richardson, *Pamela.*

1742  (Handel, *Messiah*; Hogarth, *Marriage à la Mode*.)

### Sense and Sensibility

Sense is a better watchword for the English 18th century than Reason. Sense embraces practical reason, the ability to tell true from false, common sense (from Lat. *communis sententia*, the common opinion). It was at first related rather than opposed to Sensibility, a capacity for moral feeling. When Sensibility became more aesthetic and sentimental, it came to be contrasted with sense, as in the title of Jane Austen's novel. Sense, finally, recalls Locke's influential account of the mind, in which reliable knowledge of the real comes from sense-impressions.

## Alexander Pope and 18th-century civilization

The day of Augustanism coincides with the days of Alexander Pope (1688–1744), when Addison and Swift also flourished – as did the unAugustan Defoe. The Augustan temper did not thereafter rule the roost, but characterizes the most accomplished work of the century: *Gulliver's Travels, Dunciad IV*, Gray's *Elegy* and the judgements of Johnson. Joseph Addison was a poet and tragedian, but his legacy is *The Spectator*, a daily paper which he edited and co-wrote with Sir Richard Steele, in succession to Steele's *The Tatler* (1709). Steele's paper amused, *The Spectator* educated entertainingly.

## Joseph Addison

After the excesses of faction and enthusiasm, John Locke, Isaac Newton, Christopher Wren and others had shown what human intelligence could do. Joseph Addison (1672–1719) relayed these achievements to the new middle class in a prose which Johnson thought 'the model of the middle style'. *The Spectator* sold an unprecedented ten thousand copies of each issue; its wit was edifying, unlike that of the Restoration; Addison's essays were taken as a model for more than a century.

In issue No. 1 (Thursday, March 1, 1711), the Spectator introduces himself:

I find, that I ... was always a Favourite of my School-master, who used to say, *that my Parts were solid and would wear well*. I had not been long at the University, before I distinguished my self by a most profound Silence: For during the Space of eight Years, except in the publick Exercises of the College, I scarce uttered the quantity of an hundred words; and indeed do not remember that I ever spoke three Sentences together in my whole Life. Whilst I was in this Learned Body I applied myself with so much Diligence to my Studies, that there are very few celebrated Books, either in the Learned or the Modern Tongues, which I am not acquainted with ....

This know-all then travels to Egypt to 'take the Measure of a Pyramid; and as soon as I had set myself right in that Particular, returned to my Native Country with great Satisfaction'. He is also an observer of men:

I have passed my latter Years in this City, where I am frequently seen in most Publick Places, tho' there are not above half a dozen of my select Friends that know me; of whom my next Papers shall give a more particular Account. There is no place of general Resort, wherein I do not often make my appearance; sometimes I am seen thrusting my Head into a Round of Politicians at *Will's*, and listning with great Attention to the Narratives that are made in those little Circular Audiences. Sometimes I smoak a Pipe at *Child's*; and whilst I seem attentive to nothing but the Post-Man, over-hear the Conversation of every Table in the Room ... In short, wherever I see a Cluster of People I always mix with them, though I never open my Lips but in my own Club.

The Club exists to set forth 'such Papers as may contribute to the Advancement of the Public Weal'. Its members are Sir Roger de Coverley, Sir Andrew Freeport, Captain Sentry and Will Honeycomb – country, city, army and society; the Church is not represented. The Spectator is the Club's critic: 'His Taste of Books is a little too just for the Age he lives in; he has read all, but approves of very few.' Addison maintains this mock-pomp throughout.

Instruction comes breezily from Steele: 'I do not doubt but *England* is at present as polite a Nation as any in the World; but any Man who thinks can easily see, that the Affectation of being Gay and in Fashion has very near eaten up our good Sense and our Religion.' Good Sense and Religion are interchangeable. Addison warned that 'The Mind that lies fallow but a single Day, sprouts up in Follies that are only to be killed by a constant and assiduous Culture.' This is the civil version of 'Satan finds some mischief still/For idle hands to do' (Isaac Watts, 'Against Idleness and Mischief').

Addison continues (in No. 10) to weed out folly and cultivate the mind:

It was said of *Socrates*, that he brought Philosophy down from Heaven, to inhabit among Men; and I shall be ambitious to have it said of me, that I have brought Philosophy out of Closets and Libraries, Schools and Colleges, to dwell in Clubs and Assemblies, at Tea-Tables and in Coffee-Houses. I would therefore in a very particular Manner recommend these my Speculations to all well regulated Families, that set apart an Hour in every Morning for Tea and Bread and Butter; and would earnestly advise them for their Good to order this Paper to be punctually served up, and to be looked upon as Part of the Tea Equipage.

The gentleman-Socrates offers empty-headed men sound material for conversation. He then turns to the Tea Equipage.

But there are none to whom this Paper will be more useful, than to the Female World. I have often thought there has not been sufficient Pains taken in finding out proper Employments and Diversions for the Fair ones. Their Amusements seem contrived for them rather as they are Women, than as they are reasonable Creatures; and are more adapted to the Sex than to the Species.

This combination of raillery, analysis and seriousness is Augustan. The premise is that the human is a rational animal or (in Christian terms) a reasonable creature. What is proposed with a smile is serious: assiduous daily culture will root out folly and vice from the well-regulated family, one that takes *The Spectator*. It was for the family, not just the father, that Addison wrote papers on Milton and the ballad. Pope was to remark that 'our wives read Milton, and our daughters plays'. The family were to insist that father took them to Bath, the new upper-middle-class spa.

Addison's classical *Cato* (1713) was popular, but such tragedy expressed a ruling-class interest in principle and nobility. Johnson described *Cato* as 'rather a poem in dialogue than a drama'. His own youthful *Irene* (1736) was a flop. No 18th-century tragedy has lasted. John Home's romantic *Douglas* (1756), a success in Edinburgh, is now chiefly remembered as a curiosity, and for the shout of a member of the audience: 'Whaur's your Wullie Shakespeare noo?' Neo-classical ideals did a lot for satire, translation, prose and criticism in England, but not for tragedy.

# Jonathan Swift

The smooth rise of Addison was interrupted only when the Whigs were out, which took him briefly into journalism (and so into this book). Defoe, Swift and Pope

**An establishment career**
Joseph Addison, b.1672, son of the Dean of Lichfield. Went from the Cathedral Close to Charterhouse, to Oxford, to a fellowship at Magdalen College, to a European tour. Dryden praised his Latin poems. Wrote *Dialogues on the Usefulness of Ancient Medals*, and a verse tribute to the victory at Blenheim. Under-Secretary of State, MP, fell with the Whigs in 1711, turned to journalism and play-writing, returned with the Whigs in 1715, Chief Secretary for Ireland, married the Countess of Warwick, retired with a pension of £1500, buried Westminster Abbey, 1719.

## Jonathan Swift (1667–1745)

Chief works:

1704   *The Battle of the Books; A Tale of a Tub*

1708   *The Bickerstaff Papers*

1710   *The Examiner* (ed.); *Meditations on a Broomstick*

1711   *An Argument against Abolishing Christianity; The Conduct of the Allies*

1717   *A Proposal for Correcting the English Language*

1724   *Drapier's Letters*

1726   *Gulliver's Travels*

1728   *A Short View of the State of Ireland*

1729   *A Modest Proposal*

1738   *Conversation*

1739   *Verses on the Death of Dr Swift*

did not have his advantages. Defoe (b.1660) is taken later as a novelist; he was a Dissenter, who wrote over 560 books, pamphlets and journals. Pope (b.1688), an invalid, a Catholic, and largely self-educated, also lived by the pen. **Jonathan Swift** (1667–1745), born of English parents in Dublin after his father's death, had a career as frustrating as Addison's was successful.

Educated alongside William Congreve at Kilkenny and at Trinity College, Dublin, Swift came to England and was secretary to Sir William Temple, statesman, author and proponent of naturalness in garden design. Lacking preferment, Swift was ordained in Ireland, but visited London from Dublin. He left the Whigs over their failure to support the Church against Dissent. In 1713 he became Dean of Dublin's St Patrick's Cathedral – not, as he would have preferred, a bishop in England. He lived in Dublin in indignant opposition to the Whig government in London, defending Ireland and the (Anglican) Church. He gave one-third of his income to the – usually Catholic – poor.

In 1704 Swift held up to satirical review the claims of ancient and modern authors in *The Battle of the Books*, and the claims of Rome, Canterbury, Geneva and the sects in the more complex *A Tale of a Tub*. His usually anonymous controversial works could be straightforward, as in the *Drapier's Letters*, which successfully prevented an English currency fraud in Ireland. But his lasting works argue from an absurd premise, as in *An Argument to Prove that the Abolishing of Christianity in England may, as things now stand, be attended with some inconveniences, and perhaps not produce those many good effects proposed thereby.* Swift believed that 'we need religion as we need our dinner, wickedness makes Christianity indispensable and there's an end of it.' But here he writes from a different point of view:

The system of the Gospel, after the fate of other systems, is generally antiquated and exploded; and the mass or body of the common people, among whom it seems to have had its latest credit, are now grown as much ashamed of it as their betters ... I hope no reader imagines me so weak to stand up in the defence of real Christianity, such as used in primitive times (if we may believe the authors of those ages) to have an influence upon men's belief and actions ... Every candid reader will easily understand my discourse to be intended only in defence of nominal Christianity, the other having been for some time wholly laid aside by general consent as utterly inconsistent with all other present schemes of wealth and power.

Likewise, *A Modest Proposal, for preventing the children of poor people in Ireland from being a burden to their parents or country, and for making them beneficial to the public* proposes that surplus children be eaten.

I have been assured by a very knowing American of my acquaintance in London, that a young healthy child well nursed is at a year old a most delicious, nourishing, and wholesome food, whether stewed, roasted, baked, or boiled; and I make no doubt that it will equally serve in a fricassee or a ragout. I do therefore humbly offer it to public consideration that of the hundred and twenty thousand children, already computed, twenty thousand may be reserved for breed, whereof only one fourth part to be males. … That the remaining hundred thousand may at a year old be offered in sale to the persons of quality and fortune throughout the kingdom, always advising the mother to let them suck plentifully in the last month, so as to render them plump and fat for a good table. A child will make two dishes at an entertainment for friends; and when the family dines alone, the fore or hind quarter will make a reasonable dish, and seasoned with a little pepper or salt will be very good boiled on the fourth day, especially in winter.

After enumerating the moral as well as economic advantages of his scheme, Swift ends disinterestedly: 'I have no children by which I can propose to get a single penny; the youngest being nine years old, and my wife past childbearing.' The proposal is prophetic of the 19th-century economist who, on hearing of the number who had died in the Irish Potato Famine, remarked sadly that it was not enough.

Swift exposes the inhumanity of emerging forms of rational simplification by simplifying them even further. His *Modest Proposal* solves a human problem by an economic calculus which ignores human love and treats the poor as cattle. *Gulliver's Travels* (1726) also takes new perspectives to logical conclusions. Captain Gulliver records his voyages to the lands of the tiny people, of the giants, of experimental scientists and of horses. Gulliver expects the little people of Lilliput to be delicate and the giants of Brobdignag to be gross; they are not. These first two voyages are often retold for children; the simply-told wonder-tale delights both readers who guess at Swift's purposes and readers who don't. *Gulliver* draws on the *True History* of Lucian of Samosata (*c.*125–200), an account of a voyage to the moon, straight-faced but entirely untrue. Gulliver refers to 'Cousin Dampier' (William Dampier's *Voyage round the World* and *Voyage to New Holland* were much read), and gives Lilliput a map-reference, placing it in New Holland (that is, Australia).

Gulliver is, like Defoe's Robinson Crusoe, one of the practical self-reliant seamen through whom Britannia had begun to rule the waves. As with Crusoe, the reader can identify with the hero, whose common sense gets him through his adventures. Our identification with the 'I' who tells the story is Swift's secret weapon. Late in Book II, Gulliver boasts of the triumphs of British civilization to the king of Brobdignag, who has treated him kindly. The king says that the advances Gulliver has recounted make him think of his countrymen as 'the most pernicious race of little odious vermin that nature ever suffered to crawl upon the face of the earth'. Shocked, Gulliver tries to impress him with the invention of gunpowder and the wonderful effects of artillery.

The King was struck with horror at the description I had given of those terrible engines, and the proposal I had made. He was amazed how so impotent and grovelling an insect as I (these were his expressions) could entertain such inhuman ideas, and in so familiar a manner as to appear wholly unmoved at all by the scenes of blood and desolation, which I had painted as the common effects of those destructive machines, whereof, he said, some evil genius, enemy to mankind, must have been the first contriver. As for himself, he protested, that although few things delighted him so much as new discoveries in art or in nature, yet he would rather lose half his kingdom than be privy to such a secret, which he commanded me, as I valued my life, never to mention any more. A strange effect of narrow principles and short views!

Greater surprises await Gulliver in Book IV in the land of the Houyhnhnms, noble horses endowed with reason. These humane enlightened creatures rule over the Yahoos, a savage man-like race remarkable for lust, greed and filth. The Houyhnhnms have no word for lying, and are shocked by Gulliver's accounts of civilization. He adopts the ways of these equine philosophers, but they expel him. Picked up by a Portuguese ship, he returns to London, but he so recoils from the Yahoo-like smell of humans that he prefers the stable to the marital home.

We find that we have been rationally tricked into disowning our own natures: like Gulli-ver, we have been truly gullible ('gull': fool). In each of the books Swift alters one dimension of life, beginning with magnitude. In Book 3 he removes death: the Struldbruggs are granted immortality – but without youth. As they age, they grow less and less happy. In Book 4 he reverses the traditional image of reason guiding the body as a man rides a horse. Should we prefer the society of rational horses to stinking Yahoos?

Swift defined Man not as rational animal but as an animal *capable* of reason. He had a keen sense of our capacity for self-delusion, folly and vice. His telescope gives perspectives, at first comic, then horrific, which confront us with unpleasant facets of human life, silently recommending proportion, humility and fellow-feeling. Swift misleads the complacent reader into the same traps as Gulliver. His *reductio ad absurdum* intensifies the paradoxes of existence, offending humanists from Johnson to Macaulay to F. R. Leavis. His is the intellectual ferocity of the 17th century, of Rochefoucauld or Pascal, not the cheerful brutality of the 18th century. He enjoyed spoiling men's romantic delusions about women, as in his line 'Celia, Celia, Celia sh—s'. His poems to Stella show that he was no misogynist. Those who have suggested that he was misanthropic have misunderstood his irony; he did not *believe* in eating children. But he was anti-romantic, hating false hearts and false ideals. A passionate English churchman, he showed integrity, courage and cunning in defending Catholic Ireland against English exploitation.

Swift was also very funny. In his Academy of Projectors, for instance, a scientist tries to extract moonbeams out of cucumbers. And his *Verses on the Death of Dr Swift* is a masterpiece of comic realism:

> … Here shift the scene, to represent
> How those I love, my death lament.
> Poor Pope will grieve a month; and Gay
> A week, and Arbuthnot a day.
> St John himself will scarce forbear          Bolingbroke
> To bite his pen, and drop a tear.
> The rest will give a shrug, and cry
> 'I'm sorry, but we all must die.' …
> My female friends, whose tender hearts
> Have better learned to play their parts,
> Receive the news in doleful dumps,
> 'The Dean is dead (and what is trumps?)          Dean Swift
> The Lord have mercy on his soul.
> (Ladies, I'll venture for the vole.)          in cards, a strong bid
> Six deans, they say must bear the pall.

> (I wish I knew what king to call.)  (in cards)
> "Madam, your husband will attend
> The funeral of so good a friend?" …
> He loved the Dean. (I lead a heart.)
> But dearest Friends, they say, must part.
> His time was come, he ran his race;
> We hope he's in a better place.'
> Why do we grieve that friends should die?
> No loss more easy to supply.
> One year is past; a different scene;
> No further mention of the Dean;
> Who now, alas, no more is missed
> Than if he never did exist.

Swift ends the poem with a defence of his record.

# Alexander Pope

Self-defence also concludes the retrospective *Epistle to Dr Arbuthnot* of **Alexander Pope** (1688–1744). Pope had found that 'the life of a wit is a warfare on earth'. He had achieved fame at a precocious age, and envious enemies attacked him on personal grounds. Pope is the first professional non-dramatic poet in English, dedicating his life to the art of poetry, and winning an unprecedented position for it. He lived by, as well as for, his art – a tribute both to its new status and to his determination.

Pope was the son of a cloth merchant in the City. When a law was passed forbidding Catholics to own a house within ten miles of London, the Popes moved, settling in Windsor Forest, west of London. The boy attended schools, but tuberculosis of the bone at the age of 12 kept him at home, reading, writing and drawing; and kept him small. The portrait painter Joshua Reynolds described Pope late in life as 'about four feet six high; very humpbacked and deformed'. Catholics (unlike Dissenters) could not go to university, vote or have a public position, and were taxed and penalized in other ways – they were not, for example, allowed to keep a horse worth £10.

By cultivating his talent, Pope overcame these disadvantages. At 12 he wrote a version of a poem by the Roman poet Horace. It begins:

> Happy the man whose wish and care
>     A few paternal acres bound,
> Content to breathe his native air,
>             In his own ground.

And ends:

> Thus let me live, unseen, unknown;
>     Thus unlamented let me die;
> Steal from the world, and not a stone
>         Tell where I lie.

The ease of phrase and movement here justify Pope's claim that, like Horace, he 'lisped in numbers [verse], for the numbers came.'

Oliver Goldsmith's *Account of the Augustan Age in England* (1759) placed this age in Queen Anne's reign, when parallels were drawn with arts and letters under Augustus. The order of Virgil's poems – pastoral in youth, then didactic, then epic –

## Alexander Pope (1688–1744)

| | |
|---|---|
| 1709 | *Pastorals* |
| 1711 | *An Essay on Criticism* |
| 1712 | *The Rape of the Lock* (in two Cantos) |
| 1713 | *Windsor Forest* |
| 1715 | *The Iliad* (trans.) |
| 1719 | *Verses to Lady Mary Wortley Montagu* |
| 1726 | *The Works of Shakespeare* (ed.); *The Odyssey* (trans.) |
| 1728 | *The Dunciad* |
| 1733 | *Essay on Man* |
| 1735 | *Epistle to Arbuthnot* |
| 1734– | Horatian translations, imitations, satires, *Moral Epistles* |

had been followed by Spenser and Milton. Dryden had taken the more social path of another Augustan poet, Horace, writing epistles, elegies, and occasional poems; he then translated Virgil. Pope wrote pastorals, then a didactic *Essay on Criticism* (an update of Horace's *Ars Poetica*); a mock-epic in *The Rape of the Lock*; translations of Homer's epics; then moral essays and Horatian epistles; and the anti-epic *Dunciad*. Pope had the humanist's faith in the educative role of poetry, and prized neo-classical clarity, concision and elegance. He used the profession of literature to exemplify and defend values which made humanity saner, finer and more complete. He never stopped: editing Shakespeare, annotating the *Dunciad*, and publishing a polished version of his own letters.

Pope refined every couplet, for

> True ease in writing comes from art, not chance,
> As those move easiest who have learned to dance.
> 'Tis not enough no harshness gives offence,
> The sound must seem an echo to the sense.
>
> *An Essay on Criticism*

Style matters, for the purpose of art is to show reality in so clear a light that its truth comes home:

> True wit is Nature to advantage dressed
> What oft was thought but ne'er so well expressed.

'Wit' here means poetic insight, not the cleverness which makes Pope so quotable. His polish may suggest that he was unoriginal. But his *Pastorals* and *Windsor Forest* introduced a new and picturesque landscape poetry, paving the way for the Romantic poetry of nature. In the 1800 Preface to the *Lyrical Ballads*, Wordsworth attacked the artificial diction of Pope, claiming that the poet 'is a man speaking to men'. But poets, strictly speaking, are writers who have learned to make written words speak.

Matthew Arnold said that Dryden and Pope were classics not of our poetry but of our prose. Pope's verse has the clarity and judgement of prose – in his *Essays* on *Criticism* and on *Man*, and in his *Moral Essays*. But his *Elegy to the Memory of an Unfortunate Lady* and *Eloisa to Abelard* are emotional, and his Epistles, like that *To Miss Blount, on her Leaving the Town, after the Coronation* (of George I), have a fine modulation of feeling and a poet's apprehension of particulars.

This little poem is a key to Pope's work. Teresa Blount and her sister Martha were close friends of Pope. Writing to her in the country, he begins with a Roman simile: 'As some fond virgin, whom her mother's care …'. This promises the dutiful decorum which gave 18th-century verse a bad name, but the second line of the couplet – 'Drags from the town to wholesome country air' – wrong-foots the reader. We feel Teresa's reaction and hear the mother's words. The boredom of country life – for a girl who has been presented at Court – is given in miniature:

| | |
|---|---|
| She went, to plain-work, and to purling brooks, | needlework |
| Old-fashioned halls, dull aunts and croaking rooks: | |
| She went from opera, park, assembly, play, | |
| To morning walks, and prayers three hours a day; | |
| To part her time 'twixt reading and bohea, | a costly kind of tea |
| To muse and spill her solitary tea, | pronounced 'tay' |
| Or o'er cold coffee trifle with the spoon, | |
| Count the slow clock and dine exact at noon; | an unfashionable hour |
| Divert her eyes with pictures in the fire, | |
| Hum half a tune, tell stories to the squire; | |
| Up to her godly garret after seven, | |
| There starve and pray, for that's the way to heaven. | |

After the excitements of Town, the old familiar things are different, and worse. The admirer signs off in the last couplet: 'Vexed to be still in town, I knit my brow,/Look sour, and hum a tune – as you may now.' She wants to be in town, he wants to be with her – an instance of the Augustan theme of the vanity of human wishes. This Epistle anticipates *The Rape of the Lock*, *The Dunciad* and the *Moral Essays*.

## Translation as tradition

In his *Life of Pope*, Johnson gave much attention to Pope's translation of Homer, judging the *Iliad* 'the noblest version of poetry the world has ever seen' and 'a performance which no age or nation can pretend to equal'. Homer was the basis of classical education, both the standard author in Aristotle's *Poetics* and Virgil's model for the *Æneid*. English education was Latin-based, but better Greek had brought Homer within reach. Pope wrote of Virgil in the *Essay on Criticism* that 'Homer and Nature were, he found, the same.' This was true of Pope too, whose favourite reading as a boy was Ogilby's 1660 version of the *Iliad*. He spent his best ten years translating Homer – and earned a financial independence.

At 21 he had translated the speech in which Sarpedon encourages Glaucus into battle, arguing that the first in peace should be the first in war. The idea that heroic status entails responsibility was adapted to an 18th-century society also based on rank. Public schoolboys learned Sarpedon's speech in Greek. Pope's version is:

| | |
|---|---|
| 'Cou'd all our care elude the greedy Grave, | |
| Which claims no less the Fearful than the Brave, | |
| For Lust of Fame I shou'd not vainly dare | |
| In fighting Fields, nor urge thy Soul to War. | |
| But since, alas, ignoble Age must come, | |
| Disease, and Death's inexorable Doom; | |
| The Life which others pay, let Us bestow, | |
| And give to Fame what we to Nature owe; | |
| Brave, tho' we fall; and honour'd, if we live; | |
| Or let us Glory gain, or Glory give!' | Either |

Poet-translators from Marlowe to Shelley experienced ancient literature as modern; its relevance was what made it classic. Thus, English gentlemen can be heroes too. Given this essential continuity, the task of the translator was, as Dryden said, 'to make his author appear as charming as possibly he can, provided he maintains his character.' The chief thing was 'the spirit which animates the whole'.

Pope's *Iliad* begins:

> *Achilles'* Wrath, to *Greece* the direful spring,
> Of woes unnumber'd, heav'nly Goddess, sing!
> That Wrath which hurld to *Pluto's* gloomy reign          i.e. Hades
> The Souls of mighty Chiefs untimely slain;
> Whose limbs unbury'd on the naked shore
> Devouring dogs and hungry vultures tore:
> Since Great *Achilles* and *Atrides* strove,          *Atrides*: Agamemnon
> Such was the sov'reign doom, and such the will of Jove.

Pope maintains this impetus. John Keats says that it was 'On first looking into Chapman's Homer' that he first breathed Homer's 'pure serene'. But readers of the whole thing may find Pope's idiom more breathable. His range includes stark physical action, as shown in the elegant third couplets of each of the above quotations.

Johnson was less keen on the *Essay on Man*, a work of Deist Christian philosophy, deriving from reason not revelation. It is 'what oft was thought' after Locke had proposed that 'Our business here is not to know all things, but those which concern our conduct.' Epistle II begins:

> Know then thyself, presume not God to scan;
> The proper study of mankind is Man.

Man swings between angel and animal on the scale of creation:

> Placed on this isthmus of a middle state,
> A being darkly wise, and rudely great …
> Sole judge of truth, in endless error hurled:
> The glory, jest and riddle of the world!

Human peril makes sanity and proportion essential. Epistle I had ended rather too sedately: 'One truth is clear: Whatever is, is RIGHT.' Yet the previous line is 'And, spite of pride, in erring reason's spite'.

### *The Rape of the Lock*

**The Rape of the Lock** combines the wit of the *Essay on Criticism* with the beauty of the Pastorals. It is a high-spirited masterpiece, the most entertaining longer poem in English between Dryden and Byron. It concerns the quarrel between two families caused by Lord Petre's snipping a love-lock from the head of Arabella Fermor, the Belinda of the poem.

Pope's magnification of this storm in a coffee-cup did not, as was hoped, 'laugh together' the parties. If this is satire, its tone is not harsh by the brutal standards of that elegant age, in which the critic John Dennis had already described Pope in print as a crippled papist dwarf whose physique showed that he had the mind of a toad. Where Swift used logic and optics to maximize and minimize, Pope uses epic frames to reduce trivia to their proper proportions. Epic allusions provide much of the

**The Rape of the Lock** was published in two cantos in 1712. *Rape* (Lat. *raptus*) means 'taking away by force', 'abduction'. The abduction of Helen caused the Trojan war, and the seizure of Briseis caused the wrath of Achilles. Pope expanded the poem to five cantos in 1714, adding the 'machinery' of the Sylphs and other epic furniture.

Alexander Pope, aged about 26: a fine young gentleman in a full-bottomed wig. The pose does not allow Pope's humped back to be seen. By Charles Jarvis, *c*.1714.

poem's wit. Belinda at her morning make-up session is described as ritually worshipping her own reflection:

> First, robed in white, the nymph intent adores,
> With head uncovered, the cosmetic powers.
> A heavenly image in the glass appears;
> To that she bends, to that her eyes she rears;
> Th' inferior priestess at her altar's side            i.e. the maid
> Trembling begins the sacred rites of pride.

In Homer the priest sacrifices to *cosmic* powers, and it is the hero who arms; here, the epic is feminized. Some of the satire is simple: 'The hungry judges soon the sentence sign,/And wretches hang that jurymen may dine.' But Pope's fun usually involves zeugma (the yoking of the incongruous) and anticlimax, as in line 2 of this account of Queen Anne's Hampton Court:

> Here thou, great Anna! whom three realms obey        England, Ireland and Scotland
> Dost sometimes counsel take – and sometimes tea.
> Hither the heroes and the nymphs resort,
> To taste awhile the pleasures of a court;
> In various talk th' instructive hours they passed,
> Who gave the ball, or paid the visit last;
> One speaks the glory of the British Queen,
> And one describes a charming Indian screen;
> A third interprets motions, looks and eyes;
> At every word a reputation dies.

But social life has compensations: 'Belinda smiled, and all the world was gay.' Her dressing-table is a magic carpet:

> This casket India's glowing gems unlocks
> And all Arabia breathes from yonder box.
> The tortoise here and elephant unite,
> Transformed to combs, the speckled and the white.

British trade has squeezed the world for jewels, perfumes and combs, to make a British beauty more beautiful. The disproportion is absurd, but its results are poetic. Pope's couplets make the trivial exquisite: the coffee-table, the card-table, and the fairy 'Sylphs' who fly around Belinda:

> Transparent forms too fine for mortal sight,
> Their fluid bodies half dissolved in light.
> Loose to the wind their airy garments flew,
> Thin glittering textures of the filmy dew.

The articulation of the last line 'echoes the sense'. Pope takes pleasure in refining the precious world he ridicules. The joy of the writing makes the *Rape* lighter than Pope's later heroi-comedies.

In 1717 Pope added a moral, spoken by Clarissa. It is based on Sarpedon's speech to Glaucus (see page 183): 'How vain are all these glories, all our pains,/Unless good sense preserve what beauty gains? …'

> '… But since, alas! frail beauty must decay,
> Curled or uncurled, since locks will turn to grey,
> Since painted, or not painted, all shall fade,
> And she who scorns a man must die a maid;
> What then remains, but well our power to use,
> And keep good humour still whate'er we lose?
> And trust me, dear, good humour can prevail,
> When airs, and flights, and screams, and scolding fail.
> Beauties in vain their pretty eyes may roll;
> Charms strike the sight, but merit wins the soul!'
> So spoke the dame, but no applause ensued.

Although a parody, this advice to women to use their power wisely balances older attitudes, Puritan and Cavalier, to sexual love. We hear more of good sense, good humour, merit and the soul in Pope's later *Epistle to a Lady*.

## Mature verse

The later verse is chiefly satire, in which Pope 'without method, talks us into sense' in public epistles or essays: unromantic forms which show that readers looked to poets for advice. The second of the four *Moral Essays* is the *Epistle to a Lady: Of the Characters of Women*. Pope believed that the key to character in a man was the 'ruling passion'. If so, according to the epistle's recipient, Martha Blount, 'Most women have no characters at all.' On this frail hook Pope hangs several 'characters'. Chloe fits one modern idea of an 18th-century lady:

> Virtue she finds too painful an endeavour,
> Content to dwell in decencies forever.
> So very reasonable, so unmoved,
> As never yet to love, or to be loved.
> She, while her lover pants upon her breast
> Can mark the figures on an Indian chest;
> And when she sees her friend in deep despair,
> Observes how much a chintz exceeds mohair.          fine fabrics

Pope's ideal woman is 'mistress of herself, though China fall'.

She who ne'er answers till a husband cools,
Or, if she rules him, never shows she rules;
Charms by accepting, by submitting sways,
Yet has her humour most when she obeys.

In another epistle, *Of the Use of Riches*, Pope shares his ideas on landscape design with Lord Burlington (1694–1753), the pioneer of English Palladianism. Pope reminds landowners, who were spending fortunes on their estates, that 'Something there is more needful than expense,/And something previous even to taste – 'tis sense.' The excesses of 'improvement' are illustrated in Timon's imaginary Villa: 'Two cupids squirt before: a lake behind/Improves the keenness of the northern wind ...'. In Timon's fountain: 'Unwater'd see the drooping sea-horse mourn,/And swallows roost in Nilus' [the River Nile's] dusty urn'. In his chapel: 'To rest, the cushion and soft Dean invite,/Who never mentions Hell to ears polite.'

Pope's last works were Imitations of Horace. *The First Epistle of the Second Book of Horace* is dedicated to the emperor Augustus (that is, George II). Maecenas, Augustus' political adviser, was a patron of poets, giving Horace a small estate and Virgil a house. Augustus had asked Horace why he had not written him one of his Epistles. George I did not speak English. Prime Minister Walpole was not interested in poetry. George II asked: 'Who is this Pope that I hear so much about? I cannot discover his merit. Why will not my subjects write in prose?' Pope provided neither prose nor praise, since 'Verse, alas! your Majesty disdains;/And I'm not used to panegyric strains.' The *Epistle* also reviews the literature of the kingdom. Among its memorable lines are: 'What dear delight to Britons farce affords!' This Epistle should be read alongside that to Arbuthnot, a more personal defence of Pope's record, with its acid portrait of Addison.

In the *Essay on Criticism*, Horace is commended for having 'judged with coolness, though he sung with fire'. Pope's Horatian satire is cool, but the fourth book of **The Dunciad**, a satire on the inversion of civilized values, is touched with fire. The title suggests an epic poem about a dunce or dunces. Dryden's *Mac Flecknoe* gave Pope the idea of the empire of Dullness, where now 'Dunce the second rules like Dunce the first.' The Muse is asked to 'Say how the goddess bade Britannia sleep,/And poured her spirit o'er the land and deep.' In the 1728 *Dunciad* Pope exposes the mediocity of those whom the Whigs had patronized: 'While Wren with sorrow to the grave descends,/Gay dies unpensioned with a hundred friends;/Hibernian politics, O Swift! thy fate;/And Pope's, ten years to comment and translate.'

But the fourth *Dunciad* rises above retaliation. It shows that mediocrity has become systematic; the colonization of Westminster (the seat of government and civility) by the City (the natural seat of dullness); the decline of education into pedantry, and of humane learning into the collection of facts or of butterflies; the replacement of Christian humanism by specialized research in natural philosophy; and the final triumph of Dullness. The courtiers of Dullness range from the ferocious pedant Bentley to a young milord on the Grand Tour: 'Europe he saw, and Europe saw him too.' The Queen of Dullness (i.e. Queen Caroline) blesses them all: 'Go, children of my care!/To practice now from theory repair./All my commands are easy, short, and full:/My sons! be proud, be selfish, and be dull!' She reminds the Court that 'princes are but things/Born for first ministers, as slaves for kings' (a crack at Sir Robert Walpole, the Whig First Minister).

**The Dunciad** The first *Dunciad* (1728) had as its hero Lewis Theobald, a minute critic of Pope's edition of Shakespeare. The *Dunciad Variorum* (1729) identifies in mock-scholarly notes the pedants and Grub Street hacks satirized in 1728: 'since it is only in this monument that they must expect to survive.' In *The New Dunciad* (1742), a 4th book was added. In the final 1743 revision, the new Poet Laureate, Colley Cibber, became the hero.

> More had she spoke but yawned – All Nature nods:
> What mortal can resist the yawn of Gods?
> Churches and chapels instantly it reached
> (St James's first, for leaden Gilbert preached) …
> Lost was the nation's sense, nor could be found
> While the long solemn unison went round: …
> The vapour mild o'er each committee crept;
> Unfinished treaties in each office slept;
> And chiefless armies dozed out the campaign;
> And navies yawned for orders on the main.

Pope asks the Muse to tell 'who first, who last resigned to rest.' A line of asterisks follows: the Muse is asleep. Dullness is at hand.

> In vain, in vain – the all-composing hour
> Resistless falls: the Muse obeys the pow'r.
> She comes! she comes! the sable throne behold
> Of Night primeval and of Chaos old!
>
> Thus at her felt approach, and secret might,
> Art after art goes out, and all is night,
> See skulking Truth to her old cavern fled,
> Mountains of casuistry heaped o'er her head!
> Philosophy, that leaned on Heaven before,
> Shrinks to her second cause and is no more …
> Religion blushing veils her sacred fires,
> And unawares morality expires.
> Nor public flame, nor private, dares to shine,
> Nor human spark is left, nor glimpse divine!
> Lo! thy dread empire, Chaos! is restored;
> Light dies before thy uncreating word;
> Thy hand, great Anarch! lets the curtain fall,
> And universal darkness buries all.

The 'uncreating word' inverts the Creation by the divine Logos, returning the universe to Chaos. Pope's is a 17th-century reaction to an 18th-century mechanical universe, and an apocalyptic indictment of Hanoverian obliviousness as to the role which humanism had assigned to literature. Pope, an enlightened Catholic deist, feared that wine was turning into water.

## John Gay

Pope, by his genius, and his intense cultivation of it, dominated the literary scene. His circle included his friend **John Gay** (1685–1732), who had an up-and-down career, losing in the South Sea Bubble the money made by his *Poems*. Of his works only *The Beggar's Opera* lives today, a parody of the Italian Opera, popular in London since 1705: 'an exotick and irrational entertainment, which has been always combated and always has prevailed' (Johnson). In 1716 Swift had written to Pope: 'a sett of Quaker-pastorals might succeed, if our friend Gay could fancy it. … Or what think you of a Newgate pastoral, among the whores and thieves there?' (Newgate prison held the cream of London's vast criminal population.) Gay's semi-opera, the success of 1728, was performed more often than any play in the 18th century.

For the 1723 season the *castrato* Senesino received £2000. Gay wrote to Swift:

'People have now forgot Homer, and Virgil & Caesar, or at least they have lost their ranks, for in London and Westminster in all polite conversations Senesino is daily voted to be the greatest man that ever liv'd.' In 1727 the sopranos Cuzzoni and Faustina came to blows on the stage. In Gay's mock-opera they become Polly Peachum and Lucy Lockit, two of the wives of Macheath the highwayman. His song 'How happy could I be with either/Were t'other dear charmer away' was applied to Sir Robert Walpole, his wife and his mistress. One of Gay's thieves is Bob Booty, a name which stuck to Walpole. Where Italian opera was noble, Gay's is sordid; his Peachum is based on Jonathan Wild the Thief-Taker. *The Beggar's Opera* is far more darkly satirical than Gilbert and Sullivan, but fashionable audiences were entranced by Gay's rogues and whores, and English folk-songs such as 'Over the hills and far away'.

## Lady Mary Wortley Montagu

The career and writing of **Lady Mary Wortley Montagu** (1689–1762) illustrate her age. Birth, beauty and wit made her a darling of society; she was also independent and learned. Best remembered for her letters, she wrote political prose and a play, but was first known for her verse. Her ballad 'The Lover' coolly advocates extra-marital discrimination, as had Pomfret in *The Choice* (1700). The ideal lover would be 'No pedant yet learnèd, not rakehelly gay/Or laughing because he has nothing to say,/To all my whole sex obliging and free,/Yet never be fond of any but me …./But when the long hours of public are past/And we meet with champagne and a chicken at last,/May every fond pleasure that hour endear ….' Lady Mary's friend Mary Astell had shown a reasoned disinterestedness in *Some Reflections upon Marriage* (1700), questioning masculine assumptions. But Lady Mary's *Letters* have a particularly dry quality. Those from Turkey are celebrated.

To the Countess of Mar, from Adrianople, 1 April 1717:

I wish to God (dear sister) that you was as regular in letting me have the pleasure of knowing what passes on your side of the globe as I am careful in endeavouring to amuse you by the account of all I see that I think you care to hear of. [Gives details of Turkish women's clothes.] You may guess how effectually this disguises them, that there is no distinguishing the great lady from her slave, and 'tis impossible for the most jealous husband to know his wife when he meets her, and no man dare either touch or follow a woman in the street. [She ends:] Thus you see, dear sister, the manners of mankind do not differ so widely as our voyage writers would make us believe. Perhaps it would be more entertaining to add a few surprising customs of my own invention, but nothing seems to me so agreeable as truth, and I believe nothing so acceptable to you. I conclude with repeating the great truth of my being, dear sister, etc.

# ■ The novel

## Daniel Defoe

A London butcher called Foe had a son who called himself Defoe. **Daniel Defoe** (1660–1731) was expert in acceptable truths. He had travelled much, failed as a retail hosier, welcomed William III to London, been to prison and worked as a spy before becoming a 'voyage writer', a writer who makes you see. Unwary readers have read *A Journal of the Plague Year* as an eyewitness report, and *Moll Flanders* as a moll's

---

**Lady Mary Wortley Montagu**
Mary Pierrepont was the daughter of the Duke of Kingston, and cousin of Henry Fielding. She learned Latin, and knew Congreve, Prior and Addison. Eloping with Edward Montagu, MP, she shone at Queen Anne's Court, and was friendly with Pope. Smallpox ended her days as a beauty. In 1716 she travelled to Turkey with ambassador Montagu. In London with Lord Hervey ('Sappho' and 'Sporus' in Pope). She left her husband, Montagu, in 1739 to follow an Italian, in vain; she remained abroad twenty years. Her daughter married Lord Bute, later Prime Minister.

'Crusoe saving his Goods out of the Wreck of the Ship': an illustration from a 1726 edition of Defoe's *Robinson Crusoe*, first published in 1711.

autobiography. His tellers give their experience 'straight'. When Robinson Crusoe gets back to his wrecked ship,

first I found that all the ship's provisions were dry and untouched by the water, and being very well disposed to eat, I went to the bread-room and filled my pockets with biscuit, and ate it as I went about other things, for I had not time to lose; I also found some rum in the great cabin, of which I took a large dram, and which I had indeed need enough of to spirit me for what was before me.

The credibility of this castaway's adventures (based on the account of Alexander Selkirk) seems to be guaranteed by his everyday pockets full of factual biscuit. Defoe 'had not time to lose' as he told his story full of things: a saw, planks, a knife, ropes, a raft, a cabin, how to grow crops. We experience these things; we see a footprint in the sand; and with the arrival of Man Friday, we realize with Crusoe that Man does not live by ship's biscuit alone, and that it is Providence which has saved him.

I had alas! no divine knowledge; what I had received by the good instruction of my father was then worn out by an uninterrupted series, for 8 years, of seafaring wickedness, and a constant conversation with nothing but such as were like my self, wicked and profane to the last degree: I do not remember that I had in all that time one thought that so much as tended either to looking upwards toward God, or inwards towards a reflection upon my own ways: but a certain stupidity of soul, without desire of good, or conscience of evil, had entirely overwhelmed me …

This is not Augustine's *Confessions* nor *Pilgrim's Progress*, but the passage ends: 'I cried out, *Lord be my help, for I am in great distress.* This was the first prayer, if I may call it so, that I had made for many years …'. Although Crusoe stresses his wickedness, his story is only fleetingly spiritual. Rather, he survives by his own effort, which he

---

### Daniel Defoe (1660–1731)

Chief publications:

1700  *The True-Born Englishman*

1702  *The Shortest Way with Dissenters*

1706  *The Apparition of Mrs Veal*

1709  *The History of the Union of Great Britain*

1719  *Robinson Crusoe*

1720  *Captain Singleton*

1722  *Moll Flanders; A Journal of the Plague Year; Colonel Jack*

1725  *Roxana*

1726  *Tour Thro' the Whole Island of Great Britain*

---

sees as God's guidance. He is a modern type: godfearing within reason, enterprising, self-reliant. Compared with *Gulliver*, his romance of adventure is naive. Its mythic quality has allowed it to be seen as a modern fable of various kinds, as by Jean-Jacques Rousseau and Karl Marx. On its Protestant side, it compares with the life story of John Newton, who went to sea as a boy, worked in the slave trade, and had an evangelical conversion and became a minister. Newton, the author of 'Amazing Grace', had a great effect on the poet William Cowper (1731–1800).

Earlier, in *The Shortest Way with Dissenters*, Defoe had advocated the contrary of his own views. This was misunderstood, and the Dissenting author put in prison and the pillory. Thereafter he put his views and his irony in his back pocket. A Whig, he worked underground for the Tory Lord Oxford, then wrote for the Whigs. Having discovered the effect of autobiographical perspective on gullible readers, he used the journalist's commonplace detail to make believable the reactions of ordinary people to extraordinary situations. His later romances of adventure introduced the **picaresque** into English fiction. In his roguish fiction, opportunists survive the bruises on their consciences. They are not studies in religious self-deception: Providence helps those who help themselves. After profitable sexual adventures in England and Virginia, a hard-up Moll Flanders helps herself to christening-presents and a child's gold necklace, feels guilt, becomes a professional thief, and ends up (adventures later) prosperous and penitent. Colonel Jack's career has a similar pattern. Less prosperous is the end of Roxana, a courtesan who refuses marriage. Captain Singleton is a mercenary whose chaotic adventures make him a fortune. Pluck plus penitence leads to success.

## Cross-currents

The Christianity of 18th-century literature may go unnoticed. Pope hid his Catholicism, but Nonconformity could be expressed unequivocally, as in Isaac Watts (1674–1748), author of hymns such as 'O God our help in ages past' and 'When I survey the wondrous cross'. Congregational hymn-singing was adopted by the Anglican John Wesley (1703–91) in his mission to the unchurched poor; his Methodists eventually left the established Church. Wesley was much influenced in youth by *A Serious Call to a Devout and Holy Life* by John Law (1686–1761), who refused the oath of allegiance to George I and resigned his Cambridge fellowship,

**picaresque** Full of the adventures of rogues, episodic. A *picaro* or rogue is the hero of the Spanish novels *Lazarillo de Tormes* (1553) and Aleman's *Guzman de Alfarache* (1599–1604).

**Events 1745–89**

| 1746 | Jacobites crushed at Culloden, near Inverness, in the north of Scotland. |
| 1752 | Britain changes to the Gregorian Calendar. |
| 1756 | William Pitt becomes Prime Minister. The Seven Years' War with France begins. |
| 1760 | Accession of George III. |
| 1763 | The Seven Years War ends, with Britain victorious. Wilkes freedom riots. |
| 1773 | The Boston Tea Party. |
| 1775 | American War of Independence begins. |
| 1776 | American Declaration of Independence. |
| 1780 | Anti-Catholic Gordon Riots. |
| 1783 | Britain recognizes American independence. Pitt the Younger becomes Prime Minister. |
| 1789 | French Revolution. |

becoming tutor to the father of Edward Gibbon. Law's emphasis on private prayer also influenced Samuel Johnson.

Johnson was to include Watts in the *Lives of the Poets*: hymns are poems. Literature included religion, ancient history and other non-fiction. Despite the fictional fireworks of the 1740s, the novel long remained a low form of the romance, given to indecorum and realism. Ladies might write romances, as in *The Female Quixote* (1752) by Charlotte Lennox (1720–1804), but no lady wrote a novel before *Evelina* (1778) by Fanny Burney (1752–1840). Her friend Hester Thrale, an omnivorous reader, owned thousands of books, but few novels. Once, when depressed, she wrote: 'No books would take off my attention from present misery, but an old French translation of Quintus Curtius – and Josephus's History of the Siege of Jerusalem. Romance and novels did *nothing* for me: I tried them all in vain.'

## Samuel Richardson

**Samuel Richardson** (1689–1761) was a printer-publisher-bookseller-author. Courtesy books on how to behave in society included letter-writing: the thank-you letter, the condolence. Richardson wrote sample 'familiar letters' for more complex social situations. From this grew the idea of *Pamela; or Virtue Rewarded* (1740), a young servant's account in letters and a journal of the attempts of her rich master ('Mr. B.') to isolate and seduce her. The epistolary form of the first English novel sounds artificial, yet the effect is immediate. Her resistance leads him eventually to recognize her qualities, and to marry her. To read the letters addressed to her parents is to overhear confidences and to feel sympathy: the formula of soap opera. Pamela's situation is morally interesting, as is the unfolding drama. Richardson, relying on his readers to know that virtue is its own reward, shows a good daughter becoming a very good wife, in conditions that are comic and trying. The 18th-century social order is a shock to modern readers, to whom the reward of becoming Mrs B. seems a very earthly one. The prudential subtitle was too much for Henry Fielding, who wrote a brilliant take-off, *Shamela*, in which a young prostitute's *vartue* is a sham designed to put up her price.

Richardson's advance in *Clarissa* (1747–8) is astonishing. It is a mature and complex society novel, epistolary, with several correspondents. The heroine and her oppressor are more interesting than in *Pamela*, and the action and the texture richer.

Clarissa is hounded and persecuted by the evil but attractive Lovelace. He cannot wear her down, and she fights him and his accomplices all the way, but she is out-witted, abducted and raped, and eventually dies a saintly death. This sounds sensa-tional and conventional, but the effect is otherwise. Its remorseless logic makes it the only tragedy of the 18th century which still succeeds. Those who have submitted themselves to the toils of this million-word boa-constrictor acknowledge it as the most involving English novel, perhaps even the greatest. It beats its successor, *Sir Charles Grandison*, whose hero saves women from potentially tragic situations to general satisfaction. Sir Charles, 'the best of men', was regarded in the 18th century with a complacency which readers, since Jane Austen, have not been able to reproduce.

## Henry Fielding

Richardson's psychology had an effect on the European novel. He deserves credit also for stimulating **Henry Fielding** (1705–54) into fiction. Fielding found *Pamela* so sanctimonious that he began a second burlesque of it, *Joseph Andrews*. Joseph is Pamela's virtuous brother who (like Joseph in Exodus), rejects the amorous advances of his mistress Lady B[ooby], and is sacked. Parody is forgotten in the perpetual motion of laughable adventures on the road and in the inns, and in the richly comic character of Parson Adams, a guilelessly good-hearted truth-teller in a wicked world.

Fielding had written twenty-five plays before he took up the law, driven from the stage by Walpole's censorship. He confronted London's corrupt system of justice, and tried to reform the justice meted out to the poor. In his experiments with the new form of novel, he was uninterested in realistic detail and individual psychology. Since he offers neither pictorial realism nor inner life, to read him demands a generic readjustment. He is an Augustan prose satirist, classically educated, brisk, high-spirited and discursive, a narrator who is perpetually present, outside his story, not absorbed into it. The narrative itself takes its sense of pace, scene and plot from the theatre.

Fielding is a cheerful moralist. Thus, when Joseph is robbed, stripped, beaten and thrown into a ditch,

a stage-coach came by. The postilion hearing a man's groans, stopped his horses, and told the coachman, 'he was certain there was a dead man lying in the ditch, for he heard him groan.' 'Go on, sirrah,' says the coachman, 'we are confounded late, and have no time to look after dead men.' A lady, who heard what the postilion said, and likewise heard the groan, called eagerly to the coachman, 'to stop and see what was the matter.' Upon which he bid the postilion 'alight, and look into the ditch.' He did so, and returned, 'that there was a man sitting upright as naked as ever he was born,' – 'O, J–sus,' cried the lady, 'A naked man! Dear coachman, drive on and leave him.'

When robbery is mentioned, a gentleman passenger says to drive on lest they be robbed too. A lawyer advises that the victim be taken into the coach, lest they be implicated in a court case. Not without a fare, says the coachman; and so on. To renew a good text – the parable of the Good Samaritan – while showing how another – Richardson's – is bad, is an Augustan procedure.

Fielding's *The History of Tom Jones*, though its action is also full of rumbustious roadside adventures, is planned. 'A comic epic in prose', it has eighteen books

(Homer has twenty-four, Virgil twelve). Its symmetrical timescale has at its centre an action-packed 24 hours in an inn at Upton-upon-Severn. Tom, a foundling, is expelled from Paradise Hall, the Somerset home of his foster-father Squire Allworthy, and after many adventures and discoveries marries Sophia Western in London. They return to the West. Each book has a critical prologue as vigorous as the narrative which follows. Even chapter titles are mini-essays. In Book V, Chapter X, *Shewing the Truth of many Observations of* Ovid, *and of other more grave Writers, who have proved, beyond Contradiction, that Wine is often the Fore-runner of Incontinency*, Tom throws himself down by a murmuring brook and breaks forth:

O Sophia, would heaven give thee to my arms, how blest would be my condition! … How contemptible would the brightest Circassian beauty, dressed in all the jewels of the Indies, appear to my eyes! But why do I mention another woman? … Sophia, Sophia alone shall be mine. What raptures are in that name! I will engrave it on every tree!' At these words he started up, and beheld – not his Sophia – no, nor a Circassian maid richly and elegantly attired for the Grand Signior's seraglio. No; without a gown, in a shift that was somewhat of the coarsest, and none of the cleanest, bedewed likewise with some odoriferous effluvia, the produce of the day's labour, with a pitch-fork in her hand, Molly Seagrim approached. Our hero had his pen-knife in his hand, which he had drawn for the before-mentioned purpose, of carving on the bark; when the girl coming near him cried out with a smile, 'You don't intend to kill me, Squire, I hope!' … Here ensued a parley, which, as I do not think myself obliged to relate it, I shall omit. It is sufficient that it lasted a full quarter of an hour, at the conclusion of which they retired into the thickest part of the grove. Some of my readers may be inclined to think this event unnatural. However, the fact is true; and, perhaps, may be sufficiently accounted for, by suggesting that Jones probably thought one woman better than none, and Molly as probably imagined two men to be better than one. Besides the before-mentioned motive assigned to the present behaviour of Jones, the reader will be likewise pleased to recollect in his favour, that he was not at this time perfect master of that wonderful power of reason, which so well enables grave and wise men to subdue their unruly passions, and to decline any of these prohibited amusements. Wine now had totally subdued this power in Jones.

After other robust escapades of the same sort, and proof that he did not commit the crime for which he was expelled from Paradise Hall, Sophia accepts Jones into a blissful marriage; her name means Wisdom. Fielding advertises 'no other than Human Nature' in his initial 'Bill of Fare', yet in his Dedication says that 'to recommend goodness and innocence hath been my sincere endeavour in this history'. Allworthy and Sophia accept Tom's warm humanity. The unheroically-named hero is honest and guileless, if not sexually innocent. He goodheartedly forgives those who use him ill. Fielding reconciles human nature with the recommendation of goodness by means of what Coleridge thought 'one of the three great plots of literature'.

The remarkably different *Tom Jones* and *Clarissa* were the father and mother of the English novel. Fielding's more interior *Amelia* was also more conventional, like his rival's *Grandison*.

## Tobias Smollett

**Tobias Smollett** (1721–71), a much-travelled Scottish surgeon based in London, has Fielding's robustness, but Fielding is an introvert compared with the heroically cantankerous Smollett, whose boldly drawn caricatures of public life have the hectic action of the animated cartoon. He translated the picaresque Le Sage and the witty anti-romance of Cervantes; his own novels follow suit. He sketches types and comments on social mores – on the road, in Bath or in London – with little coherent

## Fiction from Richardson to Edgeworth

1740   Samuel Richardson, *Pamela, or Virtue Rewarded*.

1741   Richardson, *Familiar Letters*.

1742   Henry Fielding, *Joseph Andrews*.

1747   Richardson, *Clarissa* (7 volumes, 1748).

1748   Tobias Smollett, *The Adventures of Roderick Random*.

1749   Fielding, *The History of Tom Jones, a Foundling*; Smollett, *Gil Blas* (trans. of Le Sage).

1750   John Cleland, *Memoirs of Fanny Hill*.

1751   Fielding, *Amelia*; Smollett, *The Adventures of Peregrine Pickle*.

1753   Richardson, *The History of Sir Charles Grandison* (7 volumes, 1754); Smollett, *Adventures of Ferdinand, Count Fathom*.

1755   Fielding (d.1754) *Journal of a Voyage to Lisbon*; Smollett, *Don Quixote* (trans. of Cervantes).

1759   Samuel Johnson, *Rasselas, Prince of Abyssinia* (Voltaire, *Candide*).

1760   Laurence Sterne, *The Life and Opinions of Tristram Shandy* (9 volumes, 1767).

1761   (Rousseau, *La Nouvelle Héloise*).

1765   Horace Walpole, *The Castle of Otranto*.

1764   Oliver Goldsmith, *The Vicar of Wakefield*.

1768   Laurence Sterne, *A Sentimental Journey*.

1771   Henry Mackenzie, *The Man of Feeling*; Smollett (d.1769), *The Expedition of Humphry Clinker*.

1773   Henry Mackenzie, *The Man of the World*.

1774   (Goethe, *The Sorrows of Young Werther*).

1778   Fanny Burney, *Evelina, or The History of a Young Lady's Entry into the World*.

1782   (Laclos, *Les Liaisons dangereuses*; Rousseau, *Confessions*).

1785   Charlotte Smith, *Manon Lescaut* (trans. of Prévost).

1786   William Beckford, *Vathek: An Arabian Tale*.

1788   Charlotte Smith, *Emmeline*.

1789   Mrs (Ann) Radcliffe, *The Castles of Athlin and Dunbayne*; Charlotte Smith, *Etheline, or The Recluse of the Lake*.

1790   Mrs Radcliffe, *A Sicilian Romance*.

1794   Mrs Radcliffe, *The Mysteries of Udolpho*; William Godwin, *Caleb Williams*.

1796   Burney, *Camilla, or A Picture of Youth*; Matthew Lewis, *The Monk*; Robert Bage, *Hermsprong*.

1800   Maria Edgeworth, *Castle Rackrent*.

story. He wrote a *Complete History of England* and much else, besides the novels between the lively *Roderick Random* and the gentler *Humphry Clinker*, the two by which he is best remembered.

## Laurence Sterne

**Laurence Sterne** (1713–68) refers to Smollett as Smelfungus, on account of his fault-finding *Travels through France and Italy*. Sterne was the most singular of the four fathers of the English novel. Clarissa and Tom Jones improve on prototypes, but *The Life and Opinions of Tristram Shandy* seems to come from nowhere. In fact, the novel had several sources: the romance and the adventure, but also philosophical tales like Swift's *Gulliver* and Voltaire's *Candide*, and non-realistic fictions like those of Rabelais and Swift's *Tale of a Tub*, and from non-fiction, such as Burton's *Anatomy of Melancholy*.

   *The Life and Opinions* disappoints all conventional expectations: Sterne, amused by fiction's pretence of combining realism with chronology, begins his hero's Life with an Opinion. The book opens: 'I wish either my father or my mother, or indeed both of them, as they were in duty both equally bound to it, had minded what they were about when they begot me ...'. After further opinions, Chapter I ends:

'*Pray, my dear*, quoth my mother, *have you not forgot to wind up the clock?—Good G–d!* cried my father, making an exclamation, but taking care to moderate his voice at the same time,—*Did ever woman, since the creation of the world, interrupt a man with such a silly question?* Pray what was your father saying?—Nothing.'

Some medical opinion held that the moment of conception affected the embryo. Why did his mother ask his father, at a moment when he was not saying anything, this particular question? Because Walter Shandy, a regular man, on the first Sunday night of the month, 'wound up a large house-clock, which we had standing upon the backstairs head, with his own hands: – And being somewhere between fifty and sixty years of age ... he had likewise gradually brought some other little family concernments to the same period.' Mrs Shandy's monthly association of the ideas of clock-winding and procreation is presented as an instance of Locke's theory of sense-impressions. Instead of G–d's 'Let there be light', the word spoken at the hero's creation is an enquiry about the clock. Clock-time and subjective experience and language are at odds.

The narrator is not born until vol. iv, his nose being damaged in the process by the obstetrical forceps of Dr. Slop, who has taken too long to undo his carefully tied-up bag of instruments. Tristram's father writes a *Tristra-paedia*, or treatise upon the education of Tristram, rather than educating him. The hero is breeched in vol. vi., but does nothing. Much of the inaction is concerned with Tristram's beloved Uncle Toby and his hobby-horse, or obsession, with making impregnable a set of military fortifications he has erected in the garden. An old soldier, he courts the Widow Wadman until informed by Corporal Trim that her curiosity about where Uncle Toby got the wound in his groin has nothing to do with the topography of Marlborough's campaigns. Much earlier, Toby takes to the window a fly he has caught: 'go, says he, lifting up the sash, and opening his hand as he spoke to let it escape; go poor Devil, get thee gone, why should I hurt thee? This world surely is wide enough to hold both thee and me.' Tristram avers that he often thinks that he owes 'one half of my philanthropy to that one accidental impression.'

Poor Tristram had, at the age of four, suffered another accidental impression, being half emasculated by the sudden descent of a sash-window. The associations of ideas in this book are irrational: life outruns all opinions in books. This one ends, with Tristram still a boy, on an inconsequential anecdote about the infertility of Shandy's bull: 'L—d! said my mother, what is all this story about?—A COCK and a BULL, said Yorick—And one of the best of its kind, I ever heard.' THE END.

Sterne, a country clergyman, gives a portrait of himself in Parson Yorick. 'Like all the best shaggy-dog stories,' says the critic Christopher Ricks of *Tristram Shandy*, 'it is somewhat bawdy, preposterously comic, brazenly exasperating, and very shrewd in its understanding of human responses.' The shaggy-dog story and cock-and-bull story are cousins of the 'Irish bull', as Ricks reminds us. The Irish Sterne took pleasure in defeating English common sense. What is the point of all this pointlessness? As the men talk for nine volumes, Tristram's poor mother says hardly a word. Yet her last question is connected to her first. All this story is (or pretends to be) about masculine decline. It is also a potent demonstration of the impotence of human language and reason. 'Nothing odd will do long,' said Johnson: '*Tristram Shandy* did not last.' But this learnedly perverse joke has appealed, chiefly to men. In this it is not unlike the post-realist work of James Joyce, himself something of a Smelfungus.

# ■ The emergence of Sensibility

Sterne's last work, *A Sentimental Journey*, ends:

> So that when I reached forth my hand, I caught hold of the Fille de Chambre's
> END OF VOL II.

Improper and experimental, this is sentimental only in that it is an old man's fancy – which stops itself. But comic pathos is one of Sterne's specialities – as in Uncle Toby's release of the fly.

The generation that followed Pope was readier to show Sensibility. Pope had censured unfeeling superiority, 'the arched eyebrow and Parnassian sneer', and wrote of his own father that he knew 'No language, but the language of the heart.' Of his own career, he claimed that 'Not in Fancy's maze I wandered long/But stooped to Truth, and moralized my song.' He moved from pastoral to larger themes, claiming that he had put wit to responsible public uses, unlike the wits of the Restoration. A move towards public acceptance and access was general: comedy after Congreve is less complex, more sentimental. The prose of Swift and Defoe is plain. Watts's hymns are clear and sincere. Although Pope did not lack moral philosophy or feeling, his finesse seems sharp in comparison with the broader taste of Hanoverian England.

Sensibility is in part a middle-class modification of upper-class cool. Although Fielding scorned Methodist enthusiasm, his wit is driven by a strong conviction of the need for truth-telling, mercy and charity. In his **Etonian** way, he is as evangelical as Richardson in his support for oppressed virtue, though he would not call it that. Horace Walpole and Thomas Gray, Etonians of the next decade, entirely lacked Fielding's moral robustness; they preferred the arts. To rob taste of its moral dimension struck Dr Johnson as irresponsible. He had no time for aesthetes and, though he responded to true feeling, scorned the cult of sensibility.

Sensibility, the capacity to feel, had many roots. Moral sensibility has Christian origins, and its 18th-century expression owes much to Dissent, Methodism and Scotch philosophy ('Scotch' was the form preferred in the 18th century). But 17th-century conflicts had made many seek a less explicit Christianity. Moral sentiment could be formulated as philanthropic benevolence, in the manner of Deists such as Shaftesbury. David Hume's *Treatise on Human Nature* (1739) and *Enquiry concerning the Principles of Morals* (1751) developed a theory of natural social sympathy and of the subordination of the self to social conditions. The tradition of rural retreat from conflict or Court corruption was modified to something more private. The antique moral harmony of Ben Jonson's *To Penshurst* was no longer an ideal. The Civil War retirement poetry which appealed to the 18th century was Denham's estate poem *Cooper's Hill*. Pope's youthful 'Ode on Solitude' is a version of Horace's daydream which became an 18th-century gentry ideal: an independent rural life, pleasant but not soft. Voltaire was to end his *Candide*, a fable on the folly of assuming that humans are naturally good, with 'Il faut cultiver son jardin' ('One should cultivate one's own garden'). This garden was the garden of the character, requiring what Addison called 'a constant and assiduous culture'.

**Eton** An English public school (a type of boarding school) for the sons of the upper classes.

The 18th-century garden expressed an ideal of the natural life, often with a literary programme. In the 1730s Lord Cobham developed at Stowe an Elysian Fields with a River Styx and Temples of Ancient Virtue and British Worthies; his family name was Temple. The garden of the poet William Shenstone (1714–63) had a much-imitated ruin. At Sir Henry Hoare's Stourhead in the 1740s the walk round the lake recreated a sequence of images from Virgil's *Aeneid VI*. Pope's poetry of the countryside was taken further by James Thomson in his popular *The Seasons* (1726–30). The Evening Walk, a late 18th-century theme, began from Milton's *Il Penseroso*, imitated in the meditations of Lady Winchilsea and Thomas Parnell. Edward Young in his *Night Thoughts* (1742) gratified a taste for morbid rumination, as did Robert Blair in *The Grave* (1743): 'the task be mine/To paint the gloomy horrors of the tomb.'

## Thomas Gray

Sensibility is distilled into something more than cultural taste in the *Elegy Written in a Country Church Yard* of **Thomas Gray** (1711–71), the most gifted poet of the generation after Pope. The celebrated *Elegy*, the most accomplished medium-length poem of the 18th century, was published in 1751. Thereafter Gray declined the Laureateship and wrote little verse; as Professor of Modern History at Cambridge, he never lectured.

His fourteen published poems are sophisticated and eclectic. In Augustan vein are his 'Lines on Lord Holland's Seat' (1769), a brilliant satire on a disgraced Paymaster-General, Henry Fox. It begins 'Old and abandoned by each venal friend,/Here H[olland] took the pious resolution/To smuggle some few years and strive to mend/ A broken character and constitution.' 'Here' is Margate, where Fox retired, building ruins on his estate. He dreams (in Gray) that had he not been betrayed he could have ruined London: 'Owls might have hooted in St. Peter's choir,/And foxes stunk and littered in St Paul's.' To his Augustan word-play and polish, Gray joined the proto-Romantic tastes shown in his letters.

Gray put the Ode, a neo-classical form imitated from the Greek lyric poet Pindar, to new purposes. It is easy to like 'Ode on the Death of a Favourite Cat Drowned in a Tub of Gold Fishes': the heroi-comic idiom of Pope is used to refine sentiment, ending in a mock-serious warning to the ladies:

> From hence, ye beauties, undeceived,
> Know, one false step is ne'er retrieved,
> And be with caution bold.
> Not all that tempts your wandering eyes
> And heedless hearts is lawful prize;
> Nor all that glisters gold.

Johnson thought the Odes a misapplication of talent. The moral of the Eton Ode – 'where ignorance is bliss,/'Tis folly to be wise' – now seems too well-turned to be taken as seriously as Gray meant. His two most ambitious Odes imitate Pindar both in form and in their lofty, condensed, and allusive style. *The Progress of Poesy* shows the Muses migrating from a conquered Greece to the free England of Shakespeare and Milton. From the sublime Milton to Gray himself there is a decline. Pindar, 'the Theban eagle', had soared high. Gray aspires to 'keep his distant way/Beyond the limits of a vulgar fate,/Beneath the Good how far – but far above the Great.' Pope had condescended to ministers, but knew them; Gray's Poesy distances herself from Power; Sterne dedicated his novel to William Pitt, the new Prime Minister.

According to Pope, English verse had improved from correctness to noble energy: 'Waller was smooth; but Dryden taught to join/The varying verse, the full-resounding line,/The long majestic march and energy divine.' In Gray's *Progress* the sublime is remote in time or place: Helicon, the frozen North, or 'Chili's boundless forests'. His note reads: 'Extensive influence of poetic Genius over the remotest and most uncivilized nations: its connections with liberty, and the virtues that naturally attend on it (See the Erse, Norwegian, and Welch Fragments, the Lapland and American songs.)' Gray interested himself in the remote origins of British poetry, and in Parry, a blind Welsh harper who visited Cambridge. In *The Bard*, a Pindaric Ode set in 1290, the last Welsh oral poet prophesies the ruin of the invader, Edward I, and the return of poetry to Britain under the (Welsh) Tudors. His appearance is dramatic:

> On a rock, whose haughty brow
> Frowns o'er old Conway's foaming flood
> Robed in the sable garb of woe,
> With haggard eyes the poet stood
> (Loose his beard and hoary hair
> Streamed, like a meteor, to the troubled air) …

Gray believed that Edward had ordered all bards to be killed. The bard's last words to the king are: '"Be thine Despair, and scept'red Care,/To triumph, and to die, are mine."/He spoke, and headlong from the mountain's height/Deep in the roaring tide he plung'd to endless night.' *Poesy* has an epigraph from Pindar: φωνᾶντα συνετοῖσιν ·ἐζ δὲ τὸ πᾶν ἑρμηνέων χᾱτίζει: 'speaking to the intelligent alone – for the rest they need interpreters'.

The Odes succeeded, and for the first time difficult poems about poetry became fashionable. 'Nobody understands me, & I am perfectly satisfied,' Gray wrote to Mason, but his sublime meaning was so misunderstood that he had to provide notes. Gray later translated from *The Goddodin*, a Welsh poem of *c*.600, and the Old Norse *Edda*. He also went on solo walking tours: in the Lake District, in 1769; and in Scotland, turning back at Killiecrankie, where the wildness of the Highlands became less pleasing.

The *Elegy*, by contrast, is about death, not the death of poets or poetry but of the rural poor: 'Each in his narrow cell for ever laid,/The rude Forefathers of the hamlet sleep.' They had not had Gray's chances: 'Knowledge to their eyes her ample page/Rich with the spoils of time did ne'er unroll.' Yet

> Full many a gem of purest ray serene,
> The dark unfathomed caves of ocean bear:
> Full many a flower is born to blush unseen,
> And waste its sweetness on the desert air.

The poet half-envies their obscurity:

> Far from the madding crowd's ignoble strife,
> Their sober wishes never learned to stray;
> Along the cool sequester'd vale of life
> They kept the noiseless tenor of their way.

Choice and placing of adjectives, and control of pace and phrasing, are finely-judged.

For Johnson, the poem's merit lay in its enforcement of moral truths. He concludes his *Life*:

In the character of his *Elegy* I rejoice to concur with the common reader; for by the common sense of readers uncorrupted with literary prejudices, after all the refinements of subtilty and the dogmatism of learning, must be finally decided all claim to poetical honours. The *Churchyard* abounds with images which find a mirrour in every mind, and with sentiments to which every bosom returns an echo. The four stanzas beginning *Yet even these bones*, are to me original: I have never seen the notions in any other place; yet he that reads them here, persuades himself that he has always felt them. Had Gray written often thus, it would be vain to blame, and useless to praise him.

The four stanzas ask whether any one has 'Left the warm precincts of the chearful day,/Nor cast one longing ling'ring look behind.//On some fond breast the parting soul relies …'. Johnson's fear of 'something after death' responded. At the poem's opening, the plowman leaves the world to darkness and to Gray, whose isolation quivers in an exquisite word: 'Now fades the *glimmering* landscape on the sight'. In the imagined ending, an illiterate rustic recalls the now buried poet as a craz'd solitary. The poem ends with a reversed perspective. The *Elegy*'s quiet exposure of poet and reader to the darkness of death has come home to many later poets and readers.

The *Elegy*'s turn from the death of others to the death of the self is symptomatic of the Romantic change to the private and personal, a clue to the minor scope of nearly all late 18th-century verse. The exceptions, Christopher Smart, Robert Burns and William Blake, were not central to English writing. But this is to anticipate, and it is necessary to note some further instances of sensibility.

## Pre-Romantic sensibility: 'Ossian'

A pre-Romantic sensibility is visible in Milton, but by the time of Pope's death it was everywhere. Poetic role-models changed: 'What are the Lays of artful *Addison,/ Coldly correct*, to *Shakespeare's* Warblings wild?' asked Joseph Warton in *The Enthusiast: or, The Lover of Nature* (1744). Joseph and his brother Thomas wrote verse imitating Spenser and Milton's *Penseroso*, where 'sweetest Shakespeare, Fancy's child,/ Warbles his native woodnotes wild'. Thomas's *History of English Poetry* (1774–81) preferred medieval and Elizabethan poetry to that of the period when 'Late, very late, correctness grew our care' (Pope). Uncorrected warbling thus preceded Wordsworth's 1798 *Lyrical Ballads* by fifty years. In his Spenserian *The Castle of Indolence* (1748), James Thomson portrayed poetic idleness as reprehensible but inviting. In a second Canto, the Knight of Industry, who had made Britannia the land of freedom, liberates (with the help of a bard) the Castle's more virtuous inmates. Gray's other themes – melancholy, marginality, craziness and extinction – are found in the lives of the poets William Collins (1721–59; melancholia), Christopher Smart (1722–71; the asylum), Thomas Chatterton (b.1753; dead at 17), William Cowper (1731–1800; suicidal melancholia) and George Crabbe (1754–1832; occasional melancholia). The triumph of sensibility, and its taste for fancy and the primitive sublime, is shown by the phenomenon of **'Ossian' Macpherson** (1736–96).

Thomson was a border Scot who, like many Irish and Scots, chose to mingle with the English epicures. He left Edinburgh before the Scottish Enlightenment of David Hume and Adam Smith. Other Enlightenment figures, David Blair and Joseph Hone, wished to preserve something of the culture of the Gaelic-speaking Highlands, sup-pressed after the Jacobite rising crushed at Culloden in 1746. In 1759, Macpherson, a young Highlander, translated a Gaelic fragment Hone had collected, a piece on the death of Oscur, beginning 'Why openest thou afresh the spring of my grief, O son of Alpin, inquiring how Oscur fell?' Sent off to collect others, Macpherson produced *Fragments of Ancient Poetry* in 1760, to instant acclaim; then *Fingal: An Epic Poem in Six Books* (1761), *Temora: An Ancient Epic Poem in Eight Books* (1763) and *The Works of Ossian* (1765). Success, repeated in London, was amplified in Europe, where Goethe found Ossian superior to Homer. Fifty years later Napoleon had scenes from Ossian painted on his bedroom ceiling. Not so Dr Johnson, who challenged Macpherson to produce the original manuscripts; he failed to do so; controversy continues. (The first extant manuscript of any Scots Gaelic verse dates from 1512, whereas the original Ossian was a 3rd-century oral *Irish* bard.) On seeing the *Fragments* Gray was '*exstasié* with their infinite beauty', a modern aesthetic reaction; authenticity or spuriousness were immaterial. Macpherson, it seems, processed scraps of oral verse into a strange English printed prose. Original translation! (The impres-sionable Boswell asked whether many men could have written such poems. Johnson: 'Many men, many women, and many children.') The *Fragments*, out of print until recently, are in a rhythmical prose reminiscent of translated Old Testament texts. Fragment 8 begins:

By the side of a rock on the hill beneath the aged trees, old Oscian sat on the moss; the last of the race of Fingal. Sightless are his aged eyes; his beard is waving in the wind. Dull through the leafless trees he heard the voice of the north. Sorrow revived in his soul: he began and lamented the dead.

However little is due to 'Ossian' and however much to Macpherson, the *Fragments* appealed – as fragments, to be completed by the fancy. All are sad and noble, all remember death, often caused by love, in landscapes of loss. Modern Gaels object that the voice supplied for them is a broken voice.

In 1726 James Thomson had called for a revival of the sublime in poetry, which had inspired mankind 'from Moses down to Milton'. **William Collins** (1721–59), author of the *Ode to Evening* (1747), refers to Thomson as a druid. (Of the druids, pagan British priests put to death by the Romans, little is known.) In the 1740s Robert Lowth lectured in Latin – to, among others, Christopher Smart – on the Sacred Poetry of the Hebrews, dwelling especially on the sublime rhythms of the prophets. In 1756 Edmund Burke argued in *The Sublime and the Beautiful* that the aesthetic pleasure of the sublime arose from pain at the sight of the immense, the obscure and the traumatic. Poetry could now inhere not only in a work of perfected art but also in the 'infinite beauty' of fragments by an inspired genius, enthusiast, druid or bard. Sophisticated 18th-century craftsmen liked to imagine wild ancestors.

The Romantics thought of **Thomas Chatterton** (1753–70) as the archetypal boy genius dead of neglect. Chatterton copied medieval manuscripts kept at St Mary Redcliffe, Bristol, and then invented a local 15th-century poet, Fr. Thomas Rowley, and wrote poems for him. His attempt to pass these off on Horace Walpole failed; Walpole had lost faith in Macpherson. Spelling which threw dust into the eyes of the Romantics can no longer hide non-medieval sentiment. Rowley's 'Mynstrelles Songe' begins: 'O! synge untoe mie roundelaie, O! droppe the brynie teare wythe mee.'

'Chatterton' by Henry Wallis, 1856. Thomas Chatterton's suicide at 17 (in 1770) made him a type of the neglected genius for Romantic poets. Wallis's model was the novelist George Meredith.

## Gothic fiction

Manuscripts were all the rage. In a preface **Horace Walpole** (1717–97) pretends to have found *The Castle of Otranto: a Gothic Story* (1764) in a manuscript by Onuphrio Muralto, Canon of Otranto in the 12th century. Horace, the fourth son of Sir Robert Walpole, brought up in the Palladian splendour of Holkham Hall, Norfolk, gradually turned a Thames-side house at Strawberry Hill, west of London, into a small Gothic castle, where he printed Gray's Odes.

His story begins with Conrad being killed at his wedding by a vast falling helmet. His father Manfred, tyrant of Otranto, imprisons the suspected murderer inside this helmet, which is able to wave its plume. Enlightened readers did not suppose that such events took place even in Latin latitudes, but their universe was short of miracles. The fantasy of *The Castle of Otranto* created a vogue for camp thrillers in which nobles drug and rape beautiful wards in the bowels of their mountain fastnesses, and statues bleed from the nose. The queen of Gothic, **Mrs Radcliffe** (1764–1823), is restrained: when in *The Mysteries of Udolpho* (1794) the heroine asks Montoni why he keeps her prisoner, he replies 'because it is my will' – a horrid reply in an Age of Reason. The oriental *Vathek* (1786) of William Beckford, written in French, is a perverse fantasy, as is *The Monk* (1796), a 'shocker' by Matthew Lewis. Heir to a fortune, Beckford built himself a huge Gothic tower, Fonthill Abbey, enclosing its park with a high wall. For all its curiosity value, the literary merit of 18th-century Gothic fiction is negligible compared with the use made of Gothic in the 19th-century novel.

## ■ The Age of Johnson

### Dr Samuel Johnson

**Samuel Johnson** (1709–84) dominated the world of letters for thirty years. The Johnson of James Boswell's sound-bites, the conversationalist who felled opponents with a sentence, was real enough. But Boswell's talker was primarily a great writer: poet, biographer, critic, editor, essayist, author of a tragedy and a philosophical tale, of political and travel books, and prayers. Unmatched as a judge of language and literature, he made permanent contributions himself in the *Dictionary*, the *Preface to*

**Samuel Johnson** (1709–84) The son of an elderly Lichfield bookseller, whose stock he read, Johnson went up to Oxford, thanks to a family friend; but the money ran out after four terms, and he left. Marrying a widow much older than himself, he started a school, where his convulsive mannerisms were a gift to his pupil, David Garrick. In London he lived by his pen, turning his hand to anything. He wrote up from memory the *Parliamentary Debates* for *The Gentleman's Magazine* (Dickens was later to use shorthand). The Grub Street life is recorded in his *Life of Mr Richard Savage*, a poet with whom Johnson walked the streets when they had nowhere to sleep. After the *Dictionary* (1755) he edited Shakespeare and wrote the *Lives*, and *A Journey to the Western Islands of Scotland* (1775). *Prayers and Meditations* was published in 1785.

*Shakespeare* and the *Lives of the Poets*. These were part of a general expansion of knowledge, the most public symbol of which was Captain Cook's South Sea voyages with the naturalist Sir Joseph Banks. Savants wrote for general readers in a clear prose, none more lucidly than the philosophers Bishop Berkeley (1685–1753) and David Hume (1711–76). A summary retrospect on English from 1760 to 1798 shows non-fictional prose taking the centre ground. Poetry withdrew, the novel wilted, but the decline of drama was halted by Goldsmith and Sheridan. Yet between 1770 and 1791 appeared the works of Johnson, Gibbon, Smith, Burney and Boswell listed below.

## Non-fictional prose: 1710–98

1710  Bishop Berkeley, *Treatise on the Principles of Human Knowledge*.

1739  David Hume, *Treatise on Human Nature* (3 volumes, 1740).

1750  Samuel Johnson (ed.), *The Rambler* (to 1752).

1751  (Diderot and D'Alembert, *French Encyclopaedia*, volume 1; 35 volumes, 1780).

1754  Hume, *History of England* (2 vols, 1762).

1755  Johnson, *Dictionary of the English Language*.

1756  Edmund Burke, *Enquiry into the Origin of Our Ideas of the Sublime and the Beautiful*.

1757  Tobias Smollett, *A Complete History of England* (4 volumes, 1758).

1758  Edward Gibbon, *Essai sur l'étude de la littérature*; David Hume, *Enquiry Concerning Human Understanding*.

1759  Adam Smith, *Theory of Moral Sentiments*.

1762  Bishop Hurd, *Letters of Chivalry and Romance*; Lord Kames, *Elements of Criticism*.

1763  Lady Mary Montagu (d.1762), *Letters*.

1765  Johnson, *Preface to Shakespeare*; Henry Fuseli, *Painting and Sculpture of the Greeks* (trans. of Winckelmann).

1769  Elizabeth Montagu, *An Essay on the Writings and Genius of Shakespeare*; Sir Joshua Reynolds, *Discourses on Art*.

1770  Burke, *Thoughts on the Cause of the Present Discontents*.

1771  John Wesley, *Collected Prose Works* (32 volumes, 1774).

1773  James Cook, *Voyage Round the World*.

1774  Lord Chesterfield (d.1773), *Letters to His Natural Son*; Thomas Warton, *History of English Poetry* (3 vols, 1781).

1775  Johnson, *A Journey to the Western Islands of Scotland*.

1776  Gibbon, *The Decline and Fall of the Roman Empire* (6 vols, 1788); Adam Smith, *The Wealth of Nations*; Thomas Paine, *Common Sense*.

1779  Hume (d.1776), *Dialogues Concerning Natural Religion*; Johnson, *The Works of the English Poets, with Prefaces, Biographical and Critical* (68 vols, 1781).

1783  David Blair, *Lectures on Rhetoric and Belles-Lettres*.

1785  James Boswell, *A Tour of the Hebrides*; Horace Walpole, *An Essay on Modern Gardening*.

1789  Charles Burney, *A General History of Music* (4 vols); Gilbert White, *Natural History of Selborne*.

1790  Burke, *Reflections on the Revolution in France*; Thomas Bewick, *General History of Quadrupeds*.

1791  James Boswell, *The Life of Johnson*; William Gilpin, *Essays on Picturesque Beauty*; Paine, *The Rights of Man*.

1792  Mary Wollstonecraft, *A Vindication of the Rights of Woman*.

1793  William Godwin, *Political Justice*.

1794  Paine, *The Age of Reason* (3 volumes, 1811).

1796  Burke, *A Letter to a Noble Lord*.

1798  Richard Brinsley Sheridan, *Collected Speeches*.

The definition for 'lexicographer' in Dr Johnson's *Dictionary* (1755).

LEXICO'GRAPHER. *n. f.* [λεξικὸν and γράφω; *lexicographe*, French.] A writer of dictionaries; a harmlefs drudge, that bufies himfelf in tracing the original, and detailing the fignification of words.

Commentators and *lexicographers* acquainted with the Syriac language, have given thefe hints in their writings on fcripture.                    *Watts's Improvement of the Mind.*

Johnson, a raw-boned uncouth provincial, short-sighted, pockmarked and melancholy, became the centre of polite letters. Members of Johnson's Literary Club included the writers Goldsmith and Boswell, the statesmen C. J. Fox and Burke, Sheridan the dramatist, Gibbon the historian, Reynolds the painter, Burney the musician, Banks the naturalist, Adam Smith the philosopher and economist, and William Jones the orientalist. Another member was Johnson's former pupil the actor David Garrick, with whom Johnson had walked to London when his little school failed in 1737.

Johnson's centrality is not an illusion caused by Boswell's version of his last twenty-one years. The solar system looks the same in earlier accounts of Johnson by Sir John Hawkins, Mrs Thrale and Fanny Burney. Most 18th-century writers were men, often unmarried men, but the widower Johnson had many women friends, including the blue-stocking Elizabeth Montagu, and Charlotte Lennox, for whom he wrote a Preface. Johnson's wholehearted character attracted people who, like Boswell, were put off by his appearance and manner. He was markedly humane, giving house-room to many unfortunates, though he did not object to dining out. He had a deep Christian faith. He told an Anglican priest that as an old man he stood bareheaded in the rain for a considerable time in Uttoxeter Market, because as a young man he had refused his father's request to look after the family's bookstall there: 'In contrition I stood, and I hope the penance was expiatory.'

## The *Dictionary*

Memory and composition were central to education, yet Johnson's mental strength and acute verbal sense were exceptional. He composed in Latin or English in his head, writing down poems when complete. The quotations in the *Dictionary* were recalled from his wide reading, often in unliterary subjects such as travel, manufacturing, agriculture and chemistry. His writing is weighty and trenchant. He examined ideas critically, considering their true meaning, relation to principles and practical consequences. His principles were Anglican and Tory, opposing American independence in *Taxation No Tyranny*, unlike his friend Burke. He attacked British injustice, as towards Ireland, and would drink 'to the next insurrection of the Negroes in the West Indies'. He disliked Americans because they owned slaves.

Johnson's prose, and heroic personality, are illustrated by a passage from his letter to Lord Chesterfield, from whom he had sought help in his early struggles on the *Dictionary*. Chesterfield now tried to associate himself with the completed work.

Seven years, My Lord, have now passed since I waited in your outward rooms or was repulsed from your door, during which time I have been pushing on my work through difficulties of which it is useless to complain, and have brought it at last to the verge of publication without one act of assistance, one word of encouragement or one smile of favour. Such treatment I did not expect, for I never had a patron before … Is not a patron, My Lord, one who looks with unconcern on a man struggling for life in the water and when he has reached ground encumbers him with help? The notice which you have been pleased to take of my labours, had it been early, had been kind; but it has been delayed till I am indifferent and cannot enjoy it, till I am solitary and cannot impart it, till I am known and do not want it.

There was no established Dictionary before Johnson, and an authority was needed to standardize spelling, to distinguish clearly between senses, and to rule on usage. He carried out the task, with secretarial help, in nine years; in which he also wrote the whole of two journals, *The Rambler* and *The Idler*; *Irene*, a tragedy; the poems *London* and *The Vanity of Human Wishes*, and a philosophical tale, *Rasselas*. The definitions established the authority of the *Dictionary*. Believing that 'the chief glory of any people arises from its authors', Johnson illustrated senses by 114,000 quotations gathered from authors since Sidney.

When first I collected these authorities, I was desirous that every quotation should be useful to some other end than the illustration of a word; I therefore extracted from philosophers principles of science; from historians remarkable facts; from chemists complete processes; from divines striking exhortations; and from poets beautiful descriptions. Such is design, while it is yet at a distance from execution. When the time called upon me to range this accumulation of elegance and wisdom into an alphabetical series, I soon discovered that the bulk of my volumes would fright away the student, and was forced to depart from my scheme of including all that was pleasing or useful in English literature, and reduce my transcripts very often to clusters of words in which scarcely any meaning is retained: thus to the weariness of copying, I was condemned to add the vexation of expunging.

Johnson's *Preface* shows that he believed in regularity but knew very well that words change their sounds and their senses, and that therefore his work, inevitably imperfect, would also become obsolete: 'I am not so lost in lexicography, as to forget that *words are the daughters of earth, and that things are the sons of heaven*.'

Johnson's *London* and *The Vanity of Human Wishes* are 'imitations', or modern applications, of satires by the Roman poet Juvenal. Like Swift, Johnson was an enemy

## Johnson's *Dictionary*: some sample definitions

ENTHU'SIASM. *n.* A vain belief of private revelation; a vain confidence of divine favour or communication. Enthusiasm is founded neither on reason nor divine revelation, but rises from the conceits of a warmed or overweening brain.—*Locke.*

TO'RY. *n.* One who adheres to the ancient constitution of the state, and the apostolical hierarchy of the church of England, opposed to a whig. The knight is more a tory in the country than the town, because it more advances his interest.—*Addison.*

WHIG. *n.* 2. The name of a faction. Whoever has a true value for church and state, should avoid the extremes of whig for the sake of the former, and the extremes of tory on the account of the latter.—*Swift.*

WIT. *n.* 1. The powers of the mind; the mental faculties; the intellects. This is the original signification. 2. Imagination; quickness of fancy. 3. Sentiments produced by quickness of fancy. 4. A man of fancy. 5. A man of genius. 6. Sense; judgment. 7. In the plural. Sound mind; intellect not crazed. 8. Contrivance; stratagem; power of expedients.

of illusion, and his poems survey the folly of human ambition. In his prayers he often reproaches himself for sloth. He had hoped to do the *Dictionary* in three years, knowing the French Academy had taken forty years. But 'Such is design, while it is yet at a distance from execution.' 'On the Death of Dr Levet', a tribute to an inmate of Johnson's house, a physician who attended the poor, begins: 'Condemned to hope's delusive mine,/As on we toil from day to day,/By sudden blasts, or slow decline,/Our social comforts drop away.' *The Vanity of Human Wishes* accordingly warns the ambitious student that in 'hope's delusive mine' there is no gold:

> Should no disease thy torpid veins invade,
> Nor melancholy's phantoms haunt thy shade;
> Yet hope not life from grief or danger free,
> Nor think the doom of man reversed for thee:
> Deign on the passing world to turn thine eyes,
> And pause awhile from letters, to be wise;
> There mark what ills the scholar's life assail,
> Toil, envy, want, the patron and the jail.
> See nations slowly wise, and meanly just,
> To buried merit raise the tardy bust.

Johnson takes a gloomy pleasure in exposing the falsity of hopes he once had shared. There is an almost tragic satisfaction in things said so tellingly in the right combination of the right words. Such verse appeals to exactness and experience, not to imagination.

In the month before his death Johnson wrote a version of Horace which has an 18th-century plain elegance of diction, but also image and rhythm:

> The snow dissolv'd no more is seen
> The fields, and woods, behold, are green,
> The changing year renews the plain,
> The rivers know their banks again,
> The spritely nymph and naked grace
> The mazy dance together trace.
> The changing year's successive plan
> Proclaims mortality to man.
> Rough winter's blasts to spring give way,
> Spring yields to summer's sovereign ray,
> Then summer sinks in autumn's reign,
> And winter chills the world again.
> Her losses soon the moon supplies,
> But wretched man, when once he lies
> Where Priam and his sons are laid,
> Is naught but ashes and a shade ...

## Literary criticism

Johnson's moral essays and *Rasselas* have long been admired, and his prayers and meditations can move atheists. His literary criticism is especially valuable, and now that criticism has few general readers, especially enjoyable. Often we do not agree – neo-classical principles can be technical or moralistic – but Johnson makes his judgements on clear grounds, obliging us to agree or disagree. He also escapes 18th-century limitations, as often in the *Lives* quoted in this History. Johnson is clearer than Coleridge, more analytic than Arnold and straighter than T. S. Eliot. He delivers

Dr Samuel Johnson, by Sir Joshua Reynolds, *c*.1775, aged about 66. Not long returned from Scotland, Johnson bends back a book in order to bring a page close to his good eye. He objected to this portrait: 'I will not be *blinking Sam*'.

the reaction not of the judging intelligence only but of the whole man. Milton 'thought woman made only for obedience, and man only for rebellion'. Pope 'never drank tea without a stratagem'; though he translated the *Iliad* he did not 'overflow with Greek'. Gray did not use his learning. But these imperfect men wrote extra-ordinary works compelling rational admiration: *Paradise Lost*, or 'the *Churchyard*'. What he thought false, he disdained: Milton's *Lycidas* or Gray's Odes.

Johnson's *Preface to Shakespeare* is the first good general account, and the last before worship set in. 'Shakespeare is, above all writers, at least above all modern writers, the poet of nature, the poet that holds up to his readers a faithful mirror of manners and of life.' Yet he was careless with plot and with moral; he rushed his end-ings; he was too wordy and obscure and fond of puns and wit-contests. He is also the writer Johnson loves and quotes most, both in the *Dictionary* and in life: to Boswell as they ride through Scotland, and to his doctor when he is dying: 'Can'st thou min-ister to a mind diseased?' Johnson thinks it undignified that Macbeth makes Heaven 'peep through the blanket of the dark': is he literal-minded, or have we been vague? He cannot bear the pain of Cordelia's unjust death: could we justify it to Johnson? His premises can be narrow, but he makes us think.

Johnson also destroyed two ruling prejudices. Critics objected to mixed or tragi-comic drama; Johnson defends it by appealing from art to nature, 'in which, at the same time, the reveller is hasting to his wine, and the mourner burying his friend'. Secondly, the prestige of the 'unity of place' had kept *Antony and Cleopatra*, in which there are many changes of scene, off the stage. Johnson:

The objection arising from the impossibility of passing the first hour at Alexandria and the next at Rome supposes that when the play opens the spectator really imagines himself at Alexandria, and believes that his walk to the theatre has been a voyage to Egypt, and that he lives in the days of Antony and Cleopatra. Surely he that imagines this may imagine more. He that can take the stage at one time for the palace of the Ptolemies may take it in half an hour for the promontory of Actium. Delusion, if delusion be admitted, has not certain limitation; if the spectator can be once persuaded that his old acquaintances are Alexander and Caesar, that a room illuminated with candles is the plain of Pharsalia …, he is in a state of elevation above the reach of reason or truth, and from the heights of empyrean poetry may despise the circumscriptions of terrestrial nature. … The truth is that the spectators are always in their senses, and know, from the first act to the last, that the stage is only a stage, and that the players are only players.

## James Boswell

This embodiment of English commonsense was not the creation of Boswell, yet Johnson's solidity is largely thanks to the memory, devotion and skill of a man very unlike himself. Boswell's *Life* (1791, 1793, 1799) is the first and perhaps the only grand life of an author.

**James Boswell** (1740–95), the son of a lowland Law Lord, made a Grand Tour. When in Switzerland he charmed both Voltaire and Rousseau, who gave him an introduction to the Corsican hero Paoli. His *Account of Corsica* made him famous: he wore the headband of a Corsican patriot, and was known as Corsica Boswell. At 23, the lion-hunter contrived an introduction to Johnson, but his introducer mentioned him as coming from Scotland.

'Mr. Johnson, (said I) I do indeed come from Scotland, but I cannot help it.' I am willing to flatter myself that I meant this as light pleasantry to sooth and conciliate him, and not as an humiliating abasement at the expence of my country. But however that might be, this speech was somewhat unlucky; for with that quickness of wit for which he was so remarkable, he seized the expression 'come from Scotland,' which I used in the sense of being of that country, and, as if I had said that I had come away from it, or left it, retorted, 'That, Sir, I find, is what a very great many of your countrymen cannot help.' This stroke stunned me a good deal …

Although including his hero's faults (for which he was much criticized), Boswell will make himself look foolish in order to draw Johnson out. Indeed, he goes out of his way to look comic: 'Amid some patriotick groans, somebody (I think the Alderman) said, "Poor old England is lost." JOHNSON: "Sir, it is not so much to be lamented that Old England is lost, as that the Scotch have found it."' Boswell adds a footnote: 'It would not become me to expatiate on this strong and pointed remark, in which a very great deal of meaning is condensed.' Such notes can reduce devotees to helpless laughter.

But the *Life* is a work of scholarship as well as affection, fully documented with letters to and from Johnson, prayers and epitaphs composed by Johnson, and his answers to moral and legal questions put to him by Boswell over twenty-one years. We get a picture of Johnson's circle and the life of the age. But we do not take our eyes off the man himself, so full of passion, humour, melancholy, fears and quirks, as well as sense, honesty and reasoned judgement.

His mind resembled the vast amphitheatre, the Colosseum at Rome. In the centre stood his judgment, which, like a mighty gladiator, combated those apprehensions, that like the wild beasts of the arena, were all around in cells, ready to be let out upon him. After a conflict, he drove them back into their dens; but not killing them, they were still assailing him.

Boswell knew Johnson as a bear-leader knew his bear, and could play upon him as well as with him. Aware that Johnson 'was sometimes a little actuated by the spirit of contradiction', he manœuvred him into a dinner where he knew his political opposite

John Wilkes would be. They talked without falling out, and Johnson thawed. Boswell: 'Mr Burke gave me much credit for this successful "negotiation"; and pleasantly said that there was nothing to equal it in the whole history of the *Corps Diplomatique*.' 'Bozzy' also persuaded Johnson at 64 to go to Scotland, to ride through the Highlands and to risk the Hebrides in autumn in an open boat. Their accounts of their experiences are now available in one volume, and the comparison improves understanding of the skill with which Boswell enlivened Johnson's life; each book is masterly. Johnson showed his ability to go from the detail to the universal after looking at the construction of windows in Banff. There follows this generalization:

The true state of every nation is the state of common life. The manners of a people are not to be found in the schools of learning, or the palaces of greatness, where the national character is obscured or obliterated by travel or instruction, by philosophy or vanity; nor is public happiness to be estimated by the assemblies of the gay, or the banquets of the rich. The great mass of nations is neither rich nor gay: they whose aggregate constitutes the people, are found in the streets, and the villages, in the shops and farms: and from them collectively considered, must the measure of general prosperity be taken.

Johnson's common touch makes 'Augustanism' real. The *Life* is a wonderful account of a deep and astonishing man, whom we come to know socially as well as anyone can be known through a book. Boswell's memory enabled him to recall lengthy conversations (he took notes afterwards), and re-create scenes, some of which he had set up. He includes prayers, which correct the bias towards the social. Boswell's self-dramatizing and self-revising can be followed in the frank journals in which for thirty years he recorded his indulgences and unhappiness. His dedication made up for his vanity, and his reputation as a writer continues to rise.

Boswell did the public relations for David Garrick's Shakespeare Jubilee of 1769 at Stratford: music by Thomas Arne, backdrops by Joshua Reynolds, an Ode by Mr Garrick, recitations galore and thousands of souvenirs sold. At this 'event' the national poet was first called the Bard, an odd title for a London dramatist neither preliterate nor Welsh.

## Non-fiction

'Non-fiction' is a library classification too drab for the prose of Burke, Gibbon and Sheridan. History was part of 18th-century literature – both Gray and Warton became professors of history – and so was oratory: all were branches of rhetoric. Literature today neglects most non-fictional prose, although history can be well written (as can literary criticism), but formal oratory has decayed. The 19th-century historian Macaulay once described Burke as 'the greatest man since Milton'. Few politicians today have read any of the three.

### Edward Gibbon

Ideals of style changed in the 18th century also, from Dryden's ease and Addison's polish to Johnson's range of manner. But the top end became more majestic and oratorical. Burke and Sheridan begin the age of British parliamentary oratory. But the prize for memory, composition and learning goes to another member of the Club, **Edward Gibbon** (1737–94). His *Decline and Fall of the Roman Empire* begins in the golden age of the 2nd-century Antonine emperors. Its end is not the barbarian invasions nor the restoration and decay of Charlemagne's western empire but the fall of Constantinople in 1453. Gibbon read and condensed the materials in ancient and modern languages for the twelve centuries connecting the ancient with the modern world, taking in the invasions of the Goths, Persians, Saracens and Turks, the rise of Christianity and Islam, and the crusades. He combined antiquarian detail with an enlightened moral and philosophical interest in human nature.

An American editor of Gibbon remarks that 'the English are at their best in the writing of the spoken word', quoting Gibbon's method of composition, which was to 'cast a long paragraph in a single mould, to try it by my ear, to deposit it in my memory, but to suspend the action of the pen 'til I had given the last polish to my work'. Gibbon is not an essayist fond of epigram: he laid marble paragraph next to long marble paragraph, and his six volumes are not to be traversed like tarmac. The finished work is as overwhelming as the Palace of Versailles when occupied, although his manner is sometimes of the kind which led to Versailles no longer being occupied.

If we carefully trace the distance from the wall of Antoninus to Rome, and from thence to Jerusalem, it will be found that the great chain of communication from the northwest to the southeast point of the empire was drawn out to the length of four thousand and eighty Roman miles. The public roads were accurately divided by mile stones and ran in a direct line from one city to another with very little respect for the obstacles either of nature or private property. Mountains were perforated, and bold arches thrown over the broadest and most rapid streams. The middle part of the road was raised into a terrace which commanded the adjacent country, consisted of several strata of sand, gravel, and cement, and was paved with large stones, or, in some places near the capital, with granite.

Gibbon's miles are Roman *millia passuum,* not English miles; he writes here not as an English but as a Roman historian. More English is his explanation of the decision not to conquer the Picts beyond the Antonine wall: 'The masters of the fairest and most wealthy climates of the globe turned with contempt from gloomy hills assailed by the winter tempest, from lakes concealed in a blue mist, and from cold and lonely heaths over which the deer of the forest were chased by a troop of naked barbarians.' He pauses in a geographical survey of eastern provinces to say that 'Phoenicia and Palestine will forever live in the memory of mankind, since America as well as Europe has received letters from the one and religion from the other.' Antithesis as a way of thinking: countries linked by Ps, continents by vowels; literature weighed against religion. Chapter XV, 'A candid but rational enquiry into the progress and establishment of Christianity', considers 'by what means the Christian faith obtained so remarkable a victory over the established religions of the earth'. Gibbon held that religion and barbarism undermined the Empire. Gibbon's editor says that he was a moderate sceptic, 'quite willing to accept the existence of a Deity, but with no stipulations about the precise mechanics of the operation of the Divine Will'. Gibbon has lasted surprisingly well as history, although his irony may make his readers suspect that they themselves may be barbarians.

## Edmund Burke

It is not for his ideas on the sublime, mentioned above, that **Edmund Burke** (1729–97) is generally remembered, but for his *Reflections on the Revolution in France* (1790), with its image of Marie Antoinette undefended, in the land of gallantry, by a single French sword. He opposed the atheism and extremism of the revolutionaries, and offered a conservative idea of society as made up of 'little platoons' of family, locality and other natural associations, and as adapting and improving organically rather than by the application of universal ideas. He stood for the liberation of the House of Commons, of Ireland, of Catholics and of the American colonies, and had opened for the prosecution against Warren Hastings, accused of corruption and ruthless government in British India. As a reformer, Burke opposed revolution. The great issue made him define his assumption that society was a living thing rather than a model run by contract or by mechanism or by ideas. Matthew Arnold thought Burke 'so great, because, almost alone in England, he brings thought to bear upon politics, he saturates politics with thought.' He influenced both Wordsworth and Coleridge.

## Oliver Goldsmith

**Oliver Goldsmith** (1730–74) was, like Dryden, Addison, Gay and Johnson, an Augustan all-rounder, writing an analytic *Essay on the Present State of Polite Letters* (1759), fiction in *The Vicar of Wakefield* (1764), poetry, notably *The Deserted Village* (1770) and, in *She Stoops to Conquer* (1773), a fine comedy, as well as much hack-work. Boswell said that Goldsmith 'wrote like an angel, but talked like poor Poll'; he was helped by Johnson, rather as Pope had helped Gay. *The Vicar of Wakefield* is about the misfortunes of an innocent clergyman and his family, a Fielding-like plot without Fielding's satire. It was a huge success, but has little in the way of insides. This 18th-century externality works better in his equally successful *She Stoops to Conquer*, a comedy of one night's mistakes: Mr Hardcastle's house is taken for an inn (thanks to a misdirection by Tony Lumpkin of The Three Jolly Pigeons), and his daughter Kate for a serving-girl, whom her supposedly shy official suitor tries to seduce. All ends well in this good-natured anti-sentimental comedy, often revived.

The title of *The Deserted Village* gives the theme. 'Sweet Auburn, loveliest village of the plain' is a rural England losing its people. When the fictional author returns to his birthplace, he finds it ruined by 'One only master', who 'rules the whole domain'.

> Ill fares the land, to hastening ills a prey,
> Where wealth accumulates, and men decay;
> Princes and lords may flourish, or may fade,
> A breath can make them, as a breath has made.
> But a bold peasantry, their country's pride,
> When once destroyed, can never be supplied.

Gone are the villagers and the schoolmaster ('And still they gazed, and still their wonder grew,/That one small head could carry all he knew') and the inn. He fondly remembers: 'The white-washed wall, the nicely sanded floor,/The varnished clock that clicked behind the door.' The empty countryside has been rearranged so that 'Its vistas strike, its palaces surprize' and 'The country blooms – a garden and a grave.' Nostalgia turns to politics: 'I see the rural virtues leave the land.' As in Gray's *Progress of Poesy*, Poetry loves Liberty. Before emigrating, she warns that States 'of native strength possest,/Tho' very poor, may still be very blest.' Fluency turns to concentration as the next lines teach

> That trade's proud empire hastes to swift decay,
> As ocean sweeps the labour'd mole away;    constructed pier
> While self-dependent power can time defy,
> As rocks resist the billows and the sky.

This conclusion was written by Johnson, the Augustan breakwater defying the rising tide of Romanticism. His values carried on into the 19th century in the journals and letters of Hester Thrale and Fanny Burney, author of *Evelina* and *Cecilia*, and the verse of the Rev. George Crabbe. Johnson hated false pastoral and admired Crabbe's *The Village* (1783) as a true picture of hard rural life. The couplet narratives of Crabbe's later *Borough* and *Tales* make a good contrast with Wordsworth's ballads on similar themes. Crabbe went on writing them until 1819.

## Fanny Burney

**Fanny Burney** (1752–1840) wrote from the age of ten, and had transcribed her father's *General History of Music*, yet she published *Evelina, or a Young Lady's Entrance into the World* anonymously. It succeeded and she was asked to Mrs Thrale's, where she was horrified to find it on display. 'I *hid* it under other Books, for I should *Die*, – or *Faint* at least – if any body was to pick it up innocently while I am here.' The well-brought-up Fanny knew that society frowned at fiction.

The innocent Evelina comes out in society in London and Bath, is pursued by dashing artful Willoughby but marries modest considerate Lord Orville. Virtue is rewarded, plot baffles, dialogue sparkles. The epistolary mode allows the machinations of men and the world to be experienced through Evelina's eyes. *Evelina* exploits an 18th-century interest in perspective and partial knowledge. It is a bridge from *Grandison* to *Pride and Prejudice*.

## Richard Brinsley Sheridan

Almost all 18th-century literature is very theatrical, in its awareness of audience and use of appearance to manipulate audience attitude. The caricatures of William Hogarth (1679–1764) and the oratorios of G. F. Handel (1685–1759) were public

Portrait of Fanny Burney as an elegant young lady, by her cousin, Edward Francesco Burney, *c.*1785.

theatre. But there had been no first-rate Hanoverian plays before Goldsmith. Garrick dominated a theatre of Shakespeare adaptations, farces and pantomimes – and Addison's *Cato*. The son of an Irish actor, **Richard Brinsley Sheridan** (1751–1816) went from Harrow School to Bath, where he eloped with a singer, fighting duels and reconciling fathers – a good start to a life in theatre management. In 1777, Johnson proposed him as a member of the Club, remarking, according to Boswell, that he had 'written the two best comedies of his age': *The Rivals* (1775), with its glorious Mrs Malaprop, a great success at Covent Garden, and *The School for Scandal* (1777). On Garrick's death in 1779, Sheridan took over the Drury Lane theatre and wrote *The Critic*. He was 28. But in 1780 he entered the Commons, where he followed the example of Burke rather than that of Gibbon, who never spoke. He spoke for six hours in the trial of Warren Hastings. Oratory led to office, and he then divided his public career, as a leader of the Whig Opposition, between speaking at elaborate length and running Drury Lane, which had to be rebuilt twice. But his neglect of detail brought him debt rather than advancement. Four Lords carried his coffin, but laid it near Garrick rather than, as he had wished, next to Fox.

The three plays of his youth show that he understood the theatre better than anyone since the decline of Restoration drama. Restoration formulations underlie his plays, which were most unlike the sentimental dramas then on London's large public stages. His masterpiece, *The School for Scandal*, concerns two brothers, Charles and Joseph Surface (theatre names in the style of Fielding: Charles II liked women, Joseph rejected the advances of Pharoah's wife). Charles seems a rake, but is good at heart; Joseph speaks of sentiment and morality. His friend old Sir Peter Teazle has a young Lady Teazle and a younger ward, Maria. In the end Charles gets Maria, whom Joseph stalks while trying to seduce Lady Teazle. All is revealed when Charles pulls down a screen in Joseph's rooms, exposing Lady Teazle, who has overheard her husband's concern for her (see illustration). She exposes the hypocrisy of her would-be

Screen episode in Act IV, scene 3, of Sheridan's *A School for Scandal*, first produced at Drury Lane in 1777.

seducer. Bath is the School of the title: scandal, whether real or invented, is better than the affectation of virtue. It is wonderfully clever and masterly – yet, compared with Congreve, or with Jane Austen, broad and formulaic.

## Christopher Smart

Sheridan's abandonment of a reworked tradition is a sign of the break-up of the Augustan consensus. William Cowper (1731–1800), the representative poet of the later period, wrote poems of radically different kinds, as had Gray and **Christopher Smart** (1722–71).

Stylistically, Smart's poems are either Augustan – dexterous and decorous, whether witty or religious – or (after his mental breakdown) biblical. Modern anthologies often include the curious and delightful 'For I will consider my Cat Jeoffrey,' a section of the unpublished *Jubilate Agno* ('Rejoice with the Lamb'). Jeoffrey is more spiritual than Mr Walpole's cat, whose drowning was deplored by Gray. Animal-lovers may find other sections stranger:

> Let Noah rejoice with Hibris who is from a wild boar and a tame sow.
> *For I bless God for the immortal soul of Mr Pigg of DOWNHAM in NORFOLK.*
> Let Abdon rejoice with the Glede who is very voracious and may not himself be eaten.
> *For I fast this day even the 31st of August N.S. to prepare for the SABBATH of the Lord.*

('N.S.' means 'New Style': in the Gregorian reform, the calendar lost 11 days in 1752.)

These productions of the madhouse were often dismissed as such. But they mimic the antiphonal structure of Psalms: the 'Let' lines are quasi-biblical in content, the 'For' lines autobiographical. This antiphonal alternation of biblical and non-biblical would have been shockingly odd rather than obscure. Smart published in 1763 *A Song to David*, a mystically-organized and wonderful work, one of the tamer stanzas of which is the 76th:

> Strong is the lion – like a coal
> His eye-ball – like a bastion's mole                outwork of masonry
>     His chest against the foes:
> Strong, the gier-eagle on his sail
> Strong against the tide, th'enormous whale
>     Emerges, as he goes.

A comparison of this with William Blake's poem 'The Tyger' makes both seem more biblical, and Smart's more Augustan. Smart's last publication was a complete version of Horace, who was in the 18th century almost an English poet.

## William Cowper

The battle between the Psalms of David and the Odes of Horace was more tragically lost by Cowper, a writer of light verse, who after a breakdown in 1763 tried to kill himself. After an evangelical conversion, Cowper wrote the *Olney Hymns*. A worse breakdown came in 1773, when he thought that God had commanded him to kill himself. Failing in his attempt, he lived the rest of his life convinced that he was damned, 'damn'd below Judas: more abhorred than he was'.

The deluded but mild and sociable poet found protectors, one of whom set him to write a Miltonic blank verse poem upon the Sofa on which they sat. Dr Johnson wrote of *Paradise Lost* that 'we desert our master and seek for companions'. *The Task* (in six books, 1785) is by contrast a very companionable poem. The Argument of the First Book begins:

Historical deduction of seats, from the stool to the Sofa.—A School-boys ramble.—A walk in the country.—The scene described.—Rural sounds as well as sights delightful.—Another walk.—Mistake concerning the charms of solitude, corrected.—Colonnades commended.—Alcove and the view from it.—The Wilderness.—The Grove.—The Thresher.—The necessity and the benefits of exercise.—The works of nature superior to and in some instances inimitable by art.—The wearisomeness of what is commonly called a life of pleasure.—Changes of scene sometimes expedient—A common described, and character of crazy Kate introduced upon it. Gipsies.—The blessings of civilized life.—etc.

Cowper discovered that walking was beneficial. He conducts our eye through the scene:

> Here Ouse, slow winding through a level plain
> Of spacious meads with cattle sprinkled o'er,
> Conducts the eye along his sinuous course,
> Delighted. There, fast rooted in his bank
> Stand, never overlook'd, our fav'rite elms
> That screen the herdsman's solitary hut;
> While far beyond and overthwart the stream
> That as with molten glass inlays the vale,
> The sloping land recedes into the clouds …

The landscape includes cattle, 'the herdsman's solitary hut', 'hedge-row beauties numberless, square tow'r,/Tall spire' and 'Groves, heaths, and smoking villages remote.' Such English scenes are found in similar combinations in Ann Finch, Pope, Thomson, Collins and Gray, but Cowper composes them best and converses most sanely. He was admired by Jane Austen and by the painter John Constable (1776–1837), and echoed by Wordsworth and Coleridge. He wrote one poem of absolute despair, 'The Castaway'.

## Robert Burns

During the 18th century writers came to the metropolis of Britain from the provinces, and from Ireland and Scotland. The second President of the United States, John Adams, came to England for a classical education. Edinburgh and Dublin had their own Enlightenments, feeding their own national literatures, but also making an impression on English literature through Edgeworth, Burns, Scott and others. Scottish enlighteners were mostly academics who mostly wrote prose. Poetry written in Scots was unknown in England, as Gaelic writing was in Edinburgh. The Reformation and the Unions of crowns and parliaments had not helped Scotland's imaginative vernacular literature.

This came to English notice for the first time with **Robert Burns** (1759–96). On the title page of his *Poems, Chiefly in the Scottish Dialect* (Kilmarnock, 1786), Burns presents himself as 'The Simple Bard, unbroke by Rules of Art'. An Edinburgh reviewer distilled this into 'a heaven-taught ploughman'. Burns did plough a poor tenant farm, but had been taught his letters, and the English Augustans, French and some Latin, by a graduate employed by his father, also a poor tenant-farmer. He wrote in English until in his twenties he discovered that the Scots he spoke had been revived as a literary medium by Allan Ramsay and especially Robert Fergusson.

He had intended this Kilmarnock publication to pay for his emigration to Jamaica. His satires on Calvinism had given offence, and he and his pregnant Jean Armour had had to do public penance in the kirk. But in Edinburgh, Henry Mackenzie, author of *The Man of Feeling* (1771), commended these Scottish dialect poems in *The Lounger*. The loungers toasted the ploughman poet, who drank in Edinburgh's taverns. The farm failing, Burns took a post in the Excise, collecting taxes for the Crown. Expanded *Poems* were published in Edinburgh in 1787, and expanded again in 1794 to include *Tam o' Shanter*. *The Scots Musical Museum*, a collection of all extant Scottish songs, now took up most of Burns's creative energy. He contributed hundreds of poems to it, often amended or rewritten.

Burns wrote variously in English and Scots, and instant fame led to some myths. Very rarely had he 'walked in glory and in joy,/Following his plough along the mountainside', as Wordsworth was to imagine, and he gave up farming with relief. He is famous as a democrat – against rank, kirk and state, and for whisky, liberty and the French Revolution – but joined the Dumfries Volunteers before his death in 1796. His versatility is seen in his exceptionally gifted songs. Not all are as beautiful and touching as 'My love is like a red, red rose', 'Ye banks and braes o' bonny Doon' or 'Ae fond kiss'. With the songs of love, patriotism and sentiment are erotic, comic, sardonic and bawdy songs. Burns embraced folk bawdy with zest, as in his subversive *The Jolly Beggars*.

Burns found his voices in the vernacular, and his Scots poems eclipse those in English. Yet he has a general debt to neo-classical tradition, and to the 18th century's reductive comic irony. He created for himself a social voice in which soliloquy sounds natural, as for example in his justly famous 'To a Mouse On Turning Her up in Her Nest with the Plough, November 1785,' ending

> But Mousie, thou art no thy-lane            alone
> In proving *foresight* may be vain:
> The best-laid schemes o' *Mice* an' *Men*
>            Gang aft agley,                        often go amiss
> An' lea'e us nought but grief an' pain,      leave
>            For promis'd joy!
>
> Still, thou art blest, compar'd wi' me!
> The *present* only toucheth thee:
> But Och! I *backward* cast my e'e,            eye
>            On prospects drear!
> An' *forward*, tho' I canna *see*,
>            I *guess* an' *fear*!

These and many other of his famous lines express sentiments to which every bosom returns an echo. This is an Augustan quality. Contemporary readers would have recognized his 'Simple bard' epigraph as from Pope, and 'The Jolly Beggars' as a miniature *Beggar's Opera*; it was also published as 'Love and Liberty. A Cantata'. He wrote satirical verse letters, and in 'Holy Willie's Prayer' joyfully converted heroi-comical techniques to the mockery of hypocritical piety. *Tam o' Shanter* itself is a mock-heroic Augustan poem in the rogue-realism tradition. This 18th-century irony is subdued in Sir Walter Scott, but bares its edge in later Anglo-Scots such as Byron, Macaulay and J. S. Mill.

The energy of the wonderful *Tam o' Shanter* allows its audience not to notice its complexity. Burns knew it was his most finished piece, and, since it is ideal for convivial social recitation, it is a suitable testament. According to Emerson, Burns offers 'the only example in history of a language made classic through the genius of a single man'. At times, however, Burns teams up his Scots with English words, as in the fourth word in the first line of 'To a Mouse': 'Wee, sleeket, cowran, tim'rous *beastie*'. One of Burns's models was James Beattie, not for his *Scoticisms, Arranged in Alphabetical Order, Designed to Correct Improprieties of Speech and Writing*, but for *The Minstrel* (1774). Burns was not a simple bard but a canny minstrel.

# Further reading

Chapman, R. W. (ed.). *Boswell's Life of Johnson* (Oxford: Oxford University Press, 1953). Gives the age as well as the man.

Fairer, D. and C. Gerrard (eds). *Eighteenth-Century Poetry: An Annotated Anthology* (Oxford: Blackwell, 1998).

Mack, M. *Alexander Pope: A Life* (New Haven and London: Yale University Press, 1985). Detailed literary biography.

Rogers, P. (ed.). *The Eighteenth Century* (London: Methuen, 1978). A good short account.

CHAPTER

7

# The Romantics: 1790–1837

## Contents

## Overview

English Romantic literature is overwhelmingly a poetic one, with six major poets writing in the first quarter of the 19th century, transforming the literary climate. Blake was unknown; Wordsworth and Coleridge won partial acceptance in the first decade; Scott and Byron became popular. The flowering of the younger Romantics, Byron, Shelley and Keats, came after 1817, but by 1824 all were dead. The other great literary artist of the period is Jane Austen, whose six novels appeared anonymously between 1811 and 1818. Other books appearing without an author's name were *Lyrical Ballads* (Bristol, 1798) and *Waverley* (Edinburgh, 1814). The novels of 'the author of *Waverley*', Sir Walter Scott, were wildly popular. There was original fiction from Maria Edgeworth and Mary Shelley, and non-fiction from Thomas De Quincey, Charles Lamb and William Hazlitt.

## The Romantic poets

### Early Romantics

#### William Blake

**William Blake** (1757–1827) was Burns's contemporary but had none of his success. He grew up poor in London, went to art school, was apprenticed to an engraver at 14, and lived by engraving. His fine teenage *Poetical Sketches* were printed but not published. He engraved his later poems by his own laborious method, hand-colouring each copy of the little books in which he published them. Eventually, his art gained him a few admirers, notably the painter Samuel Palmer (1805–81).

Blake had begun his *Songs of Experience* with 'Hark to the voice of the Bard!' – but the age did not hearken to this truly 'heaven-taught' genius. Self-educated and mis-understood, he opposed the ruling intellectual orthodoxies, political, social, sexual and ecclesiastical, with a marked contempt for Deist materialists, censorious priests and the President of the Royal Academy, Sir Joshua Reynolds. A revolutionary who briefly shared Milton's hope that paradise might be restored by politics, he came to regard the political radicals, his allies, as blind rational materialists: 'Mock on, mock on, Voltaire, Rousseau;/Mock on, mock on, 'tis all in vain./You throw the sand against the wind,/And the wind throws it back again.' For Blake, human reality was political, spiritual and divine. A material ideal of advancement showed 'Single vision, and Newton's sleep' (Isaac Newton's prophetic writings were then unknown). A religious visionary driven by Deism to unorthodox extremes, Blake was also, unlike most mystics, a satirical ironist and a master of savage aphorisms, as in *The Marriage of Heaven and Hell.*

Blake's *Songs of Experience* (1794) contain what have become his most celebrated poems, such as 'The Sick Rose', 'The Tyger' and 'London', which begins:

> I wander thro' each charter'd street,
> Near where the charter'd Thames does flow,
> And mark in every face I meet
> Marks of weakness, marks of woe.

Blake uses the rhythmical quatrains of Isaac Watts's *Divine Songs for Children* (1715), repeating and twisting words and sounds to make a discord with the childhood vision of his earlier *Songs of Innocence.* Concentration lends his images a surreal intensity: 'the hapless Soldier's sigh/Runs in blood down Palace walls' and 'the youthful Harlot's curse … blasts with plagues the Marriage hearse'.

When read, he was not understood. Wordsworth said later: 'There was no doubt that this poor man was mad, but there is something in the madness of this man which interests me more than the sanity of Lord Byron and Walter Scott.' In the time of the French Revolution there were many who saw signs that the Judgement of the Apocalypse was at hand, but Blake was isolated and his thought was esoteric. He drew on unfamiliar theological traditions of biblical prophecy. Blake's thought evolved in his later prophetic books, often inverting conventional religious values in a way deriving from 18th-century satirical traditions of reversed perspective. Thus, Milton's God the Father is parodied as 'Old Nobodaddy aloft' who 'farted and belched and coughed'. He invented new and complex myths with allegorical strands of meaning, as in the *Vision of the Daughters of Albion*, featuring Oothoon, Theotormon and Bromion. Scholarship has made the later Blake less obscure, but it will never communicate as other Romantic poetry does. If keys can never fully unlock these prophetic myths of political and sexual liberation, yet lightning can strike from their most impenetrable clouds. A brief History cannot do justice to Blake's later work, which is a study in itself.

Blake illustrated a book by Mary Wollstonecraft (1759–97), the indomitable author of *A Vindication of the Rights of Woman* (1792), who married the radical social philosopher William Godwin (1756–1836), author of an *Inquiry concerning Political Injustice* (1793) and a programmatic Gothic novel, *Caleb Williams* (1794). She died after giving birth to a daughter, later to become Mary Shelley. Godwin's belief that humanity, since it was reasonable, could be made perfect by rational persuasion persuaded many in the early 1790s.

## Subjectivity

The ingredients of Romantic sensibility had existed before 1798, but the new poets found for it an authentic voice, touch and intensity. The novel elements in the *Lyrical*

---

**The Romantic poets**

**First Romantics**
William Blake (1757–1827); William Wordsworth (1770–1850); Samuel Taylor Coleridge (1772–1834).

**Younger Romantics**
George Gordon, Lord Byron (1788–1824); Percy Bysshe Shelley (1792–1822); John Keats (1795–1821).

---

**William Wordsworth**
(1770–1850) Son of steward of the Lonsdale estate, Westmorland. 1778 mother dies, Wordsworth becomes a boarder at Hawkshead School. 1790 walks 2000 miles through France and Alps in the Cambridge Long Vacation. 1791 in France. 1792 a daughter born to Annette Vallon. Wordsworth returns home for funds; war prevents a reunion. 1794 the Terror (mass executions) cools Wordsworth's enthusiasm for French Revolution; he 'yielded up moral questions in despair'. 1795 a bequest allows him to live in Dorset; meets Coleridge, and moves to live near him, with his sister Dorothy. 1798 *Lyrical Ballads*. 1799 returns to the Lakes for good. 1802 inherits money Lord Lonsdale owed his father. Marries Mary Hutchinson. 1807 *Poems in Two Volumes*. 1810 estranged from Coleridge. 1813 appointed Stamp Distributor (tax collector) for Westmorland. 1843 appointed Poet Laureate. 1850 *Prelude* published.

*Ballads* were defined and given impetus by the *Preface* Wordsworth added in 1800 (without mention of Coleridge). The quality and impact of the best poems were such that lyric poetry and imaginative literature were permanently altered, especially by the new emphasis on subjective experience. This subjectivity is exemplified in a famous Wordsworth lyric:

> She dwelt among th' untrodden ways
> Beside the springs of Dove,
> A maid whom there were none to praise,
> And very few to love.
>
> 5   A violet by a mossy stone
> Half-hidden from the eye! –
> Fair as a star, when only one
> Is shining in the sky.
>
> She lived unknown, and few could know
> 10   When Lucy ceased to be;
> But she is in her grave, and oh!
> The difference to me.

The ending illustrates a principle of the *Preface* that in these poems 'the feeling therein developed gives importance to the ... situation, and not the ... situation to the feeling.' This inverts the Augustan idea that literature's object is 'just representations of general nature', or general truth. The comic impulse of the 18th century also recedes. Had Pope written lines 3–4 or 7–8 above, irony might have been suspected; but social irony has no place in Wordsworth's graveside manner. Lines from Gray's *Elegy* approach Wordsworth's position: 'Full many a flower is born to bloom unseen/And waste its sweetness on the desert air.' Gray's churchyard lies betweeen London and the Lakes, whence the half-hidden violet and the first star (the planet Venus) can be seen. Yet it takes a poet's eye to see a Lucy, and a poetic reader to respond. The poet is becoming a special interpreter of special truths to a special reader, not of general truths to common readers. This relationship is more personal, and can be deeper and more intense than what it replaced, but – as the rhyme on 'oh!' illustrates – it can also be more risky.

As poetry became more subjective, literature began to be defined as imaginative. Thus the post-Romantic prose of Carlyle, and of Ruskin, Newman and Pater, is more 'literary' than the rational prose of J. S. Mill, which relies less on rhythm and imagery. In fiction, too, the keynote is often set by imaginative natural description, as in the novels of the Brontës.

## Romanticism and Revolution

There had been a European Romanticism or pre-Romanticism since the 'Ossian' craze of the 1760s. Rousseau's *Julie, ou la Nouvelle Héloïse* (1761) and Goethe's *The Sorrows of Young Werther* (1774) added passionate love to the ingredients of sensibility sketched in the last chapter. Thus it was that **Robert Southey** (1774–1843), expelled from Westminster School, could say that he went up to Oxford with 'a heart full of poetry and feeling, a head full of Rousseau and Werther, and my religious principles shaken by Gibbon.' He makes out here that he was a typical student of the generation that shared Wordsworth's reaction to the French Revolution: 'Bliss was it in that dawn to be alive,/But to be young was very heaven.' Southey became very popular, and eventually a strong Tory.

The idea of the American Revolution excited European intellectuals. French Romantics were radical and liberal, but English Romantics divided. Early 18th-century French thinkers had admired the English for having already curbed the royal power; mid-18th-century French thinkers identified repression with king, nobles and clergy. Things were not so clear in England, where the French Revolution had a mixed and changing reception. Youthful rapture was modified by the Terror, when thousands were killed. **Tom Paine** (1737–1809), a hero of the American Revolution and radical author of *The Rights of Man* (1791), was welcomed in France. Yet his opposition to the execution of Louis XVI put him in prison and near the guillotine. In 1793 France declared war on England, whose government as a result became more repressive – and had much to repress. Napoleon set about his 'liberating' conquest of Europe; Britain resisted and at length succeeded. But her own reforms had to wait until after 1824, when Byron, Shelley and Keats, young radicals at the end of a long and severe period of national reaction against the Revolution and Napoleon, were dead. Blake was the only Romantic to stay true to his vision in middle age. Coleridge and Wordsworth lost faith in utopian solutions, and by 1815 had turned to the Church of England.

## William Wordsworth

Wordsworth's early radicalism went quiet, yet a democratic tone is clear in the *Advertisement* to *Lyrical Ballads, with Pastoral and Other Poems* (1798), which advises that most of the poems were 'to be considered as experiments' to determine 'how far the language of conversation in the middle and lower classes of society is adapted to the purposes of poetic pleasure'. In line with this programme, a few *Lyrical Ballads* recount incidents of unsophisticated rural life, using a language close to common speech. The *Preface* attacks the artificial 'poetic diction' used in conventional 18th-century verse (and suggests that 18th-century verse is conventional). The *Preface* proclaims that, at this moment of crisis, the poet is the defender of human nature.

For a multitude of causes, unknown to former times, are now acting with a combined force to blunt the discriminating powers of the mind and, unfitting it for all voluntary exertion, to reduce it to a state of almost savage torpor. The most effective of these causes are the great national events which are daily taking place, and the increasing accumulation of men in cities, where the uniformity of their occupations produces a craving for extraordinary incident, which the rapid communication of intelligence [news] hourly gratifies. To this tendency of life and manners, the literature and theatrical exhibitions of the country have conformed themselves. The invaluable works of our elder Writers, I had almost said the works of Shakespeare and Milton, are driven into neglect by frantic novels, sickly and stupid German tragedies, and deluges of idle and extravagant stories in verse. When I think upon this degrading thirst after outrageous stimulation, I am almost ashamed to have spoken of the feeble effort with which I have endeavoured to counteract it …

Wordsworth's analysis of how the media excited bored urban audiences is republican and idealist, not populist. It also shows the 18th-century austerity which kept extravagance out of his work. A sentence in the *Preface*, however, claims that 'all good poetry is the spontaneous overflow of powerful feeling'. Untrue of most previous kinds of poetry, this described his own poetic process, which involved 'emotion recollected in tranquillity'. But the overflow model has not helped his reputation. Despite lyrics such as 'My heart leaps up when I behold/A rainbow in the

## Events 1789–1824

| 1789 | French Revolution. The Third Estate becomes the National Assembly. |
|------|-------------------------------------------------------------------|
| 1791 | Louis XVI accepts a new Constitution. |
| 1792 | France is declared a Republic. Royalists massacred. |
| 1793 | Reign of Terror in France. France and Britain at war. |
| 1794 | Pitt suspends the law of *habeas corpus*, curbs the press. Robespierre guillotined. |
| 1796 | French invasion of Ireland fails. |
| 1797 | Naval mutinies are suppressed. Naval victories. |
| 1798 | The French intervene in the Low Countries, Austria, Italy, Egypt. Rebellion against British rule in Ireland. Nelson wins Battle of the Nile. |
| 1799 | Combinations Act forbids trade unions. |
| 1800 | Ireland is united to England. Irish MPs come to Westminster. |
| 1803 | Irish rebellion is suppressed. |
| 1804 | Napoleon is crowned Emperor. |
| 1805 | Nelson defeats the French fleet at Trafalgar. |
| 1807 | Abolition of the slave trade in the British Empire. |
| 1808 | Britain opposes France in the Peninsular War in Spain. |
| 1809 | Napoleon conquers the Papal States, and occupies Vienna. |
| 1811 | George III is insane. The Prince of Wales becomes Regent (to 1820). Luddites break machines in the Midlands. |
| 1812 | The French army invading Russia is destroyed by winter. |
| 1813 | Wellington victorious in Spain. |
| 1814 | The Allies invade France. Napoleon abdicates. |
| 1815 | Napoleon returns; he is defeated by Wellington at Waterloo. |
| 1816–17 | Riots. |
| 1818 | Parliamentary motion for universal suffrage is defeated. |
| 1819 | 'Peterloo Massacre': eleven radicals killed at a mass meeting in Manchester. |
| 1820 | George III dies. George IV reigns (to 1830). |
| 1821 | Failure of the Cato Street Conspiracy, a plot to murder the Cabinet. |
| 1822 | The Greeks revolt against Turkish rule. |
| 1823 | Prime Minister Peel begins legal reforms. |
| 1824 | Combinations Act of 1799 repealed. |

sky', he rarely gushes, especially in comparison with other Romantics. Matthew Arnold rightly praised his ability to face the worst with terrible calm – as in 'A slumber did my spirit seal', which attains moral grandeur in eight uneffusive lines.

Of the chief *Lyrical Ballads*, only Coleridge's *Rime of the Ancient Mariner* is a ballad, and *Lines written some miles above Tintern Abbey, Michael, Nutting* and 'There was a boy, ye knew him well' are not lyrics. But the volume claims in its hybrid title that the finer qualities of song-like lyrics, such as 'A slumber did my spirit seal', can inhere in rough 'folk'-verse tales. The experimental poems partially succeed, or fail interestingly. More significant are the anecdotes from everyday life, such as 'We are Seven' and 'Simon Lee', which successfully mix genres and offer unresolved viewpoints. Less experimental are the central *Lines written some miles above Tintern Abbey*, which follow in Cowper's conversational mode.

Coleridge's earlier *Frost at Midnight* was a model for *Tintern*, giving landscaped reflection a new poetic intensity and psychic depth. The thought of the two friends was at this time almost indistinguishable. Both poems offer the doctrine of Nature now associated with Wordsworth, Coleridge's in a finely articulated psychological, philosophical and religious form. Wordsworth felt 'A presence that disturbs me':

> a sense sublime
> Of something far more deeply interfused,
> Whose dwelling is the light of setting suns
> And the round ocean and the living air,
> And the blue sky, and in the mind of man.

These are the accents of faith – but in what? Coleridge is always Christian, but Wordsworth as yet acknowledges no God outside natural phenomena: 'the mighty world/Of eye and ear, – both what they half create,/And what perceive.' The Nature which asks his co-operation is his anchor, nurse, guide, guardian, and the 'soul/Of all my moral being.' *Tintern* has an emotional weight which makes Coleridge's more perfect poem seem magically light.

In *Frost at Midnight*, Coleridge's gaze at the fire in the cottage in Devon turns back to a daydream of his schooldays in London, where he had dreamed of his infancy in Devon; and then forward to the hopes he has for his sleeping child. In this imaginative reverie, 'Fancy' makes 'a toy of Thought'. Imagination was for the Romantics a means of access to truths which were psychic not rational. As *Tintern* ends, Wordsworth confides his hopes to his sister Dorothy. In a spellbinding opening verse-paragraph of natural description, each poet confides in the reader. We are drawn into intimacy and identification with the poet-speaker.

*Poems in Two Volumes* (1807) has memorable poems: *Resolution and Independence*, the *Immortality Ode*, 'The Solitary Reaper', the *Elegiac Stanzas on Peele Castle*, and some Miltonic sonnets, but also the ominous *Ode to Duty*, 'Stern Daughter of the Voice of God!' Wordsworth asks Duty to give him 'the spirit of self-sacrifice' and 'the confidence of reason.' His return to Grasmere in 1799 after 'five years,/And the

William Wordsworth, aged 48, a portrait in pencil and chalk by Benjamin Robert Haydon, 1818. Known in the Wordsworth family as 'the Brigand'.

length of five long winters' (*Tintern*) was a retreat to base to recover from the crushing of his political dreams by the Terror and of his first love by the war with France. At home, he reconstructed himself, renewing memories of his natural upbringing and dealing with other traumatic memories. In 1802 he had already asked 'Whither is fled the visionary gleam? Where is it now, the glory and the dream?' (*Immortality Ode*). But as, after 1807, public recognition arrived, poetic inspiration departed. He wrote new poems and rearranged old poems, publishing in 1814 a Prospectus to an intended philosophical poem, *The Recluse*. It begins 'On Man, on Nature, and on Human Life,/Musing in solitude …', lines heavy with dutiful unenthusiasm for philosophy. In his great decade, Wordsworth had always preferred prosiness to 'inane and gaudy phraseology'. One 1806 poem begins 'Spade! with which Wilkinson hath tilled his lands'. But his verse now became almost uniformly flat.

Wordsworth's reputation was transformed by a poem published in 1850 as *The Prelude, or Growth of a Poet's Mind*; its working title had been 'the poem to Coleridge'. It is a blank-verse memoir in fourteen books, first drafted in two parts in 1799, expanded to thirteen books by 1805 and tinkered with for forty-five years. Critics usually prefer 1805 to 1850, and readers rightly respond to the freshness of the two-part *Prelude* of 1799, with its boat-stealing and night-skating episodes. In either of its elaborated versions, it is the most worthwhile long poem of the 19th century (Byron's *Don Juan* being the most entertaining). Wordsworth records his mental and psychic growth with dogged integrity. Those who do not find the growth of this poet's mind as absorbing as he did should traverse the books dealing with Cambridge, London, mountain-climbing and France to reach the great passage of Book XII beginning 'There are in our existence spots of time', with its memory of traumatic experiences endured. Wordsworth's faith in humanity is less impressive than the honesty with which he faces loss and his inability to explain it all.

> Oh! mystery of Man, from what a depth
> Proceed thy honours! I am lost, but see
> In simple childhood something of the base
> On which thy greatness stands; but this I feel,
> That from thyself it comes, that thou must give,
> Else never canst receive. The days gone by
> Return upon me almost from the dawn
> Of life: the hiding-places of Man's power
> Open; I would approach them, but they close.
> I see by glimpses now; when age comes on
> May scarcely see at all, and I would give,
> While yet we may, as far as words can give,
> Substance and hope to what I feel, enshrining,
> Such is my hope, the spirit of the past
> For future restoration: –

He then adds baldly 'Yet another of these memorials', and recalls waiting to return home from Hawkshead school for Christmas 1783. He climbs a hill to see on which road the horses are coming for him and his brothers to ride home; but 'ere we had been ten days/Sojourners in my Father's House, he died.' He returns to his memory of the wait.

> And afterwards, the wind and sleety rain
> And all the business of the elements,
> The single Sheep, and the one blasted tree,

> And the bleak music of that old stone wall,
> The noise of wood and water, and the mist
> That on the line of each of those two roads
> Advanced in such indisputable shapes;
> All these were kindred spectacles and sounds
> To which I oft repaired, and thence would drink
> As at a fountain ...

Wordsworth ends this sublime and musical passage by saying that a strong wind still causes in him inward agitations –

> Whate'er their office, whether to beguile
> Thoughts over-busy in the thought they took,
> Or animate an hour of vacant ease.

The Wordsworth who recreates, confronts and draws upon his most painful memories was no lyric simpleton. Although in 1812 he felt 'no need of a Redeemer', his trust in the providence of Nature, and his sustained transcription of its traces on his memory, is religious. An even more striking instance of Wordsworth's moral originality and of his acceptance of the harshest providence comes in his aged narrator's astonishing words at the conclusion to *The Ruined Cottage*, a tale of heart-breaking bleakness: 'I turned away/And walked along my road in happiness.' This early draft of a narrative included in *The Excursion* was published in 1949. Wordsworth is a stranger poet than is usually realized.

## Samuel Taylor Coleridge

**Samuel Taylor Coleridge** (1772–1835) had every poetic talent but discipline. It has been said that his greatest masterpiece was Wordsworth, but his own exceptional gifts produced five absolutely remarkable poems: *The Ancient Mariner* in *Lyrical Ballads*; from the same period *Frost at Midnight*, and the fragments *Kubla Khan* and *Christabel*, unpublished until 1816. Finally, *Dejection: An Ode* (1802), drafted the night he heard Wordsworth read the *Immortality Ode*. Wordsworth later added a conclusion to his own *Ode*, declaring that: 'To me the meanest flower that blows can give/Thoughts that do often lie too deep for tears.' STC, as he called himself, could not make the same act of faith. He fluently suggests the beauties of the night that surround 'Yon crescent Moon, as fixed as if it grew/In its own cloudless, starless lake of blue', but ends, 'I see them all so excellently fair,/I see, not feel, how beautiful they are.' He 'may not hope', he says, 'from outward forms to win/The passion and the life, whose fountains are within.' *Dejection* ends with a stifled prayer that Joy will attend a Lady (namely, Sara Hutchinson). He published it on the fourth anniversary of Wordsworth's marriage, and the seventh of his own.

The image of a fountain recurs in *Kubla Khan*, and in Wordsworth's commemoration of STC's death, when 'every mortal power of Coleridge/Was frozen at its marvellous source.' Coleridge conceived the mind as active, not as in Locke's passive model in which ideas derive from sense-impressions on a blank mental plate. Coleridge also went beyond the physiological turn given to Locke's theory of the association of ideas by David Hartley (1705–57). Coleridge called his first child Hartley, but his second after the idealist philosopher Berkeley, who placed the source of knowledge in the divinely-inspired human mind. For Coleridge, association of ideas could only lead to the combinatory power of Fancy, as he defined it in *Biographia Literaria*, whereas the poet imitates the divine creativity by the power of

**Samuel Taylor Coleridge**
(1772–1835) Youngest son of the vicar of Ottery St Mary, Devon. Educated at Christ's Hospital, London. Leaves Cambridge to join Light Dragoons, as Silas T. Comberbache; bought out under insanity clause. Marries Sara, Robert Southey's sister-in-law, as part of the scheme for Pantisocracy, an ideal commune in Pennsylvania. 1795 meets Wordsworth; friendship, *Lyrical Ballads*. 1798–9 in Germany. 1799 in love with Sara Hutchinson, sister of Wordsworth's future wife. Addicted to (medically prescribed) opium. 1804–6 in Malta; returns to London in despair. 1810 quarrel with Wordsworth. Lecturing, play-writing, writing *The Friend*. 1813 spiritual crisis. Recovers from addiction at Dr Gillman's, in Highgate, London. 1816 *Christabel and Other Poems*, *Lay Sermons, Statesman's Manual*. 1817 *Biographia Literaria, Sybilline Leaves*. 1825 *Aids to Reflection; Church and State*.

primary Imagination. This is the centre of Coleridge's critical thinking, in which literature is less a work of art than a natural product of the imagination. His applied criticism is philosophical and comprehensive, as when in *Biographia Literaria* he enlarges Wordsworth's ideas of poetic diction and rhythm. It can be psychological, as in his notable Shakespeare criticism. Most branches of knowledge contribute to Coleridge's criticism, which he carried on endlessly in letters, notebooks, lectures and in the margins of books.

*Biographia Literaria* is an attempt to give his 'literary life and opinions' on poetry more systematically. Intended as an autobiographical preface to his *Christabel and other Poems* (1816), it outgrew its function. Too long for a preface, it was too short for the two volumes allotted by the publisher. Masterly pages on, for example, 'The Poets before and since Mr Pope', are filled out by secondary matter. He has often been blamed for unacknowledged borrowing from the German Romantic thinkers whom he had studied at Gottingen in 1799. Coleridge's criticism is never uninteresting though it can be frustrating: autobiographical, speculative, comprehensive, unpredictable and enriched by his range of reading. He thought aloud, and his writing resembles his talk, which, as Hazlitt and Carlyle testify, was marvellous and boundless. His later works on social and religious questions combine Romantic conservatism with Christian radicalism, and had a lasting effect. As J. S. Mill wrote, 'By Bentham [the founder of Utilitarianism], beyond all others, men have been led to ask themselves, in regard to any ancient or received opinion, Is it true? and by Coleridge, What is the meaning of it?' STC's insights into symbol, understanding and development influenced John Henry Newman; his cultural criticism, Matthew Arnold. Modern criticism of poetry begins with Coleridge.

The musical and psychological modulation of *Frost at Midnight* and *Dejection* is found in improvised epistolary poems such as *This Lime-tree Bower my Prison*, but also in his 'demonic' poems, of which only *The Rime of the Ancyent Marinere* is complete. It is an experimental ballad narrative of a voyage to the South Pole, of the mariner's arbitary killing of an albatross, and of psychic punishment, a death-in-life, which lifts when the beauty of nature suddenly impels the mariner to bless God's creation. This symbolic supernatural romance was decorated with archaisms. Coleridge later modernized the 'medieval' spelling and inserted pseudo-archaic marginal glosses instead. The poem's popular success is due to its narrative drive, and its packing of nightmarish images and homely morals into a rhymed doggerel hard to forget: 'Water, water, everywhere,/Nor any drop to drink' and 'A sadder and a wiser man/He rose the morrow morn.'

The completed poem has weak passages, unlike *Kubla Khan* and *Christabel*. These are the first entirely successful experiments in modes which had been attempted for half a century: the imaginary exotic and the medieval romance. 'In Xanadu did Kubla Khan' is an incantation; each name says backwards the vowels of the other. The magic mounts as the rhythm rises. Then (as his headnote tells), STC was interrupted in writing down this vision he had had in a dream by the call of 'a person on business from Porlock'. The breaking-off improves the mystery. If Coleridge had never touched opium, this symbolic account of poetic possession shows that he had 'drunk the milk of Paradise' – and that such intense experience was a burden. This is the first supra-rational poem in English, what De Quincey called a poem of power rather than a poem of knowledge, though its fuel is STC's extraordinary reading. *Christabel*, his most organized and sinister Gothic poem, breaks off: he never provided the happy ending he intended. The innocent Christabel is possessed by a beautiful demon, in spite of the poem's 'medieval' Christianity. It is a flesh-creeping verse romance, 'extravagant' and 'sickly' in its subject-matter – to take terms from Wordsworth's *Preface* – but disciplined and subtle in execution.

The Romantic Revival often drew on Percy's *Reliques of Ancient English Poetry* (3 volumes, 1765; 4th edn, 1794). Bishop Percy (1729–1811), who translated from Chinese, Old Icelandic, Spanish and Hebrew, collected old songs, ballads and romances in English and in Scots, often in 'improved' versions. His *Reliques* had a huge influence. 18th-century antiquarianism, the romancing of the past, was the source of 19th-century Romanticism.

## Sir Walter Scott

*The Lay of the Last Minstrel* (1805) was the first of the verse romances by which **Sir Walter Scott** (1771–1832) made his name. He had begun by translating German imitation-romances, and collecting the *Minstrelsy of the Scottish Border*, continuing the work of Percy and of *The Scots Musical Museum*. The battlefields of the Borders of Scotland and England produced ballads such as the 15th-century *Chevy Chase*, a romance admired by Sidney, praised by Addison and printed by Percy. Scott spent much of his boyhood in the Borders with his grandparents. The *Lay*, sung at a noble Scott household in Tudor times, is a medieval tale of feud and magic, taking clues from *Christabel*, which Scott had seen in manuscript, and from Spenser. It has a shape-changing dwarf, and a wizard, Michael Scott, from whose tomb a magic book is taken to provide a curse. It also has feasting, a tournament, horses, armour and picturesque country. But a tragic outcome to this tale of lovers from feuding families is averted – by love, chivalry and magic, not by divine grace. The *Lay* is recited in a flexible and pleasing minstrel verse-form. Scott followed up its huge success with other verse-romances including *Marmion* and *The Lady of the Lake*, until Byron captured this market. He then wrote novels, anonymously.

# Younger Romantics

## Lord Byron

George Gordon, **Lord Byron** (1788–1824) had a wild ancestry, a Calvinist child-hood, handsome looks and a club foot. Inheriting his title unexpectedly, he lived noisily at Harrow and Cambridge, creating an image by athletic and libertine exploits. The 'craving for extraordinary incident' noted by Wordsworth could be 'hourly gratified' in the Regency by spoilt noblemen, among them the Prince Regent. The Romantic Poet, spontaneously producing poems as a tree does leaves or a thundercloud lightning, was more intruiging to journalists and to society than mere poems. A composite image of poet-as-flawed-genius took elements from the opium addiction of Coleridge; from Byron and Shelley scattering wives, lovers, children and debts across Europe; and from the younger Romantics' early deaths. Rousseau and Napoleon preceded Byron, but he was the first British poet to become the hero-villain of a publicity cult.

On leaving Cambridge, Byron pursued adventure in Iberia, Malta and the Turkish empire. These travels contributed to the first two cantos of *Childe Harold's Pilgrim-age*, published in 1812:

> Whilome in Albion's isle there dwelt a youth,  Britain once upon a time
> Who ne in virtue's ways did take delight;  not at all
> But spent his days in riot most uncouth,

> And vex'd with mirth the drowsy ear of Night.
> Ah, me! in sooth he was a shameless wight          creature
> Sore given to revel and ungodly glee;
> Few earthly things found favour in his sight
> Save concubines and carnal companie,
> And flaunting wassailers of high and low degree.

> Childe Harold was he hight.                        called

*Childe* is a medieval title of chivalry, and Byron (for it is transparently himself) claims a lineage stained with ancestral crime. The revels he boasts of took place at Newstead Abbey, Nottinghamshire, his inherited seat. He takes his Spenserian stanzas from Thomson's *The Castle of Indolence* (1748), in which Indolence seems a venial sin. Childe Harold is unrepentant:

> Apart he stalk'd in joyless reverie,
> And from his native land resolv'd to go,
> And visit scorching lands beyond the sea;
> With pleasure almost drugg'd he almost long'd for woe,
> And e'en for change of scene would seek the shades below.

'I awoke one morning and found myself famous,' Byron wrote, but the fame was no accident. He never stopped writing, nor being guilty, unrepentant and famous. The poetic autobiographer mentions his love for his daughter and his half-sister, but chiefly displays his sensibility via a travelogue. 'Europe he saw,' wrote Pope of an earlier milord on his Grand Tour, 'and Europe saw him too.' The later Cantos 3 and 4 have set-pieces reflecting at Waterloo or in Venice. In Switzerland, Byron writes:

> I live not in myself, but I become
> Portion of that around me, and to me
> High mountains are a feeling, but the hum
> Of human cities torture …

This is Wordsworth on a brass instrument. Harold writes in his farewell:

> There is a pleasure in the pathless woods,
> There is a rapture on the lonely shore,
> There is society, where none intrudes,
> By the deep Sea, and music in its roar:
> I love not Man the less, but Nature more …

Wordsworth internalized the external topics of 18th-century sensibility into a new personal poetry; Byron processed the result for export. Comparison makes clear the broadness of Byron's attitudinizing. 'Roll on, thou deep and dark blue ocean – roll!', he declaims. Rhetoric, the persuasive rational discourse of Burke and Gibbon, was now amplified by emotional emphasis, simplification and repetition, in writers as various as Sheridan, Mary Shelley and Macaulay, and in parliamentary oratory. Winston Churchill was the last in this style.

Byron worked the crowd with romances and dramatic poems in fluent verse, posing as himself. Only his liberalism, egotism and scepticism were sincere. Notable among his doomed self-projections is *Manfred* (1817), in which the superman refuses a deathbed repentance, telling the Abbot, 'Old man! 'tis not too difficult to die.' Byron's sensational romances continued with *Cain* in 1821. But his verse journalism also had a more intimate and epistolary side, glimpsed above in 'Save concubines and carnal companie' and the irony of 'E'en for change of scene would seek the shades below' – a prophecy of *Don Juan*.

Having woken up famous, Byron became more than famous. After flinging herself at him, Lady Caroline Lamb described him as 'mad, bad, and dangerous to know'. In 1814 his half-sister gave birth to a child said to be his. In 1815 he married a rich, serious and unlucky wife. Ostracized for incest, he left England for good in 1816, travelled to Lake Geneva, stayed with the Shelleys, and then moved to Italy. Most days Byron was a drawing-room milord, but he had wild periods: his debauches in Venice involved two hundred women; he was also bisexual. He sealed his European reputation as a rebel by his death while supporting the Greek revolt against the Turks.

Byron's distinction and originality is found in his anti-romantic *Don Juan*. He tired of his own poses and of 'cant', the sanctimonious expression of sentiment. His new irony is much closer to the self he reveals in his sparkling letters. Like Scott, Edgeworth, Peacock, Landor and Austen, Byron did not think that the Romantic revolution invalidated rational criticism. Pope he thought far better than any of the Romantics. His mature voice is first heard in *Beppo* and *The Vision of Judgement*. *Don Juan* (1818) begins

> I want a hero: an uncommon want,
> > When every year and month sends forth a new one,
> Till, after cloying the gazettes with cant,
> > The age discovers he is not the true one;
> Of such as these I should not care to vaunt,
> > I'll therefore take our ancient friend Don Juan,
> We all have seen him in the pantomime
> Sent to the devil, somewhat ere his time.

Byron's *Don Juan* (pronounced in the English way), the legendary womanizer who ends in hell, the Don Giovanni of Mozart's 1787 opera, is, among other things, a humorous self-portrait: a passive youngster who falls in with the amorous wishes of a series of beautiful women in Seville, Greece, St Petersburg and England. But *Don Juan*, like *Tristram Shandy*, is not read for the Life but for the Opinions, which include: 'What men call gallantry, and the gods adultery,/Is much more common where the climate's sultry' and 'Thou shalt believe in Milton, Dryden, Pope;/Thou shalt not set up Wordsworth, Coleridge, Southey;/Because the first is crazed beyond all hope,/The second drunk, the third so quaint and mouthey ...'. Although it rises to satire, most of *Don Juan* is a long-running joke. Insofar as it is self-display, the mature milord is more interesting than the self-regarding Childe. 'It may be profligate,' Byron wrote to a friend, 'but is it not *life*, is it not *the thing*?' He exposes hypocrisy with a wonderfully varied use of anticlimax which disarms as it unmasks.

> Some have accused me of a strange design
> > Against the creed and morals of the land,
> And trace it in this poem every line:
> > I don't pretend that I quite understand
> My own meaning when I would be very fine,
> > But the fact is that I have nothing plann'd,
> Unless it were to be a moment merry,
> A novel word in my vocabulary.

**Percy Bysshe Shelley**
(1792–1822) Son of Sir T.
Shelley, MP. Hates Eton;
publishes two Gothic novels.
1811 sent down from Oxford
for distributing his *The
Necessity of Atheism*. Elopes
with Harriet Westwood (16).
1812 a radical activitist in
Dublin and Wales. 1813
*Queen Mab*. 1814 to Geneva,
with Mary Wollstonecraft
Godwin (16). Son is born to
Harriet. 1815 receives legacy.
Mary's child dies. *Alastor*.
1816 with Byron on Lake
Geneva. Mary begins
*Frankenstein*. *Hymn to
Intellectual Beauty*; *Mont
Blanc*. Harriet drowns herself;
Shelley marries Mary. 1817
meets Keats. 1818 moves to
Italy. *The Revolt of Islam*;
translates Plato's *Symposium*.
*Julian and Maddalo*. 1819
*Prometheus Unbound*; *Ode to
the West Wind*. 1820 at Pisa.
*The Cenci* (performed 1886).
1821 *Defence of Poetry*;
*Adonais*; *Hellas*. 1822 *The
Triumph of Life*; translations.
Drowns. 1824 *Posthumous
Poems* (ed. Mary Shelley).
1839 *Poetical Works* (ed. Mary
Shelley).

# Percy Bysshe Shelley

**Percy Bysshe Shelley** (1792–1822) was, like Byron, an aristocratic radical with the money to flout convention. But Byron was a Regency buck and milord, fêted by society before his exile, whereas Shelley was already an exile at Eton, a revolutionary thinker, an intellectual for whom to think was normally to do. He believed in vegetarianism, pacifism, and free love – for marriage, he thought, enslaved women. The philosophical anarchist William Godwin thought so too, but found himself Shelley's father-in-law. Both held that Man, as reasonable, was perfectible. Expelled from Oxford for challenging the authorities to refute atheism, Shelley was soon known as a revolutionary who had absconded with two 16-year-olds in two years. The second, the daughter of Godwin and Mary Wollstonecraft, was later to write: 'That man could be perfectionized as to be able to expel evil from his own nature, and from the greater part of the creation, was the cardinal point of his system.' When his body was washed up on the shore of Italy with an Aeschylus in his pocket, Shelley displaced Chatterton as the Romantic poet-as-victim. Most of his work was published posthumously.

Wordsworth said that 'Shelley was one of the best *artists* of us all: I mean in workmanship of style.' He wrote in several styles – revolutionary satire, philosophical vision and urbane verse letters – but posterity preferred his lyrics to his radical philosophical and political poems – strong stuff in 'Men of England' and 'England in 1819'. Scholarly recovery of the historical context of these poems has not repaired the damage done to poetry in general by the overuse of Romantic nature lyrics in primary school. It is still rumoured that Wordsworth's heart danced only with daffodils. Shelley is not only the author of 'Hail to thee, blithe Spirit!/Bird thou never wert' ('To a Skylark'). His writing is intellectually abstract, and 'Considerably uninviting/To those who, meditation slighting,/Were moulded in a different frame.' This is one of his own cracks at Wordsworth in *Peter Bell the Third*. Wordsworth 'had as much imagination/As a pint-pot: – he never could/Fancy another situation,/ … Than that wherein he stood.' Equally unetherial are the versatile verse letters Shelley wrote to Byron, Maria Gisborne and Jane Williams. His major achievement lies in his philosophical poems such as *Mont Blanc*, *Prometheus Unbound* and *The Triumph of Life*, in the pastoral elegy *Adonais*, and in such lyrics such 'When the lamp is shattered' and the Choruses from *Hellas*.

Philosophically, Shelley was a Platonist, holding the world of appearances less real than the world of underlying Forms and Ideas. An omnivorous reader, he was keenly interested in empirical science, and eventually became sceptical about earlier revolutionary fantasies, such as that in *The Masque of Anarchy* where 'ankle-deep in blood,/Hope, that maiden most serene,/Was walking with a quiet mien'. The atheist constructed new myths, as in his ambitious lyric drama, *Prometheus Unbound*. In this completion of Aeschylus's *Prometheus Bound*, the Titan who can foresee the future is given the traits Shelley found admirable in Milton's Satan. A cosmic explosion releases Prometheus from the tortures imposed by a jealous God. The play ends with prophecies of the liberation of mankind. It has lyric variety and fine passages, but the mythology is obscure. More impressive are the bleakly apocalyptic visions of *The Triumph of Life*, incomplete at his death.

Critics who complain that Shelley's world lacks solidity and oxygen should reckon with his serious Platonic belief that words are inadequate to express the ultimate, which is ineffable. Shelley deploys his music and rhetoric to enact a mind racing in pursuit of complex and evanescent truths. The energy, vision and music of the most exciting of English lyric poets are exemplified in this stanza from *Adonais*, an elegy for John Keats:

> The one remains, the many change and pass;
> Heaven's light forever shines, Earth's shadows fly;
> Life, like a dome of many-coloured glass,
> Stains the white radiance of Eternity,
> Until Death tramples it to fragments. – Die,
> If thou wouldst be with that which thou dost seek!
> Follow where all is fled! – Rome's azure sky,
> Flowers, ruins, statues, music, words, are weak
> The glory they transfuse with fitting truth to speak.

Shelley here is near to despair – as a pastoral elegist should be – but self-pity obtrudes when he 'Made bare his branded and ensanguined brow,/Which was like Cain's or Christ's.'

This poet-as-victim also appears in that wonderful performance, his *Ode to the West Wind*,

> Oh! lift me as a wave, a leaf, a cloud!
> I fall upon the thorns of life! I bleed!

The *Ode* combines extreme formal complexity with rhythmic energy and a cosmic scale of reference. The final stanza is a prayer to the wind of inspiration to

> Make me thy lyre, even as the forest is:
> What if my leaves are falling like its own!
> The tumult of thy mighty harmonies
>
> Will take from both a deep, autumnal tone,
> Sweet though in sadness. Be thou, Spirit fierce,
> My spirit! Be thou me, impetuous one!
>
> Drive my dead thoughts over the universe,
> Like withered leaves to quicken a new birth!
> And, by the incantation of this verse,
>
> Scatter, as from an unextinguished hearth
> Ashes and sparks, my words among mankind!
> Be through my lips to unawakened Earth
>
> The trumpet of a prophecy! O Wind,
> If Winter comes, can Spring be far behind?

Hope is wrested from despair. The prophesied Spring is not physical nor simply political, but moral and spiritual.

This too is the argument of Shelley's eloquent *Defence of Poetry*, that love and imagination, the sources of moral feelings, can be developed by poetry. The *Defence* is a ranging and categorical answer to an ironic essay *The Four Ages of Poetry* (1820), in which his friend Thomas Love Peacock (1785–1856) argued that the Romantics' claims for poetry were brazenly exaggerated, and that modern poetry had declined from the Silver Age poetry of the 18th century, itself feebler than the poetry of primitive Golden Ages. Poetry naturally turns backwards: 'While the historian and the philosopher are advancing in, and accelerating, the progress of knowledge, the poet is wallowing in the rubbish of departed ignorance. Mr Scott digs up the poachers and cattle-stealers of the ancient border. Lord Byron cruises for thieves and pirates on the shores of the Morea and among the Greek islands … Mr Wordsworth picks up village legends from old women and sextons ….' Shelley's unfinished *Defence* combines Sidney's arguments with the fervour of Wordsworth's *Preface*, declaring finally that 'Poets are the unacknowledged legislators of the World.' It was itself unacknowledged, being published only in 1840. The most influential British philosopher of the 19th century, the Utilitarian Jeremy Bentham (1772–1832), thought poetry trivial and unnecessary. (Bentham wrote in an unpublished manuscript of *c.*1780: 'The difference between prose and poetry [is that] … prose begins at the left-hand margin and continues to the right … while in poetry some of the lines fall short'.)

## John Keats

**John Keats** (1795–1821), son of the manager of a London livery stables, attended not Eton or Harrow but Enfield School, a Dissenting academy. Here he learned much English poetry before leaving at 15, already the head of his family. At 20 he qualified at Guy's Hospital as an apothecary-surgeon, but decided to be a poet. Through Leigh Hunt (1784–1859), editor of the liberal *Examiner*, he met Hazlitt, Lamb and Shelley. His 4000-line *Endymion* (1817) was censured in the Tory quarterlies. His *Poems* appeared in 1820. He died in Rome in 1821, of tuberculosis.

Keats's reputation rose at his death and has not fallen. His gift is clear in 'On First Looking into Chapman's Homer' (1816). His notable trials in the sonnet form helped him devise the stanzas used in his Odes. In the couplets of *Endymion* and the blank-verse of the unfinished *Hyperion*, his fertile mind tends to run on: his imagination responded impetuously to sensuous beauty, in women, in nature or in art, and in verse and language themselves. Stanza-form controlled his sentences and concentrated his thought, and his late unstanzaic poems, *Lamia* and *The Fall of Hyperion*, are less diffuse. The first critics of *Endymion* wanted him to control his aestheticism –

John Keats (1795–1821) after a sketch by B(enjamin) R(obert) Haydon, a pen-and-ink drawing, above *An(no) 1816,* and a more classically idealized sketch, crossed out.

'A thing of beauty is a joy for ever', it begins. They found his explicit sensuousness cloying. But Keats did not need to be told that aesthetic joy passes. In 1816 he had asked in *Sleep and Poetry*, 'And can I ever bid these joys farewell?/Yes, I must pass them for a nobler life,/Where I may find the agonies, the strife/Of human hearts.' He had already lost his mother to the tuberculosis which was later to claim his brother Tom and himself.

*Sleep and Poetry* is a title which points to Keats's lasting concern about the morality of imagination, and the complex relationships between art and experience. In his last major work, *The Fall of Hyperion*, he is told that 'The poet and the dreamer are distinct,/Diverse, sheer opposite, antipodes./The one pours out a balm upon the world,/The other vexes it.' In *The Eve of St Agnes* he produced perhaps the most coherent of all the symbolic legends invented by the Romantic poets. Using a medieval romance setting and the Spenserian stanza, Keats brings together young lovers from feuding families, a situation found in *The Lay of the Last Minstrel* and *Christabel*. The end is neither tragic, as in *Romeo and Juliet*, nor, as in Scott or in Coleridge's intended ending, happy. Unlike Scott's lovers, Madeline and Porphyro consummate their love in her stained-glass bedchamber, though she may not know what is happening:

> Into her dream he melted, as the rose
> Blendeth its odour with the violet, –
> Solution sweet: meantime the frost-wind blows
> Like Love's alarum pattering the sharp sleet
> Against the window-panes; St. Agnes' moon hath set.

The element of mutual wish-fulfilment is clear, but the sleet tells us that it does not last. Unlike his masters, Keats sees medieval society and religion critically, but he also shows that a sweet modern solution does not bring happiness ever after:

> And they are gone: ay, ages long ago
> These lovers fled away into the storm.

This medieval romance is more serious than Scott's and more balanced than Coleridge's. Keats once again perfected a genre pioneered by others in *La Belle Dame Sans Merci*, the first lyrical ballad to have the qualities of both forms – and much imitated by poets down to W. B. Yeats.

Between April and September 1819 Keats wrote six Odes. This lofty Greek lyric form, revived in the 18th century and favoured by the Romantics, often addresses abstract entities. In his Odes to the Nightingale, the Grecian Urn and Autumn, Keats has much of the grandeur of Wordsworth's 'Immortality Ode', the evocativeness of Coleridge's 'Dejection Ode' and the intensity of Shelley's apostrophe to the West Wind. He brings to this demanding form his sensuous apprehension and a new poetic and intellectual economy. His Odes dramatize the struggle between longing and thinking. Odes tempted Romantic poets to use capital letters – as in Schiller's 'Ode to Joy'. Especially tempting letters were 'I' and 'O!'. Keats resists.

He had advised Shelley to 'load every rift with ore'. His own gift was to imagine particularly a desired sensation: 'O, for a draught of vintage! that hath been/Cool'd a long age in the deep-delved earth,/Tasting of Flora and the country green,/Dance and Provençal song, and sunburnt mirth!' Provençal troubadours sang of the nightingale. Thus, for the myth-hungry Keats, the song of the nightingale he heard on Hampstead Heath was love-poetry. (The Symbol, wrote Coleridge, 'always partakes of the Reality which it renders sensible.') On first hearing the bird sing 'of summer in full-throated ease', his 'heart aches': not only for the girl he loved but because he desires oblivion. He wishes to drink, and 'with thee fade away unto the forest dim':

> Fade far away, dissolve, and quite forget
>     What thou amongst the leaves hast never known,
> The weariness, the fever, and the fret
>     Here where men sit and hear each other groan;
> Where palsy shakes a few, sad, last gray hairs,
>     Where youth grows pale, and spectre-thin, and dies;
>         Where but to think is to be full of sorrow
>             And leaden-eyed despairs,
>     Where Beauty cannot keep her lustrous eyes,
>         Or new love pine at them beyond to-morrow.

Keats's images of illness and death would be just as concrete if we did not know that he was an apothecary-surgeon who had nursed his dying brother Tom. This concreteness is the 'ore' he recommended to Shelley.

The struggle continues: 'Now more than ever seems it rich to die,/To cease upon the midnight with no pain,/While thou art pouring forth thy soul abroad/In such an ecstasy!/Still would'st thou sing, and I have ears in vain –/To thy high requiem become a sod.'

> Thou wast not born for death, immortal Bird!
>     No hungry generations tread thee down;
> The voice I hear this passing night was heard
>     In ancient days by emperor and clown.

This is a strong version of the classical and Renaissance claim – one which gives this history what interest it may have – that human song is heard across human generations impatient to replace their predecessors.

The same contest between the beauty of art and the pain of life runs through the *Odes* to Psyche, Indolence, Melancholy and the Grecian Urn. For the Romantics, the glory of Greece surpassed the grandeur of Rome, and Keats's Odes turn Greek myths into new English myths. Thus the Urn is a 'still unravish'd bride of Quietness', a 'foster-child of Silence and slow Time.' Autumn is addressed as a 'Season of mists and mellow fruitfulness,/Close bosom friend of the maturing Sun/Conspiring with him.' These involuted apostrophes have an intelligence, poise and richness equal to those of Renaissance verse. The models which the Romantics emulated were Shakespeare and Milton. Their best lyrics survive the comparison, much as the lyric music of Schubert (1797–1828) and Chopin (1810–49) survives comparison with that of Mozart (1756–91). But no English Romantic poet was able to combine intensity with major form on the scale of Milton and Beethoven.

Keats envies the perfection of the scenes on his 'still unravish'd' urn. He turns to her again as he ends:

> Cold Pastoral!
> When old age shall this generation waste,
>     Thou shalt remain, in midst of other woe
> Than ours, a friend to man, to whom thou say'st,
> ' "Beauty is Truth, Truth Beauty," – that is all
>     Ye know on earth, and all ye need to know.'

Keats did not always think that what the urn says is all we need to know, for he once wrote in a letter that 'an eagle is not so fine a thing as a truth'. In another letter he wished for a life of sensations rather than of thoughts. He created a correlative to this wish in 'To Autumn', the most perfect English poem of the 19th century. The mental struggle of earlier Odes is over, and an apparently artless natural symbolism tells us all we need to know – that as 'gathering swallows twitter in the skies' in September 1819, he accepted that winter was not far behind.

The spontaneous mode of Romantic poetry relies, in extended works, upon unusual powers of syntax and form, and also on organization, which cannot be improvised. Keats's major Odes are superbly organized, but his earlier *Hyperion*, like some of the ambitious myths of Byron and Shelley, gets lost. The new sublime, what Keats called 'the wordsworthian or egotistical sublime', needed a world, a myth, an intelligible form if it was to communicate more than the feelings and experience of one person. Turning away from Christianity to a 'religion of humanity' led the younger Romantics to create provisional truths in historical legend and literary myth. They found some of these difficult to finish, as have their readers. The 'low' rural narratives of Wordsworth succeed by understating their symbolic values. The grandiose Titanic myths of his successors are less coherent. In Keats's later *The Fall of Hyperion: A Dream* he sees a ladder leading upwards and is told by the Prophetess Moneta: 'None can usurp this height …/But those to whom the miseries of the world/Are misery, and will not let them rest.' This fragment has a maturity which suggests that Keats might have equalled Wordsworth in magnitude as he did in quality. Tennyson thought Keats the greatest 19th-century poet, and T. S. Eliot, no friend of the personal cult in poetry, judged Keats's letters 'certainly the most notable and most important ever written by any English poet'. A few quotations may suffice to indicate their lively quality. In a letter to a friend he wrote, thinking of Wordsworth: 'We hate poetry that has a palpable design upon us – and if we do not agree, seems to put its hand in its breeches pocket. Poetry should be great & unobtrusive …' Elsewhere he wrote: 'axioms in philosophy are not axioms until they are proved upon our pulses.' In another letter, he mentions to his brothers: '… that quality which Shakespeare possessed so enormously – I mean *Negative Capability*, that is when man is capable of being in uncertainties, Mysteries, doubts, without any irritable reaching after fact & reason –'.

Romantic poetry changed priorities in English literature. Poetry is henceforth about personal experience rather than the public and moral concerns of a classical/Christian Augustanism. In this general cultural shift to finding meaning in personal rather than collective experience, poetry showed the way. And whereas the 18th-century novel of Fielding focused on moral action, the 19th-century novel chronicles the emotional development of characters – or of a leading character with whom we are expected to identify. The first-person narrator is no longer an ironist.

# ▉ Romantic prose

## *Belles lettres*

Romantic poetry invites a reverence which Romantic prose essayists, for all their 'fine writing', rarely show. In the year in which Keats addressed the nightingale as a 'light-winged Dryad of the trees' on Hampstead Heath, Thomas Love Peacock wrote

## Men of letters

**Charles Lamb** (1775–1834) *Specimens of the English Dramatic Poets who Lived about the Time of Shakespeare* (1818), *Essays of Elia* (1823).

**William Hazlitt** (1778–1830) *Characters of Shakespeare's Plays* (1817), *English Comic Writers* (1819), *The Spirit of the Age* (1825).

**Walter Savage Landor** (1775–1864) *Imaginary Conversations* (1824–9).

**Leigh Hunt** (1785–1859) (ed.) *The Examiner* and others.

**Thomas Love Peacock** (1785–1866) *Headlong Hall* (1816), *Melincourt* (1817), *Nightmare Abbey* (1818), *Crochet Castle* (1831), *Gryll Grange* (1861).

**Thomas De Quincey** (1795–1859) *Confessions of an English Opium-Eater* (1821).

that 'We know … that there are no Dryads in Hyde-park nor Naiads in the Regent's-canal. But barbaric manners and supernatural interventions are essential to poetry. Either in the scene, or in the time, or in both, it must be remote from our ordinary perceptions.' This last is an 18th-century judgement on Romantic poetry, to be read with Wordsworth's *Preface* and Shelley's *Defence.*

## Charles Lamb

Charles Lamb (1775–1834) was indifferent to ideas, to politics and to the Lake District. His anthology of the older dramatists was a contribution to later Romantic tastes. Although his comments are often shrewd, Lamb treated Renaissance plays as cabinets of poetic gems and curiosities. His preference for reading plays rather than seeing them is only partly due to the low state of the theatre. Playwrights were for him 'dramatic poets', whereas the Romantics were specimens of humanity who lived about the time of Lamb. The purpose of his own familiar essays is to display his idiosyncratic sensibility. The charm valued by his friends lingers in *Old China* and in *The Two Races of Men* – these are 'the men who borrow' and 'the men who lend'. Coleridge appears as 'Comberbatch, matchless in his depredations'; those books that he returns are 'enriched with annotations'.

## William Hazlitt

A humorous phrase was not the highest ambition of the lifelong radical, **William Hazlitt** (1778–1830). His literary and theatrical criticism consists of random lively 'impressions'. He wrote one wonderful essay, *My First Acquaintance with Poets* (1823), an unforgettable account of his meeting with his heroes of twenty-five years earlier. Wordsworth 'sat down and talked very naturally and freely, with a mixture of clear gushing accents in his voice, a deep guttural intonation, and a strong tincture of the northern burr, like the crust on wine. He instantly began to make havoc of the half of a Cheshire cheese on the table …'. STC's 'forehead was broad and high, light as if built of ivory, with large projecting eyebrows, and his eyes rolling beneath them, like a sea with darkened lustre … His mouth was gross, voluptuous, open, eloquent; his chin good-humoured and round: but his nose, the rudder of the face, the index of the will, was small, feeble, nothing – like what he has done.'

Vigorous caricature made Hazlitt an effective journalist and public speaker, but his politics overrode his critical judgement. The premium which Romanticism gave to sincerity leaves a criticism which is merely autobiographical at the mercy of whim and prejudice. Lamb, for example, so 'gentle', so fond of old books, old China and his old schoolfriend Coleridge, had a philistine contempt for the music of Mozart and Handel. Leigh Hunt (1784–1859) was a benign exponent of descriptive-cum-appreciative criticism, a man of letters of liberal energy and sympathy. He will be remembered less for his own writing than as the editor who published Keats, Shelley, Byron, Hazlitt, Hogg and Tennyson.

## Thomas De Quincey

Thomas De Quincey (1785–1859) is best remembered for the elaborate prose of *Confessions of an English Opium-Eater*, an autobiography full of hallucinatory dreams, notably one of an Easter Sunday when he recognizes the face of Ann, a 17-year-old prostitute who had helped him when he was down and out in London. The psychological configuration given by De Quincey to his compelling memories is reminiscent of those in *Frost at Midnight* and in Wordsworth's 'spots of time'. It prefigures the imaginative use of the Gothic made by the Brontës.

# Fiction

### Thomas Love Peacock

Thomas Love Peacock (1785–1864), who worked beside Lamb in the East India Office under John Mill, was a fine satirist. Like the gifted poet Walter Savage Landor, Peacock was a long-lived 18th-century gentleman Radical. Both wrote imaginary conversations between writers, but Landor's historical conversations have none of the quickness of Peacock's ironic country-house dialogues between 'perfectibilians, deteriorationists, status-quo-ites ... transcendentalists, political economists, theorists in all sciences ... lovers of the picturesque, and lovers of good dinners.'

*The Misfortunes of Elphin* (1829), set in 6th-century Wales, contains 'The War Song of Dinas Vawr', a parody of the dark-age battle-poem idealized by the Romantics: 'The mountain sheep are sweeter/But the valley sheep are fatter;/We therefore deemed it meeter/To carry off the latter.'

### Mary Shelley

If Peacock's dialogues are modelled upon Plato's, *Frankenstein, or the Modern Prometheus* by **Mary Shelley** (1797–1851) is a cross between the Gothic tale and the fable of ideas; neither is realistic. *Frankenstein* began as a literary experiment within a social experiment – as a 'ghost story' in a game proposed by Byron at the Villa Diodati on Lac Leman, Switzerland, in 1816, while Mary's half-sister Claire Clairmont was having an affair with Byron. Two years earlier Mary, aged 16, had eloped with Shelley from the home of her father, the philosopher-novelist William Godwin. Her mother, the feminist Mary Wollstonecraft, had died after her birth in 1797. Mary herself lost a daughter at 17, bore a son at 18, and, after the suicides of another of her half-sisters and of Shelley's wife, married the poet at 19. She had lost another child before she was widowed at 24. She dedicated *Frankenstein* to Godwin. Shelley wrote a preface, supposedly by Mary, and also a disingenuous pre-publication review in which he refers to the author as male and as showing the influence of Godwin. Men were the midwives of this myth-breeding text.

*Frankenstein* is an epistolary narrative with three narrators, the English Arctic explorer Capt. Walton, the German scientist Victor Frankenstein, and the nameless 'man' which Frankenstein 'creates' out of human body-parts by electrical experiment. The Creature wants a mate, which Frankenstein assembles but destroys. It then kills its creator's brother, his friend and his wife; he tries to kill it, but it escapes into the Arctic. The sensational contents and moral ideas of *Frankenstein* are conveyed in a mechanical style. Its interest is cultural, moral, philosophical and psychological: it is a nightmare of alienation; a sentimental critique of the victorious intellect to which Shelley and Godwin trusted; and a negative critique of a Faustian overconfidence in natural science.

## Maria Edgeworth

Women make a notable contribution to fiction from early in the 19th century. The historical novel was perfected by Scott, but he did not invent it. In *Waverley* he wrote 'so as in some distant degree to emulate the admirable portraits drawn by Miss Edgeworth'. He refers to the anonymous *Castle Rackrent: An Hibernian tale taken from facts and from the manners of the Irish squires before the year 1782*, an edited oral memoir of the steward of the Rackrent estate. Its editor remarks in his Preface that

the race of the Rackrents has long since been extinct in Ireland; and the drunken Sir Patrick, the litigious Sir Murtagh, the fighting Sir Kit, and the slovenly Sir Condy, are characters which could no more be met with at present in Ireland than [Fielding's] Squire Western or Parson Trulliber in England. There is a time, when individuals can bear to be rallied for their past follies and absurdities, after they have acquired new habits, and a new consciousness. Nations as well as individuals gradually lose attachment to their identity, and the present generation is amused rather than offended by the ridicule that is thrown upon its ancestors.

This historian-editor is R. L. Edgeworth, an enlightened County Longford landowner who despite his 'new consciousness' was attached to his Irish identity, and in 1800 voted against the Union of the short-lived Irish Parliament with that of Great Britain. When his eldest daughter Maria left her English boarding school, he gave her Adam Smith's *Wealth of Nations*. This gave her the term *Rackrent*, a title which suggests both extortionate rent and the rack and ruin of the estate. The 'oral' style was new.

Having, out of friendship for the family, upon whose estate, praised be Heaven! I and mine have lived rent-free, time out of mind, voluntarily undertaken to publish the MEMOIRS of the RACKRENT FAMILY, I think is is my duty to say a few words, in the first place, concerning myself. My real name is Thady Quirk, though in the family I have always been known by no other than '*honest Thady*', – afterwards in the time of Sir Murtagh, deceased, I remember to hear them calling me '*old Thady*', and now I'm come to 'poor Thady'; for I wear a long great coat winter and summer, which is very handy, as I never put my arms into the sleeves; they are as good as new ...

   **Maria Edgeworth** (1768–1849) took Thady's idiom from the speech of her father's steward. To this passage is added a long note on the Irish greatcoat, and a Glossary explaining customs and terms. Thus, 'An *English tenant* does not mean a tenant who is an Englishman, but a tenant who pays his rent the day that it is due.' Successive Rackrents die of drink, apoplexy, gaming and drink, loyally helped by Honest Thady, whose nephew buys up Sir Condy's estate. The 'long ... extinct' *facts* and *manners* of the Rackrent squires have since formed the staple of Anglo-Irish fiction, as has the illogical rattle in which they are reported: 'not a man could stand after supper but Sir Patrick himself, who could sit out the best man in Ireland, let alone the three kingdoms itself'. As for Sir Kit, 'unluckily, after hitting the tooth pick out of his adversary's finger, he received a ball in a vital part, and was brought home, in little better than an hour after the affair, speechless on a handbarrow, to my lady'.

The anecdotes are in lively Irish English, the Notes and Glossary in dry Anglo-Irish. Beneath the comedy is a sharp analysis of the supposedly stupid servile Irishman and the feckless folly of the old squires. *Castle Rackrent* is, like *Tristram Shandy*, a tale of sharp decline, but with Swift's command of perspective. It is also the first of various kinds of novel: historical, Anglo-Irish, regional, colonial. With her father, Maria Edgeworth championed the education of daughters, and wrote other tales, but the Irish tales stand out: *Ennui*, *The Absentee* and *Ormond*. She sent Scott examples of Irish talk; Miss Austen sent her a copy of *Emma*.

## Sir Walter Scott

The *Quarterly Review*, founded by Scott, greeted the anonymous *Waverley* (1814) as 'a Scotch *Castle Rackrent*' but 'in a much higher strain'. *Waverley; Or, 'Tis Sixty Years Since* deals with a larger subject more directly, the Jacobite Rising of 1745, in which Bonnie Prince Charlie, backed by Highland clans loyal to the deposed House of Stuart, advanced as far as Derby before retreat and defeat.

Scott's initial approach is oblique, establishing Edward Waverley as a decent young English gentleman who has spent his youth, like Cervantes' Don Quixote, reading romances of chivalry. He is an innocent blank page. Finding himself in Scotland with his detachment of Dragoons, he is charmed by Scottish hospitality and manners, and by Rose Bradwardine. He is then captivated by Highland life, and smitten with Flora MacIvor, whom he sees in the glen in a scene of 'romantic wildness':

Here, like one of those lovely forms which decorate the landscapes of Poussin, Waverley found Flora gazing at the waterfall. Two paces further back stood Cathleen, holding a small Scottish harp, the use of which had been taught to Flora by Rory Dall, one of the last harpers in the Western Highlands. The sun now stooping in the west, gave a rich and varied tinge …

Eventually he joins Flora's bold brother Fergus in the Prince's army. He orders a pair of tartan *trews* (a compromise between English trousers and Highland kilt), and sees bloody action. He gradually sees that he is being used by Fergus. Captured, Fergus and his clansmen face death bravely. Flora becomes a Benedictine nun in Paris. Waverley marries Rose Bradwardine: a happy Union! But the orotund prose is not naively Romantic: the too-picturesque vision by the waterfall is presented with some irony. Like Don Quixote and Flaubert's Emma Bovary, Waverley falls for images from books. The making of the *trews* by James of the Needle is a parody of the arming of an epic hero. The tragic Highland romance is set inside a British novel about a young Englishman who wisely marries a Lowland Scot.

Scott's success was immediate, immense, international. *Waverley* was followed by twenty-five Scottish historical novels, notably *The Antiquary* (1816), *Old Mortality* (1816), *The Heart of Midlothian* (1818) and *Redgauntlet* (1824), and English medieval romances, beginning with *Ivanhoe* (1819); also numbers of plays, biographies, essays, and editions. Thanks to Scott, Edinburgh saw the Prince Regent in a kilt (and pink tights) taking a dram of whisky: a swallow which made the summer of Scottish tourism. Scott, the first Briton to be made a baronet for writing books, may be the most influential of all British novelists. His historical novels use a new social history to recreate the past through characters imaginary and real. He combined wide reading in 18th-century antiquarians with fluent composition and narrative. Leisurely and detailed in exposition, he sets up several centres of interest; the action then develops energy and drama. He made the past imaginable, with a sympathetic grasp of the motives and influences shaping the actions of groups and individuals. His characterization is benign, detached, shrewd, humorous, owing much to 18th-century theatrical traditions of external representation, but very wide in its social scope, with pungent low-life characters. His reconstruction of how things happen in history is broad, penetrating and subtle, and his plots are expertly managed. In his Scottish novels he sought to make the differing versions of Scottish history mutually intelligible to their inheritors, using a new relativistic historical and anthropological approach to reconcile sectarian traditions, so that a Scotland who understood herself could be known to England. Scott was a patriot and a Unionist.

The greatest commercial success of 'the Wizard of the North' was *Ivanhoe*, the first of the English romances which succeeded his Scottish novels. It created the costume-drama industry which turns out 'good reads' and bodice-rippers. In Scott's English medieval pageants, drawn from reading rather than local knowledge, the use of theatrically-posed scenes, as of Flora MacIvor at the waterfall, loses both irony and Scottish iron. His popularity and reputation eventually faded, and his generosity of style means that he seems long-winded compared with his snappier imitators. The success of *Ivanhoe* and its sequels should not conceal the achievement of the author of *Waverley*, a historical novelist of range, grasp and balance.

## Jane Austen

**Jane Austen** (1775–1817) grew up in the quiet country parish of her father, the Rev. George Austen, in a family where literature was the chief amusement. One of her five elder brothers became her father's curate and successor. She wrote for pleasure in childhood, and as an adult chose to work on '3 or 4 families in a country village': the world she knew. Her wit, workmanship and background are not Romantic but Augustan and 18th-century Anglican, like the ideals of the older country gentry she depicts.

Despite its sudden spring in the mid-18th century, the novel became a major form again only after 1800. Before Austen, there were Gothic tales, novels of sensibility like Mackenzie's *The Man of Feeling*, the social entertainments of Fanny Burney and Charlotte Smith, and Godwin's experiments of ideas, but the novel reached perfection with Jane Austen. It went on to popularity, periodical publication, and bigger things.

**Jane Austen** (1775–1817) Born at Steventon, Hampshire. 1801: Moved to Bath. 1806: Moved to Southampton. 1809: Moved to Chawton, Hampshire. 1817: Died at Winchester. Novels, in order of composition (with publication dates): *Sense and Sensibility* (1811), *Northanger Abbey* (1818), *Pride and Prejudice* (1813), *Mansfield Park* (1814), *Emma* (1816), *Persuasion* (1818).

'And what are you reading Miss —?' 'Oh, it is only a novel', replies the young lady; while she lays down her book with affected indifference, or momentary shame. – 'It is only Cecilia, or Camilla, or Belinda'; or, in short, only some work in which the greatest powers of the mind are displayed, in which the most thorough knowledge of human nature, the happiest delineation of its varieties, the liveliest effusion of wit and humour are conveyed to the world in the best-chosen language.

Thus Jane Austen in *Northanger Abbey*. (*Cecilia* and *Camilla* are novels by Fanny Burney; *Belinda*, a novel by Maria Edgeworth.)

In her brilliant fragment, *Love and Friendship*, the 14-year-old Austen mocks the novel of feminine sensibility, and in *Northanger Abbey*, begun in 1798, the silliness of Gothic. Catherine Morland reflects: 'Charming as were all Mrs Radcliffe's works, and charming even as were the works of all her imitators, it was not in them perhaps that human nature, at least in the Midland counties of England, was to be looked

'Tales of Wonder' (1802), by James Gillray, a print caricaturing the Gothic craze. *Tales of Wonder* was the title of a collection of verse tales of horror published by M. G. Lewis in 1801. The ladies listen to Lewis's *The Monk*.

for.' She learned from Fanny Burney, but preferred Cowper, Crabbe and the moral essays of Johnson to the fiction of wish-fulfilment.

After juvenilia written to entertain her family, she dedicated herself to the novel. Her novels are cast in the form of the comedy of manners: accuracy of social behaviour and dialogue, moral realism, elegance of style, and ingenuity of plot. For all her penetration and intelligence, Austen is distinctly a moral idealist. The mistress of irony unfolds a Cinderella tale ending in an engagement. The heroine, typically of good family but with little money, has no recognized prospect but marriage; no wish to marry without love; and no suitable man in sight. After trials and moral discoveries, virtue wins. Of the few professional novelists before her, none is so consistent. Formally, Austen's fiction has the drastic selectivity of drama, and, like Racine, gains thereby. The moral life of her time is clear in her pages, although the history is social not national. Two of her brothers, however, became admirals; and in *Persuasion*, amid the vanities of Bath, she rejoices in the challenge of naval officers to the old social hierarchy. Her comedy of manners accepts the presence or absence of rank, wealth, brains, beauty and masculinity as facts, and as factors in society, while placing goodness, rationality and love above them. Such comedy is not trivial, unless a woman's choice of husband is trivial. For all her fun and sharp-edged wit, Austen's central concern is with the integrity of a woman's affections. Her novels become increasingly moving.

The bright *Northanger Abbey* and the dark *Sense and Sensibility* are preparatory to the well-managed gaiety of *Pride and Prejudice*, which the author came to find 'too light, bright and sparkling'. It is certainly simpler than the serious *Mansfield Park*, the classical *Emma* and the autumnal *Persuasion*. It is hard to choose between these. *Mansfield Park* is not about the education of its heroine: her example educates others. Amidst complex social comedy, the plain and simple Fanny Price, a poor niece brought up at Mansfield in its splendid park but not sophisticated by it, resists the predatory charm of visitors from London. Edmund, her admired cousin, eventually realizes the beauty of her nature.

Moral worth is recommended less directly in *Emma*, a work of art designed with economical symmetry. 'Emma Woodhouse, handsome, clever, and rich, with a comfortable home and happy disposition, seemed to unite some of the best blessings of existence; and had lived nearly twenty-one years in the world with very little to dis-

Jane Austen aged *c*.35. A pencil and watercolour sketch made by her sister Cassandra in *c*.1810, the only likeness to show Jane Austen's face.

tress or vex her.' Emma, the queen of the village, prides herself on her perceptiveness, and decides that Harriet Smith, a pretty seventeen-year-old of unknown birth whom she takes up, is too good to marry a local farmer. Emma invites her to the house to meet the new parson, who misinterprets the encouragement and proposes to Emma. This is only the first, however, of Emma's mistaken efforts to marry off Harriet. Austen so manages appearances that the reader shares Emma's dangerous delusions. Virtually everybody in the book is misled by their imagination. In this sense, Austen is squarely anti-Romantic.

Emma, doted upon by her old father, believes that she herself will not marry. 'But still, you will be an old maid!' says Harriet, 'and that's so dreadful!' 'Never mind, Harriet,' Emma replies, 'I shall not be a poor old maid; and it is poverty only which makes celibacy contemptible to a generous public!' Both may be thinking of a garrulous old spinster in the village, the good-hearted Miss Bates, an old friend of the family who is neither handsome, clever nor rich. The normally considerate Emma is later carried away by the playfulness of Frank Churchill at a picnic, and in a chance remark publicly ridicules the dullness of Miss Bates. For this cruelty she is rebuked by Mr Knightley, a worthy family friend who has the judgement Emma's father lacks. Further misunderstandings ensue: Harriet Smith fancies that Mr Knightley is interested in her; Knightley thinks that Emma is taken with Frank Churchill. But Mr Churchill suddenly reveals that he has been secretly engaged to the mysterious Jane Fairfax.

Emma is walking in the garden when Knightley calls. 'They walked together. He was silent. She thought he was often looking at her, and trying for a fuller view of her face than it suited her to give.' In Jane Austen's tightly-governed world, this is intimacy and drama. After Knightley has chivalrously consoled Emma for the pain caused her by Mr Churchill's engagement, and has been undeceived, he declares his love and entreats her to speak. Miss Austen now teases her reader: 'What did she say? – Just what she ought, of course. A lady always does.' Reticence resumes. Yet Knightley comments on Mr Churchill's secret engagement: 'Mystery; Finesse – how they pervert the understanding! My Emma, does not every thing serve to prove more and more the beauty of truth and sincerity in all our dealings with each other?' Although Miss Austen smiles at the man's vehemence, she too admires truth, sincerity and plain-dealing. This is both Augustan, Romantic and romantic.

*Persuasion* is for devotees her most touching and interesting novel. Eight years before the novel begins, the 19-year-old Anne Elliott was persuaded by Lady Russell, a friend of her dead mother, to break off her engagement with Wentworth, a man whom she loved, accepting Lady Russell's view that he was: 'a young man, who had nothing but himself to recommend him, and no hopes of attaining affluence, but in the chances of a most uncertain profession [the navy], and no connexions to secure even his farther rise in that profession …'. Captain Wentworth returns rich, and, he tells his sister, 'ready to make a foolish match. Any body between fifteen and thirty may have me for asking. A little beauty, and a few smiles, and a few compliments to the navy, and I am a lost man.' Nevertheless, 'Anne Elliot was not out of his thoughts, when he more seriously described the woman he should wish to meet with. "A strong mind, with sweetness of manner," made the first and last of the description.'

Wentworth is persuaded that a woman who broke her engagement does not have a strong mind; and Anne is persuaded that Wentworth cannot think of her. He is soon involved with Louisa Musgrove, but when Louisa has a fall, it is Anne who is calm and useful. Earlier, Wentworth had silently relieved Anne of the attentions of a troublesome two-year-old while she is engaged in looking after the child's sick brother. In a letter to a friend, Maria Edgeworth comments on this passage: 'Don't you see Captain Wentworth, or rather, don't you in her place feel him, taking the boisterous child off her back as she kneels by the sick boy on the sofa?'

In this short novel – concluded as the author became very ill – gesture and silence develop emotional expressiveness. At the climax, Anne takes her opportunity to make it clear to Wentworth – indirectly, but persuasively – that she loves him still. Wentworth is sitting writing at a table in a room full of people as Anne is engaged in debate by a naval officer who claims that men's love is more constant than women's love. Wentworth listens to her reply, which ends: 'All the privilege I claim for my own sex (it is not a very enviable one, you need not covet it) is that of loving longest, when existence or when hope is gone.' When compared with the plot of *Emma*, that of *Persuasion* is theatrically conventional, especially on its 'wicked' side; but the central relationship is magically managed.

No 19th-century successor in the novel or the theatre approaches the economy in dialogue and action Austen developed by formal discipline and concentration of theme. (Her novels offered 'an admirable copy of life', but lacked imagination, according to Wordsworth, who lacked the kind of imagination she relied on in a reader.) She also seems to be the first English prose writer since Julian of Norwich who is clearly superior to male contemporaries in the same field. A finer novelist than Scott, she confirmed the novel as a genre belonging significantly to women writers as well as women readers.

## Towards Victoria

The literary lull which followed the early deaths of Keats, Shelley and Byron is a true age of transition, the period of the Great Reform Bill of 1832. Features of the Victorian age began to appear: liberal legislation, a triumphant middle class, industrial advance, proletarian unrest, religious renewal. When Victoria came to the throne,

## Chief events and publications of 1823–37

| Events | | Notable publications | |
|---|---|---|---|
| 1823 | Peel begins penal reforms. | 1824 | James Hogg, *Memoirs and Confessions of a Justified Sinner*; Walter Savage Landor, *Imaginary Conversations*; Mary Russell Mitford, *Our Village*; Walter Scott, *Redgauntlet*; Lord Byron (d.1824), *Don Juan* xv–xvi; Percy Bysshe Shelley (ed. Mary Shelley), *Posthumous Poems*. |
| 1825 | Stockton–Darlington Railway is opened. | 1825 | S. T. Coleridge, *Aids to Reflection*; William Hazlitt, *The Spirit of the Age*. |
| 1826 | University College, London, is founded. | 1826 | Benjamin Disraeli, *Vivian Grey*; Mary Shelley, *The Last Man*. |
| 1828 | Duke of Wellington becomes Prime Minister. The Test and Corporation Acts, which had kept Catholics and Nonconformists from high office, are repealed. | 1827 | John Clare, *The Shepherd's Calendar*; John Keble, *The Christian Year*; Alfred and Charles Tennyson, *Poems by Two Brothers*. |
| 1829 | Catholic Emancipation Act; Daniel O'Connell elected to Parliament. Peel establishes the Metropolitan Police. Stephenson's *Rocket* runs on Liverpool–Manchester railway. | | |
| 1830 | George IV dies. William IV reigns to 1837. | 1830 | William Cobbett, *Rural Rides*; Coleridge, *On the Constitution of Church and State*; Alfred Tennyson, *Poems, Chiefly Lyrical*. |
| 1832 | Reform Bill is passed: the end of 'rotten boroughs'; the franchise is extended. | 1832 | Alfred Tennyson, *Poems*. |
| 1833 | Parliament abolishes slavery in the Empire. Education and Factory Acts are passed. John Keble's sermon 'National Apostasy' begins Oxford Movement. | 1833 | Thomas Carlyle, *Sartor Resartus*; Keble, Newman, *et al. Tracts for the Times* (–1841); Robert Browning, *Pauline*. |
| 1834 | New Poor Law Act is passed. The 'Tolpuddle Martyrs'. The Houses of Parliament burn down. | 1834 | George Crabbe (d.1832), *Poetical Works*. |
| | | 1835 | Coleridge (d.1834), *Table Talk;* Charles Dickens, *Sketches by Boz*; Capt. Marryat, *Mr Midshipman Easy*; R. H. Froude, Keble, John Henry Newman and others, *Lyra Apostolica*. |
| 1836 | Barry and Pugin design new Houses of Parliament. | | |
| 1837 | William IV dies. Victoria reigns (to 1901). | 1837 | Carlyle, *French Revolution*; Charles Dickens, *The Pickwick Papers*; William Makepeace Thackeray, *The Professor*; John Gibson Lockhart, *The Life of Sir Walter Scott*. |

the warning voices of Keble and Carlyle were audible. Among the young writers were Tennyson, the Brownings, Thackeray and Dickens.

## Further reading

Barnard, J. (ed.). *The Complete Poems of John Keats*, 2nd edn (Harmondsworth: Penguin, 1977).

Butler, M. *Romantics, Rebels and Reactionaries: English Literature and its Background 1760–1830* (Oxford: Oxford University Press, 1982).

Macrae, A. D. F. (ed.). *P. B. Shelley* (London: Routledge, 1991). A good student selection.

Wu, Duncan (ed.). *Romanticism*, 2nd edn (Oxford: Blackwell, 1998). An annotated anthology.

**PART 4**

# Victorian Literature to 1880

# The Age and its Sages

# CHAPTER 8

## Overview

Victoria's long reign saw a growth in literature, especially in fiction, practised notably by Dickens, Thackeray, the Brontës, George Eliot, Trollope, James and Hardy. Poetry too was popular, especially that of Tennyson; Browning and (though then unknown) Hopkins are also major poets. Thinkers, too, were eagerly read. Matthew Arnold, poet, critic and social critic, was the last to earn the respectful hearing given earlier to such sages as Carlyle, Mill, Ruskin and Newman. Many Victorians allowed their understanding to be led by thinkers, poets, even novelists. It was an age both exhilarated and bewildered by growing wealth and power, the pace of industrial and social change, and by scientific discovery. After the middle of the reign, confidence began to fade; its last two decades took on a different atmosphere, and literature developed various specialist forms – æstheticism, professional entertainment, disenchanted social concern. These decades, which also saw an overdue revival of drama, are treated separately.

## Contents

## ▉ The Victorian age

'Victorian' is a term that is often extended beyond the queen's reign (1837–1901) to include William IV's reign from 1830. Historians distinguish early, middle and late Victorian England, corresponding to periods of growing pains, of confidence in the 1850s, and of loss of consensus after 1880, a date which offers a convenient division: Charles Dickens (1812–70) and Oscar Wilde (1854–1900) belonged to different ages.

Under Victoria, a Britain transformed by the Industrial Revolution became the world's leading imperial power and its most interesting country. Fyodor Dostoevsky, Mark Twain, Henry James and even French writers came to see London. New Yorkers waited on the dockside to hear if Dickens's Little Nell, of *The Old Curiosity Shop*, was still alive. But were England's authors as taken up with their rapidly-changing age as the term 'Victorian literature' can suggest? Many were. The historian T. B. Macaulay praised the age's spirit of progress. Thomas Carlyle and John Ruskin prophesied against the age, as sometimes did Dickens. Tennyson

The Albert Memorial, Kensington Gardens, Hyde Park, London. Albert had died in 1861; George Gilbert Scott's Gothic monument (1864–7) celebrates the achievements of the age, and the Prince's patronage of the arts and sciences.

periodically tried to make sense of it; Matthew Arnold criticized it; Mrs Gaskell reflected it and reflected on it. Anthony Trollope represented it.

## Moral history

Although literature is never merely history, the novel becomes a moral history of modern life with Dickens and Thackeray, elaborately so in George Eliot's *Middle-march*, a novel exemplifying a principle Eliot derived from Scott: 'there is no private life which has not been determined by a wider public life'. Yet the wider life was interesting to George Eliot (the pen-name of Mary Ann Evans) because it shaped the moral and emotional life of single persons. In keeping with this Romantic priority, her characters are more personal than Scott's.

George Eliot (1819–80) was one of many who sought after wisdom in an age of shaken certitudes and robust consciences. Clergymen, sages and critics wrote lessons and lectures for the breakfast-table and the tea-table. These were later bound up in tomes with marbled endpapers. Few are unshelved today, except in universities. The Victorian books living today are chiefly novels, and these novels (despite the 'authenticity' of their modern film versions) do not hold up a mirror to the age. Victorians produced impressive reports on the London poor, on the factories of Manchester and on urban sanitation, but a documentary social realism was not the rule in Victorian fiction.

One reason for this lies in the subjective and imaginative character of Romantic literature of the years 1798–1824, which altered the nature of non-factual writing. The simple pleasure of vicarious egotism died with Byron, but books, annuals and

## Events and publications of 1837–80

| Events | Notable publications |
|---|---|
| | 1837 Thomas Carlyle, *The French Revolution*; Charles Dickens, *The Pickwick Papers*. |
| 1838 Chartist movement, demanding votes for workers, begins. | 1838 Dickens, *Oliver Twist*; Elizabeth Barrett, *The Seraphim, and Other Poems*. |
| | 1839 Dickens, *Nicholas Nickleby*; Mrs Hemans (d.1835), *Collected Works*; Charles Darwin, *The Voyage of HMS Beagle* (J. M. W. Turner, *The Fighting Téméraire*; Stendhal, *The Charterhouse of Parma*). |
| 1840 Victoria marries Prince Albert. Penny Post is begun. | 1840 Robert Browning, *Sordello*. |
| 1841 Sir Robert Peel's Conservative ministry. | 1841 Carlyle, *On Heroes and Hero-Worship*; Dion Boucicault, *London Assurance*. |
| | 1842 T. B. Macaulay, *Lays of Ancient Rome*; Alfred Tennyson, *Poems*. |
| | 1843 Carlyle, *Past and Present*; John Ruskin, *Modern Painters* (5 vols 1860). |
| | 1844 Dickens, *Martin Chuzzlewit*; Benjamin Disraeli, *Coningsby*; Elizabeth Barrett, *Poems*; William Barnes, *Poems of Rural Life, in the Dorset Dialect*; William Makepeace Thackeray, *The Luck of Barry Lyndon*. |
| 1845 Potato Famine in Ireland (to 1850). | 1845 Disraeli, *Sybil, or the Two Nations*; John Henry Newman, *Essay on the Development of Christian Doctrine*; R. Browning, *Dramatic Romances and Lyrics* (Edgar Allan Poe, *Tales of Mystery and Imagination*). |
| 1846 Repeal of Corn Laws protecting landowners: this splits the Conservatives. Russell's Liberal ministry (to 1852). | 1846 Charlotte, Emily and Anne Brontë, *Poems by Currer, Ellis and Acton Bell*; Edward Lear, *Book of Nonsense*. |
| | 1847 Anne Brontë, *Agnes Grey*; Charlotte Brontë, *Jane Eyre*; Emily Brontë, *Wuthering Heights*; Anthony Trollope, *The Macdermots of Ballycloran*; Tennyson, *The Princess*. |
| 1848 Revolutions in Paris, Berlin, Vienna, Rome, etc. Marx and Engels: *The Communist Manifesto*. The Pre-Raphaelite Brotherhood is founded. | 1848 Anne Brontë, *The Tenant of Wildfell Hall*; Dickens, *Dombey and Son*; Gaskell, *Mary Barton*; Mill, *Principles of Political Economy*; Thackeray, *Vanity Fair*; Arthur Hugh Clough, *The Bothie of Tober-na-Vuolich*. |
| | 1849 Charlotte Brontë, *Shirley*; Macaulay; *The History of England* (5 vols to 1861); Ruskin, *The Seven Lamps of Architecture*; Thackeray, *Pendennis*. |
| | 1850 Dickens, *David Copperfield*; Elizabeth Barrett Browning, *Sonnets from the Portuguese*; Dante Gabriel Rossetti and others, *The Germ*; Tennyson, *In Memoriam*; William Wordsworth, *The Prelude*. |
| 1851 Great Exhibition at the 'Crystal Palace'. | 1851 Ruskin, *The Stones of Venice* (3 vols 1853); E. B. Browning, *Casa Guidi Windows*. |
| 1852 Victoria and Albert Museum opened. | 1852 J. H. Newman, *Discourse on the Scope and Nature of University Education*; Thackeray, *The History of Henry Esmond*. |
| | 1853 Charlotte Brontë, *Villette*; Dickens, *Bleak House*; Elizabeth Gaskell, *Cranford*; Matthew Arnold, *Poems*. |
| 1854 Crimean War against Russia (to 1856). | 1854 Dickens, *Hard Times*; Thackeray, *The Newcomes*; Tennyson, *The Charge of the Light Brigade*; Coventry Patmore, *The Angel in the House* (4 parts 1862). |
| | 1855 Gaskell, *North and South*; Trollope, *The Warden*; R. Browning, *Men and Women*; Tennyson, *Maud* (Walt Whitman, *Leaves of Grass*). |

## Events and publications of 1837–80 *Continued*

| | |
|---|---|
| | 1856 James Anthony Froude, *History of England* (12 vols 1870). |
| 1857 Indian Mutiny. | 1857 Charlotte Brontë, *The Professor*; Dickens, *Little Dorrit*; Gaskell, *The Life of Charlotte Brontë*; Carlyle, *Collected Works* (16 vols 1858); Thomas Hughes, *Tom Brown's Schooldays*; Trollope, *Barchester Towers*; E. B. Browning, *Aurora Leigh*; George Eliot, *Scenes of Clerical Life* (Gustave Flaubert, *Madame Bovary*; Charles Baudelaire, *Les Fleurs du Mal*). |
| | 1858 Carlyle, *Frederick the Great* (8 vols 1865); Clough, *Amours de Voyage*. |
| | 1859 Dickens, *A Tale of Two Cities*; Eliot, *Adam Bede*, 'The Lifted Veil'. |
| | 1860 Wilkie Collins, *The Woman in White*; Eliot, *The Mill on the Floss*. |
| 1861 American Civil War (to 1865). Prince Albert dies. | 1861 Dickens, *Great Expectations*; Thackeray, *The Four Georges*; Trollope, *Framley Parsonage*; Francis Turner Palgrave (ed.), *The Golden Treasury*; D. G. Rossetti (trans.), *Early Italian Poets*. |
| 1862 Prince Bismarck becomes Prussian Chancellor (to 1890). | 1862 E. B. Browning, *Last Poems*; George Meredith, *Modern Love*; Christina Rossetti, *Goblin Market*. |
| 1863 London Underground begun. | 1863 Eliot, *Romola*; John Stuart Mill, *Utilitarianism*. |
| | 1864 Newman, *Apologia Pro Vita Sua*; Trollope, *Can You Forgive Her?*; R. Browning, *Dramatis Personae*. |
| | 1865 Arnold, *Essays in Criticism*; Lewis Carroll, *Alice's Adventures in Wonderland*; Dickens, *Our Mutual Friend*; Newman, *The Dream of Gerontius*. |
| | 1866 Eliot, *Felix Holt*; Elizabeth Gaskell (d.1865), *Wives and Daughters*; Algernon Charles Swinburne, *Poems and Ballads*. |
| 1867 Benjamin Disraeli's Second Reform Bill. | 1867 Trollope, *The Last Chronicle of Barset* (Leo Tolstoy, *War and Peace*). |
| 1868 W. E. Gladstone PM (to 1874). First Trades Union Congress. | 1868 Collins, *The Moonstone*; Browning, *The Ring and the Book*; William Morris, *The Earthly Paradise* (3 volumes, 1870). |
| 1869 Anglican Church disestablished in Ireland. | 1869 Matthew Arnold, *Culture and Anarchy*. |
| 1870 Prussians defeat Napoleon III at Sedan. | 1870 Disraeli, *Lothair*; Newman, *A Grammar of Assent*. |
| 1871 Paris Commune suppressed. Non-Anglicans allowed to attend Oxford and Cambridge. | 1871 Eliot, *Middlemarch* (4 vols 1872). |
| | 1872 Hardy, *Under the Greenwood Tree*. |
| | 1873 Arnold, *Literature and Dogma*; Hardy, *A Pair of Blue Eyes*; Walter Pater, *Studies in the Renaissance*. |
| 1874 Disraeli becomes PM (to 1880). | 1874 Hardy, *Far From the Madding Crowd*; James (B. V.) Thomson, 'The City of Dreadful Night' |
| 1875 Public Health Act. | 1875 Trollope, *The Way We Live Now*. |
| 1876 Invention of the telephone. | 1876 Eliot, *Daniel Deronda*; Henry James, *Roderick Hudson*. |
| 1877 Victoria Empress of India. | 1878 Hardy, *The Return of the Native* (Leo Tolstoy, *Anna Karenina*). |
| 1879 Gladstone denounces the Imperialism of the Conservative Government. | 1879 James, *Daisy Miller*, *The Europeans*. |
| | 1880 (Fyodor Dostoevsky, *The Brothers Karamazov*). |

periodicals brought a regulated Romanticism into Victorian homes – via, for example, Jane Austen's novels. In this simple sense, all subsequent literature – even the anti-Romantic literature of the modernists – is post-Romantic. Victorian narrative history has much in common with novel-writing. Scott's wish to tell the tale of the tribe was felt by Thackeray, Dickens and George Eliot, who re-create the worlds surrounding their childhoods. In an age of disorienting change, historical thinking was incited by the blasts of Carlyle's trumpet in his *French Revolution, Heroes and Hero-worship* and *Past and Present.* The effects of Carlyle can be read in Ruskin, Dickens and William Morris.

## Abundance

An eager reading public, larger than before, was regularly fed with serials and three-decker novels. Collected editions of popular novelists and best-selling prophets, and of fastidious prose-writers such as John Henry Newman and Walter Pater, run to many volumes. In an age when engineering miracles appeared every month and London had several postal deliveries a day, Dickens was thought hyperactive. Trollope wrote 2–3000 words daily before going to work at the Post Office. He invented the pillar box, rode to hounds midweek and Saturday, and wrote seventy books. The verse of a Tennyson, a Browning or a Morris is not contained in a thousand pages. Lesser writers such as Benjamin Disraeli, Bulwer Lytton, Charles Kingsley, Mrs Oliphant and Vernon Lee were equally prolific. Victorian vim continued less cheerfully in Thomas Hardy, Henry James, Joseph Conrad and the Edwardian Ford Madox Ford. Thereafter, serious novelists became less productive, though D. H. Lawrence (1885–1930) and the American William Faulkner (1897–1962) are exceptions.

To some, such abundance already seemed oppressive long before 1914. But by the time Lytton Strachey's *Eminent Victorians* came out in 1918, most of what the Victorians had believed, assumed and hoped had died. Strachey's debunkings of Cardinal Manning, Dame Florence Nightingale, Dr Thomas Arnold and General Gordon sold well. Victorians enjoyed laughing at themselves with Dickens, Lewis Carroll, Edward Lear, W. S. Gilbert and Oscar Wilde, and had a genius for light verse and for nonsense verse (not the same thing). But the modernists ridiculed the Victorians, who are still not always taken seriously, even by academics. Although universities have reinvested heavily in Victorian literary culture, quality remains the criterion in a critical history. Much of this literary abundance is of human or of cultural interest. How much of it is of artistic value?

Queen Victoria opening the Great Exhibition in the Crystal Palace, Hyde Park, London, 1 May 1851.

Before attempting this question, a change in the position of the writer must be noted. The novel became a major public entertainment at the same time that books became big business. The writer now worked for the public, via the the publisher. Whereas Wordsworth had a government sinecure, and the Prince Regent had obliged the reluctant Miss Austen to dedicate *Emma* to him, Victorian writers pleased the public. It is true that the Queen liked Tennyson to read to her, and that she ordered Lewis Carroll's complete works. When she wished to meet Dickens, he declined to be presented. Dickens was a commercial as well as a literary wizard, but not every writer could trade in letters. Edward Lear, a twentieth child, acted as tutor to Lord Derby's children. Robert Browning, Edward Fitzgerald and John Ruskin had private incomes. Lewis Carroll was a mathematics don, Trollope a civil servant, Matthew Arnold an Inspector of Schools. But commercial publication and writers' personal finances meant that few Victorians treated literature as an art – unlike Jonson, Milton, Austen or Keats, none of whom was rich. There were perfectionists – W. S. Landor, Emily Brontë, Christina Rossetti, J. H. Newman, Matthew Arnold, Gerard Hopkins, Walter Pater, Henry James, and more in the Nineties. Other perfectionists, Tennyson and Wilde, prospered greatly, and George Eliot earned millions in modern money, though less than Dickens.

But few Victorian novels are as well made as *Wuthering Heights* or *Middlemarch*, and few Victorian poems are perfect. What was perfection in comparison with imaginative and emotional power, moral passion, and the communication of vision, preferably to a multitude? The popularity of Romanticism, combined with the need of the press for a rapid and regular supply, had an inflationary effect on the literary medium. The quality of the writing of Carlyle, Thackeray, Ruskin and Dickens is more grossly uneven than that of their 18th-century predecessors. In retrospect, and in comparison with today, Victorian confidence in the taste of a middle-class public is impressive. The quality of novels published in monthly serials is high if not consistent. Ordinary talents were strained by the hectic pace of serial publication, but Dickens exulted in it. His novels could be shorter, but few would wish them fewer. The abundance and unevenness of Victorian writing do not suit the summary generalizations of a brief literary history. To the curious reader with time, however, there is compensation in its immense variety, and the unprecedentedly full and individualized set of pictures it gives of its age. The reader of Christopher Ricks's *New Oxford Book of Victorian Verse* (1988) will have some pleasant surprises.

## Why sages?

The lasting influence of Victorian thinkers such as Carlyle, Mill, Ruskin, Newman, Darwin and Arnold requires some preliminary attention. Why did this new animal, the Victorian Sage, appear? Why did secular literature assume such importance? Why did the saintly Newman write two novels and the politician Disraeli sixteen? Why did another prime minister, Gladstone, publish three books on Homer, and a third, Lord Derby, translate Homer? Why did Matthew Arnold believe that poetry would come to replace religion?

Deism and scepticism had in the 18th century reduced both what educated Christians believed, and the strength with which they believed it. By the time of the French Revolution, some intellectuals (not all of them radicals) were not Christians. Public meetings gave new chances to speakers, and Dissent became political rather than religious. In the liberal reforms of 1828–33, the Church of England lost its legal monopoly. Most Victorians went to church or chapel, although the factory towns of the Midlands and North had fewer churches, which did not always provide convincing leadership. In an age of rapid change and disappearing landmarks, guides to the past, present and future were needed, and lay preachers appeared. Some were Dissenters, others sceptics, others penny-a-liners.

Carlyle and Ruskin came from Scots Calvinist backgrounds to set up pulpits in the English press. Unchurched intellectuals like George Eliot looked for and provided guidance. The Oxford Movement renewed the Catholic inheritance of the Church of England. Most preachers preached, of course, from Anglican pulpits, like the Broad Church Charles Kingsley, who also preached from university lecterns, as did his Christian Socialist friend the Rev. F. D. Maurice. These thinkers were the first to see and to seek to understand the effects of industrial capitalism on social and personal life, effects which continue. Their often valid analyses are rarely read today, for the tones in which Carlyle and Ruskin address their audiences sound odd today. Yet they had a deep influence, so long assimilated as to be forgotten, on many significant currents of national culture, among them the Gothic Revival, Anglo-Catholicism, Christian Socialism, British Marxism, 'Young England' Toryism, the Trade Union movement, the Arts and Crafts movement, the National Trust, the Society for the Preservation of Ancient Monuments, and the cults of the environment, of the arts, and of literature. The society and conditions shaped by the Industrial Revolution met their first response in these thinkers.

## Thomas Carlyle

The voice of **Thomas Carlyle** (1795–1881) was heard soon after the Romantic poets fell silent. Edinburgh University enlightened this stonemason's son out of the Presbyterian ministry for which he was intended, but left him dissatisfied with scepticism. Religion was created by humanity to meet human needs: its old clothes should be discarded, updated, replaced by new man-made beliefs. This is the theme of *Sartor Resartus* ('The Tailor Re-clothed'), which purports to be the autobiography of a mad German philosopher edited by an equally fictitious editor. A Romantic heart is similarly 'edited' by an Enlightened head in Edgeworth's *Castle Rackrent* (1800) and Hogg's *Justified Sinner* (1832), but Carlyle's work is far more extraordinary in form and style. Once devoured for its message, the book's chaotic style makes it hard reading.

After arduous years studying German thought and translating Goethe, Carlyle moved from Craigenputtock, Dumfries, to Chelsea, where his *History of the French Revolution* made him famous. Scornful of metaphysical and materialist thinkers, he forged a faith in Life, in intuition and action, and in historical heroes who transcended human limitation. His great man – statesman, priest, man of action, captain of industry, man of letters – achieves his vision with energy. Earnest action is itself good; the vision itself is secondary. Carlyle's shrewdness, trenchancy and conviction cannot hide a want of mind, a substitution of means for ends. It is an attitude which prepared the way for the 'world-historical' man, the Hitlers and Stalins of the religion of humanity.

Carlyle was one of the first to diagnose the ills that industrial capitalism brought to society. He saw the plight of the factory hand whose labour was the source of wealth: with no stake or pride in the processes to which he was enslaved; exploited, underpaid, discarded (unemployment was high in the 1840s) and condemned to the workhouse. Carlyle's analysis was admired by Karl Marx when he took refuge in

**Thomas Carlyle** (1795–1881)
*Signs of the Times* (1829), *Characteristics* (1831), *Sartor Resartus* (1833–4), *History of the French Revolution* (1837), *Heroes and Hero-Worship* (1841), *Chartism* (1839), *Past and Present* (1843), *Oliver Cromwell's Letters and Speeches* (1845), *Occasional discourse on the nigger question* (1849), *Latter-day Pamphlets* (1850), *Life of John Sterling* (1851), *Life of Frederick the Great of Prussia* (1858–65).

liberal England. Marx's solution was political: class war, and the victory of the proletariat. The warning of Carlyle was moral: those to whom evil is done do evil in return. The remedy, in *Past and Present*, lies in renewing old arrangements: leaders who work, a renewed feudalism. Carlyle argues that Gurth, the Saxon swineherd of Scott's *Ivanhoe*, knew his master, his place, and the value of his work. Unlike the factory hand, the serf Gurth was spiritually free. This idealization of the mutual respect between the different ranks of pre-industrial society, found in Burke, Scott, Cobbett's *Rural Rides* (1821–) and Pugin's *Contrasts* (1836), is found again in Disraeli, Ruskin and even Morris. Anti-capitalist, it more often took a paternalist than a progressive form. Carlyle's political legacy was mistrust of revolution and fear of the mob, given unforgettable expression in his *French Revolution*, a source of Dickens's *A Tale of Two Cities*.

## John Stuart Mill

**John Stuart Mill** (1806–73) was the son of James Mill (1773–1836), a Scot intended for the ministry who came to London, like Carlyle. A friend of the economist David Ricardo and the philosopher Jeremy Bentham, James forced his infant son through a famously stiff educational programme.

At 16, J. S. Mill founded the Utilitarian Society to study Bentham's idea that all policy should be judged by the criterion of what furthered 'the greatest happiness of the greatest number' by the use of a 'felicific calculus'. As Mill recounts in his *Autobiography* (1873), he had as a young adult 'felt taken up to an eminence from which I could see an immense mental domain, and see stretching out into the distance intellectual results beyond all computation.' This biblical metaphor recalls both Swift's Academy of Projectors, and Bentham's Panopticon, a design for a workhouse where every inmate could be supervised by a single all-seeing person. (All inmates could see the supervisor's elevated observation-room, but could not tell whether he was there watching them.) British reformers used Bentham's planning throughout the 19th century, but his reductive and mechanistic model of society was anathema to Carlyle and Dickens (see the illustration on page 255).

At 20, Mill suffered a depression from which he was rescued by reading Wordsworth's poetry – 'the very culture of the feelings which I was in quest of'. Mill's lucid essays on Bentham and Coleridge balance rational material improvement with emotional and spiritual growth. They are a good starting-place for an understanding of post-Romantic culture, and an advertisement for the 19th-century liberal mentality. Intellectual clarity marks the prose of *On Liberty* (1859), *Principles of Political Economy* (1848) and *Utilitarianism* (1863).

## John Ruskin

The most Romantic prose of the Victorian sages is found in **John Ruskin** (1819–1900). His eloquent reaction to social problems had a spellbinding effect on the thought and lives of the young: on William Morris and Oscar Wilde, on Gandhi, who read him on trains in South Africa, and on Marcel Proust, who translated him (with some help) into French. Ruskin, untrained in aesthetics, was to be England's great art critic. He next turned from art and architecture to society, denouncing the ugly greed of England, and eventually, in apocalyptic tones, the pollution of the natural world by 'the Storm-Cloud of the Nineteenth Century'.

Ruskin's greatness is as striking as his singularity, an instance of the effect of Evangelicalism and Romanticism on an only child. Of his first sight (at 14) of the Swiss Alps at sunset, he wrote (at 70) that 'the seen walls of lost Eden could not have been more beautiful'. Like the Alps at sunset, Ruskin's works are vast, awe-inspiring and easy to get lost in. He is like Coleridge in his range, but less metaphysical and more moral in his discursiveness. He has passages of rhythmical harmony almost as beautiful as Tennyson's verse: of rapt perception and analytic description, of social insight and prophetic force. Of his passages of description, Virginia Woolf wrote that it is as if 'all the fountains of the English language had been set playing in the sunlight'. He was an enchanting public lecturer, but could run self-persuaded into oddity or obsession. Ruskin, like Carlyle and Dickens, confronted by the brutality and waste of industrial society and by the amoral neutrality of political economists, felt outrage. He proposed radical and collective human solutions both in the arts and in politics. He lost the narrowness of his upbringing, but regained Christian belief. He called himself a Tory of the school of Homer and Sir Walter Scott *and* a 'communist, reddest of the red'.

Ruskin's first major work, *Modern Painters* (5 volumes, 1843–60), was interrupted by *The Seven Lamps of Architecture* and *The Stones of Venice* (3 volumes,

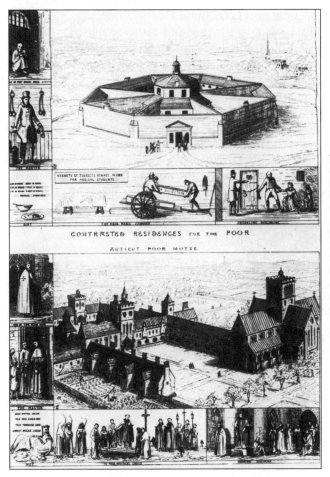

'Contrasted Residences for the Poor', one of the architect A. W. Pugin's polemical *Contrasts* (1830; revd edn 1841). The modern poorhouse is a rational House of Correction, like Bentham's Panopticon (see page 254); its turnkey and dissectionist's suppliers anticipate Dickens. The medieval almshouse, by contrast, supplies food, loving care and Christian burial.

1851–3). He turned aside from his defence of the English Romantic painter J. M. W. Turner to preserve in prose the medieval architecture of Europe then being destroyed. He drew and measured the major Gothic buildings in Venice like a geologist, studying the components of their architecture and ornament. Volume 1 analyses the results of this original research, classifying good and bad. Volume 2 cleanses Venice of its post-medieval reputation, and famously defines, after an imagined overview of Europe from the air, 'the Nature of Gothic'. He derived the health of Gothic architecture from the condition of its producers in craft guilds, in contrast with the uniform dead finish of British factory ware, and the condition of *its* producers. (The Gothic revival architect, A. W. Pugin, had anticipated these views in *Contrasts* (1836). Ruskin did not acknowledge this, perhaps because Pugin wanted to undo the Reformation as well as the Renaissance.)

Ruskin's perception that the workman was being turned into a machine led him to denounce competition and commercialism. After 1860 he plunged into furious propaganda on art and craft, on social, political and economic theory. He poured out money, lectures, tracts, and public letters, and set up schools, organizing the Guild of St George, and teaching at the Working Men's College. He was the first Slade Professor of Art at Oxford, resigning twice. Increasingly isolated, he had periods of delirium. After 1889 he withdrew to Brantwood, his house on Coniston Water, spoke little and wrote nothing. (His career was to be curiously paralleled by that of the 20th-century American poet Ezra Pound.)

Before falling silent, Ruskin wrote an enchanting autobiography, *Praeterita*, a lucid vision of the lost paradise of his childhood: his protected upbringing, learning the Bible by heart with his mother; private education; reading Byron; Oxford (not much use to him); learning to draw (very well). Travel opened his eyes: in a carriage specially built with a seat for young John to see out from, the Ruskins visited the houses of clients (his father was a sherry-importer, a partner of Pedro Domecq), and then toured Normandy, Switzerland and northern Italy. He studied geology, walked and sketched in the Alps or in Scotland. In *Praeterita*, the reformer's remaining wish is to recompose his youthful visions and make us see – the Rhone, the Alps, a single tree. This calm after the storm is not ruffled by any word of his arranged marriage, which ended in public scandal; his infatuation with Rose La Touche; his court case against Whistler.

Ruskin's principles, in art, craft, architecture and ecology, have outlasted his immediate causes. *Praeterita* ('Things Past'), ends:

Fonte Branda I saw with Charles Norton, under the same arches where Dante saw it. We drank of it together, and walked together that evening on the hills above, where the fireflies among the scented thickets shone fitfully in the still undarkened air. How they shone! moving like fine-broken starlight through the purple leaves. How they shone! through the sunset that faded into thunderous night as I entered Siena three days before, the white edges of the mountainous clouds still lighted from the west, and the open golden sky calm behind the gate of Siena's heart, with its still golden words, *Cor magis tibi Sena pandit*, and the fireflies everywhere in sky and cloud rising and falling, mixed with the lightning, and more intense than the stars.

*Cor magis tibi Sena pandit* is the city's motto: 'More than her gates, Siena opens her heart to you'.

Sunset and valediction coincide in Wordsworth's *Tintern*, Coleridge's *Dejection*, Keats's *Autumn* and Shelley's *West Wind*. Soaring skies and sad clouds are a Victorian combination.

# John Henry Newman

Romanticism, on one view, is 'spilt religion', a definition which suggests that religion is an emotion. This was not the view of **John Henry Newman** (1801–90), the master of Victorian non-fictional prose. The departure of rationalists from Christian belief, and the first moves to separate Church and State in England, provoked John Keble, a Fellow of Oriel College, Oxford, to preach a sermon in 1833 on 'national apostasy': the prospect of an atheist England. This began the Oxford or Tractarian Movement, so called from *Tracts for the Times*, founded by Newman and contributed to by Keble and Pusey, also Fellows of Oriel. The tracts argued that the Church of England kept the faith of the apostles and of the early Church. In 1841 Newman, vicar of the University Church of St Mary the Virgin, published Tract 90, which maintains that the 39 Articles in which the Church of England had formulated its faith under Edward VI were those of the historic and universal Catholic Church. Newman, originally an Evangelical and then a liberal, came to believe that Broad Church liberalism would first dilute and then dissolve Christian belief.

Bishops denounced Tract 90, and Newman had to consider the possibility that the Church of England was not apostolic, and that the Roman Catholic Church was what it claimed to be. He resigned St Mary's and his Fellowship, and in 1845 was received into the Catholic Church. As Oxford was the intellectual centre of the country's religious life, Newman's conversion was a landmark in post-Reformation history. Other clergy and undergraduates turned to Rome. Was this a 'Second Spring' of English Catholicism? In 1846 Newman left Oxford, paying a last visit to his tutor at his undergraduate college:

Trinity had never been unkind to me. There used to be much snap-dragon growing on the wall opposite my freshman's rooms there, and I had for years taken it as the emblem of my own perpetual residence even unto death in my University. On the morning of the 23rd I left the Observatory. I have never seen Oxford since, excepting its spires, as they are seen from the railway.

This passage comes from *Apologia Pro Vita Sua*, a vindication of his life, composed in 1864 in response to Charles Kingsley, who had casually remarked in a review that Newman, like the Catholic clergy generally, did not hold truth to be a necessary virtue. (Alexander Macmillan, publisher of the magazine in which the remark appeared, sincerely enquired of Newman whether this was not the Catholic position.) Newman's scrupulous history of his religious opinions showed the falsity of Kingsley's charge and convinced a sceptical audience of his own good faith. The *Apologia* remains a convincing spiritual and intellectual autobiography.

Newman had studied the Church Fathers and 17th-century Anglican divines, and like them he composed for the ear, taking pains over rhythmic and syntactic organization as well as clear argument and distinct diction. Some of his sermons, hymns, prayers, poems and lives of English saints have outlived their occasions; as have his Church history, theology and fiction. An early hymn suggests his modesty:

> Lead, kindly Light, amid the encircling gloom.
>     Lead thou me on;
> The night is dark and I am far from home;
>     Lead thou me on.
> Keep thou my feet; I do not ask to see
> The distant scene; one step enough for me.

**John Henry Newman** (1801–90) *The Arians of the Fourth Century* (1832), *Tracts for the Times* (1833–41), *The Tamworth Reading Room* (1841), *Essay on the Development of Christian Doctine* (1845), *Loss and Gain* (1847), *Discourses on the Scope and Nature of University Education* (1852), *Apologia Pro Vita Sua* (1864), *The Dream of Gerontius* (1865), *An Essay in Aid of a Grammar of Assent* (1870), *The Idea of a University* (1873).

Too dim for Kingsley, this hymn was a favourite of Thomas Hardy's. Newman's major work in verse is *The Dream of Gerontius*, made into an oratorio by Elgar. It dramatizes the destiny of the soul after death.

The most valuable of Newman's other works are his *Development of Christian Doctrine*, which relates the historical evolution of Christian dogma to the Church's teaching authority, and his *Grammar of Assent*. Another classic is his *Idea of a University*, his discourses as first Rector of University College, Dublin. He defines and defends the liberal idea of education against Edinburgh Utilitarianism and an Irish hierarchy which assumed that its new College was there to teach Catholic doctrine. Newman's 'Idea' is that a university is not to teach useful knowledge or dogmatic truth, nor to pursue research, but to educate philosophically and critically, to discipline and enlarge the mind.

In his *Apologia* Newman approaches Christian belief along converging arguments from history and personal experience as well as from scripture, philosophy and theology. His view that Providence has guided the historical development of Christian revelation brings a British empiricism into theology. His argument from experience draws on the educated imagination, developing a Romantic doctrine. Newman also thought that the Oxford Movement developed from Romanticism. In retrospect, he understood that Movement as

a reaction from the dry and superficial character of the religious teaching and the literature of the last generation, or century; and as a result of the need which was felt both by the hearts and the intellects of the nation for a deeper philosophy; and as the evidence and as the partial fulfillment of that need, to which even the chief authors of the then generation had borne witness. First, I mentioned the literary influence of Walter Scott, who turned men's minds in the direction of the middle ages ...

He then mentioned Coleridge, who 'made trial of his age, and succeeded in interesting its genius in the cause of Catholic truth'; Southey's fiction; and Wordsworth's philosophical meditation. He thus anticipates Mill on Wordsworth's culture of the feelings, and the role assigned to imaginative literature by Matthew Arnold. A central passage of the *Apologia* is from 'Position of My Mind Since 1845':

To consider the world in its length and breadth, its various history, the many races of man, their starts, their fortunes, their mutual alienation, their conflicts; and then their ways, habits, governments, forms of worship; their enterprises, their aimless courses, their random achievements and acquirements, the impotent conclusion of long-standing facts, the tokens so faint and broken, of a superintending design, the blind evolution of what turn out to be great powers or truth, the progress of things, as if from unreasoning elements, not towards final causes, the greatness and littleness of man, his far-reaching aims, his short duration, the curtain hung over his futurity, the disappointments of life, the defeat of good, the success of evil, physical pain, mental anguish, the prevalence and intensity of sin, the pervading idolatries, the corruptions, the dreary hopeless irreligion, that condition of the whole race, so fearfully yet exactly described in the Apostle's words, 'having no hope and without God in the world' – all this is a vision to dizzy and appall; and inflicts upon the mind the sense of a profound mystery which is absolutely beyond human solution.

What shall be said to this heart-piercing, reason-bewildering fact? I can only answer that either there is no Creator, or this living society of men is in a true sense discarded from His presence ... And so I argue about the world – *if* there be a God, since there is a God, the human race is implicated in some terrible aboriginal calamity. It is out of joint with the purposes of its Creator. This is a fact, a fact as true to me as the fact of its existence; and thus the doctrine of what is theologically called original sin becomes to me almost as certain as that the world exists, and as the existence of God … Supposing then it to be the Will of the Creator to interfere in human affairs, and to make provision for retaining in the world a knowledge of Himself, so definite and distinct as to be proof against the energy of human scepticism …

This last is the argument which leads him to belief in the teaching authority of the Catholic Church.

## Charles Darwin

In *The Voyage of the Beagle* (1845), **Charles Darwin** (1809–82) recounts his experience as ship's naturalist on an expedition to South America in 1831–6. Like poets from Wordsworth to Thomas Hardy, he felt he was 'superior to the common run of men in noticing things which easily escape attention, and in observing them carefully'. Observation led to the theory systematically demonstrated in *The Origin of Species* (1859), that species evolve by retaining the characteristics of their most successful members.

The *Descent of Man* (1871) assembled new evidence for the old idea that humans descend from apes; Darwin wrote cautiously but had a great effect. Geology had shown the earth to be millions of years old. The 'Higher Criticism', as it was called to distinguish it from textual criticism, doubted the historical basis of supernatural events in scripture. Geology, evolution and scientific history combined to show that the Bible was not scientific history. Many British Protestants had both an empirical model of truth and an implicit faith in the literal truth of the Bible. These two simple notions were now in conflict. If the account of Creation in Genesis was neither scientific nor historical, could it be true? If not, was the New Testament true? Evolution challenged Christian ideas of the origin and end of mankind. Some, like Tennyson, modified their belief in the existence of God and the special destiny of humanity. Others, like Thomas Hardy, were left feeling defrauded. Darwin was not a social critic, but his work had much influence, clearly seen in the novels of George Eliot.

## Matthew Arnold

The last central Victorian thinker is **Matthew Arnold** (1822–88), son of Dr Thomas Arnold, the reforming headmaster of Rugby School. Matthew had his father's sense of obligation, but chose to conduct his own mission to educate the middle class in a cooler tone, more French than British, or – to adopt the terms of *Culture and Anarchy* – more Hellenic than Hebraic. He turned his talents away from the writing of poetry to bear on the value of European and of biblical literature.

Arnold's prose is, with Newman's, among the most persuasive Victorian writing. Arnold writes as a man of the world rather than a prophet; a critic, not a sage. Wearing this urbane manner, he travelled the provinces for thirty-five years as an Inspector of Schools. But the smiling public lecturer had a serious concern: he saw a new ruling class obsessed with profit, use and morality, unnoticing of ugliness, untouched by large ideas or fine ideals. In his polemical *Culture and Anarchy* he dismisses the aristocracy as Barbarians, and ridicules the middle class as Philistines – a name offensive to puritan belief in the English as a chosen race. His terms 'culture' and 'Philistine' gained lasting currency. His literary criticism will be mentioned later, but his forecast that the consolations of religion would in future be supplied by poetry

**Matthew Arnold** (1822–88)
*The Strayed Reveller and Other Poems* (1849), *Empedocles on Etna* (1852), *Essays in Criticism* (1865, 1868), *Schools and Universities on the Continent* (1868), *On the Study of Celtic Literature* (1867), *Culture and Anarchy* (1869), *Friendship's Garland* (1871), *Literature and Dogma* (1873).

deserves the final mention in an account of Victorian sages. His successor, **Walter Pater** (1839–94), discussed in Chapter 11, was a critic not of society but of art and letters and the individual life.

## ■ Further reading

Holloway, J. *The Victorian Sage: Studies in Argument* (London: Macmillan, 1953).

Houghton, W. E. *The Victorian Frame of Mind: 1830–1870* (New Haven: Yale University Press, 1957).

Young, G. M. *Victorian England: Portrait of an Age* (Oxford: Oxford University Press, 1936; annotated edn by G. K. Clark, Oxford: Oxford University Press 1977).

# Poetry

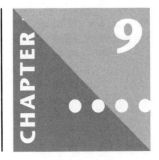

# CHAPTER 9

## Overview

This survey of Victorian poetry to 1880 restricts itself to the major figures listed below, ignoring considerable minor poets such as Emily Brontë, William Barnes, Edward Fitzgerald, William Morris, George Meredith, Coventry Patmore, and C. S. Calverley. The copious variety of Victorian verse is well sampled in the anthologies which are listed in 'Further reading' (page 271). Although Victorian verse is broadly post-Romantic, giving new inflections to the personal, subjective, emotional and idealistic impulses of the Romantics, it is more various than this suggests. Expressive and plangent, it is also descriptive, of nature and of domestic and urban life. Often it half-dramatizes figures from history, legend and literature. Browning, Clough and Hopkins suggest an idiosyncrasy of subject, language and metre equally pronounced in less serious and less major poets.

## Contents

# Victorian Romantic poetry

## Minor verse

### John Clare

Of minor verse between Byron and Tennyson, we admire the best of Walter Savage Landor, George Darley and Thomas Lovell Beddoes and may respond to the sentimental lyrics of Tom Moore and Mrs Felicia Hemans, but the poetry of **John Clare** (1793–1864) has value as a whole. His *Poems Descriptive of Rural Life and Scenery* (1820) and later volumes are a faithful account of the old rural life. Clare, a farm labourer, describes in a simpler voice than Crabbe and in more detail than Wordsworth: 'I peeled bits of straw and I got switches too.' His innocence is seen in 'I Am'. Unsettled by a move from his native village in Northamptonshire, Clare spent decades in asylums.

If Wordsworth clothed Nature with piety and philosophy, the things described by his successors are more actually present to imagined sight and touch than those in

## Poets

Alfred, Lord Tennyson (1809–92)

Elizabeth Barrett (1806–61)

Robert Browning (1812–89)

Matthew Arnold (1822–88)

Arthur Hugh Clough (1819–61)

Dante Gabriel Rossetti (1828–82)

Christina Rossetti (1830–94)

Algernon Charles Swinburne (1837–1909)

Fr Gerard Hopkins (1844–89)

his own recollections. Natural detail comes to have an authenticating role in many poems of Alfred Tennyson, Robert Browning, Gerard Hopkins, Thomas Hardy and Edward Thomas. Thanks to the advance of natural science, particularity increased; but Tennyson also had the power 'of creating scenery, in keeping with some state of human feeling so fitted to it as to be the embodied symbol of it'. So J. S. Mill wrote of Tennyson's early poems, *Mariana* and *The Lady of Shallott*.

## Alfred Tennyson

**Alfred Tennyson** (1809–92) succeeded Wordsworth as Poet Laureate in 1850. He became almost universally popular, and at his death in 1892 was mourned as 'the voice of England'. The widowed Queen liked him to read *Maud* to her, and he wrote grand public poems such as 'The Charge of the Light Brigade' and 'Ode on the Death of the Duke of Wellington'. In an Edison recording of the former, he can be heard 'mouthing out his hollow o's and a's' – his description of himself reading *Morte d'Arthur*. It fits such sonorous lines as:

> And slowly answered Arthur from the barge
>
> > *Morte d'Arthur*
>
> The moan of doves in immemorial elms,
> And murmuring of innumerable bees
>
> > 'Come Down, O Maid'
>
> The long day wanes; the slow moon climbs; the deep
> Moans round with many voices.
>
> > *Ulysses*

Tennyson hailed Virgil as 'wielder of the stateliest measure moulded by the lips of man'. His own orchestral musicality was admired by later writers, though they mocked him. James Joyce called him 'Alfred Lawn Tennyson'. Tennyson is the central poet of the 19th century.

Eliot did not join in the modernist reaction against Tennyson, but W. H. Auden thought him 'the stupidest of our poets' (if with 'the finest ear'); Auden shrank from his family-mindedness. Tennyson was ruminative rather than clever, yet he was well-read in science and religion, and *In Memoriam A. H. H.* dramatizes the struggle of Faith and Doubt better than any other work. Tennyson subdued everything to his craft, and ideas often melt into music in his verse. His primary interest was in feelings, as in this Song from *The Princess*:

> Tears, idle tears, I know not what they mean,
> Tears from the depth of some divine despair
> Rise in the heart, and gather to the eyes,
> In looking on the happy autumn-fields,
> And thinking on the days that are no more.

'These lines,' Tennyson said, 'came to me on the yellowing autumn-tide at Tintern Abbey, full for me of its bygone memories.' (Tintern is on the Wye, a tributary of the Severn, on the shore of which his friend Arthur Hallam was buried.) The poems echo with voices and memories. Tennyson both created landscape and inscribed emotion on real landscapes.

He was the sixth of twelve children of the Rector of Somersby, Lincolnshire. The disinherited eldest son of a landowner, the Rector was an unwilling clergyman. Melancholia, drunkenness, violence, opium and madness visited the Rectory, yet it

Alfred Tennyson, aged about 30, an engraving after an oil painting by Samuel Laurence, 1838.

produced three poets among its sons. Alfred, taught Greek by his father, imagined Troy on a North Sea beach: 'Here often, when a child, I lay reclined;/I took delight in this fair strand and free:/Here stood the infant Ilion of my mind,/And here the Grecian ships did seem to be.'

At Cambridge, Alfred became a friend of the brilliant Arthur Hallam, eldest son of Henry Hallam, a historian predeceased by all twelve of his children. Arthur, who had published theology and literary criticism and was to have married Tennyson's sister, died of a brain hæmorrhage at twenty-two. This event darkened Tennyson's life. Rejected by his first love for a richer suitor, the poet drifted, staying with friends, writing:

> … for the unquiet heart and brain
> A use in measured language lies;
> The sad mechanic exercise,
> Like dull narcotics, numbing pain.

He married late and lived in the country, on the Isle of Wight and in Surrey. After *Poems, Chiefly Lyrical* (1830), collections came every few years, notably in 1832 and 1842. Larger works include *In Memoriam* (1850); *Maud* (1855), *Enoch Arden* (1864), and the Arthurian *Idylls of the King* (1859–88).

Critical opinion divides over the long poems, except *In Memoriam*. This elegy for Hallam, expressing agonized doubts about Christianity and human destiny, is the most emotional English poem of its length. Its 132 lyrics, all in the same stanza, were not written as a sequence, but finally arranged to span three Christmasses. The keynote is pure loss:

> Old Yew, which graspest at the stones
> That name the under-lying dead,
> Thy fibres net the dreamless head,
> Thy roots are wrapt about the bones …            II

> Dark house, by which once more I stand
> Here in the long unlovely street,
> Doors, where my heart was used to beat
> So quickly, waiting for a hand …            VII

> … My Arthur, whom I shall not see
> Till all my widowed race be run;
> Dear as the mother to the son,
> More than my brothers are to me.                    IX

The loss becomes generalized:

> … Behold, we know not anything;
> I can but trust that good shall fall
> At last – far off – at last, to all,
> And every winter change to spring.
>
> So runs my dream; but what am I?
> An infant crying in the night;
> An infant crying for the light,
> And with no language but a cry.                     LIV
>
> Are God and Nature then at strife,
> That Nature lends such evil dreams?
> So careful of the type she seems,
> So careless of the single life …                   LV
>
> Man, her last work, who seemed so fair,
> Such splendid purpose in his eyes,
> Who rolled the psalm to wintry skies,
> Who built him fanes of fruitless prayer,           temples
>
> Who trusted God was love indeed
> And love Creation's final law –
> Though Nature, red in tooth and claw
> With ravine, shrieked against his creed – …        LVI
>
> There rolls the deep where grew the tree.
> O earth, what changes hast thou seen!
> There where the long street roars hath been
> The stillness of the central sea.                  CXXV

Tennyson was the first poet to come to terms with geological time and Evolution. *In Memoriam* climbs slowly, moaning, towards a hard-won Christian faith. It dramatizes inner feelings and projects them onto an outer world of landscape, space and time. Notable lyrics of natural symbolism act as points of emotional transition on the journey to the third Christmas: 'Calm is the morn without a sound'; 'Tonight the winds begin to rise'; 'Witch-elms that counterchange the floor'; 'The time draws near the birth of Christ'; 'Ring out, wild bells, to the wild sky'; 'Now fades the last long streak of snow.' The cycle makes its effect from repetition as much as from arrangement. Its composer's gift was for song, scene and soliloquy rather than narrative or architecture. Like Wordsworth before him and Hardy and Eliot after him, he 'sees by glimpses' and 'remembers'. His best work is from the first half of his career, but he kept his lyric gift.

The Romantics had turned poetry towards autobiography, real, pretended or disguised. The Victorians often avoided self-disclosure by the use of a first-person speaker, historical, legendary or invented. Tennyson's best poems outside *In Memoriam* include dramatic monologues such as *Ulysses* and *Tithonus*. Without context, monologue is open to various interpretation. In *Ulysses*, Odysseus plans a last voyage into the western ocean; he hopes, if he dies, 'to see the great Achilles, whom we knew'. Tennyson said that the poem expressed his own 'need of going forward and braving the struggle of life' after the death of Hallam; the need can be felt more than the braving. The ghosts of Homer, Virgil, Shakespeare and Milton speak in the rhythms and phrasing of *Ulysses*. Tennyson was steeped in the classical, and, more than any predecessor, in the whole of the English poetic tradition also. As an undergraduate he had translated a little of *Beowulf*, the first English poet to do so. He chose the lines in which Beowulf 'his wordhoard unlocked'.

*Tithonus*, like *Tiresias*, *The Lotos-Eaters* and other poems drafted after 1833, longs for death. Its speaker was loved by the goddess Aurora (Dawn), who gave him eternal life but not eternal youth. Nothing is more Tennysonian than the opening:

> The woods decay, the woods decay and fall,
> The vapours weep their burthen to the ground,
> Man comes and tills the field and lies beneath,
> And after many a summer dies the swan.
> Me only cruel immortality
> Consumes; I wither slowly in thine arms ...

## Elizabeth Barrett and Robert Browning

When in 1846 **Robert Browning** (1812–89) secretly married **Elizabeth Barrett** (1806–61), she was the more popular poet. Only after her death in 1861, when he returned to England from Italy, did his reputation eclipse hers. Her *Sonnets from the Portuguese* (not translations, but her own love-poems) were much admired – 'How do I love thee? Let me count the ways' – but they now seem too declamatory. The lower-pitched reaches of her verse-novel *Aurora Leigh* make better reading.

Browning lacks Tennyson's beauty of verse and language, but the poets apply the Romantic legacy in ways that can be compared. After his early verse was criticized as self-obsessed, Browning chose not to wear his heart on his sleeve. Turning outwards, he wrote a number of unsuccessful plays – melodramatic acting vehicles – then went back to the dramatic monologue. Whereas Tennyson spoke indirectly through classical myth and literary legend, Browning's speakers are, or seem, historical. He had read much out-of-the-way Renaissance history, as demonstrated in the romance *Sordello*. He perfected the monologue in 'My Last Duchess': the Duke, who speaks, has had his last wife killed because she smiled at everyone. Browning develops the form further in *Men and Women* (1855), *Dramatis Personae* (1864), and others. 'The Bishop Orders his Tomb', a compact and energetic short story, is a fine representative of the form.

Browning's artists, humanists and clerics, ancient and modern, talk as compulsively as Coleridge's Ancient Mariner. Like characters in the 'humour' comedy of Ben Jonson, they sacrifice proportion, humanity and morality to a ruling passion. Spirit and strong will can seem self-justifying in these confessions, for the author does not offer context or judgement. Yet in Browning, as in Dickens, the fascination of egotism is to be read against a humane and undogmatic Christianity. When authorial judgement is explicit, as in 'The Lost Leader', 'Prospice' and the Epilogue to *Asolando*, Browning's attitudes are strong, even crude. Browning needed his masks. He insisted that his poems were dramatic, not personal, as did Tennyson and Hardy. The modern speakers are often lovers, dissatisfied, possessive or obsessive. 'Porphyria's Lover' tells of strangling Porphyria with her own hair, ending 'And yet God has not said a word.' The grotesque fascinates Browning, who rarely satisfies the curiosity he arouses. But he did not want to satisfy: 'a man's reach should exceed his grasp/Else what's a heaven for?' ('Andrea del Sarto').

His later years produced *The Ring and the Book*, a verse-novel of monologues about a 17th-century Roman murder, in which twelve participants tell what happened. This use of separate perspectives, found in the old epistolary novel, became a formal principle in the work of Browning's admirer, the American novelist Henry James. It remains a formula of the detective story. Browning had a novelist's fascination with the inscrutability of motives and the unpredictability of their combined effects. The monologue was a gift to Thomas Hardy, Rudyard Kipling, Ezra Pound and T. S. Eliot. In the hands of its master, however, the monologue offers the fascination of a feat or a puzzle. Like many 19th-century musical virtuosi, for example the Abbé Liszt, Browning enjoys drawing attention to his own skill, and manner upstages matter. 'Irks care the crop-full bird?' asks the speaker of 'Rabbi Ben Ezra': 'Frets doubt the maw-crammed beast?'

Browning's striking talent is put to better use in short poems such as 'Home-Thoughts from Abroad', 'Meeting at Night' and 'Parting at Morning', and in some of his modern love poems, such as 'Two in the Campagna', which ends:

> No. I yearn upward, touch you close,
>     Then stand away. I kiss your cheek,
> Catch your soul's warmth – I pluck the rose
>     And love it more than tongue can speak –
> Then the good minute goes.
>
> Already how am I so far
>     Out of that minute? Must I go
> Still like the thistle-ball, no bar,
>     Onward, whenever light winds blow,
> Fixed by no friendly star?
>
> Just when I seemed about to learn?
>     Where is the thread now? Off again!
> The old trick! Only I discern –
>     Infinite passion, and the pain
> Of finite hearts that yearn.

This was a gift that he did not lose with his wife's death, as testified by many late poems, including one, 'Inapprehensiveness', from 1889, his last year.

## Matthew Arnold

English Romantic poetry was not always romantic. Keats was the first strongly to associate Romantic yearning with love, the ideal of post-Romantic life and literature. The only Victorian poem both great and perfect – as Matthew Arnold's 'Dover Beach' has been called – opens with Nature:

> The sea is calm tonight.
> The tide is full, the moon lies fair
> Upon the straights – on the French coast the light
> Gleams and is gone; the cliffs of England stand,
> Glimmering and vast, out in the tranquil bay.
> Come to the window, sweet is the night air!

The second subject, Love, returns in the final verse-paragraph: 'Ah, love, let us be true/To one another!' But nature and love, beauty and passion, are not at the heart of the poem. There is a new reason why the lovers must be true to one another:

> for the world which seems
> To lie before us like a land of dreams,
> So various, so beautiful, so new,
> Hath really neither joy, nor love, nor light,
> Nor certitude, nor peace, nor help for pain;
> And we are here as on a darkling plain
> Swept with confused alarms of struggle and flight,
> Where ignorant armies clash by night.

From this island once brightly girdled by 'the Sea of Faith', Arnold can 'only hear its melancholy, long, withdrawing roar'. He had gone from his father's Rugby School to an Oxford torn between Tractarianism and liberalism, and from his father's Broad Church liberal faith to realizing that the Bible was only partly historical. A. H. Clough, Arnold's friend and his father's prize pupil, resigned his college fellowship in 1848, unable to subscribe to the Thirty-Nine Articles of the Church of England.

This crisis of faith in Christianity lent Arnold a keen sense of human isolation, expressed in the poetry of his earlier career. 'I have less poetical sentiment than Tennyson,' he was to write to his mother, 'and less intellectual vigour and abundance than Browning; yet, because I have perhaps more of a fusion of the two than either of them, and have more regularly applied that fusion to the main line of modern development, I am likely enough to have my turn.' Arnold's self-analysis is clear-sighted, as is his forecast that 'the movement of mind' would bring him readers. His diagnosis of the moral ailments of modern life is sound, but he saw also that his poems lack the tonic effect of true tragic poetry. They are intensely sad, whereas his later prose, forging new roles for literature and religion in society, sparkles with wit.

Arnold's best poetry is personal, a category which in his case includes intellectual autobiography ('Stanzas from the Grande Chartreuse' and 'The Buried Life') and poems to other writers, as well as the love poems to Marguerite and the academic pastorals, *The Scholar Gipsy* and *Thyrsis*. In all these poems, land, water and sky lend symbolic power and plangency. His literary criticism is impersonal, 'seeing life steadily and seeing it whole', applying the moral and intellectual criterion of 'high seriousness', asserting that great literature is 'a criticism of life', and quoting briefly to show what is classic. Arnold's poetic criticism has not been improved upon, even by Eliot, who borrowed much from him. His command of classical, European, English and biblical literature shows the quality of high Victorian culture. Scholar-critics such as W. P. Ker or Eric Auerbach can match his knowledge, but they do not quote so tellingly.

His own poetry meets the tests he proposed, but its style and rhythm can seem too studied. Here is the conclusion to the pastoral elegy *Thyrsis*:

> Too rare, too rare, grow now my visits here!
>   'Mid city noise, not, as with thee of yore,
>     Thyrsis! in reach of sheep-bells is my home.
>   – Then through the great town's harsh, heart-wearying roar,
>     Let in thy voice a whisper often come,
>       To chase fatigue and fear:
>     *Why faintest thou? I wandered till I died,*
>     *Roam on! The light we sought is shining still.*
>     *Dost thou ask proof? Our tree yet crowns the hill,*
> *Our Scholar travels yet the loved hillside.*

### Arthur Hugh Clough

'Thyrsis' is **Arthur Hugh Clough** (1819–61). Clough's squibs are often quoted to illustrate Victorian Doubt, but his long poems now hold our attention. In *Amours de Voyage* and *Dipsychus*, his frankness, irony, conversational texture and play of mood seem very modern. His most perfect work is the early verse-novel, *The Bothie of Tober-na-Vuolich*, a high-spirited mock-epic romance, in Homeric hexameters, of the adventures of a 'reading party' of Oxford men in the Highlands.

## Dante Gabriel Rossetti and Christina Rossetti

In 1848 **Dante Gabriel Rossetti**, son of an Italian political refugee, founded the Pre-Raphaelite Brotherhood, a group of young artists including John Millais and Holman Hunt, sworn to an anti-academic realism, a simple directness unmodified by classical norms, and so 'medieval'. The Pre-Raphaelite Brotherhood lasted five years, but Rossetti later worked with or close to William Morris, Ford Madox Brown and Edward Burne-Jones. J. M. Whistler and A. C. Swinburne stayed with him in Chelsea.

Rossetti's often unfinished paintings and uneven poems have a willed emotional intensity. An admirer of Keats, he had at eighteen written 'The Blessed Damozel' in which a beauty 'leaned out/From the gold bar of Heaven', longing to be reunited with her earthly lover. The poem jumbles sensuous with spiritual imagery; the Damozel leans 'until her bosom must have made/The bar of heaven warm.' Rossetti's symbolism, and his association of erotic love with death, anticipate Aestheticism and Decadence. When his wife, a former model, committed suicide, he buried with her a book of poems which he later exhumed. His bohemian lifestyle gave scandal, and his verse was attacked in a pamphlet, *The Fleshly School of Poetry*.

His sister **Christina Rossetti** (1830–94) retained a Pre-Raphaelite truth to nature,

'Buy from us with a golden curl': the frontispiece to a volume of Christina Rossetti's verse, *Goblin Market* (1862), published by Morris, Marshall, Faulkner and Co. Dante Gabriel Rossetti's illustration is based on a line from the title poem.

with bright colours and clear edges. A devout Anglo-Catholic, she renounced two engagements on religious grounds, cared for her family, and wrote poetry. For ten years she did voluntary work to help ex-prostitutes. Her poem 'In An Artist's Studio' reflects upon her brother's doomed world: 'One face looks out from all his canvases,/ One selfsame figure sits or walks or leans … Not as she is, but was when hope shone bright;/Not as she is, but as she fills his dream.' Songs such as 'When I am dead, my dearest', 'My heart is like a singing bird' and 'Does the road wind up-hill all the way?' show her fine lyric gift – the best English woman poet, thought Virginia Woolf. Delicacy and a wan fancy are her characteristics, and she wrote well for children, though 'An Apple-Gathering' is more than girlish. Her masterpiece, *Goblin Market*, is a richly-charged fairy story of forbidden fruit, of two sisters, of innocence lost and redeemed. Its adult themes, close to her brother's, are managed with a tact and discipline beyond him, and a sensuous verbal and rhythmic energy.

## Algernon Charles Swinburne

Algernon Charles Swinburne (1837–1909) was an anti-Victorian immoralist; he referred to Tennyson's *Morte d'Arthur* as the *Morte d'Albert*. A libertarian aristocrat and amateur of Greek lyric poetry, he followed Shelley and Landor. Victorian restrictiveness produced in him an extreme reaction. Swinburne was a hedonist, a literary aesthete and an expert in Greek impropriety, favouring the ecstatic Greek cults above that of 'the pale Galilean', Jesus Christ. Metrically he was a virtuoso, and his *Songs and Ballads* were in vogue in the 1860s, but his appeal lay in his inversion of respectability and of moral 'uplift'. In him, the Victorian cult of the dead takes a post-erotic tinge. To intone, in appropriate circumstances, the chants by which he is represented in anthologies, 'When the hounds of spring are on winter's traces' and 'I will go back to the great sweet mother' and 'The Garden of Proserpine', can be fun. But re-reading shows them to be vague in sense, fond of their own manner, and designed to induce maudlin despair. His versions of the 15th-century criminal poet Villon have lasted better. The octosyllabics of the original curb the translator's fluency, fatally evident in his elegy to his idol, the French poet Charles Baudelaire (1821–67).

Masochism and alcohol led to Swinburne's collapse. In his last thirty years, under voluntary restraint, he poured out verse, plays, pornography, prejudiced literary criticism and an odd novel. 'We Poets in our youth begin in gladness', wrote Wordsworth, 'But thereof come in the end despondency and madness.' Swinburne's heirs flowered and fell in the 1890s.

## Gerard Hopkins

The poetry of **Gerard Hopkins** (1844–89) – he disliked his middle name, Manley – was first published by his friend Robert Bridges in 1918. Converted at Oxford (and cut off by his family), Hopkins was received into the Catholic Church by J. H. Newman, and entered the Society of Jesus in 1868. Courageous, sensitive, often ill, he worked in industrial parishes, then as a conscientious Professor of Greek at University College, Dublin, dying of typhoid.

Hopkins put aside his early verse, but in 1877 a casual remark by his Rector prompted him to write *The Wreck of the Deutschland*, and to submit it to a Jesuit journal. It was rejected. Hopkins thereafter thought that the Society might regard

Gerard Hopkins SJ (1844–89).
A late photograph.

poetry as inconsistent with his profession. He exchanged poems privately with Robert Bridges and R. W. Dixon; his were extremely unconventional in style. Even in the 1930s they seemed experimental and modern – *The Wreck of the Deutschland* begins *The Faber Book of Modern Verse* (1936) – and were imitated. The shock has worn off, the astonishing achievement remains.

'A horrible thing has happened to me,' Hopkins wrote in 1864, 'I have begun to *doubt* Tennyson.' His instinct, he said, was 'to admire and do otherwise'. Hopkins avoided smooth movement and harmony of language in order to make the reader see and think. He believed with Coleridge that Nature is 'the language that thy God utters'. His tutor at Balliol, Walter Pater, would have encouraged a scrupulous articulation of moments of perception. Hopkins believed further that the Incarnation meant that 'the world is charged with the grandeur of God', and he tried therefore to catch the selfhood of each created thing in matching words. To do this in an age slipping into what Blake called 'single vision and Newton's sleep', he had to awaken the forces in language – spring in rhythm, grasp in syntax, quickness in diction – to sharpen its apprehension of reality.

God creating nature is his first theme, as in 'Hurrahing in Harvest':

> Summer ends now; now, barbarous in beauty, the stooks rise
> Around; up above, what wind-walks! what lovely behaviour
> Of silk-sack clouds! has wilder, wilful-wavier
> Meal-drift moulded ever and melted across skies?
>
> I walk, I lift up, lift up heart, eyes,
> Down all that glory in the heavens to glean our Saviour:
> And éyes, heárt, what looks, what lips yet gave you a
> Rapturous love's greeting of realer, of rounder replies?

The flour of cloud-fragments is gleaned for a reply to the priest's uplifted heart. Nature-mysticism becomes almost eucharistic. This transforming intensity is such that the alliteration on *mould* and *melt* and on *glory* and *gleam*, and the extraordinary rhyming on *Saviour*, seem functional. He liked things 'original, counter, spare, strange', but his idiosyncrasy never became predictable. His diamond condensation makes Browning seem an Ancient Mariner. Pascal's apology, for writing a long letter as he had not time to write a short one, is not required for Hopkins's poetry. Only four of his fifty-three completed poems are of more than two pages in length, and few of them are less than intense. Even the musical 'Binsey Poplars *felled 1879*' ends with a significant discord on 'únselve'. He has a higher proportion of outstanding poems than any contemporary; he must rank as a poet with Tennyson and Browning.

Hopkins began his adult writing with the words 'Thou mastering me/God!' *The Wreck of the Deutschland, to the happy memory of five Franciscan nuns exiled by the Falck Laws drowned between midnight and morning of Dec. 7th, 1875* is a terrifying work. His often lyrical vision of the world as incarnating divine glory includes tragedy and suffering at its centre. His ecstatic vision 'The Windhover' ends: 'and blue-bleak embers, ah my dear,/Fall, gall themselves, and gash gold-vermilion.' The late 'terrible' sonnets (addressing God as 'O thou terrible') wrestle bitterly with God and with despair. 'No worst, there is none' is out of the world of *King Lear*. 'I wake and feel the fell of dark, not day' is a Christian nightmare. It is wrong, however, to see these anguished poems outside a tradition of spiritual conflict which goes back to the Old Testament Book of Job. Hopkins' range is not wide, but he touches the depths and the heights.

# Further reading

Armstrong, I. *Victorian Poetry, Poetics and Politics* (London: Routledge, 1993).

Richards, B. (ed.). *English Verse, 1830–1890* (Harlow: Longman, 1980). An annotated anthology.

Ricks, C. (ed.). *The New Oxford Book of Victorian Verse* (Oxford: Oxford University Press, 1990). A fresh new selection.

# CHAPTER 10

# Fiction

## Contents

### Novelists

## Overview

The super-productive Dickens is the dominant figure of the Victorian novel, combining elements of the Gothic – a genre made serious by the Brontë sisters – with a remarkably imagined account of the social institutions of Victorian London. The mode of his novels owes much to popular stage and melodrama, though language and character-creation are his own. His rival, Thackeray, is represented here by *Vanity Fair*. A less theatrical realism comes in with Mrs Gaskell and Trollope, and with the historian of imperfect lives in their fullest social settings, George Eliot.

## The triumph of the novel

Modern images of 19th-century English life owe much to novels, and versions of novels. By 1850, fiction had shouldered aside the theatre, its old rival as the main form of literary entertainment. As with the drama at the Renaissance, it took intellectuals some time to realize that a popular form might be rather significant. Human beings have always told stories, but not always read the long prose narratives of the kind known as novels. The reign of the novel has now lasted so long as to appear natural. There had been crazes for the Gothic novel and for Scott's fiction, yet it was only in the 1840s, with Charles Dickens, that the novel again reached the popularity it had enjoyed in the 1740s. Between 1847 and 1850 appeared *Jane Eyre*, *Wuthering Heights*, *Vanity Fair* and *David Copperfield*. In 1860, Dickens was still at his peak, Mrs Gaskell and Trollope were going strong, and George Eliot had begun to publish. Poetry was popular, but prose more popular. The popularity of broadly realistic novels seems to go with the broadening basis of middle-class democracy.

For the sake of clarity, this cornucopia of fiction is treated author by author, at the expense of chronology, interrelation, context. Dickens coincidentally published his first novel in the year of Victoria's accession. Although the Brontë sisters wrote ten years later, they are here treated first, not in chronological order. Their novels are closer to the genres of Romantic poetry than to the realism of the mainstream novel; fantasy and family are more relevant to their work than the currents of national history. This also allows Mrs Gaskell, Dickens and Thackeray, who are closer to historical developments, to be taken together.

## Two Brontë novels

### Jane Eyre

Elizabeth Gaskell's *Life of Charlotte Brontë* (1857) tells this family story of misery and splendour, dwelling on the misery. The eldest sister, impresario, editor and survivor, impressed first, and her *Jane Eyre* is a first-person autobiography of emotive, narrative, and at times mythic power. The orphan heroine suffers, is tried many times, and triumphs. We are to feel for and with her; insofar as we are asked to judge, she acts rightly. She opposes the misuse of authority, whether by an aunt, a clergyman, an employer or an admirer. She puts conscience before love, refusing to become Rochester's mistress and declining marriage to a clergyman less interested in her than the support she would give his mission. She returns to a Rochester now free to marry, and in need. Jane *deserves* her final happiness, whereas the plucky young protagonists who win through in Dickens's novels are lucky as well as good. Jane's righteousness is at times reminiscent of that in Jane Austen's teenage parody of Mrs Radcliffe, *Love and Friendship*. Some readers suspect that Jane is used by her creator as a fantasy vehicle; others enjoy the trip. Matthew Arnold wrote that Charlotte's mind contained 'nothing but hunger, rebellion, and rage', a view which suggests that the psychology of the book is at odds with its external Christianity – a charge which had also been brought against Richardson's *Pamela; or Virtue Rewarded* (1740), in which a poor girl also marries a gentleman.

*Jane Eyre* works as much through its atmospheric writing as through the moral

**Charlotte Brontë** (1816–55) and **Emily Brontë** (1818–48) were daughters of Rev. Patrick Brunty, an Irishman. Their mother dying, they boarded at a Clergy Daughters' School, returning after sickness had cut short the lives of two elder sisters. They were educated at home, the parsonage of Haworth, a village on the Yorkshire moors, with their sister **Anne** (1820–49) and brother Branwell. As adolescents they wrote fantasies set in the worlds of Gondal and Angria. The girls taught, acted as governesses, and wrote. Charlotte: *Poems by Currer, Ellis and Acton Bell* (ed., 1846); *Jane Eyre* (1847), *Shirley* (1849), *Villette* (1853), *The Professor* (1857). Emily: *Wuthering Heights* (1847). Anne: *Agnes Grey* (1847), *The Tenant of Wildfell Hall* (1848). Branwell drank himself to death. Charlotte married, dying a few months later in pregnancy. Patrick survived.

The Brontë Sisters, by their brother Branwell Brontë, *c.*1834. Oil on canvas, later much folded. Left to right: Anne, Emily, Charlotte.

urgency of its narration. The Brontës are the first novelists, or romance-writers, to endow landscape with Wordsworth's sensitivity and burden of meaning. *Jane Eyre* uses description with a new symbolic suggestion and delicacy, as in the description of the horse-chestnut tree in Rochester's park and of the red room at aunt Reed's. The nightmarish red room signals the Gothic key of a work which steers by the stars of passion, ordeal, and trauma. Jane's 'master', his mad Creole wife locked in the attic, the foiled bigamy, Jane's surprise legacy, the telepathic call across the moor, and the blazing Hall, are all machines of Gothic romance, a genre which the Brontës had adopted in childhood. For some readers, these archetypes are appropriate to romance and psychologically powerful. The Gothic trades in fantasy, which can be used playfully, as by Horace Walpole, or intellectually, as by Mary Shelley. If its conventions are taken seriously, it can only escape absurdity by avoiding cliché. The seriousness of Charlotte Brontë's effort to define emotional integrity is compromised by a Gothic tradition debased in its stock devices and their stock responses. Thus the blind Rochester is 'a sightless Samson' and 'a caged eagle whose gold-ringed eyes cruelty has extinguished'. Untransmuted archetype and autobiography loom also through the later, more realist novels. Of these, *Villette* is the best, though the reformer Harriet Martineau thought it too concerned with 'the need for being loved'. Anne Brontë's *The Tenant of Wildfell Hall* successfully blends realism and the Gothic. In the Brontë family, real life was Gothic.

### Wuthering Heights

Those who come to Emily Brontë's *Wuthering Heights* having seen a film version are shocked by the complexity of a narration which even seasoned admirers find enigmatic. That this is no simple first-person love story is clear from the opening comedy of errors, in which Lockwood's attempts to interpret his Northern landlord's goblin household by genteel southern English conventions prove grimly wide of the mark: Heathcliff's house, Wuthering Heights, is a demonic menagerie. The Romantic habit of adopting the narrator's point of view is dealt a rabbit-punch. The bewildered Lockwood is put in a room with a closet bed; in a nightmare, Cathy's spirit tries to enter at the window. He 'pulled its wrist on to the broken pane, and rubbed it to and fro till the blood ran and soaked the bedclothes; still it wailed, "Let me in!"' Emotional extremity also characterizes Emily's uncanny poems, published by Charlotte as independent lyrics but originally composed for characters in the 'Gondal' saga of their childhood.

At the end of *Wuthering Heights*, Lockwood stands in the graveyard where Cathy is buried between Linton and Heathcliff:

the middle one grey, and half buried in heath: Edgar Linton's only harmonized by the turf and moss creeping up its foot: Heathcliff's still bare. I lingered round them, under that benign sky; watched the moths fluttering along the heath and harebells, listened to the soft wind breathing through the grass, and wondered how anyone could ever imagine unquiet slumbers for the sleepers in that quiet earth.

Attention to the word 'heath' here suggests that Lockwood still does not understand what he sees.

Some of the intervening narration by the housekeeper Nelly Dean is as unreliable as Lockwood's. It unfolds a tale of three generations of two families whose relations are wrecked by the 'suitable' but fatal marriage of Catherine Earnshaw of Wuthering Heights to Edgar Linton of Thrushcross Grange. An opposition between wild passion and civil gentility is found in the names of houses and their owners (Earnshaw is Old Norse for Eagleswood). The passion of Catherine and her adopted brother, the orphan Heathcliff (a significantly unChristian name), is an elemental affinity rather than a romantic sexual love. As children, they play together on the moor in a poetic landscape more firmly visualized than any before those of Thomas Hardy. Catherine likens her love for Heathcliff to 'the eternal rocks beneath', telling the housekeeper, 'Nelly, I *am* Heathcliff!' Spurned, Heathcliff makes a fortune abroad and returns to dispossess Edgar of Catherine, engineering two loveless marriages in order to inherit Thrushcross Grange. But his long revenge turns sour, and he starves himself to death in order to be reunited to Catherine – underground! The saga ends in a love-match between the families in the next generation, thwarting Heathcliff's will. Heathcliff's hatred dies with him, but the book's madness and cruelty, though carefully unendorsed by the author, remain disturbing.

Despite Heathcliff's wolfish teeth, Emily's writing is not hackneyed, and she transmutes the grotesqueness of her Gothic materials far better than Charlotte. Her complex narrative is filtered through several viewpoints and timeframes, and her attitudes remain inscrutable. In its combination of ferocity, imagination, perspective and control, *Wuthering Heights* is unique.

## Elizabeth Gaskell

It is convenient, if achronological, to take next Charlotte's biographer, **Elizabeth Gaskell** (1810–65) the wife of a Manchester Unitarian minister and mother of a large family, who began at thirty-seven to write *Mary Barton: A Tale of Manchester Life* (1848). Dickens then secured her for his magazines.

Her work has the virtues of 19th-century realist fiction, of Jane Austen and Anthony Trollope. *Cranford* (1853), set among the ladies of a small town near Manchester, is small, well observed, gently penetrating. Apparently her least serious book, its deserved popularity may diminish ideas of her true merit. Her most distinguished book is the not-quite-finished *Wives and Daughters* (1866), which anticipates George Eliot in its steadily built-up exploration of family and provincial life shaped by historical contingencies which are less obviously thematic than those of *Ruth* (1853), about a seduced milliner, and *North and South* (1855). An age in which a Mrs Gaskell is in the second rank is healthy.

## Charles Dickens

The bubble of reputation that floats above writers seems to be more volatile above novelists and dramatists than above poets. Lord Lytton, Harrison Ainsworth, Benjamin Disraeli and George Meredith are hardly read today. Trollope thought George Eliot's novels impossibly intellectual, but she has lately had a popular as well as her long-standing critical success. Trollope's own popularity has recently been accompanied by a developing critical reputation.

The 19th-century novel itself achieved full respectability only with George Eliot. Newman, in *Loss and Gain* (1848), had used it to explore religious issues. Cardinal Manning said 'I see that Newman has stooped to writing novels.' Some Anglicans thought that Newman had thus 'sunk lower than Dickens'. Fiction was to be consciously raised to the status of art by Henry James. Yet the master of the early

**Charles Dickens** (1812–70)
Born in Portsmouth, Dickens
moved to Chatham. His father,
a clerk in the Navy pay office,
was imprisoned for debt in
Marshalsea prison. Charles
was taken out of school, aged
12, to work in a blacking
warehouse, but returned to
school, and was a legal office
boy at 15, and then a
shorthand reporter of
Parliamentary debates for the
*Morning Chronicle*. Works
include: *Sketches by 'Boz'*
(1836–7), *The Pickwick
Papers, Oliver Twist* (1837),
*Nicholas Nickleby* (1838), *The
Old Curiosity Shop* (1840–1),
*Barnaby Rudge* (1841),
*American Notes* (1842), *Martin
Chuzzlewit* (1843–4), *A
Christmas Carol* (1843),
*Pictures from Italy* (1844),
*Dombey and Son* (1847–8),
*David Copperfield* (1848–50),
*Bleak House* (1852–3), *A
Child's History of England*
(1851–3), *Hard Times* (1854),
*Little Dorrit* (1855–7), *A Tale of
Two Cities* (1859), *Great
Expectations* (1860–1), *Our
Mutual Friend* (1864–5), *The
Mystery of Edwin Drood*
(1870). He married Catherine
Hogarth in 1837; they had ten
children. Founding editor of the
*Daily News, Household Words*,
and *All the Year Round*, he
travelled in America and
Europe, and was a
philanthropist, and amateur
actor. He left his wife in 1858,
defying scandal; maintained a
secret friendship with Ellen
Ternan, an actress. He died
worn out by public reading
tours.

Victorian novel, **Charles Dickens** (1812–70), had no interest in the theory of fiction. The success of his early books owed much to the immediate popular appeal of their comedy and pathos, and their attacks on notorious public abuses. For Trollope in *The Warden* (1855), Dickens was still 'Mr Popular Sentiment'. First impressions are not easily dislodged: Dickens so entertained everybody that it was a century before he was taken seriously. Academics have since remedied this.

Dickens's novels came out originally not in book form but in parts in illustrated monthly magazines – the 19th-century equivalent of a television series. They were read aloud in families, and Dickens gave semi-dramatic readings by gaslight to large audiences. The novels were staged, and are often adapted to film and musical performance. There had been crazes before – Richardson in the 18th century, Scott and Byron in the 1810s and 1820s – but Dickens's public was much larger. His success in popular media continues, both with readers and with audiences, usually in forms different from those of their first incarnation – as has happened to Shakespeare.

Dickens's mother, when she and her husband were released from the Marshalsea prison, wanted Charles to stay on at the blacking factory. The trauma, retold in *David Copperfield*, toughened Dickens. He early learned Mr Micawber's lesson:

'Annual income twenty pounds, annual expenditure nineteen nineteen six, result happiness. Annual income twenty pounds, annual expenditure twenty pounds ought and six, result misery. The blossom is blighted, the leaf is withered, the god of day goes down upon the dreary scene, and – and in short you are forever floored. As I am!'

### The Pickwick Papers

The experience had also given young Dickens what Chesterton called 'the key of the street'. The office boy contrived to get a job as reporter on a London daily newspaper. He travelled England by coach, writing news reports to deadlines, and also sketches. *Sketches by 'Boz' and Cuts by Cruikshank*, a famous illustrator, was commissioned; then *The Posthumous Papers of the Pickwick Club*. Chapter 2 begins:

That punctual servant of all work the sun, had just risen, and begun to strike a light on the morning of the thirteenth of May, one thousand eight hundred and twenty-seven, when Mr. Samuel Pickwick burst like another sun from his slumbers, threw open his chamber window, and looked out upon the world beneath.

Mr Pickwick is soon on the stage-coach to Rochester with a Mr. Jingle:

'Head, heads – take care of your heads!' cried the loquacious stranger, as they came out under the low archway, which in those days formed the entrance to the coach-yard. 'Terrible place – dangerous work – other day – five children – mother – tall lady, eating sandwiches – forgot the arch – crash – knock – children look round – mother's head off – sandwich in her hand – head of a family off – shocking, shocking! Looking at Whitehall, sir? – fine place – little window – somebody else's head off there, eh, sir? – he didn't keep a sharp look-out enough either – eh, sir, eh?'
    'I am ruminating,' said Mr. Pickwick, 'on the strange mutability of human affairs.'
    'Ah! I see – in at the palace door one day, out at the window the next. Philosopher, sir?'
    'An observer of human nature, sir,' said Mr. Pickwick.
    'Ah, so am I. Most people are when they've little to do and less to get. Poet, sir?'

The shorthand reporter in London's streets, inns and courts had kept 'a sharp look-out enough'. But the caricaturist, mimic, and raconteur also invents: Mr Jingle is a version of Dickens himself, a Cockney Byron; he talks himself into our

Charles Dickens, acting the part of Captain Bobadil in Ben Jonson's *Every Man in his Humour* in 1845; a painting by C. R. Leslie.

confidence. *Pickwick* is not a novel, 'merely a great book', as George Gissing said, and full of writing which begs to be read aloud, to be shared. Not all its successors are great books, though all have passages in which the language bounds and cavorts like a tumbler. Not all are novels, if the novel has both to tell a coherent story, and render social reality. The approach is too theatrically stylized to be realistic. Dickens loved comic acting. The novelist he admired was Fielding, the play in which he most often acted was Jonson's *Every Man in his Humour*: tough satiric models, like the caricaturists of the 18th century and early 19th: Hogarth, Rowlandson – and George Cruickshank, Dickens's own illustrator. But Dickens also loved melodrama, the source of some of his own memorable effects and less memorable plots. As Ruskin said, Dickens's action takes place within 'a circle of stage fire'.

Some who laughed at *Pickwick* over its nineteen-month appearance also exclaimed over a serial he brought out simultaneously, one in which Oliver asked for more, and Nancy was murdered. *Oliver Twist* presents Dickens the hagiographer of martyred innocence – in workhouse, school, factory, prison and law court – the Dickens who makes us feel the cruelty of injustice and the pinch of poverty. His witness to the life of the back streets is not documentary but symbolic, fabulous, moral: privation, constriction, dirt; hypocrisy, servility, meanness; devotion, philanthropy. We weep less easily than the Victorians, yet in the comedy and pathos of Dickens's first decade, the comic writing seems absolutely better: the outrageous *Martin Chuzzlewit*, not the winsome *Nicholas Nickleby*. Reading early Dickens is like travelling in a coach, careering along in roughly the right direction, at very variable speed, pulled along by emotional drive and personal energy, jostled by vividly defined idiosyncratic characters. Critics praising Dickens are reduced to listing favourite characters: Mr Jingle, Pecksniff, Micawber, Mrs Gamp, Wemmick and his Aged P, Mrs Jellyby and her Telescopic Philanthropy, Flora Finching, Mr Podsnap. This habit, mysterious to those who have not read Dickens (*everyone* should read Dickens), simply acknowledges the delight given by his astonishing fertility of invention. He is a dramatic

'Fagin in the condemned cell', an illustration by George Cruikshank for Dickens's *Oliver Twist* (1837–9). The book on the shelf may be a Bible. Black and white, guilt and punishment, life and death!

writer, and the hundreds of characters are stage creatures, defined by a humour or an extraordinary habit; often caricatures or puppets, often magnificent, sometimes malign. Few have internal consciousness and three dimensions. All have life, few grow.

### David Copperfield

There is no answering the question whether this rich and copious writer is at his best early or late, in parts or wholes, in comedy or drama. Only a few dishes can be sampled here. His most delightful book may be *David Copperfield*, a lucid auto-biographical fairy tale. By a trick of narration we fully share the viewpoints both of the child and of the adult looking back. We experience Steerforth's seductiveness to David, and see the casual rapacity behind it. We see with Dickens's smile and Dickens's pity the child-bride Dora offering to help David by holding his pens. The career of Steerforth, however, tests our ability to feel as Dickens wishes after the ruin of Little Emily. Interest weakens.

The first writing in which everything tells is the brief *A Christmas Carol*. After the elaborate *Dombey and Son* (1006 pages), the novels are designed and have thematic ambition. Academic opinion admires the three huge novels, *Bleak House*, *Little Dorrit* and *Our Mutual Friend*, 1000-pagers more serious and complex than those which had made his name. Post-*Dombey* Dickens certainly repays re-reading, if there is time. The comic conjurer retires, the tragic artist advances. Stakes are raised, there is loss and gain.

### Bleak House

Of these big three, *Bleak House* is the best integrated, if hard to summarize. The plot has two main lines, the Chancery case of the estate of Jarndyce and Jarndyce, so long drawn out that costs absorb all the benefits; and the discovery that the orphan Esther Summerson is the illegitimate child, supposed dead, of Lady Dedlock. The saintly Esther is to marry John Jarndyce, for whom she keeps house; he nobly releases her to marry a young doctor. Of the minor characters, Skimpole is wonderful. Summary, however, conveys even less than usual. In late Dickens, although we vividly experi-ence the outsides of many characters, there is none whose life we share fully from within – not even Esther, who is nearest to its centre, and whose narrative conveys much of the story. The home Esther is to set up with her doctor is the symbolic anti-type of the various bleak houses of the novel. Yet it is hard to care for Esther's doctor, or, as much as Dickens might wish, for Esther.

For all its crowded canvas, the book is not about people, but about mentalities, feelings, institutions, the experience of living in a phantasmagoria: a bleak world which relates to life in Victorian London, yet is too personally imagined to be a mirror held up to life. Late Dickens is not character-centred but visionary, full of metaphors, symbols and fables of good and evil, of sympathy and cunning. One indicator of this is the symbolic suggestiveness of the opening set-pieces, such as 'The floods were out in Lincolnshire' or Chapter 1, 'In Chancery':

London. Michaelmas Term lately over, and the Lord Chancellor sitting in Lincoln's Inn Hall. Implacable November weather. As much mud in the streets as if the waters had but newly retired from the face of the earth, and it would not be wonderful to meet a Megalosaurus, forty feet long or so, waddling like an elephantine lizard up Holborn Hill. Smoke lowering down from chimney-pots, making a soft black drizzle with flakes of soot in it as big as full-grown snowflakes – gone into mourning, one might imagine, for the death of the sun. Dogs, undistinguishable in mire. Horses, scarcely better; splashed to their very blinkers. Foot passengers, jostling one another's umbrellas in a general infection of ill temper, and losing their foot-hold at street-corners …

Fog everywhere. Fog up the river, where it flows among green aits and meadows; fog down the river, where it rolls defiled among the tiers of shipping and the waterside pollutions of a great (and dirty) city. Fog on the Essex marshes, fog on the Kentish heights. Fog creeping into the cabooses of collier-brigs; fog lying out on the yards and hovering in the rigging of great ships; fog drooping on the gunwales of barges and small boats. Fog in the eyes and throats of ancient Greenwich pensioners …

## Our Mutual Friend

The late novels can open three subjects in the first three chapters, as does *Our Mutual Friend*: the recovery of a body from the Thames; the Veneerings' dinner party; Silas Wegg with his wooden leg. The themes do not always hold together, but Dickens's parts are better than other writers' wholes. There is Mr Podsnap, for instance, who 'considered other countries … a mistake, and of their manners and customs would conclusively observe, "Not English!"', clearing them away with 'a peculiar flourish of his right arm'. He instructs a visiting Frenchman in English pronunciation:

'We call it Horse,' said Mr. Podsnap, with forbearance. 'In England, Angleterre, England. We Aspirate the "H," and We Say "Horse." Only our Lower Classes Say "Orse!"'

'Pardon,' said the foreign gentleman; 'I am alwiz wrong!'

'Our Language,' said Mr. Podsnap, with a gracious consciousness of being always right, 'is Difficult. Ours is a Copious Language, and Trying to Strangers. I will not Pursue my Question.'

That could be early Dickens. This is late Dickens:

A certain institution in Mr. Podsnap's mind which he called 'the young person' may be considered to have been embodied in Miss Podsnap, his daughter. It was an inconvenient and exacting institution, as requiring everything in the universe to be filed down and fitted to it. The question about everything was, would it bring a blush into the cheek of the young person?

The last sentence is immortal and Victorian. The first sentence has the more abstract wit of the later novels, with no loss of acrobatic mock-grandiloquence.

The clearest of Dickens's books is *Hard Times*, a satire upon the hard-hearted regimes governing industrial life in a northern Coketown. It is a fable lacking the specificity and nightmare of Dickens's London. The critic Leavis agreed with its analysis and relished the bite of its caricatures: industrialism in Bounderby, utilitarianism in Gradgrind. Yet its love story has a weak pitifulness which lets energy leak from the novel.

### Great Expectations

Dickens best combines narrative and analysis in *Great Expectations*, a story with a single focus of consciousness. Expectations are thrust on 'Pip', a boy brought up by his harsh sister, the wife of a simple village blacksmith. Pip is suddenly given money from a mysterious source, supplied via a lawyer, Jaggers. Pip imagines his benefactor to be Miss Havisham, an heiress jilted on her wedding day, who has trained up the beautiful Estella to take revenge on men. Pip's rise in the world turns his head. In London he is embarrassed by his blacksmith brother-in-law, the good-hearted Joe. Estella chooses to marry a rival suitor who is Pip's social superior. The story takes few holidays, one being Pip's visits to the eccentric home of Jaggers's kindly clerk, Wemmick. But this holiday is, like Homer's similes in the *Iliad*, a reminder of the normal human simplicities left behind. Everything in the novel hangs together, even the melodrama which usually weakens the effects it is supposed to intensify.

A disciplined beginning helps:

Ours was the marsh country, down by the river, within, as the river wound, twenty miles of the sea. My first most vivid and broad impression of the identity of things, seems to me to have been gained on a memorable raw afternoon towards evening. At such a time I found out for certain, that this bleak place overgrown with nettles was the churchyard; and that Philip Pirrip, late of this parish, and also Georgiana wife of the above, were dead and buried; and that Alexander, Bartholomew, Abraham, Tobias, and Roger, infant children of the aforesaid, were also dead and buried; and that the dark flat wilderness beyond the churchyard, intersected with dykes and mounds and gates, with scattered cattle feeding on it, was the marshes; and that the low leaden line beyond was the river; and that the distant savage lair from which the wind was rushing, was the sea; and that the small bundle of shivers growing afraid of it all, and beginning to cry, was Pip.

'Hold your noise!' cried a terrible voice, as a man started up from among the graves at the side of the church porch. 'Keep still, you little devil, or I'll cut your throat!'

This is a convict escaped from the prison hulks moored in the Thames. The terrified boy brings him food he purloins from home. In recompense the convict Magwitch, having made good in Australia, magically becomes Pip's secret benefactor. When he returns to inspect the young gentleman his wealth has created, Magwitch is proud but Pip is ashamed.

Dickens wrote an ending in which Estella had found that 'suffering had been stronger than Miss Havisham's teaching' and Pip is single. But the published ending, changed at Lytton's suggestion, reads:

I took her hand in mine, and we went out out of the ruined place; and, as the morning mists had risen long ago when I first left the forge, so, the evening mists were rising now, and in all the broad expanse of tranquil light they showed to me, I saw no shadow of another parting from her.

This chastened marital ending, recalling *Paradise Lost*, does not take away the pain of *Great Expectations*, a Romantic 'autobiography' in which the reader is more aware than the hero-narrator. Here Dickens best combines his myth-making with a world of experience. Its critique of worldly success succeeds because it is not too explicit.

## 'The Inimitable'

Dickens was 'the Inimitable' – a word from his own circus style. His extraordinary talent is uniquely a communicative one. In his best scenes, his words seem to be actors, gesticulating and performing on their own. Yet he can be over-praised or wrongly praised. In the contests run by critics, single novels by Dickens have won in fields including *Wuthering Heights*, *Vanity Fair* and *Middlemarch*. A general comparison shows him as less fine than Jane Austen, less compelling than Richardson in *Clarissa*, less profound than Tolstoy or Dostoevsky, less terrible than Flaubert. If the comparison with Shakespeare, offered by partisans of the English novel or of the Victorian age, is taken seriously, the quality and range of character and of language in Shakespeare's poetic drama makes the comparison a damaging one. Dickens's vision is peculiar; his cultural traditions, though vital, are, compared with Shakespeare's, too often sentimental or melodramatic. His women leave much to be desired. Thackeray threw the number in which Paul Dombey dies onto the desk of Mark Lemon at *Punch* with the words: 'There's no writing against such power as this ... it is stupendous.' That particular pathos is no longer quite so stupendous.

# William Makepeace Thackeray

William Makepeace Thackeray (1811–63) was born in India but, after his father's death and mother's remarriage, educated in England. He enjoyed Cambridge and a dilettante period in Europe as a painter, gambling away his money. He married, but his wife became insane, and he lived by his pen, supporting his daughters, who lived with his mother in Paris.

These were the miseries from which, financially at least, he emerged in the 1840s as a brilliant sketch-writer and caricaturist for *Punch*. After *The Luck of Barry Lyndon* (1844) and *The Book of Snobs* (1846), *Vanity Fair* appeared monthly in 1847–8; then *Pendennis* (1848–50), *The History of Henry Esmond* (1852), *The Newcomes* (1853–4) and *The Virginians* (1857–9); also *English Humourists of the Eighteenth Century* (1851) and *The Four Georges* (1855–7). Thackeray is not as other Victorian novelists: he does not show people behaving well. A gifted parodist and a worldly ironist, sardonic if not heartless, his reputation was once as wide as it was high. It now hangs on *Vanity Fair*, the later novels being little read, perhaps because their focus is on a gentleman's conduct. Fewer novel readers today are prepared to see the middle class from above, as Thackeray did, than from below – as did Thackeray's 'Mr Dickens in geranium and ringlets'. As this phrase suggests, both men saw it from the outside.

## *Vanity Fair*

Thackeray illustrated his own books. His *Book of Snobs* sketches with zest a variety of social climbers. The increasing wealth of the middle classes created an unhappy interface with the gentry. The ancient theme of upward social mobility is emergent in Jane Austen, buoyant in Disraeli, and thoroughly canvassed by Trollope. The classic satire on this famous English preoccupation is *Vanity Fair*, subtitled *A Novel without a Hero*, rather as Fielding called *Tom Jones* a 'comic epic in prose'. It follows the fortunes of Becky Sharp, a fearless social mountaineer. These are contrasted throughout with those of Amelia Sedley, the daughter of a stockbroker; Becky is the

'Mr Joseph entangled': Joseph Sedley helps Becky Sharp wind a skein of green silk. One of W. M. Thackeray's illustrations for his *Vanity Fair*, published in monthly parts, 1847–8.

orphan child of an artist and a French opera dancer. In Chapter 1, as Becky sits in her friend Amelia's carriage outside Miss Pinkerton's Academy for young ladies, she is presented with Johnson's *Dictionary*. As they leave, Becky tosses it out of the window; she does not intend to be a governess. The first man Becky enchants is Amelia's brother Jos, the wealthy, witless and cowardly Collector of Boggley Wallah. Becky is sharp and unscrupled, Amelia mild, decent, and silly. Amelia hopes to wed the handsome Lt George Osborne, a merchant's son. Then, 'in the month of March, Anno Domini 1815, Napoleon landed at Cannes, and Louis XVIII fell, and all Europe was in alarm, and the funds fell, and old John Sedley was ruined.' Against his father's will, George Osborne marries the penniless Amelia, shamed into doing the decent thing by his honourable friend Dobbin, who loves Amelia. It is a mistake. Becky begins as governess in the family of Sir Pitt Crawley, a Hampshire baronet, so bewitching him that the old boor actually proposes.

'I say agin, I want you,' Sir Pitt said, thumping the table. 'I can't git on without you. I didn't see what it was till you went away. The house all goes wrong. It's not the same place. All my accounts has got muddled agin. You must come back. Do come back. Dear Becky, do come.'

'Come – as what, sir?' Rebecca gasped out.

'Come as Lady Crawley, if you like,' the Baronet said, grasping his crape hat. 'There! will that zatusfy you? Come back and be my wife. Your vit vor't. Birth be hanged. Your're as good a lady as ever I see. You've got more brains in your little vinger than any baronet's wife in the county. Will you come? Yes or no?'

'Oh, Sir Pitt!' Rebecca said, very much moved.

'Say yes, Becky,' Sir Pitt continued. 'I'm an old man, but a good'n. I'm good for twenty years. I'll make you happy, zee if I don't. You shall do what you like; spend what you like; an' 'av it all your own way. I'll make you a zettlement. I'll do everything reg'lar. Look year!' and the old man fell down on his knees and leered at her like a satyr.

Rebecca started back a picture of consternation. In the course of this history we have never seen her lose her presence of mind; but she did now, and wept some of the most genuine tears that ever fell from her eyes.

'Oh, Sir Pitt!' she said. 'Oh, sir – I – I'm *married already*.'

Becky is sorry because she has misplayed her hand. She has secretly married Sir Pitt's spendthrift younger son Rawdon, hoping that he will inherit his rich aunt's estate. As Sir Pitt's wife, she would have been rich now, and could soon hope to be his widow. As Mrs Crawley, she drives her gambling husband higher and higher in society on less and less money. Regency society may have been driven by money and pleasure, but cannot have been so breathtakingly heartless as this.

Few novels move so well as *Vanity Fair*. We watch Becky climb ever higher without visible support. The Fair's social scenes, topical details and theatrical effects spin round in an action similar to that of a comedy by Ben Jonson, but accompanied by a rapid commentary and appeals to the middle classes. Thackeray has a whip-crack style. Wives follow their men to Brussels and to the Countess of Richmond's Ball on the eve of Waterloo. Amelia persists in loving George, who writes proposing elopement with Becky, who is bewitching a general. At last 'no more firing was heard at Brussels – the pursuit rolled miles away. Darkness came down on the field and city: and Amelia was praying for George, who was lying on his face, dead, with a bullet through his heart.'

At the climax, Rawdon discovers Becky compromisingly alone with her protector the Marquis of Steyne. 'He tore the diamond ornament out of her breast, and flung it at Lord Steyne. It cut him on his bald forehead. Steyne wore the scar to his dying day.' Becky claims she is innocent, 'but who could tell what was truth which came from those lips; or if that corrupt heart was in this case pure?' Further anticlimax follows: Steyne pre-empts Rawdon's challenge to a duel by having the bankrupt gambler appointed Governor of Coventry Island, a fever spot. Becky pursues her luck in Paris and then in Pumpernickel, where she shows Amelia George Osborne's letter proposing elopement, so that Amelia will marry the faithful Dobbin. Whether Becky was technically innocent and whether she had some feeling for Amelia are intriguing moral questions but less clear than the brevity of life and the rarity of goodness in *Vanity Fair*. In its spirited narrative, drama alternates with irony, feeling with cynicism, hilarity with sadness. Thackeray's dash and wit create effects which are hard to define, but seem to be more moral and humane than he pretends, and curiously moving. His disillusioned exposure of conventional sentiment and morality implies that there are truer standards.

Mrs Lynn Lynton wrote that 'Thackeray, who saw the faults and frailties of human nature so clearly, was the gentlest-hearted, most generous, most loving of men. Dickens, whose whole mind went to almost morbid tenderness and sympathy, was infinitely less plastic, less self-giving, less personally sympathetic.' Thomas Babington Macaulay made a different comparison: 'Touching Thackeray and Dickens, my dear,/Two lines sum up critical drivel,/One lives on a countess's sneer,/And one on a milliner's snivel.' The historian may have been piqued by their popularity.

# Anthony Trollope

Like Thackeray, **Anthony Trollope** (1815–82) came down in the world and wrote. Each week he wrote 40 pages, each of 250 words, often while travelling for the Post Office by train or ship. His *Autobiography* says that he began a new novel the day after finishing the last. In twenty years his novels earned £68,939 17s. 5d., which he thought 'comfortable, but not splendid'.

Trollope presents himself as a workman proud of his work, but his demystification

**Anthony Trollope** (1815–82) Son of a failed barrister and Frances Trollope, author of *The Domestic Manners of the Americans* (1832). Educated at Winchester and Harrow. A clerk in the General Post Office from 1834, he moved to Ireland in 1841, returned in 1859, and retired in 1867. *The Macdermots of Ballycloran* (1847). *The Warden* (1855), *Barchester Towers* (1857), *Dr Thorne* (1858), *Framley Parsonage* (1861), *The Small House at Allington* (1864) and *The Last Chronicle of Barset* (1867) are the Barsetshire Novels. *Can You Forgive Her?* (1864), *Phineas Finn* (1869), *The Eustace Diamonds* (1873), *Phineas Redux* (1876), *The Prime Minister* (1876) and *The Duke's Children* (1880) are the Palliser Novels. Others include *The Way We Live Now* (1875).

of the business of writing upset the sensitive. He was robustly English, devoted to fox-hunting and cigars, taking his own bath with him on his travels. By 1900, when highbrows and middlebrows had drawn apart, aesthetes and intellectuals shrank from Trollope's confidence. Yet Newman and George Eliot had admired him. His affectionate, temperate, good-humoured picture of an innocent rural social order has today a nostalgia which gilds its original charm. But Trollope was no naïf: he did not live in a cathedral close, and should not be confused with Septimus Harding, Barchester's Warden, still less with Archdeacon Grantly. Most of his books are set in London. He lived in Ireland for eighteen years, and travelled more than any other 19th-century writer, in Europe, Africa, the Americas and the Pacific. He was a worker, a go-ahead civil servant and a moderate reformer, standing for Parliament as a Liberal in 1869.

A sample of Trollope's comedy comes early in *Barchester Towers*. At the inaugural reception organized by his wife, the Evangelical Bishop Proudie is accosted by Bertie, the son of the Reverend Vesey Stanhope, whom the new bishop has recalled from long residence in Italy. Proudie, mistaking Bertie for an Italian Prince, is initially impressed: 'There was just a twang of a foreign accent, and no more.'

'Do you like Barchester on the whole?' asked Bertie.

The bishop, looking dignified, said that he did like Barchester.

'You've not been here very long, I believe,' said Bertie.

'No – not long,' said the bishop, and tried again to make his way between the back of the sofa and a heavy rector, who was staring over it at the grimaces of the signora.

'You weren't a bishop before, were you?'

Dr Proudie explained that this was the first diocese he had held.

'Ah – I thought so,' said Bertie; 'but you are changed about sometimes, a'nt you?'

'Translations are occasionally made,' said Dr Proudie; 'but not so frequently as in former days.'

'They've cut them all down to pretty nearly the same figure, haven't they?' said Bertie.

To this the bishop could not bring himself to make any answer, but again attempted to move the rector.

'But the work, I suppose, is different?' continued Bertie. 'Is there much to do here, at Barchester?' This was said exactly in the tone that a young Admiralty clerk might use in asking the same question of a brother acolyte at the Treasury.

'The work of a bishop of the Church of England,' said Dr Proudie, with considerable dignity, 'is not easy. The responsibility which he has to bear is very great indeed.'

'Is it?' said Bertie, opening wide his wonderful blue eyes. 'Well; I never was afraid of responsibility. I once had thoughts of being a bishop, myself.'

'Had thoughts of being a bishop!' said Dr Proudie, much amazed.

'That is, a parson – a parson first, you know, and a bishop afterwards. If I had begun, I'd have stuck to it. But, on the whole, I like the Church of Rome best.'

The bishop could not discuss the point, so he remained silent.

'Now, there's my father,' continued Bertie; 'he hasn't stuck to it. I fancy he didn't like saying the same thing over so often. By the bye, Bishop, have you seen my father?'

This conversation at cross-purposes matches Bertie's idle enquiries about the work and rewards of the spiritual life against the offended sense of caste of the supposed reformer. Trollope's Olympian calm and humour are winningly displayed at Barchester, but he can be more than amusing. Trollope renders his hundreds of characters, often country gentry or people in the learned professions, with unobtrusive patient care. His moral realism has Jane Austen's value for integrity and Thackeray's eye for the operation of interest, with a far less evident irony. Unlike Dickens, he has no violently good or evil characters, and less melodrama than George Eliot. After Barset, his benign tone darkens in the Palliser novels. The late *The Way We Live Now* is a satire upon speculative finance.

Trollope's readership has grown, full sets of his forty-seven novels appearing in the 1990s from five publishers. The Palliser novels of high politics and marital intrigue, after *Can You Forgive Her?*, are more ambitious in their moral explorations. As the novel must entertain, Trollope may be a major novelist. He is certainly a master of the form whose supreme master, Leo Tolstoy, said of him, 'He kills me with his excellence.' The realism in which he excels is broad and everyday rather than deep or intense. Trollope and Hopkins are opposites, both as writers and as Christians.

# George Eliot

**George Eliot** (1819–80) was born Mary Ann Evans, daughter of the steward of a Warwickshire estate, a circumstance which informs all her work.

Life did change for Tom and Maggie; and yet they were not wrong in believing that the thoughts and loves of these first years would always make part of their lives. We could never have loved the earth so well if we had had no childhood in it, – if it were not the earth where the same flowers come up again every spring that we used to gather with our tiny fingers as we sat lisping to ourselves on the grass – the same hips and haws on the autumn hedgerows – the same redbreasts that we used to call 'God's birds', because they did no harm to the precious crops. What novelty is worth that sweet monotony where everything is known, and *loved* because it is known?

The wood I walk in on this mild May day, with the young yellow-brown foliage of the oaks between me and the blue sky, the white starflowers and the blue-eyed speedwell and the ground ivy at my feet – what grove of tropic palms, what strange ferns or splendid broad-petalled blossoms, could ever thrill such deep and delicate fibres within me as this home-scene? These familiar flowers, these well-remembered bird-notes, this sky, with its fitful brightness, these furrowed grassy fields, each with a sort of personality given to it by the capricious hedgerows – such things as these are the mother tongue of our imagination, the language that is laden with all the subtle inextricable associations the fleeting hours of our childhood left behind them. Our delight in the sunshine on the deep-bladed grass to-day, might be no more than the faint perception of wearied souls, if it were not for the sunshine and the grass in the far-off years which still live in us, and transform our perception into love.

This is from early in *The Mill on the Floss*. The 'capricious' hedgerows recall the 'little lines of sportive wood run wild' above Tintern Abbey. Wordsworth found in the recollection of early experience a moral influence from nature, an organic process. The complex inwardness of Romantic poetry here reaches the novel, a form largely shaped by theatrical outwardness, especially in novels dealing with social questions. Mary Ann Evans too held that nature nourishes moral emotions through the imagination, but doubted that 'One impulse from a vernal wood/May teach you more of man,/Of moral evil and of good,/Than all the sages could' (Wordsworth, 'The Tables Turned'). She read all the sages, and became one. She thirsted for understanding, and all her life educated herself in ancient and modern literature, religious history, philosophy and science. At twenty-one she lost the passionate literal belief of the Evangelicalism which had seized her in childhood. She sought then to reinterpret human life and history by the light of a humane imagination and the human sciences, retaining Christian values of love, sympathy and duty.

**positivism** The creed of Auguste Comte (1789–1857), who taught that sociology and other human sciences would lead to definitive knowledge which would explain human behaviour, as the physical sciences explained matter. Captains of industry would rule, the religion of humanity would be established, women would encourage the growth of altruism.

Determination and mental stamina enabled her to translate Strauss's *Life of Jesus* (1846) and Feuerbach's *Essence of Christianity* (1854), radical new works reducing Christianity to history and psychology. She helped to edit *The Westminster Review*, a learned journal founded by J. S. Mill. She became emotionally attached to its publisher, John Chapman, and then to Herbert Spencer, the apostle of scientism, before forming a lifelong union with the versatile G. H. Lewes, biographer of Goethe and advocate of the **positivist** philosophy of Comte, and of phrenology. Lewes, a married man with several children, could not divorce his wife, having acknowledged a son of hers conceived in adultery with a friend of his. Miss Evans found the illegality of her union painful, and called herself Mrs Lewes. George Eliot was loved by readers, including the Queen, but Mary Ann, or Marian, Evans was not asked to dinner. Gradually the great world came to call on her and Lewes on Sunday afternoons in their London home. Her beloved brother Isaac, however, never spoke to her; he wrote to her only when she married, after Lewes's death in 1878. She died soon after.

The intellectual who had grown up on Walter Scott began to write stories herself, encouraged by Lewes. In a set of the *Waverley* novels which he gave her, Lewes described Scott as 'her longest-venerated and best-loved Romancist'. When *Scenes of Clerical Life* appeared in 1857, 'George Eliot' was thought to be a clergyman, or a clergy wife. There followed *Adam Bede* (1859), *The Mill on the Floss* (1860), *Silas Marner* (1861), *Romola* (1862–3), *Felix Holt, The Radical* (1866), *Middlemarch* (1871–2), *Daniel Deronda* (1874–6), and the short story, 'The Lifted Veil'. All but *Deronda* and *Romola* are rooted in provincial England; *Romola* is set in 15th-century Florence. At her death, Eliot was admired, even revered. After a reaction against the intellectuality of the later novels, she has been accounted one of the two or three great 19th-century novelists, and *Middlemarch* the classic Victorian realist novel.

The passage above from *The Mill on the Floss* suggests George Eliot's commitment to the experience of living, accompanied by an earnest effort to understand its processes and convey its value. The final words '… the sunshine and the grass of the far-off years which still live in us and transform our perception into love' echo Wordsworth's *Immortality Ode*. This formulation, which is also close to the mood of Tennyson's *In Memoriam* and the terms of Arnold's *Dover Beach*, trusts to a scientific metaphor: the sunlight stored in memory has transforming moral power. As value and meaning become problematic, the need to define them becomes urgent, and the vocabulary more complex, elaborate and provisional.

Dickens and Thackeray begin with *Sketches*, George Eliot with *Scenes*. Thereafter she named five of her seven novels after their protagonists, adopting the post-Romantic narrative mode of virtual autobiography, as in *Oliver Twist*. Dickens's attack on social abuses draws its emotional power not from an accurate representation of the Yorkshire Board Schools but from the reader's identification with the protagonist, a convention borrowed from romance, adventure and fantasy. After Byron, the Romantic protagonist is often transparently the author as hero and victim. *Jane Eyre* shows how hard it is to avoid vicarious self-pity in this mode, where protagonist, author and reader are all to share the same point of view and to pull together, a problem better managed in *David Copperfield* and better still in *Great Expectations*. George Eliot's seven novels develop the strengths of the mode without entirely overcoming its weakness.

### Adam Bede

In *Adam Bede* the pretty, vain Hetty Sorrell prefers the young squire Arthur to the worthy Adam, a carpenter. She is to marry Adam but finds herself pregnant, and kills the baby. Hanging is commuted to transportation after Arthur intervenes. In prison, Hetty is comforted by the Methodist preacher Dinah Morris, loved by Seth Bede. Seth stands aside to allow his brother Adam to marry her. This tragicomedy of moral choices is set in a quaintly idyllic rural society. Mrs Poyser, Hetty's aunt, was thought a comic creation equal to Sam Weller. Sam's creator, Dickens, was not taken in by George Eliot's manly pseudonym: 'no man ever before had the art of making himself mentally so like a woman'.

## The Mill on the Floss

The narrator of *The Mill on the Floss* is Maggie Tulliver, who has a childhood like that of Mary Ann Evans: she is a sensitive, intelligent, awkward girl, chafing at the bonds of rural society, though its domesticities are again described in loving detail. The narrative in the passage quoted initially passes from 'they' (Tom and Maggie), to 'we' (who used to call robins 'God's birds'), into 'I' musing in a wood, and out again to 'we' the readers, Humanity. Third-person narrative melts into collective auto-biography and normative reflection. The tale ends in catastrophe: Maggie saves her alienated brother Tom from a flood; they drown, reconciled in a final embrace. The ugly duckling has turned into a swan, but must die. We are to identify with Maggie in her stands against family prejudice and pride, and in the suffering caused her by the mutual attraction between her and Stephen Guest, a handsome youth engaged to her cousin. The drama is played out against the background of a 'real' social panorama, of painful choices between family, love and friendship. It is experienced through the acute sensibility of Maggie, seen above in richly reflective mode. The moral intelligence of the heroine-narrator's commentary is characteristic of George Eliot's fiction. In the catastrophe, Maggie lays down her life for her brother, a martyr to Christian family love. The moral is less bleak than those of Wordsworth's peasant tragedies, *Michael* and 'The Ruined Cottage'.

Illustration to George Eliot's *The Mill on the Floss* (1860), by W. J. Allen. Tom and Maggie Tulliver foresee their fate.

### Silas Marner

A Christian symbolic dimension dominates *Silas Marner, The Weaver of Raveloe*. Silas, falsely accused of theft, is excluded from his Protestant sect. His solitary pursuit of his craft makes him prosper, but one day his gold is stolen from his cottage. An orphan whose mother has died in the snow comes to his door; in bringing her up, he recovers happiness. This parable of redemptive love stands against a melodramatic narrative. The girl chooses to stay with Silas when the squire's elder son acknowledges that he is her true father. His younger brother's body, found with the stolen gold in a drained pond, reminds him of the fate of the girl's mother, whom he had never acknowledged. The rural comedy shrinks, and the themes play out more darkly as the chosen situation evolves.

*Romola* seems a departure. In a picturesquely historical Florence, with the Medici facing Savonarola and popular unrest, Tito, a plausible Greek, weaves an intrigue. Romola, however, is one of George Eliot's sorely-tried heroines who finds her destiny in sacrifice. Noble in birth as well as character, this daughter of a blind old scholar is tricked into marriage by Tito; who betrays her, her father, and his own benefactor. A picture by Tintoretto is the source of Eliot's next work, the dramatic poem *The Spanish Gypsy* (1868).

After prose about Coventry, why Italy and poetry? George Eliot wrote poetry because she felt that her writing lacked symbolic power. *Silas Marner* shows her universalizing her concerns by using religious parable. *Romola* tries to elevate its theme by using a Florentine setting sanctified by art and literature. The result, however, is not grand tragedy but a historical novel based on research. The more authentically historical such a novel, the less the use of a remote or glamorous setting escapes the limits of documentary realism. Eliot's research rebuilt the literal prison she was trying to escape.

*Felix Holt, the Radical* is the most dispensible of the English novels, a historical recreation of 1832, the eve of the Reform Bill. Esther chooses the austere idealist Felix rather than Harold Transome, the heir to the estate. By an expedient device of the Victorian stage, Esther turns out to be the true heir, and Harold's father a mean lawyer.

### Middlemarch

These experiments paved the way for *Middlemarch*, a major novel by any standard. The historical canvas is very wide. The several storylines of the multiple plot are traced from their beginnings, gradually combining into a drama which gathers intense human and moral interest. Themes emerge naturally out of believable families and marriages, and final outcomes do not depend upon gratuitous interventions from melodrama or authorial providence. *Middlemarch: A Study of Provincial Life* is set, like *Felix Holt*, in a Midlands manufacturing town towards 1832. It shows the attrition of ideals by experience. The young, unworldly and ardent Dorothea Brooke, against the advice of her uncle, sister and gentry connections, accepts the Reverend Dr Isaac Casaubon, a dry middle-aged scholar, aspiring to serve him in his life's task, a 'Key to All Mythologies'. Discovering that her husband is petty and that he is secretly unsure of his great work, and will never complete it, she pities and cares for him. He dies suddenly, leaving a will which shows his true meanness. The intelligent Dr Tertius Lydgate, a medical pioneer, has been trapped into marrying the town beauty, Rosamund Vincy, a manufacturer's daughter hoping to rise out of Middlemarch. She is not interested in his research but in the distinction of his social origins. Rosamund has a beautiful neck, good manners, a strong will, a small mind and a smaller heart. Established Middlemarch doctors make sure that Lydgate's new ideas do not prosper; the young couple come close to giving up the fine house he has imprudently bought her – but are rescued by a loan. Lydgate, like Dorothea, is loyal to a selfish spouse.

Casaubon's lively young cousin, Will Ladislaw, a friend of Lydgate, admires Dorothea, who is innocently friendly towards him. In his will, Casaubon forbids Dorothea to marry Ladislaw on pain of losing her inheritance. Fred, the immature brother of Rosamund, loves Mary Garth, daughter of a land agent, Caleb. The Garths' home has the love and integrity George Eliot valued from her childhood. Mary is too sincerely religious to allow Fred to become a clergyman, a genteel profession, and Fred joins Caleb to learn the land agent's trade. Mrs Vincy's sister is married to the banker Bulstrode, a Calvinist hypocrite, who before coming to Middlemarch and marrying Harriet Vincy, had made his pile by pawnbroking and receipt of stolen goods in London, marrying the boss's widow and defrauding her grandson, lost and supposed dead, but still alive. This turns out to be Will Ladislaw. Bulstrode is blackmailed by Raffles, a reprobate, whom he allows to die by silently varying Dr Lydgate's instructions. But Raffles had talked, and Lydgate has innocently accepted a loan from Bulstrode. When this reaches the gossips of Middlemarch, the doctor is ruined along with the banker. Mrs Bulstrode stands by her husband. These lives are baffled, but Dorothea gives up Casaubon's money to marry Ladislaw.

We learn in a diminishing Finale that Fred and Mary marry and are good and happy and live to be old if not rich. 'Lydgate's hair never became white': he takes a fashionable London practice which thrives, but 'he always regarded himself as a failure'. Dying at fifty, he leaves Rosamund rich. She marries an elderly physician, regarding her happiness as 'a reward'. 'But it would be unjust not to tell, that she never uttered a word in depreciation of Dorothea, keeping in religious remembrance the generosity which had come to her aid in the sharpest crisis of her life.' Will becomes a Liberal MP for Middlemarch, and Dorothea a wife, mother and minor benefactress – one who performs the 'little, nameless, unremembered, acts/Of kindness and of love' which Wordsworth in *Tintern Abbey* calls 'that best portion of a good man's life'. Dorothea is a good woman who lived in a society which did not allow her to make the great contribution her nature sought, a point made in the Prelude to *Middlemarch* with a comparison to the career of St Theresa of Avila, and repeated in the Finale:

Her finely-touched spirit had still its fine issues, though they were not widely visible. Her full nature, like that river of which Cyrus broke the strength, spent itself in channels which had no great name on the earth. But the effect of her being on those around her was incalculably diffusive: for the growing good of the world is partly dependent on unhistoric acts; and that things are not so ill with you and me as they might have been, is half owing to the number who lived faithfully a hidden life, and rest in unvisited tombs.

(Cyrus, founder of the Persian Empire, who released the Jews from captivity, was admired by Christians as well as by the classical author Plutarch. Mary Garth 'wrote a little book for her boys, called *Stories of Great Men, taken from Plutarch*'. Cyrus also diverted the Euphrates for irrigation.)

George Eliot's temperate use of catastrophe and happy ending allow a rich if subdued realism in presentation and a satisfying realism of assessment: life is imperfect. By prevailing standards, the incidence of illegitimacy, mistaken identity, legacies, letters going astray, improbable coincidence and drownings (this author's favoured form of natural disaster) is tiny; the lurid Raffles is a well-calculated exception. George Eliot moderates the excesses of sentiment and irony found in her more 'Victorian' predecessors. In structure and theme, her parallelling of unhappy marriages, with one woman finally repaying the other's generosity with a helpful hint which makes a marriage, may owe something to *Vanity Fair*. The moral and mechanical complexities of a story with several continuing centres of interest are managed with steady clarity and subtlety. Here the comparison with Dickens is to George Eliot's advantage. These complexities are more numerous than is suggested in the plot summary above, which leaves out Dorothea's comical uncle, Brooke of Tipton, a confused candidate in the Liberal interest; her worldly sister Celia, conventionally married to Sir James Chettam; two gentry/clergy families, the Cadwalladers and the Farebrothers; and other relationships of family, class and business interest. The dense social web built up yields an extraordinarily rich representation of provincial life in middle England. The picture is also an analysis – 'study' in the subtitle has both senses – and the pettiness and prejudices of Middlemarch can be seen eventually to limit or stifle all but the Garths, whose worth is related not to the town but to the land, work, and the family. Their integrity is Christian in its derivation.

George Eliot's running commentary does not please every reader. Some prefer novel as drama to novel as moral essay. Those who do not wish to be so explicitly guided will grant the quality and scope of her understanding. The insight into motive towards the end of *Middlemarch* produces wonderful writing. The steady pace, compared with Thackeray and Dickens, does not lessen interest in the evolving destinies of the Bulstrodes, of Dorothea and Lydgate, Rosamund and Ladislaw, the Garths. The mounting tension of the penultimate stages is dramatic or operatic, with the motives of the principals in full view. Human imperfection, even in the chilling instance of Casaubon, is presented with understanding, though he receives more sympathy from his wife than from his creator. Some critics think Dorothea too good, and Ladislaw less interesting than she finds him.

This English novel, however, has fewer blemishes than others of its scope in the 19th century. In 1874, the American Henry James (1843–1916), beginning his career as a novelist, noticed some, yet concluded that *Middlemarch* 'sets a limit … to the development of the old-fashioned English novel'. All the Victorian novels so far reviewed were old-fashionedly inclusive in their readership, though *Middlemarch* would strain the attention of some educated people today. The conscious procedures of James's own art, following French examples, make George Eliot's openness look solidly provincial. James's handling of narrative propriety and of point-of-view is more discriminated. Yet he fully shared Eliot's root concern with the future of innocence in a civilization growing ever more complex. He thought the old-fashioned English novels 'loose and baggy monsters'. Yet there is always an appeal from art to life and human import. James's refinement set a different limit to the development of the novel.

### Daniel Deronda

*Daniel Deronda*, Eliot's last novel, has had a mixed reception. In order to save her family and herself from poverty, Gwendolen Harleth marries the rich Grandcourt, who has had children by a mistress known to Gwendolen. Grandcourt's selfishness and his mistress's reproaches isolate Gwendolen, who relies increasingly on the soulful Daniel Deronda – an idealist of a type dear to Eliot, who in the Preface to *Middlemarch* had dwelt on the modern problem of the martyr without a cause. Deronda turns out to be the son of a Jewish singer, who sacrificed him to her own career. When Grandcourt is drowned, Deronda marries Mirah, a young singer, and devotes himself, with Mirah's brother Mordecai, to founding a Jewish national home in Israel. Many readers find that the Jewish theme is presented uncritically.

*Daniel Deronda* does not show English virtue and foreign duplicity, rather the reverse. Its international perspectives on the fate of idealists in a sophisticating world are those of Henry James and Conrad. After George Eliot's death in 1880, the Novel's achievements and audiences became more specialized, as common culture further diversified.

## Nonsense prose and verse

### Lewis Carroll

The rest of the 19th century is treated separately, but before leaving the Victorian uplands, mention must be made of a rare flower which grew there: Lewis Carroll's *Alice's Adventures in Wonderland*. The author, Charles Lutwidge Dodgson, was a deacon at Christ Church, Oxford, a mathematics don and a pioneer of portrait photography. Alice Liddell was the daughter of the Dean of Christ Church, joint editor of the standard Greek dictionary. *Alice* was originally made up by Dodgson for her and her sisters while he was rowing them up the Thames in 1862, when she was ten. Alice's adventures occur when in a dream she falls down a rabbit-hole. In a series of odd and threatening situations, creatures engage her in 'curiouser and curiouser' conversations and sing nonsensical songs. Alice's unintimidated common sense saves her.

Children still like *Alice*'s fantasy, surprise, and logical and verbal jokes, as in 'The Mad Hatter's Tea Party'. The action often shows the absurd arrangements whereby large animals eat small ones (weeping in pity as they do so), and big people boss little people about without compunction. Adults enjoy the stream of riddles and logical games, such as 'How do I know what I mean until I see what I say?', and the Cheshire Cat's grin, 'which remained some time after the rest of it had gone.'

The Mad Hatter's Tea Party. An illustration by John Tenniel for Lewis Carroll's *Alice's Adventures in Wonderland* (1865), showing Alice, the March Hare, the Dormouse and the Hatter.

There are also verse parodies. Alice tries to repeat Isaac Watts's 'Against Idleness and Mischief': 'How doth the little busy bee/Improve each shining hour'. It comes out as 'How doth the little crocodile/Improve its shining tail', with a second verse:

> How cheerfully he seems to grin,
> How neatly spreads his claws,
> And welcomes little fishes in,
> With gently smiling jaws!

Further parodies are found in a sequel, *Through the Looking-Glass* (1871), notably 'Jabberwocky', a version of a German Romantic ballad into mock Anglo-Saxon: ''Twas brillig, and the slithy toves/Did gyre and gimble in the wabe ....' Humpty Dumpty, a literary critic, explains:

'"Brillig" means four o'clock in the afternoon – the time when you begin *broiling* things for dinner.'
    'That'll do very well,' said Alice: 'and "slithy"?'
    'Well, "slithy" means "lithe" and "slimy". "Lithe" is the same as "active". You see it's like a portmanteau – there are two meanings packed up into one word.'
    'I see it now,' Alice remarked thoughtfully: 'and what are "toves"?'
    'Well, "toves" are something like badgers – they're something like lizards – and they're something like corkscrews.'

Another parody, 'The White Knight's Song' ('I'll tell you everything I can;/There's little to relate') brings out the illogic of Wordsworth's ballads. The Alice books, wonderfully illustrated by Tenniel, had a great success, and have entered the language. Unlike other Victorian children's books, they teach no lessons.

### Edward Lear

The gentler nonsense verse of **Edward Lear** (1812–88), a gifted watercolourist, has less logical bite and point than Carroll's, more whimsy, and a melancholy charm.

> He reads, but he cannot speak, Spanish,
> He cannot abide ginger beer:
> Ere the days of his pilgrimage vanish,
> How pleasant to know Mr Lear!

Nonsense verse, England's answer to French symbolism, thrived before the 19th century, but its flowering then may be the other side of Arnold's proposition that 'all great literature is, at bottom, a criticism of life'. Victorians also had more time for their children.

## ▇ Further reading

Gaskell, E. *Life of Charlotte Brontë*, ed. E. Cleghorn (Harmondsworth: Penguin, 1975).

Haight, G. *George Eliot: A Life* (Harmondsworth: Penguin, 1968).

Wheeler, M. *English Fiction of the Victorian Period*, 2nd edn (Harlow: Longman, 1994).

# Late Victorian Literature: 1880–1900

# CHAPTER 11

## Overview

The last decades of the reign saw a disintegration of the middle ground of readership. Writers went along with or rose above a broadening mass market, as did Hardy and James respectively. These were major talents, but it was a period of transition without a central figure, although Wilde briefly took centre stage in a revival of literary theatre, with Shaw as the other leading figure. The old Victorian poets went on writing, but their juniors were retiring or minor, consciously aesthetic or consciously hearty. There was a new professional minor fiction, in Stevenson and Conan Doyle.

## Differentiation

The two decades of 1880–1900, with the next decade, lie between the mid-Victorian uplands and the peaks of modernism. For a long time, Joyce, Pound, Eliot, D. H. Lawrence and Virginia Woolf hid their predecessors. If literary history is written by the victors, as with the Romantics and the Renaissance humanists, a longer view can bring revision. As the Modernist revolution revolves into the distance, and dust settles, it is easier to see origins in the eighties and nineties, and to try an evaluative sketch.

A sketch it is, for major writers are few. Confidence in the cultural stamina of the general reader, and in the direction of society, waned. Serious writers dealt with a middlebrow market by some simplification or specialization, or else went into covert or open opposition to majority views, as some poets did. The first mass-circulation newspaper claiming to be the organ of democracy, the *Daily Mail*, began in 1896. Its owner bought *The Times* in 1908. 'The newspaper is the roar of the machine', declared W. B. Yeats. A less oracular truth is that paper and printing were cheaper and that new technology found a new market in the newly literate.

### Thomas Hardy and Henry James

Drama revived, with Wilde and Shaw; poets shrank; sages went into aesthetics or

## Contents

## Events and publications 1881–1901

| Events | Chief publications |
|---|---|
| | **1881** Revised Version of the New Testament (Old Testament, 1885); Henry James, *Portrait of a Lady, Washington Square*; Oscar Wilde, *Poems*. |
| **1882** The Irish Secretary is assassinated in Dublin. | **1882** Robert Louis Stevenson, *Treasure Island*. |
| **1884** Third Reform Act extends franchise. | **1884** James Murray (ed.), *A New English Dictionary on Historical Principles* (125 parts, 1928). |
| **1885** Prime Minister Gladstone resigns on the defeat of his Irish Home Rule Bill. | **1885** Sir Richard Burton (trans.), *Arabian Nights* (16 volumes, 1888); H. Rider Haggard, *King Solomon's Mines*; George Meredith, *Diana of the Crossways*; Walter Pater, *Marius the Epicurean*; John Ruskin, *Praeterita* (3 volumes, 1888); Alfred, Lord Tennyson, *Tiresias, and Other Poems*. |
| | **1886** Thomas Hardy, *The Mayor of Casterbridge*; James, *The Bostonians, The Princess Casamassima*; R. L. Stevenson, *Dr Jekyll and Mr Hyde, Kidnapped*; Rudyard Kipling, *Departmental Ditties*; Tennyson, *Locksley Hall, Sixty Years After*. |
| | **1887** Hardy, *The Woodlanders* (August Strindberg, *The Father*). |
| | **1888** James, *The Aspern Papers*; Kipling, *Plain Tales from the Hills*. |
| | **1889** Stevenson, *The Master of Ballantrae*; Robert Browning, *Asolando*; W. B. Yeats, *The Wanderings of Oisin*; Pater, *Appreciations*. |
| | **1890** Sir James Frazer, *The Golden Bough* (12 volumes, 1915); William Morris, *News from Nowhere*. |
| **1891** Assisted Education Act provides free elementary education. | **1891** Hardy, *Tess of the d'Urbervilles*; Wilde, *The Picture of Dorian Gray*. |
| | **1892** Arthur Conan Doyle, *The Adventures of Sherlock Holmes*; Wilde, *Lady Windermere's Fan*; Yeats, *The Countess Kathleen*. |
| **1893** Second Irish Home Rule Bill is defeated. | **1894** George Moore, *Esther Waters*; Kipling, *The Jungle Book*; Stevenson, *The Ebb-Tide*; George Bernard Shaw, *Arms and the Man*. |
| | **1895** Hardy, *Jude the Obscure*; H. G. Wells, *The Time Machine*; Wilde, *An Ideal Husband, The Importance of Being Earnest*. |
| | **1896** Stevenson (d.1894), *Weir of Hermiston*; A. E. Housman, *A Shropshire Lad*. |
| | **1897** Joseph Conrad, *The Nigger of the Narcissus*; James, *What Maisie Knew*. |
| | **1898** James, *The Turn of the Screw*; Shaw, *Mrs Warren's Profession*; Hardy, *Wessex Poems*. |
| **1899** Boer War against the Dutch South Africans (to 1902). | **1899** Kipling, *Stalky and Co.* |
| **1900** Labour Party is founded. | **1900** Conrad, *Lord Jim*. |
| **1901** Queen Victoria dies. Edward VII reigns (to 1910). | **1901** Kipling, *Kim* (Anton Chekhov, *The Three Sisters*). |

into politics. There was plenty of fiction, some of it short, as from R. L. Stevenson, George Moore, George Gissing and Arthur Conan Doyle, who show the specialization of the age. An author who had intellectual prestige for fifty years was the versatile and productive George Meredith (1828–1909), now remembered for *The Egoist* (1879) and *Diana of the Crossways* (1885). But the only novelists so substantial that several of their works are still read are **Thomas Hardy** (1840–1928) of Upper Bockhampton, Dorset, and **Henry James** (1843–1916) of New York.

In subject-matter and approach, they are worlds apart. James patronized 'poor little Thomas Hardy', as later did T. S. Eliot, of St Louis, Missouri. In *The Great Tradition* (1948), the critic F. R. Leavis, weeding the garden of English fiction for Cambridge students, kept George Eliot, James and Conrad, but threw out this 'provincial manufacturer of gauche and heavy fictions that sometimes have corresponding virtues'. But Hardy has proved to be a perennial. From Dorset, James's field and approach must have looked very rarefied.

Hardy's novels did not fit Leavis's idea of fiction as moralized realism; they are pastoral, romance, or tragic drama, not studies of provincial life. James spent most of his adult years in England, an observer, writing often about the islanders. He is a great practitioner of the art to which he devoted his life, and he influenced the ways in which that art was later analysed. An American who influenced the English novel, he is treated more marginally than in a history of literature in English he would deserve.

Henry James came from a family of speculative intellectuals, his father a theologian, his brother William a philosopher of religion and psychology. Educated in the US and Europe, he set his scenes in New York, Boston, Paris, Switzerland, Florence, Rome or London. His people are sometimes artistic, more often moneyed people staying in villas or country houses: the floating society of a new international civilization, superior in tone rather than substance. The central figure is often a young woman, the victim of subtle manoeuvres to do with money. An urbane narrative voice focuses the subject, attending to exactly what each character knows. The reader has to infer motive, and to wait. Despite the subtlety of his narration, psychology, and syntax – famously drawn out in his later work – James's fundamental interest is in innocence, and in those who exploit it.

Thomas Hardy's father was a Dorset mason, his mother a domestic servant who gave him for his twelfth birthday a copy of Dryden's Virgil. His background was tangled, and less respectable than he made out in *The Life of Thomas Hardy*, the biography published posthumously over his second wife's name, but written by him. Leaving school early, he was apprenticed to architects in Dorchester, then in London. He went on educating himself, much as George Eliot did. He married above himself (so they both felt), a vicar's niece from Cornwall. They were happy at first, but she resented his success as a novelist, which allowed him to build a house outside Dorchester, in which they spent many unhappy and childless years. James's major novels are listed above; Hardy's are taken later.

The gulf between Hardy and James indicates a trend. It is at this juncture, or disjuncture, that a weakening assent to gospel truths in the literal forms offered by the Protestant churches began to take effect in divergent and more partial ideals. In her novels George Eliot had kept her agnosticism quiet behind a Christian morality. Hardy, losing his beliefs suddenly, proclaimed his atheism, then his agnosticism. A churchgoer unable to forgive God for not existing, he also blamed God for a lack of compassion. James, too well-bred to mention the divine, shows a post-Calvinist interest in evil spirits, as does Stevenson, whom he admired. Many were taken up with spiritualism and the occult: W. B. Yeats, H. Rider Haggard, Andrew Lang, Arthur Conan Doyle, J. M. Barrie, Rudyard Kipling. Many put their faith in secular politics: William Morris, founder of the Socialist League (and the Arts and Crafts movement), and George Bernard Shaw, a founder of the **Fabian Society**. After hearing

**Henry James** A selection: *Roderick Hudson, The Americans* (1877), *Daisy Miller* (1879), *Portrait of a Lady, Washington Square* (1881), *The Bostonians* (1886), *The Aspern Papers* (1888), *What Maisie Knew* (1897), *The Turn of the Screw* (1898), *The Wings of the Dove* (1902), *The Ambassadors* (1903), *The Golden Bowl* (1904).

**Fabian Society** Founded in 1884, the Fabian Society was dedicated to the gradual achievement of socialism. It was called after Quintus Fabius Maximus, the Roman general who defeated Hannibal by avoiding battle until the favourable moment (he was nicknamed Cunctator, the Delayer). Among its artistic members were Edward Carpenter (1844–1929), sexologist, environmentalist, vegetarian, and author of the poem *Towards Democracy* (4 volumes, 1883–1902); and later the poet Rupert Brooke (1887–1915) and the children's writer, E. Nesbit (1858–1924).

Shaw speak, Oscar Wilde wrote *The Soul of Man under Socialism*, which is, however, a plea for artistic individualism. Some were strongly patriotic: W. E. Henley, Rudyard Kipling and Sir Henry Newbolt for England, others for a Celtic identity. As beliefs diverged, codes became important.

## Aestheticism

The period saw a cult of beauty or Aestheticism, now remembered for the Decadent illustrations of Aubrey Beardsley (1872–98) and for the life of Oscar Wilde, imprisoned for homosexuality in 1895. It was not only or even chiefly a literary movement. Its importance lies not in the lifestyle of the Decadents, nor in their own work, but in a new idea: that literature was an art, and worth living for. This idea shaped the lives of Yeats, and of Joyce, Pound, Eliot and Virginia Woolf. Keats's Grecian Urn had said: 'Beauty is Truth, Truth Beauty', but Keats had weighed Beauty against ideas of the good life. Tennyson too adhered to the view that beauty served truth by making wisdom or noble conduct attractive. But the Aesthetes separated art from morality. They quoted from Walter Pater's Conclusion to *The Renaissance* (1873) – 'the desire of beauty, the love of art for art's sake', a formula found in Théophile Gautier (1811–72), who had in 1835 denied that art could be useful.

### Walter Pater

Ruskin's lectures on beauty and the dignity of labour inspired the undergraduate Oscar Wilde to manual work on the roads. After Oxford, Wilde left work to William Morris and pursued beauty, taking his cue from Walter Pater, another Oxford don, who had turned Keats's wish for a life of sensations rather than thoughts into a programme. The Conclusion to Pater's *The Renaissance* contains this passage:

Every moment some form grows perfect in hand or face; some tone on the hills or the sea is choicer than the rest; some mood of passion or insight or intellectual excitement is irresistibly real and attractive to us – for that moment only. Not the fruit of experience, but experience itself, is the end. A counted number of pulses only is given to us of a variegated, dramatic life. How may we see in them all that is to be seen in them by the finest senses? How shall we pass most swiftly from point to point, and be present always at the focus where the greatest number of vital forces unite in their purest energy? … To burn always with this hard, gemlike flame, to maintain this ecstasy, is success in life.

Oxford's young men had heard of 'a healthy mind in a healthy body' at their public schools. Their still largely clerical University wished to put 'a Christian gentleman in every parish'. Ecstasy upon ecstasy was a new ideal. Which were 'the finest senses'? The Conclusion was dropped in a second edition, shutting the stable door after the horse had gone, as 'it might possibly mislead some of those young men into whose hands it might fall'. Pater made his own idea clearer in *Marius the Epicurean* (1885), a historical novel commending an austere epicureanism in 'the only great prose in modern English' (W. B. Yeats), and very readably. Yet this austere critic's discussion of Leonardo da Vinci's *Mona Lisa* breathes strange longings. Leonardo's painting (also called *La Gioconda*, 'The Smiling Lady'), Pater wrote, embodies 'the animalism of Greece, the lust of Rome, the mysticism of the Middle Age with its spiritual ambition and imaginative loves, the return of the Pagan world, the sins of the Borgias. She is older than the rocks among which she sits.…'

Matthew Arnold had said that it was the task of Criticism 'to see the object as in itself it really is'. Taking Pater's subjectivity to a logical conclusion, Wilde argued that 'the highest Criticism' aims 'to see the object as in itself it really is not' (*The Critic as Artist*, 1890), and indeed Leonardo's lady and what Pater saw in her are not at all the same thing. Yet Yeats chose 'She is older than the rocks' as the first item in his *Oxford Book of Modern English Verse* in 1936 – a grandly perverse gesture. It is not verse, but for Yeats it was modern; he was eight when it was published.

Pater relates art to life in 'Style', an essay in *Appreciations* (1889). Art must first be beautiful, then true:

> I said, thinking of books like Victor Hugo's *Les Misérables*, that prose literature was the characteristic art of the nineteenth century, as others, thinking of its triumphs since the youth of Bach, have assigned that place to music. Music and prose literature are, in one sense, the opposite terms of art; the art of literature presenting to the imagination, through the intelligence, a range of interest, as free and various as those which music presents to it through sense. And certainly the tendency of what has been here said is to bring literature too under those conditions, by conformity to which music takes rank as the typically perfect art. If music be the ideal of all art whatever, precisely because in music it is impossible to distinguish the form from the substance or matter, the subject from the expression, then literature, by finding its specific excellence in the absolute correspondence of the term to its import, will be but fulfilling the condition of all artistic quality in things everywhere, of all good art.
>
> Good art, but not necessarily great art, the distinction between great art and good art depending immediately, as regards literature at all events, not on its form, but on the matter ... Given the conditions I have tried to explain as constituting good art – then, if it be devoted further to the increase of men's happiness, to the redemption of the oppressed, or to the enlargement of our sympathies with each other, or to such presentment of new or old truth about ourselves and our relation to the world as may ennoble and fortify us in our sojourn here, or immediately, as with Dante, to the glory of God, it will be also great art; if, over and above those qualities I summed up as mind and soul – that colour and mystic perfume, and that reasonable structure, it has something of the soul of humanity in it, and finds its logical, architectural place, in the great structure of human life.

A song from the comic opera *Patience* (1881), with words by W. S. Gilbert and music by Sir Arthur Sullivan, shows that Wilde had been noticed in London. Gilbert and Sullivan operas had the confident rapport with a broad public which serious writers were losing. 'If You're Anxious for to Shine in the High Aesthetic Line' ends:

> Then a sentimental passion of a vegetable fashion must excite your languid spleen,
> An attachment *à la Plato* for a bashful young potato, or a not-too-French French bean!
> Though the Philistines may jostle, you will rank as an apostle in the high aesthetic band,
> If you walk down Piccadilly with a poppy or a lily in your medieval hand.
> > And everyone will say,
> > As you walk your flowery way,
> 'If he's content with a vegetable love which would certainly not suit *me*,
> Why, what a most particularly pure young man this pure young man must be!'

This satire proved accurate.

# A revival of drama

## Oscar Wilde

Oscar Fingall O'Flahertie Wills Wilde (1854–1900), son of a famous Dublin surgeon, had gone from Trinity College to Oxford, then to London, to publicize aestheticism

Oscar Wilde (1854–1900), photographed in
London between 1890 and 1894.

and himself. A brilliant talker, he put his art into his lifestyle. Fascinating as Wilde's
act is, his writing looks thin when compared with that of the comparably flamboyant
Byron. Serious emotion comes out as sickly sentiment in his early poems and fiction,
and in *The Ballad of Reading Jail* (1898) and *De Profundis* (1905), written after his fall.
(Lord Queensbury had accused Wilde of homosexual practices, a serious legal
offence – Wilde was sleeping with Queensbury's son, Lord Alfred Douglas. Wilde
sued for libel, lost, and went to jail, dying in exile in France.) The Romantic movement is sometimes dated from 'Ossian' MacPherson's 'The Death of Oscar' (1759).
Ossian provided Wilde with his first and second names. The death of Wilde began a
legend of Saint Oscar, which has been better for newspapers than for literature.

Wilde is a brilliantly provocative critic, but his distinction lies in his comedies,
*Lady Windermere's Fan*, *A Woman of No Importance*, *An Ideal Husband* and *The
Importance of being Earnest*, staged in 1892–5. The last has been rated the best English
comedy since Sheridan, Goldsmith or even Congreve, and is more quoted than any
play not by Shakespeare. Only Bernard Shaw was unamused. The play on Ernest and
'earnest' is resolved in the play's last line, in which Jack Worthing discovers that he is
in fact Ernest Moncrieff, and is thus able to marry Gwendolen Fairfax, who will only
marry him if he is called Ernest. He releases his ward, Cicely Cardew, to marry Algernon Moncrieff. The cleverly managed plot is a pretext for absurd dialogue full of
paradox. Lady Bracknell, Gwendolen's mother, questions Worthing about his background, and finds that he has money.

LADY BRACKNELL: And now to minor matters. Are your parents living?

JACK: I have lost both my parents.

LADY B: Both? To lose one parent may be regarded as a misfortune – to lose *both* seems like
carelessness. Who was your father? Was he born in what the Radical papers call the purple
of commerce, or did he rise from the ranks of aristocracy?

JACK: I am afraid I really don't know. The fact is, Lady Bracknell, I said I had lost my parents. It
would be nearer the truth to say that my parents seem to have lost me … I don't actually
know who I am by birth. I was … well, I was found.

LADY B: Found?

JACK: The late Mr Thomas Cardew, an old gentleman of a very charitable and kindly disposition, found me, and gave me the name of Worthing, because he happened to have a first-class ticket for Worthing in his pocket at the time. Worthing is a place in Sussex. It is a seaside resort.

LADY B: Where did the charitable gentleman who had a first-class ticket for this seaside resort find you?

JACK [*gravely*]: In a handbag.

LADY B: A handbag?

JACK [*very seriously*]: Yes, Lady Bracknell, I was in a handbag – a somewhat large, black leather handbag, with handles to it – an ordinary handbag, in fact.

LADY B: In what locality did this Mr James, or Thomas, Cardew come across this ordinary handbag?

JACK: In the cloak room at Victoria Station. It was given to him in mistake for his own.

LADY B: The cloak room at Victoria Station.

JACK: Yes. The Brighton line.

LADY B: The line is immaterial. Mr. Worthing, I confess I feel somewhat bewildered by what you have told me. To be born, or at any rate, bred in a handbag, whether it had handles or not, seems to me to display a contempt for the ordinary decencies of family life that reminds one of the worst excesses of the French Revolution. And I presume you know what that unfortunate movement led to? As for the particular locality in which the handbag was found, a cloak room at a railway station might serve to conceal a social indiscretion – has probably, indeed, been used for that purpose before now – but it could hardly be regarded as an assured basis for a recognised position in good society … You can hardly imagine that I and Lord Bracknell would dream of allowing our only daughter – a girl brought up with the utmost care – to marry into a cloak room, and form an alliance with a parcel? Good morning, Mr Worthing!

[*Lady Bracknell sweeps majestically from the room*]

This comedy of manners is not satire, for it is not mimetic. 'Good society' is a pretext for an imaginary world, though Wilde's wit relies upon social nuance for some of its effects. Though he acknowledged W. S. Gilbert, Wilde's comedy is personal and extraordinarily verbal, perfecting the techniques of his own conversation.

Lady Bracknell later tries to prevent her nephew Algernon from marrying Cicely Cardew, but on learning that she has £130,000 'in the Funds', observes: 'Miss Cardew seems to me a most attractive young lady, now that I look at her. Few girls of the present day have any really solid qualities, any of the qualities that last, and improve with time. We live, I regret to say, in an age of surfaces.' She commends the eighteen-year-old Cicely's habit of admitting to twenty at evening parties: 'You are perfectly right in making some slight alteration. Indeed, no woman should ever be quite accurate about her age. It looks so calculating …'. The assumption that society depends upon untruth is the basis of this logic: 'In matters of grave importance, style, not sincerity is the vital thing.' Echoes of Wilde can be found in the parodist Max Beerbohm (1872–1956). His aunts, butlers, bachelors and debutantes reappear in the weightless world of P. G. Wodehouse (1881–1975).

Wilde reunited literature and theatre after a century in which poets from Shelley to Tennyson wrote poetical plays, little staged and largely forgotten. After Sheridan, the theatre fell into the hands of stock companies, doing farces or sub-literary melodrama, vehicles for actors such as Edmund Kean and William Macready. After making his name in *The Bells* (1870), the actor-manager Henry Irving dominated in London, putting on lavish Shakespeares with Ellen Terry. In Lyceum productions, acting came first, staging second, text last. Act V of *The Merchant of Venice* was dropped so that Irving (Shylock) could achieve maximum pathos.

In comedy, *London Assurance* (1841) by the Irishman Dion Boucicault was an effective piece, but ripped-off French farces were the staple fare. The work of the great Norwegian, Henrik Ibsen (1828–1906), was first performed in England in 1880 in translation by William Archer. Recovery began with Sir Arthur Pinero (1855–1935), whose *The Second Mrs Tanqueray* (1893) Shaw compared to the 'culminating chapters of a singularly powerful and original novel'; Mrs Patrick Campbell played Mrs T., a 'woman with a past' (that is, the mistress of rich men). But Ibsen is more than social-realism-with-moral-problem, and the plays of Wilde and Shaw are minor compared to some of the foreign plays that were beginning to be seen in London. Reading the plays of the Russian Anton Chekhov (1860–1904), Shaw said, made him want to tear up his own; he resisted the temptation.

## George Bernard Shaw

**George Bernard Shaw** (1856–1950) was an honest if perverse man who made the most of his talent, contributing to British cultural life long and vigorously. In 1876, with his music-teacher mother, he came to London from Dublin, where he had been a clerk for seven years. He worked long as a critic of music and then of drama, a champion of Wagner and Ibsen. A follower of Carlyle and the Life Force, he combined socialism with hero-worship of strong men and emancipated women. After five novels, he wrote many plays, beginning with *Widowers' Houses* (1892), an attack on slum landlords, and *Mrs Warren's Profession*, a comic satire exposing the economic incentives to prostitution in a capitalist society. Mrs Warren runs a chain of brothels; her Cambridge-educated daughter Vivie happily becomes a cigar-smoking actuary. Mrs Warren defends social convention, Vivie wins the arguments. The play could not be legally staged in England until 1926.

Shaw used the theatre as a tool of social reform, presenting situations which challenged conventional attitudes, directing a stream of ideas at audiences, provoking while entertaining. The published plays have long argumentative prefaces and lengthy stage directions. A foe of Victorian pieties, he attacked theatrical censorship, medical fraud, the English devotion to class and accent, the British treatment of Ireland, and so on. As his ideas have gained ground, his plays have lost their challenge. We admire his versatile technique in tickling the middle class while attacking

George Bernard Shaw, in London in about 1890.

its preconceptions, but his topicality has dated. He attacked the dreaminess of W. B. Yeats, who retaliated by dreaming of Shaw as a smiling sewing-machine. He was perhaps more of a mechanical tin-opener, opening minds with paradoxes.

Shaw was not modest – he thought himself better than Shakespeare, or said so. But time and his own success have turned the tireless craftsman, wit and educator into an entertainer. The English tend to regard Irishmen who make jokes as fundamentally unserious. The 'dreamy' W. B. Yeats (1865–1939), who spent more than half his life in England, took a long way round to a more lasting achievement. Yeats and Rudyard Kipling (1865–1936) are dealt with later, as is Hardy's poetry.

# Fiction

## Thomas Hardy

The art of **Thomas Hardy** (1840–1928) was his poetry, but after his marriage he put it aside to earn a living as a novelist. He finished with fiction in *Jude the Obscure* (1896). The six novels listed after *Under the Greenwood Tree* are considered major, but there are fine things in the three Romances; the classes are not exclusive. *A Pair of Blue Eyes* was the favourite of the French novelist Marcel Proust (1871–1922); it also provides a background to the poems Hardy wrote after his wife's death.

Hardy's first novel, *The Poor Man and the Lady*, was declined by Macmillan as too fiercely satirical. He wrote *Desperate Remedies* (1871), a heavily-plotted Novel of Ingenuity, and then the pastoral *Under the Greenwood Tree*. Ingenuity, fantasy and romance are found in the more serious Novels of Character and Environment. Like Dickens, he borrowed from folklore, popular theatre, and broadsheet ballad tragedies. Despite this 'stagy' quality, he visualizes settings topographically (he was trained as an architect) so that their firm features are readily envisaged, as with the famous description of Egdon Heath which opens *The Return of the Native*. In *The Mayor of Casterbridge*, the town (based on Dorchester) is so laid out that the reader locates

Thomas Hardy sits with his second wife, Florence, on the shaft of a 'bathing machine' on the beach at Aldeburgh, 1915.

each scene in street, tavern, house or workplace. Hardy lived much of his life out of doors. Improbable or coincidental scenes can be visualised because he has made sure we see them clearly, often setting them against natural backgrounds. He places human figures against a world which has been inhabited for immense periods of time. In his tragic novels he endows his puppets with nobility, consciously following Greek models. Environment and action are often more important than character. His characters, rather than showing psychological development, are made of simple elements and experience a variety of emotions as plot and situation act upon them. His novels build up to climactic scenes. His mixing of genres invokes a greater variety of dimensions than other novelists.

Hardy's obscure birthplace 'far from the madding crowd's ignoble strife' (Gray's *Elegy*) gave him a long perspective, increased by the longevity of his family. His grandmother told him of 'that far-back day when they learnt astonished/Of the death of the king of France' ('One We Knew (M. H. 1772–1857)'). Hardy observed that Wordsworth could have seen him in his cradle, as Gray could have seen Wordsworth in his. Hardy's last visit to London was to attend the wedding of Harold Macmillan to the daughter of the Duke of Devonshire. When he died in 1928, two years before D. H. Lawrence, he had not written a novel for thirty-three years. That career had ended in a storm of protest: *Tess of the d'Urbervilles*, and especially *Jude the Obscure*, shocked a public Hardy had earlier wooed with rustic humour, and such winning characters as Gabriel Oak in the abundant tragicomedy of *Far From the Madding Crowd*. The middle novels which end unhappily, *The Mayor of Casterbridge* and *The Woodlanders*, do not depart absolutely from what may befall star-crossed lovers in romantic tragedy. He had concealed his views from the pious and the prudish in a career as a popular novelist, buying a financial independence. He then booby-trapped the Wessex of the endpaper maps with the corpses of Tess and Jude and their symbolically-named children, repaying the public for the accommodations he had had to make.

### Tess of the d'Urbervilles

All the novels have moments of grandeur, and *The Mayor of Casterbridge* is a balanced tragedy, but his most powerful book is *Tess of the d'Urbervilles: A Pure Woman*. Tess Durbeyfield is the hope of her poor family. After the horse on which her father's work depends is killed in an accident, she goes to work for a rich relative, Alec, who seduces her. Tess improvises a baptism for the child, who dies; the vicar is reluctant to bury the child (called Sorrow) in consecrated ground. In a later summer, as a dairymaid, she becomes engaged to Angel Clare, the agnostic son of an evangelical clergyman. On her wedding night she tells her husband about her past. Disgusted, although he has been no angel himself, he leaves her. Things at her home get worse. Working on a harsh upland farm, she meets Alec, who has become an itinerant preacher but gives it up to pursue her. Her letters to Angel unanswered, she becomes Alec's mistress for the sake of her family. She kills him, then spends a hidden 'honeymoon' in the woods with Angel, who has returned. She is arrested at Stonehenge and hanged, leaving Angel with her younger sister. '"Justice" was done, and the President of the Immortals, in Aeschylean phrase, had ended his sport with Tess.' This outraged readers: the book not only attacked social hypocrisy, double standards, the Church, the law and God, but seemed by its subtitle to condone adultery and murder. Hardy expressed surprise.

The 'faults and falsity' in *Tess* (Henry James's phrase) come from Hardy's ambiguous use of popular methods. The crude plot and simple characterization of the 'shocker' lured the public into an ambush where conventional values were upended. The pure woman's confession that she has been 'ruined' by the devilish Alec causes her impure Angel to abandon her. Her innocent fineness then causes the 'reformed' Alec to abandon evangelism. The Victorian reader sees that the conventional norms of class, gender, morality and the supernatural do not work; and that it is natural for Tess to attract Alec and Angel, and may be natural for her to kill Alec. The use of paradox in the Nineties is not confined to Shaw and Wilde.

*Tess* is crude in plot and in the character of Alec, but not in its natural and imaginative style, although at times there are awkwardly learned references. After the Chaseborough dance, a village beauty jealous of Tess challenges her to a fight. She strips off her bodice and

bared her plump neck, shoulders, and arms to the moonshine, under which they looked as luminous and beautiful as some Praxitelean creation, in their possession of the faultless rotundities of a lusty country girl. She closed her fists and squared up to Tess.

Alec rides up and rescues her: 'Jump up behind me,' he whispered, 'and we'll get shot of the screaming cats in a jiffy!' Although a female punch-up is subject for neo-classical laughter in Fielding's *Tom Jones*, the Greek sculptor Praxiteles has not much to do with this episode, omitted from *Tess*'s serialization in the popular *Graphic*. The mention of Aeschylus, as the curtain comes down on Tess, forces a comparison with Tragedy. But 'the President of the Immortals' was not a familiar phrase even to classicists, and is less well introduced than the mention of Cyrus at the end of *Middlemarch*. Hardy may have thought his pure suffering woman a more realistic modern counterpart to St Theresa than Eliot's martyr to idealism, Dorothea.

Having rescued Tess from the frying-pan, and the 'screaming cats', Alec loses his way in the night. Tess is tired, and he stops to give her a rest, lending her his over-coat. He finds out where they are, and returns.

The Chase was wrapped in thick darkness, although morning was not far off. He was obliged to advance with outstretched hands to avoid contact with the boughs, and discovered that to hit the exact spot from which he had started was at first entirely beyond him. Roaming up and down, round and round, he at length heard a slight movement of the horse close at hand; and the sleeve of his overcoat unexpectedly caught his foot.

'Tess!' said d'Urberville.

There was no answer. The obscurity was now so great that he could see absolutely nothing but a pale nebulousness at his feet, which represented the white muslin figure he had left upon the dead leaves. Everything else was blackness alike. D'Urberville stooped; and heard a gentle regular breathing. He knelt and bent lower, till her breath warmed his face, and in a moment his cheek was in contact with hers. She was sleeping soundly, and upon her eyelashes there lingered tears.

Darkness and silence ruled everywhere around. Above them rose the primeval yews and oaks of The Chase, in which were poised gentle roosting birds in their last nap; and about them stole the hopping rabbits and hares. But, might some say, where was Tess's guardian angel?

The Chase speaks better of innocence and wrong than this last question. Hardy is best when he allows description to interpret itself, as in the visionary scenes of courtship at Talbothays Dairy. He is a great visual and symbolic storyteller, rather than a social analyst in the tradition of the 19th-century realistic novel. The red-mouthed pure-hearted Tess is a memorable symbolic figure.

In *Jude the Obscure*, a child called Old Father Time hangs the two babies and then

**dystopia** An imaginary world in which everything is wrong; the opposite of 'eutopia' (a good place). *Erewhon* is an anagram of *Nowhere*, 'utopia' (no place).

himself, leaving a note: 'Done because we are too menny'. Grotesque! But it reflects Hardy's idea of life as determined, not by heredity, environment and economics but by 'crass Casualty'. Chance, in logic, cannot be cruel, although it can feel so. Such a pathos makes one think less about the victims than about their creator, Hardy.

## Minor fiction

### Samuel Butler

Hardy's assault on Victorian morality was anticipated by **Samuel Butler** (1835–1902), the author of *Erewhon* (1873), a **dystopian** novel. Butler was a professional heretic, attacking the Resurrection (Darwin applauded), Canadian prudery (Montreal would not exhibit naked statues), Darwinian evolution (Butler preferred Lamarck's theory), and the Homeric problem (*The Authoress of the Odyssey*, 1897). His heartlessly entertaining satirical novel, *The Way of All Flesh* (1903), is based on his own upbringing in a clerical family.

### Robert Louis Stevenson

Robert Louis Stevenson (1850–94) was once famous enough to be known as RLS, but his work faded, leaving an adventurous legend. He sailed much in childhood – his Edinburgh family built lighthouses – and, despite weak health, travelled far from Scotland, dying in Samoa. He wrote plays, travel, a historical novel and *A Child's Garden of Verses* (1885), with much else that has dated. Still vivid are his full-length romances, begun in Bournemouth: *Treasure Island* (1883), *Kidnapped* (1886) with its sequel *Catriona* (1893), *The Master of Ballantrae* (1889), and, more seriously engaging with the past, *Weir of Hermiston* (1896), unfinished. *The Strange Case of Dr Jekyll and Mr Hyde* (1886) makes a bonny film, but, like the horror of Bram Stoker's *Dracula* (1879), disappoints adult re-reading. Later short stories, *The Ebb-Tide* and *The Beach at Falesà*, lightly anticipate Conrad. RLS spins excellent yarns in an economically picturesque style. Another Scot who developed a genre in England was **Arthur Conan Doyle** (1859–1930), with his Sherlock Holmes detective stories, beginning with *A Study in Scarlet* (1887).

### Wilkie Collins

The perfection of genre for a middlebrow market had begun with Dickens's friend, **Wilkie Collins** (1824–89), who made a career out of a new kind of minor fiction in *The Woman in White* (1860) and *The Moonstone* (1865). These detective novels combine murder mystery with problem-solving in a kind of parlour Gothic. In true Gothic novels, such as *Memoirs and Confessions of a Justified Sinner* (1824) by James Hogg or *Wuthering Heights*, horror and the problems of interpretation are infinite. Dickens's last book, *The Mystery of Edwin Drood* (unfinished) would have transmuted the detective story.

### George Moore

George Moore (1852–1933) wrote much and variously. A major figure in Anglo-Irish literature, he is noted here for pioneering French fictional styles in English, and remembered chiefly for *Esther Waters* (1894), a novel in the naturalist manner of Emile Zola, combining a clinical physical realism deriving from natural science with a pathos lacking in glamour. Esther is a religious girl driven from home to work in a racing stable; she becomes pregnant, and endures many ordeals. **George Gissing**

(1857–1903) also wrote about poverty and failure, but from personal experience; especially, in *New Grub Street* (1891), of the life of a struggling writer.

#  Poetry

## Aestheticism

The old men wrote until they died: Browning in 1889, Tennyson in 1892, Morris in 1896, Swinburne in 1909. Of their juniors, on the basis of verse published before 1901, none is a major poet: William Ernest Henley (1849–1903), Lionel Johnson (1867–1902), Ernest Dowson (1867–1900), W. B. Yeats (1867–1939), John Davidson (1857–1909), A. E. Housman (1859–1936). Prose and verse taken together show Rudyard Kipling (1865–1936) as a major talent. The great poetry of Hardy and Yeats came after 1900. Looking back over the 19th century, it seems that, after the death of Byron, Shelley and especially Keats, poetry suffered a loss in quality and in centrality.

In 'The Tragic Generation' (in *Autobiographies*) Yeats wrote of Johnson and Dowson and other 'companions of the Cheshire Cheese', a pub off Fleet Street where the Rhymers' Club met. Some Rhymers are cameo'd in Ezra Pound's *Hugh Selwyn Mauberley*: 'Dowson found harlots cheaper than hotels'; Johnson died 'by falling from a high stool in a pub'. Affecting dandyism, standing away from a prevailing English heartiness – Gilbert's *Patience* is again a guide – they became as precious as they had pretended to be, emigrating inwards to dissipation and early death. Arthur Symons (1865–1945) and John Gray (1866–1934) survived. Some were Decadents as well as Aesthetes; many of them were dandies, many homosexual, most became Catholics. Judged by continental standards, few were truly decadent. The mood and subject-matter of the group is best caught in a line of Dowson's, 'They are not long, the days of wine and roses', and his 'Cynara', which ends:

> I cried for madder music and for stronger wine,
> But when the feast is finished and the lamps expire,
> Then falls thy shadow, Cynara! and the night is thine;
> And I am desolate and sick of an old passion,
>     Yea, hungry for the lips of my desire:
> I have been faithful to thee, Cynara! in my fashion.

These poets, like Swinburne and the painters Whistler and Sickert, often pursued their French aesthetic ideals, sometimes in French cafés. In *The Importance of Being Earnest*, the fictitious brother Ernest, killed off by Jack, is 'said to have expressed a desire to be buried in Paris.' 'In Paris!', exclaims Canon Chasuble. 'I fear that hardly points to any very serious state of mind at the last.' Lionel Johnson is the only one of this wasted group to write more than ten poems of interest, notably 'The Dark Angel' and 'On the Statue of Charles I at Charing Cross'. His art imposed economy on the Swinburnian tendency to swoon. Both Yeats and Ezra Pound were related by marriage to Johnson.

## A. E. Housman

A. E. Housman's *A Shropshire Lad* (1896), the most distinct volume of the decade, later became very popular. Housman, the son of a Worcestershire solicitor, had feelings for a fellow student at Oxford which were not reciprocated, as is suggested in an unpublished poem: 'Because I liked you better/Than it suits a man to say …'. A classical scholar, he failed his Finals and became a clerk in the Patent Office, yet in

1892 his learning earned him the Chair of Latin at University College, London. A great textual critic of Latin poetry, he kept his own verse quite separate, his second volume, *Last Poems*, appearing in 1922.

*A Shropshire Lad* is set in a timeless country inhaled from the pages of Horace as much as in Shropshire, a county not well known to Housman. Its short lyrics, simple in form and refined in diction, turn on youth and death. A note of stoic, contained despair is struck plangently and often. Some of the poems have been set to music: 'Loveliest of trees, the cherry now', 'In summertime on Bredon', 'Is my team ploughing?', 'On Wenlock Edge the wood's in trouble'. Much of Housman is in this short poem:

> Into my heart an air that kills
>     From yon far country blows:
> What are those blue remembered hills,
>     What spires, what farms are those?
>
> That is the land of lost content,
>     I see it shining plain,
> The happy highway where I went
>     And cannot come again.

Pastoral nostalgia rarely has this painful economy. In Hardy, Wilde and Housman there is a temptation to self-pity which is not always resisted.

## Rudyard Kipling

Most of the notable poems of the time are not at all aesthetic. An earlier, remarkable work, 'The City of Dreadful Night' by **James Thomson** (1834–82), pen-name 'B.V.', and John Davidson's pseudo-Cockney 'Thirty Bob a Week' are poems of the urban wasteland, both by Scots. Some are ruggedly earnest, such as W. E. Henley's 'Invictus' ('I am the master of my fate;/I am the captain of my soul') and 'England, my England'. His 'Madam Life's a piece in bloom/Death goes dogging everywhere', a realistic sketch of urban life, uses the figure of the prostitute not for stock pathos but to make an unromantic moral point.

But the master of the hearty mode was **Rudyard Kipling** (1865–1936), born in India, schooled in England. A journalist back in India, his prose reputation began with *Plain Tales from the Hills* (1888) and the *Jungle Books* (1894, 1895). *Barrack Room Ballads* (1892) come in the Cockney accents of the soldier who knows nothing of 'the Widow of Windsor', Queen Victoria, and the policy of her empire: all he knows is the army. The rollicking vigour of this verse made it welcome in houses without bookshelves. Kipling became the favourite writer of millions in the Empire, with poems like 'Gunga Din', 'Ladies', 'If', 'Tommy', 'Danny Deever' and 'The Road to Mandalay'. His quotability has been used against him: 'A woman is only a woman,/But a good cigar is a smoke', for example, but these are the words of a nervous man, not of his creator.

Kipling's popularity fell with that of the Empire, but his imperialism was never uncritical. In 1897, he warned the British of their fate in 'Recessional', written for Victoria's Diamond Jubilee; a recessional hymn is sung as the priest processes out of church at the end of the service.

> God of our fathers, known of old,
>     Lord of our far-flung battle-line,
> Beneath whose awful Hand we hold
>     Dominion over palm and pine –
> Lord God of Hosts, be with us yet,
> Lest we forget – lest we forget.

The end of empire is foreseen: 'The tumult and the shouting dies;/The Captains and the Kings depart' … 'Far off, our navies melt away.' Kipling's final petition is: 'For frantic boast and foolish word – Thy mercy on Thy People, Lord!' Few of the Queen-Empress's subjects would have been surprised by the idea that the English were God's people.

# Further reading

Innes, C. *Modern British Drama, 1880–1990* (Cambridge: Cambridge University Press, 1992).

Raby, P. (ed.). *The Cambridge Companion to Oscar Wilde* (Cambridge: Cambridge University Press, 1997).

Thornton, R. K. R. (ed.). *The Decadent Dilemma* (London: Edward Arnold, 1983).

# PART 5

# The Twentieth Century

# Ends and Beginnings: 1901–19

# CHAPTER 12

## Overview

The war of 1914–18 made the England of Edward VII (1901–10) and of the start of George V's reign seem forever 'pre-war', and a pendant to the 19th century. Those years were rich in good writing of many kinds, old and new, major and minor, but established masters and modes were dominant: poetry by Hardy, drama by Shaw. In 1910 Swinburne died, and Yeats' *Collected Poems* appeared. The fiction of James and Conrad, and of Kipling, was more ambitious and far-reaching than that of younger writers such as Arnold Bennett. Ford Madox Ford's career is representative of the changes to come. Yet by 1918, the impression made by 'modernist' writing before 1914 had faded, and writers later famous as modernists or as war poets were little known.

## Contents

## The new century

Queen Victoria's death in 1901 renewed the novelty of the century. Her elderly, cigar-smoking son, Edward VII, diffused a far more relaxed atmosphere. In clubs, men left the bottom buttons of their waistcoats undone, as the new King did; there was talk of Votes for Women. In 1910 the accession of George V again promised fresh beginnings: the new Georgian era would differ from the Edwardian ... but all is dwarfed in retrospect by how the Great War altered everything. The old world of social rank, of (unequal) prosperity, and of horses and railways, had a liberal hope: the way of life of Britain, of Europe and America, and of the Empire, would gradually improve – materially, politically, morally. The world would grow more civilized. It did not. The words put to Sir Edward Elgar's 'Pomp and Circumstance' march, 'Land of Hope and Glory', have a chorus, still lustily sung each year at the Last Night of the Promenade Concerts in the Albert Hall: '... wider still, and wider, may your bounds be set./God that made thee mighty, make thee mightier yet!' How strange this must have sounded in 1919, and again in 1947, when India became independent and the Empire became the Commonwealth.

We can read about the pre-war English world in the novels of John Galsworthy, Arnold Bennett, H. G. Wells and E. M. Forster; in light fiction such as G. K. Chesterton's *The Innocence of Father Brown* (1911) and E. C. Bentley's *Trent's Last Case*

## Events and publications of 1900–19

| Events | | Publications | |
|---|---|---|---|
| | | 1900 | Joseph Conrad, *Lord Jim*; G. B. Shaw, *You Never Can Tell*. |
| 1901 | Victoria dies. Edward VII reigns (to 1910). | 1901 | Rudyard Kipling, *Kim*. |
| 1902 | Boer War ends. | 1902 | Henry James, T*he Wings of the Dove*; W. B. Yeats, *Cathleen Ni Houlihan*; Beatrix Potter, *The Tale of Peter Rabbit*. |
| | | 1903 | Conrad, *Typhoon*, *Romance* (with F. M. Hueffer); James, *The Ambassadors*. |
| | | 1904 | G. K. Chesterton, *The Napoleon of Notting Hill*; Conrad, *Nostromo*; James, *The Golden Bowl*; M. R. James, *Ghost Stories of an Antiquary*; J. M. Barrie, *Peter Pan*; J. M. Synge, *Riders to the Sea*; Shaw, *John Bull's Other Island*; Thomas Hardy, *The Dynasts* (3 parts, 1908). |
| | | 1905 | E. M. Forster, *Where Angels Fear to Tread*. |
| | | 1906 | John Galsworthy, *The Man of Property*; Rudyard Kipling, *Puck of Pook's Hill*. |
| | | 1907 | Conrad, *The Secret Agent*; Edmund Gosse, *Father and Son*; Synge, *The Playboy of the Western World*; Hilaire Belloc, *Cautionary Tales for Children*. |
| 1908 | H. H. Asquith (Liberal) becomes Prime Minister. 'Votes for Women' rally in Hyde Park, London. | 1908 | Arnold Bennett, *The Old Wives' Tale*; Kenneth Grahame, *The Wind in the Willows*; Yeats, *Collected Works* (Anton Chekhov (d.1904), *The Cherry Orchard*). |
| 1910 | Edward VII dies. George V reigns (to 1936). Post-Impressionist exhibition held in London. | 1910 | E. M. Forster, *Howards End*; H. G. Wells, *The History of Mr Polly*. |
| 1911 | Delhi Durbar. | 1911 | Rupert Brooke, *Poems*; Chesterton, *The Ballad of the White Horse*; D. H. Lawrence, *The White Peacock*. |
| 1912 | Suffragettes active. Loss of *TheTitanic*. | 1912 | Edward Marsh (ed.), *Georgian Poetry I*; Walter de la Mare, *The Listeners*. |
| | | 1913 | D. H. Lawrence, *Sons and Lovers*; Compton Mackenzie, *Sinister Street*. |
| 1914 | First World War begins. | 1914 | Hardy, *Satires of Circumstance*; James Joyce, *Dubliners*; Shaw, *Pygmalion*; Yeats, *Responsibilities*; Ezra Pound *Lustra*, (ed.) *Des Imagistes* (anthology). |
| 1915 | Battle of Ypres; Gallipoli landings. | 1915 | Ford Madox Ford, *The Good Soldier*; Conrad, *Victory*; D. H. Lawrence, *The Rainbow*; Ezra Pound, *Cathay*. |
| 1916 | Battle of the Somme. David Lloyd George (Liberal) becomes Prime Minister. The Easter Rising in Dublin. | 1916 | James Joyce, *A Portrait of the Artist as a Young Man*. |
| 1917 | Battle of Passchendaele. Bolshevik Revolution in Russia. | 1917 | T. S. Eliot, *Prufrock*; Conrad, *The Shadow Line*. |
| 1918 | Armistice ends fighting: Germany defeated. | 1918 | Brooke, *Collected Poems*; Lytton Strachey, *Eminent Victorians*. |
| 1919 | Treaty of Versailles. | 1919 | Eliot, *Poems*; Siegfried Sassoon, *The War Poems*; Yeats, *The Wild Swans at Coole*. |

(1913); and in Edwardian children's books: E. Nesbit's *New Treasure Seekers*, Beatrix Potter's *The Tale of Peter Rabbit*, Kipling's *Puck of Pook's Hill*, Kenneth Grahame's *The Wind in the Willows*, Hilaire Belloc's *Cautionary Tales* – and J. M. Barrie's play *Peter Pan*, a theatrical whimsy first performed in 1904, published in 1911, and still on the London stage every Christmas. Shaw dominated the stage, and Barrie was the only new theatrical talent, with *The Admirable Crichton* (1902) and *What Every Woman Knows* (1908). The Abbey Theatre opened in Dublin in 1904 to the plays of

Synge and Yeats. A wider world appears in the novels of Henry James and Joseph Conrad, with more knowledge of good and evil.

# ▌Fiction

## Edwardian realists

### Rudyard Kipling

In Kipling's *Kim* a wide world is seen through the eyes of a street-wise unprejudiced child: 'He sat, in defiance of municipal orders, astride the gun Zam-Zammah on her brick platform opposite the old Ajaib-Gher – the Wonder House, as the natives call the Lahore Museum.' Readers of the Empire's favourite author were delighted by this novel of adventure, with its glimpses of India's human and religious variety. Kipling, like his Irish-Indian orphan, Kim, could say 'Thanks be to Allah who gave me two/Separate sides to my head'. Many heads can be inhabited by readers of his five adult short story collections, and many different worlds experienced – in, for example, 'Regulus', 'Aunt Ellen', 'Dayspring Mishandled', 'The Church that was at Antioch' and 'The Janeites'. Many of the stories are dramatic monologues voicing unfamiliar prejudices without authorial censorship.

The label 'imperialist' means that Kipling is still neglected, though his uncanny skills make him 'a writer impossible to belittle' (T. S. Eliot). He is as clear as but less simple than H. Rider Haggard, Henry Newbolt and John Masefield. *Puck of Pook's Hill* is original, combining the fairy Puck with the lives of those who worked a Sussex valley under each invader over two millennia. There was a new southern pastoralism: Sussex was home to Kipling and Belloc, Kent to James, Conrad, Ford and Wells.

### John Galsworthy

The domestic novel was dominated by John Galsworthy, Arnold Bennett and H. G. Wells. **John Galsworthy** (1867–1933), the son of a solicitor – like Housman and Bennett – is known for a series of novels, beginning with *A Man of Property* (1906), about the stockbroking Forsyte family, tracing their fortunes, financial, marital and artistic, through changing times. This detached chronicle became less satirical over twenty-three years. His plays, *The Silver Box*, *Strife* and *Justice*, address social issues in a moral spirit. His conventional decency can be judged from his impression of Conrad (see below).

### Arnold Bennett

**Arnold Bennett** (1867–1931) was the best businessman of letters since Dickens: he wrote journalism, reviewed fiction for the *Evening Standard*, turned out entertainments like *The Grand Babylon Hotel*, and composed sensitive novels of provincial life in French realist detail, notably *The Old Wives' Tale*. He bought a steam yacht, which to Henry James, W. B. Yeats, Ezra Pound and Virginia Woolf was the mark of the beast. Kipling and Wells drove large new motor cars. In Kenneth Grahame's *The Wind in the Willows* the 'Poop, poop!' of the motor car driven by Mr Toad embodies the unwelcome in modern life.

### H. G. Wells

**Herbert George Wells** (1866–1946), the son of a small tradesman and professional cricketer, won a scholarship to study science in South Kensington, and soon burst

**Joseph Conrad** (1857–1924)
Selected novels: *Almayer's Folly* (1896), *Lord Jim* (1901), *Youth, Heart of Darkness* (1902), *Nostromo* (1904), *The Secret Agent* (1907), *Under Western Eyes* (1911), *The Shadow Line* (1917).

into print. He wrote pioneering science fiction in *The Time Machine* (1895) and others; a feminist novel, *Ann Veronica* (1909); a spoof on advertising in *Tono-Bungay* (1910); and a social comedy in *The History of Mr Polly* (1910), about being a draper. The unhappy Polly, trying to burn himself to death, becomes frightened of the flames and runs out of the house – and out of his marriage, and his shop, to happiness: a riverside pub. Wells's belief in progress turned him to tracts and popularization (*The Outline of History*, 1920). His last book was *Mind at the End of its Tether* (1945), as might have been predicted by G. K. Chesterton, who mistrusted salvation by the corporate state.

## Joseph Conrad

**Josef Teodor Konrad Korzeniowski** (1857–1924) was the son and grandson of Polish gentlemen who dedicated their lives to resisting Russian rule of the Ukraine. His mother died in exile in northern Russia when he was seven, his father when he was eleven; at sixteen he went to sea, joining a French ship at Marseilles. There are rumours of gun-running, attempted suicide, of having killed a man. After ten years at sea, he became a master mariner and a British subject.

In 1893 a young product of Harrow, Oxford and the Bar wrote home from the *Torrens*, sailing to Adelaide:

The first mate is a Pole called Conrad and is a capital chap, though queer to look at; he is a man of travel and experience in many parts of the world, and has a fund of yarns on which I draw freely. He has been right up the Congo and all around Malacca and Borneo and other out of the way parts, to say nothing of a little smuggling in the days of his youth …

The writer was Galsworthy, who was to help Conrad. In 1895, after twenty years at sea, this aristocratic Pole published *Almayer's Folly* and married an English typist. He explained in his Preface to *The Nigger of the Narcissus* (1897) that 'My task … is by the power of the written word to make you hear, to make you feel – it is, before all, to make you see.' As 'before all' suggests, Conrad still thought in French; 'above all' would be more natural in English. He soon suggested to Ford Madox Ford that they should collaborate; they wrote *The Inheritors* and *Romance*. Ford shared Conrad's view that the English novelist

does not go about building up his book with a precise intention and a steady mind. It never occurs to him that a book is a deed, that the writing of it is as an enterprise as much as the conquest of a colony. He has no such clear conception of his craft.

Conrad's books were admired rather than bought; his narration was unstraightforward and his style was not idiomatic. An exile from nation, language and family, writing in his third language, he wrote of lonely lives, on ships or in outposts, or of exiles in London. Family history and personal experience had made Conrad mistrust political idealists. His writing is torn between a proud sense of honour and a sardonic sense of irony.

### *Heart of Darkness*

The first words of Conrad encountered by many students are 'Mistah Kurtz – he dead,' the epigraph T. S. Eliot used for 'The Hollow Men'. They are spoken in *Heart of Darkness*, a long short story or novella based on Conrad's trip up the Congo in 1890 to become a river pilot for the Belgians, who ran the trade on the river. To reach the heart of the dark continent had been a dream of Conrad's boyhood; the experience undermined his health and changed him. Kurtz is the company agent at the Inner Station, a colonialist intellectual corrupted by the pursuit of ivory and of power; he is worshipped in 'unspeakable rites' involving human sacrifice. Marlow, Conrad's narrator, unfolds his tale to three men in a yawl at the mouth of the Thames. His nightmare experience has affected him more seriously than he realizes. Impressed against his will by Kurtz's intensity, he found that, back in Brussels, he could not tell Kurtz's 'Intended' the truth of his last words, 'The horror! The horror!' He says instead that Kurtz's last words were 'your name', whereupon he hears 'an exulting and terrible cry, of inconceivable triumph and of unspeakable pain. "I knew it – I was sure!"' These are the words of the Intended, yet it is not clear that the cry comes from her only, for the story is also a fable about evil, and Marlow too has been partly possessed by it. The story ends with the Thames 'leading into the heart of an immense darkness'.

That darkness is the darkness of the human heart, but also that of London and of the future of empires. Marlow has three hearers: a Director of Companies, an Accountant and a Lawyer. '"And this also," said Marlow suddenly, "has been one of the dark places of the earth."' Britannia, he explains, would have looked 'dark' to a young Roman naval commander waiting to invade. London is like imperial Rome, but also like commercial Brussels, directed by companies, accountants and lawyers. The conquest of Britannia, as described by Tacitus in his *Agricola* (AD 98), is paralleled with the exploitation of the Congo: a defiant African queen on the banks of the river is described in terms which echo Tacitus' account of the British queen Boadicea; and Kurtz's enclosure, decorated with human heads, is like Tacitus' grove of the druids in Anglesea. Conrad did not like the Russian empire, and he had spent twenty years carrying goods about the French, British and Dutch empires. Marlow tells his friends that the Roman administration was 'merely a big squeeze', and that

The conquest of the earth, which mostly means the taking it away from those who have a different complexion or slightly flatter noses than ourselves, is not a pretty thing when you look into it too much. What redeems it is the idea only … something you can set up, and bow down before, and offer a sacrifice to …

This portentous talk is true in ways that Marlow (and the reader at this point) cannot see. Besides its dramatic irony, *Heart of Darkness* is a parable with moral, psychological and spiritual aspects. Its stiff narration generates claustrophobia. Dickens's drama is looser, James's scrutiny is more refined, but English prose had not seen anything of this dense universality before. In Conrad's maturer work, gesture and narrative become less obtrusive.

## *Nostromo*

Other noted works are *Victory* and *The Shadow Line*, with three major novels, *Nostromo*, *Under Western Eyes* and *The Secret Agent*, of which *Nostromo* is the acknowledged masterpiece. Its opening shows Conrad's rhythmical balance:

In the time of Spanish rule, and for many years afterwards, the town of Sulaco – the luxuriant beauty of the orange gardens bears witness to its antiquity – had never been commercially anything more important than a coasting port with a fairly large local trade in ox-hides and indigo. The clumsy deep-sea galleons of the conquerors that, needing a brisk gale to move at all, would lie becalmed, where your modern ship built on clipper lines forges ahead by the mere flapping of her sails, had been barred out of Sulaco by the prevailing calms of its vast gulf.

Some harbours of the earth are made difficult of access by the treachery of sunken rocks and the tempests of their shores. Sulaco had found an inviolable sanctuary from the temptations of a trading world in the solemn hush of the deep Golfo Placido as if within an enormous semicircular and unroofed temple open to the ocean, with its walls of lofty mountains hung with the mourning draperies of cloud.

This picture is sumptous but not decorative, for the grand indifferent natural setting puts human activity into the perspective Conrad wants. It is a big book, in which the temptations of trade do indeed violate the peace of the gulf and alter the history of the South American republic of Costaguana. The San Tomé silver mine, inherited by Charles Gould, is financed by an American idealist. Its expansion slowly changes lives in the country, including that of the honourable Gould, who believes that 'material interests' and hard work will make Costaguana more peaceful and prosperous. Means become ends, limiting the value of human activity, even the heroic feats of the charismatic Nostromo – 'our man', the agent of the better party in the Revolution.

A varied cast of strongly-marked characters cross and recross a wide and beautiful landscape to sad or tragic ends. There is much irony, and some comedy: the dutiful unimaginative harbourmaster Captain Mitchell enjoys the historic importance of every event. There are time shifts in the narration, so that even the most picturesque actions fall into patterns from which meaning can be made out, though there is much final suspense. Conrad's interest here is not in individual psychology but in the complex web of human action and in moments of grand and petty drama. It is a deeply satisfying work, epic in scale and of a similar standing to *Middlemarch*, more visual, less parochial, and involving our sympathies less immediately.

Political complexities also preoccupy the other two major novels, where Conrad's sense of human absurdity becomes more intimate and Dickensian. James and Conrad were to be models for T. S. Eliot in his effort to regain for poetry some of the ground it had lost to the novel.

## E. M. Forster

An Edwardian novelist appreciated in England is **Edward Morgan Forster** (1879–1970), who wrote four pre-war novels, *Where Angels Fear to Tread* (1905), *The Longest Journey* (1907), *A Room with a View* (1908) and *Howards End* (1910). Forster was brought up by his mother; a great-aunt left him money. After Kings College, Cambridge, he acted as a tutor and a private secretary, and became associated with the Bloomsbury group (see page 340).

Forster's first short story shows his mastery of the comedy of manners: 'The Story of a Panic' (1904) sets conventional English tourists against natural Greeks. *A Room with a View* has several panics, in a comic Florence *pensione* and then in Surrey, setting inhibited upper- against liberated lower-class characters. Under the motto 'Only connect', *Howards End* offers a liberal hope for the future in the marriage of the sensitive Helen Schlegel to the businessman Henry Wilcox in the house of the title. Both novels offer an analysis of an evolving England which might be saved by tolerance, forbearance and sympathy in personal relations, often presented through female characters. *A Passage to India* (1924), however, though advocating the same virtues through Mrs Moore and Mr Fielding, shows English and Indian differences as irreconcilable, thanks largely to English prejudice. Adela Quested, hoping to see the 'real' India, is taken to the famous Marabar Caves by the anglophile Muslim Dr Aziz.

E. M. Forster (1879–1970).

The caves have a strange echo – 'ou-boum'. She panics, accusing him of a sexual approach. At the trial, she withdraws the charge, but Aziz turns away from Fielding's friendship towards an India without the British. Connection is not only a personal matter.

This ambitious novel in three parts, Mosque, Caves and Temple, has Forster's clear shaping of theme, and a plot cleverly balanced on the fault-line of interracial sexual contact and the incident of the cave. What 'happened' is left unclear – probably nothing. We are shown the Brahmin Professor Godbole serene amid the festival at the Hindu temple, but Forster is more indulgent to non-Christian mysticism than to the possibility of the divine. 'Ou-Boum', the echo in the Caves, says to the Hindu sacred word 'Om' what 'Hocus Pocus' says to the Latin words of consecration, *Hoc est corpus meum*. Much ado, little connection.

Forster may have been a 'thesis' novelist who lost his thesis. Though he had used his gift with tact and charm, he wrote no more fiction. The posthumously published *Maurice* was completed in 1910. His *Aspects of the Novel* (1927), 'intellectually null' for F. R. Leavis, is useful to the more modest.

## Ford Madox Ford

Ford Madox Ford (1873–1939) presided over the transition towards modernist writing, as typefied in Joyce's *Ulysses* and T. S. Eliot's *The Waste Land* (both 1922). Ford was grandson to the Pre-Raphaelite painter Ford Madox Brown and nephew to W. M. Rossetti, the brother of D. G. and Christina. His father was Dr Francis Hueffer, music critic of *The Times* and author of *The Troubadours*; Ford changed his name from Hueffer after the war. In 1906–8, he wrote *The Fifth Queen*, a picturesque Tudor trilogy about Henry VIII's Catherine Howard. Conrad called it 'the swan song of Historical Romance'. In 1908, Ford founded *The English Review*, editing it for fifteen months and making literary history.

Number 1 included contributions from Hardy, James ('The Jolly Corner'), Conrad, Wells, W. H. Hudson, R. B. Cunninghame Graham, W. H. Davies, Galsworthy and Tolstoy – 'The Raid', translated by Constance Garnett. Later issues had contributions from Bennett, Yeats, Chesterton, Belloc and George Moore. Ford also introduced Ezra Pound, Wyndham Lewis, Rupert Brooke, E. M. Forster, Lowes Dickinson and

Norman Douglas to a wider public, and published on sight a story submitted by post, 'Odour of Chrysanthemums' by an unknown D. H. Lawrence.

Ford bridged the generations, but after the war some of these names were 'modern', others were not. Ezra Pound, the chief modernizer of English poetry, said that it was Ford who modernized him, by laughing at the stilted language of his third slim volume – laughing till he rolled on the floor. Ford, half a Pre-Raphaelite, knew where Pound's medieval stilts had come from. He could now describe his *Fifth Queen* as 'a fake more or less genuine in inspiration and workmanship, but none the less a fake'. *The English Review* was a turning point in his own development.

Ford's best novel, *The Good Soldier* (1915), is a feat of narration. It uses indirect disclosure on a subject to which it is peculiarly suited: the discovery by a seemingly foolish narrator, John Dowell, that his wife Florence, an invalid with a 'bad heart', has betrayed him with his friend Edward Ashburnham, the soldier of the title; Florence and Edward commit suicide, and Edward's ward goes mad. Dowell bumblingly unwraps a many-sided horror, in Henry James's manner, but with less tissue-paper.

More attractive if less economical is *Parade's End* (1924–8), a quartet also known as the Tietjens tetralogy, after its hero Christopher Tietjens, a Yorkshire squire rooted in an old idea of England. At the war's end, Tietjens leaves his treacherous wife Sylvia for the suffragette schoolteacher Valentine Wannop. The inner volumes draw on Ford's own war experiences. Also very attractive are Ford's fictionalized literary reminiscences, *Return to Yesterday* (1931) and *It Was the Nightingale* (1933), his travel book *Provence* and his wonderful *The March of Literature* (1938). In all the later books, the reader can hear Ford's voice speaking. This is significant, since after a cultural transition, writing has to regain a vital relation with the speech of the day, and such a shift had begun before 1914. The last of Ford's eighty books to appear (in 1988) was *A History of Our Own Times, I (1875–95)*, written in 1930.

# Poetry

## Pre-war verse

After 1900, the Romantic impulse became less rhetorical and its subjects became simpler. Apart from Hardy and Yeats, great talents were few. Kipling's 'The Way through the Woods' is an example of a successfully nostalgic Edwardian poem:

> They shut the road through the woods
> Seventy years ago.
> Weather and rain have undone it again,
> And now you would never know
> There was once a road through the woods
> Before they planted the trees.
> It is underneath the coppice and heath
> And the thin anemones.
> Only the keeper sees
> That, where the ring-dove broods,
> And the badgers roll at ease,
> There was once a road through the woods.

John Masefield, W. H. Davies and Walter de la Mare were Edwardians who also appeared in the first of Edward Marsh's five anthologies of *Georgian Poetry*, which came out between 1912 and 1922. Successful anthologies establish poetic taste. Palgrave's *Golden Treasury* (1861), embodying Tennyson's taste, sold well for a century; it was enlarged in 1896. Marsh preferred something more modest: Abercrombie, Drinkwater, Gibson. Less dim names are Rupert Brooke, J. E. Flecker, D. H. Lawrence, James Stephens, Robert Graves, Siegfried Sassoon, Isaac Rosenberg, and Harold Monro, whose Poetry Bookshop in Devonshire Street, London, offered readings (and beds) to many poets.

Headline literary history sometimes pretends that 'Georgian Poetry' (hedgerows, tweed and cider) was deservedly replaced by 'War Poetry' or by 'Modernist Poetry'. Yet war poets and modernist poets appeared in *Georgian Poetry*, and Ezra Pound in *The Oxford Book of Victorian Verse* (1912).

## Thomas Hardy

Thomas Hardy wrote the most ambitious Edwardian poetry in *The Dynasts* (1904, 1906, 1908), an epic verse drama on the Napoleonic wars, set in various continental theatres and in Wessex, where Bonaparte was expected to land. There are Choruses of the Spirits of the Years and the Pities, as in Greek tragedy and Wagner's opera. It rewards, but rarely gets, a reading. Its epic historical panorama and lofty viewpoint suggest a comparison with Pound's *Cantos* and Eliot's *The Waste Land*; from this Hardy emerges with some solid qualities. But by common consent his best work is found scattered through the six volumes from *Wessex Poems* (1898) to *Winter Words* (1928). He wrote nearly a thousand poems.

Hardy, Yeats and Eliot, who dominate 20th-century English poetry, differ hugely. Hardy can be read without preface or note. He discouraged theorizers by remarks such as 'there is no new poetry', 'unadjusted impressions have their value' and 'no harmonious philosophy is attempted in these pages – or in any bygone pages of mine, for that matter' (1928). His unadjusted impressions are miscellaneous, and the collections, apart from the *Poems of 1912–13*, are unshaped. Many were written before 1900, but his style did not change. Although Hardy deepened, no critic could make a career out of explaining his 'development'. He wrote workmanlike poems, from 'Domicilium' in his teens, to 'During Wind and Rain' in his eighties, hundreds of them excellent. His quality is acknowledged by subsequent poets as very English. Having no intellectual, political or artistic programme, he is easier to anthologize than to write about. But unpretentiousness should not be misprized; sketches and watercolours make a strong contribution to English art. In Helen Gardner's *New Oxford Book of English Verse* (1972), only Shakespeare and Wordsworth had more poems than Hardy; in Philip Larkin's *Oxford Book of Twentieth-Century Verse* (1973), Hardy had more than anyone.

Apart from a few ballads, the poems are apparently personal and occasional, prompted by place, time and mood. The title *Moments of Vision* (1917) suggests Hardy's tradition from Wordsworth, Shelley and Browning. He owed much to his friend the Rev. William Barnes (1801–86), a gifted writer of verse in standard English and Dorset dialect. Barnes's example (in poems such as 'Woak Hill' and 'Linden Lea') showed how local speech could ground a lyric in everyday life. To Hardy no word or thing was in itself unpoetic or poetic: his poems range from the tiny to the great. The interest of Hardy lies not in his attempted 'philosophy', but in his religious regard for the universe and its inhabitants, a country supernaturalism. His landscapes are full of omens and presences, and he wished to be remembered for his habit of noticing them, as he says in 'Afterwards':

> … If, when hearing that I have been stilled at last, they stand at the door,
>     Watching the full-starred heavens that winter sees,
> Will this thought rise on those who will meet my face no more,
>     'He was one who had an eye for such mysteries'?
>
> And will any say when my bell of quittance is heard in the gloom,
>     And a crossing breeze cuts a pause in its outrollings,
> Till they rise again, as they were a new bell's boom,
>     'He hears it not now, but used to notice such things'?

There is a surprising amount of rising here, but Hardy is a surprising writer. The strong metrical tune of his verse carries his 'unadjusted' diction well.

As Pound said, Hardy's *Poems of 1912–13* 'lift him to his apex, sixteen poems from "The Going" to "Castle Boterel", all good, and enough for a lifetime.' They are plangent elegies for his wife, who had died suddenly, and for the love they had at first enjoyed. Alongside the poems Pound mentions, 'The Voice', 'Beeny Cliff' and 'After a Journey' stand out.

> I see what you are doing: you are leading me on
>     To the spots we knew when we haunted here together,
> The waterfall, above which the mist-bow shone
>     At the then fair hour in the then fair weather,
> And the cave just under, with a voice still so hollow
>     That it seems to call out to me from forty years ago,
>         When you were all aglow,
> And not the thin ghost that I now fraily follow!
>
> ('After A Journey')

## War poetry and war poets

In 1915 Hardy published 'In Time of "The Breaking of Nations"':

> Only a man harrowing clods
>     In a slow silent walk
> With an old horse that stumbles and nods
>     Half asleep as they stalk.
>
> Only thin smoke without flame
>     From the heaps of couch-grass;
> Yet this will go onward the same
>     Though Dynasties pass.
>
> Yonder a maid and her wight
>     Come whispering by:
> War's annals will fade into night
>     Ere their story die.

This poem, Hardy says, was prompted by farm workers he saw in Cornwall in 1870 during the Franco-Prussian War, but he 'did not write the verses till during the war with Germany of 1914'. Hardy was thus a war poet; as was Kipling, who lost his son, and wrote a sombre set of Epitaphs of the War. The 1914–18 war also lies behind Pound's poetry from 1915, and Eliot's *The Waste Land.* Eliot said that Ford's 'Antwerp' was the only good poem he had met with on the subject of the war.

Popularly, however, war poetry is about the Front, and by young combatants: typically, **Siegfried Sassoon** (1886–1967), who protested against the mechanized slaughter of the trenches; supremely, his friend **Wilfred Owen** (1893–1918), who was killed; as were **Isaac Rosenberg** (1890–1918) and **Edward Thomas** (1878–1917). Accounts which focus on anti-war poems usually employ **Rupert Brooke** (1887–1915) as a foil. Brooke had welcomed the war in a spirit of patriotic idealism: 'If I should die, think only this of me,/That there's some corner of a foreign field/That is forever England' ('The Soldier'). After his death on the way to Gallipoli, the handsome young Brooke was held up as a symbolic type of the myriad of young officers lost in the war. After the battle of the Somme in 1916, the losses of the trenches blighted the idea of heroic sacrifice. Poems such as Sassoon's 'The General', Owen's 'Anthem for Doomed Youth', Rosenberg's 'Break of Day in the Trenches' and 'To His Love' by Ivor Gurney immerse us in that stalemate in the mud for which even professional soldiers were unprepared. The last battle anywhere near Britain had been Waterloo in 1815. The poems of Sassoon and Owen came to the fore after 1918, and came to express national mourning. The outraged sense that the wastage of the trenches must not be forgotten gave a symbolic value to Sassoon's savagely effective protest verse and to Owen's pathos. Both men returned to the front, Owen to die; Sassoon survived, to write *Memoirs of a Fox-Hunting Man* (1928) and *Memoirs of an Infantry Officer* (1930).

In 1914 poetry was still a natural medium for the expression of public feelings; the newspapers printed many patriotic poems. Survivors also wrote prose about the war: the novel *Death of a Hero*, by Richard Aldington (1892–1962), and the memoir *Goodbye to All That*, by Robert Graves (1895–1985), both 1929. The 'home front' is commemorated in the popular *Testament of Youth* (1933), by Vera Brittain (1893–1970). Of the scores of books about the war, the account by Edmund Blunden (1896–1974) of going to the front in *Undertones of War* (1928) should be read with *In Parenthesis* (1937) by David Jones (1895–1974) and Ford's *No More Parades* (1924–8).

'Over the top': British troops climb out of a trench towards the barbed wire, in 1916.

The best poet who came to light in the war, and fell in it, is the Anglo-Welsh **Edward Thomas** (1878–1917). Thomas had lived by writing 'countryside' prose and reviewing verse, until, encouraged by the American poet Robert Frost, he turned poet late in 1914. Poems such as 'Adlestrop', 'The Owl' and 'As the Team's Head Brass' approach the war indirectly through the life of rural England in peacetime, a contrast with the shock tactics of the protest poems. They have the effect of the similes in Homer which liken wartime to peacetime sights or activities. Natural observation accrues an understated symbolic suggestion in a poem like 'Lights Out', which, like another fine poem, 'Old Man', makes no reference to war but accepts death. Later English poets have seen Hardy and Edward Thomas as continuing an English tradition.

Yeats dismissed Owen with the words 'Passive suffering is not a theme for poetry'; his own poems on the Easter Rising in Dublin in 1916 strike a more heroic note. Although Owen's pathos can cloy, his poems speak immediately, and are set for school examinations. The Owen-Sassoon story was often recycled later, but the literary merit of the poems has been exaggerated. Precious witness to a traumatic national experience, they are not major modern poems, though their simple emotions are easier to respond to than the adult poetry of the modernists.

## ◾ Further reading

Bergonzi, B. *Heroes' Twilight: A Study of the Literature of the Great War*, 2nd edn (London: Constable, 1980).

Fussell, P. *The Great War and Modern Memory* (Oxford: Oxford University Press, 1975).

# CHAPTER 13

## Overview

Two pieces of writing published in 1922, James Joyce's *Ulysses* and T. S. Eliot's *The Waste Land*, differed in form from the novels and poems that had preceded them. This was the crest of a new wave in English literature, from Ezra Pound's *Lustra* and Joyce's *Dubliners* in 1914 to Virginia Woolf's *To the Lighthouse* in 1927. The modern writing of Joyce, Pound, Eliot and D. H. Lawrence came when Hardy, Conrad, Shaw, Kipling and Ford were still writing, and Yeats was becoming a powerful poet. This writing, new and old, makes the period 1914–27 the richest in 20th-century English literature. It may be the richest since the Romantics, and certainly since the years about 1850, when many novelists and poets flourished.

## Contents

## ◼ 'Modernism': 1914–27

These modern writers are often called modernists. The word 'modernism' is a convenience term, for the '-ism' of the new is hard to define; it therefore appears in this text without a capital letter. Although the present had begun – before 1914 – to feel more than usually different from the past, there were no agreed principles for an artistic programme. Rather, the old ways would not do any more. Behind this cultural shift were changes in society, politics and technology, and slackening family, local and religious ties. As the value for the human person fostered by Christianity and continuing in liberal humanism weakened, Marx, Freud and Nietzsche, the fathers of modern atheism, were read. But these general factors do not point to an obvious formulation which fits these writers as a group. Ambitious, they broke with prevailing formal conventions. 'Modern Art', meaning the painting of Picasso, the music of Stravinsky and the poetry of Eliot, soon became a historical label.

After a war won at a dire cost in blood, spirit and money, London was no longer the centre to which Pound and Eliot had come, in the steps of Henry James. Younger Americans went to Paris. Pound left for Paris and Italy, Ford for Paris and the US, Lawrence for wilder shores, leaving Virginia Woolf as the sole remaining Anglo-modernist who was entirely English. Modernist literature was not very English, and was largely written by exiles. *Exiles* is the name of a play by James Joyce, who avoided England. When the Irish Free State was created in 1921, Joyce had been thirty-nine years a British citizen. Yeats, who was then fifty-seven, continued to spend much of his time in England. **Samuel Beckett** (1906–89), sometimes called the last modernist, left Ireland in 1937 for Paris. (Yeats and Pound get less space here than they would in histories of Irish or American literature.)

# D. H. Lawrence

D(avid) H(erbert) Lawrence (1885–1930) had a prophet's lack of interest in aesthetics. His first mature work, *Sons and Lovers* (1913), like his play *The Widowing of Mrs Holroyd* (1914), has a 19th-century base – a slice of domestic life – and purpose: to make a strong emotional impact. When the Son (Paul Morel) has escaped from his mother's suffocating love and two love-affairs – one spiritual, one carnal – the narrative stops. It is autobiographical: Lawrence grew up in a Nottinghamshire pit village; at home, his high-minded non-conformist mother cherished him; his father, a miner, felt out of place.

    Although Lawrence came later to repudiate his mother's ideals and to sympathize with his father, he retained an evangelical true-or-false model of what is good, a moral intelligence and a St Paul-like temperament. His writing is powered by

## Publications of the modernist period

1913  D. H. Lawrence, *Sons and Lovers*; Compton Mackenzie, *Sinister Street*.

1914  James Joyce, *Dubliners*; W. B. Yeats, *Responsibilities*; Ezra Pound (ed.), *Des Imagistes*; Thomas Hardy, *Satires of Circumstance*; George Moore, *Hail and Farewell*; George Bernard Shaw, *Pygmalion*.

1915  Ford Madox Ford, *The Good Soldier*; Lawrence, *The Rainbow*; Richard Aldington, *Images*; Rupert Brooke, *1914 & Other Poems*; Ezra Pound, *Lustra, Cathay*.

1916  James Joyce, *A Portrait of the Artist as a Young Man*.

1917  T. S. Eliot, *Prufrock and Other Observations*; Norman Douglas, *South Wind*.

1918  Gerard Hopkins, *Poems* (ed. Robert Bridges); D. G. Wyndham Lewis, *Tarr*; Lytton Strachey, *Eminent Victorians*; Siegfried Sassoon, *Counter-Attack*.

1919  Eliot, *Poems*; W. B. Yeats, *The Wild Swans at Coole*; Pound, *Homage to Sextus Propertius*.

1920  Ezra Pound, *Hugh Selwyn Mauberley*; Lawrence, *Women in Love*; Eliot, *Poems, 1920, The Sacred Wood*; Wilfred Owen, *Poems* (ed. Siegried Sassoon); Shaw, *Heartbreak House*.

1921  Aldous Huxley, *Crome Yellow*; Lawrence, *Women in Love*.

1922  Eliot, *The Waste Land*; A. E. Housman, *Last Poems*; John Galsworthy, *The Forsyte Saga*; Isaac Rosenberg, *Poems* (ed. Bottomley); Joyce, *Ulysses*; Katherine Mansfield, *The Garden Party*.

1923  Lawrence, *Kangaroo*; Huxley, *Antic Hay*.

1924  Ford, *Some Do Not*; E. M. Forster, *A Passage to India*; Sean O'Casey, *Juno and the Paycock*.

1925  Ford, *No More Parades*; Lawrence, *St Mawr*; Virginia Woolf, *Mrs Dalloway*; W. B. Yeats, *A Vision*; Hugh MacDiarmid, *Sangschaw*.

1926  MacDiarmid, *A Drunk Man Looks at the Thistle*; Ford, *A Man Could Stand Up*; T. E. Lawrence, *The Seven Pillars of Wisdom*; Yeats, *Autobiographies*.

1927  Virginia Woolf, *To the Lighthouse*; Wyndham Lewis, *Time and Western Man*; Elizabeth Bowen, *The Hotel*; T. F. Powys, *Mr Weston's Good Wine*.

1928  Yeats, *The Tower*; Lawrence, *Lady Chatterley's Lover*; Sassoon, *Memoirs of a Fox-Hunting Man*; Edmund Blunden, *Undertones of War*; Huxley, *Point Counter Point*; Evelyn Waugh, *Decline and Fall*.

---

tensions between the classes or the sexes or mind and body or, more apocalyptically, between natural life and a civilization of death. His better books enact these struggles, which are reduced to a simple formula in his last novel, *Lady Chatterley's Lover*, in which Sir Clifford Chatterley, paralysed below the waist by a war wound, is in a wheelchair; his gamekeeper, Mellors, satisfies the needs of Lady Constance in clearly described sexual scenes, sacred in intention. It is the woman who admires and needs the man. Lawrence's mission to make the word 'fuck' holy meant that this intensely serious book was banned. Its trial for obscenity in 1960 crowned a history of misunderstandings between Lawrence and official England. The 'permissive' consequences of the 'not guilty' verdict were not what Lawrence would have wanted. *Lady Chatterley's Lover* is a fable lacking the rich density of his major novels, *The Rainbow* (1915) and *Women in Love* (1921), and their prophetic burden.

In some 19th-century French novels, the test of integrity is the willingness of lovers to act on their (extramarital) love. Not so in Nottingham in 1912, when Lawrence ran off with Frieda, the German wife of his old tutor at the University College. She left Professor Ernest Weekley with their three children, went to Germany with Lawrence, and came back to England and married him in 1914; shortly after, her cousin became the leading fighter pilot, Baron von Richthofen. Lawrence was a pacifist, and when police kept an eye on his Cornish cottage, he felt persecuted. He

David Herbert Lawrence, in 1908, at Nottingham University College, aged 23.

was already alienated – by education from his family, by marriage from his friends at home, by intransigence from friends in London. His novels and paintings were often banned for indecency. He travelled incessantly from 1919 to his death – to Italy, Australia, Mexico, New Mexico, Italy and France – pouring out travel books, essays and sketches, as well as *Kangaroo* (1923), *The Plumed Serpent* (1926) and other novels and novellas, and seeking a natural life untainted by modern consciousness. Travel made his alienation and his views more extreme, so that those who were not for him were against him.

As some of his ideas have been accepted (and others rejected: 'The root of sanity is in the balls', for example, or Dostoevsky as 'a rat slithering along in hate'), partisanship has cooled. His writing is alive, uneven: the fresh accuracy of the first impression of Sydney in *Kangaroo* turns to turgidity and an incredible plot. His talent flames out in his poems and travel books, yet often he could not leave well alone. His efforts to raise consciousness of sexuality have succeeded so well that his theories and symbols can now seem over-insistent. (The modern disease was 'sex in the head', he said; yet he wanted no children.) His preaching is curbed in his short stories, and often absent from his informal free-verse sketches, which are autobiographical and of birds, beasts and flowers; these will last. In such glimpses, and some late essays, he is more playful and self-conscious than in his long fictions.

### The Rainbow

His best novel is *The Rainbow* (1915), a saga of three generations of a farming family, the Brangwens. Social life gives way to individual personality; sexual relations are made to express both historical and emotional developments; and there is much symbolism.

Three of his modes – realism, symbolic projection and an exploratory expressionism – are shown in the following passage. Anna Brangwen finds she is expecting a child, but cannot tell her husband, though she loves him. She goes to tell her parents. Her husband walks in:

Tom Brangwen, blue-eyed and warm, sat in opposition to the youth.
  'How long are you stopping?' the young husband asked his wife.
  'Not very long,' she said.

'Get your tea, lad,' said Tom Brangwen. 'Are you itchin' to be off the moment you enter?'

They talked of trivial things. Through the open door the level rays of sunset poured in, shining on the floor. A grey hen appeared stepping swiftly in the doorway, pecking, and the light through her comb and her wattles made an oriflamme tossed here and there, as she went, her grey body was like a ghost.

Anna, watching, threw scraps of bread, and she felt the child flame within her. She seemed to remember again forgotten, burning, far-off things.

'Where was I born, mother?' she asked.

(The 'oriflamme' was a pennon on a lance, in form like a gold flame.) After the men's antagonism, the sun shining through the old hen's crest awakes in Anna a flickering trace of her own birth, and she asks her question. This almost subconscious symbolism, legible today, was subtle in 1915.

*The Rainbow* lies between the realism of *Sons and Lovers* and the symbolism of *Women in Love*, itself a sequel to *The Rainbow*, but more ambitious and intellectually schematic. It is also typically modernist in its alienation, dislike of modern life, and satire on literary, social and intellectual élites. *The Rainbow* makes structural use of the symbolism of the rainbow after the Flood in Genesis. Lawrence made several efforts to replace the Christian story.

## James Joyce

James Joyce (1882–1941) is the central figure in modernist prose, as Eliot is in modernist verse. He makes a contrast with Lawrence: both were rebels, exiles, and victims of censorship, but they had little else in common. Joyce is an artist, deeply interested in the medium and form of his art. Each of his chief works – *Dubliners* (1914), *Portrait of the Artist as a Young Man* (1916), *Ulysses* (1922) and *Finnegans Wake* (1939) – differs in language and approach from its predecessor. Joyce's aim was to leave an impersonal and objective work of art for the reader to interpret, an aim he shared with Eliot, James and Flaubert, but not with Lawrence. 'The artist,' Stephen Dedalus pronounced in *Portrait of the Artist*, 'like the God of creation, remains within or behind or beyond or above his handiwork, invisible, refined out of existence, indifferent, paring his fingernails.'

### *Portrait of the Artist as a Young Man*

Joyce was well educated at Jesuit schools and at University College, Dublin. He became an ex-Catholic (as Lawrence became an ex-Protestant) and an exile, but not an ex-Irishman. He kept away from Dublin, in Trieste and Paris, to remember it the more clearly in his art. Joyce's family were ex-middle class. In *Portrait of the Artist as a Young Man*, Stephen Dedalus (the Artist) is asked what his father was.

Stephen began to enumerate glibly his father's attributes.
—A medical student, an oarsman, a tenor, an amateur actor, a shouting politician, a small landlord, a small investor, a drinker, a good fellow, a storyteller, somebody's secretary, something in a distillery, a taxgatherer, a bankrupt and at present a praiser of his own past.
Cranly laughed, tightening his grip on Stephen's arm, and said:
—The distillery is damn good.

It is characteristic of Dublin's appreciation of speech that Cranly attends to the phrase 'something in a distillery' rather than to what Stephen has said. Joyce himself, in adopting the French convention of a dash rather than quotation marks to introduce direct speech, erased the distinction between words and things. When Joyce told his father that he was marrying, his father asked for the woman's name. On hearing it was Nora Barnacle, he replied, 'She'll stick to you, then.' Such a father had his educational side. Stephen's own wit is appreciated by Cranly, but both are earnest enough young men. '—It is a curious thing, do you know, Cranly said dispassionately, how your mind is supersaturated with the religion in which you say you disbelieve.'

Joyce studied languages, learning enough Norwegian to write to Ibsen. Though he read Yeats and others, much of his modern reading was European. He left Dublin at twenty-one, returning for his mother's death, and leaving shortly afterwards with Nora, a Galway girl who stuck to him but never read his 'dirty books'. Stephen gives Cranly his reasons for leaving:

—I will not serve that in which I no longer believe, whether it call itself my home, my fatherland, or my church: and I will try to express myself in some mode of life or art as freely as I can and as wholly as as I can, using for my defence the only arms I allow myself to use – silence, exile and cunning.

Joyce lived obscurely, teaching English, helped eventually by a number of patrons. Although the first story of *Dubliners* was written in 1904, publication was delayed, so that Joyce's three masterpieces appeared within eight years. *Dubliners* consists of realistic sketches of the lives of ordinary Dubliners, largely of the lower middle class. Each fails to break out of habitual routines, and the cumulative effect is depressing, as in Maupassant's tales of little urban lives and George Moore's *The Untilled Field* (1903). *Dubliners* deals first with children, then gradually with older people; in Joyce's plan, twelve stories in a style of 'scrupulous meanness' would show a Dublin paralysed by family, poverty, bigotry and provincial small-mindedness. Each story is organized through thematic symbols. All Joyce's works have this multi-dimensionality.

Such systematic art, common in Renaissance verse, is previously approached in English fiction only in Austen (who hides it better) and in the late James; and Joyce works in a wider world than theirs. Like Flaubert, he wears gloves of antiseptic irony, but some warmth comes through from such wincing stories as 'A Little Cloud' and 'A Painful Case', where human feelings are given greater purchase. When his omission of Dublin's hospitality was pointed out to him, Joyce added a final longer story, 'The Dead'. This richly elaborate story is set at a Christmas party, where Gabriel Conroy presides at the table of his musical old aunts. The unheroic Gabriel, a wearer of goloshes who takes holidays in Belgium, feels culturally above the company. At the end of the evening he hears from his wife that she had once been loved by a boy from the West who had died for love of her.

Generous tears filled Gabriel's eyes. He had never felt like that himself towards any woman but he knew that such a feeling must be love. The tears gathered more thickly in his eyes and in the partial darkness he imagined he saw the form of a young man standing under a dripping tree. Other forms were near. His soul had approached that region where dwell the vast hosts of the dead. He was conscious of, but could not apprehend, their wayward and flickering existence. His own identity was fading out into a grey impalpable world: the solid world itself which these dead had one time reared and lived in was dissolving and dwindling.

Gabriel is sympathetic, yet remains a spectator. In the next, final paragraph Joyce allows himself to write lyrically and imaginatively about the island he was leaving.

In *A Portrait of the Artist*, first drafted as *Stephen Hero*, Stephen Dedalus tells of his growing up, always in the language and range of sensations suited to each stage of infancy, boyhood, adolescence and student life. He is sensitive and short-sighted, and his experiences are negative: family politics, nationalist and clerical; school tyrannies; sexual experience and ascetic reaction; an invitation to the priesthood; fruitless romantic love; family impoverishment. His wit and learning earn him some respect from fellow students. He has an exalted vision of a girl wading offshore, whom he sees in the likeness of a sea-bird: 'A wild angel had appeared to him, the angel of mortal youth and beauty, an envoy from the fair courts of life, to throw open before him in an instant of ecstasy the gates of all the ways of error and glory.' This is an 'epiphany', a revelation. After it, Stephen

climbed to the crest of the sandhill and gazed about him. Evening had fallen. A rim of the young moon cleft the pale waste of skyline, the rim of a silver hoop embedded in gray sand; and the tide was flowing in fast to the land with a low whisper of her waves, islanding a few last figures in distant ponds.

5

He drained his third cup of watery tea to the dregs and set to chewing the crusts of fried bread that were scattered near him, staring into the dark pool of the jar. The yellow dripping had been scooped out like a boghole …

Transposition of his 'high' into a low register undercuts Stephen, who is less heroic than in *Stephen Hero*; the artist revised the portrait of his younger self.

The private Stephen is less assured than in the epigrams he fires at his fellows. The book ends in diary form, concluding:

Welcome, O life! I go to encounter for the millionth time the reality of experience and to forge in the smithy of my soul the uncreated conscience of my race.
*April 27.* Old father, old artificer, stand me now and ever in good stead.

Stephen is about to fly Dublin; his 'old father' is Dedalus the smith who with his son Icarus flew away from the island of Crete on wings he had made. But Icarus fell, and although Stephen hopes to forge a conscience for his race, the bags his mother has packed for him contain 'new secondhand clothes'. How to take this aspirant to art is unclear, but there is an ambiguity in 'forge' of which he is unaware. It is a portrait of a self-absorbed young man.

## Ulysses

The case is changed in *Ulysses*, in which Stephen Dedalus plays second fiddle to Leopold Bloom, a Jewish advertising agent, who acts as a father figure to him. Much of the book consists of Bloom's mingled impressions and reflections as he wanders round Dublin, going to a funeral, a pub, a newspaper office and other locations. He meets Stephen, whose stream of consciousness is more elevated, and helps him.

Unity of place and time is observed in this unclassical book, all of which takes place in Dublin on 16 June 1904. *Ulysses* ends with Molly Bloom's soliloquy in bed saying 'Yes', and opens in the Martello Tower, south of Dublin, where Stephen is staying.

Stately, plump Buck Mulligan came from the stairhead, bearing a bowl of lather on which a mirror and a razor lay crossed. A yellow dressing-gown, ungirdled, was sustained gently behind him by the mild morning air. He held the bowl aloft and intoned:
　　—*Introibo ad altare Dei.*

Mulligan plays the priest beginning the Latin mass, a comic blasphemy which is to be matched by a closing parody. For Mrs Bloom, who is talking as the book ends, is a comic inversion of the Penelope to whom Odysseus returns at the end of Homer's

*Odyssey*. Unlike the faithful Penelope, Molly (a singer) awaits a lover, 'Blazes' Boylan. Bloom is unheroic, indecent and unlike Odysseus; and Stephen is unlike Telemachus, Odysseus' faithful son. 'Ulysses' (pronounced '*Oo*-liss-ays' by Joyce) is the modern form of 'Odysseus' in later Western literature; *Ulysses* parodies much of that tradition.

This encyclopædic tendency makes it an epic (of a heroi-comical sort) as much as a novel. Its chapters shadow episodes of the *Odyssey*, and Joyce used 'Proteus', 'Nausicaa' etc. as working titles for chapters, and charted the correspondences with Homer's story. These names do not appear in the text – which can be read without Homer, although one misses some of the jokes. Mulligan looks out to sea.

—God, he said quietly. Isn't the sea what Algy calls it: a grey sweet mother? The snotgreen sea. The scrotumtightening sea. Epi oinopa ponton. Ah, Dedalus, the Greeks. I must teach you. You must read them in the original …

'Algy' is Algernon Charles Swinburne, who wrote 'I will go back to the great [*not* grey] sweet mother'. The Greek phrase means 'on the wine-dark sea'. Mulligan (based on the wit Oliver St John Gogarty) coins new Homeric compound epithets, indecent in their naturalism. Dedalus reads Greek. Joyce has his revenge on Mulligan when he has an old woman ask him 'Are you a medical student, sir?'

To read *Ulysses* it is not necessary to know Homer, Shakespeare's biography, the history of the English language, Dublin's geography or Ireland's history, though all of these are part of its matter, as are newspapers, dirty postcards and a nightmare in the brothel area. But *Ulysses* cannot be read without a relish for words, a sense of fun, and a tolerance for jokes, including allusions once clear but now obscure. The Latin Mass, for example, was dropped in the 1960s by the Second Vatican Council, and its opening can no longer be effectively parodied. Readers cannot look for steady progress in a single mode and an ordered syntax. Nor can *Ulysses* be read for the story, for the texture of many of its 933 pages is so intricate or discontinuous that the text becomes a world of its own. Today it is read in universities, often in selection. Bits of it are brilliantly, outrageously comic. All of it is clever, most repays rereading, much has to be puzzled out, some is simply showing off.

*Ulysses* is difficult but not intellectual. The chief conduit for its 'stream of consciousness' is Leopold Bloom, who is not high-minded. M'Coy asks him about Paddy Dignam's funeral just when Bloom had been hoping to catch a glimpse of the legs of a lady getting into a carriage opposite.

Watch! Watch! Silk flash rich stockings white. Watch!
A heavy tramcar honking its gong slewed between.
Lost it. Curse your noisy pugnose. Feels locked out of it. Paradise and the peri. Always happening like that. The very moment. Girl in Eustace street hallway. Monday was it settling her garter. Her friend covering the display of. *Esprit de corps*. Well, what are you gaping at?
—Yes, yes, Mr Bloom said after a dull sigh. Another gone.
—One of the best, M'Coy said.
The tram passed. They drove off towards the Loop Line bridge, her rich gloved hand on the steel grip. Flicker, flicker: the laceflare of her hat in the sun: flicker, flick.
—Wife well, I suppose? M'Coy's changed voice said.
—O yes, Mr Bloom said. Tiptop, thanks.
He unrolled the newspaper baton idly and read idly:
>    *What is home without*
>    *Plumtree's Potted Meat?*
>    *Incomplete.*
>    *With it an abode of bliss.*
—My missus has just got an engagement. At least, it's not settled yet.

Eliot welcomed *Ulysses* as a masterpiece, Forster and Virginia Woolf turned up their noses. Although it has a medical student's sense of humour – frank, smelly, even disgusting – it lacks disdain for contemporary common life. The unedifying Bloom has finer feelings too, chiefly for his family, and is kind to Stephen. Regarding his wife's adultery, he feels 'the futility of triumph or protest or vindication'. Posterity has agreed with Eliot.

*Finnegans Wake*, the work of seventeen years, extends the half-asleep monologue into a phantasmagoria of names and initials who change identity. Much of it is dreamed by a drunken Dublin publican called H. C. Earwicker (HCE, 'Here Comes Everyone'). Another character is Anna Livia Plurabelle (ALP), who is also the river Liffey. A long inter-lingual pun on world literature, it is a good write rather than a good read. The right book for those who believe that there is no right reading, it is also a long joke played on its readers.

## Ezra Pound: the London years

In his years in London, 1908–20, **Ezra Pound** (1885–1972) collaborated with W. B. Yeats, published Joyce, 'discovered' T. S. Eliot and edited *The Waste Land*. In thanks, Eliot dedicated the poem to him in a phrase from Dante, *il miglior fabbro* ('the better workman'). In compliment to his translations in *Cathay*, Eliot called Pound 'the inventor of Chinese poetry for our time'. Pound also invented the influential poetic movement which he called 'Imagism'. 'In a very short time,' Ford wrote of Pound, recalling the palmy days of *The English Review*, 'he had taken charge of me, the review and finally of London.' '*Most important influence since Wordsworth*' was the headline in the London *Observer* on Pound's death. Yet in 1965, at Eliot's memorial service in Westminster Abbey, few recognized Pound. In the intervening years, he had returned to London only in the memories recorded in the *Pisan Cantos* (1948). But his London years are part of this story.

Pound's Imagism called for verbal concentration, direct treatment of the object and expressive rhythm – as against the long-winded rhetoric and metrical regularity of the Victorians, the style in which he had himself grown up. Other Imagists were the American poet H. D. (Hilda Doolittle) and her husband Richard Aldington; echoes can be heard in the poems of T. E. Hulme and in Eliot's *Preludes*. Pound's critical impetus is recognized better than the poetry he wrote in England: *Personae* (1909), *Ripostes* (1912), *Lustra* and *Cathay* (1914), *Homage to Sextus Propertius* (1917), *Hugh Selwyn Mauberley* (1920).

An Imagist fragment in the volume *Lustra* is 'Fan-Piece, for her Imperial Lord', written by a Chinese emperor's courtesan:

> O fan of white silk,
> > clear as frost on the grass-blade,
> You also are laid aside.

The eloquence of this comparison lies in what is not stated but implied. To temper emotion, Pound often uses remote literary masks or modes, from Provençal, Latin or Chinese, or the Anglo-Saxon 'Seafarer'. His translations were to be imitated, but the new poetry was pushed aside by the war, as can be felt in the background of 'Exile's Letter' in *Cathay* and the defence of love in *Propertius*:

Dry wreaths drop their petals,
their stalks are woven in baskets,
To-day we take the great breath of lovers,
to-morrow fate shuts us in.

Though you give all your kisses

you give but few.

*Mauberley* traces the stultifying treatment given to art and poetry in Victorian England, which produced the marginal imaginary poet Mauberley. The English reaction to Pound's *Propertius* appears as 'Better mendacities/Than the classics in paraphrase'. English advice to Pound appears as 'Accept opinion. The "Nineties" tried your game/And died, there's nothing in it.' Pound took his epic *Cantos* elsewhere. He described them as a mystery story trying to solve the historical crime of the First World War. *The Cantos* offered a model for *The Waste Land*, but the splendours and delusions of Pound's later work lie outside English literature.

## T. S. Eliot

T(**homas**) S(**tearns**) **Eliot** (1887–1965) was born in St Louis, Missouri, where his grandfather had founded the university. The family came from New England, to which an English ancestor had emigrated in the 17th century. After school in Boston, and Harvard University, he studied philosophy in Marburg, Paris and Oxford. In London when war began, he married an Englishwoman and stayed on. After the success of *The Waste Land* and his criticism, he edited *The Criterion*, a review, and joined the publisher, Faber. In 1927 the daring modern became a British subject, and proclaimed himself 'classicist in literature, royalist in politics, and anglo-catholic in religion'.

Eliot's pre-eminence was critical as well as poetic. In the discipline of English, new at Cambridge in the 1920s, there was no god but Eliot, and the critics I. A. Richards and F. R. Leavis were his prophets. Disciples passed the word to the English-studying world. In 1948 Eliot was awarded the Nobel Prize and the Order of Merit. *The Waste Land* was 'modern poetry'; his wartime *Four Quartets* were revered; his plays ran in the West End. *Cats* (1981), a musical based on *Old Possum's Book of Practical Cats*

From the left, Ford Madox Ford, James Joyce, Ezra Pound and John Quinn (1923). Quinn, a New York lawyer, bought the manuscript of T. S. Eliot's *The Waste Land*.

(1939), has earned millions, with lyrics rewritten to turn Eliot's nonsense for intelligent children into singable whimsy for tired parents.

## The Love Song of J. Alfred Prufrock

The poetry Eliot chose to publish is perfected; he grouped some of the work in his *Collected Poems* as 'Minor Poems'. His non-dramatic work has fewer weak poems than that of any poet of the 19th century. Most notable are *The Love Song of J. Alfred Prufrock* (written in 1911 and published by Pound in *The Egoist*, 1915); *The Waste Land* (1922); and *Four Quartets* (completed in 1942). Between the first two came disconcerting but chillingly polished quatrain poems such as 'Sweeney Among the Nightingales' (1918); between the second, a series of poems recording painful progress towards a rather ghostly Christianity, notably *Ash Wednesday*. (At this time Eliot's wife became mentally ill; he and her brother signed the order to place her in an asylum in 1938; she died in 1947. A second marriage in 1957 was happy.)

> Let us go then, you and I,
> When the evening is spread out against the sky
> Like a patient etherised upon a table;
> Let us go, through certain half-deserted streets,
> The muttering retreats
> Of restless nights in one-night cheap hotels
> And sawdust restaurants with oyster shells;
> Streets that follow like a tedious argument
> Of insidious intent
> To lead you to an overwhelming question …
> Oh, do not ask, 'What is it?'
> Let us go and make our visit.

So begins Prufrock's love song. The twisting of meaning in 'spread out' is characteristic of Eliot's doubleness: the romantic evening is displayed as for surgery. The likeness of the evening clouds to a supine patient is more than visual, for the passive sufferer never makes his visit nor asks 'the overwhelming question'. Images of heroic martyrdom suggest that the question might have been 'To be or not to be'; images of distant sexual attraction, 'Could you love me?' Absurd rhymes make it clear that Prufrock is capable of neither love nor sacrifice; insistent rhythms suggest a ritual approach to a climax that syntax always defers. Accepting that the visit would not have been 'worth it after all', Prufrock faces the future:

> Shall I part my hair behind? Do I dare to eat a peach?
> I shall wear white flannel trousers, and walk upon the beach.
> I have heard the mermaids singing, each to each.
>
> I do not think that they will sing to me.

## The Waste Land

Dramatic monologues are multiplied in *The Waste Land*, an earlier title for which was 'He Do the Police in Different Voices' (words found in Dickens's *Our Mutual Friend*). The poem collates modern voices and ancient beauty and wisdom; its lives are incoherent, shabby, incomplete, unloving, lost. But not all is lost.

> O City city, I can sometimes hear
> Beside a public bar in Lower Thames Street,
> The pleasant whining of a mandoline

And a clatter and a chatter from within
Where fishmen lounge at noon: where the walls
Of Magnus Martyr hold
Inexplicable splendour of Ionian white and gold.

The men have finished work, bringing fish up from the Thames to Billingsgate market. Magnus Martyr, near which Eliot then worked in Lloyd's Bank, is one of Christopher Wren's churches in the City of London. After the war, it was proposed that nineteen of them should be demolished as redundant. 'St Magnus Martyr', says Eliot's note, has 'to my mind one of the finest among Wren's interiors'. Its columns are Ionic, which Eliot varies to evoke the Ionian Sea. Whatever its interior, the church is dedicated to a hero who preferred to be killed rather than to shed blood. 'Martyr' and 'Ionian' contribute inexplicable qualities. Words, said Eliot, have 'tentacular roots … reaching down to our deepest fears and desires'.

It is easier to write about *The Waste Land*'s themes than its words, images, sounds and rhythms. Yet Eliot's favourite line in the poem was 'drip drop drip drop drop drop drop'. He insisted that 'a poem has to be experienced before it is understood'. His is a poem of images placed side by side, a multiplex version of an Imagist poem such as Pound's 'Fan-Piece'. The ending is prefaced by 'these fragments I have shored against my ruins'. Fragments had long been potentially sublime in poetry, but less romantic fragments had recently been in the air.

What is that sound high in the air
Murmur of maternal lamentation
Who are those hooded hordes swarming
Over endless plains, stumbling in cracked earth
Ringed by the flat horizon only
What is the city over the mountains
Cracks and reforms and bursts in the violet air
Falling towers
Jerusalem Athens Alexandria
Vienna London
Unreal.

This is from the last part, 'What the Thunder Said', where (Eliot notes) 'three themes are employed: the journey to Emmaus, the approach to the Chapel Perilous (see Miss Weston's book), and the present decay of eastern Europe'. (Emmaus is the city to which disciples walked after the death of Jesus; Jessie L. Weston's book is *From Ritual to Romance*; and the 'present decay' is the break-up of Austria-Hungary.) Themes are not stated but 'employed', like motifs in music. The 'maternal lamentation' of mothers in Vienna and London are entwined with those of the women of Jerusalem whom Christ told to weep not for him but for themselves and for their children. Their city was to be destroyed, but would re-form above the mountains: blown sky-high and reconstituted as a heavenly Jerusalem.

In editing the poem, Pound had cut out half of it, increasing fragmentation and intensity. He wrote to the author that at nineteen pages it was now 'the longest poem in the English language'. But the publisher wanted something for the blank pages at the back, and Eliot supplied notes explaining that the poem's title and plan were suggested by Miss Weston's book on the Grail legend. A devastated world is presented as a Waste Land where no crops grow, no children are born, and sex is unlovely. Eliot's fragments illustrate this theme, looking finally to religious texts for answers,

T(homas) S(tearns) Eliot (1887–1965), a studio portrait. This was the man whom Arthur Waugh compared to 'a drunken Helot' (see page 345).

Christian and Hindu: 'Prison and palace and reverberation/Of thunder of spring over distant mountains'. Is the thunder at the death of Christ the thunder that brings rain for the sacred river Ganges? Eliot uses many languages to pose unanswered questions in inclusive mythological forms bearing several senses.

In his essay 'The Metaphysical Poets' (1921) Eliot credited Donne with a 'unified sensibility' in which thoughts and feelings were not dissociated, as they were to become. In 'Tradition and the Individual Talent' (1919), he separated the man that suffers from the mind that creates, recommending impersonal art rather than romantic self-expression. Like Joyce, T. E. Hulme, Pound and Wyndham Lewis, and unlike Lawrence, Eliot opposed the idea that good poetry is the spontaneous over-flow of powerful feeling. Poetry, he says, may arise from emotion and can arouse emotion, but its composition is an art guided by intelligence. This fits his own work. *The Waste Land* is an agonizing poem, written after a nervous breakdown arising from overwork and marital unhappiness. Lines can be linked to places Eliot visited – 'On Margate Sands/I can connect/Nothing with nothing' and 'By the waters of Leman I sat down and wept' – but this tells little of a poem which transcends its occasions, and whose apparent incoherence is composed with care. It is planned as a musical drama for male and female voices in a represented world to which a reason-able reaction would be agony.

Eliot later pooh-poohed the idea that *The Waste Land* had articulated post-war disillusion, describing it as 'a fit of rhythmical grumbling'. But by the late 1920s he had became central to English literary culture. Undergraduates quoted with delight lines expressive of a modern emptiness: 'This is the way the world ends/Not with a bang but a whimper' ('The Hollow Men'); 'birth and copulation and death', and 'Any man has to, needs to, wants to/Once in a lifetime, do a girl in' (*Sweeney Ago-nistes*). But Eliot turned away from Sweeney – a modern savage, Prufrock's opposite – towards something graver. He came to believe that the comparative anthropology underlying *The Waste Land*, which relativized the higher religions and seemed to explain them away as sophistications of nature-cults and vegetation ceremonies, was mistaken, and that truth lay in the opposite direction. After his Anglican conversion, Dante replaced Donne as his model. His later poetry is less agonized and dramatic.

His play *Murder in the Cathedral* (1935), commissioned by Canterbury, is success-ful; Becket's martyrdom in defence of Christian claims was close to Eliot's new position. *The Family Reunion* (1939) was the first of four mysterious dramas, disguised as bright West End comedies in ever less noticeable verse. The implicit themes, dedication, sacrifice, transfiguration, healing, are at a strange angle to their 'amusing' drawing-room settings.

### *Four Quartets*

'Burnt Norton' (1936), a fragment unused in *Murder in the Cathedral*, was followed by 'East Coker' (1940), 'The Dry Salvages' (1941) and 'Little Gidding' (1942), gathered as *Four Quartets*. The title suggests chamber music played by four players. Each quartet has five parts, of which the first establishes a personal theme and the fourth is short and lyrical; *The Waste Land* also has this shape. *Four Quartets* is less intense and dramatic, more meditative, repeating and varying themes on different 'instruments' or quietly self-communing voices, one of which is pedantically clear: 'There are three conditions which often look alike/Yet differ completely, flourish in the same hedgerow:/Attachment to self and to things, and to persons, detachment/From self and from things and from persons; and, growing between them, indifference/Which resembles the others as death resembles life ...' – a manner self-mocking yet seriously didactic. In 'Little Gidding', Eliot takes farewell of his poetic gift and meditates the value of his life.

> 'Let me reveal the gifts reserved for age,
> And set a crown upon your lifetime's effort.
> First the cold friction of expiring sense ...'

So speaks a 'familiar compound ghost/Both intimate and unidentifiable', echoing Dante, Shakespeare, Yeats and Swift, and also the forefathers of a poet haunted by family ghosts.

Eliot's family were Unitarians – believing, as he put it, that there was 'at most, one God' – but he came to a faith more incarnational and sacrificial, immanent and mystical. His marital life had made romantic disappointment and 'detachment ... from persons' a painful reality, which he cast in the terms of the Buddhist and Brahmin philosophy he had studied for two years at Harvard. Detachment does not grab every reader. Nor does a return to the England of Charles I's execution, and 'the tattered arras woven with a silent motto' (reversing the motto of the executed Mary Queen of Scots): 'In my end is my beginning'. Yet each Quartet opens with a directly personal experience at a named place, and the thinking is consecutive, though it concerns 'the intersection of the timeless moment with time', the presence of the divine in experience and in history. The mode is intimate: 'My words echo/Thus in your mind' ('Burnt Norton'). The language is ascetic, returning always to the perfection and limits of poetic language: 'As the Chinese jar still/Turns perpetually in its stillness' so 'the communication/Of the dead is tongued with fire beyond the language of the living.'

As in *The Waste Land*, Eliot achieved what he admired in Dante, a depth of language yielding levels of meaning. A simple example is: 'If I think of a king at nightfall,/Of three men, and more, on the scaffold/And a few who died forgotten/In other places, here and abroad,/And of one who died blind and quiet/Why should we celebrate/These dead men more than the dying?' The men are Charles I, his supporters Laud and Strafford, and the blind John Milton; but also Jesus, the thieves, the apostles, and St John the Divine. Eliot's allegory is usually less referential. History and experience are open to a realm where language stops but meaning continues, a realm to which language can only point. Less striking than *The Waste Land*, *Four Quartets* is an even more ambitious poem. As the subject is more difficult, the style is simpler.

## Eliot's criticism

Eliot's early criticism of Renaissance drama and the Metaphysicals is highly intelligent, incisive, elegant and subtle. Although learned, it is pre-academic and more personal than its manner suggests. It is also strategic, creating the taste by which his own poetry would be appreciated. What Eliot later called 'effrontery' worked a velvet revolution, winning him an authority comparable to that of Matthew Arnold. As he aged, his literary criticism became less piercing and more general. He also wrote social criticism in support of a restored Christian society in England, a hope outlived in *Four Quartets*.

Eliot's critical dominance has passed, but his poetry still echoes. When Lawrence died in 1930, high modernism was over, its practitioners dispersed or absorbed in projects marginal to English audiences. *Apes of God*, Wyndham Lewis's 1930 attack on 'Bloomsbury' and the cult of youth, is distinctly retrospective. Modernism had conquered the peaks, at the cost of excluding middlebrows from a minority culture and alienating non-modernist writers. The poet Robert Graves attacked Pound and Eliot in 'These be your gods, O Israel!'

Eliot was indeed a god for some of the new English generation of Evelyn Waugh (1903–66), George Orwell (1903–50) and W. H. Auden (1907–73), but he was not for W. B. Yeats, as is clear from Yeats's 1936 *Oxford Book of Modern English Verse*. The old man meanwhile had become a living master for Eliot and for Auden.

## W. B. Yeats

W(illiam) B(utler) Yeats (1865–1939) is introduced belatedly, for it was after 1920 that he made his major impact on English poetry. Pound had liked the Pre-Raphaelite Yeats of the 1910 *Collected Poems*.

> The woods of Arcady are dead,
> And over is their antique joy;
> Of old the world on dreaming fed;
> Grey Truth is now her painted toy.

The dreams which fed this short-sighted, vague-seeming man were of the wisdom of the East, the heroes and heroines of Ireland's past, and the peasants of the West. Early poems such as 'The Lake Isle of Innisfree', 'Down by the Salley Gardens', 'The Stolen Child', 'The Song of Wandering Aengus', 'The Man Who Dreamed of Faeryland', though beautifully made, did not alter the impression of a dreamer; nor did love poems interweaving 'pale brows, still hands and dim hair'. Wilde and Shaw were not taken very seriously, and Yeats's pre-war concerns – folklore, the Abbey Theatre in Dublin, Irish nationalism – were discounted in London. After a transit of the metropolitan sky, his star was setting in the West.

But the dreamer had worked very hard, 'All his twenties crammed with toil'. J. B. Yeats, a fine painter, left his son a fine example of how not to conduct a career, and also taught him to believe only in art. Chesterton once said that 'a man who doesn't believe in God, doesn't believe in nothing: he believes in anything'. A need to believe and to worship fuelled Yeats's devotions: to Blake, Irish mythology and folklore, the

Willam Butler Yeats
(1865–1939).

theatre, national causes, the Rhymers' Club, poetry readings, committee meetings, public meetings, journalism, his own plays and poetry – and to the beautiful Irish nationalist Maud Gonne. He invested almost as much time in the occult and the esoteric – seances, spirit-rappings, theosophy, reincarnation, automatic writing – and especially in visions. *A Vision* (1925) outlines a system in which human history follows a cycle linked to (among other things) the phases of the moon. He played at and half-believed in these ideas, but needed them.

After working hard for an Irish literary revival and the Irish National Theatre, he returned to London disgusted. In 1890 Catholic sentiment had brought down Parnell, and in 1907 Dublin demonstrated against Synge's *The Playboy of the Western World* at Yeats's Abbey Theatre, for showing Irish people as imperfect. Then in 1913 Dublin's Municipal Gallery rejected Impressionist pictures left to it by Hugh Lane, a nephew of Yeats's ally Lady Gregory. In Sussex in 1914 and 1915, Yeats worked with Ezra Pound on translating Japanese plays. Then in 1916 'a terrible beauty was born', as Yeats was to put it, in the Easter Rising, badly handled by Britain: executions, martyrs, struggles, and in 1921 the Irish Free State. Yeats became a Senator in a Catholic-dominated Ireland, but was to pay a new attention to Anglo-Irish ancestors and historical heroes.

From 1913 onwards his poetry had extended its range: of subjects, to politics; of diction, to the colloquial; of moods, to realism and even bitterness. He began to address others besides himself. Always he maintained his devotion to form, which for him (unlike Pound) meant 'a complete coincidence of sentence and stanza'. But now he had more ways of saying, and more to say. In 1917 he stopped adoring Maud Gonne and married; he had children. His poetry become more powerful and declarative, filled with his own voice, binding and provoking a large audience. The Romantic poets and their heirs, with rare exceptions such as Browning and Hardy, had tended to dry up after the age of thirty-five. When Yeats was 'close on forty-nine', he began to write his greatest poetry. He has thirty or forty outstanding poems, more than any other poet of the 20th century, chiefly in *The Tower* (1928) and *The Winding Stair* (1933). Eliot was astonished, Auden and Dylan Thomas awestruck. In the next generation, Philip Larkin (1922–85) began by trying to write like Yeats.

In prose, some of Yeats's opinions, spiritual and political, today seem very strange. In the poems they are held as dramatized ideas, often in dialogue within a volume. In style and form, his poems dramatize the tradition of the Romantic ode. Some of those set at Lady Gregory's house at Coole, and 'Among School Children', are comparable to Keats's odes, and the most splendid of 20th-century poems. His paradox of soul and body finds classical expression in 'Sailing to Byzantium':

> That is no country for old men. The young
> In one another's arms, birds in the trees
> – Those dying generations – at their song,
> The salmon-falls, the mackerel-crowded seas,
> Fish, flesh or fowl, commend all summer long
> Whatever is begotten, born, and dies.
> Caught in that sensual music all neglect
> Monuments of unageing intellect.

'We were the last Romantics', he claimed of his friends in the Irish Literary Revival. He has since been claimed also as a modernist, partly on the strength of extremist later poems which express, often with epigrammatic force, his sense that his soul was growing younger as his body aged: 'Love has pitched his mansion in/The place of excrement.'

The last poems are full of self-destruction and renewal, as in 'The Circus Animals' Desertion', where his old symbols desert him: 'it was the dream itself enchanted me.'

> Those masterful images because complete
> Grew in pure mind, but out of what began?
> A mound of refuse or the sweepings of a street,
> Old kettles, old bottles, and a broken can,
> Old iron, old bones, old rags, that raving slut
> Who keeps the till. Now that my ladder's gone,
> I must lie down where all the ladders start,
> In the foul rag-and-bone shop of the heart.

As filthy rags and bones are boiled down to make fine paper, and as the physical assimilation of food feeds the mind, so the spirit is fed by gross appetite. Some critics find the rhetoric of the larger poems strained. Others dwell on how modernist poets were attracted to authoritarian attitudes. Although this is not true of European modernists generally, it is evident that Yeats, Pound and Eliot were doubtful of the future of high art in a popular democracy in which, to quote Pound in *Mauberley*, 'the age demanded/An image of its accelerated grimace' made 'to sell, and sell quickly'.

## Hugh MacDiarmid and David Jones

This is true also of two other modernists, C. M. Grieve ('**Hugh MacDiarmid**', 1892–1978) and **David Jones** (1895–1974). MacDiarmid, a Scottish nationalist who rejoined the Communist party after the Soviet invasion of Hungary in 1956, would not want house-room in a Sassenach literary history: not for his fine early lyrics in a Lowland dialect enriched by words from the older Scottish tongue; nor for *A Drunk Man Looks at the Thistle* (1926), a Dostoevskian *Tam O'Shanter* (though Burns was not his model); nor for his later 'poetry of fact' in English. Jones, a Londoner whose mother was Welsh, went the other way. An artist who converted after the war to Catholicism, he took up the pen only when in 1931 he could not paint, writing a rhythmical prose which uses poetic techniques found in Hopkins, Joyce and Eliot. *In Parenthesis* (1937), the only modernist book about the war, was too belated and too considered to catch many readers. Eliot thought it a work of genius, Auden the best long poem of the 20th century. It has a narrative drive lacking in *The Anathemata* (1956), a richly imagined Catholic myth of Britain from prehistory and archaeology to Arthur and (more thinly) the present. Jones's humility is unique, but his work has the long historical perspective and universal ambition of major modernist poetry. This is true also of the nuggets of Basil Bunting (1900–85), a disciple of Pound who won late recognition with *Briggflatts* (1966). This sequence applied modernist techniques to his Northumbrian subjects with fierce economy. Modernist poetry asks and gives more than many readers want. Its ambitions live on in the verse of Donald Davie (1922–95), Charles Tomlinson (1927–) and Geoffrey Hill (1931–).

## Virginia Woolf

**Virginia Woolf** (1882–1941) was the daughter of Sir Leslie Stephen, critic, rationalist, scholar and founder of the *Dictionary of National Biography*. Its pages contain other

Virginia Woolf (1882–1941), in 1936.

Stephens, as well as Huxleys, Darwins, Stracheys, and Trevelyans: families of gentry, evangelical or professional background, who had abolished the slave trade, pioneered science, reformed the Civil Service, and climbed mountains. Having administered Britain and its Empire, and written its history, they would now question its rationale.

After her father died in 1904, Virginia lived with her sister and brothers in Bloomsbury Square, London, north of the British Museum, a quarter which gave its name to the Bloomsbury Group, a group of intellectuals, critics and artists: Lytton Strachey, the biographer; John Maynard Keynes, the economist; Roger Fry and Clive Bell, art critics; E. M. Forster and others. All the men had been at Cambridge. Virginia's sister Vanessa, a painter, married Bell and settled nearby. Virginia Stephen – or Woolf, for in 1912 she married Leonard Woolf, civil servant and author – had become central to the Group. Bloomsbury memoirs, letters and diaries show both wit and intelligence, and an uncommon frankness about sexual behaviour, homosexual, bisexual, adulterous, or incestuous.

The lasting interest their lifestyle holds for Sunday journalists may be unfair to the Group's intellectual, critical and artistic achievements. Keynes's economics were to have worldwide influence. In art, Bloomsbury critics introduced Post-Impressionism and a new formalist criticism. In literature, Strachey pioneered a new kind of biography in *Eminent Victorians* (1918), reversing Victorian priorities by holding morally energetic public figures up to ridicule by innuendo. If no man is a hero to his valet, Strachey may be said to have created a valet school of biography – which has now found plenty to pick over in Bloomsbury. Strachey was a conspicuous conscientious objector, and Bloomsbury became generally associated in the public mind with the attitude later expressed by E. M. Forster: 'If I had to choose between betraying my country and betraying my friend, I hope I would have the guts to betray my country.'

Although their techniques are different, Virginia Woolf's post-war novels share a creed with Forster's pre-war novels: the good is to be found in pleasurable states, transient since death is final, to be found in private life: love, friendship and art. These ideas, set forth by the Cambridge philosopher G. E. Moore, did not lead to any interest in God, history, public politics or conventional morality. Reason, clarity, exclusivity and a certain refined sensitivity outranked moral rules – but could not be expected of most people. Virginia Woolf wrote of Clive Bell's *Civilisation* (1928), that 'in the end it turns out that civilisation is a lunch party at No. 50 Gordon Square.'

Virginia Woolf's novels ignore external social reality except as it constitutes the phenomena of personal consciousness. She attacked the 'materialism' of Galsworthy and Bennett: their heaped-up facts designed to clothe in credibility a theatrical plot-with-characters and an action leading to a resolution. 'We want to be rid of realism, to penetrate without its help into the regions beneath it', she wrote in 1919 in a review of one of thirteen stream-of-consciousness novels by Dorothy Richardson (1873–1957), eventually grouped together as *Pilgrimage* in 1938. Woolf explored a world of finely registered impressions – an interior, domestic, feminine world – impressions often worked into patterns, as in the paintings of Pierre Bonnard, and of her sister Vanessa. Beside the examples of Richardson and Joyce, she had that of Marcel Proust's *À la recherche du temps perdu* (1913–27). Her first 'impressionist' novel (to borrow Ford's term) was *Mrs Dalloway* (1925), devoted to a day in the life of Clarissa Dalloway, the wife of an MP, as she prepares for a party where old flames of hers are to reappear. Her interior monologue is set against those of others, including that of a shell-shocked survivor of the war.

### To the Lighthouse

Woolf's subjective apprehension of time is imposed through the tripartite structure of *To the Lighthouse* (1927), in which two long days are separated by ten short years. In the first act the Ramsay family are at their holiday home on Skye. This is the opening of Part I, 'The Window':

'Yes, of course, if it's fine to-morrow,' said Mrs Ramsay. 'But you'll have to be up with the lark,' she added.

To her son these words conveyed an extraordinary joy, as if it were settled the expedition were bound to take place, and the wonder to which he had looked forward, for years and years it seemed, was, after a night's darkness and a day's sail, within touch. Since he belonged, even at the age of six, to that great clan which cannot keep this feeling separate from that, but must let future prospects, with their joys and sorrows, cloud what is actually at hand, since to such people even in earliest childhood any turn in the wheel of sensation has the power to crystallize and transfix the moment upon which its gloom or radiance rests, James Ramsay, sitting on the floor cutting out pictures from the illustrated catalogue of the Army and Navy Stores, endowed the picture of a refrigerator as his mother spoke with heavenly bliss. It was fringed with joy. The wheelbarrow, the lawn-mower, the sound of poplar trees, leaves whitening before rain, rooks cawing, brooms knocking, dresses rustling – all these were so coloured and distinguished in his mind that he had already his private code, his secret language, though he appeared the image of stark and uncompromising severity, with his high forehead and his fierce blue eyes, impeccably candid and pure, frowning slightly at the sight of human frailty, so that his mother, watching him guide his scissors neatly round the refrigerator, imagined him all red and ermine on the Bench or directing a stern and momentous enterprise in some crisis of public affairs.

'But,' said his father, stopping in front of the drawing-room window, 'it won't be fine.'

Had there been an axe handy, a poker, or any weapon that would have gashed a hole in his father's breast and killed him, there and then, James would have seized it.

The length and falling-forward gait of the long sentences either side of 'It was fringed with joy' pull the reader into James's six-year-old consciousness. We too see the joy-fringed refrigerator, smiling at the adjective, and at his mother's picture of him in the future. There is wit in the wording of James's extreme reaction to his father's devotion to truth. Mrs Ramsay, we know, will try to shield James against this disappointment. Woolf's writing is often as carefully-flighted as this, informal yet composed, judiciously adding a detail – much as, at the end of the book, the painter Lily Briscoe adds a brush-stroke to consummate her painting, just at the moment when Mr Ramsay reaches the lighthouse with James and his sister. Reality (for that, in some form, is what is conveyed to a novel's readers) is aesthetic in form.

Woolf is not a crude realist – the scenes and people of *To the Lighthouse* are not those of the Isle of Skye. But the Ramsays are based on her mother and father, and are more real than her other characters – if not than the consciousness of her own consciousness. People who are not members of the Ramsay family are real only as outsiders; Charles Tansley, for instance, is witnessed by Mrs Ramsay with kindly condescension. But her kindliness is missed when it is gone.

Part II, 'Time Passes', is very short. The house ages:

Nothing stirred in the drawing-room or in the dining-room or on the staircase. Only through the rusty hinges and swollen sea-moistened woodwork certain airs, detached from the body of the wind (the house was ramshackle after all) crept round corners and ventured indoors.

A little later we read:

[Mr Ramsay stumbling along a passage stretched his arms out one dark morning, but, Mrs Ramsay having died rather suddenly the night before, he stretched his arms out. They remained empty.]

There is the plot, sidelined in parentheses but indispensable. Mrs Ramsay's absence fills Part III, 'The Lighthouse', in which the lighthouse is reached. Lily and her picture symbolize the role of art, and verbal composition, as consolation. The Mrs-Ramsay-shaped void in their lives is an ache characteristic of this writer, who suffered sudden losses in her life; which she ended by suicide in 1941.

*To the Lighthouse* rewards attention: it is a moving book. Yet it asks a high degree of attention, like a modernist poem. In *The Waves* (1931), Woolf's most schematically experimental novel, six consciousnesses become conscious at intervals through their lives. Like most modernists, Woolf has been appreciated, admired and loved rather than very widely liked. As her subject-matter is that which is left out of other novels, novel-readers miss things that they like, some of which (with much that they might not) are to be found in *Ulysses*.

Fine writer as Woolf is, her work may not seem very substantial, and she was not rated one of the greater modernists until the 1970s. Her revived status has to do with the rise of literary and academic feminism, on which her theory and practice have been influential for good reasons. Her fiction has a mode of sensibility which she thought distinctively feminine, though its intense self-consciousness can also be found in Eliot and Joyce. Her Mrs Ramsay, like Forster's Mrs Wilcox and Mrs Moore, is a new kind of character – maternal, wise, detached from, superior to, protective of the childish men around her. They are tributes to the authors' mothers – a class rather taken for granted in utilitarian Britain. Woolf's literary criticism, too, in *The Common Reader* and other essays, is quick, informal, sensitive in rendering impressions, always personal and in her own voice (qualities Woolf thought feminine); often they are more revealing of herself than of the work, like some of Pater's appreciations. Her polemic, *A Room of One's Own* (1928), traces the history of women's contributions to English literature with fine judgement. It set a course for academic literary feminism, and can be recommended to all students of English for its sustained irony.

A more ambiguous feminism informs *Orlando: A Biography* (1928). As its hero changes sex and has lived for nearly four hundred years, the subtitle is a spoof. It also parodies the obituaristic, external style of the *Dictionary of National Biography*. Yet the key to *Orlando* is its dedication to Vita Sackville-West, with whom Woolf was infatuated (see *Portrait of a Marriage* (1973) by Nigel Nicolson, Vita's son). *Orlando* is a fantasy love-letter to its aristocratic dedicatee, and to her ancient house. It put a new 'bi-' into biography.

## Katherine Mansfield

The Woolfs' Hogarth Press, founded 1917, also published **Katherine Mansfield** (1888–1923) and other new writers, often in translation, especially Russians and eastern Europeans. Mansfield's notable short stories, many set in her native New Zealand, are firmer than those of Woolf, who thought Mansfield's 'hard' and 'shallow'. The work of Lawrence, Woolf and Mansfield should be compared with that of the master of the short story, the humane Anton Chekhov.

# ◼ Non-modernism: the Twenties and Thirties

A caution. Most of the authors now to be dealt with (and some already discussed) lived well into the lifetime of the writer of this history. Its judgements will be more affected by its author's partialities, and by the preoccupations of the day. Such judgements are provisional. An observer of reputations rising and falling over twelve centuries becomes cautious in predicting future fame. Time edits contemporary reputations severely: the star playwright of the post-war years, Christopher Fry (1907–), is now in total eclipse, and the poetry of Dylan Thomas, the popular poet of that period, is no longer highly rated. Many thousands of books are now published annually. Which will last? The way chosen here is to say something of the probables rather than to give each of the possibles one sentence.

A second caution. The national criterion which, as the Introduction explains, has become unavoidable (see page 5), excludes foreign writers much read in Britain. Foreign-language writers have always been read in Britain, for European and Biblical literature has from the first informed English writing. But non-native writers of English were first read in England in Victorian times, when the American **Henry Wadsworth Longfellow** (1807–82) was a poet almost as popular as Tennyson. From the 1930s, as the US began to dominate the world's media, F. Scott Fitzgerald, Ernest Hemingway, John Steinbeck, William Faulkner, Eugene O'Neill, Tennessee Williams and Arthur Miller were read in England – and studied. In the 1960s, novelists such as Saul Bellow, Norman Mailer, Joseph Heller, Philip Roth and John Updike, and the poet Robert Lowell, were as popular in the UK as any native writer. US literary influence has waned. But many leading Anglo writers have not been British: the West Indians V. S. Naipaul and Derek Walcott; Seamus Heaney, an Ulsterman with an Irish passport, Oxford Professor of Poetry, succeeded in that chair by another Ulster poet, Paul Muldoon; the Australian Les Murray, winner of the Queen's Medal for poetry in 1999. The transatlantic novelists Margaret Atwood and Toni Morrison have been read enthusiastically in Britain. As the American commercial empire has succeeded the British Empire, writing in English (like much else in the world economy) is now global. The majority of Nobel Prizewinners for Literature writing in English have not been British. Other writing in English will continue to enrich English culture and literature. It comes from former colonies, from political and cultural exiles in Britain, and, increasingly, from the descendants of more recent immigrants.

The years of economic difficulty following 1927 saw high modernist examples ignored more often than assimilated, except by Auden, the major talent to emerge in Eliot's shadow. The distinct achievements of the domestic novel were modest and conservative. Little in English drama was of interest to literary history. Non-fiction was increasingly dominated by politics.

Though winning the Great War, Britain lost by it. This is shown as much in the gay Twenties as in the glum Thirties. The post-war slump led to mass unemployment and a General Strike; the Wall Street Crash led to a Labour–Conservative co-alition and the 'National Government' of 1929–31. Promises to alleviate social injustice and economic problems proved false. Some liked the idea of the Communist experiment in Russia. In 1930, 107 Nazis were elected to the Reichstag.

The end of high modernism was also the end of the irresponsible years of the Bright Young Things. Brightness was also to be found in Strachey's Bloomsbury, where the Charleston was not danced, and in the writings of Aldous Huxley, the Sitwells, Rose Macaulay, William Gerhardie, the plays of Noël Coward and the cynical Somerset Maugham. That spray-on brightness has made even Huxley's novels of ideas seem dated, though his scientific *Brave New World* (1932) can be read against George Orwell's political *Nineteen Eighty-Four* (1949). They breathe the moods of the Twenties and of the Thirties respectively. The timeless world of P. G. Wodehouse

## Publications 1929–1939

1929  Richard Aldington, *Death of a Hero*; Robert Graves, *Goodbye to All That*; Richard Hughes, *A High Wind in Jamaica*; Henry Green, *Living*.

1930  T. S. Eliot, *Ash-Wednesday*; Evelyn Waugh, *Vile Bodies*; W. H. Auden, *Poems*; Noël Coward, *Private Lives*.

1931  Anthony Powell, *Afternoon Men*; Siegfried Sassoon; *Memoirs of an Infantry Officer*; Virginia Woolf, *The Waves*.

1932  Lewis Grassic Gibbon, *Sunset Song*; Aldous Huxley, *Brave New World*.

1933  W. B. Yeats, *The Winding Stair*; George Orwell, *Down and Out in Paris and London*.

1934  Graves, *I, Claudius*; Dylan Thomas, *Eighteen Poems*; Waugh, *A Handful of Dust*.

1935  Ivy Compton-Burnett, *A House and its Head*; Louis MacNeice, *Poems*; Eliot, *Murder in the Cathedral*; W. H. Auden and Christopher Isherwood, *The Dog Beneath the Skin*; Isherwood, *Mr Norris Changes Trains*.

1936  Eliot, *Burnt Norton*; J. C. Powys, *Maiden Castle*; Auden, *Look, Stranger!*; Yeats (ed.), *The Oxford Book of Modern Verse*; Michael Roberts (ed.), *The Faber Book of Modern Verse*.

1937  David Jones, *In Parenthesis*; J. R. R. Tolkien, *The Hobbit*.

1938  Samuel Beckett, *Murphy*; Elizabeth Bowen, *The Death of the Heart*; Graham Greene, *Brighton Rock*.

1939  Joyce Cary, *Mister Johnson*; Eliot, *The Family Reunion*; James Joyce, *Finnegans Wake*; MacNeice, *Autumn Journal*; Dylan Thomas, *The Map of Love*.

(1881–1975), who kept his brightness under a bushel for 120 volumes, has not dated; he is not a novelist of ideas. Much of what was enjoyable in these authors is distilled and superseded in *Decline and Fall* (1928), the first novel of a latecomer to the party, **Evelyn Waugh** (1903–66).

His father, Arthur Waugh, a publisher and critic, had likened T. S. Eliot to a drunken Helot: 'It was a classic custom [in ancient Sparta] in the family hall, when a feast was at its height, to display a drunken slave among the sons of the household, to the end that they, being ashamed at the ignominious folly of his gesticulations, might determine never to be tempted into such a pitiable condition themselves.' The philosopher Bertrand Russell (1872–1970) noticed Eliot's 'Etonian manners' on meeting him at Harvard, and Virginia Woolf noted that he wore 'a three-piece suit, there being no four-piece suits'. What made Arthur Waugh liken this urbane poet to a drunken slave exhibited as a warning to the ruling class? His reaction, shared by Robert Graves, needs to be understood, for modernism did not conquer or transform English literature: it modified it and was assimilated.

*The Waste Land* was unlike previous poems: metrically irregular and discontinuous in sense, it was not all in English. Poetry that is 'simple, sensuous and passionate', as Milton prescribed, has to be in the mother tongue. *The Waste Land* uses three languages before it reaches English, and later uses three more. Dr Johnson's saying that 'a man should should show as much of his Greek as he does of his lace' still has a point in England: why say '*œuvre*' when you can say 'work'? Virginia Woolf admired Eliot's work, but lamented its neglect of the literary 'decorums' of her youth. *The Waste Land* also fails to convey what Pound called 'beautiful thoughts in flowery language'. Arthur Waugh's reaction to the pretensions of these young Americans was widely shared; it overtook the far from stuffy early Imagist, Richard Aldington, Eliot's junior. There was a dislike of the thought that the future was going to be American.

Arthur Waugh's anti-modern irony descended in lethal form to his son Evelyn, who as an undergraduate liked to outrage the fathers of households, though he preferred to be drunk as a lord rather than as a Helot. He thought Eliot's *Poems, 1909–1925* 'marvellously good, but very hard to understand' and picked their 'most impressive flavour of the minor prophets'. The title of his darkest novel, *A Handful of Dust* (1934), comes from *The Waste Land.*

*Interviewer:* Have you found a professional criticism of your work illuminating or helpful? Edmund Wilson, for example?
*Evelyn Waugh:* Is he an American?
*Interviewer:* Yes.
*Waugh:* I don't think what they have to say is of much interest, do you?

Evelyn Waugh liked to make the provoking claim that he and Graham Greene and Anthony Powell were craftsmen producing well-made novels of classic form for civilized readers, as if Queen Anne were still on the throne. Waugh was successful from 1928, Greene hugely so from 1932. Powell was the dark horse of the trio, emerging as the others faded. All three were products of select boarding schools – 'public school men' – as were Auden and his circle in the Thirties. Their achievements in the novel now stand out, with those of Elizabeth Bowen, above those of the less conventional Henry Green, the Powys brothers, Richard Hughes, Ivy Compton-Burnett, Sylvia Townsend Warner or the popular J. B. Priestley and Compton Mackenzie.

## Modernism fails to catch on

The modernist novel, it seems, made little impact in England, a country avoided by its later practitioners, **Samuel Beckett** (1906–89), **Malcolm Lowry** (1909–57) and **Christine Brooke-Rose** (1926–). Despite the art novels of James and Conrad, the social and entertaining tradition of the English Victorian novel persisted. The successors to these 'loose, baggy monsters' (James's phrase) are neater, yet have a family resemblance. Their natural imitation of life, rather than of art, lacks the intensity and ambition of modernist poetry, though this may in part be a matter of style. For whatever reason, *Women in Love* and *Ulysses* had no major successor, whereas in European fiction modernism continued. It may be England's insularity which makes her exceptional, though it is normal for a revolution to be followed by some settlement. The English stage was finally boarded by modernism in 1955, with Beckett's *Waiting for Godot*, translated by an Irishman from his original French. Only in poetry did modernism have an evident effect.

## The poetry of the Thirties

W(ystan) H(ugh) **Auden** (1907–73) and his Oxford friends Stephen Spender (1909–9?), Louis MacNeice (1907–63) and Cecil Day-Lewis (1904–72) were briefly left-wing poets; their rapid success provoked the South African poet Roy Campbell to attack a composite monster, MacSpaunday. They had missed the war and had no jobs to lose. Guilty about privilege, the idea of equality, even of revolution, appealed.

### Political camps

A little political sketch is required here, for attitudes to Nazism and Communism still affect accounts of the literature of these generations. Enlightened opinion favoured the Russian experiment, overlooking its atrocities. Better-known was the Nazi suppression of the Communists, especially to Auden and his friends Christopher Isherwood (1904–86) and Spender, who had visited Berlin and Weimar Germany, the frenetic life of which is caught in Isherwood's novel, *Mr Norris Changes Trains*. Several of the Auden group visited Spain; they supported the Republicans. But Auden noticed that the Republicans had closed the churches, and asked himself why he felt that this was wrong. A second question, about the source of his certainty that Hitler was evil, eventually led him back to Christianity.

In 1939, the year of the Nazi-Soviet Pact, Auden and Isherwood left for New York, amid jeers. Many in the Auden circle were homosexual: he joked about the 'Homintern' (a reference to Comintern, the Communist International movement). Cecil Day-Lewis published a sonnet in *Left Review* in 1934 beginning, 'Yes, why do we all, seeing a communist, feel small?' By 1936 some did not. Most reverted from Communism to liberalism. Of the early Thirties, MacNeice was to write, 'Young men were swallowing Marx with the same naive enthusiasm that made Shelley swallow Godwin' (*The Strings are False*, 1965). Day-Lewis is remembered for his versions of Virgil. He became Laureate in 1968, and Spender was knighted for services to literature. Isherwood was clever, MacNeice talented, Auden major.

### W. H. Auden

MacNeice wrote an open, journalistic, colloquial verse of his own, notably in *Autumn Journal*, about 1938–9. The others did some 'Pylon poetry' – so called after a futuristic poem of Spender's – full of pistons and aerodromes. Their modern ballads were better, especially MacNeice's 'It's no go the Yogi-Man, it's no go Blavatsky,/All we want is a bank-balance and a bit of skirt in a taxi' ('Bagpipe Music'). In 'Spain', Auden wrote: 'To-morrow the bicycle races/Through the suburbs on summer evenings. But to-day the struggle.' Marxism apart, the tone of this is strikingly unlike that in which Yeats, thinking of Pegasus, the winged horse of poetry of Greek mythology, wrote: 'But all is changed, that high horse riderless,/Though mounted in that saddle Homer rode/Where the swan drifts upon a darkening flood' ('Coole Park and Ballylee, 1931'). It is worth listening to recordings of Yeats, Eliot and Auden reading their own verse: Yeats chants, Eliot enunciates with precision, Auden is fast, flat, metrical, 'unpoetic'.

Auden described a poem as 'a verbal contraption', and the poet's duty as to tell the truth. He was a virtuoso, writing in any style or form except free verse, and reading geology, history, psychology, Old and Middle English, Icelandic, Kierkegaard, Niebuhr, musicology – all was grist to his mill. In his longest works, the verse-plays and oratorios in which he worked out his ideas, his sophistication palls. He found verse so easy that he used it for thinking in, like Dryden. He was happier in shorter forms.

Auden put new wine in old bottles. Unlike Yeats, Eliot, Pound, Lawrence, Jones and early Joyce, he did not believe in a Fall from a previous golden age. Not having grown up before 1914, he was used to the idea that mankind had fallen, himself included. He masked his anxiety with humour, but his first poems betray it in their ellipses, private language and electricity. Yet if the phrasing is perverse, the forms are traditional: 'Sir, no man's enemy' is a prayer, 'Look, stranger' an epitaph. An engaging way into early Auden is his light verse 'Letter to Lord Byron'. Later, 'A Thanksgiving' (1973) listed his poetic mentors: Hardy, Thomas, Frost, Yeats, Graves, Brecht, Horace, Goethe. As a modern European he found it natural, as the modernists did not, to write discursively in a connected and completed syntax, and to use forms which allow the poem to breathe as a social animal.

His work falls into three phases. First there is the pre-war personal lyricist alive to the ills of the time ('Look, stranger', 'Out on the lawn I lie in bed', 'Lullaby'), looking to psychological or political solutions ('Spain'). Then, the Christian existentialist

W(ystan) H(ugh) Auden (1907–73), by
Erich Auerbach, 1961.

and New York moralist of the middle style ('Musée des Beaux Arts', 'The Shield of Achilles'). Lastly, the chatty Horatian joker back in Europe ('Thanksgiving for a Habitat'). He left England to escape his role as spokesman for the Left. On 'September 1, 1939' (as Germany invaded Poland) he wrote: 'I sit in one of the dives/On Fifty-Second Street/Uncertain and afraid/As the clever hopes expire/Of a low dishonest decade'. A lonely individual, he was to sit in 1961 in a Cadena Café in Oxford, a Professor of Poetry doing the *Daily Telegraph* crossword. He died in a hotel room in Vienna in 1973.

Yeats died in January 1939, a crucial year for Auden, who wrote

> He disappeared in the dead of winter:
> The brooks were frozen, the airports almost deserted,
> And snow disfigured the public statues;
> The mercury sank in the mouth of the dying day.

As the mercury sinks in the oral thermometer, disfiguring the poet's noble pose, the brooks are frozen in sympathy – a convention of pastoral elegy, as is the opening discord of grief. Auden makes the great man 'disappear' among the dead. His words live, no longer his: 'The death of the poet was kept from his poems', as the death of a parent is kept from children. 'A few thousand will think of this day/As one thinks of a day when one did something slightly unusual'. Unlike Yeats, Auden depersonalizes and understates. Part 2 of 'In Memory of W. B. Yeats' begins 'You were silly, like us' and tells that 'poetry makes nothing happen' – politically. Part 3 is hymn-like: 'With your unconstraining voice/Still persuade us to rejoice' and 'In the deserts of the heart/Let the healing fountain start.' This redeploys the imagery of *The Waste Land* within the conventions of elegy; yet all seems modern. He domesticates Eliot's sharp reversals of tone.

Earnest critics held that Auden was trivial, that he did not apply his talent, that he preferred to 'ruin a fine tenor voice/For effects that bring down the house' ('In Praise of Limestone'). This ignores his simple ethical basis: 'Those to whom evil is done, do evil in return'. Or, in 'The Shield of Achilles',

> A ragged urchin, aimless and alone,
>     Loitered about that vacancy; a bird
> Flew up to safety from his well-aimed stone:
>     That girls are raped, that two boys knife a third,
>     Were axioms to him, who'd never heard
> Of any world where promises were kept
> Or one could weep because another wept.

That seems grave enough. Auden did not try to be great all the time. If poetry is 'memorable speech', his unconstraining voice will survive. He wrote a modern poetry for a wider audience, the civilized and the ordinary as well as the avant-garde.

In 1936, from the heights of T. S. Eliot's firm, Michael Roberts launched *The Faber Book of Modern Verse* (1936), canonizing the 'modern' for some decades. It began with Hopkins (who had died in 1889!), Yeats, Pound and Eliot, but omitted 'Georgians', even Edward Thomas, and the unsmart Edwin Muir. In the Thirties, a progressive criterion was applied: Spender's 'I think continually of those who were truly great/... Whose lovely ambition/Was that their lips, still touched with fire,/Should tell of the Spirit' is as unmodern as the poetry Wilfred Owen wrote before 1917. Without politics, Spender might have been a neo-Romantic like Dylan Thomas, autobiographical, emotional, rhetorical: yet Spender is in Roberts's anthology. Ever since Pound's Imagist anthology, 'little magazine' poets have tried to overthrow ruling poetic regimes by the tendentious use of anthologies. Even the literary historian, listening to the poem rather than the hype, cannot quite do without the groups and movements seeking to patent themselves in an anthology. But the only tendency that counts is the tendency to write good poems.

## The novel

### Evelyn Waugh

**Evelyn Waugh** (1903–66) seemed at the time the opposite of Auden. His eminence among novelists was less absolute and briefer than Auden's among poets, yet the careers have similarities. At Oxford Waugh gained some Wildean friends and a third-class degree in history. Like Auden, he then taught in a preparatory school for boys to the age of 13.

*Decline and Fall* traces the fortunes of Paul Pennyfeather, innocent victim of an undergraduate prank, sent down from Oxford, teaching at Llanabba Castle, a boarding school staffed by miscreants, notably the bigamous Captain Grimes. On sports day, young Lord Tangent is shot in the foot. Paul is taken to bed by the glamorous Margot Beste-Chetwynde, the widowed mother of a pupil. About to marry her, he is sent to Egdon Heath Penal Settlement for unwitting complicity in her white slave trade. There he reflects on 'the undeniable cogency of Peter Beste-Chetwynde's "You can't see Mamma in prison, can you?" The more Paul considered this, the more he perceived it to be the statement of a natural law.' Margot, now Lady Metroland, arranges his release and return to Oxford and theology.

In 1928 Waugh married. Divorced in 1930, he was received into the Catholic Church. *Decline and Fall*, *Vile Bodies* (1930), *Black Mischief* (1932), *A Handful of Dust* (1934) and *Scoop* (1938) are often described as satire. *Scoop* is a satire on Fleet Street, and the Mayfair creatures of *Vile Bodies* are certainly worthless and silly. But these novels are black comedies about an absurd world, written with detachment and a

Evelyn Waugh (1903–66), about 1949.

demonic joy: they are not realistic. It is the Wodehouse world as seen by a man whom Belloc described as 'possessed'. Thus the death of Lord Tangent, the imprisonment of Paul, and the shipping off of girls to brothels in South America seem as funny as the devices by which Jeeves preserves Bertram Wooster from wearing the wrong tie, or from marrying girls who think that the stars are God's daisy-chain. Grimes seems no more sinister than Wodehouse's Black Shorts movement.

Waugh's world is mad as well as depraved, but he does not convey a hope that it may change for the better. The idea that rank involves responsibility, presupposed however ironically in *Persuasion* or *Our Mutual Friend*, has gone – a casualty of war and of the author's temperament. His acceptance of Catholicism was a reasoned one. He sought a fidelity and clarity which life rarely offers. In *A Handful of Dust*, Tony Last inherits Hetton, a Gothic stately home which is a memorial of Victorian chivalry. Another hero-victim, he is an honourable but feeble anachronism. His wife Brenda leaves him for Beaver, a drone. He telephones her in London, but is answered by Beaver. 'Oh dear,' says Brenda, 'I feel rather awful about him. But what *can* he expect, coming up suddenly like this. He's got to be taught not to make surprise visits.' Tony leaves for South America, where he is enslaved by a Mr Todd, who makes him read Dickens aloud. *Tod* is German for death, and Tony's surname is also allegorical. As well as eschatology, Waugh wrote hagiography – with dash in *Campion*, with humility in *Ronald Knox*. *Helena* is a witty historical romance about the saint who found the True Cross in Jerusalem.

Like Auden, Waugh travelled, to Africa, South America, Abyssinia. He married in 1937 a member of the Herbert family, and set up as a West Country squire, playing outrageous practical jokes. *Brideshead Revisited* (1945) is a romantic novel about a Catholic noble family and the operation of divine grace. The former is the outward and visible site of the latter. The agnostic artist Charles Ryder is charmed by the old Catholic family of an Oxford friend Sebastian Flyte, nearly marrying his sister Julia, who is recalled to her marriage vows by her father's good death. The bitter situations of *A Handful of Dust* are reversed; the novels are poles apart, as are their critics. Wartime deprivation, its author later conceded, lent enchantment to this dream of England as it ought to have been, a purple *Four Quartets*. Sebastian's final innocence is presumed in circumstances which earlier would have been treated mercilessly. Waugh's war service in the Marines informs *Sword of Honour* (1965): Guy Crouchback, from an old Catholic family, joins up on hearing of the Nazi-Soviet pact but is disillusioned in three volumes. The trilogy is more tired than Powell's corresponding trio.

Waugh's reputation has outlived the offence caused by the real-life charades in which he acted like a Duke with gout, an act which got out out hand (see his *The Ordeal of Gilbert Pinfold*). George Orwell, who had the opposite snobbery to Waugh's, admired his courage and the clarity and discipline of his English. He was a professional writer of unique vision, force and bite.

### Graham Greene

Theology has a more explicit impact on the writings of Waugh's ally, **Graham Greene** (1904–91). Writing of the French novelist François Mauriac, and his theme of the misery of man without God, Greene observed that 'with the death of Henry James the religious sense was lost to the English novel, and with the religious sense went the sense of the importance of the human act. It was as if the world of fiction had lost a dimension....' For him, the characters of Woolf and Forster drift 'like cardboard symbols through a world that is paper-thin'.

Greene's first success was his fourth novel, *Stamboul Train* (1932), later classified as an 'entertainment' as distinct from his more serious novels. Greene was a journalist, a film critic, an Intelligence officer and a traveller, and usually set his fictions in far-off theatres on political fault-lines: Vienna, Mexico, Liberia, Cuba. All are written with chameleon skill, keeping to the rules of the genre and taking on the colouring of the place, though the place is never a good place. Greene writes sparely with a firm narrative line.

Some prefer the unintellectual entertainments, which make good films. But his distinctiveness rests on his 'Catholic' novels, from *Brighton Rock* (1938) to *A Burnt-Out Case* (1961), which rest on a theology of the gamble, carried to unorthodox extremes. Since good-and-evil is a more important axis than right-and-wrong (for divine grace trumps human morality), a (Catholic) sinner who sacrifices himself to redeem another may be saved, even if the rules say that he should lose his soul. This 'good' Faustian bargain, related to Greene's suicidal despair before his 1926 conversion, is seen at its simplest in his unconvincing play *The Potting Shed* (1958) and at its best in *The Power and the Glory* (1940) and *The Heart of the Matter* (1948). The enigmatic Greene worked the media of his day with the mastery of an older raconteur, Daniel Defoe, but a Defoe who had read Pascal.

## Anthony Powell

A similar novelist, in a more artfully realist vein, is **Anthony Powell** (1905–2000), who wrote five drily satirical pre-war novels, notably *Afternoon Men* and *Venusberg*. These were well reviewed by L. P. Hartley (1895–1972), author of *Eustace and Hilda* and *The Go-Between*. Powell is now known, however, as the author of the twelve-novel sequence, called *A Dance to the Music of Time* after a painting by Nicolas Poussin. He had discovered Proust while at Oxford, as had a fellow-Etonian, Henry Yorke (1905–73). As 'Henry Green', Yorke too wrote a series of novels, from *Blindness* (1929) to *Doting* (1962), including *Living* (1929) and *Loving* (1945). Like their titles, these novels are elliptical and stylish, combining a patterned surface with the social curiosity and clipped reportage of the 1930s. The slimming effect of modernism on English fiction is taken further by Ivy Compton-Burnett, whose novels consist of dialogues between the heads of Victorian houses and their juniors, conducted in a mood of courteous hatred.

Powell's panorama, from *A Question of Upbringing* (1951) to *Hearing Secret Harmonies* (1975), shows with remarkable objectivity the criss-crossing lives of a group of schoolfriends, their wives and associates, from 1920 to 1970, via the narrative voice of the self-effacing Nicholas Jenkins. Eton, Oxford, London, publishing, the arts – an upper-class world, professional rather than rich. Among those who dance to time's music are a socialist peer, a critic on the make, a Freudian general, a tragic composer, a South American diplomat, a tycoon (Sir Magnus Donners), and the women around whom their lives revolve. There are pubs and parties, smart, respectable or bohemian, with alcoholic and erotic casualties, but the navigation is steady. At first the breadth of the canvas, the self-effacement of Jenkins, and the lack of immediate purpose or subject, diffuses interest. The pace is even and the tone quiet compared with the whip-crack Waugh. But the web of family and friendship builds up a satisfying density, especially with the wartime volumes. The reader looks forward to the appearances of the pompous Widmerpool, a youth disliked at school, whose drive takes him ever higher in social, industrial and political circles, as he trims his sails to the next wind. Each success of this toady is crowned with a social humiliation which spurs him on to his next incarnation; he falls at last for a sinister occultism. The twelve novels follow the signs of the zodiac, a circle not an advance. Unlike Proust, Powell is neither inward nor philosophical: he perseveres in a tempered observation of the oddity of individual lives and their apparently random regroupings. But the composition gives the gossip-column materials a strange sense of pattern. Time yields slow-burning comic sequences and tragic revelations. The acceptance of marital breakdown and of cynicism about the public world shows 'the disintegration of society in its traditional forms', and, eccentric as the dancers are, the Dance has its representative value. It lives through its curiosity, quiet humour and skilful composition.

Powell's tenacity is demonstrated in his Memoirs, which open with a family history of stupefying ramification. They offer judgements of his fellow Etonians, Cyril Connolly and Eric Blair ('George Orwell', 1904–50), who became influential journalists, Connolly as reviewer and editor of the journal *Horizon* (1939–50), Orwell as a campaigning reporter and political commentator.

## George Orwell

The cult of Orwell, like that of Connolly, has faded, but his name will live through *Animal Farm* (1945), a political allegory of the Russian Revolution which became a modern classic. The animals depose Farmer Jones, but the pigs (the Party), led by Napoleon, take over the farmhouse, while the other animals stay in their pens. The noble carthorse Boxer is the revolutionary worker, sent off to the knacker's yard. Orwell had an acute understanding of the role of propaganda. The slogan 'All animals are equal', having effected the revolution, is modified: 'but some are more equal than others'. Likewise in *Nineteen Eighty-Four*, a dystopian novel, Big Brother, the Thought Police and Newspeak remain in the mind; the hero, Winston Smith, fades. Experience in the Burma Police had turned Blair into Orwell, who embraced a life of poverty in order to attack injustice. He called the Left to democratic socialism and away from communism. His essays on popular culture and on Dickens are models of the plain style.

## Elizabeth Bowen

The Anglo-Irish **Elizabeth Bowen** (1899–1973) can be placed with these novelists. Educated in England, she grew up in a Big House in County Cork, experiencing directly the disintegration of a privileged world. She tells its story in *Bowen's Court* (1942), after she had failed to keep it going. The Troubles inform *The Last September* (1929), in which the isolated heroine has her engagement to a young English soldier broken off, and the house where the dining, dancing and tennis parties continue is about to be burned down. Her detached art is compared to that of *The Real Charlotte* (1894), the Anglo-Irish masterpiece of Sommerville and Ross.

Bowen writes of society from a feminine point of view, with sensitivity and humour, implying raw emotional truths through social nuance. Often she writes of a young woman's loss of happiness and innocence, as did Henry James. Her idea of a novel was 'a non-poetic statement of a poetic truth'. If Woolf registers personal impressions in poetic prose, Bowen's conception of a novel modifies the tradition in which social externals can convey personal relations. Her first novel, *The Hotel* (1927), concerns a young woman lost among the drifters at an Italian resort. Similar themes can be found in *The House in Paris* (1936) and *The Death of the Heart* (1938), studies in the misfortunes of the children of extramarital love-affairs. The last is the best-reputed of her novels, though its painful realizations have a too visibly calculated refinement. *The Heat of the Day* (1949), set in the London of the Blitz, has a Greene-like scenario of treasons, private and public, with an attractive heroine in Stella Rodney and some hope emerging from the wreckage. The novel is memorably atmospheric, and Bowen's writing is generally remarkable for its touch. She sometimes had difficulty with plots, and was a great hand at the short story. If she is in the tradition of the Anglo-Irish novel, one can also place her work at a mid-point between two talented contemporaries, the frankly confessing tone of the sensitive

## Events and publications of 1940–55

| Events | Publications |
|---|---|
| **1940** North-west Europe, except Britain, falls to Germany. The Battle of Britain. The London Blitz. Winston Churchill becomes Prime Minister. Advance in the Western Desert. | **1940** T. S. Eliot, *East Coker*; Graham Greene, *The Power and the Glory*; Arthur Koestler, *Darkness at Noon*. |
| **1941** Germany invades the USSR. Japan bombs the US Fleet in Pearl Harbor. The US joins the Allies. Blitz on Coventry. Income tax is 10s. 0d. in the £. | **1941** Eliot, *The Dry Salvages*; Noël Coward, *Blithe Spirit*. |
| **1942** Singapore falls to Japan. The Battles of Midway, Stalingrad, El Alamein. | **1942** Eliot, *Little Gidding*. |
| **1943** The Allies land in Sicily. The fall of Mussolini. | **1943** David Gascoyne, *Poems*. |
| **1944** The Normandy landings. Butler Education Act. | **1944** Joyce Cary, *The Horse's Mouth*; L. P. Hartley, *The Shrimp and the Anemone*; Eliot, *Four Quartets*. |
| **1945** The Allies conquer Germany. Atomic bombs are dropped on Japan. War dead total *c*.55 million. Clement Attlee (Labour) becomes Prime Minister. | **1945** Sidney Keyes, *Collected Poems*; Nancy Mitford, *The Pursuit of Love*; George Orwell, *Animal Farm*; Evelyn Waugh, *Brideshead Revisited*; Henry Green, *Loving*; Flora Thompson, *Lark Rise to Candleford*. |
| **1946** Institution of the National Health Service. Labour begins to nationalize industries. | **1946** Dylan Thomas, *Deaths and Entrances*; Mervyn Peake, *Titus Groan*. |
| **1947** Economic crisis. The Marshall Aid Plan. India granted independence; partition creates Pakistan. | **1947** L. P. Hartley, *Eustace and Hilda*; Malcolm Lowry, *Under the Volcano*. |
| **1948** Russians blockade Berlin. Communist coup in Czechoslovakia. | **1948** Graham Greene, *The Heart of the Matter*; W. H. Auden, *The Age of Anxiety*; Christopher Fry, *The Lady's Not for Burning*; Winston Churchill, *The Second World War*; F. R. Leavis, *The Great Tradition*; Robert Graves, *Collected Poems*; Edwin Muir, *The Labyrinth*. |
| **1949** NATO is created. | **1949** Elizabeth Bowen, *The Heat of the Day*; Eliot, *The Cocktail Party*; Orwell, *Nineteen Eighty-Four* (Ezra Pound, *The Pisan Cantos*). |
| **1950** Korean War (to 1953). | **1950** C. S. Lewis, *The Lion, the Witch and the Wardrobe*; William Cooper, *Scenes from Provincial Life*. |
| **1951** Churchill becomes Prime Minister. The Festival of Britain. | **1951** Samuel Beckett, *Malone Dies, Molloy*; Greene, *The End of the Affair*; Anthony Powell, *A Question of Upbringing*; C. P. Snow, *The Masters*. |
| **1952** George VI dies. | **1952** David Jones, *The Anathemata*; Waugh, *Men at Arms*; Dylan Thomas, *Collected Poems*. |
| **1953** Coronation of Elizabeth II. | **1953** Kingsley Amis, *Lucky Jim*; Beckett, *Watt*; Hartley, *The Go-Between*. |
| **1954** Food rationing ends. **1955** Anthony Eden becomes Prime Minister. | **1954** William Golding, *Lord of the Flies*; Dylan Thomas, *Under Milk Wood*; Iris Murdoch, *Under the Net*; J. R. R. Tolkien, *The Fellowship of the Ring*; Muir, *Autobiography*; Terence Rattigan, *Separate Tables*. |

Rosamund Lehmann and the firmer ideas-driven fiction of 'Rebecca West' (1892–1983), an Anglo-Irishwoman who took her name from the feminist heroine of Ibsen's *Rosmersholm*. Elizabeth Bowen did not turn her life or opinions too simply into fiction.

## Fairy tales

### C. S. Lewis

The Anglo-Irish **C. S. Lewis** (1898–1963), the scholar of medieval and renaissance literature who wrote *The Allegory of Love* (1936), also developed an other-worldly fiction in *The Screwtape Letters* (1942), an infernal correspondence-course on How to Tempt, and *Perelandra* (1943), one of three cosmic allegories about technology and human pride. Later, *Surprised by Joy* and *A Grief Observed* dealt impressively with experiences of love and loss. *The Lion, the Witch and the Wardrobe* and the other 'Narnia' books for children have since proved very popular. Narnia is full of the romance, parable and folklore Lewis had harvested. Such genres are found in every literature, but advanced opinion used to neglect them as fairy stories suitable for children, thinking of realist novels as serious and 'adult'. Yet childhood reading is the only access to literature many people get, and, to children, adult experience is not real.

### J. R. R. Tolkien

This may be why in the 1950s a worldwide popularity came to the South African philologist **J. R. R. Tolkien** (1892–1973) for his trilogy *The Lord of the Rings*, a heroic romance of vast mythological scope, drawing on *Beowulf* and northern legend, symbolic rather than (as Narnia is) parabolic. Tolkien's cycle grew out of his early romance *The Hobbit*, written for his children. He inscribed his wife's gravestone in Elvish, an invented language used in *The Lord of the Rings*.

Tolkien was one of Lewis's 'Inklings', a group who read stories in an Oxford pub. The first Inkling to become known, Charles Williams (1886–1945), author of Arthurian romances and theological thrillers, is now unknown. But there was a demand for supernatural fiction.

## Poetry

### The Second World War

Like the Napoleonic Wars, the Second World War (1939–45) is remembered in novels rather than in poems; partly because German bombing meant that the 'Home Front' was part of the battle zone. The war was entered with fewer illusions. The Home Front was the scene of two memorable Second World War poems: 'Naming of Parts' by Henry Reed, partly a parody of Auden's 'Spain', and 'In Westminster Abbey', by **John Betjeman** (1906–84), which begins

> Let me take this other glove off
>  As the *vox humana* swells,          Latin: a throbbing organ stop
> And the beauteous fields of Eden
>  Bask beneath the Abbey bells.
> Here, where England's statesmen lie,
> Listen to a lady's cry.

> Gracious Lord, oh bomb the Germans.
>> Spare their women for Thy Sake,
> And if that is not too easy
>> We will pardon Thy Mistake.
> But, gracious Lord, whate'er shall be,
> Don't let anyone bomb me.

Of three young poets who fell in the war, Alun Lewis, Sidney Keyes and Keith Douglas, Douglas wrote at least two fine poems, '*Vergissmeinnicht*' and 'Simplify Me When I'm Dead'. Reed, F. T. Prince (1912–95), a South African, and **Roy Fuller** (1912–91) wrote well about war and peace to the end of their long lives. Literature also played a part in the war through the oratory of **Winston Churchill** (1874–1965), encouraging Britons on 18 June 1940 to 'their finest hour':

I expect that the battle of Britain is about to begin. Upon this battle depends the survival of Christian civilisation. Upon it depends our own British life, and the long continuity of our institutions and our Empire. The whole fury and might of the enemy must very soon be turned upon us. Hitler knows that he will have to break us in this island or lose the war. If we can stand up to him, all Europe may be free and the life of the world may move forward into broad, sunlit uplands. But if we fail, then the whole world, including the United States, including all that we have known and cared for, will sink into the abyss of a new dark age made more sinister, and perhaps more protracted, by the lights of perverted science. Let us therefore brace ourselves to our duties, and so bear ourselves that, if the British Empire and its commonwealth last for a thouand years, men will still say, 'This was their finest hour.'

Shakespeare too was recruited to the war effort in Laurence Olivier's memorable film of *Henry V*.

## Dylan Thomas

**Dylan Thomas** (1914–55) was the most famous poet of his day, and a sonorous public reader of poems such as 'The force that through the green fuse drives the flower', 'And death shall have no dominion' and 'Do not go gentle into that good night'. As these first lines suggest, he wove phrases musical with alliteration and assonance into rhythmic lines. These were then worked into rhythmical stanzas, which in Thomas's 'poetry voice' sounded good to audiences. Yet if his best poem, 'Fern Hill', is compared with his model, Hopkins, a consciously 'lovely' manner has melted the meaning – it is almost as if Swinburne had seen the light and taken up hymn-writing. Thomas could also exploit and mock the folk-poetry of Welsh speech, as in his delightful radio play, *Under Milk Wood* (1954), set in the village of Llareggub. His prose *Portrait of the Artist as a Young Dog* (1940) and his short stories show a gift for comedy.

# Drama

From the demise of Wilde until his own death in 1950, Shaw was the leading English dramatist and, with the exceptions of Sean O'Casey and T. S. Eliot, the only literary dramatist of stature. In 1904 he had answered Yeats's request for 'a patriotic contribution to the repertory of the Irish Literary Theatre' with *John Bull's Other Island*. At a command performance, King Edward VII laughed so much that he broke his chair. The playwright Henry Arthur Jones wrote of the first English perfomance in 1924 of *The Cherry Orchard* that it gave him 'the impression of someone who had entered a lunatic asylum and taken down everything the lunatics said'. Chekhov was too far from English theatrical norms to be realistic. The theatre in 20th-century England remained conservative, and old conventions survived. In the year 2000, the Festival Theatres in Malvern and Pitlochry had the audiences Shaw knew. These theatres revived plays by the sentimental Barrie, the solid Galsworthy, the cynical Maugham, the bright Coward, the workmanlike Priestley and the stylish Rattigan. The 20th-century English novelists reviewed above had a remarkably uniform background, but their fictional world is more varied than is found in the middle-class moral-problem plays of **Terence Rattigan** (1911–77), educated at Harrow and at Trinity College, Oxford: *French Without Tears, The Winslow Boy, The Browning Version, The Deep Blue Sea, Separate Tables.* A master of theatrical narrative, Rattigan perfected a highly stylized and understated mode of dialogue. Introducing his *Collected Works* (1953), he invented an 'Aunt Edna' whom playwrights ignore at their peril, for there are things she would not like.

In a preface to *The Playboy of the Western World*, **J. M. Synge** (1871–1909) opposed 'countries where the imagination of the people, and the language they use, is rich and living' (his native Ireland?) to 'the modern literature of towns' (Paris or London?), where we find 'Ibsen and Zola dealing with the reality of life in joyless and pallid words. On the stage, one must have reality, and one must have joy.' An English drawing-room does not address a moral problem in the language of joy.

### Sean O'Casey

If the language of Synge is too joyful to be true, except of the Aran islands, **Sean O'Casey** (1880–1964) used incantatory rhythms in tragicomedies of the Dublin slums such as *Juno and the Paycock* (1924) and *The Plough and the Stars* (1926), in which old gunmen strut their political formulas and memories, and women take the strain. After nationalist riots against this unfavourable portrayal, O'Casey left for London, where *The Silver Tassie* was produced in 1929.

If pacifism was unwelcome in Dublin, non-realistic expressionism was puzzling in London. Auden helped found a Group Theatre which in 1935 put on plays in styles which combined German expressionist techniques with English music-hall routines. Minority audiences saw their first drama by **Bertold Brecht** (1898–1956), full of Marx and Freud; the joy was supplied by music-hall*isch* songs. Eliot's verse drama was more radically experimental in approach than in effect. He had thought 'to take a form of entertainment and subject it to a process which would leave it a form of art. Perhaps the music hall comedian is the best material ...'. The 'form of entertainment' he opted for was West End comedy, dressing Greek tragedy in lounge suits. First he had tried the music hall comedian, in *Sweeney Agonistes* (1932), but this remained a fragment. The experiment he had proposed was performed in 1955 by Samuel Beckett in *Waiting for Godot*. Christopher Fry had much success with plays such as *The Lady's Not for Burning*, written in a cleverly decorative verse. Rattigan has since been revived, but not Fry.

## ■ Further reading

Bergonzi, B. *Reading the Thirties: Texts and Contexts* (London: Macmillan, 1978).

Brown, K. (ed.) *Rethinking Lawrence* (Milton Keynes: Open University Press, 1990).

Cunningham, V. *British Writers of the Thirties* (Oxford: Oxford University Press, 1988).

Ellmann, R. *James Joyce*, 2nd edn (Oxford: Oxford University Press, 1982).

Innes, C. *Modern British Drama, 1880–1990* (Cambridge: Cambridge University Press, 1992).

Macmillan's *Studies in Twentieth-Century Literature*. (Basingstoke: Macmillan). A useful series.

Moody, A. D. (ed.). *The Cambridge Companion to T. S. Eliot* (Cambridge: Cambridge University Press, 1994).

# CHAPTER 14

# New Beginnings: 1955–80

## Contents

## Overview

The change after 1955 is clearest in drama, where Beckett's impact overturned conventions. The marked change from Rattigan and Waugh to Pinter and provincial fiction was as much to do with social class as literary approach. The original talent of William Golding stood aside from conventional social realism. Muriel Spark, too, is an inventive moralist rather than a social chronicler. The dominant poetic voice was Philip Larkin's, his social irony concealing a disappointed hope in human love. Although mocking the Establishment (a word of the 1960s), he and others stood back from the sexual and social liberation of that decade.

About 1955 the post-war era was ending, both in politics and in literature. For most, the war had come as less of a shock than in 1914, and British casualties had been fewer, but reserves were low. Bomb-sites still marked some cities. In the post-war reconstruction a Labour government built up a Welfare State, unchallenged until 1979. On Churchill's overdue retirement in 1955, Eden succeeded as Prime Minister. Hopes were dashed when Eden's attempt to reverse Nasser's takeover of the Suez Canal divided British opinion. In forcing a Franco-British withdrawal from Suez, the US made it clear that Europe should give up its colonies. Russian tanks crushed a Hungarian rising; the Cold War intensified. After 1958, the anti-nuclear movement rallied forces of protest which played a part in politics for twenty years. Eden's successor announced in 1960 that Britain would give up her African colonies.

The leading writers of the post-war decade were well known in 1939: Eliot, Auden, Thomas; Hartley, Bowen, Waugh, Greene, Powell; Rattigan, Fry. In 1955–6, Beckett, Osborne and Pinter altered drama. In 1954, William Golding published his non-realist *Lord of the Flies.* Novels by Kingsley Amis and others made less established voices heard. In 1955 came Philip Larkin's *The Less Deceived*, and other poets began to publish: Thom Gunn, Donald Davie, Elizabeth Jennings, Ted Hughes. They were Oxbridge-educated but from grammar schools; Evelyn Waugh hailed them with delight as 'these grim young people coming off the assembly lines in their hundreds every year and finding employment as critics, even as poets and novelists.' Their tone was stricter, less social, more mocking. New breezes blew, and in the 1960s a storm went through. Its harbingers, Beckett and Golding, were not young.

## Events and publications 1955–

| Events | | Publications | |
|---|---|---|---|
| | | 1955 | Samuel Beckett, *Waiting for Godot*; Brendan Behan, *The Quare Fellow*; William Golding, *The Inheritors*; Philip Larkin, *The Less Deceived*; William Empson, *Collected Poems*. |
| 1956 | President Nasser of Egypt nationalizes the Suez Canal. Israel attacks Egypt. Britain and France send troops, but the US imposes a ceasefire. Russia invades Hungary. | 1956 | Rebecca West, *The Fountain Overflows*; John Osborne, *Look Back in Anger*; Angus Wilson, *Anglo-Saxon Attitudes* (Eugene O'Neill, *Long Day's Journey into Night*). |
| 1957 | Harold Macmillan (Conservative) becomes Prime Minister. | 1957 | Evelyn Waugh, *The Ordeal of Gilbert Pinfold*; Lawrence Durrell, *Bitter Lemons, Justine*; Ted Hughes, *The Hawk in the Rain*; Stevie Smith, *Not Waving but Drowning*; Thom Gunn, *The Sense of Movement*; Rebecca West, *The Fountain Overflows* (Boris Pasternak, *Dr Zhivago*). |
| 1958 | Charles de Gaulle President of France. | 1958 | Brendan Behan, *The Hostage*; Harold Pinter, *The Birthday Party*; Iris Murdoch, *The Bell*; T. H. White, *The Once and Future King*; Samuel Beckett, *Endgame, Krapp's Last Tape*; Alan Sillitoe, *Saturday Night and Sunday Morning*; John Betjeman, *Collected Poems* (Giuseppe Di Lampedusa, *The Leopard*). |
| | | 1959 | John Arden, *Serjeant Musgrave's Dance*; Muriel Spark, *Memento Mori*; Geoffrey Hill, *For the Unfallen*. |
| 1960 | Macmillan's 'Wind of Change' speech: African colonies to be independent. | 1960 | John Betjeman, *Summoned by Bells*; Philip Larkin, *The Whitsun Weddings*; Harold Pinter, *The Caretaker*; D. H. Lawrence, *Lady Chatterley's Lover*; Olivia Manning, *The Balkan Trilogy* (to 1965). |
| | | 1961 | *The New English Bible*; Richard Hughes, *The Fox in the Attic*; V. S. Naipaul, *A House for Mr Biswas*; Muriel Spark, *The Prime of Miss Jean Brodie*; Evelyn Waugh, *Unconditional Surrender*; John Osborne, *Luther*; Thom Gunn, *My Sad Captains*. |
| 1962 | Immigration from black Commonwealth restricted. Second Vatican Council of the Catholic Church (to 1968). | 1962 | Anthony Burgess, *A Clockwork Orange*; Doris Lessing, *The Golden Notebook*; A. Alvarez (ed), *The New Poetry*; Samuel Beckett, *Happy Days*. |
| 1963 | Alec Douglas-Home (Conservative) becomes Prime Minister. | 1963 | Anthony Burgess, *Inside Mr Enderby*; John le Carré, *The Spy Who Came in from the Cold*; Sylvia Plath, *The Bell Jar*. |
| 1964 | Harold Wilson (Labour) becomes Prime Minister. | 1964 | Joe Orton, *Entertaining Mr Sloane*; Keith Douglas, *Selected Poems*. |
| | | 1965 | Sylvia Plath, *Ariel*; John Heath-Stubbs, *Selected Poems*; Robert Graves, *Collected Poems*; Harold Pinter, *The Homecoming*; N. F. Simpson, *The Cresta Run*. |
| 1966 | Adult homosexual acts decriminalized. | 1966 | Jean Rhys, *Wide Sargasso Sea*; W. H. Auden, *Collected Shorter Poems*; Seamus Heaney, *Death of a Naturalist*; Paul Scott, *The Jewel in the Crown* (vol. 1 of *The Raj Quartet*, 1975). |
| | | 1967 | Tom Stoppard, *Rosencrantz and Guildenstern are Dead*; Elizabeth Jennings, *Collected Poems*. |
| 1968 | Student riots in Paris. | 1968 | Bryan Moore, *I am Mary Dunne*; Victor S. Pritchett, *A Cab at the Door*; Tom Stoppard, *The Real Inspector Hound*; Basil Bunting, *Collected Poems*. |
| 1969– | Northern Irish 'Troubles'. | 1969 | John Fowles, *The French Lieutenant's Woman*; Douglas Dunn, *Terry Street*. |
| 1970 | Edward Heath (Conservative) becomes Prime Minister. | 1970 | E. M. Forster, *Maurice*; Ted Hughes, *Crow*. |
| | | 1971 | Geoffrey Hill, *Mercian Hymns*; Edward Bond, *Lear*. |

## Events and publications 1955– *Continued*

| Events | | Publications | |
|---|---|---|---|
| | | 1972 | Tom Stoppard, *Jumpers*; Seamus Heaney, *Wintering Out*; Donald Davie, *Collected Poems*. |
| 1973 | UK enters Common Market. Ceasefire in Vietnam. | 1973 | R. S. Thomas, *Selected Poems*; Alan Ayckbourn, *The Norman Conquests*. |
| 1974 | US President Richard Nixon resigns. | 1974 | Beryl Bainbridge, *The Bottle Factory*; Tom Stoppard, *Travesties*; Philip Larkin, *High Windows*. |
| | | 1975 | Malcolm Bradbury, *The History Man*; Seamus Heaney, *North*; Charles Causley, *Selected Poems*; David Lodge, *Changing Places*. |
| 1976 | James Callaghan (Labour) becomes Prime Minister. | 1976 | Tom Stoppard, *Professional Foul*. |
| | | 1977 | Barbara Pym, *Quartet in Autumn*; Paul Scott, *Staying On*. |
| 1978 | Pope John Paul II elected. | 1978 | Tony Harrison, *The School of Eloquence*; Geoffrey Hill, *Tenebrae*; Charles Tomlinson, *Selected Poems*; A. S. Byatt, *The Virgin in the Garden*. |
| 1979 | Margaret Thatcher (Conservative) becomes Prime Minister. | 1979 | William Golding, *Darkness Visible*; Seamus Heaney, *Field Work*. |
| | | 1980 | William Golding, *Rites of Passage*; Paul Muldoon, *Why Brownlee Left*; Brian Friel, *Translations*. |
| | | 1981 | Salman Rushdie, *Midnight's Children*; Molly Keane, *Good Behaviour*. |
| | | 1982 | Caryl Churchill, *Top Girls*. |
| | | 1984 | Seamus Heaney, *Station Island*; Angela Carter, *Nights at the Circus*; Douglas Dunn, *Elegies*. |
| 1989 | Collapse of Eastern European regimes. The end of the Cold War. | 1985 | Peter Ackroyd, *Hawksmoor*. |
| 1990 | Fall of Margaret Thatcher. | 1990 | Brian Friel, *Dancing at Lugnasa*. |
| 1997 | Tony Blair (Labour) becomes Prime Minister. | | |
| 1999 | Devolution to Scotland and Wales. | | |

# ◼ Drama

## Samuel Beckett

**Samuel Beckett** (1906–89) had the career of an Irish exile. A Protestant, he was educated at Wilde's old school – captaining the cricket XI – and lectured in philosophy at Trinity College, Dublin. He left for Paris, still hostess to international modernism, wrote on Proust, translated *Finnegans Wake* into French, became Joyce's disciple. After the war he wrote three novels – in French rather than his native language, in order to write 'without style'. In 1952 Beckett wrote *En attendant Godot*. After its success in Paris, he translated it. As *Waiting for Godot* it came to London, following plays by Jean Cocteau, Jean-Paul Sartre and Albert Camus. In *The Myth of Sisyphus* (1942) Camus had put forward the idea of 'the absurd', a philosophical reaction to the unintelligibility of life, which under the German occupation of Paris had become greater than usual. *La Cantatrice Chauve* (1948) by Eugène Ionesco was the first comedy of the Theatre of the Absurd (*The Bald Prima Donna*, London, 1958). Brecht's Berliner Ensemble visited in 1956, the year of Osborne's *Look Back in Anger*.

In 1957 came Pinter's *The Birthday Party*. But London had seen nothing like *Godot*. Beckett's comic, experimental novels had been ignored. He now became the West's leading literary dramatist.

*Waiting for Godot* can be misunderstood – as Chekhov can – as merely bleak, especially by students who have not seen it. Subtitled 'a tragicomedy in two acts', its mood is one of gaiety, and the characters are clowns as well as tramps. 'Life is first boredom, then fear,' Larkin was to write later. Beckett would think that formulation too solemn.

Modernist nihilism of a theatrical kind had been prominent in Eliot's *The Waste Land*:

> 'What is that noise?'
> >The wind under the door.
> 'What is that noise now? What is the wind doing?'
> >Nothing again nothing.
> 'You know nothing? Do you see nothing? Do you remember
> Nothing?'

A drama, said Aristotle, is the imitation of an action. In *Waiting for Godot* nothing happens. Indeed, famously, nothing happens twice. Vladimir and Estragon await the arrival of Godot, a name which adds a French diminutive ending to 'God' (in France, Charlie Chaplin was called 'Charl*ot*'). But, whoever he is, he doesn't arrive. The play ends:

VLADIMIR: We'll hang ourselves tomorrow. (*Pause.*) Unless Godot comes.
ESTRAGON: And if he comes?
VLADIMIR: We'll be saved.
*Vladimir takes off his hat (Lucky's), peers inside it, feels about inside it, shakes it, knocks on the crown, puts it on again.*
ESTRAGON: Well? Shall we go?
VLADIMIR: Pull on your trousers.
ESTRAGON: What?
VLADIMIR: Put on your trousers.
ESTRAGON: You want me to pull off my trousers?
VLADIMIR: Pull ON your trousers.
ESTRAGON: (*realizing his trousers are down*). True.
*He pulls up his trousers.*
VLADIMIR: Well? Shall we go?
ESTRAGON: Yes, let's go.
*They do not move.*
*CURTAIN*

No thing happens, but words happen. Attempted reasoning replaces plot, and language becomes supreme. Set directions read: 'Act I. A country road. A tree. Evening', and 'Act II. Next day. Same time. Same place.' To this tree come Vladimir and Estragon, with their music-hall boots, trousers and bowler hat. Vladimir is the funny man and Estragon the straight man (like the British television comedians, Morecambe and Wise). Their cross-talk also comes from the music hall:

VLADIMIR: Did you ever read the Bible?
ESTRAGON: The Bible … (*He reflects.*) I must have taken a look at it.
VLADIMIR: Do you remember the Gospels?

ESTRAGON: I remember the maps of the Holy Land. Coloured they were. Very pretty. The Dead Sea was pale blue. The very look of it made me thirsty. That's where we'll go, I used to say, that's where we'll go for our honeymoon. We'll swim. We'll be happy.

VLADIMIR: You should have been a poet.

ESTRAGON: I was. (*Gesture towards his rags.*) Isn't that obvious?

*Silence.*

VLADIMIR: Where was I … How's your foot?

ESTRAGON: Swelling visibly.

VLADIMIR: Ah yes, the two thieves. Do you remember the story?

ESTRAGON: No.

VLADIMIR: Shall I tell it to you?

ESTRAGON: No.

VLADIMIR: It'll pass the time. (*Pause.*) Two thieves, crucified at the same time as our Saviour. One –

ESTRAGON: Our what?

VLADIMIR: Our Saviour. Two thieves. One is supposed to have been saved and the other … (*he searches for the contrary of saved*) … damned.

ESTRAGON: Saved from what?

VLADIMIR: Hell.

ESTRAGON: I'm going.

*He does not move.*

VLADIMIR: And yet … (*pause*) … how is it – this is not boring you I hope – how is it that of the four Evangelists only one speaks of a thief being saved. The four of them were there – or thereabouts – and only one speaks of a thief being saved. (*Pause.*) Come on, Gogo, return the ball, can't you, once in a way?

As well as action and set, Beckett dispenses with the convention that the redundancy and inconsequence of everyday conversation is purged from stage dialogue. Vladimir's attempt to debate the chances of salvation is held under difficult conditions, for weak reason is at the mercy of a weaker physique. The gushing stream of consciousness of James Joyce divides into two trickles. The absence of context means that the audience's consciousness begins to stream, filling the void with possible meanings. The text, and the tree, suggest at times the Crucifixion and the Garden of Eden.

VLADIMIR: Christ! What's Christ got to do with it? You're not going to compare yourself to Christ!

ESTRAGON: All my life I've compared myself to him.

VLADIMIR: But where he lived it was warm, it was dry!

ESTRAGON: Yes. And they crucified quick.

But even less than in *Prufrock* are these grand comparisons lived up to, as urgent or trivial physical needs lower the tone spectacularly, rather as in the Heath scenes in *King Lear*, or the medieval play of Cain and Abel. Man without God is farcical as well as miserable. Beckett brings modernist literature home to an audience by inverting the relation between text and audience found in *Finnegans Wake*: instead of too much meaning there is too little. The audience has to make sense of a verbal and visual text as spare as an Imagist poem and as basic as a music-hall sketch. By letting in audience imagination, Beckett made extremist minority art immediate, involving, universal. His early tragicomic novels appeal to intellectuals. But another early work, a tribute to the silent film comedian Buster Keaton, was the route to the music-hall solution Eliot had tried and abandoned in *Sweeney Agonistes*.

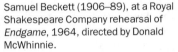

Samuel Beckett (1906–89), at a Royal Shakespeare Company rehearsal of *Endgame*, 1964, directed by Donald McWhinnie.

Beckett's later work further reduces the dramatic elements: the number of actors, of their movements, of their moving parts, of their words. Words achieved a stage role they had not had for centuries. Beckett used directors, but liked to gauge every detail of his plays, every word, movement, gesture, syllable and tone of voice. In 1962 the television actress Billie Whitelaw was sent a script to read, entitled *Play*. It was by 'a fairly bizarre writer called Samuel Beckett … On paper, it seemed to be about a man, his wife and his mistress, all of whom were stuck in urns.' She became Beckett's favourite actress, and her performance can be seen in a videotape of the BBC television version of *Not I*, a play in which a spotlit mouth speaks continuously and at breathless speed for sixteen minutes, often recycling its topics and words. Lips, teeth and tongue can be seen, not nose, chin or eyes. It gives 'soliloquy' a new meaning. The effect is intense.

## John Osborne

The impact of *Look Back in Anger* (1956), by the actor **John Osborne** (1929–94), was due to its content rather than any novelty of form. The working-class Jimmy Porter, married to Alison, a young woman of conventional upper-middle-class background, delivers colourful tirades directed equally at the limitations of their lives and the pieties of her family, representing what was soon called 'the establishment', a term originally referring to the legal position of the Church of England but now extended to the inherited social set-up. The remembered social cohesion of the war years gave a

**Harold Pinter** (1930–)
Selected plays: *The Room, The Dumb Waiter, The Birthday Party* (1957), *The Caretaker* (1959), *The Homecoming* (1965), *Old Times* (1971), *No Man's Land* (1975), *Betrayal* (1978), *One for the Road* (1984), *Mountain Language* (1988).

dramatic edge to Jimmy's frustration at social inequality and the futility of individual action. Osborne made the grotty flat with its Sunday newspapers and ironing-board an image of its time: 'kitchen-sink realism' was at hand. *The Entertainer* (1957) is his next-best play, though protest has a good day out in *Luther* (1961).

## Harold Pinter

Another actor, **Harold Pinter** (1930–), son of a tailor in the East End of London, learned from Beckett and the Theatre of the Absurd. His verbal surface has a peeling realistic veneer, each character being identified by a memorable trick of speech; but the characters' relation to what is ordinarily taken as real life is tenuous and oblique. In *The Caretaker* three men pursue their delusions: Aston, who has had electro-convulsive brain treatment, takes Davies, an evasive tramp, to a ramshackle room in an derelict house, used both by Aston and his brother Mick, a fantasist. Each manages his world passably enough, talking it into existence, though references to the real world become unreal. Davies is not going to 'get to Sidcup', any more than Chekhov's Three Sisters will go to Moscow; but Sidcup is a less grand ambition. Inconsequential cross-talk, less logical than Beckett's, with pauses and silences, gives way occasionally, as also in Beckett, to operatic arias of banality expressing the loneliness of the speaker. Though found in O'Casey and Beckett, these verbal rigmaroles became a Pinter trademark. Audience laughter turns to pity.

Pinter's other speciality is undefined ominousness. The neurosis of Beckett's speakers has a metaphysical dimension, a fear of death, eternity, nothingness. Pinter's are scared of being found out or of being beaten up. In *The Birthday Party*, the nervous lodger, Stanley, is visited by old friends, who turn out to be from an organization which they say he has betrayed. As in Franz Kafka's *The Trial*, nothing is clear, every-

Donald Pleasance and Alan Bates in Harold Pinter's *The Caretaker*, directed by Clive Donner, 1963.

thing is menacing. In summary, Pinter's plays sound formulaic; in performance, they are gifts to actors, directors and audiences. But his style is easier to imitate than Beckett's, and dialogue in which the interlocutors speak past each other became standard.

Already by 1960, the theatre of Beckett and Pinter had triumphed. Yet *The Waste Land* had already left the themes of the meaninglessness of life and the impossibility of communication with limited scope for development. Pinter's *Betrayal* concerns a married couple and their best man, who has a love-affair with the wife. The time-sequence of scenes is reversed, so that the consequences of telling and living a lie become, as in a detective story, progressively more intelligible and less comic. Imitated everywhere, Pinter remains an unsurpassed craftsman of spoken dialogue. His later plays are less mysterious and more political.

## Established protest

The theatrical revolution of 1956–60 established the stage as a platform for anti-establishmentarianism, directorial, political and sexual-political. The Theatre of the Absurd gave way to the Theatre of Cruelty, in which audiences were spat at by actors and sprayed with pig's blood. An admired production of *King Lear* by Peter Brook omitted Cornwall's servant and all other signs of hope from the text. Sexual liberation was pursued with anarchic laughter by Joe Orton, more thinkingly by Caryl Churchill; Marxist theatre by John Arden and more grimly by Edward Bond, Howard Brenton, David Hare, David Edgar and Trevor Griffiths. The anti-capitalist attitudes of the student riots in Paris in 1968 took up residence on state-subsidized stages. The most skilled dramatists of the period were Alan Bennett (1934–), Dennis Potter (1935–97), Alan Ayckbourn (1939–), Tom Stoppard (1937–) and Caryl Churchill (1938–). Among the best plays were Bennett's *An Englishman Abroad* (BBC TV 1983), Stoppard's *The Real Inspector Hound* (1968) and *Travesties* (1974), and Churchill's *Top Girls* (1982). But it was not a great literary period in the theatre. Irish English came once again to the rescue, with Brian Friel (1929–), whose *Translations* (1980), *Making History* (1988) and *Dancing at Lugnasa* (1990) brought language back to the English stage.

### Other dramatists

Brendan Behan, *The Quare Fellow* (1956), *The Hostage* (1958).

N. F. Simpson, *A Resounding Tinkle* (1957).

John Arden, *Live Like Pigs* (1958), *Serjeant Musgrave's Dance* (1959).

Joe Orton, *Entertaining Mr Sloane* (1964), *Loot* (1966), *The Ruffian on the Stair*, *The Erpingham Camp* (1967), *What the Butler Saw* (1969).

Tom Stoppard, *Rosencrantz and Guildenstern are Dead* (1966), *The Real Inspector Hound* (1968), *Jumpers* (1972), *Travesties* (1974).

David Pownall, *Masterclass* (1985).

Michael Frayn, *Copenhagen* (1999).

**William Golding** (1911–93)
Educated at Marlborough
Grammar School and Oxford;
worked in theatre and
teaching. Novels: *Lord of the
Flies* (1954), *The Inheritors*
(1955), *Pincher Martin* (1956),
*Free Fall* (1959), *The Spire*
(1964), *The Pyramid* (1967),
*Darkness Visible* (1979), *Rites
of Passage* (1980), *Close
Quarters* (1987), *Fire Down
Below* (1989), *The Paper Men*
(1984). Winner of the Nobel
Prize for Literature (1983).

## ■ Novels galore

In 1960, 30,000 new titles appeared in the UK. In 1990 England's leading second-hand bookseller, Booth of Hay-on-Wye, calculated that the gross number of new titles of all kinds published since 1960 exceeded the number published before 1960. This is bad news for a historian of contemporary literature, who in a different way is also a valuer of secondhand books. Readers cannot keep up, although books are still often given as presents.

Dr Johnson's question 'Do you read books *through*?' might be put to the celebrities who list the Books of the Year, to the judges of the growing number of literary prizes, and to the academic assessors of the research quality of English departments. The growth in direct mail, newsprint and publishing prompts a self-defence reaction: 'Do I need to read this?' At Book Weeks, actors read books aloud to people who can read.

Acclaimed novels of the 1960s, 1970s and even 1980s do not very often stand up well to re-reading. In such conditions, an account of the volcanic state of the contemporary novel must choose between providing an annotated list, marking the card of runners with summary comments, and an unannotated list with some discussion of a few names. The second seems more honest.

## William Golding

Leading post-war novelists

See also 'Publications 1940–55'
(page 353) and 'Publications
1955–' (pages 359–60).
Joyce Cary (1888–1957)
Rebecca West (1892–1983)
Jean Rhys (1894–1979)
Arthur Koestler (1905–83)
Malcolm Lowry (1909–57)
William Golding (1911–93)
Lawrence Durrell (1912–90)
Barbara Pym (1913–80)
Angus Wilson (1913–91)
Anthony Burgess (1917–93)
Olivia Manning (1918–80)
Muriel Spark (1918–)
Iris Murdoch (1919–99)
Doris Lessing (1919–)
Paul Scott (1920–78)
Brian Moore (1921–)
Kingsley Amis (1922–93)
John Fowles (1926–)
Malcolm Bradbury (1932–)
David Lodge (1934)
A. S. Byatt (1936)

**William Golding** (1911–93) is a name likely to last, and not only for *Lord of the Flies*, a fable about a party of boys from a Cathedral Choir School marooned on a Pacific island. A teacher, Golding knew something of boys, and his strong tale is believably reported through the eyes and idioms of Piggy, Ralph, Simon, Jack and Co. As commander of a rocket ship in the Royal Navy, Golding also knew something of how people behave in emergencies. At the end of the novel, Ralph, running for his life from the spear-wielding boys, runs smack into a naval officer who has just landed on the beach. 'Ralph wept for the end of innocence, the darkness of man's heart, and the fall through the air of the true, wise friend called Piggy.' The officer, looking out to his trim cruiser, says, 'I should have thought that a pack of British boys . . . would have been able to put up a better show than that.' The text has just mentioned R. M. Ballantyne's *The Coral Island* (1857), a jolly adventure in the self-reliant happy-ending tradition of Defoe's *Robinson Crusoe* (1719), and still a boys' book in 1954.

The officer's appearance emphasizes the fictiveness of happy endings. His 'pack' recalls the Boy Scouts, as do the rituals the boys invent; but the pack had gradually become tribal and savage, worshipping a pig's head on a stake: the 'lord of the flies' is Beelzebub, a name for the Devil. Simon, an 'oversensitive' boy, disbelieves in the idol; he is put to death. The book is a moral and Christian fable. The metaphysical pessimism of Conrad and the early Eliot is here delivered to the schoolroom, more tellingly than in Richard Hughes's *A High Wind in Jamaica* (1929). The spiritual void and moral relativism sensed before 1914 had not prevented the evil of genocide in Europe's most 'scientific' country. The sacrifice of the Jews as scapegoats for the ills that had befallen Germany became fully known only after 1945; the killing of Simon may not refer to this evil, but the intolerability of good is one of Golding's themes.

Golding is not a simple moral fabulist like Lewis or Tolkien. *Lord of the Flies* adopts the frictionless simplicity of a boy's book only to challenge the assumptions

(Sir) William Golding 1970.

of boys' books. His other allegories are embedded in temporal as well as physical settings. Such an allegory is executed boldly in *The Inheritors*, set in the imagined sensory world of a group of Neanderthals, 'the people':

The sun dropped into the river and light left the overhang. Now the fire was more than ever central, white ash, a spot of red and one flame wavering upwards. The old woman moved softly, pushing in more wood so that the red spot ate and the flame grew strong. The people watched, their faces seeming to quiver in the unsteady light. Their freckled skins were ruddy and the deep caverns beneath their brows were each inhabited by replicas of the fire and all their fires danced together. As they persuaded themselves of the warmth they relaxed limbs and drew the reek into their nostrils gratefully. They flexed their toes and stretched their arms, even leaning away from the fire. One of the deep silences fell on them, that seemed so much more natural than speech, a timeless silence in which there were at first many minds in the overhang; and then perhaps no mind at all. So fully discounted was the roar of the water that the soft touch of the wind on the rocks became audible. Their ears as if endowed with separate life sorted the tangle of tiny sounds and accepted them, the sound of breathing, the sound of wet clay flaking and ashes falling in.

Then Mal spoke with unusual diffidence.

'Is it cold?'

Drawn slowly into their collective and undifferentiated language, we come to know the people and see old Mal succeeded as leader by Lok. The people become aware of some 'new men', whom they watch with interest. The narrative viewpoint then switches to that of the new men; for them, Lok is 'the red creature', an animal to be killed. The language of the new men is a more modern English. Such dramatic switches of viewpoint, language and morality are structural in Golding's novels.

The precision, density and ambition of Golding's imaginings, and his searching moral sense, make him unusually demanding and potentially rewarding. He can be tempted by the mimetic fallacy which thinks that the best way of staging madness is to put a real madman on the stage. He can veer into Gothic, and also into a stiff playfulness reminiscent of Conrad; his writing also has Conrad's deliberate beauty. Perhaps his most successful later novel is *Rites of Passage*, set on an ex-man-of-war taking some emigrants to Australia after the Napoleonic wars. The action is presented via the contrasting journals of young Talbot, jarringly self-important and with powerful aristocratic connections, and the Reverend Colley, a wretched Christian minister who plays the holy fool in a very unholy ship, and dies of humiliation and shame. If Simon in *Lord of the Flies* is perhaps too clearly the Christian innocent, Colley is both genuinely irritating and genuinely abased by a sexual act which he performs when the sailors get him drunk in the ceremonies of Crossing the Line. The embarrassing impracticability of the Christian ideal leaves a horrible conundrum at the heart of this sombre tragedy, which is lit theatrically at times by moments of surprise and laughter. This strange and impressive achievement, both very literary (it alludes both to Coleridge's *Ancient Mariner* and to Jane Austen) and painfully real, begins a trilogy. Although Golding is more in the tradition of Dostoevsky and Conrad than a social novelist, he is a recognizably English one, and makes his juniors seem light in comparison.

Greene's remark that the loss of the religious sense deprives the human act of importance bears on the form of the novel. As English life further loosens from Christian ideals which have historically shaped its self-understanding, the social order – which is the canvas, when it is not the subject, of the realist novel – is less easily used to convey larger meanings. A novelist with Golding's need to reach towards the heights and the depths has to borrow the symbolic potential of poetic drama. The price of a more extreme shift of the English novel away from its natural territory is seen in *Under the Volcano* by Malcolm Lowry (1909–57), a novel about the fall into alcoholic madness of a British consul in Mexico; its hallucinatory quality is compromised by its too evident mythic reinforcement. It is hard to move the English novel far from its role of social entertainment. The work of Barbara Pym (1913–80) and Kingsley Amis (1922–93) shows how good at social comedy English novelists can still be. Angus Wilson (1913–91) wrote in that tradition with more ambition, but his work at its best remains painful and sophisticated.

## Muriel Spark

A lighter writer who shares some of Golding's concerns (she wrote a dystopian novel called *Robinson*) is **Muriel Spark** (1918–). Brought up in Edinburgh, half-Jewish but a Catholic convert, and the survivor of a marriage to a husband who became deranged, she lived in London and Italy. Her engaging, ingenious novels are often set in largely female institutions – a hostel, a school, a convent – where personal destiny and value are at stake, and bizarre happenings are recounted with a cool amusement which brings out a comic Gothic pattern. Her best-known novel, thanks to a film, is *The Prime of Miss Jean Brodie*: a charismatic mistress at an Edinburgh girls' school uses her hold over her pupils to make them fulfil her heroic and romantic fantasies. When one of the girls is killed on her way to the Spanish Civil War, Miss Brodie is reported by a member of the set and dismissed. In putting a stop to Miss Brodie, however, her betrayer has imitated her mistress in trying to play God. The costs and benefits of moral choices remain sharply unreconciled.

**Muriel Spark** (1918–)
Selected novels: *Memento Mori* (1959), *The Ballad of Peckham Rye* (1960), *The Prime of Miss Jean Brodie* (1961), *Girls of Slender Means* (1963), *The Abbess of Crewe* (1974).

## Iris Murdoch

Iris Murdoch (1919–99), author of valuable essays in moral philosophy and aesthetics, was another novelist who dealt with serious moral questions in a mode touched by fantasy, though without Spark's economy. Born in Dublin and educated in England, she lived in Oxford. Her first novel, *Under the Net* (1954), is a beguiling exploration of love, touched with the philosophical issues that preoccupied Jean-Paul Sartre and Samuel Beckett. In it the narrative enchantment of romance contains her strong intellectual impulse. This stylish balance between spirit and intelligence is sometimes strained in the twenty novels that followed, in which ingenious and arbitrary set-up situations, involving permutations of relationships, act as a code for the mysterious operation of free will. Iris Murdoch's verve and charm won for her a large audience, but the novels are more sophisticated than satisfying.

Some will dispute this judgement, and its implied preference for a more solid realization of character and event. The paradoxes arising from the differences between fiction and fact, realism and reality, have come to fascinate writers and critics. But novelists who dispense with imaginative human engagement with character, and who interrupt what Coleridge called 'that willing suspension of disbelief', run the risk that the reader may not care what happens to their characters. The author's ideas have then to be very interesting indeed – as, with Iris Murdoch, they often are.

## Other writers

The early novels of **John Fowles** (1926–) mesmerized a readership which expanded with *The French Lieutenant's Woman* (1969), a neo-Victorian romance based on Hardy locales and situations but lit by the light of a modern awareness of Freud and of Victorian improprieties. Following the ideas of Alain Robbe-Grillet and Roland Barthes, Fowles provides more than one ending: luckier than the readers of 1869, those of 1969 were free to choose. A simple interest in the dilemmas of the Victorian love-triangle is trumped by a modern understanding which the reader is invited to share with the author. The double perspective is piquant but less satisfying than a real Hardy novel. Similar perspectives work better in two recent 'Victorian' novels, *Possession* (1990) by A(ntonia) S(usan) **Byatt** (1936–), about the dangers of poetic research, and *Oscar and Lucinda* (1988) by the Australian Peter Carey, based on Edmund Gosse's *Father and Son* and episodes of colonial history.

Jim Dixon, of Kingsley Amis's first novel, *Lucky Jim* (1953), Jimmy Porter of *Look Back in Anger* (1956) and Joe Lampton of John Braine's *Room at the Top* (1957) were called 'Angry Young Men' by journalists. Whether they rose like Joe or stuck like Jimmy, they did not accept inferiority. Anti-establishment voices were heard in the novels of **Alan Sillitoe** (1928–) and **John Wain** (1925–95). The significance of these writers is a broadly social one; a lower- is substituted for an upper-middle-class point of view. Amis's Dixon, however, is a genuine comic invention, a lower-middle-class provincial lecturer incurably hostile to all forms of pretension, especially the painfully high culture of his madrigal-singing Professor. *Lucky Jim* is excellent farce. Amis's later novels developed Dixon's talent for taking off pseuds and bores. He was a verbal caricaturist of wicked accuracy, a craftsman of the grotesque, but increasingly a curmudgeon, though *Lucky Jim* remains the most vigorous of university novels.

The more lasting revolution of the 1960s came in sexual rather than class attitudes, as picked by Philip Larkin in his '*Annus Mirabilis*':

> Sexual intercourse began in 1963,
> Which was just too late for me,
> Between the end of the *Chatterley* ban
> And the Beatles' first LP.

This joke offers dates for some changes: the introduction of the female contraceptive pill; leave to print four-letter words; the triumph of pop music. The notion that sexual inhibition is bad and explicitness good has had consequences. The spread of female contraception coincided with a new claim for equality of opportunity for women, both in employment and in relationships outside or without marriage; there was also an explicit claim for parity of esteem for literature devoted to women's experience. The radical South African writer Doris Lessing (1919–) was angrier about men and race than the young men were about class. A challenge to heterosexuality as the norm, and a plea for same-sex relationships to be accepted, is heard in the plays of Joe Orton (1933–67). Some feminists aspired to women-only social arrangements.

## ■ Poetry

Philip Larkin and Kingsley Amis, friends at St John's College, Oxford, were suspicious of high culture. They preferred jazz, beer and mockery to madrigals, wine and Romanticism. *Lucky Jim* ends with Jim Dixon's attack on the myth of Merrie England. Larkin's poem 'Church Going' probes uneasily the reasons why churches are visited. Larkin also questioned the authenticity of a poetic 'myth kitty', the religion and myth drawn on by Eliot, Yeats and earlier poets. For him those myths were dead. These Oxford English graduates doubtful of high culture were soon among its trophies: Amis a Cambridge lecturer, Larkin the librarian of Hull University. Their suspicion of pretension turned into a general irony.

Poetry has become a minority taste. The only true poets who have approached popularity between John Betjeman and Seamus Heaney have been Larkin, Hughes (and, posthumously, his wife Sylvia Plath), and Tony Harrison. There have been many good poets, and a fine anthology could be made of English verse 1955–2000. But the position of poetry within literature has been weakened, like literature itself, by media competition and social change in an age of celebrity. Few people spend an evening reading. Poets who require the highest kinds of attention, such as Geoffrey Hill, find few readers. The enthusiasm with which identifiable groups responded to the American 'Beat' poets, or to John Betjeman or Sylvia Plath or Tony Harrison, is due to the predispositions of readers as well as to merit in the poets. Subject matter can generate interest: the Holocaust, Northern Ireland, the death of one person, minority politics. Other poetry has had to be sold hard to reach a readership of any size. Few general publications carry any verse; poetry magazines are little magazines. 'All the literati keep/An imaginary friend' (Auden, 'The Fall of Rome'). In a period when novelists have received advances of half a million pounds, none of the poets

### Leading British poets: 1955–

| | |
|---|---|
| Stevie Smith (1902–71) | Thom Gunn (resident in California) (1929–) |
| Sir John Betjeman (1906–84) | Peter Porter (born in Australia) (1929–) |
| R. S. Thomas (1913–) | Ted Hughes (1930–99) |
| C. H. Sisson (1914–) | Geoffrey Hill (1932–) |
| Philip Larkin (1922–85) | Tony Harrison (1937–) |
| Elizabeth Jennings (1926–) | Seamus Heaney (1939–) |
| Charles Tomlinson (1927–) | |

named above has lived off the sales of poems. Larkin said of Amis, a poet turned successful novelist, 'He has outsoared the shadow of our night'. In 1998 Oxford University Press axed its poetry list. But popularity isn't everything, and good poetry deserves no less space than good fiction or drama.

**Philip Larkin** (1922–85)
Novels: *Jill* (1946), *A Girl in Winter* (1947). Verse: *The North Ship* (1945), *The Less Deceived* (1955), *The Whitsun Weddings* (1964), *High Windows* (1974), *Collected Poems* (1988).

## Philip Larkin

Of post-war English poets, the reputation of **Philip Larkin** (1922–85) seems most assured. His *Collected Poems* has many of the best poems of its time. The title of the slim volume that made his name, *The Less Deceived*, inverts a phrase from Shakespeare, 'I was the more deceived'. Not to be deceived was one of Larkin's chief aims in a life in which he protected himself. His father, who had a bust of Adolf Hitler on his mantlepiece, was Town Clerk of Coventry, destroyed by German bombs while young Larkin was at Oxford. He hid a wounded Romantic temperament behind a mask of irony, and became known as an anti-romantic, thanks to poems of disgust and despair, such as *Annus Mirabilis*, 'This Be the Verse', 'The Old Fools' and 'Aubade'.

A better way into Larkin is 'Cut Grass':

> Cut grass lies frail:
> Brief is the breath
> Mown stalks exhale.
> Long, long the death
>
> It dies in the white hours
> Of young-leafed June
> With chestnut flowers,
> With hedges snowlike strewn,
>
> White lilac bowed,
> Lost lanes of Queen Anne's lace,
> And that high-builded cloud
> Moving at summer's pace.

This is a Georgian poem, Shakespearean in its final gesture, a last breath of English pastoral, the syntax dancing carefully in its tiny metres. He joked that deprivation was to him what daffodils were to Wordsworth. Yet, like Wordsworth's, Larkin's poetry at its best is 'heart-breaking'. It is with suppressed anger, pity and humour that he views the degraded circumstances in which people live their lives, 'loaf-haired' secretaries amid 'estates full of washing' or shopping for 'Bri-Nylon Baby Dolls and Shorties' (Modes for Night), in the poem 'The Large Cool Store'. In 'The Whitsun Weddings', Larkin, travelling to London by train, looks out idly, recording sensations:

> now and then a smell of grass
> Displaced the reek of buttoned carriage-cloth
> Until the next town, new and nondescript,
> Approached with acres of dismantled cars.

The last line has the anticlimax of Eliot's 'I have measured out my life with coffee-spoons', but here the coffee is instant. Larkin's use of regular stanzaic forms, artful syntax and diction masks the originality of his subject-matter. At stations, wedding parties put newly-weds on the train, 'an uncle shouting smut':

Philip Larkin (1922–85), in about 1965.

> A dozen marriages got under way.
> They watched the landscape, sitting side by side
> – An Odeon went past, a cooling tower,
> And someone running up to bowl –.

He watches, separate from them but drawing nearer. A distance between self and others, especially married others, is preserved. He values ordinary collective institutions – marriage, seaside holidays, British trains, 'Show Saturday', hotels, churches, Remembrance Day, even 'An Arundel Tomb' – but he is outside them all. In 'Dockery and Son' he wonders why a contemporary of his already has a son at university. 'Why did he think adding meant increase?/To me it was dilution.' His own idea of happiness is 'Unfenced existence:/Facing the sun, untalkative, out of reach' ('Here'), or

> 　　　　　　　　　　　the thought of high windows:
> The sun-comprehending glass,
> And beyond it, the deep blue air, that shows
> Nothing, and is nowhere, and is endless.　　　'High Windows'

Larkin's own reputation, established early and not fading, was contested by those who disliked his grouchy anti-modernism, xenophobia and attitudes to sex. That fine poet Charles Tomlinson thought Larkin self-limiting and formulaic; Ezra Pound had the same view of A. E. Housman. Larkin took Hardy rather than Yeats as his model; he mocked Picasso and Pound. Of Margaret Thatcher's remark, 'If you can't afford it, you just can't have it', Larkin said with delight: 'I thought I would never hear anyone say that again.' An ironic connoisseur of the boring and the banal, Larkin was more modernist, cultivated and literary than he pretended; his poems are intensely if quietly allusive. But the mask grew on him as he played the Little Englander, more morosely than his adopted poetic uncle, John Betjeman. He was an inveterate joker. The poet-librarian did not truly think, like the man in his 'A Study of Reading Habits', that 'Books are a load of crap.'

## Ted Hughes

**Ted Hughes** (1930–99) A selection: *The Hawk in the Rain* (1957), *Lupercal* (1960), *Wodwo* (1967), *Crow* (1970), *Birthday Letters* (1999).

**Ted Hughes** (1930–99) did not share Larkin's interest in human beings, nor his horrified urbanity. *The Hawk in the Rain* contains memorable poems about birds and fish, such as 'Hawk Roosting' and 'Pike', based on boyhood experience of fishing and shooting in his native Yorkshire. He fills these poems with the animals' physical presence, endowing their natural strength with mythic power. These taut muscular poems are his best. The anthropology he read at Cambridge enabled him to systematize his approach in *Crow*, an invented primitive creation cycle which glorifies a brutal life-force. He wrote a repulsive version of Seneca's *Œdipus* for Brook's Theatre of Cruelty. His later work is quieter and more topographical. Hughes accepted the Laureateship in succession to Betjeman, perhaps attracted to the mythic aspect of the role. His life was darkened by the suicide in 1963 of his wife Sylvia Plath, the American poet. Her intense verse eventually took a turn, as in her father-hating poem 'Daddy', which led some admirers to blame Hughes for her death. Before he died in 1999, he released in *Birthday Letters* poems which concern that time.

# Geoffrey Hill

According to a poem by the Australian Peter Porter, 'Great British poets begin with H'. The least known but not the least of these is **Geoffrey Hill** (1932–), a teacher in universities in England and latterly the US. He is concerned with the public responsibility of poetry towards historical human suffering, injustice and martyrdom. His meditated verse has the tight verbal concentration, melody and intelligence of Eliot, Pound and early Auden, adroitly using a variety of verse-forms and fictional modes. He is agonized, intense, ironical, scornful. Condensation and allusiveness lend his work a daunting aspect, softened in his more narrative later sequences.

His most approachable volume is *Mercian Hymns*, a sequence of memories of his West Midlands boyhood, figured in a series of imaginary Anglo-Saxon prose poems about Offa, the 8th-century king of Mercia and England. Its serious play domesticates and makes intimate the ancient and modern history of England.

> The princes of Mercia were badger, and raven. Thrall
>  to their freedom, I dug and hoarded. Orchards
>  fruited above clefts. I drank from honeycombs of
> chill sandstone.
>
> 'A boy at odds in the house, lonely among brothers.'
>  But I, who had none, fostered a strangeness, gave
>  myself to unattainable toys.
>
> Candles of gnarled resin, apple-branches, the tacky
>  mistletoe.
>
> from Hymn 6

Hill is a classic with a small audience which will surely grow.

**Geoffrey Hill** (1932–)  *For the Unfallen* (1959), *King Log* (1968), *Mercian Hymns* (1971), *Tenebrae* (1978), *The Mystery of the Charity of Charles Péguy* (1983), *The Triumph of Love* (1998).

**Tony Harrison** (1937–)  Born and educated in Leeds. Poetry collections: *The School of Eloquence* (1978), *v.* (1985); translations: *The Mysteries* (1985), *The Trackers of Oxyrhyncus* (1990).

# Tony Harrison

**Tony Harrison** (1937–), on the other hand, has been a public poet, writing a clanking pentameter line with punchy rhymes. His degree was in classics, but he also learned from stand-up comics in Leeds about pace, timing and delivery. He has written, translated and adapted a number of theatrical and operatic scripts for international companies.

This theatrical extroversion lends a performative impact to his own verse, which shows a bleakly Gothic range of emotions and a proclaimed and campaigning commitment to the Northern working class. His upbringing contributes richly to his idiom, which is often vulgar in the good sense of the word. Alienation from family by education is rawly recorded in telling poems to his parents in *The School of Eloquence*, as in 'A Good Read', 'Illuminations' and 'Timer':

> Gold survives the fire that's hot enough
> to make you ashes in a standard urn.
> An envelope of coarse official buff
> contains your wedding ring which wouldn't burn.
>
> Dad told me I'd to tell them at St James's     *a crematorium*
> that the ring should go in the incinerator.
> That 'eternity' inscribed with both their names is
> his surety that they'd be together, 'later'.

I signed for the parcelled clothing as the son,
the cardy, apron, pants, bra, dress –      cardigan

the clerk phoned down: *6–8–8–3–1?*
*Has she still her ring on?* (Slight pause) *Yes!*

It's on my warm palm now, your burnished ring!

I feel your ashes, head, arms, breasts, womb, legs,
sift through its circle slowly, like that thing
you used to let me watch to time the eggs.

Harrrison's long spectacular *v.*, made into a television film, became famous. The title *v.* is short for *versus*, Latin 'against', as used in football fixtures such as 'Leeds *v.* Newcastle'; it also means 'verse'. It is one of several letters sprayed on his parents' gravestone by skinheads after a Leeds United defeat. The poem dramatizes personal and cultural conflicts, giving poetry a rare public hearing. A less socially committed poem, more finely expressive of Harrison's relished gloom, is *A Kumquat for John Keats*:

Then it's the kumquat fruit expresses best
how days have darkness round them like a rind,
life has a skin of death that keeps its zest.

## Seamus Heaney

**Seamus Heaney** (1939–)
*Eleven Poems* (1965), *Death of a Naturalist* (1966), *Door into the Dark* (1969), *North* (1975), *Field Work* (1979), *Station Island* (1980), *The Haw Lantern* (1987), *Seeing Things* (1991), *The Spirit Level* (1996), *Beowulf* (1999).

The fourth 'H' is **Seamus Heaney** (1939–), who won the Nobel Prize in 1997. Heaney considers himself no longer British, but Irish. He was born into a rural Catholic family in Protestant Northern Ireland. Poems written out of the experience of his own people can reflect this, as in 'Requiem for the Croppies' or 'The Ministry of Fear', but he is not simply partisan. The Loyalist–Republican conflict in the North brought Ulster writing to wider notice. Heaney has taken an Irish passport and lives in the Republic. His voice is Irish, as are most of his subjects. But he writes in English, and, like many in Ireland, he partook in the everyday culture of the English-speaking British Isles. His poems mention London's Promenade Concerts, BBC

Seamus Heaney (b.1939).
Peter Edwards, 1987–8.

radio's Shipping Forecast – and British army checkpoints in Northern Ireland. He was a popular Professor of Poetry at Oxford and has for two decades been the most widely-read poet in Britain.

Early poems re-creating sights, sounds and events of his childhood won him many readers; he writes well of his farming family, from whom his education at Queen's College, Belfast, did not separate him, and he still makes his living from the land metaphorically. Where his fathers dug with spades, he digs with his pen ('Digging'), uncovering layers of Irish history, Gaelic, Viking and pre-historic. He has extended his range to politics and literary ancestry without losing his way with language; for him words are also things. Despite the Troubles, to which he attends, he is never merely political. The memorable poem 'Punishment', likening a sacrificial body found in a Danish bog to a victim of Republican punishment squads, echoes also to cast stones and numbered bones from the Gospels.

Modern poets in English are more discreet with their literary allusions than the modernists, and gentler on their readers. Heaney has always learned from other writers – 'Skunk', for instance, humanizes a Robert Lowell poem with the same starting-point. The volume *Seeing Things* deals with the death of parents, marital love and the birth of children. It is much concerned with the validity of the visionary in reaching towards life after death. It opens with Virgil's Golden Bough and ends with Virgil explaining to Dante why Charon will not take him across the Styx. These translations and preoccupations return poetry to classical sources and central concerns with human destinies: a contrast with Larkin's mistrust of the 'myth-kitty' and his sense of 'solving emptiness'.

It is striking that Heaney, with other leading Anglo poets, Geoffrey Hill, the Australian Les Murray and the West Indian Derek Walcott, looks towards the realities of metaphysics, of religion, of presence. In defending the possibilities of the sacred, the poets are quite opposed to the scepticism of Franco-American literary theorists who have much affected the academic climate in which literature is often studied. A generation of post-Marxist intellectuals came to the fore in France after 1968, sceptical towards metaphysics and the possibility of meaning in language. Their competing discourses – political, psychological and philosophical: far too complex to be briefly summarized – belong to a chapter in the history of criticism rather than of literature. They have, however, influenced American and to an extent British academic criticism into trying to cleanse its language of any intimations of the immortal or of the divine. This push towards provisionality and indeterminacy is linked with what is often called postmodernism.

## ▮ **Further reading**

Armitage, S. and R. Crawford (eds). *The Penguin Book of Poetry from Britain and Ireland since 1945* (Harmondsworth: Penguin, 1998). An up-to-date anthology.

Bradbury, M. *The Modern British Novel* (Harmondsworth: Penguin, 1994).

Corcoran, N. *English Poetry since 1940* (Harlow: Longman, 1993). A full and reliable account.

Hewison, R. *Culture and Consensus: England, Art and Politics Since 1940* (London: Methuen, 1995).

---

**Some Irish poets**

Austin Clarke (1896–1974)
Patrick Kavanagh (1904–67)
Brendan Kenelly (1936–)
Seamus Heaney (1939–)
Michael Longley (1939–)
Seamus Deane (1940–)
Derek Mahon (1941–)

---

**Some Scottish poets**

Edwin Muir (1887–1959)
'Hugh MacDiarmid' (C. M. Grieve) (1892–1978)
Robert Garioch (1909–81)
Norman MacCaig (1910–96)
Sorley Maclean (1911–96)
Edwin Morgan (1920–)
George Mackay Brown (1921–96)
Iain Crichton Smith (1928–98)
Douglas Dunn (1942–)

# Postscript on the Current

## Overview

In the last decades of the 20th century, the UK edged closer to Europe and away from the USA. Literature in English became (like the world economy) ever more international.

## Internationalization

England has become 'an anglophone culture within an English-speaking world,' write the editors of the *Penguin Book of Poetry from Britain and Ireland since 1945* (1999); or is it an American-speaking world? By the year 2000, the national criterion adopted for this *History* had begun to seem restrictive, when the Americans Toni Morrison and Don DeLillo, the Russian Joseph Brodsky, the Canadian Margaret Atwood and the Australian Les Murray may have been read and taught in Britain as much as contemporary Britons such as Tom Stoppard, born in Czechoslovakia (which no longer exists), Kazuo Ishiguro from Japan, Peter Carey from Australia, Brian Friel and Seamus Heaney from Ireland, or Douglas Dunn from Scotland – not to mention works in translation, from South America or Italy. This internationalization is parly a market phenomenon. Or so it seems: the reader should be aware also that contemporary history is made up of currently acceptable impressions. Even when accurate, it is not scholarship or criticism, but journalism trying to discriminate in a barrage of 'hype'. A postscript does not prescribe.

## Postmodernism

The much-used term 'postmodernism' indicates what came after modernism, but also has a suggestion (like 'post-Marxist' or 'post-structuralist') that it upstages or supersedes the -*ism* which it post-dates. Since 'modern' means 'new', and modernist literature defined itself chiefly as different from what went before, it had no clear identity. If modernists were ambitious, reaching towards the universal, whether real or ideal, and towards the grandly historical, postmodernist writing is less ambitious, settling for less. But the high modernists, Pound, Eliot, Joyce and Lawrence, knew very well that their efforts to formulate absolutes were inadequate. Postmodernism mistrusts the ambition of these ancestors (as John Fowles did that of the Victorians), and sometimes claims to be more democratic. But the political analogy is dubious. It

**Novelists from other literatures read in the late 20th century**

**Nadine Gordimer** (1923–) Born in South Africa. *July's People* (1981). (Nobel Laureate, 1991.)

**Tony Morrison** (1931–) Born in US. *The Bluest Eye* (1970), *Beloved* (1987). (Nobel Laureate, 1993.)

**Margaret Atwood** (1939–) Born in Canada. Feminist poet and novelist. *The Edible Woman* (1969); *Surfacing* (1972); *Bodily Harm* (1982); *The Handmaid's Tale* (1986).

**Vikram Seth** (1952–) Born in India. *A Suitable Boy* (1993), *An Equal Music* (1998).

is safer to take 'postmodernist' as a label of convenience rather than a term of substance or a movement. Insofar as it has a definite reference, it may apply to self-consciously experimental writing of the post-1968 period.

Politics are clearer: Britain edged uneasily closer to Europe just as Soviet economic collapse left the US as the world power, and liberal capitalism as a global model. The policies of the New Labour government of 1997 modified and ratified Margaret Thatcher's changes. Gone was the post-war consensus that economics come second to social security and full employment. Home industries were not protected from foreign competition. Some power was devolved to Wales and Scotland; extremists in Northern Ireland neared exhaustion. The pattern of social life was increasingly influenced by international technology, finance and competition; literary culture was modified by the currency of visual and electronic media. For the mass of people, the human liking for self-representation in story and drama was increasingly satisfied by television or video, where words are subordinate to images. Playwrights such as Stoppard and Pinter and novelists such as Ruth Prawer Jhabvala have successfully adapted classic novels for film and television; in such adaptations, 90 per cent of the original dialogue has to go. The desire for rapid impact began to affect most forms of writing.

# Novels

Novels are published, promoted and reviewed, but public agencies also affect the reputation and dissemination of literature: University English departments, and government bodies such as the Arts Council and the British Council. All for a time supported the campus novel pioneered by Larkin and Amis, and worked by **Malcolm Bradbury** (1932–) and **David Lodge** (1935–), English professors who have read Evelyn Waugh. Campus novels are comic studies of English university life in the days before 'research' became all-consuming, a world which may soon be as remote as Trollope's Barchester. Bradbury is farcical, Lodge more systematic. Bradbury's *The History Man* is, however, an original and comic-horrific study of the sociologist Howard Kirk, author of *The Defeat of Privacy*, for whom the self is a delusion abolished by Marxism, and the secret of History is to co-operate with it by manipulating others.

Lodge's most serious novel is *How Far Can You Go?*, a case study of a group of Catholics living through the changing morality of the decades before and after the Second Vatican Council. *Changing Places* is a well-crafted job-exchange between Philip Swallow of Rummidge (Birmingham), who prides himself on his setting of

**Malcolm Bradbury** (1932–) Novelist. *Eating People is Wrong* (1959), *Stepping Westward* (1965), *The History Man* (1975), *Rates of Exchange* (1983), *Why Come to Slaka?* (1986).

**David Lodge** (1935–) Novelist. *Changing Places* (1975), *How Far Can You Go?* (1980), *Small World* (1984), *Nice Work* (1988), *Paradise News* (1991).

exam questions, and Maurice Zapp of Euphoria State, who plans to be the best-paid English professor in the world. Professor Lodge has also explained continental literary theory, while reserving his own position; he likes binary structures. *Nice Work* is an internal Rummidge exchange, between Dr Robyn Penrose, feminist materialist semiotician, and Vic Wilcox, managing director of an engineering firm. An older educationalist, Anthony Burgess (1917–93), turned from linguistics to novel-writing with a Malayan trilogy (1956–9), an Enderby trilogy (1963–74) and the long *Earthly Powers* (1980). The violence of *A Clockwork Orange* (1962) made Burgess famous, but verbal energy is not enough.

There has been perhaps a levelling-out of the realistic novel, which has skilled practitioners whose names are not listed below. Anita Brookner, Penelope Lively, Penelope Fitzgerald and Susan Hill, for example, write sensitive novels of a familiar realistic kind, dealing with middle-class private lives. They maintain good writing, as do the broader comic treatments of current marital or social predicaments by Fay Weldon and Beryl Bainbridge. These topical novels shade into genre fiction, such as the spy novels of John le Carré and literary biography.

There have been fine literary biographies of Thomas Hardy and George Eliot, and good lives of Keats, Shelley, Wordsworth and Virginia Woolf, although the best of these, such as the scholarly *James Joyce* (1959, 1982) by Richard Ellmann or the stylish *Ford Madox Ford* (1990) by Alan Judd, are not Boswell's *Johnson*. Literary biography seems to promise a full understanding of another human being, combining the fact of scholarship with the depth of psychology. Fact and fiction seem to have become closer. Talented writers such as Richard Holmes and Peter Ackroyd have written novelistic biographies and biographical novels, Holmes of the Romantics, Ackroyd on Nicholas Hawksmoor and Thomas Chatterton. Ackroyd has also written straight biographies of T. S. Eliot and Sir Thomas More, but his *Charles Dickens* has interchapters which imagine Dickens's thoughts, and he has tried to imagine John Milton in America. Susan Hill has recreated the world of Owen and Sassoon, a vein which has been further reworked by others. This adoption of documentary and historical material, a source of fiction since the time of Defoe, recurs in recent historical novels about slavery, and, more literally, in a series of maritime novels by Patrick O'Brian (1972–99). Literary biography offers some of the pleasures of the realist novel.

## Notable recent novels

Alastair Gray (1934–) *Poor Things* (1982).

A. S. Byatt (1936–) *Possession* (1990).

Julian Barnes (1946–) *Metroland* (1981), *Flaubert's Parrot* (1984).

Salman Rushdie (1947–) *Midnight's Children* (1981), *Shame* (1983), *The Satanic Verses* (1988), *The Moor's Last Sigh* (1997).

Ian McEwan (1948–) *The Cement Garden* (1978), *The Comfort of Strangers* (1981).

Peter Ackroyd (1949–) *Hawksmoor* (1985).

Martin Amis (1949–) *Money* (1986), *London Fields* (1989).

Graham Swift (1949–) *Waterland* (1983), *Last Orders* (1996).

Angela Carter (1940–92) *The Bloody Chamber* (1979), *Nights at the Circus* (1984), *Wise Children* (1991).

Kasuo Ishiguro (1954–) *An Artist of the Floating World* (1986), *The Remains of the Day* (1989).

Jeannette Winterson (1959–) *Oranges Are Not The Only Fruit* (1985).

Novelists in the late-20th-century limelight were Angela Carter (1940–92) and Salman Rushdie (1947–), who wrote with panache about dangerous issues, and Kasuo Ishiguro (1954–), who stalks large subjects with subtlety. Rushdie's extravagant prose has a cosmopolitan glitter. *Midnight's Children* is a novel or romance of a new type sometimes called historical fabulism, presenting history via 'autobiographical' fantasy. It begins with the narrator's birth at midnight on 15 August 1947, when Pakistan and India were born as separate independent states: parturition as partition. Entangled lives of that generation are made vivid, unfamiliar things perceived with cultural difference.

Rushdie (born in Bombay in 1947, but educated at Rugby School) has adopted magic realism, now an international mode, in which realist narrative includes episodes of symbolic fantasy. *The Satanic Verses*, for example, opens with two entwined characters singing rival songs as they fall from an airliner to land on a snowy British beach unharmed. Similar things are found in Latin American writing and earlier in the Central European novel, as in Günter Grass's *The Tin Drum* (1959). 'Magic realism' was a term invented for German expressionism of the late 1920s, traumatic times in which ordinary realism would not do.

A British upbringing has alienated Rushdie from the religious culture of Islam; the sending of the blasphemous *Satanic Verses* to the Ayatollah Khomeini in Iran invoked a sentence of death. Former colonies continue to educate Britain in fiction as in politics. Lively Anglo writing comes from writers such as the Nigerian political exile Wole Soyinka, or from second-generation immigrants such as Hanif Kureishi. The multicultural nature of current writing in English is increasingly reflected, on social as well as artistic grounds, in the syllabus at schools and colleges.

An expressionism similar to that of Grass is found in the late poetry of the American Sylvia Plath, and in the sexual polemics of Angela Carter. Carter's *Nights at the Circus* (1984) is so zestfully written that its narrative surprises keep its pornographic affinities under control. The heroine, Fevvers, a gorgeous artiste of the flying trapeze, spent her childhood in a Whitechapel brothel. After international erotic adventures, it is confirmed that the plumage which enables her to fly is genuine, for she is a bird as well as a woman. The gender-bending, species-blurring comedy is, like that of

Kazuo Ishiguro (b.1954).

Woolf's *Orlando*, not all good fun: the frustration Fevvers causes the men she attracts is part of the point. Carter's influence is seen in *Sexing the Cherry* (1989) by Jeannette Winterson, in which the narration erases male/female differences. Her earlier 'autobiography' *Oranges Are Not the Only Fruit* (1985), less deliberate, is more original.

*Waterland* (1983) by Graham Swift is a formidable achievement. A carefully-mounted narrative, it combines fictional autobiography, family saga and a history of the Fens. Likened to Eliot's *The Mill on the Floss* and to Hardy for its slow naturalistic build-up and determined pattern, its doomed rural lives and multiple narration also recall William Faulkner's *As I Lay Dying*. Its highly conscious narrative method is modern rather than Victorian. Swift's *Last Orders* is highly praised.

*The Remains of the Day* (1989) by Kasuo Ishiguro (born in Japan in 1954) is narrated by a retired butler, a man rather similar to the old Japanese painter who narrates *An Artist of the Floating World* (1986). In both, an old man remembers a life in which he has made dubious accommodations with authority in order to retain an honoured role. For both, the radical revision of perspectives after 1945 is too painful to admit. If the Japanese setting is slightly opaque to outsiders, the English country house is convincing. The butler's quaintly dignified language does not hide from us what he has trained himself not to see: that his admired master was host to pre-war Anglo-German appeasement talks. This finely managed serious comedy shows clearly how sticking to social roles and rules can lead to self-deception and self-betrayal. Ishiguro draws no attention to this, nor to his skill. Japanese reticence could be recommended to a Britain where the postmodernist often rings twice.

## Contemporary poetry

Contemporary poetry is a small area full of prospectors for gold. Since the humane *Elegies* for his first wife by Douglas Dunn (published in 1985), no British collection has imposed itself in the same way.

> And I am going home on Saturday
> To my house, to sit at my desk of rhymes
> Among familiar things of love, that love me.
> Down there, over the green and the railway yards,
> Across the broad, rain-misted, subtle Tay,
> The road home trickles to a house, a door.
> She spoke of what I might do 'afterwards'.
> 'Go, somewhere else.' I went north to Dundee.
> Tomorrow I won't live here any more,
> Nor leave alone. *My love, say you'll come with me.*
>
> from 'Leaving Dundee'

Dunn's reticence packs a punch.

The Northern Irishman **Paul Muldoon** (1951–) and the English **James Fenton** (1949–) are major figures, and **Carol-Ann Duffy** (1955–) seems a major talent now and for the future. Muldoon is a poet of magical imagination and verbal adroitness, with an oblique economy which dazzles, puzzles and delights, though he can punch when he wants to, simply, as in 'Blemish' or 'Why Brownlee Left', or eerily, as in 'Duffy's Circus':

Once Duffy's Circus had shaken out its tent
In the big field near the Moy
God might as well have left Ireland
And gone up a tree. My father had said so.

…

I had lost my father in the rush and slipped
Out the back. Now I heard
For the first time that long-drawn-out cry.

It came from somewhere beyond the corral.
A dwarf on stilts. Another dwarf.
I sidled past some trucks. From under a freighter
I watched a man sawing a woman in half.

**Notable poets**

John Fuller (1937–)
Ian Hamilton (1938–)
Craig Raine (1944–)
Wendy Cope (1945–)
Paul Muldoon (1951–)
Andrew Motion (1952–)
Sean O'Brien (1952–)
Glyn Maxwell (1962–)
Simon Armitage (1963–)

Fenton is highly versatile in a traditional range of prosodic and rhetorical skills, applying an old-fashioned use of metre and sonority to painfully contemporary subjects, such as Cambodia, where he was a foreign correspondent, and Jerusalem. Duffy's powerful gift for ventriloquism is evidenced in 'Warming her Pearls':

Next to my own skin, her pearls. My mistress
bids me wear them, warm them, until evening
when I'll brush her hair. At six, I place them
round her cool, white throat. All day I think of her …

Andrew Motion, appointed Poet Laureate in 1999, is a mannerly and accomplished writer. Great claims are made for the Northerner, Simon Armitage, whose *Zoom* (1989) retails muscular anecdotes from his experience as a social worker. Seamus Heaney's successive volumes make him seem still the poet most worth attending. He has gone on, with *The Spirit Level*, and in 1999 translated *Beowulf*, taking English literature back to its origins.

# Further reading

Hamilton, I. (ed.). *The Oxford Companion to Twentieth-Century Poetry in English* (Oxford: Oxford University Press, 1994). A well-edited and balanced reference book.

Parker, P. (ed.). *The Reader's Companion to Twentieth-Century Writing* (London: Helicon, 1995).

Stringer, J. (ed.). *The Oxford Companion to Twentieth-Century Literature in English* (Oxford: Oxford University Press, 1996). Another well-edited and balanced reference book.

# *Index*